The Congress of Carlowitz (1698/99)

Legal History Library

VOLUME 82

Studies in the History of International Law

Series Editor

Randall C.H. Lesaffer (*KU Leuven and Tilburg University*)

VOLUME 29

The titles published in this series are listed at *brill.com/shil*

The Congress of Carlowitz (1698/99)

Supra-cultural Diplomatic Norms and Practices of Peacemaking at the End of the Seventeenth Century

By

Konstantinos Poulios

BRILL | NIJHOFF

LEIDEN | BOSTON

Cover illustration: François-Gerard Jollain the Elder, *La Paix générale conclue par l'Empereur, la Pologne, la Moscovie et la République de Venise avec le Grand Turc à Carlowitz le 29 janvier 1699*. [Almanach. 1700] Bibliothèque de l'Institut de France, Fol AA 66 P f.72.

The Library of Congress Cataloging-in-Publication Data is available online at https://catalog.loc.gov
LC record available at https://lccn.loc.gov/2025048255

Typeface for the Latin, Greek, and Cyrillic scripts: "Brill". See and download: brill.com/brill-typeface.

ISSN 1874-1793
ISBN 978-90-04-45611-2 (hardback)
ISBN 978-90-04-45849-9 (e-book)
DOI 10.1163/9789004458499

This book is printed on acid-free paper and produced in a sustainable manner.

Στην Παναγιώτα

Contents

Acknowledgments XIII
List of Figures and Tables XIV
Abbreviations XV
Notes on Transliteration, Names, Dates, Translation and Specific Terminology XVI

Introduction 1
1 Early Modern Peace Congresses: a Widespread, Supracultural Phenomenon 2
2 A Western/Central European Apanage 5
3 The Carlowitz Congress Historiographic State-of-the-Art 8
4 Challenging Eurocentrism 10
5 Confronting Cultural Essentialism, Provincialising Westphalia and Demythologising Carlowitz 11
6 Approaching an Early Modern Congress: a Methodological Guide 16
7 'The Carlowitz Congress Theatre of Peace': the Libretto 18

Prelude 25
1 Alexandros Mavrocordatos 27
2 The Failed Vienna Congress and the Concept of the 'Honourable Peace' 30
3 War and Peace in the 1690s 36

ACT I
The Preliminaries (Late December 1697–Early October 1698)

Dramatis Personae 43

Narration Part I: Embarking on the Road to Peace 45
1 The First Steps 45
2 A Mini Interlude: the Concept of *Uti Possidetis* 54
3 The Play Resumes 58

Narration Part II: a Mistrust Caused by Distance 64

Narration Part III: Laying Down the Foundation of Peace 69
1 First Scene: Adrianople 69
2 Second Scene: Vienna 73
3 Third Scene: Following Peter I's 'Grand Embassy' 79
4 Fourth Scene: Adrianople 82
5 Fifth Scene: Warsaw 90
6 Sixth Scene: Vienna 94

Interlude I: Mediation 99
1 Mediation, Arbitration, Bons Offices 100
2 The Evolution and Proliferation of Peacemaking by Mediation in the Seventeenth Century 105
3 Mediators and Mediating Undertakings during the Sixteen Years' War 107
4 Smooth the Negotiation but Do Not Intervene in It? The (Fluid) Position and Duties of a Mediator 109
5 Efforts to Win Over the Mediators and Complaints of Their 'Partisanship' 113
6 An Impartial Peacemaker: the Self-Fashioning of a Mediator 116
7 The Tangible Material and Symbolic Benefits of a Mediator 117
8 The Various Types of Mediation at the Carlowitz Congress 118

Narration Part IV: on the Way to the Congress 121
1 Quarrels among the Mediators 121
2 The Ottoman Response to the Imperial-Venetian Instrument of the Foundation of Peace 122
3 The Tsar in Vienna and the Developments in the Allied Camp 132
4 Searching in the Archives 139
5 The Final French 'Mediation Gambit' 141
6 Apprehension on the Ottoman Side: Prevarications in Vienna 142
7 The Arrangement of the Final Details 147

ACT II
The Congress Begins (October–Middle November 1698)

Dramatis Personae 151

Narration Part I: the Arrival of the Delegations 153
1 'We Have Gathered Here in the Plain of Carlowitz' 153
2 'All Is Quiet around Carlowitz' 155

3 The First Ceremonial Visits 158
4 The Exchange of the Plenipotentiaries' Credentials 159
5 The Drafting of the Congress Regulation 161

Interlude II: the Ceremonial 165
1 What Is the Ceremonial? 167
2 Terminology 168
3 Ceremonial Regulations in Seventeenth-Century Peace Congresses Prior to Carlowitz 170
4 The Pioneering Ceremonial Ordering of the Carlowitz Congress 172
5 The Carlowitz Participants' Hierarchical Conception of the 'Society of Polities' 174
6 Status Projection Instances and Means 179
7 The (Disputed) Ceremonial Equality of the Principal Members of an Embassy 181
8 The Ceremonial Forms Retained during the Talks 183
9 The Ceremonial of the Signing of the Instruments of the Peace Treaties 186
10 The Farewell Visits 187
11 Ceremonial Strife during the Congress: a Short Prelude 188
12 'Worse than a Fight of Cats and Mice': the Fierce Muscovite–Commonwealth Ceremonial Dispute 189
13 The 'Tents Incident' No. 2 193
14 Who Is to Sit First at the Table with the Ottomans? 195
15 'Faked' Ceremonial Disputes? 197

Narration Part II: the *Arcana Congressus* 199
1 The Secret Negotiations between Voznitsyn and the Ottoman Delegation 199
2 Polish Secret Dealings 203
3 Venetian Anxieties 204
4 Count Marsigli's Moves 206
5 And the Mediators … 207
6 The Spy 208

Interlude III: Being a Plenipotentiary Ambassador 210
1 Clarifying the Terms 212
2 The Portraits of the Carlowitz Plenipotentiaries 214
3 The Supra-cultural Traits of an Ambassador 219
4 Crash-Courses for Newly Appointed Plenipotentiaries 223
5 The Various Social Roles of an Early Modern Ambassador 225

6 Striving for Partaking in the Glory of Peace 229
7 More and Less Innocent 'Gifts' 230
8 The Daily Routine and Obligations of a Plenipotentiary Ambassador 235
9 Ambassadorial Self-Portrayal 244
10 How Plenipotentiary Was a Plenipotentiary? 249

ACT III

The Central Phase of the Congress (*13 November–20 December 1698*)

Dramatis Personae 257

Narration Part I: Sur la manière de négocier entre les plénipotentiaires 259
1 How to Set About the Congress Negotiations and in Which Mode to Pursue Them? 259
2 The Fate of Transylvania Is Sealed 262

At the Negotiating Table I: Territorial Claims, Possession and Border Making 266
1 The Territorial Aspirations of the Participants of the Carlowitz Congress 267
2 '*Uti Possidetis* Sequel': the Congress Playing Out 272
3 Who Possesses What? 280
4 Borders: Some Preliminary Thoughts 285
5 The Terms 290
6 'Natural' and Artificial Boundaries 292
7 Border-Making Tools 299
8 No-Man's-Land and the Issue of Fortresses 302
9 Controlling the Borderlands 305
10 A 'Closing' of the Frontier? 307

At the Negotiating Table II: Smaller South-Eastern European Polities as Discussion Topics during the Congress 311
1 Ragusan Manoeuvrings 313
2 What Is to Be Done with the Tatars? 322

Interlude IV: the Physical and Social Environment of the Congress 335
1 The Practical Choice of the Plain of Carlowitz 336

2 Transforming the 'Wilderness' 343
3 A Multicultural Social Environment 347
4 The Congress's 'Public Opinion' 350
5 Instances of *Ensemble* Social Interaction 352
6 The 'Other' 353

Narration Part II: Peace Is Ostensibly Drawing Near ... at Least for Most 356
1 The Imperials 356
2 Venice 359
3 The Polish-Lithuanian Commonwealth 365
4 Muscovy 371
5 New Rapproachments in the Allied Camp 374
6 The Ottomans 374

Interlude V: the Composition of an Embassy 377
1 'The More the Better': the General Structure and Size of a Congress Embassy 377
2 Family Members 378
3 Noblemen 379
4 The Secretary 379
5 Interpreters 384
6 Special Advisers 391
7 Physicians and Priests 393
8 Postmen, Cooks, Provisioners, Hajduks, Servants and Others 395

Narration Part III: Meanwhile in Vienna ... 397
1 'You Take It, or You Leave It' 397
2 Francesco Loredano at the Imperial Court 401

ACT IV
***The Grand Finale* (*20 December 1698–5 February 1699*)**

Dramatis Personae 407

Narration Part I: 'The Ultimate Great Obstacle for Peace' 409
1 Setting the Stage for the Final Act 409
2 The Unsuccessful Restart of the Ottoman–Venetian Talks 413

At the Negotiating Table III: Peace or Truce/Armistice? The Duration of the Treaties 416
1 Religion: the 'X Factor'? 418
2 Terminology 422
3 Temporal Validity of the Agreements 426
4 Which Type of Agreement to Pick? 429

Narration Part II: the Deadline 437
1 Ruzzini Remains Firm; the Imperials Actively Intervene 438
2 Voznitsyn's Moves 440
3 Apprehension at the Imperial Court 442
4 Time Is Running Out 443

Narration Part III: the Finale 449
1 Reconciliation in Public Display: the Signing Ceremonies 449
2 When Is Peace Considered Concluded? 453
3 The Last Days of the Congress 456

Conclusions 460

Archival Material 467
Published Sources 469
Bibliography 472
Webpages 491
Index of Names and Places 492

Acknowledgments

While it is generally accurate that a monograph is, first and foremost, the product of hard personal toil, it is equally accurate that, in many respects, it is also a collective endeavour. Without the assistance, remarks, suggestions, and encouragement of numerous individuals, this work would never have come into fruition. The central arguments of this book owe much to the lengthy conversations I have enjoyed over the past six years with Giancarlo Casale, Güneş Işıksel and Jan Hennings. Their invaluable input prompted me to radically rethink or (re)frame my research questions at critical junctures throughout the 'writing-process journey'.

Given the complexity of a topic that requires expertise across various subfields, certain parts of the book could not have been completed without the inestimable help and guidance of Olga Katsiardi-Hering, Gábor Kármán, Natalia Królikowska–Jedlińska, Lovro Kunčević, Vedran Stojanović, Nikolas Pissis and Vigdis Evang. Moreover, I couldn't provide a comprehensive account of the Congress of Carlowitz using material from every one of its multiple participants without the immense aid of Russian and Polish-speaking colleagues. Nikolas Pissis and Lana Martysheva assisted me with translating Russian sources and secondary bibliography, while Jan Blonski did the same with the Polish archival material and Natalia Królikowska–Jedlińska came eagerly to my succour with regard to the Carlowitz-related bibliography in Polish.

I would also like to extend my gratitude to the two anonymous reviewers whose critical remarks and suggestions helped considerably in improving the final text. Any deviation from their recommendations burdens me and me alone.

Last but not least, I would not have borne six years of sometimes stressful research and writing without the unconditional backing of my wife, Panagiota. She always stood by my side, patiently enduring my constant badgering to read every sentence, paragraph, or part of this book I deemed paramount, and spending countless hours listening to my thoughts and anxieties about the whole project while helping me to keep my spirits high. In a sense, this monograph belongs to her as much as it does to me.

Figures and Tables

Figures

1 Plan of the spatial arrangement of the Failed Vienna Congress joint conferences 31
2 Detail of a Venetian map portraying the geography and spatial arrangement of the Carlowitz Congress venue 40
3 Unknown painter. The Negotiations at Zsitvatorok 128
4 *Theatrum Pacis*. The geography and spatial arrangement of the congress venue 338
5 Detail of the allied encampment 339
6 A depiction of the three tents that housed the negotiations at the beginning of the congress 345
7 Detail of the Conference House 346
8 Detail of the plan of the Conference House 347

Tables

1 Number and relative frequency of the relations to the emperor sent by the Habsburg embassy per month during the congress 239
2 Official conferences held at the Carlowitz Peace Congress from 13 November to 20 December 1698 263
3 Official conferences held at the Carlowitz Peace Congress from 21 to 31 December 1698 414
4 Official conferences held at the Carlowitz Peace Congress during January 1699 438

Abbreviations

A.DVNS.MHM.d	Divan-ı Hümayun Sicillatı Mühimme Defterleri
A.DVNS.NMH.d	Divan-ı Hümayun Sicillatı Name-i Hümayun Defterleri
AGAD	Archiwum Główne Akt Dawnych
BayHStA	Bayerisches Hof-, und Staatsarchiv
BNM	Biblioteca Nazionale Marciana
DABOA	Devlet Arşivleri Başkanlığı Osmanlı Arşivi
HHStA	Haus, Hof-, und Staatsarchiv
İE. DH	İbnülemin Dahiliye
MÖStA	Mitteilungen des Österreichischen Staatsarchivs
MPEPIL	Max Planck Encyclopedia of Public International Law
PUF	Presses Universitaires de France
OGIZ	Ob"edinenie gosudarstvennykh izdatel'stv
ÖStA	Österreichisches Staatsarchiv
SK	Süleymaniyye Kütüphanesi
SP	State Papers
TDVİA	Türk Diyanet Vakfı İslam Ansiklopedisi
TNA	The National Archives
TSMK	Topkapı Sarayı Müzesi Kütüphanesi

Notes on Transliteration, Names, Dates, Translation and Specific Terminology

1 Transliteration and Spelling

The transliteration of Ottoman texts, words, and names follows the MEB (Milli Eğitim Bakanlığı) İslam Ansiklopedisi system, whereas the Russian and Greek ones adhere to the Library of Congress system. Ottoman names are rendered in their transliterated Ottoman form rather than Modern Turkish (e.g., *Rāmī Meḥmed* instead of *Rami Mehmet*). For Turkish terms which have acquired a standard form in English, such as *pasha* or *padishah,* I will mostly follow this form (e.g. the *pasha* of Bosnia), except in cases when the full Ottoman name plus title is given (e.g., *ʿAmcazāde Köprülü Ḥüseyin Paşa*). Russian, Polish, and Hungarian names are retained in their original spellings, except when a variant has become common in English (e.g., Peter I). Regarding place names that are not standard in English, I generally follow their modern spellings with the following exceptions:

1) Adrianople (Edirne)
2) Carlowitz (Sremski Karlovci)
3) Castello di Rumelia (Antirrio)
4) Constantinople (Istanbul)
5) Lepanto (Nafpaktos)
6) Ṭemeşvar (Timişoara)

2 Dates and Translation

All dates are given in the Gregorian Calendar unless specified otherwise (*see* J.C. [Julian Calendar] and A.H. [Anno Hegirae]). In some instances, when the protagonists use dual calendars in their correspondence, both dates are kept (e.g., 10/20 December 1698). January 1 is uniformly regarded as the beginning of the year. All translations are my own unless otherwise indicated.

3 Specific Terms

Since terms such as *diplomat, diplomacy, diplomatic,* and *foreign policy* were not used by late seventeenth-century contemporaries, I employ them only expansively for the sake of clarity and linguistic diversity. Although, in theory, the words *ambassador*, *plenipotentiary*, and *plenipotentiary ambassador* had distinct connotations among most Carlowitz participants, these terms are often used interchangeably in the sources. To avoid tedious repetition, I will adopt the same practice while clarifying their terminological differences in Interlude IV regarding the plenipotentiary ambassador.

State constitutes a highly problematic term when it comes to its possible semantics for the diverse participants of the Carlowitz Congress. Although I privilege the use of the terms polity or political entity, when I do employ the term or translate specific words as such (for instance, the Ottoman Turkish *devlet*), I intend an impersonal political entity (*dominium*), which, in the case of hereditary monarchies (such as the Austrian Habsburgs, the Ottoman Empire or Muscovy), was, in tandem, closely associated with the ruling dynasty.

The Austrian Habsburg side is referred to as the Habsburgs or the Imperials – a term frequently encountered in the sources – since, at this period, the Habsburg monarch in Vienna was the Emperor of the Holy Roman Empire of the German Nation. The Ottoman Empire will also be referred to as the Porte or the 'Exalted State' – the Ottomans' predominant appellation by the late seventeenth century when referring to their empire. Russia, as a name, was not used by the Carlowitz contemporaries to designate the tsar's polity; they instead spoke of Muscovy and the Muscovites. I will follow this terminology unless I am speaking about the language (Russian).

Finally, regarding one of the largest political formations of Eastern Europe in the early modern period, its correct designation would be the Polish-Lithuanian Commonwealth or the *Rzeczpospolita Obojga Narodów* (Republic of the Two Nations), or simply the *Rzeczpospolita* (Commonwealth/Republic). This is the terminology I primarily follow. However, since the terms Pole, Polish or Poland also appear in the primary material, I sporadically use only the first two to avoid linguistic repetitions.

Introduction

> The revisionism of diplomatic history is now in full swing, and this is in itself a global historical project.
>
> ANDRÉ J. KIRCHER AND HILLARD VON THIESSEN, 'Diplomacy in a Global Early Modernity: The Ambiguity of Sovereignty', 1100

> Research on early modern foreign relations needs a more holistic approach that not only concentrates on Western Europe.
>
> LENA OETZEL, 'A Diplomatic Sphere of Its Own: Early Modern Peace Congresses', 466, fn. 9

∴

Around the end of October 1698, a desolate plain near the ruins of the town of Carlowitz (Sremski Karlovci), in modern-day northern Serbia, became the site of an unusual amount of activity. Numerous cavalcades made an appearance, accompanied by the roll of drums and the peal of trumpets. Boats anchored on the banks of the river and unloaded provisions and building materials. Soon, the plain was transformed into a busy construction site as different encampments and provisional residences were raised to house the many newly arrived 'guests' from afar. In place of the silence previously covering the debris of Carlowitz, one could now hear a cacophony of various languages and admire the equally varied attire of their speakers. This was the stage of the peace congress that was to take place for close to four months (from mid-October 1698 to early February 1699). Its primary purpose: to put an end to the grinding conflict that had started fifteen years before, in 1683, when the Ottoman Porte declared war on the Austrian Habsburgs and unsuccessfully attempted to conquer their capital, Vienna. A year after this monumental and ultimately siege, under the auspices of the Pope, an anti-Ottoman coalition of the Habsburg emperor, the Polish-Lithuanian Commonwealth, and the Republic of Venice was formed under the name of 'The Holy League', transforming the Habsburg-Ottoman conflict into a multi-front-war engulfing much of central, south-eastern, and eastern Europe. Its zone would expand further east as Muscovy also joined the Christian alliance, first informally in 1686 and then formally in 1697.

 | DOI:10.1163/9789004458499_002

The subject of the present study is not the 'theatre' of this gigantic military confrontation, known since the time of the actual fighting by various names.[1] Instead, it constitutes the first comprehensive analysis of the endeavours of its multiple participants to bring the conflict to an end through their final and most successful effort: the Peace Congress of Carlowitz. In doing so, it explores what this congress reveals about the nature of diplomatic norms and practices of peacemaking during the late seventeenth and early eighteenth centuries, and how it can serve as a paradigmatic case study for challenging the dominant west-European centred narrative on the origins and evolution of multilateral diplomacy, a cornerstone of modern international law.

1 Early Modern Peace Congresses: a Widespread, Supra-cultural Phenomenon

Multilateral diplomatic gatherings aimed at ending military conflicts – especially those fought by coalitions of multiple belligerents – became a standard peacemaking mechanism across Europe from the 1640s onwards.[2] Their proliferation across religious and cultural divides is most clearly evidenced by

1 Most prevalent in contemporary Christian sources and subsequent historiographical works are those of 'The War of the Holy League', 'The Great Turkish War' (*Der Große Türkenkrieg*), or, in the Venetian context, 'The Morea War' (*La Guerra di Morea*) – stemming from the primary theatre of the Ottoman–Venetian struggle, the Peloponnese (Morea). In this study, without disregarding either contemporary terminology or established scholarly usage, I have chosen the term "Sixteen Years' War" as a more neutral and inclusive label, although technically only the Imperial/Polish-Ottoman conflict lasted the full sixteen years. Such historiographical decisions are not unprecedented; a parallel example is that of the "Nine Years' War" (1689–97), alternatively known as the 'War of the League of Augsburg': J.S. Bromley (ed.), *The New Cambridge Modern History*, vol. 6, The Rise of Great Britain and Russia, 1688–1715/25 (Cambridge: Cambridge University Press 1971) 223. Furthermore, the term "Sixteen Years' War" can also be grounded in late seventeenth-century sources. For instance, the preambles of the Latin and Ottoman versions of the Ottoman–Imperial Treaty at Carlowitz refer equally to the 'sixteen years of war/fighting' (*per sedecim annos* [...] *bellu* // *onaltı seneden berü şikāk*): *Gründ- und umständlicher Bericht von denen römisch-kayserlichen wie auch ottomannischen Groß-Bothschafften, wodurch der Friede oder Stillstand zwischen dem aller-durchleuchtigst-großmächtigst- und unüberwindlichstem römischen Kayser Leopoldo Primo und dem Sultan Mustafa Han III. den 26. Januarii 1699. Zu Carlowiz in Sirmien auf 25. Jahre geschlossen und darauff auch denen respective Höffen zu Wienn und Constantinopel bestätiget worden* (Vienna: Schönwetter 1702) 10; Silāḥdār Fındıḳlılı Meḥmed Aga, Mehmet Topal (ed.), *Nusretnâme: inceleme – metin (1106–1133–1695–1721)* (Ankara: Turkish Academy of Sciences 2018) 496.

2 Lena Oetzel, 'A Diplomatic Sphere of Its Own: Early Modern Peace Congresses', in Goetze and Oetzel, *Early Modern European Diplomacy*, 465–82; Johannes Burkhardt and Benjamin Durst, 'Friedenskongresse', in Irene Dingel et al. (eds.), *Handbuch Frieden im Europa der*

the widespread adoption of similar terminology to describe such assemblies throughout this vast region. In western and central European languages, such assemblies, predominantly, but not exclusively, came to be referred to as congresses (*Congresso*, *Kongress*, *Congrès*). The word stems from the classical Latin verb *congredior*, meaning 'a coming or going together, in a friendly or hostile manner'.[3] By the sixteenth century, it was already used to describe a (bilateral) gathering of princes or their representatives.[4] However, even in the late seventeenth century, the French diplomat and writer François de Callières (d. 1717) deemed the term too impure to serve as a label for multilateral diplomatic gatherings. Instead, he preferred terms like *Assemblée* or *Conférence de Ministres* (ambassadors).[5] Still, by 1698, 'congress' was generally accepted as a designation, although, indicative of its continuing semantic fluidity, some of Callières' contemporaries applied it equally to the multilateral diplomatic assembly as a whole and the bilateral sessions within it.[6]

At the same time, the Ottomans adopted a semantically related term, *cemiʿyyet*. The renowned late-seventeenth-century Ottoman-Latin dictionary of François de Mesgnien, alias Franciszek Meninski (d. 1698?), defined this word stemming from the Arabic primarily as "the action of gathering together (*collectio & recollectio*) one's thoughts", or, in a social context, as the assembling of troops (*ʿasker cemiʿyyeti, collectio exercitus*).[7] However, it appears that the word underwent a semantic expansion as the Ottomans began participating in multilateral diplomatic gatherings during the 1683–99 war. The first recorded use of the term in this context dates to 1689–90.[8] By 1698, it had become the prevalent Ottoman equivalent of 'congress,' as demonstrated by the account of the Carlowitz talks written by Rāmī Meḥmed, the first plenipotentiary

---

Frühen Neuzeit / Handbook of Peace in Early Modern Europe (Berlin/Boston: De Gruyter 2020) 437–53.

3 University of Chicago, *Logeion: A Digital Dictionary*, 'Congressus', available at: https://logeion.uchicago.edu/congressus.

4 Burkhardt and Durst, 'Friedenskongresse', 437.

5 Niels F. May, *Zwischen fürstlicher Repräsentation und adliger Statuspolitik. Das Kongresszeremoniell bei den westfälischen Friedensverhandlungen* (Stuttgart: Thorbecke 2016) 74, fn. 81.

6 For example, BNM, Ms. It. VII 407 (=7594), Narratio conventus caroloviciani, quam dedit quidam a secretis Carolo Ruzzini, veneti cum summa potestate ad eum conventum legati, fol. 15^r, 57^r (henceforth *Narratio*). To avoid terminological confusion, this study adopts the terminology most commonly used by participants at Carlowitz: 'congress' refers to the gathering as a unified body. In contrast, the individual meetings between the warring parties are referred to as 'conferences'.

7 Franciszek Meninski, *Thesaurus linguarum orientalium turcicae, arabicae, persicae* (Vienna 1680) 1652.

8 *See* below, Prelude, 30.

ambassador of the Porte.[9] Further east, the Muscovites spoke of *s"ezd*. Originally describing a gathering, assembly, or meeting (primarily for commercial purposes), the term was used to designate bilateral diplomatic encounters by at least the fifteenth century.[10] Similarly to 'congress', with the rise of multilateral diplomacy in the 1600s, *s"ezd* seems to have gradually expanded its scope to incorporate the novel reality, constituting the predominant appellation to describe the Carlowitz negotiations.[11]

Although the origins and gradual evolution of various terms in different languages to designate multilateral diplomatic assemblies can be partially traced, the historical circumstances behind the emergence of the 'congress phenomenon' are still not fully understood. Nonetheless, it seems highly plausible that multilateral diplomacy sprang primarily out of the practical need to terminate large-scale wars involving multiple participants – a coalition of powers against another coalition of powers or a coalition against a single polity.[12] Hence, it is perhaps no coincidence that the first multilateral congress was convened to terminate the Thirty Years' War (1618–48), a conflict encompassing large parts of the European continent in an unprecedented manner, and that this peacemaking format proliferated with subsequent geographically extensive multi-party confrontations such as the Second Northern War (1655–60),'The War of Holland' (1672–9), The Nine Years' War (1688–97) and, of course, the Sixteen Years' War.

Determining which early modern gatherings for the purpose of conflict-resolution constituted a congress, and which did not, remains somewhat unclear in the current literature, as seems to have been the case also for late-seventeenth-century contemporaries.[13] At the most basic level, one could argue that for an early modern congress to be considered as such, it typically required

9 TSMK, Revan, no. 1311, Ta'rīḫ-i Ṣulḥ-nāme-i ʿAmcazāde Ḥüseyin Paşa, fol. 37[b], 40[b], 95[b], 101[a] (henceforth *Ta'rīḫ-i Ṣulḥ-nāme*). Moreover, the word seems to have further broadened its meaning during this period. For example, the late-seventeenth/early-eighteenth century Ottoman bureaucrat and historian Muṣṭafā Naʿīmā (d. 1716) would use it to describe a human community organised itself as a political entity: Mustafa Naʿîmâ, Mehmed İpşirli (ed.), *Târih-i Naʿîmâ: Ravzatü'l-Hüseyn Fî Hulâsati Ahbâri'l-Hâfikayn*, vol. 1 (Ankara: Turkish Historical Association 2007) 26 (henceforth *Târih-i Naʿîmâ*).

10 V.B. Krys'ko (ed.), *Slovar' russkogo jazyka XI–XVII vv.*, vol. 29 (Moscow: Nauka 2012) 125–6.

11 For example, *see Pamiatniki diplomaticheskih snoshenij drevney Rossii s derzhavami inostrannymi*, vol. 9 (Saint Petersburg 1868), 3–4, 31–2, 53–4 (henceforth *Pamiatniki*). Interestingly, *s"ezd* seems to have continued to refer to bilateral, peacemaking-oriented meetings as well (ibid., 518). This dual usage suggests that early modern diplomats did not always clearly differentiate between bilateral and multilateral 'congresses'.

12 Oetzel, 'Diplomatic Sphere', 465.

13 Burkhardt and Durst, 'Friedenskongresse', 438.

more than two negotiating parties sending delegates with plenipotentiary powers to a mutually agreed location to discuss and conclude a peace treaty.[14] Despite their usual overarching multilateral character, however, the negotiation format of early modern congresses was nevertheless predominantly bilateral; that is, each participant conducted separate talks and signed separate agreements with its primary adversary(-ies).[15] This means that a congress' diplomatic practices were a mixture of long-established customary norms between two polities and more improvised, ad hoc solutions to accommodate the multilateral aspects of the negotiations (for instance, the ceremonial).[16]

2 A Western/Central European Apanage

Occupying such a central role in early modern peacemaking mechanisms, congresses have long captivated the attention of historians and IR specialists. This is particularly the case for the Congress of Westphalia (1643–8), traditionally heralded as a landmark in the history of international law, being the initiator of the modern system of sovereign states, although this narrative has been criticised during the past few decades.[17] In particular, a significant regeneration in the study of early modern congresses took place starting in the late 1990s and accelerated into the first two decades of the twenty-first century, with the advent of the so-called New Diplomatic History (even if, today, it is no longer so 'new').[18] Scholars of this school moved steadily away from a strictly political

---

14 Oetzel, 'Diplomatic Sphere', 465; Burkhardt and Durst, 'Friedenskongresse', 438.

15 Ibid., 439; Randall Lesaffer, 'The Lore and Laws of Peacemaking in Early Modern and Nineteenth-Century European Peace Treaties', in Marc Weller, Mark Retter and Andrea Varga (eds.), *International Law and Peace Settlements* (Cambridge: Cambridge University Press 2021), 46. This dual and simultaneous multilateral and bilateral nature of early modern congresses is perfectly encapsulated in the Ottoman Sultan's decree authorising the grand vizier to appoint the plenipotentiary ambassadors of the Porte to the Carlowitz Congress. The two men were instructed to negotiate 'with all the allies together and with each one of them separately' (*cümleten ve başḳa başḳa müttefiḳleriyle mükāleme* [...] *ėdüb*): *Taʾrīḫ-i Ṣulḥ-nāme*, fol. 39[a].

16 May, *Repräsentation und Statuspolitik*, 73–90.

17 Christoph Kampmann, 'The Treaty of Westphalia as Peace Settlement and Political Concept. From a German Security System to the Constitution of International Law', in Weller, Retter and Varga, *International Law*, 64–85. Also, special mention should be made to a recent attempt to challenge the dominant 'Westphalian Paradigm' in the field of IR: Ayşe Zarakol, *Before the West. The Rise and Fall of Eastern World Orders* (Cambridge: Cambridge University Press 2022).

18 For the principal tenets, methodological tools, and main research directions of 'New Diplomatic History', *see* the comprehensive article of Tracey Sowerby, 'Early Modern

and systemic oriented understanding of such multilateral gatherings and, similarly to other historical fields, influenced by cultural studies, sociology and anthropology, turned towards the investigation of diplomatic practices, the cultures of war and peacemaking and the re-interpretation of diplomatic sources as an archive of cultural history.[19]

Nonetheless, despite the proliferation of monographs and collected volumes on early modern congresses that have emerged from this new approach, one must search very hard to find any reference within them to Carlowitz, or, for that matter, any other congress taking place east of Westphalia. Hitherto, the research field remains, to an overwhelming extent, a western/central European apanage, and this has had an enormous influence on how early modern congresses are generally perceived. In other words, it still remains a dominant view that seventeenth-century multilateral diplomatic gatherings were a western/central European phenomenon per se, and emerged from a particular set of specifically western European cultural and religious underpinnings, which, under the ascendancy of powers such as France, England or the Austrian Habsburgs, were then disseminated, or rather, imposed by them and grudgingly adopted by cultural outliers (and for that reason, in term of diplomatic practice, backward) polities in the east and south-east of the continent.[20] In addition, a special 'congress genealogy' was conjured up, starting with the Westphalian watershed and passing then to the so-called 'Netherlandish Period' with the congresses of Nijmegen (1676–8), Ryswick (1697) and finally that of Utrecht (1713–5).[21] Any other similar gathering during the same period

---

Diplomatic History'. *History Compass* 14/9 (2016), 441–56. Also, Toby Osborne, 'Whither Diplomatic History? An Early-Modern Historian's Perspective'. *Diplomatica* 1 (2019), 40–5.

19 Notable examples include the monographs of May, *Repräsentation und Statuspolitik*; Matthias Köhler, *Strategie und Symbolik. Verhandeln auf dem Kongress von Nimwegen* (Cologne/Weimar/Vienna: Böhlau 2011); Derek Croxton, *Westphalia. The Last Christian Peace* (New York: Palgrave Macmillan 2013) and Lucien Bély, *Espions et ambassadeurs au temps de Louis XIV* (Paris: Fayard, 1990). From the various collective volumes dedicated to a new study of early modern congresses, one could also signal out the following: Christian Windler (ed.), *Kongressorte der Frühen Neuzeit im europäischen Vergleich: Der Friede von Baden (1714)* (Cologne/Weimar/Vienna: Böhlau 2016); Renger de Bruin et al. (eds.), *Performances of Peace: Utrecht 1713* (Leiden/Boston: Brill 2015); Christoph Kampmann et al. (eds.), *L'art de la paix. Kongresswesen und Friedensstiftung im Zeitalter des Westfälischen Friedens*, (Münster: Aschendorff 2011).

20 For such an approach, *see*, for instance, Heinz Duchhardt, 'Peace Treaties from Westphalia to the Revolutionary Era', in Randall Lesaffer (ed.), *Peace Treaties and International Law in European History. From the Middle Ages to World War One* (Cambridge/New York: Cambridge University Press 2004) 45–58.

21 Ibid.; Hillard von Thiessen, 'Diplomacy in a Changing Political Order: An Actor-Centred View of European Diplomats at the Time of the Spanish Succession', in Matthias Pohlig

was considered simply not worthy of extensive mention since it couldn't rival the magnitude of these four 'sacred monsters'.[22]

But what are the primary reasons behind the resilience of such a western-European-centred approach? Certainly, the linguistic barriers to studying congresses beyond western-central Europe, such as Carlowitz or Oliva-Copenhagen (1659–60), are an important consideration. Objectively speaking, it is much easier for a researcher in European Diplomatic History to work with sources in Italian, Spanish, French or German than in Ottoman (and modern) Turkish, Polish, Swedish or Russian. But just as important is the general perception, unfortunately still prevalent among historians of early modern European diplomacy, that political entities like the Ottoman Empire, Muscovy or even the Polish-Lithuanian Commonwealth, were too culturally and/or religiously distant from the states of western Europe to be considered full members of the 'European State System' – becoming so, to a greater or lesser extent, only over the course of the eighteenth century, as they (willing or begrudgingly) accepted western European diplomatic norms, one of which was of course, congresses.

Even more regrettably, the contemporary politics of memory play an equally cardinal role in shaping the research landscape since funds are typically channelled to projects that align with the historical narratives that those in power seek to disseminate in the contemporary public sphere. Thus, the supposedly 'first pan-European' Congress of Westphalia served and continues to serve the attempts to forge a common European identity based on peaceful cooperation among sovereign states. In contrast, as the Polish historian Dariusz Kołodziejczyk asserted perspicaciously, none of the current political entities associated with the Congress of Carlowitz finds today any compelling reason to actively remember or celebrate it.[23]

---

and Michael Schaich (eds.), *The War of the Spanish Succession: New Perspectives* (Oxford: Oxford University Press 2018) 69.

22 As the French historian Géraud Poumarède framed it, the Congress of Carlowitz does not have the *ampleur* of the 'grandes rencontres qui servent à terminer les guerres européennes, qu'il s'agisse des réunions de Westphalie, de Rijswick ou d'Utrecht': Géraud Poumarède, *L'Empire de Venise et les Turcs XVIe–XVIIe siècle* (Paris: Classiques Garnier 2020) 281.

23 Dariusz Kołodziejczyk, 'The Treaty of Carlowitz in Polish Memory – a Date Better Forgotten?', in Colin Heywood and Ivan Parvev (eds.), *The Treaties of Carlowitz (1699). Antecedents, Course and Consequences* (Leiden/Boston: Brill 2020) 201.

3 The Carlowitz Congress Historiographic State-of-the-Art

Although Carlowitz has not attracted much attention from specialists in early modern congress diplomacy, that does not mean it is a historiographic terra incognita. The 1698–9 diplomatic gathering on the banks of the Danube has been the subject of multiple monographs, articles and collective volumes ever since the late nineteenth century, and a significant part of the primary sources used in the present volume have already been explored by various previous scholars.[24] Nevertheless, despite their indispensability as starting points for any attempt to (re)address the topic, the majority of these studies either focus on specific bilateral relations and negotiations during the congress,[25] or, when they adopt a more general perspective, rely on a particular corpus of primary material related to one or two main participants, rather than a genuinely 'multilateral' use of available sources.[26] Still other studies are little more than short, generic accounts of the negotiations, with some of them primarily based on

24 One of the least known but significant earlier works on the congress which is mainly based on the correspondence of the second Imperial ambassador at the congress, Count Leopold von Schlik, is the short study of Robert van Zuijlen van Nijevelt, *De Vrede van Carlowitz* (Utrecht: J. van Boekhoven Publishing House 1883). Another older but still valuable scholarly work, especially for the Dutch side of the negotiations, is the extensive article of J.H. Hora Siccama, 'De Vrede van Carlowitz en wat daaraan voorafging'. *Bijdragen voor Vaderlandsche Geschiedenis en Oudheidkunde* 4/8 (1910), 43–185. Mention should also be made to an anthology of sources on the Carlowitz Congress (mainly from the HHStA in Vienna and other less-known western-central European archival collections as well), unfortunately available only in their Hungarian translation: Szita Laszlo and Gerhard Seewann (eds.), *A karlócai béke és Európa: dokumentumok a karlócai béke történetéhez 1698–1699* (Pécs: Gálos Nyomdász 1999).

25 Among the most recent studies: Poumarède, *L'Empire de Venise*, 283–91; Andrei G. Guskov, 'Uchastie Rossii v Karlovitskom Kongresse (1698–1699 Gody): Russkaja Diplomatija v rannee novoe vremja'. *Novaja i novejshaja istorija* 3 (2018), 119–41; Güner Doğan, *"Venediklü ile dahi sulh oluna". 17. ve 18. Yüzyıllarda Osmanlı-Venedik İlişkileri* (Istanbul: İletişim 2017) 109–39; Mónika F. Molnár, 'The Treaty of Karlowitz in the Venetian sources. Diplomacy and ceremony', in Hasan Celal Güzel. C. Cem Oğuz and Osman Karatay (eds.), *The Turks*, vol. 3 (Ankara 2002) 405–14; Maciej Serwański, 'Dyplomacja polska wobec zasady uti possidetis w negocjacjach karłowickich 1698–1699', in Ilony Czamanskiej and Witolda Szulca (eds.), Traktaty Karlowickie z 1699 roku i ich następstwa (Poznan: Adam Mickiewicz University Press 2003) 15–24.

26 In this category, apart from the earlier works of the two Dutch historians cited above (fn. 24), one could also ascribe the unpublished Ph.D. thesis of Rifa'at Abou-El-Haj, 'The Reisülküttab and Ottoman Diplomacy at Carlowitz' (Ph.D. thesis, Princeton University 1963), and the first part of William B. Slottman's posthumously published dissertation, dedicated to diplomatic negotiations during the Sixteen Years' War: William B. Slottman, *Ferenc II Rákóczi and the Great Powers* (New York: Columbia University Press 1997).

a selective secondary bibliography.[27] Overall, with few notable exceptions,[28] most follow a narrow approach that places extreme emphasis on the unfolding of the negotiations rather than the diplomatic norms and practices underpinning them.[29]

On the other hand, espousing, sometimes uncritically, the western-European-centred narrative, they generally interpret the congress predominantly as 'a *Zeitenwende*, a *plaque tournante*', marking the end of the Ottoman Imperial Age of territorial expansion, the beginnings of the Eastern Question (the dismantling of the Ottoman Empire by the European powers, grosso modo), the meteoric rise in prominence of the Austrian Habsburgs, and the transition of 'non-European' polities, mainly the Ottoman Porte and Muscovy, from their distinctive pre-Carlowitz peacemaking norms and practices to an era of western European style 'New Diplomacy'.[30] As English historian Colin Heywood framed it in dramatic tones with his undoubtedly gifted pen,

---

27 For instance, Marija Kocić and Nikola Samardžić, 'Porta na Kongresu u Karlovcu (1698.–1699.): kraj ad hoc diplomatije'. *Historijski Zbornik* 68 (2015),15–30; Nuri Yurdusev, 'Karlofça Antlaşması ve Diplomasi Tarihi'. *Çanakkale Araştırmaları Türk Yıllığı Dergisi* 4 (2006), 1–16; Ernst D. Petritsch, 'Rijswijk und Karlowitz. Wechselwirkungen europäischer Friedenspolitik'. In Heinz Duchhardt et al. (eds.), *Der Friede von Rijwick 1697* (Mainz: Philipp von Zabern 1998) 291–312; Ivan Parvev, *Habsburgs and Ottomans between Vienna and Belgrade (1683–1739)* (New York: Columbia University Press 1995) 128–36.

28 Dariusz Kołodziejczyk's short but informative article, 'Between the Splendor of Barocco and Political Pragmatism: The Form and Contents of the Polish-Ottoman Treaty Documents of 1699'. *Oriente Moderno, Nuova serie* 22 (83)/3 (2003), 671–9, is one of them. So is the latest contribution of Ali Yaycıoğlu, 'On the Ottoman Arguments during the Congress of Karlowitz (1699)', in Kären Wigen (ed.), *Territorial Imaginaries: Beyond the Sovereign Map* (Chicago: University of Chicago Press 2025) 61–76.

29 Such is the case, for instance, with undoubtedly one of the most complete overviews of the congress, both in terms of sources and bibliography – although it unfortunately does not address the Polish and Muscovite perspectives: Mónika F Molnár, 'Der Friede von Karlowitz und das Osmanische Reich'. In Arno Strohmeyer and Norbert Spannenberger (eds.), *Frieden und Konfliktmanagement in interkulturellen Räumen* (Stuttgart: Franz Steiner 2013) 197–220.

30 *See*, for example, Yaycıoğlu, 'Ottoman Arguments'; Colin Heywood and Ivan Parvev, 'Introduction', in Heywood and Parvev, *Treaties of Carlowitz*, 2–5; Ali Yaycıoğlu, 'Karlofça ânı: Osmanlı İmparatorluğu 18. yüzyıla nasıl başladı?'. *Tarih ve Toplum Yeni Yaklaşmalar* 18 (2021), 8–56; Daniel O'Quinn, *Engaging the Ottoman Empire. Vexed Mediations 1690–1815* (Philadelphia: University of Pennsylvania Press 2019) 39–88; Kocić and Samardžić, 'Porta na Kongresu u Karlovcu'; Jean Bérenger, 'Conclusions générales', in Jean Bérenger (ed.), *La paix de Karlowitz 26 Janvier 1699. Les relations entre l'Europe centrale et l'Empire Ottoman* (Paris: Honoré Champion 2010) 235–42; Yurdusev, 'Karlofça Antlaşması', Vladimir Matveyev, *The Karlowitz Congress and the Debut of Russia's Multilateral Diplomacy (1698–99)* (Leicester 2000).

Carlowitz 'marks the bringing of the Ottomans, unwillingly, into the western European congress system from which they were fated never to escape'.[31]

In this brief bibliographic overture, a final special remark deserves to be made on three collective volumes on the congress – or, more accurately, on the broader period of the Congress and the Sixteen Years' War – that have appeared over the last twenty years. Two of these are proceedings from special conferences held in France and Poland in 1999 to mark the 300th anniversary of the Carlowitz Treaties,[32] while the third and most recent was a volume produced from a conference held in Sofia in 2014.[33] What these three volumes share is the surprising fact that although Carlowitz features conspicuously in their respective titles, the majority of their contributions are only marginally related to the Congress itself.[34] Such comments are not meant, by any means, to diminish the value of the collective volumes in question, which contain authoritative and genuinely informative contributions.[35] They rather reconfirm that despite the Carlowitz Congress being a fertile research field, many of its plots have been left fallow, and the ones already worked require new methods of cultivation.

4 Challenging Eurocentrism

Despite the enduring resilience of a western-European-centred historiographical paradigm regarding early modern congresses in general and the Congress of Carlowitz in particular, in the last decade or so the spread of a new 'global approach' has introduced some quite innovative perspectives into the historiographic fields of inter-polity relations during the early modern period and the history of international law. Although the term 'global' remains somewhat nebulous, serving as an umbrella to cover a variety of methodologies and interpretations, its proponents among diplomatic and legal historians share the ambition of introducing an alternative to the (western) European-dominated narratives

31 Heywood and Parvev, 'Introduction', in Heywood and Parvev, *Treaties of Carlowitz*, 5.

32 Bérenger, *La paix de Karlowitz*; Czamanskiej and Szulca, *Traktaty Karlowickie.*

33 Heywood and Parvev, *Treaties of Carlowitz.*

34 If we take as a paradigmatic example the latest book edited by Colin Heywood and Ivan Parvev, a quick look at its contents reveals no paper on the congress per se. Most of its chapters are instead devoted to negotiations preceding or following the conference, to other Sixteen Years' War-related themes or to overviews of bilateral relations between some of its participants in a broader late-seventeenth to early-eighteenth-century time frame.

35 I refrain from enumerating them here since many of them frequently appear in the following pages.

and understandings of how diplomacy and norms governing inter-polity relations evolved from the sixteenth to the late eighteenth centuries.

Such scholars have shifted their focus away from the 'Old Continent' and into Asia, Africa, or the Americas, prioritising the study of encounters between European and non-European powers. They have forcefully asserted that although cultural differences did often cause intentional or unintentional misunderstandings during intercultural diplomatic encounters, and therefore need to be taken seriously, they were, in general, far less critical than the traditional Eurocentric approaches would have us believe. Early modern societies were generally hierarchical and stratified, sharing similar perceptions of protocol, jurisdiction and protection.[36] Thus, intercultural diplomatic encounters, far from being marked by complete cultural estrangement, were instead defined by a minimum of 'cultural commensurability', often gradually 'constructed' through the very process of frequent diplomatic contacts. Hence, they have effectively demonstrated that the dissemination of diplomatic practices and the formation of inter-polity law(s) was not a one-way process, but a relational one, resulting in the gradual construction of a shared vocabulary of communication. Such views have contributed to reshaping the understanding of early modern diplomacy and the origins of modern international law, both geographically and thematically.[37]

5 Confronting Cultural Essentialism, Provincialising Westphalia and Demythologising Carlowitz

Following in the footsteps of such ground-breaking approaches, this study seeks to provide a new lens through which to reexamine the nature of the early modern norms and practices governing inter-polity relations, the origins and

36 Lauren Benton and Adam Clulow, 'Legal encounters and the origins of global law', in Jerry H. Bentley, Sanjay Subrahmanyam and Merry E. Wiesner-Hanks (eds.), *The Cambridge World History*, vol. 6/2 (Cambridge: Cambridge University Press 2015) 80–100.

37 Some prominent examples of the truly copious literature: Nadine Amsler, Henrietta Harrison and Christian Windler, 'Introduction: Eurasian Diplomacies Around 1800: Transformation and Persistence'. *The International History Review* 41/5 (2019), 943–6; André J. Krischer and Hillard von Thiessen, 'Diplomacy in a Global Early Modernity: The Ambiguity of Sovereignty'. *The International History Review* 41/5 (2019), 1100–07; Will Smiley, *From Slaves to Prisoners of War: The Ottoman Empire, Russia, and International Law* (Oxford: Oxford University Press 2018); Jan Hennings, *Russia and Courtly Europe. Ritual and the Culture of Diplomacy, 1648–1725* (Cambridge: Cambridge University Press 2016); Laurence Badel and Stanislas Jeannesson, 'Introduction: Une histoire globale de la diplomatie?'. *Monde(s)* 5/1 (2014), 6–26; Bardo Fassbender and Anne Peters (eds.), *The Oxford Handbook of the History of International Law* (Oxford: Oxford University Press 2012).

development of the rules and conventions of congress diplomacy, as well as the significance of Carlowitz for the history of central, south-eastern, and eastern Europe. The analysis is structured around three principal assertions, which could be summarised as: 1) confronting cultural essentialism, 2) provincialising Westphalia, and 3) demythologising Carlowitz.

To begin with, this study contends that early modern diplomatic norms of peacemaking were neither primarily culturally nor religiously determined, nor confined to specific geographical zones from which they were forcibly disseminated to the Others. For this reason, I privilege the term 'supra-cultural' rather than 'intercultural' to refer to the key norms and practices of peacemaking. The difference between the two terms is crucial. Whereas 'inter-cultural' highlights interactions grounded in cultural difference and the attempt to bridge distinct traditions, 'supra-cultural' describes norms and practices that transcend cultural barriers and are thus widely recognisable and operative across diverse political communities. I contend that these supra-cultural norms emerged as shared practices, gradually developed through reciprocal compromises and practical needs during sustained interactions between two or more polities.[38] As such, frequent contact between neighbouring or distant political entities increased the likelihood of forming a joint diplomatic vocabulary. In the geographical context of Europe and the western part of Asia (namely the Ottoman Empire), the development of a unified 'big law' of peacemaking[39] was further facilitated by the high degree of commensurability between certain aspects of otherwise distinct legal systems governing interpersonal relations, such as third-party mediation and boundary-making, which were adapted to an inter-polity level. The Carlowitz Congress exemplifies this process, illustrating that by the late seventeenth century, a shared vocabulary of reconciliation extended from the British Isles to the Russian steppes and beyond. This underscores the extensive political entanglements and the intensification of inter-polity relations across this vast region.

Moreover, the maturing of such a unified diplomatic lexicon relied heavily on the contributions of various actors involved in negotiations, from chief negotiators to simple scribes. These individuals (re)shaped, enriched, and reinterpreted peacemaking norms and practices not only during oral

38 A similar argument for the gradual development of shared ceremonial practices in seventeenth-century Habsburg-Ottoman diplomatic exchanges is convincingly put forward by Özgür Kolçak in his recent article, 'A History of Learned Courtesy: Habsburg–Ottoman Diplomatic Encounters in the 17th Century (1606–83)'. *Turkish Historical Review* 15 (2024), 223–51.

39 I am borrowing the term 'big law' from Lauren Benton's recent book, *They Called It Peace. Worlds of Imperial Violence* (Princeton/Oxford: Princeton University Press 2024) 13.

discussions but primarily through the paperwork they generated, particularly treaty texts.[40] These treaties, carefully preserved in the archives of different chanceries, served as indispensable guides for negotiators and primary sources of 'legal' argumentation. Quite interestingly, references to the works of early modern jurists often regarded as the 'fathers' of modern international law – such as Grotius, Gentili, and Pufendorf – are nowhere to be found at Carlowitz, nor, for that matter, in most of the other seventeenth-century congresses.[41]

Coming now to the second principal argument of this study, although the first diplomatic gatherings widely recognised as multilateral were held in western Europe,[42] the practice didn't remain restricted in this geographical area. For instance, negotiations with multilateral elements (presence of more than two negotiating parties and special ceremonial/spatial regulations to accommodate them) are encountered in peace discussions between the Porte and its Christian neighbours dating back at least in the early seventeenth century, such as at those taking place at Zsitvatorok (1606) between the Habsburgs, the Ottomans and the rebellious Hungarian Estates under the leadership of the Transylvanian Prince István Bocskai.[43] As will be discussed later, many of the ceremonial and spatial regulations first adopted during the negotiations at Zsitvatorok would exert a strong influence on some of those later applied during the Carlowitz Congress.

Therefore, for the post-1648 era, instead of perceiving congress diplomacy as culturally foreign to them, the supposed Others were quick both to accommodate themselves to the multilateral environment of congresses and to actively promote pioneering negotiating methods as these meetings unfolded. If we take the Ottoman case as an example, most scholars tend to disregard that the first time a delegation of the Porte participated in a congress – as the

40 Randall Lesaffer, 'Peace Treaties and the Formation of International Law', in Fassbender and Peters, *History of International Law*, 71–94. However, for the early modern period, the author restricts his analysis to western Europe.

41 *See*, for instance, Markus Laufs, *In viam pacis. Praktiken niederländischen und päpstlicher Friedensvermittlung auf den Kongressen von Münster (1643–1649) und Nimwegen (1676–1679)* (Vandenhoeck & Ruprecht 2022)148–53.

42 Joycelyne Gleghill Dickison, *The Congress of Arras 1435. A Study in Medieval Diplomacy* (New York: BIBLO and TANNEN 1972).

43 *See* a detailed discussion of the topic in Gábor Kármán, 'A Third Party: Gábor Bethlen, Prince of Transylvania and the Habsburg–Ottoman Peace Negotiations 1624–1627', in Rubén González Cuerva and Francesco Caprioli (eds.), *Beyond European Courts. Models of Indirect Diplomacy in Imperial Borderlands* (forthcoming). I deeply thank Gábor Kármán for sharing with me his manuscript as well as for his instructive comments and suggestions regarding the multilateral aspects of the negotiations at Zsitvatorok.

participants themselves referred to it[44] – was not in 1698 but ten years earlier in a failed diplomatic gathering in Vienna, the intent of which was to put an end to the war with the Holy League.[45] While unsuccessful, this congress was one of the first (if not the very first) in which some of its initial sessions were truly multilateral, with the simultaneous presence of all its participants, a format that the Ottoman side firmly endorsed. Similarly, in 1698, it was the Muscovite plenipotentiary ambassador Prokopii Voznitsyn who proposed a similar format, a proposal that was, however, rejected by the Habsburg delegation, which, for its own reasons, privileged the 'traditional' bilateral mode. However, even this 'traditional' model was not strictly adhered to throughout the congress. It was modified at times, resulting in quite unique and unprecedented variations that blended bilateral and multilateral elements. For instance, formal and informal mediators were sometimes simultaneously present at bilateral meetings (with informal mediators also being a negotiating party themselves!). Similarly, the peace articles for Venice were finally negotiated collectively by its allies with the Ottomans without Venice's participation. Lastly, at Carlowitz, with active Ottoman participation, several other innovative features, particularly in ceremonial regulations, were introduced, many of which are wrongly attributed to later congresses. Simply put, the concept of equality between sovereign polities was upheld to a far greater extent than during the Congress of Westphalia, often credited as the first to introduce it. Viewed in this light, Westphalia and other western European congresses appear less pivotal to the overall evolution of multilateral diplomacy. Instead, the latter takes on a far more polycentric character, with the alleged 'peripheries' playing equally a role in its development alongside the traditionally recognised 'nucleus'.

Thirdly, the present study argues that contrary to popular 'myths', the Congress of Carlowitz did not have the long-term impact often attributed to it as a political agreement.[46] As it didn't mark the first Ottoman encounter with

---

44 *See*, for example, Eudoxiu Humurzaki (ed.), *Documente privitóre la istoria românilor*, vol. 5, part 1 (Bucharest 1885) 204, 212, 214–5; Girolamo Venier, 'Relazione del Nob. Ec. s. Girmo. Venier Cr. fù ambasciator in Germania', in *Fontes Rerum Austriacarum, Diplomataria et Acta*, vol. 27 (Vienna: Imperial and Royal Printing House 1867) 309–44, 338–9 (henceforth Venier, *Relazione*).

45 The first scholar to correctly refer to those negotiations as a congress was William Slottman: Slottman, *Ferenc II Rákóczi*, 38. However, he didn't fully assess the significance of his reference.

46 Some characteristic examples: Yaycıoğlu, 'Ottoman Arguments'; Heywood and Parvev, 'Introduction'; Yaycıoğlu, 'Karlofça ânı'; O'Quinn, *Engaging the Ottoman Empire*; Kocić and Samardžić, 'Porta na Kongresu u Karlovcu'; Bérenger, 'Conclusions générales'; Yurdusev, 'Karlofça Antlaşması'; Matveyev, *The Karlowitz Congress*.

multilateral diplomacy, it also didn't signal the starting point of a straight downward path leading the Ottoman polity from the status of a 'World Empire' to that of the 'Sick Man of Europe'. If, during the Sixteen Years' War, the Ottoman armies performed poorly on many occasions, the congress could be genuinely considered a resounding success for Ottoman diplomacy. Playing skillfully on the disunion and diverse interests among the Holy League allies, the Ottoman delegation succeeded not only in imposing favourable negotiating rules during the preliminary phase of the peace talks but also in dictating its own terms on some of the Christian allies, notably on the Republic of Venice. Thus, the Ottomans left the congress having managed not only to avoid the appearance of being the overtly losing party but also, in practical terms, to considerably alleviate the hard reality of the significant territorial losses suffered during the war years. Such an argument has in fact already been articulated by the late Rifaʿat Abou-El-Haj, who was the first to study the Ottoman side of the 'Carlowitz story'[47] but without a detailed analysis of how these results were practically achieved during the course of the multi-lateral negotiations themselves (and, indeed, during preceding talks, when the 'rules' of the congress were established in ways that already favoured the Ottomans' position).

Following from this point, there are several other respects in which Carlowitz's place as a political *plaque tournant* in traditional scholarship must also be re-evaluated. Although it confirmed Habsburg hegemony over most of the lands once comprising the medieval kingdom of Hungary, it did not usher in a long-term, uninterrupted *Drang nach Süden* territorial expansion of the Vienna-based monarchy. Similarly, the significant Venetian territorial gains, mostly in southern Greece, far from marking an 'Imperial come-back' for the Serenissima, proved short-lived, as the Ottomans were successful in liquidating much of Venetian presence in eastern Mediterranean (apart from the Ionian islands) less than twenty years after the conclusion of the Carlowitz Treaties. As for Muscovy, the Carlowitz Congress neither constituted its first encounter with the concept of multilateral diplomacy nor Muscovy's *grand point d'entrée* in the European 'system' of inter-state relations.[48] And despite the tsar's first attempts to get direct access to the Black Sea or to claim the right of protection for the Greek Orthodox subjects of the sultan, we are yet far removed from the truly radical alterations in the Russian–Ottoman balance of power brought during the second half of the eighteenth century. On the other hand, if there

47 The archival backbone of his study was the account of the congress written by the first Ottoman plenipotentiary ambassador, Rāmī Meḥmed (*Taʾrīḫ-i Ṣulḥ-nāme*), which also serves as the principal Ottoman source for the negotiations in the present book.

48 As it is argued in Guskov, 'Uchastie Rossii' and Matveyev, *The Karlowitz Congress*.

is any genuine political turning point in the Carlowitz Treaties, that is to be found in the relations between the Ottoman Porte and the Polish-Lithuanian Commonwealth. The treaty signalled the end of a series of struggles between the two polities that had spanned much of the 1600s, ushering in a stable, peaceful relationship that lasted until the Commonwealth disappeared from the political map of Europe at the end of the eighteenth century.

While not an all-out political watershed, however, Carlowitz should still be considered one of the most unique multilateral diplomatic gatherings of the seventeenth century, mainly because it formed the first truly multi-religious early modern congress. If Westphalia managed to gather – in separate cities, don't forget – Catholics, Calvinists and Protestants, Carlowitz brought together all the above in addition to Muslims and Orthodox Christians. No other early modern congress before or after it could boast the same.

6 Approaching an Early Modern Congress: a Methodological Guide

Finding the best way to comprehensively approach the study of an early modern congress such as Carlowitz is an arduous task. In developing an appropriate methodology, an indispensable and genuinely helpful guide has been Derek Croxton's monograph on the Congress of Westphalia.[49] Although Westphalia has been the subject of an enormous amount of previous scholarship, Croxton effectively combined the 'traditional' events-oriented approach with analytical sections heavily influenced by the 'New Diplomatic History', thus providing a compelling and gripping holistic analysis not only of the proceedings of the congress itself but also of the broader diplomatic norms and practices of the middle seventeenth century and the influences the latter received from what he refers to as the 'Baroque' psychological and intellectual background of their practitioners.[50] Leaving aside the somewhat problematic idea of 'Baroque concepts', the present study closely follows Croxton's synthesis of narration and analysis. The former does not lead to broader conclusions and cannot be understood without the latter, and the latter looks equally incomprehensible and decontextualised without the former. Hence, I am trying to strike a balance between an actor-centred approach,[51] catalytic for the unfolding of events, and the larger 'structures' in which the actors thought and operated.

49 Croxton, *Westphalia*.

50 Ibid., 6–11.

51 By 'actor-centred', I mean a focus on individuals – their unique thinking, interests, and strategies – as the primary drivers of historical events. This approach is masterfully

Regarding the narrative parts of this study, I have deliberately opted for a less rigid and laconic writing style. Siding wholeheartedly with the recently rediscovered idea that history is as much a form of literature as it is a scientific undertaking,[52] my principal aim has been, like that of a novelist, to lead the reader deep into the world of the novel's protagonists, and explore their diverse interests, complex thinking and mentalities. I have also deemed it essential to provide frequent quotations from the sources, thereby allowing my actors to speak by themselves, in their own words, using their own concepts. Hence, my narration, while at some points quite detailed, is not meant to be an exhaustive (and potentially tedious) day-to-day account of the talks, but rather another analytical tool to understand the intricate workings of late seventeenth-century diplomacy.

Passing now to the explicitly analytical as opposed to narrative parts of this book, I have attempted to bring together normative topics of both the 'old school' – border-making, the concept of mediation or the types and duration of peace settlements – as well as other subjects, such as the diplomatic ceremonial, which form privileged themes of the 'New Diplomatic History'. In making that choice, one unavoidably has to deal with many of the most cardinal and complex topics of early modern diplomatic history. For instance, border-making and the use of cartography to achieve it could form a separate monograph of its own. Thus, it is only natural that certain strategic choices had to be made for practical reasons of space and coherence. I do not pretend to have covered all such topics in the depth they perhaps deserved, but merely used my primary material and a selective, digestible and representative amount of the available bibliography to offer some (novel) insights from my case study and contribute to the already rich historiographical landscape.

Speaking of primary sources and secondary bibliography, while the present study does not claim to offer a definitive account of the Carlowitz Peace Congress, it aspires to be the first comprehensive, systematic, and multi-perspective analysis of the event. This has been made possible primarily

---

exemplified by Australian historian Christopher Clark in his thought-provoking yet controversial book on the origins of the First World War: Christopher Clark, *The Sleepwalkers: How Europe Went to War in 1914* (London/New York: Penguin 2013). I thus extend the concept introduced by German historian Hillard von Thiessen, who describes an 'actor-centred view' of early modern diplomacy as 'the history of diplomats, their practices, social status, and political roles': Thiessen, 'Diplomacy', in Pohlig and Schaich, *The War of the Spanish Succession*, 64.

52 Ivan Jablonka's book, *L'histoire est une littérature contemporaine. Manifeste pour les sciences sociales* (Paris: Éditions du Seuil 2014) constitutes the rallying-cry for such a more literature-oriented historical writing.

by the extensive and in-depth use of archived documents consulted during the research for this book. Accessing the vast archival material related to the Carlowitz Congress requires proficiency and palaeographical skills in at least ten different languages – and even more for the available bibliography. Acquired knowledge of many of these languages (Ottoman Turkish, French, Latin, Italian, German, English, and Greek) proved invaluable in tackling this linguistic challenge. For the remaining languages (Polish, Russian, and Dutch), as well as the secondary literature in Hungarian, I relied on the invaluable assistance of several colleagues and supplementary support from recent advancements in digital translation tools. So, while I don't claim to have been the first to examine all this Carlowitz-related material,[53] the result is the first monograph on an early modern congress to integrate and analyse together both published and unpublished primary sources pertaining to all its participants.

7 'The Carlowitz Congress Theatre of Peace': the Libretto

The present book follows a rather particular layout. Given its intricate construction, the multiple topics addressed, and the substantial length of the text itself, it is essential at the outset to provide the reader with a clear roadmap, signposting the principal points they will encounter along the way. Instead of the classical division into chapters, this study is presented in the form of a theatrical oeuvre in four Acts, 'The Carlowitz Congress Theatre of Peace'. This peculiar layout is inspired by the combination of two further analytical approaches.

The first is the conception of early modern peacemaking, in general and peacemaking via a congress, in particular, as a process that must pass through certain phases to be completed.[54] This process, however, is not predetermined;

53 To name but a few examples, Güner Goğan and Mónika F Molnár extensively used Venetian material in their respective studies. William Slottman relied heavily on parts of the *Haus-, Hof- und Staatsarchiv* collections in Vienna. Andrei Guskov provided an excellent overview of the congress based on the available Russian sources, while Colin Heywood used much of the available English documentation in the National Archives (NA) in London for his unpublished Ph.D. thesis, 'English Diplomacy Between Austria and the Ottoman Empire in the War of the Sacra Liga, 1684–1699, with Special Reference to the Period 1688–1699' (Ph.D. thesis, University of London 1970). Rifa'at Abou-El-Haj's pioneering use of Ottoman sources has already been mentioned.

54 Maria-Elisabeth Brunert and Lena Oetzel, 'Verhandlungstechniken und -praktiken', in Irene Dingel et al., *Frieden im Europa*, 455–72; Franz Bosbach, 'Verfahrensordnungen und Verhandlungsabläufe auf den Friedenskongressen des 17. Jahrhunderts. Überlegungen zu

rather, it is always liable to fail at any given moment, and although it commences with the direct or indirect initial tentative talks of the different parties to end the war between them, its ending is far more challenging to determine. When is peace considered concluded? With the signing by the plenipotentiaries of Peace Instruments containing the treaty terms at the negotiations' venue? With the ratification of those terms by the respective sovereigns? Or maybe with the completion of the demarcation of the new borders resulting from the agreements? Here, I have opted to make the de facto peace finale coincide with the conclusion of the congress.[55] It was a deliberate choice, driven by the need to create a cohesive narrative and avoid producing an even longer book. On the other hand, many contemporary accounts of the talks follow the same path.[56]

The second analytical approach that catalytically shapes the present study's structure is the idea of the peacemaking process as a 'theatre'. The 'theatre simile' to describe or refer to social realities originated in Classical Greece.[57] Still, it was during the early modern period that the metaphor found its greatest application and dissemination.[58] Many Carlowitz participants also referred to the congress as a theatre and to themselves as actors taking part in it.[59] And,

---

einer vergleichenden Untersuchung der äusseren Formen frühneuzeitlicher Friedensverhandlungen', in Christoph Kampmann et al., *L'art de la paix*, 93–118.

55 I stress the de facto because, as we shall see, for most of the Congress of Carlowitz contemporaries, a treaty was considered de jure concluded only with the exchange of the rulers' ratifications.

56 For instance, the account of the first Ottoman ambassador plenipotentiary Rāmī Meḥmed (*Ta'rīḫ-i Ṣulḥ-nāme*) as well as the relation of the secretary of the Polish-Lithuanian embassy, Andrei Gorkowski: *Compendium legationis jaśnie wielmożnego* [...] *Stanisława Małachowskiego, woiewody poznańskiego, od* [...] *Krola Imci y stanow Rzeczypospolitey Polskiey ad tractandam pacem z Portą Otomańską deputowanego commissarza* [...] *zebrane przez* [...] *Andrzeia Gorkowskiego* [...] ([Place of publication unknown]: [Publisher unknown], [n.d.]).

57 Monique Trédé, 'Le téâtre comme métaphore au IIe siècle ap. J. -C. : survivances et metamorphoses'. *Comptes rendus des séances de l'Académie des Inscriptions et Belles-Lettres* 146/2 (2002), 581–605; Elena Penskaya and Joachim Küpper, 'Introduction', in Elena Penskaya and Joachim Küpper (eds.), *Theater as Metaphor* (Berlin/Boston: De Gruyter 2019) 1.

58 Ibid., 1–2; Flemming Schock, Oswald Bauer and Ariane Kolle (eds.), *Dimensionen der Theatrum-Metapher in der Frühen Neuzeit. Ordnung und Repräsentation von Wissen/ Dimensions of the Early Modern Theatrum-Metaphor. Order and Representation of Knowledge* (Hannover: Wehrhahn 2008).

59 One of the most telling examples is the following: The second plenipotentiary ambassador of the Habsburg delegation, Count Leopold Schlik, was a general. In one of his letters from the congress venue to his superior and patron, the influential minister Count Franz Urlich von Kinsky, Schlik humbly requested that the latter not address him with the ambassadorial title because it 'does not suit the state from which I exited (the military)

although some negotiating parties, like the Ottomans, were not so culturally familiar with the concept, they equally perceived the unfolding of peacemaking, as much as the Christians, as a staged and 'theatrical' proceeding, with carefully choreographed moves by the leading actors and an audience, commonly referred to as 'the World', which was highly interested in the development of the plot as well as the performance of the protagonists of the play.

All that said, the principal ramification in turning the present book into a 'theatrical play', is that each Act does not correspond to a central argument per se but instead to a different stage of the peacemaking process, collectively illustrating how, by the turn of the eighteenth century, each one of those stages came to be linked to standardised features and requirements accepted and shared by all participants of the Carlowitz Congress. Thus, Act I narrates the story of the highly consequential phase of the Preliminaries (Late December 1697–Early October 1698), which paved the way for the diplomatic gathering on the banks of the Danube. At this stage, the different warring sides accepted the mediation of third parties, laid down the so-called Foundation of Peace – a pre-agreement regulating the way the territorial questions would be addressed during the main talks – appointed their delegations and agreed on the negotiations' venue. Act II corresponds to the congress's opening chapter before the start of the official talks between its participants (October–mid-November 1698). Its principal features consisted in the promulgation of an armistice around the area the congress was to take place, the exchange of the delegates' credentials so that each side could confirm that their interlocutors had sufficient power to negotiate a treaty, the agreement on general regulations regarding the technicalities of the talks (e.g., were they to be conducted multilaterally or bilaterally) and delicate ceremonial issues and matters pertaining to the maintaining of order at the congress venue. With Act III, we enter the core period of the negotiations, which cleared the road to peace for most but not all of the warring parties (13 November–20 December 1698). Act IV relates the climactic finale of the congress culminating in the signing of the various bilateral treaties, which brought the Sixteen Years' War de facto to an end (20 December 1698–5 February 1699).

Moving now to the internal structure of the different Acts, these are divided into 'Narration Parts', which recount the main 'play', with particular emphasis on the processual character of its unfolding and the complex strategies and

---

and in which I must soon re-enter after I lay down the [ambassadorial] costume (or ornamentation) of this theatre (*aprez avoir poseé la parûre de ce teatre*)': ÖStA, HHStA, Türkei I, Turcica Box 168, Folder 1 (November 1698, 1st half), fol. 41^r, Schlik to Kinsky, 5 November 1698.

aims of its multiple actors and 'Interludes', which constitute the analytical pieces, focusing on a specific topic related to the broader diplomatic norms of the age or the general environment of the congress.[60] It is precisely these analytical parts that mostly correspond to the traditional definition of a chapter and contain some of the study's most cardinal micro-arguments. Taken together, these constitute the book's overarching arguments regarding diplomatic culture, namely the consolidation of a common supra-cultural repertoire of peacemaking norms and practices across Europe and the western part of Asia (the Ottoman Empire) by the twilight of the seventeenth century, and the multicentric evolution of early modern multilateral diplomacy.

More specifically, Interlude I studies the concept of third-party(-ies) mediation. It argues that, in contrast to the prevailing notion within current literature that mediation's role in peace congresses waned during the late seventeenth century, the Carlowitz case vividly demonstrates that the phenomenon of mediation was far from fading away. Instead, it remained a crucial hallmark of the peacemaking process, capable of advancing, influencing, and significantly shaping it. Moreover, despite minor differences, which only underscore its diverse nature, mediation constituted a supra-cultural practice with a shared lexicon and well-recognised attributes across a vast geographical expanse, spanning from the British Isles and the Iberian Peninsula to the Euphrates and the Russian steppes.

Interlude II takes as its main subject the ceremonial. The Carlowitz Peace Congress was the first early modern peace congress in which ceremonial regulations were officially removed for the duration of the talks. Thus, it holds the potential to significantly enhance our comprehension of their long-term evolution in the diplomatic arena. However, it also underscores that questions related to ceremony and precedence remained prominently relevant in the late seventeenth century. These questions continued to occupy the thoughts of congress participants and could pose significant obstacles to successful negotiations. Lastly, the Carlowitz case also reveals that polities with seemingly disparate ceremonial traditions actually had more similarities than previously believed. Interlude III touches on the topic of the general profile of an early modern plenipotentiary ambassador, a topic that has experienced a rejuvenation in the last two decades, largely thanks to the emergence of the 'New Diplomatic History'. The Carlowitz Congress offers a unique opportunity to examine the early modern ambassadorial phenomenon from a comparative and comprehensive perspective, transcending cultural and religious divisions

60 However, small interludes can also be found inside a 'Narration Part' wherever needed.

typically assumed to result in entirely distinct diplomatic cultures. It equally demonstrates that despite variations stemming from distinct societal structures or other cultural nuances, including within a supposedly homogeneous 'Christianity', the fundamental characteristics of a plenipotentiary ambassador were identifiable to all participants of the congress.

After passing through the plenipotentiaries, with Interlude V, we move to the various individuals composing the congress embassy, from the ambassadors' kin down to the simple but indispensable servants. The numerous ambassadorial suits transformed the desolate Carlowitz plain into a vibrant social hub, where people speaking varied languages, holding different religious beliefs and stemming from dissimilar cultural backgrounds had the occasion to come together and socialise with one another in the same setting. This social interaction reinforced or reshaped their perceptions of the various Others, a process that was not always unrelated to political motives and personal animosities (Interlude IV).

From the standpoint of the thesis's overall organisation, the systematic alternation of 'Narration Parts' and 'Interludes' described above is designed to avoid the tediousness that could be caused by prolonged and sometimes extensively detailed chronicling. Furthermore, this zooming in-and-out helps the reader to contextualise and comprehend not only the 'play' itself but also the rules and the overarching atmosphere of the 'theatre' that determines the conduct of its 'actors'.

As a final element, I have also included an additional section, labelled 'At the Negotiating Table', at three different moments during the two final acts of the congress. These resemble the 'Interludes' in the sense that they are more analytical than narrational, but they are distinguished by being dedicated to specific topics discussed at the congress. Since it would be impossible to extensively examine every one of the major issues debated at Carlowitz, I opted to focus on three specific ones that were considered of paramount importance for the participants themselves: 1) the question of territorial possession and border-making, 2) the future of particular vassal or tributary polities of southern and eastern Europe, and lastly, 3) the different types and durations of the treaties.

Regarding the first, in contrast to pre-modern border-making, where a state could opt to clearly define or leave undefined specific portions of its borders with neighbouring political entities, I show that the contemporaries of the Carlowitz Congress insisted on meticulous territorial delineation as a fundamental requirement. They categorised borders into two groups: natural boundaries (such as rivers and mountain ranges) believed to be divinely or naturally ordained, and artificial boundaries, which required human intervention. To establish the latter, they all turned to a combination of archival records, maps, and designated commissioners on the ground. Each side advocated for one method or the other based on their convenience and interests. Additionally, I argue that contrary to the dominant view, Carlowitz was not a watershed for inter-polity border delimitation or the introduction of 'territoriality' into the political consciousness of south-eastern and eastern Europe. Thus, regarding the congress border-making practices, the prevailing mode was one of continuity rather than innovation.

Moving now to the second topic addressed 'At the Negotiating Table', we will here encounter the exhilarating efforts of smaller political entities in south-eastern and eastern Europe, all caught between stronger neighbours and their diverse interests, to navigate between them, balancing one against the other, to safeguard their existence, privileges, and way of life. The example of the Republic of Dubrovnik showcases how these secondary, less prominent powers could endeavour to harness the interests of their larger neighbours. Nevertheless, it will also become apparent that the ultimate decisions regarding to whom they would finally owe their allegiance remained the exclusive prerogative of the 'great princes' and their delegates in the peace congress. On the other hand, the feverish discussion at Carlowitz of yet another, 'second-tier' eastern European power, the Crimean Khanate, serves as an excellent case study to illustrate the unified vocabulary but also the highly volatile and ambiguous conception of 'sovereignty' among the participants of the Congress of Carlowitz. For the latter, the question of who was considered a 'sovereign' was constantly (re)negotiated and depended, especially for lesser polities, on the interests of the 'big players' to recognise them as such.

Finally, the third 'At the Negotiating Table' section serves as an invitation to reconsider the still prevalent view among scholars with respect to a key 'law' element of intercultural diplomacy in Early Modern Europe, namely that the types of negotiated settlements were primarily based on diametrically different precepts, heavily influenced by religion, held by the opposing parties. From the extensive available documentation, it becomes clear that all Carlowitz participants recognised a distinction between two categories of inter-polity reconciliation agreements based on their duration: those without a time limit and those with a specified time frame. The former could or could not bind the successors of a ruler and typically indicated that both sides had resolved their most contentious issues. The latter, on the other hand, could be extended from a few years to several decades. In the latter case, they did not differ significantly from the format of an everlasting peace treaty, except for their non-permanent nature. The choice between these two types of agreements was not determined by religious or cultural principles but rather by a combination of strategic considerations and established norms. These strategic considerations were primarily linked to territorial arrangements. For instance, a truce or armistice was mainly associated with an agreement based on the status quo post bellum, exemplified by the supra-cultural concept of *uti possidetis* or *ʿalā ḫālihi* in Ottoman Turkish.

Prelude

The Background of the Carlowitz 'Theatre of Peace' from the Failed Vienna Congress (1689–90) to the Threshold of the Preliminaries (Early Autumn 1697)

Süleymān II (r. 1687–91) ascended to the Ottoman throne in late 1687 amidst chaos. Four years had passed since the crushing defeat of the Porte's armies at the gates of Vienna, and the formation of a coalition of Christian powers, known as the Holy League, which included the Habsburg emperor, the Polish-Lithuanian Commonwealth, and the Republic of Venice (1684).[1] Throughout this period, the Ottoman armies suffered continuous defeats on almost every war front, stretching from the plains of Hungary and those of Podolia (a region in present-day western Ukraine) in the north down to the Morea peninsula in modern-day Greece in the south. In 1687, the Ottoman troops on the Hungarian front decided that they had had enough. They revolted, marched to the Ottoman capital, deposed the ruling Sultan Meḥmed IV (r. 1648–87), and brought his brother Süleymān into power. The new monarch was determined to reverse the ill fortunes of the war. According to the palace official and chronicler Silāḥdār Fındıḳlılı Meḥmed Aga (d. 1726–7),

> When His Majesty the Glorious Emperor ascended to the throne, he decided to join the campaign himself on the necessity [to uphold] the honour and reputation of the dynasty and to protect the religion and the state. [A decision taken] because of the many losses suffered by the subjects and of the removal from the thread of the lands possessed by the Exalted State of so many castles conquered by the great power of his ancestors.[2]

Yet, simultaneously, news reached the Ottoman government, coming directly from the war front, from the head of the Ottoman troops in Belgrade, Ḫazīnedār Ḥaṣan Paşa, and the governor of Várad (in modern-day southern Hungary), Çavuşbaşı Meḥmed Paşa. They claimed to have received letters from the Imperial commander, General Antonio Caraffa (d. 1693), indicating the Habsburg readiness to discuss peace, provided the Ottomans would agree

1 Parvev, *Habsburgs and Ottomans*, 43–5; Petritsch, 'Rijwijk und Karlowitz', 297–8.

2 Silāḥdār Fındıḳlılı Meḥmed Aga, *Silāḥdār Ta'rīḫi*, vol. 2 (Istanbul: Orḫaniye Maṭba'ası 1928) 365.

 | DOI:10.1163/9789004458499_003

to send emissaries to negotiate its terms. The Dutch seconded this proposal, offering at the same time their mediation to bring about the termination of hostilities.[3] This was not the first time peace talks had taken place between the two sides, nor was it the first time an aspiring mediator had stepped forward to facilitate them. Diplomatic channels remained open even in the immediate aftermath of the Ottoman Vienna debacle, and the year 1685 was dominated by reconciliation efforts mainly sponsored and facilitated by the Prince of Transylvania, Mihály Apafi (r. 1661–90).[4] However, these efforts bore no fruit. The Imperials, the factual leaders of the Christian coalition, judged the Ottoman proposals too vague and marching from one victory to the next, they had little interest in immediately halting the fighting. In the following two years, further peace overtures by the Porte proved equally futile.[5] Yet, faced with additional crushing defeats and territorial losses and eager to restore internal order after the mutiny of its own troops that had brought a violent end to Meḥmed IV's reign, the new Ottoman government was determined to once again risk its chances of ending the war through the force of diplomacy.

Still, the Porte did not wish to appear overtly as the party suing for peace, a maxim that would henceforth guide its policy in every negotiation until the end of the war. And so, an accommodating idea emerged: the use of the 'old custom' (*dīrīn-i kadīme*) of sending an embassy to foreign rulers every time a new sultan ascended to the throne 'in order to strengthen the friendship with those friendly [to us] and turn enmity into amity with those hostile [to us]'.[6] Accordingly, letters were dispatched to India, Persia, the Uzbeks, the Imam of Yemen, France, England, the Netherlands and last but not least, the Habsburg emperor.[7] With this stratagem, the Porte aimed, on the one hand, to present the embassy to Vienna not as extraordinary but as one of the many that it simultaneously sent to every corner of its frontiers. On the other hand, it set a specific background for the instructions it was going to hand out to the two men heading to the Habsburg capital as plenipotentiaries (*me'ẕūn u muraḫḫaṣ*):[8] the bureaucrat Zülfikār Efendi

3 *Ta'rīḫ-i Ṣulḥ-nāme*, fol. 3b–4a; Defterdar Sarı Mehmet Paşa, Abdülkadir Özcan (ed.), *Zübde-i Vekayiât: Tahlil ve Metin (1066–1116/1656–1704)* (Ankara: Printing House of the Turkish Historical Society 1995) 291. For a discussion of the Dutch mediating efforts to terminate the Sixteen Years' War and the motivations behind them, refer to Act I, Interlude I below.

4 Konstantinos Poulios, 'Αναζητώντας την ειρήνη εν μέσω πολέμου. Η οθωμανική διπλωματική δραστηριότητα του έτους 1685 και ο ρόλος του Αλέξανδρου Μαυροκορδάτου'. *Mnimon* 38 (2021), 11–32.

5 Ibid.

6 Defterdar, *Zübde-i Vekayiât*, 291; *Ta'rīḫ-i Ṣulḥ-nāme*, fol. 4a.

7 Ibid.

8 Mustafa Güler (ed.), *Zülfikâr Paşa'nın Viyana Sefâreti ve Esâreti. Cerîde-i Takrirât-ı Zülfikâr Efendi [1099–1103/1688–1692]* (Istanbul: Çamlıca 2008) 22 (henceforth *Cerîde-i Takrirât*).

(d. 1696)[9] and the Chief Interpreter of the Porte, Alexandros Mavrocordatos.[10] The Ottoman ambassadors were to 1) report the sultan's ascension and express his inclination and desire to renew the 'ancestral friendship' (*baba dostlugu*) and 2) if the other side shared the same inclination and desire, then to engage in peace talks.[11]

1 Alexandros Mavrocordatos

It would perhaps have been the most common and easiest way to introduce one of the central figures of Ottoman diplomacy throughout the Sixteen Years' War and one of the primary actors in the ensuing Carlowitz 'Theatre of Peace' with a *dramatis persona*-style couple of lines before the main text or by dedicating one or two paragraphs within it. However, since he left us a curriculum vitae written at precisely the same time that the events of the present part were unfolding, I deemed it better to allow him to present himself directly to the audience. As with every self-presentation, it is not objective but instead reflects how he wished to fashion himself at a particular moment, addressing a specific group of people.[12] Since his multifaceted self-fashioning[13] will be discussed numerous times in the following pages, I confined myself to adding

9 Demetrius Cantemir, *Incrementorum et Decrementorum Aulae Othoman[n]Icae Sive Aliothman[n]Icae Historiae a Prima Gentis Origine Ad Nostra Usque Tempora Deductae Libri Tres* (Timisoara: Amarcord 2001) 225, 463; Songül Çolak, 'Zülfikar Paşa', in TDVİA, vol. 44 (Istanbul: Turkish Religious Foundation 2013) 557–9.

10 Initially, the chief accountant (*baş-muḥāsebeci*), Ḥamdī Efendi, was appointed as ambassador. Yet, he declined the position, allegedly saying, 'I cannot carry out this difficult task. It is likely that at the end of the mission I would be the object of reproach' (Defterdar, *Zübde-i Vekayiât*, 292). For his refusal, he was immediately executed: Silāḥdār, *Silāḥdār Tarīhi*, 365.

11 Ibid.

12 He most likely composed this curriculum vitae in September 1689 to be accepted in the *Academia Caesareo-Leopoldina Naturae Curiosorum* in Vienna: Stefano Saracino and Vasilios N. Makrides, 'Die Aufnahme des Alexandros Mavrocordatos ex Aporriton in die Academia Naturae Curiosorum (1689). Die Quellen aus dem Archiv der Leopoldina'. *Ο Ερανιστής* 30 (2021), 33–114. An interesting detail: it is likely that Mavrocordatos first dictated the text to one of his secretaries. Then the Ottoman ambassador read and amended the text, as evidenced by the corrections he made on it: Ibid., 45.

13 The term was coined by Stephen Greenblatt to describe the two-way process by which individuals construct their persona by conforming to cultural norms and perceptions tied to their social position while simultaneously reshaping those norms and perceptions: Stephen Greenblatt, *Renaissance Self-Fashioning: From More to Shakespeare* (Chicago/London: University of Chicago Press 1980).

only a few clarifying footnotes and dates to assist readers in better understanding and framing the text. Let's leave the floor to him, then:

> Alexandros Mavrocordatos. Of the Greek nation (*Natione Graecus*).[14] He was born in Constantinople in the year 1641 [...] to illustrious parents, Nikolaos Mavrocordatos from Chios, and Roxandra Bodina,[15] former wife of Alexander, Prince of Moldavia and Wallachia.[16] He was first initiated into the Greek letters in his adolescence. From a desire to widen [his] knowledge horizons [he] went to Venice and afterwards to Rome [1656] – profiting from [the patronage of] Pope Alexander VII – where, having been initiated in the [fields of] philosophy and theology, he perfected his Latin and [his] higher-level humanistic studies. Indeed, due to the intensive studies, the proper mixture [of the humours] in his body was perturbed. [And so] to regain his health, he left [Rome], and he returned once again to Venice [1660], and for ten years,[17] he eminently cultivated his spirit in philosophy, medicine, anatomy, and other disciplines [...] In the year 1664, when he was 23 years old, he published a little work on the movement [of blood] and use of lungs with which he primarily incited many to [search] beyond the usage which the previous authors were attributing to them and to skillfully investigate [them] in a completely different manner, exposing [this view] to the community of the literati.[18] Although he could have benefited the Republic of Letters by continuing these kinds of studies at the same place (Bologna), [offering] many more elucidations, he was summoned [back] due to the death of his oldest brother and returned to his homeland [1665]. There, after taking care of the domestic affairs for a short time, he publicly taught philosophy in the Greek language, not only having been entreated by his entourage but [also] entirely constrained by their supplications [...] [By his teachings

14 While *natio* should not be confused with its modern meaning, it is clear that Mavrocordatos uses the term – likely a Latin translation of the Greek word γένος – to refer to a distinct ethnoreligious group.

15 The female form of *Boda*, that is, lord or prince, in Romanian.

16 Alexandru Coconul, prince of Wallachia (1623–7) and Moldavia (1629–30).

17 In fact, it was only four. He initially enrolled at the University of Padova but was forced to leave following an unspecified incident and continued his doctoral studies at the University of Bologna: Dimitris Tzelepis, *Τὰ Ῥωμαϊκὰ τοῦ Ἀλέξανδρου Μαυροκορδάτου τοῦ « Ἐξ Ἀπορρήτων »*, vol. 1 (Athens: Irodotos 2023) 34–6.

18 He is referring to his doctoral dissertation entitled, *Pneumaticum instrumentum circulandi sanguinis, sive de motu, & usu pulmonum dissertatio philosophico-medica* (Bologna: Ferroni 1664).

and scholarly activities] Greek eloquence was revived [and] Greek philosophy was restored [...] In the meantime, he truly acquired full knowledge of all oriental languages to such a degree that he was declared by the emperor of the Turks, Chief Interpreter of the Ottoman Porte with all the related to [her] [Christian] nations, endowed with the most outstanding annual incomes. And because in the [Ottoman] Empire, this office has not much to do with translation and clarification [of one's sayings] in a negotiation, but with all those issues that arise between the Turkish Porte and the Christian princes, it concerns for the most part administrative matters and so it's very arduous both because of the workload and the Turkish tyranny. Although he verily tried to avoid such an obnoxious position, he [finally] accepted [it] and with extraordinary patience, he sustained it firmly for twenty years[19] [during which], praised for [his great] prudence, as a deputy of the Porte, he negotiated and concluded peace with the Polish ambassador in Constantinople[20] and after three years with the Muscovite one.[21] Profiting from such occasions, he eminently returned to his nation [and] to God's worship, two churches in Constantinople that were entirely destroyed by fire. He frequently endured too much significant damage, having been accused of favouring his coreligionists. Especially, seven years ago [1683],[22] he was charged again and was thrown into jail in chains [...] stripped of all ancestral fortune.[23] During this period, he endured for a year the loss of his goods and the extreme filthiness of the jail with great perseverance, and he rejected the

19 The twenty-year period mentioned by Mavrocordatos here is somewhat problematic. We know that he firmly remained in office for ten years (1673–83) and, as he narrates himself below, shortly after the Ottoman disaster in Vienna, he was relieved of his duties and was thrown into jail, where he remained for almost a year. So, either he exaggerates deliberately (highly improbable), or he counts approximately his period of service up to late 1689 (when he most likely composed the curriculum vitae, Saracino and Makrides, 'Die Aufnahme', 45), although, as mentioned, for a brief period (late 1683–early 1685), he was not in office.

20 He alludes to the coming to the Ottoman capital of the ambassador of the Polish-Lithuanian Commonwealth, Jan Gniński (1677–8), to ratify the Treaty of Żurawno (1676), terminating the 1672–6 war between the Ottoman Empire and the Commonwealth.

21 He refers to Prokopij Bogdanovic Voznitsyn's 1681 embassy to the Ottoman capital to ratify the Treaty of Bakhchisarai, which ended the Muscovite–Ottoman war (1676–81 or 1672–81, depending on the various scholarly interpretations).

22 Here we once more encounter an approximation of dates, since, strictly speaking, seven years had not passed from 1683 until the most possible date of the composition of the curriculum vitae (September 1689). For this date inconsistency, *see* also Saracino and Makrides, 'Die Aufnahme', 54–6.

23 For the reasons for his imprisonment, *see* Poulios, 'Αναζητώντας την ειρήνη', 15.

Turkish allure to escape [these misfortunes] by renouncing his Christian faith. After being afflicted with such torments, when he obtained his liberty with the payment, for the second time, of [a] money [sum], he would opt for private life. [However], called again, he was dragged back to his previous office [1685]. And when Meḥmed IV was expelled, and Süleymān II ascended to the throne of the Ottoman Empire [1688], he was sent, alongside his Turkish colleague, a man with high dignity among the Ottomans, as ambassador plenipotentiary (*Minister Plenipotentiarius*) to the August Emperor of the Romans, Leopold I, both to announce the new reign and to renew the peace. So, now [1689], he remains in Vienna for the continuation of the [peace] negotiations.[24]

2 The Failed Vienna Congress and the Concept of the 'Honourable Peace'

The Ottoman embassy arrived in Vienna in late 1688. After awaiting for an audience with the emperor for about three months, peace talks with the representatives of the powers of the Holy League (The Habsburg emperor, the Polish-Lithuanian Commonwealth and Venice)[25] finally commenced, with the extraordinary Dutch ambassador Jacob Hop offering his *bons offices* to facilitate communication between the negotiating parties.[26] This marked the first time the term *cemʿiyyet* (gathering) would be encountered in an Ottoman text to designate simultaneous peace negotiations involving more than two parties occurring in the same venue.[27] The uniqueness of the Failed Vienna Congress lies in the fact that, contrary to all previous and subsequent such diplomatic gatherings until 1815, which were primarily based on bilateral discussions among each of their various participants, at least its three initial sessions were joint ones (Figure 1).[28] It was only due to insistence from the Imperial side and against the wishes of the Ottoman delegation, who preferred this

24 The full Latin text is published by Saracino and Makrides, 'Die Aufnahme', 100–2.

25 Muscovy was not yet present since only in 1696 it officially became a member of the Christian alliance.

26 For a detailed discussion of the term *bons offices* as a designation for a specific form of informal mediation, refer to Act I, Interlude I below.

27 *Cerîde-i Takrirât*, 109.

28 *Cerîde-i Takrirât*, 35–49. Subsequently, the congress reverted to a hybrid format combining direct bilateral sessions and indirect negotiations, mainly through the exchange of letters and messages between the Ottoman and the three allied Christian delegations through Hop: Ibid., 49–114.

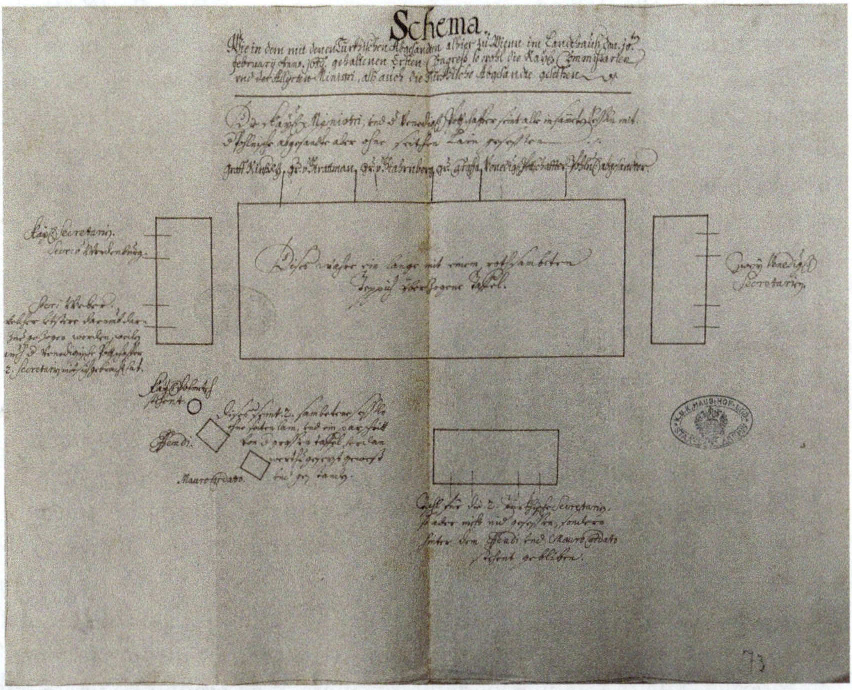

FIGURE 1 Plan of the spatial arrangement of the first joint session of the Failed Vienna Congress (10 February 1689). At the top, from left to right: 1) the Imperial representatives, Count Kinsky, Strattman, Stahrenberg, and General Caraffa; 2) the Venetian ambassador; and 3) the extraordinary Polish envoy. The two Ottoman ambassadors face them at the bottom left. The secretaries of the various delegations are seated on each side, with the Venetian secretaries on the right and the Imperial secretaries on the left, while the two Ottoman secretaries stand (as the text specifies) directly behind the Ottoman delegates
ÖSTA, HHSTA, TÜRKEI I, TURCICA BOX 154 (FEBRUARY 1689), FOL. 73

joint-conferences-model, or *külliyetli meclis* in Ottoman Turkish, that the talks subsequently reverted to a bilateral level.[29]

Regrettably, we cannot examine in detail the 1689–90 negotiations, as that would have required a separate monograph.[30] However, they will serve as a

29 Ibid., 97–8. Note here that at Carlowitz, it will again be the Imperial side, which would vehemently reject any proposal of a joint-session form with the participation of all plenipotentiaries.

30 Although several studies address the 1689–90 Failed Vienna Congress, a comprehensive monograph incorporating archival material from all parties involved has yet to be written. Among the existing works on the topic are Yasir Yılmaz, 'An Ottoman Peace Attempt at the Habsburg Court during the Ottoman-Holy League War: Zülfikâr Efendi in Vienna,

constant point of reference for various matters concerning the Carlowitz Congress. Nonetheless, let us provide some general lines on how the events unfolded. The task faced by the Ottoman plenipotentiaries in 1688 was challenging. When the de facto Dutch mediator Jacob Hop first met with Zülfikār and Mavrocordatos in Vienna, he attempted to persuade them to accept the Imperial peace proposals – at least that is how the two ambassadors perceived his intention – by confronting them with the highly adverse position in which the Porte was presently finding herself in the war.

> The armies of the German emperor are everywhere victorious. And whatever goal they set, they carry it through. His troops are warlike; his captains and generals are prudent and efficient. There is no constraint [for him] in any matter [...] You, on the other hand, did not achieve anything in between. Your troops could not withstand anywhere, and your pashas were broken. You are left with no battle-hardened janissaries any more [...] Presently, victory is totally on the German side and defeat on yours.[31]

Still, despite the adverse position it found itself in, the Ottoman side was not at all willing to concede to just any kind of peace. As Mavrocordatos would categorically state to the imaginary interlocutors of an oration he wrote but never delivered during his stay in Vienna, 'do not deceive yourselves] that [the Ottoman State] would purchase its tranquillity whatever the price nor that it would exchange the current dangers it faces for inglorious and dishonourable treaties'.[32] The role reputation and honour (*ʿırż* and *nāmūs* in Ottoman Turkish)[33] played in early modern foreign relations has long attracted the attention of scholars.[34] While inextricably linked to the interests and strategic

---

1688–1693' (MA dissertation, Bilkent University 2008); Slottman, *Ferenc II Rákóczi*, 38–82; Lothar Höbelt, 'Die Sackgasse aus dem Zweifrontenkrieg: Die Friedensverhandlungen mit den Osmanen 1689'. *Mitteilungen des Instituts für Österreichische Geschichtsforschung* 97 (1989), 329–80; Hora Siccama, 'De Vrede van Carlowitz', 54–74.

31 *Cerîde-i Takrirât*, 46–7.

32 Alexandros Mavrocordatos, 'Πρευσβευτικός πρὸς Γερμανοὺς Λόγος Ὑπὲρ Εἰρήνης', in *Ἐπιστολάριον ἐκ Διαφόρων Ἐρανισθέν* (Constantinople: Patriarchal Printing House 1804), 322–3.

33 In his famous late seventeenth-century Ottoman-Latin dictionary, Franciszek Meninski defined both *ʿırż* and *nāmūs*, among others, as reputation, honour and fame: Meninski, *Thesaurus*, 3246, 5117. This highlights the close semantic relationship between reputation and honor among contemporaries of the Congress of Carlowitz.

34 Christoph Kampmann, 'Der Ehrenvolle Friede als Friedenshidernis: Alte Fragen und neue Ergebnisse zur Mächtepolitik im Dreißigjährigen Krieg', in Inken Schmidt-Voges, Siegrid Westphal, Volker Arnke and Tobias Bartke (eds.), *Pax perpetua. Neuere Forschungen zum*

concerns of the various parties in a negotiation, both terms could be better understood if also placed into the context of the 'community' of early modern political entities, a strictly hierarchical society very similar to what Luc Boltanski and Laurent Thévenot define as *la cité de l'opinion*.[35]

In this community, one's position on the [societal] hierarchical ladder is measured according to the opinion the others have of a specific person, of how strong they think this person is. This opinion is primarily, though not solely, shaped by external indicators, such as the number of servants in a person's possession, the clothing one wears, and so forth. All those indicators constitute the *grandeur* of an individual.[36] The latter, those external signs of power, also defined to a great extent the reputation and honour of a prince in early modern times and allowed him to occupy a specific place within the community of opinion of political entities.[37] For instance, the late-seventeenth-century Ottoman self-perception of greatness relied primarily upon the empire's glorious past, vast territorial reach and purportedly limitless financial and military resources.[38] A peace that could allegedly tarnish this self-image of one's power in the eyes of the 'world', to the other members of the early modern 'Society of Princes',[39] or even to the internal audience of a polity[40] was thus deemed unacceptable.

In an influential article, Christoph Kampmann has effectively demonstrated how the idea of an 'honourable peace' (*Ehrenvolle Friede*) played a catalytic role in delaying the termination of the Thirty Years' War (1618–48). Of course, there was considerable elasticity and flexibility during the negotiations. Yet, in the end, all parties agreed to engage seriously in talks only after exhausting every other possible alternative for a 'victorious peace', as each side conceived

---

Frieden in der Frühen Neuzeit (Munich: De Druyter Oldenbourg 2010) 141–56; Michael Rohrschneider, 'Reputation als Leitfaktor in den internationalen Beziehungen der Früher Neuzeit'. *Historische Zeitschrift* 291/2 (2010), 331–52; J.H. Elliott, 'Foreign Policy and Domestic Crisis: Spain, 1598–1659', in J.H. Elliott, *Spain and Its World 1500–1700. Collected Essays* (New Haven and London: Yale University Press 1989) 114–36.

35 Luc Boltanski and Laurent Thévenot, *De la justification: les économies de la grandeur* (Paris: Gallimard 2008) 126–37.

36 Ibid.

37 For the symbolic signs that mirrored a ruler's position in the early modern inter-polity pecking order, manifested via the ceremonial refer below to Act II, Interlude II.

38 Poulios, 'Αναζητώντας την ειρήνη', 20–6.

39 This highly pertinent term for the period it describes, was coined by French historian Lucien Bély in his now classic oeuvre, *La société des princes. XVI*e*–XVIII*e *siècle* (Paris: Fayard 1999).

40 By 'internal audience', I am here referring to both the ruling élite as well as to broader segments of the population.

it.[41] Kampmann's analysis is very pertinent to our case because it perfectly captures the realities of the Sixteen Years' War as well: constant negotiations throughout the hostilities that were not consummated due to the refusal of the various players to accept terms that would compromise their honour, with a final peace settlement occurring only when the belligerents realised they had run out of alternatives for achieving their goal of 'honourable peace'. Late seventeenth–early eighteenth-century Ottoman bureaucrat-cum-historian Muṣṭafā Naʿīmā (d. 1716) precisely pointed to this when he claimed that the Ottoman officials were often sceptical during the war of signing a peace treaty, hoping instead to achieve a 'victorious peace' (*ṣulḥ-i gālibāne*) through a heroic assault.[42] We should keep in mind the concept of the 'honourable peace', or 'peace based on moderation' (*iʿtidāl üzere ṣulḥ*), as the Ottomans referred to it,[43] as its impact on the unfolding of the negotiations at the Carlowitz Congress will be paramount.

For the time being, the excessive and dishonourable for the sultan demands of the Holy League powers – as the Porte's plenipotentiaries considered them – were instrumental in causing the failure of the Vienna Congress, as is plainly illustrated by a dialogue that took place on late December 1689 between Mavrocordatos and an old acquaintance of his, Bishop Don Giuseppe Camilo, a native of the island of Chios.[44] It is reported by Cardinal Leopold Karl von Kollonitsch (d. 1707), quite an influential figure in the Imperial Court, who assumed the informal chief negotiating role on behalf of Leopold I with the Ottoman ambassador after the official congress conferences in the spring and summer of 1689 failed to procure results.[45] To gain Mavrocordatos's trust, the cardinal enlisted the services of Camilo, with whom the Porte's representative had studied at the Papal College of Saint Athanasius in Rome. The two men met at the residence of the Ottoman embassy.[46] The initial part of their conversation, as reported by Kollonitsch, is presented here in the form of direct dialogue to capture something of its vividness:

41 Kampmann, 'Ehrenvolle Friede'.

42 *Târih-i Naʿîmâ*, 46.

43 For instance, *Taʾrīḫ-i Ṣulḥ-nāme*, fol. 42a.

44 His bishopric is unknown.

45 Yılmaz, 'Ottoman Peace Attempt', 71–2.

46 ÖStA, HHStA, Türkei I, Turcica Box 155, Folder 3 (December 1689), fol. 23r, Kollonitch to (?), 12 December 1689. Mavrocordatos's old acquaintance with certain allied ambassadors or other individuals in their suite would also be crucial in facilitating informal negotiations during the Carlowitz Peace Congress. *See* extensively below, Act II, Narration Part II.

MAVROCORDATOS: I hope to bring peace back home, but it is impossible.
DON GIUSEPPE: Why?
MAVROCORDATOS: The Christians are asking for things without precedent.
DON GIUSEPPE: [Such as]?
MAVROCORDATOS: As practised in similar occasions of war and peace in the past, everybody held what he had taken from the other.[47] Nothing else. But now, [even though] we have already offered this, they are not content. I don't know what else they want. Sometimes they say they want [lands] as far as the Black Sea, other times as far as the Adriatic. And in this way, they never propose anything concrete.[48]

In his *Relazione Finale* to the Venetian Senate, the Serenissima's second ambassador at the congress, Girolamo Venier, would explain for his part, the infelicitous outcome of the negotiations by pointing to the confidence of the Habsburgs' further successes in Hungary and the belief that the troops there would be better kept busy by war rather than left idle in peace.[49] He would share the blame, though, with the Porte's delegation as well: 'Mavrocordatos, refined in sagacity, made everyone expect things that he could not [ultimately] agree to, and in the same blossoming of the negotiation, he destroyed the fruit that could have been gathered'.[50]

Finally, in late 1689, Emperor Leopold I permitted the Ottoman embassy to return home.[51] The Ottomans departed from Vienna in early February 1690 but did not travel far. When they reached the town of Komárno, in modern-day Slovakia, they were detained for several months. Thus began a period of semi-captivity that lasted nearly two more years, during which the two men desperately and incessantly pleaded with the Imperial authorities to allow

47 He refers here to the principle of *uti possidetis*, which would equally be adopted as a basis of peace during the preliminary talks of the Carlowitz Congress. For the *uti possidetis*, per extensum, refer below to Act I, Narration Part I, 54–8.

48 ÖStA, HHStA, Türkei I, Turcica Box 155, Folder 3, fol. 23^{r-v}, Kollonitch to (?), 12 December 1689.

49 Venier, *Relazione*, 337. Interestingly enough, in a letter to Cardinal Kollonitsch, Mavrocordatos voiced his fears that the Habsburg emperor may not incline to peace 'either due to the reason of state or due to the yearning for new conquests': Humurzaki, *Documente*, vol. 2, part 1, 315.

50 Venier, *Relazione*, 336.

51 Hurmuzaki, *Documente*, vol. 2, part 1, 293.

them to depart.[52] One of the possible reasons for their lengthy detention appears to have been the desire of the Habsburg side to utilise the embassy for further peace talks in the future.[53] And verily, negotiations continued, at least until the summer of 1690, with Kollonitsch and the Porte's representatives exchanging various letters, and the cardinal himself, alongside one of the Imperial secretaries, Werdenberg, visiting Komárno for direct discussions.[54] By September 1690, the Ottoman delegation was back in Vienna. However, until its ultimate departure from there in December 1692, it ceased to play a decisive role in the 'Theatre of Peace'. This was practically the end of the Failed Vienna Congress. The central stage moved now to the Ottoman Domains, where the ambassadors of England and the United Provinces endeavoured to mediate an end to the conflict.

3 War and Peace in the 1690s

The primary reason the two northern maritime powers undertook this role was to disengage the Holy Roman Emperor from his war in the east so that he could focus all his forces on what they regarded as the most crucial conflict: the one against the King of France in the west. As the Ottoman embassy was making its way to Vienna, Ottoman diplomacy scored a significant victory by establishing an informal yet de facto alliance with Louis XIV. In 1688, as the Imperial forces marched triumphantly across northern Serbia, the French launched an attack on the Imperial lands from the west, forcing the emperor to fight a two-front war. Similar to the formation of the Holy League in the east, a large coalition, including the Holy Roman Empire, England, the United Provinces and Spain, emerged to counter the French territorial ambitions in the west during the so-called Nine Years' War (1688–97).[55] From that point onwards, every

52 Ibid., 311–99; *Cerîde-i Takrirât*, 146–78.

53 Although, according to the Ottoman bureaucrat and chronicler Üsküdarī Abdullāh Efendi, the Imperials detained the two ambassadors as a form of reprisal to avenge the humiliating way Ḳara Muṣṭafā Paşa treated the Imperial internuncio Count Caprara in 1683: Üsküdarî Abdullah Efendi, Erhan Afyoncu (ed.), *Vâkı'ât-ı Rûz-Merre*, vol. 3 (Ankara: Turkish Academy of Sciences 2017) 275–6.

54 Hurmuzaki, *Documente*, vol. 2, part 1, 321–2.

55 For an overview of the conflict, *see* John A. Lynn, *The Wars of Louis XIV 1667–1714* (Abingdon/New York: Routledge 2013) 191–265; Lucien Bély, *Les relations internationales en Europe, XVII*[e]*–XVIII*[e] *siècle*, 4th edn (Paris: PUF 2007) 355–81.

development in one of the two simultaneous conflicts had significant repercussions on the other.[56]

Profiting from the war in the west, the Ottoman armies, commanded by the energetic Grand Vizier Köprülüzāde Fāżıl Muṣṭāfā Paşa (in office, 1689–91), scored some significant victories over the Habsburg forces with the recapture of the fortress of Niš on 9 July 1690 and Belgrade on 9 November of the same year.[57] These successes explain the relative 'freezing' of peace talks during this period.[58] However, this Ottoman stroke of luck was not to last long. On 20 August 1691, a massive battle took place in the vicinity of Slankamen in present-day northern Serbia. It ended with a crushing defeat for the sultan's armies. Fāżıl Muṣṭāfā Paşa lay dead on the battlefield.[59] Negotiations commenced anew and lasted until 1693, also without success.[60] One of the key figures during the final stages of the talks was Lord William Paget, who was appointed resident ambassador of the English King at the Ottoman Court in 1693 and was tasked with mediating a peace settlement.[61] However, the allied terms he brought to the Porte were deemed preposterous by the Ottoman officials. A contemporary of the events, the Ottoman chronicler and member of the scribal élite, Üsküdarī ʿAbdullāh Efendi, documented the presentation and reading of the terms in the presence of Paget and his Dutch colleagues Jacob Colyer (d. 1725)[62] and Coenraad van Heemskerck[63] at an expanded

56 Konstantinos Poulios, 'From the Palace of Ryswick to the Sultan's *Seraglio*: The Ottoman Translation and Interpretation of a Christian European Peace Treaty'. *Legatio* 6 (2022), 101–3.

57 İsmail Hakkı Uzunçarşılı, *Osmanlı Tarihi*, 8th edn, vol. 3, part 1 (Ankara: Turkish Historical Society 2011) 524–8.

58 That did not deter the Dutch and English ambassadors at the Porte from trying at the same period to convince Fāżıl Muṣṭāfā Paşa to sit at the peace table: Hora Siccama, 'De Vrede van Carlowitz', 82–99.

59 Uzunçarşılı, *Osmanlı Tarihi*, 533–5.

60 For a detailed narration of these negotiations, taking place mainly in the Ottoman camp in Belgrade and then at the sultan's court, through Dutch archival sources, *see* ibid., 99–117. Also, Colin Heywood, 'An undiplomatic Anglo-Dutch dispute at the Porte: the quarrel at Edirne between Coenraad van Heemskerck and Lord Paget (1693)', in Colin Heywood, *The Ottoman World, the Mediterranean and North Africa, 1660–1760* (London/New York: Routledge 2016) 59–94.

61 Ibid.

62 Colyer was the resident ambassador of the United Provinces at the Ottoman Court since 1686 and one of the main protagonists of the 'Carlowitz Theatre of Peace'.

63 In 1692, Van Heemskerck was appointed extraordinary ambassador of the King of England, William III, to represent him at the sultan's court and to mediate a peace settlement between the Ottomans and the Christian allies. After abortive first talks with the Ottoman officials in Belgrade, he was taken to Edirne, the seat of the sultan's government, and kept there in semi-captivity until the arrival of Paget: Heywood, 'An Anglo-Dutch dispute'.

session of the Ottoman Imperial Council on 24 March 1693.[64] According to him, the terms included, among other 'unimaginable' demands, the surrender of the Danubian Principalities, Wallachia and Moldavia, to the Polish Lithuanian Commonwealth, based on the alleged historical rights of the latter over the former, and even the subordination of the Greek Orthodox Patriarchate to Rome![65] In exasperation, the Ottoman chronicler commented that 'the pride of the Infidels reached its summit', while he described their proposals as 'haughty' (*mağrûrâne*) and 'cosmocratorical' (*sâhib-kırânîye*).[66] And thus, the Englishman's initial mediation attempt ended miserably.

Meanwhile, in 1695, a new sultan ascended to the Ottoman throne. Muṣṭafā, the second of his name (r. 1695–1703), young and dynamic, wanted, like his late uncle Süleymān II, to restore the military fortunes of his empire by leading his troops into battle personally. Although not spectacular, his first two campaigns against the Imperials, in 1695 and 1696, were crowned with relative success.[67] Combined with the recapturing from the Venetians of the Island of Chios in 1695, and despite the significant loss of Azov to the Muscovites in 1696, the Ottoman fortunes seemed to turn felicitous again. With the wind in her sails, the Porte was no longer inclined to peace talks on her enemies' terms. She would instead impose her own with the force of arms. Writing to the Bohemian Chancellor Count Franz Urlich von Kinsky (d. 1699),[68] from the Ottoman capital on 22 September 1697, Paget succinctly captured the prevailing spirit among the chief dignitaries of the 'Exalted State' in the following manner: 'Presently, it is highly certain that they don't want to see reason at all [...] a decisive [military] encounter, well-handled [from your part], from which they could experience [the maximum] of blows and inconveniences, would dispose them far better towards a peace treaty'.[69]

64 Paget sustained, though, that those were terms that 'I had not spoke of, nor had been mentioned to mee'. It rather seems that they were the ones presented to the Ottomans earlier by Van Heemskerck in Belgrade: Ibid., 85.

65 Üsküdarî 'Abdullāh Efendi, Mahmut Ak (ed.), *Vâkı'ât-ı Rûz-Merre*, vol. 4 (Ankara: Turkish Academy of Sciences 2017) 270–1.

66 Ibid., 271–2. Heywood sustains that the whole occasion was 'a carefully planned propaganda exercise' by the grand vizier in order to arouse the feelings of the Ottoman dignitaries against peace: Heywood, 'An Anglo-Dutch dispute', 85. If that was indeed his aim, he totally succeeded, as Üsküdarī's comments reveal.

67 Uzunçarşılı, *Osmanlı Tarihi*, 556–63.

68 Yet another of our principal actors. He was Chancellor of Bohemia from 1683 and one of the most influential Imperial ministers during the late 1680s and until his death in 1699, just two months after the end of the Carlowitz Congress.

69 ÖStA, HHStA, Türkei I, Turcica Box 164, Folder 5 (1697), fol. 44^{r-v}, Paget to Kinsky, 12/22 September 1697.

He could well have been a prophet. Eleven days before this letter was composed, on 11 September 1697, the Ottoman armies, with the sultan at their head, were annihilated by the Imperial troops led by Prince Eugene of Savoy in the battle of Zenta in modern-day northern Serbia.[70] The grand vizier and most of the commanders perished on the field; the sultan barely escaped, and his and the army's treasury, along with the whole Ottoman camp, fell into the hands of the Habsburgs.[71] It was a disaster proportionate only to the defeat at Vienna in 1683. It is at this precise moment that the Carlowitz Peace Congress's 'Theatre of Peace' commences. The stage is set. The main actors have already taken their positions on it. The curtains rise, and the play begins.

---

70 Parvev, *Habsburgs and Ottomans*, 126–7; Petritsch, 'Rijswijk und Karlowitz', 294–96.

71 Uzunçarşılı, *Osmanlı Tarihi*, 566–70.

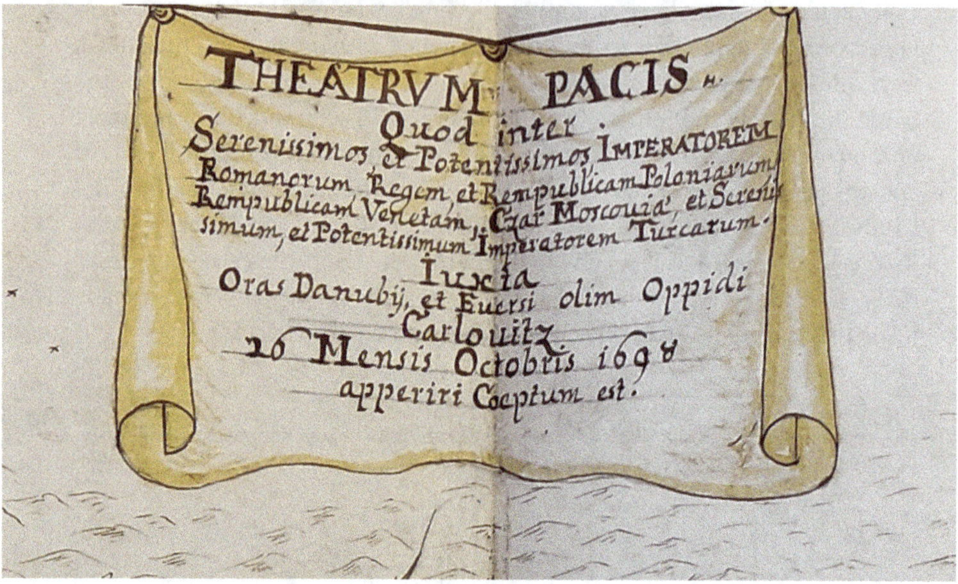

FIGURE 2 Detail of a Venetian map portraying the geography and spatial arrangement of the Carlowitz Congress venue

BNM, MS.IT VII 381 (7782), C. [1]R. SU CONCESSIONE DEL MINISTERO DELLA CULTURA – BIBLIOTECA NAZIONALE MARCIANA. DIVIETO DI RIPRODUZIONE

ACT I

The Preliminaries (Late December 1697–Early October 1698)

Even in political negotiations, the immature fruits are ripened only at the appropriate time, at favourable conjectures of interests and accidents.

> FEDERICO CORNER, Venetian Ambassador at the Imperial Court, *Relazione Finale*, 1690

Dramatis Personae

The Protagonists

ALEXANDROS MAVROCORDATOS: Ottoman Grand Gragoman (Interpreter).
ʿAMCAZĀDE KÖPRÜLÜ ḤÜSEYİN PAŞA: Ottoman Grand Vizier.
AUGUST II: King of Poland and Elector of Saxony.
CARLO RUZZINI: Resident ambassador of the Republic of Venice at the Imperial Court.
COUNT FRANZ URLICH VON KINSKY: High Chancellor of Bohemia and influential Imperial minister.
EMETÜLLĀH RĀBİʿA GÜLNŪŞ SULṬĀN: Muṣṭafā II's mother.
FEYZÜLLĀH EFENDİ: Head of the Ottoman religious-juridical establishment (*Şeyhü'l-islām*) and the most trusted advisor of Muṣṭafā II.
JACOB COLYER: Resident ambassador of the United Provinces at the Ottoman Court.
LEOPOLD I: Holy Roman Emperor.
LORD WILLIAM PAGET: Resident ambassador of the English King at the Ottoman Court.
MUṢṬAFĀ II: Ottoman Sultan.
PETER I (THE GREAT): Tsar of Muscovy.
PHILIPP GEORG SCHREYER (or the 'Hermes of Carlowitz'): Lord Paget's secretary.
RĀMĪ MEḤMED: Head of the Ottoman chancery (*Re'isü'l-küttāb*).
SELĪM I GİRAY: Crimean Khan.

Second Roles

CHRISTOPH DIETRICH BOSE: August II's Saxon envoy in spring 1698 to England and the United Provinces.
JAN GOMOLINSKI: Extraordinary envoy of the Polish King and the Commonwealth at the Imperial Court (late July–August 1689).
PROKOPII BOGDANOVICH VOZNITSYN: One of the three chief members of Peter I's 'Great Embassy' (1697–1698) and great and plenipotentiary ambassador of Muscovy at the Carlowitz Congress.
(?) SEDLNITZKY: Resident Imperial ambassador at the Polish Court.

 | DOI:10.1163/9789004458499_004

One could reasonably suggest that the 'Theatre of Peace' begins to unfold upon the arrival of the plenipotentiaries in the commonly agreed 'stage' and the formal opening of the congress. Yet, for the early modern peacemaking process to reach this level, it was essential to pass through an initial phase, which was sometimes much lengthier but carried perhaps even greater significance than the subsequent Acts of the 'play'. During this phase, the preliminaries, the opposing parties usually made known to the other side their intentions to bring an end to the fight by a peaceful reconciliation; accepted the mediation [if offered] of a third power(s); put forward their general peace-terms; established the foundation of the future peace (upon which commonly accepted general principle(s) peace was to be made); and came to an agreement on the venue and the format of the peace-congress.[1]

That the preliminaries were considered by the contemporaries an essential part of the peacemaking process is attested by the prominent place they occupy in many of the different post-congress ambassadorial relations. Thus, the chief Ottoman ambassador Rāmī Meḥmed dedicated nearly half of his account to them and only the other half to narrating the negotiations at the congress venue.[2] The preliminaries could last for several months, even for whole years. For instance, those of the Westphalian Peace Congress took seven years, whereas those of the Congress of Ryswick dragged on for nearly four (1694–7).[3] In the Carlowitz case, their duration was much smaller in comparison, eleven months, more or less (late December 1697–early October 1698) but, still, far longer than the main phase of the congress (October 1698–early February 1699).

1 Brunert and Oetzel, 'Verhandlungstechniken', 456–8.

2 *Ta'rīḫ-i ṣulḥ-nāme*, fol. 2^{a}–70^{b}.

3 Konrad Repgen, 'Friedensvermittlung und Friedensvermittler beim Westfälischen Frieden', in Franz Bosbach and Christoph Kampmann (eds.), *Dreissigjähriger Krieg und Westfälischer Friede: Studien und Quellen*, 3rd edn. (Paderborn: Ferdinand Schöningh 2015) 939–66, 940; Lucien Bély, 'Négocier la Paix, de Westphalie au Temps des Révolutions', in Franck Petiteville et al. (eds.), *Négociations Internationales* (Paris: Presses de Sciences Po 2013) 179.

Narration Part I: Embarking on the Road to Peace

> The beginnings of important negotiations are surely small in weight, yet they carry a great amount of virtue.[1]
>
> ALEXANDROS MAVROCORDATOS to the Transylvanian Prince Mihály Apafi, 1685

∴

1 The First Steps

By early October 1697, the news of the disaster at Zenta reached the Ottoman capital. Writing on the 19th, Lord Paget would commend that 'it is the most considerable and the most total [victory] that was won against them [the Ottomans] during this century [...]'. And he added, 'When the sultan will arrive in Adrianople, he is [...] expected [to be there] in eight days, we will see what effect this disgrace had upon these stiff and high-elevated minds'.[2] Indeed, the Zenta debacle seems to have stricken a considerable psychological blow to the sultan as much as to the Ottoman public opinion.[3] Upon his arrival at the then de facto Ottoman seat of government, Adrianople (Edirne), the sultan, according to Dimitrie Cantemir,

> being unrecognised, travestied, was frequenting assemblages of ordinary people, listening to numerous voices both from the citizens and from the army [saying]: 'It's impossible for the Ottomans to obtain victory against the Germans'. [...] 'God has publicly attested to be on the side of the Infidels, making his decision in the matter clear to us by his decree with sufficient evidence. Hence, all the torrents of so much Muslim blood that had been shed will be shed in vain if must simultaneously fight with both God and men'.[4]

---

1 Quoted in Poulios, 'Αναζητώντας την ειρήνη', 16.

2 ÖStA, HHStA, Türkei I, Turcica Box 164, Folder 5 (1697), fol. 53^{r}, Extrait d'une lettre de my Lord Paget dattée du 19 Octob. S.V. de Pera.

3 For the radical change in the sultan's psychology after Zenta, *see* the still pioneering article of Abou-El-Haj, 'The Narcissism of Mustafa II (1695–1703): A Psychohistorical Study'. *Studia Islamica* 40 (1974), 115–31.

4 Cantemir, *Incrementorum et Decrementorum*, 270.

 | DOI:10.1163/9789004458499_005

Despite this general climate of pessimism, the official Ottoman narrative denied that there was even the slightest thought for peace during this 'dark hour'. As Defterdār Sarı Meḥmed Paşa claims in his chronicle, when the new grand vizier, ʿAmcazāde Köprülü Ḥüseyin Paşa (d. 1702), took office after the defeat, 'in no way did he want to make peace with the Infidels' but instead he immediately embarked on a hectic preparation of the Ottoman forces for revenge.[5] Yet, it seems highly plausible that the new vizier had already made up his mind on the course he was about to take, and that course would not lead to a continuation of the war.[6] 'As the Turkish Monarchy was witnessing such a destruction of its armies', narrates an early eighteenth-century Greek chronicler, 'it started deliberating on what is [henceforth] to be done. The grand vizier summoned the Chief Interpreter Alexandros and asked him what they should do now. And [the latter] replied that peace is to be made'.[7]

ʿAmcazāde wanted to negotiate, but not from a position of weakness. The empire's enemies would first have to see that the Ottoman war machinery did not collapse but had, on the contrary, such huge capacities to quickly make up for the losses suffered. Appearing solid and resilient would have increased the Ottoman bargaining position and preserved the empire's reputation and honour. Still, if the Grand Dragoman was counselling the vizier for peace, this was not only based on a realistic assessment of the Ottoman situation but also on a prompt reading of essential developments occurring in the western half of Europe. Developments which once again revealed the interconnectedness of events on a large geographical scale, constantly manifesting themselves since the beginning of the Sixteen Years' War.[8] On 30 September 1697, peace was finally signed between the German Emperor and the French King at Ryswick.[9]

---

5 Defterdar, *Zübde-i Vekayiât*, 639. One encounters a similar narrative in *Taʾrīḫ-i ṣulḥ-nāme*, fol. 16a–b.

6 He would later claim to the English and Dutch mediators that he opted for peace 'from the beginning of my viziership' (*vezāretimiñ ibtidāsından*): Ibid., fol. 68a.

7 Kaisarios Dapondes, 'Χρονογράφος', in Konstantinos Sathas (ed.), *Μεσαιωνική Βιβλιοθήκη*, vol. 3 (Venice: Chronos Publishing House 1872) 58–9.

8 Mavrocordatos was fully aware of the political constellation in Western Europe: Cantemir, *Incrementorum et Decrementorum*, 271. According to the Venetian plenipotentiary at the Carlowitz Congress, Carlo Ruzzini, during the negotiations, the Ottoman ambassador remained eager to receive news on the health of the Spanish king: 'Relazione del Congresso de Carloviz e dell' Ambasciata di Vienna di Sr. Carlo Ruzini Cavr.' in *Fontes Rerum Austriacarum*, 371 (hereafter Ruzzini, *Relazione*). This is corroborated by Count Ferdinando Marsigli, member of the Imperial delegation in the congress: ÖStA, HHStA, Türkei I, Turcica Box 167, Folder 2 (October 1698, 2nd half), fol. 97v, Marsigli to Kinsky, 22 October 1698.

9 Hitherto, there is only one collective volume dedicated to the Congress of Ryswick: Heinz Duchhardt et al (eds.), *Der Friede von Rijwick 1697* (Mainz: Philipp von Zabern 1998).

The Imperial government could thus feel free to concentrate all its forces on the eastern front against the Ottomans, who suddenly found themselves deprived of the 'informal' military alliance they had with the French.[10] And yet, the signing of peace in the West also brought closer the prospects of an end to the war in the East.

The Peace of Ryswick, which some late-seventeenth-century contemporaries labelled as a mere truce,[11] was undermined from the outset since it left unresolved the main point of contention between Louis XIV and the Habsburgs: the question of the Spanish succession. Given the unstable health of the Spanish King Carlos II, conflict could recommence at any moment. Leopold and his ministers, as soon as the drums of war felt silent in the West, desired that the same would happen in the East in order to have a chance to regroup and be ready for the next round of confrontation with France without the nuissance of a war on two fronts.[12] This strategy coincided with the aspirations of the main allies of the Holy Roman Emperor against the 'Sun King', William III of England and the United Provinces. Bearing that in mind, it comes as no surprise that in a letter to Paget, dated 20 November 1698, Count Kinsky, after remarking that it would take years for the Ottomans to redress the losses in personnel suffered at Zenta, instructed the Englishman that, 'if they mention [peace] Your Lordship may hear them with the hope of good success if they form their propositions in the manner that all the previous treaties with us were concluded'.[13]

As the resident Dutch ambassador at the Porte, Jacob Colyer, reported, news of the events taking place at Ryswick reached the Ottoman capital in early

10 Jean Bérenger, 'La politique ottomane de la France de Vienne à Carlowitz (1683–1699)', in Czamanskiej and Szulca, *Traktaty Karlowickie*, 45–8.

11 'Avant-Propos'. *Mercure Historique et Politique*, vol. 26 (January-June 1699). For a synopsis of the principal terms of the various bilateral treaties signed at Ryswick, *see* Bély, *Les relations internationales*, 371–2.

12 *Narratio*, fol. 3^r. A short note concerning the author of this important source. The description of the manuscript vaguely identifies him as one of Ruzzini's secretaries. If that is correct, we have two possible candidates for its authorship: The secretary of the Venetian embassy, Gian Battista Nicolosi and the ambassador's personal secretary, Giran Alberto Colombo. Given this uncertainty, I will refer to its composer throughout the book as the Anonymous Venetian. Lastly, it should be mentioned that this unique account of the negotiations, rich in engrossing details usually left unattended by other sources (especially on material culture), has also been translated into German by Almut Bues, 'Ein venezianischer Bericht zu den Friedensverhandlungen von Karlowitz 1698/99'. *Münchner Zeitschrift für Balkankunde* 10/11 (1996), 163–243.

13 ÖStA, HHStA, Türkei I, Turcica Box 164, Folder 5 (1697), fol. 57^v–58^r, Kinsky to Paget, 20 November 1697.

December 'from all sides' (*de tous côtez*).[14] The Ottoman government was not only orally informed of the agreement between the emperor and France but also acquired a printed copy of it.[15] It was probably from this exact printed copy that an Ottoman translation of the peace articles was inserted by the contemporary Ottoman chronicler and palace official, Silāḥdār Fındıklılı Meḥmed Aġa, in his chronicle entitled, *Nuṣretnāme*, 'The Book of Victory'. This inclusion, unprecedented until that time in Ottoman historiography, clearly illustrates the increased intertwining of political and military developments across the European continent and its full appreciation by members of the Ottoman élite.[16]

On the same day the copy of the articles of the Peace of Ryswick reached the Porte, a meeting of the *Dīvān-ı Hümāyūn* (the Imperial Council) took place,

> in which it was discussed if it would be better [for them] to conclude a truce on reasonable conditions as well; but those present in the council could not agree to the acceptance and the conditions of such a truce because, if petitioning it, it would run to a great extent contrary to the respect of their empire and the authority of the Grand Seigneur. Thus, in the end, it was decided to pursue the war with all imaginable rigour until a better conjuncture presents itself or [until such time as] novel propositions would be offered from the part of His Majesty of Great Britain and the States General as mediators, which would be in accord with their law and the respect of their empire.[17]

And as Colyer further recounted,

> this last point was confided to me by a confidant friend, a sheikh highly esteemed and favoured by the mufti [...], and the same friend added to me that if the conditions for a truce of 20[10?] years between the Porte and the Roman Emperor and his allies based on the *uti possidetis* had not been altered, he would be ready to solicit it, although the possession of the Morea would pose great obstacles to it.[18]

14 TNA, SP 97–20, fol. 389ᵛ, Colyer to Van Heemskerck, 27 December 1697.
15 Ibid.
16 For this translation and its significance, *see* Poulios, 'From the Palace of Ryswick'.
17 TNA, SP 97–20, fol. 389ᵛ, Colyer to Van Heemskerck, 27 December 1697.
18 Ibid., fol. 390ʳ.

Various crucial points arise from this reporting of events by the Dutch ambassador. First, it becomes evident that the principal Ottoman officials, despite their rhetoric for a continuation of the war, had already decided, in fact, to explore the possibility of peace. As noted above, such deliberation preceded the arrival of news of the signing of peace in the west. However, the latter still provided further support for ʿAmcazāde's decisions and perhaps undermined the designs of elements in the Ottoman government who could have counted on a continuation of French support.[19] Second, the decision to ask for peace becomes a matter of honour and reputation. In the Prelude, we briefly touched upon the issue of how the quest for an honourable peace prolonged the war and how the concepts of honour and reputation permitted the early modern 'Society of Princes'. Such perceptions would have a direct impact on the decision-making process. And although authors such as Cantemir or other Christian European observers like Paget attributed such a stance to Ottoman 'superstition' or 'superbness', they failed (perhaps purposely) to acknowledge that this was a common trait of their era.[20] As much as the Habsburg emperor wanted peace, nobody could expect him to ask it from the Ottoman side.

As Mavrocordatos could discern the Habsburg desire for peace, the same seemed to have happened with Paget and the Ottoman Court. From the Ottoman capital, Constantinople (İstanbul), Paget appeared to have grasped that after the defeat at Zenta, there could be a change in attitudes inside the sultan's government.[21] He asked permission from the Ottoman officials to travel to Adrianople ostensibly to congratulate the new vizier on his appointment and present some grievances regarding the affair of an English ship kept by the Ottoman authorities in Smyrna.[22] As for Colyer – the latter sending his interpreter Theyls to the Ottoman Porte to congratulate ʿAmcazāde – his fellow mediator-companion since 1693, he promised him 'en foi de gentilhomme' to

19 Those same elements would later try again to explore the possibility of French assistance, but this time via a peace mediation. *See* below.

20 Croxton, *Westphalia*, 17. Similar concerns with peace petitioning and third-party solutions to resolve the deadlock can be observed during the Ottoman-Venetian negotiations of 1573, which concluded the Cyprus War (1570–3): Güneş Işıksel, 'Barbaro's Glass Ball and Soḳollu Meḥmed's Finesse Ottoman–Venetian Peace in 1573'. *Librosdelacorte.es* 26 (2023), 295–311.

21 ÖStA, HHStA, Türkei I, Turcica Box 164, Folder 5 (1697), fol. 60r, Paget to Kinsky, 29 December 1697 (J.C.).

22 *Taʾrīḫ-i ṣulḥ-nāme*, fol. 16b; Hora Siccama, 'De Vrede van Carlowitz', 132. Heywood claims that Paget received an order from the grand vizier 'to proceed immediately to Edirne for consultations': Colin Heywood, '"This Great Work": Lord Paget and the Processes of English Mediating Diplomacy in the Latter Stages of the Sacra Lega War, 1697–1698', in Heywood and Parvev, *The Treaties of Carlowitz*, 43.

keep him informed of everything.[23] En route to the Ottoman seat of government, Paget received, just in time, the letter from Kinsky, instructing him to explore the Ottoman intentions.[24] That could have further boosted the ambassador's optimism. The constellation of events somehow fully vindicated his moves. He arrived at the Porte at precisely the right time when the Ottoman government was waiting for the mediators to make their move.

Upon reaching Adrianople, Paget was visited by Mavrocordatos, who, together with presents from the vizier, brought the Englishman a 'strange' question. Was he the one, the vizier asked, that had earlier brought terms for peace? As silly as this question appeared to Paget – a view that present-day historians tend to reproduce[25] – it was actually a very subtle and clever way to explore Paget's intentions and insinuate to him that if he had come to propose something, the Porte was willing to listen. Mavrocordatos didn't fail to point this out to Paget, suggesting, supposedly on his own initiative, that it might not have been inappropriate for the ambassador to remind the vizier of these earlier peace initiatives of his.[26]

Paget did precisely that. In his audience, he declared that 'being his king also a friend of the German side' as much as of the Ottoman Porte, he thinks that 'it is not appropriate to reduce the subjects to misery and to cause so many men from both sides to perish with the continuation of the war'. He had offered his mediation before, and was still waiting for an answer.[27] These were normative claims of *arguing* or 'common superior principles' stemming from the vocabulary of the late seventeenth-century universal peace culture.[28] It is in this way that Paget presented his conversation with the vizier to Count Kinsky and

23 Hora Siccama, 'De Vrede van Carlowitz', 132.

24 Basil C. Gounaris, "'The Turks are Like Women; quidquid volunt, valde volunt.' Alexandros Mavrocordatos, William Paget, and the Preliminaries of the Karlowitz Treaty (1697/98)". *Südost-Forschungen* 71 (2012), 5.

25 Ibid.; Heywood, "'This Great Work'", 43.

26 Ibid.

27 *Ta'rīḫ-i ṣulḥ-nāme*, fol. 16b; ÖStA, HHStA, Türkei I, Turcica Box 164, Folder 5 (1697), fol. 60r, Paget to Kinsky, 29 December 1697 (J.C.).

28 Sociologists define *arguing* as the invocation of shared normative concepts and ideas among all participants in a negotiation, aimed at enhancing mutual understanding. Luc Boltanski and Laurent Thévenot refer to these shared ideas as 'common superior principles': Boltanski and Thévenot, *De la justification*, 43, 60–61. In contrast, bargaining involves 'negotiating a compromise based on the interests of the participants', where 'private motives and exit options' play a central role: Matthias Köhler, 'Argumentieren und Verhandeln auf dem Kongress von Nimwegen', in Arndt Brendecke (ed.), *Praktiken der Frühen Neuzeit. Akteure-Handlungen-Artefakte* (Cologne/Weimar/Vienna: Böhlau 2015) 524–5. As we shall see in the following Acts, however, this distinction is not always clear-cut, and negotiators often combined both tactics in their discourse.

even to his superiors.[29] Yet the Ottoman version of his oration continues quite differently, with Paget actually counselling the Ottoman side.

According to the ambassador, the English King suggested to the Ottomans that peace was needed for the subjects and the soldiers to rest for a while (*bir miḳdār rāḥat olurlar*). After the pause, war could be again at hand (*yine sefer etmek ellerindedir*).[30] Peace was highly recommendable for the Ottoman side in the present circumstances. Firstly, because of the treaty signed that year between the 'Christian Kings' (*mülūk-i Naṣārā*), the German Emperor would be able to disengage and transfer from the western to the eastern front 40.000 troops. Secondly, with such an increase in their forces, the Imperials would try to capture the fortress of Ṭemeşvar (Timişoara) to gain control of the Danube and thus drive the Ottomans out of Hungary completely. And thirdly, because after that, they would try to cut off Belgrade from its hinterland in order to force it to surrender.[31]

After this exposé of concrete arguments, Paget requested that if an Ottoman answer was to be delivered to him, it had to be given in writing to act as proof of the Porte's 'good intentions'.[32] The vizier replied that such difficult decisions required time for deliberation.[33] What followed was a series of conferences between Mavrocordatos and Paget in which the former, applying a combined negotiation strategy of *arguing* and *bargaining*, tried to induce from the ambassador what were the demands of the other side and to solicit his support for the Porte's positions, while the latter attempted to mitigate some of the Ottoman claims and to gain the Ottomans' confidence by constantly switching 'roles' between a *ministre public* and an *honnête homme*.

According to early modern treatises on the 'ideal ambassador', the latter possessed two 'selves' or was supposed to perform two roles. On the one hand, that of *ministre public*, a mirror image of his sovereign, with the task to promote his interests at a foreign court or a peace congress and follow his instructions to the letter. On the other hand, that of *honnête homme*, a member of the courtly society with his own particular aims and cliental networks, as well as with a specific ethical code of behaviour towards other *honnêtes hommes*. Hence,

---

29 Paget to Kinsky, 29 December 1697, fol. 60^{r-v}; TNA, SP 97/21, fol. 5^{r}, Paget to Shrewsbury, 23 January 1697 (1698) (J.C.).

30 *Ta'rīḫ-i ṣulḥ-nāme*, fol. 16^{b}. It is quite interesting to note that Paget used here an argument also found in contemporary Ottoman historical sources: *Târih-i Na'îmâ*, 45. Perhaps – but one cannot be absolutely certain – these could have been Mavrocordatos's words, who was interpreting Paget and not the ambassador's.

31 *Ta'rīḫ-i ṣulḥ-nāme*, fol. 17^{b}–18^{a}.

32 Ibid., 18^{a-b}; TNA, SP 97/21, fol. 5^{r-v}, Paget to Shrewsbury, 23 January 1697 (1698) (J.C.).

33 Ibid.

the main challenge for an ambassador was to keep these two roles, these two 'selves' of his, in balance. In practice, this multiplicity of roles provided the ambassador/negotiator with a considerable space of manoeuvre, as he could switch roles according to the circumstances, ultimately facilitating the negotiation process.[34] For instance, Mavrocordatos, as we remarked above, advised Paget, as *honnête homme*, not as *ministre public*, to remind the vizier about the former peace overtures. The Ottoman Chief Interpreter adopted this seemingly independent move to win Paget's confidence and facilitate peacemaking. As we shall see, Paget adopted the same strategy vice-versa.

From the outset, it was evident that the future of Transylvania would be a thorny problem. This autonomous principality, tributary to the Ottomans since the late sixteenth century, was conquered – or liberated, according to the perspective – by Habsburg forces in the late 1680s and early 1690s.[35] The Ottomans were not reconciled to that loss. The strategic importance of the principality as a 'buffer zone' between the Ottoman Domains – as well as the other, much more significant tributaries of the Porte, Wallachia, and Moldavia – and both the Habsburg dominions and the Polish-Lithuanian Commonwealth was too great to be overlooked. Not to say anything of the loss of prestige.[36] Already during the 1689–90 Failed Vienna Peace Congress, the Ottoman side had requested the return of Transylvania to its antebellum status.[37] The Imperial side had then vehemently opposed such a request by stating that the principality belonged to the emperor by ancestral right, as King of Hungary, and by the right of conquest.[38]

Paget had already warned Ḥüseyin Paşa during his first audience against bringing up this issue again by reminding him that in past negotiations, 'when the issue of Transylvania came into discussion, the emperor's minister Count

34 For this issue, *see* extensively, Köhler, *Strategie und Symbolik*, 159–76, 293–7.

35 From the extensive bibliography on the early modern Principality of Transylvania, notable works include: Gerald Volkmer, *Siebenbürgen zwischen Habsburgermonarchie und Osmanischem Reich. Völkerrechtliche Stellung und Völkerrechtspraxis eines ostmitteleuropäischen Fürstentums 1541–1699* (Munich: De Gruyter Oldenborg 2015); István Keul, *Early Modern Religious Communities in East-Central Europe: Ethnic Diversity, Denominational Plurality, and Corporate Politics in the Principality of Transylvania (1526–1691)* (Leiden/Boston: Brill 2009).

36 I extend my sincere thanks to Gábor Kármán for his valuable suggestions regarding the importance of Transylvania to the Ottomans. He also expressed the opinion that the loss of the tribute paid by the Principality – 40,000 florins (80,000 thalers) since 1658 – was not of minor significance.

37 *Cerîde-i Takrirât*, 71, 75–76.

38 Ibid., 56, 71.

Kinsky replied that, 'our emperor can forfeit himself, but not Transylvania'.[39] The Porte, though, was still not ready to do away with the principality. Looking into Mavrocordatos's argumentation on this issue, as presented by Paget, it becomes clear that the Ottoman side was trying to win the Englishman's support by recycling the same arguments already voiced by its ambassadors ten years before in Vienna.[40] The further arguments (or *arguing*) about the 'ancient law' of the country and its religious freedoms may well have been orchestrated to strike a sensitive chord with Paget as an Englishman – we should remember here the 'Glorious Revolution' – and a Protestant. The Ottomans didn't want Transylvania for themselves but to save her from the absolutist policies and the Counter-Reformation 'storm' that was to be brought by Leopold I and his government.[41]

As oxymoron as it may seem to historians working with early modern Western European history, the self-portrayal of the Ottomans as supporters of 'ancient laws' and religious freedoms against 'absolutist policies' of neighbouring Christian polities was a constant justification for Ottoman involvement in central and eastern Europe during the second half of the seventeenth century.[42] Besides, one of the main causes of the Sixteen Years' War was the Ottoman support for the Calvinist ruler of 'Upper Hungary', Imre Thököly, and the creation in 1682 of a new protestant Ottoman vassal state, that of Orṭa Macar (Middle Hungary), with Thököly as its 'king'.[43]

Nonetheless, Mavrocordato's effort to win over Paget came to no avail.[44] It was also evident that although the Porte was willing to accept the principle of *uti possidetis* – or *ʿalā ḥālihi* in Ottoman Turkish – as a basis for the treaty, he demanded some compensation because, as the grand vizier would remind

39 *Taʾrīḫ-i ṣulḥ-nāme*, fol. 17[a].

40 *Cerîde-i Takrirât*, 76.

41 TNA, SP 97/21, fol. 6[r], Paget to Shrewsbury, 23 January 1697 (1698) (J.C.).

42 *Taʾrīḫ-i ṣulḥ-nāme*, fol. 2[b]; Victor Ostapchuk, 'Cossack Ukraine In and Out of Ottoman Orbit, 1648–1681', in Gábor Kármán and Lovro Kunčević (eds.), *The European Tributary States of the Ottoman Empire in the Sixteenth and Seventeenth Centuries* (Leiden/Boston: Brill 2013), 123–52; Dariusz Kolodziejczyk, 'The Orthodox Exarchate of Little Rus': A few remarks on the Ottoman confessional policy in the late seventeenth century'. *Archivum Ottomanicum* 33 (2016), 247–55; idem, 'Native Nobilities and Foreign Absolutism: a Polish-Ottoman case'. *Studia Caroliensia* 3–4 (2004), 303–8.

43 Gábor Kármán, 'King Thököly in Chains: The Fall of the Ottoman Tributary State of Upper Hungary', in Gábor Kármán (ed.), *Tributaries and Peripheries of the Ottoman Empire* (Leiden/Boston: Brill 2020) 264–89.

44 Paget to Shrewsbury, 23 January 1697 (1698) (J.C.), fol. 5[v].

Paget on a later meeting between them, 'a truce/armistice (*terk-i cidāl*)[45] [has its] advantages, but it should not benefit only the German side. It has to be equally beneficial for the Exalted State so that all will praise this work'.[46] This interpretation of the *uti possidetis* by the Ottoman side would create many problems in the peacemaking process, as we shall encounter later on.

2 A Mini Interlude: the Concept of *Uti Possidetis*

At this point, a small intermission from the narration is necessary in order to examine more closely the principle of *uti possidetis*, a term which dominated the discourse of the various parties throughout the preliminary phase of the peace negotiations and, as we shall see, formed, in the end, the foundation of the eventual peace treaties. As its meaning denotes, *uti possidetis* has mostly to do with the possession of territory, the principal issue of inter-polity negotiations. It wasn't the first time it appeared as a proposed basis for a peace agreement to end the Sixteen Years' War. It was put forward by the Ottoman side in 1689–90 during the negotiations in Vienna and again in 1693 by the Christian allies via Paget in his first attempt as a mediator to end the conflict.[47]

As with the concept of mediation, which we shall later encounter, *uti possidetis* (at least in its Christian, not Ottoman version) originated in the realm of private law. In ancient Rome, its purpose was to guarantee the ownership of one's immovable property against outside interference.[48] From this context of interpersonal litigation, it was transferred to the inter-polity level, where it affirmed, by treaty, the territorial status quo resulting from the war.[49]

---

45 As will be discussed in detail in Act IV, 'At the Negotiating Table III', the Carlowitz participants did not clearly differentiate between a 'truce' and an 'armistice'. Therefore, I chose to employ both terms together and to translate the Ottoman term *terk-i cidāl*, the Russian *peremir'e*, and the German *Stillstand* as truce/armistice.

46 *Ta'rīḫ-i Ṣulḥ-nāme*, fol. 18^{a-b}.

47 *Ceride-i Takrirât*, 63–4, 74; For the *uti possidetis* as a basis for the treaty negotiations in 1693, *see Ta'rīḫ-i ṣulḥ-nāme*, fol. 19^{b}.

48 Giuseppe Nessi, 'Uti possidetis Doctrine', in Rüdiger Wulfrum (ed.), MPEPIL, vol.10 (Oxford: Oxford University Press 2018).

49 Lesaffer, 'Lore and Laws of Peacemaking', 53; Despite the fact that one can encounter numerous studies on the *uti possidetis* in contemporary International Law – a basic search on the Internet can attest that – there is no specific work centring on its meaning and application in the early modern peace treaties but only cursory and rather vague references. *See*, for instance, Lesaffer, ibid., and Izidor Janžekovič, 'The Balance of Power from the Thirty Years' War and the Peace of Westphalia (1648) to the War of the Spanish Succession and the Peace of Utrecht'. *History of European Ideas* (2022), 4.

Ironically, in that sense, it strongly differed from the Roman Law *uti possidetis*, which safeguarded a property acquired *nec vi, nec clam, nec praecario* (not by force, stealth, or license).[50]

And yet, despite the Roman origins of this specific term, the notion of agreeing to a peace settlement based on a territorial status quo created by the war was not confined to a particular legal tradition but transcended cultural barriers as a practice. By the late seventeenth century, there were various expressions in Ottoman Turkish to name that very concept. For instance: *herkesin elinde bulunan yerlerin bulunduğu üzere olmağla, tarafeyn bulunduğu hâl üzere kala, hâli üzerine* etc.[51] It was the result of the extended usage of the principle in multiple treaties signed between the sultan and its Christian neighbours.[52] In respect to terms, the Ottomans appear more pluralistic than their contemporary Christians. Still, by the time of the Carlowitz peace negotiations, a new term was coined and gained preeminence over all the others, that of *ʿalā ḥālihi*.[53] It is interesting to point out that this is a purely Arabic expression in contrast to previous expressions, which were Turkish or a mixture of Arabic and Turkish.[54] It might be only a tentative hypothesis, but it is intriguing to see in the adoption of *ʿalā ḥālihi* an attempt by the Ottoman chancery to transform what was until then a customary practice into a 'law' by creating an Arabic term which conveyed an aura of Islamic legal authority, in the same way as the Latin term *uti possidetis* convened a Roman one in the western Christian European context.[55]

Such a hypothesis is further strengthened if one pays attention to how the different sides justify the adoption of the principle as a basis for the territorial

50 Nessi, 'Uti possidetis'.

51 Cerîde-i Takrirât, 63–6.

52 The treaty between the sultan and the Habsburg emperor at Vasvar in 1664 or the treaty of 1669 between the Ottomans and Venice, to name but a few: Özgür Kolçak, 'Vasvar Antlaşması', in TDVİA, vol. 42 (Istanbul: Turkish Religious Foundation 2012) 560–2; *Taʾrīḫ-i Ṣulḥ-nāme*, fol. 40^{b}–41^{b}.

53 One does not encounter the term in Zülfikār's 'Final Relation' of his embassy in Vienna (1688–92), so it could be guessed that the term was coined somewhere between 1692 and 1698.

54 Although in Rāmī Meḥmed's account, one could still find the expressions in Turkish. For instance, *Taʾrīḫ-i ṣulḥ-nāme*, fol. 40^{a}.

55 It is perhaps no coincidence that, although *uti possidetis* was customarily accepted as a basis for territorial regulation in previous Ottoman-Christian peace treaties, it was only at Carlowitz (and possibly in 1693) that it was clearly and officially named as the governing principle of peacemaking. For a similar argument regarding the refashioning of *uti possidetis* as an 'international legal norm' during the final decades of the seventeenth century, *see* also Yaycıoğlu, 'Ottoman Arguments', 64.

arrangement during the Carlowitz negotiations. In his account of the congress, Rāmī Meḥmed provides a fascinating section in which he analyses the concept. He commences as follows: 'If there was a war with one of the Christian rulers, and especially with the German one, when peace was made, it was made on the principle of *'alā ḥālihi*. It is a principle that was used as a basis [for peace treaties] and has remained in force for 150 years now.[56] On the other hand, Count Kinsky, one of the most influential Imperial ministers during the peace negotiations, simultaneously described *uti possidetis* as 'an uninterrupted principle, retained with respect and [frequently] used' (*haud interrupta observantia recepta et usitata Regula*) between the ancestors of the two emperors.[57]

Such statements reveal the force that such supra-cultural customary principles exerted upon the peacemaking process and decision-makers, and the way they could effectively be used as normative argumentation. It also says a lot about their elevation to the level of an ancient 'law of peace' from a remote past, which supplied them with authority and 'sanctity'. As the Ottoman delegation in Vienna in 1689 would state to the Imperial ministers, if the *uti possidetis* was applied as a peacemaking principle since the time of Süleymān the Magnificent, why should it change now?[58] Thus, on a more general level, one observes that, as in other practices of conflict resolution, the argumentation on the *uti possidetis* attests that when it came to intercultural (or even those inside the same cultural sphere) peace negotiations, established custom and not religious precepts held the upper hand. In analysing the *'alā ḥālihi* principle, Rāmī Meḥmed doesn't seek to justify it based on Islamic Law but instead explains it by making recourse to previous treaties, taking as his primary example the one signed in 1669 with the Republic of Venice.[59]

Still, despite its general acceptance, the *uti possidetis* didn't always adequately solve the territorial issues between the belligerents. One of the greatest preoccupations of late-seventeenth-century decision-makers (or at least many of them) was to achieve a clear separation of land – and increasingly a clearly defined border – which would make their territory easily defendable and deter future enemy incursions.[60] That was the ideal. But in practice, the territorial

56 *Ta'rīḫ-i Ṣulḥ-nāme*, fol. 40^{b}.

57 ÖStA, HHStA, Türkei I, Turcica Box 165, Folder 2 (April 1698), fol. 85^{r}, Kinsky to Paget, 24 April 1698.

58 *Cerîde-i Takrirât*, 65–6. Interestingly, the 150 years mentioned by Rāmī almost coincide with the first Ottoman-Habsburg treaty, signed in 1547, differing by only a year: Ernst D. Petritsch, 'Der habsburgisch-osmanische Friedensvertrag des Jahres 1547'. *MÖStA* 38 (1985), 49–80. Rāmī's sense of historicity was indeed astounding.

59 *Ta'rīḫ-i Ṣulḥ-nāme*, fol. 40^{b}–41^{b}.

60 For this issue, refer below to Act III, At the Negotiating Table I.

status quo at the end of the war was much more complicated, leaving, for example, enclaves in control of one side in a territory which was conquered for the most part by the other. That was mostly the situation in 1698. For example, the Ottoman province of Temeşvar was, for the most part, in Imperial hands, but the Ottoman troops still held its main homonymous fortress.

In such instances, it was evident that the principle of a mere *uti possidetis* was not enough, and that the latter should be further 'explained', that is, supplemented with other arrangements in order either to achieve a clear separation of territory or to allow the side who suffered the most territorial losses to save face by getting back a portion of the lands it had lost. The former was mainly a preoccupation of the Imperial side.[61] The latter, on the other hand, was chiefly entertained by the Ottomans. As the Grand Vizier ʿAmcazāde Ḥüseyin Paşa stated in his letter to the English King William III in 1698, referring to the peace negotiations in 1693, 'the abstract assertion *ʿalā hālihi* that was [then] discussed to be the basis of the peace settlement was not congruent with the honour of the Exalted State'.[62]

Typical arrangements to further supplement the *uti possidetis* were demolitions or evacuations of specific fortresses and permutations of territory.[63] For example, the Treaty of Ryswick between the Holy Roman Emperor and the King of France contained all these different territorial settlements.[64] Nevertheless, trying to 'explain' the *uti possidetis* was not an easy task. Here 'the controversy springs' (*nacque la controversia*), as Count Kinsky explained.[65] The Vienna Congress of 1689–90, as well as the subsequent negotiations at the Ottoman Court (1692–3), mainly failed because the allies tried, according to the Ottoman plenipotentiaries, to acquire more lands than they currently held. One of the greatest issues faced in the first meeting of the Imperial ministers in February 1698 to discuss the issue of the peace was, '[…] whether it would be more advisable to stay as hitherto in the general [sense] of *uti possidetis* or by giving in advance quasi-conditions, as France has gone twice with the allies,[66]

61 ÖStA, HHStA, Türkei I, Turcica Box 166, Folder 1 (August 1698), fol. 220^{r-v}, Kinsky to Caprara, 24 August 1698.

62 *Taʾrīḫ-i Ṣulḥ-nāme*, fol. 19^{b}–20^{a}.

63 Kinsky to Caprara, 24 August 1698, fol. 220^{r-v}.

64 I have consulted the following: *Traité de paix entre l'Empereur, la France, et l'Empire conclu à Rysvvick le trentiéme Octobre 1697* (Paris: Frederic Leonard 1697).

65 Kinsky to Caprara, 24 August 1698, fol. 220^{v}.

66 They probably refer here to the members of the anti-French coalition during the Nine Years' War (1688–97).

to explain it in detail?'[67] Finally, they decided not to show their cards from the outset and left the issue to be clarified later.[68]

In the end, although the *uti possidetis* was agreed upon as the foundation of the Carlowitz peace negotiations, it was attenuated to a great extent by demolitions and evacuations of fortresses. It did not even serve as the main principle in the talks between the Ottomans and the Polish-Lithuanian Commonwealth. But this discussion belongs to a different Act. Let us resume our narration.

3 The Play Resumes

Already four days after his first audience with the grand vizier, Paget wrote to Kinsky. 'The merry success [of the Imperial forces] during the last campaign rendered them [the Ottomans] slightly more negotiable', he claimed.[69] After going on to narrate the audience he had with ʿAmcazāde – omitting, of course, the advice he gave to the Ottomans – he optimistically reported to the Imperial minister that 'from the manner I see the court's standing, one could hope that the affair is practicable, provided that a way will be found [for them] to save appearances, an issue on which the Turks are obstinate'.[70] In addition, he requested further directions from Kinsky and asked him how the allies' issue was to be touched upon. And he concluded that if the emperor would, by his grace, offer something to facilitate this treaty, he could have the glory and satisfaction to end the current war 'if not with a regular peace (*une Paix reguliere*), then at least with a truce of a number of years (*une Treve d'années*)'.[71]

After this first round of conferences between Mavrocordatos and Paget, the time had come for the Ottoman government to deliberate and make resolutions. On 10/20 January 1698, the Imperial Council (*Dīvān-i Hümāyūn*) was summoned. According to the English ambassador, its meeting lasted three to four hours.[72] Although one could not discern any hint of disagreement in the Ottoman sources, the unfolding of subsequent events seems to indicate that there was indeed a consensus among the main Ottoman powerholders on the necessity of peace. And indeed, the council decided in favour of it on the

67 ÖStA, HHStA, Turcica I Box 165, Folder 1 (January-March 1698), fol. 10^{r-v}, relation of the members of the 'Turkish Deputation' to Leopold I, 13 February 1698.

68 Ibid., fol. 14^{r-v}.

69 ÖStA, HHStA, Türkei I, Turcica Box 164, Folder 5 (1697), fol. 60^{r}, Paget to Kinsky, 29 December 1697 (J.C.).

70 Ibid., fol. 60^{v}.

71 Ibid.

72 TNA, SP 97/21, fol. 6^{v}, Paget to Shrewsbury, 23 January 1697 (1698) (J.C.).

following grounds: it was evident that victory was difficult (*ẓafer müteʿaẕẕir olduġu ẓāhir olmaġla*) against such a firmly united and robust coalition of Christian powers; peace was needed to bring the Ottoman Domains back in order; the termination of hostilities would be the only way to break the coalition and alliance of the 'Infidels'; "and because of many more advantages of that nature to the benefit of Muslims, [and] in any case, peace was necessary according to the exigencies of the moment, by both reason and tradition and [lastly] according to the Holy Saying 'if they incline towards peace, incline yourself as well and put your trust in God' (*in ceneḥüvā li's-selāmi fācnaḥ lahā ve tevekkel ʿali'l-llāh*)".[73] As the grand vizier would repeat in a letter to the *Vālide Sulṭān*, the sultan's mother, in late May 1698, 'Indeed, because of the long duration of these campaigns, no strength and ability remained either with the subjects and the treasury or with the soldiery. No other way was left but peace to bring them all again in order'.[74]

The restoration of internal order through external peace would form the kernel of ʿAmcazāde Ḥüseyin Paşa's policy and the rallying cry of his supporters and eulogisers. On the other hand, the breaking of the Christian coalition would constitute one of the main goals of the Ottoman ambassadors at Carlowitz, although, as we will see, they received ample assistance in this matter from the allies themselves. Still, the argument of economic exhaustion deserves some more attention. After sixteen years of endless war, the Ottomans were not the only ones to suffer from it. The Habsburgs and the Venetians were facing similar difficulties.[75] The following example is telling. In a meeting with Count Kinsky in Vienna in July 1698, the Muscovite Tsar Peter I (r. 1682–1725) complained to the Imperial minister about the peace negotiations with the Porte with the argument that his new Black Sea fleet had cost him millions.[76] The Bohemian Chancellor promptly replied that for the emperor, 'it would have [probably] cost millions and millions throughout these fifteen years' to finance this war.[77] One could discern from these references the limits imposed upon the early modern 'fiscal-military' state to withstand long-lasting

73 *Taʾrīḫ-i Ṣulḥ-nāme*, fol. 18^{b}–19^{a}.

74 DABOA, TS. MA.e 523,15, Ḥüseyin Paşa to the Vālide Sulṭān, 29 Ẕi'l-ḥicce 1109 (8 July 1698). The date for the letter given in the online register of the DABOA, is probably erroneous. The letter is undated, but given its content, it should have been written in the second half of May 1698.

75 *Narratio*, fol. 3^{r-v}; Jean Bérenger, 'La politique de l'empereur Léopold 1er face à l'Empire Ottoman (1689–1699)', in Bérenger, *La paix de Karlowitz*, 9–24, 19–24.

76 ÖStA, HHStA, Türkei I, Turcica Box 165, Folder 5 (July 1698), fol. 45^{v}, Kinsky to Leopold I, 5 July 1698.

77 Ibid., fol. 47^{r}.

conflicts. In the Ottoman case, this realisation led to much longer periods of peace during the eighteenth century.[78]

The day following the gathering of the Ottoman Imperial Council, Mavrocordatos visited Paget once again. He asked him what papers he had to support his proposition.[79] Obviously, good intentions would have to be ascertained reciprocally. Paget resorted to the 'switching of roles' strategy, 'I told him that I had no orders to shew it, and therefore that I had it not, then, with mee, neither would I shew it as a minister, but in familiar conference with him, to content his curiosity, and to let him see the sincerity of my dealing, I would meet him the next day, and let him see a copy of it'.[80] Of course, his 'sincerity' only extended to a certain point. 'Having copied so much of the letter, as I thought he might see without any inconvenience', he presented it to the Ottoman Chief Interpreter.[81] The strategy of supposedly disclosing written (or oral) information as *honnête homme* in order to prove one's 'sincerity' and win the trust of his interlocutor was commonly applied by late-seventeenth century 'diplomats'. For instance, the English ambassador in Vienna, Lord Sutton, having received in early February 1698 a letter from Adrianople, wrote to Kinsky to confide in him, 'the important news, that I received lately from Lord Paget; It's for this reason that I send to Your Excellency the most faithful translation, that I could make of his letter so that You can truly see and know, what he sends concerning the inclination, that the Porte professes for peace'.[82]

Still, it was likely the same ambassador, Sutton, who 'faithfully' translated Paget's important letter detailing his conferences with the grand vizier and Mavrocordatos as it passed through Vienna, and 'shared' its contents with Kinsky.[83] And yet, comparing the English original and the French translation, one could clearly see that all parts where Paget provides the Ottomans with counsel are diligently removed. In order not to cause 'any inconvenience', it would seem. Such a strategy of allegedly providing someone with full

78 During the seventeenth century, the Ottoman Empire witnessed solely seventeen years of peace without engaging in a war with a limitrophe polity. In the eighteenth, they were substantially raised to seventy-four.

79 TNA, SP 97/21, fol. 6v, Paget to Shrewsbury, 23 January 1697 (1698) (J.C.).

80 Ibid., fol. 7r.

81 Ibid.

82 ÖStA, HHStA, Türkei I, Turcica Box 165, Folder 1 (January–March 1698), fol. 5r, Sutton to Kinsky, 7 February 1698.

83 One translated copy could be found in BNM, Ms.it VII 399(8625), Congresso di Carlowitz (1699) e Carte Relative e Missione di Carlo Ruzzini, fol. 7r–17r. Another is located in ÖStA, HHStA, Turcica I Box 167, Folder 1 (October 1698, 1st half), 166r–167v. The English original: Paget to Shrewsbury, 23 January 1697 (1698) (J.C.), fol. 5r–8r.

information, when in fact, it was a controlled disclosure, appears to have been so widespread that certain ambassadors were always suspecting it. In a letter to the tsar just before the start of the Carlowitz Congress, Prokopii Bogdanovich Voznitsyn, the Muscovite plenipotentiary, accused his allies, mainly the Imperials, of not providing him with the full letters coming from the Ottoman side, or from the mediators, but only with abstracts of them, thus deliberately concealing information from him.[84]

Nevertheless, the precautious information disclosure appeared to have worked in the case of Paget since Mavrocordatos was left satisfied, and he assured the Englishman that the vizier would draft him a formal letter to the English King as well as the Ottoman peace proposals concerning the emperor and his allies.[85] Would, though, the Ottomans reveal in their turn their true sentiments? According to Rāmī Meḥmed, 'for this beneficial matter to commence, [it was deemed that] if the genuinely thought propositions were to be revealed from the outset, maybe the affair will not go anywhere, since the enemy [might] react with great arrogance and hostility'.[86] Hence, what was decided to be sent to England was 'the matter [of the terms] supposedly intended by the Exalted State, to explore to secret thoughts [of the enemy]'.[87]

Such a statement leaves open to speculation whether the actual Ottoman demands were greater or lesser. Yet, from the supposed terms, one could perceive that it was a combination of both. The principle of *ʿalā ḥālihi/uti possidetis* was accepted as a negotiation basis for the Habsburg emperor and Venice. Yet, for the Polish-Lithuanian Commonwealth, a permutation was suggested between the Ottoman-held fortress of Kamianets-Podilskyi in present-day western Ukraine,[88] which had to be demolished, and the Commonwealth-controlled areas in northern Moldavia. Concerning the emperor, against the advice of Paget, the Porte insisted on her demands on Transylvania, her full possession of the region of Ṭemeşvar, the demolition of significant Imperial fortresses

84 M.M. Bogoslovskii, *Petr I. Materialy dlia biografii*, vol. 3 (Moscow: OGIZ 1946) 366.

85 TNA, SP 97/21, fol. 7r, Paget to Shrewsbury, 23 January 1697 (1698) (J.C.).

86 *Taʾrīḫ-i ṣulḥ-nāme*, fol. 19a.

87 Ibid., fol. 20a.

88 Kamianets-Podilskyi (Ott. Tr.: Ḳamaniçe, Pol.: Kamieniec Podolski) was the most important fortress in the region of Podolia, which in 1672 was conquered from the Polish-Lithuanian Commonwealth by the armies of Sultan Meḥmed IV and until 1699 formed an Ottoman province (*eyālet*) with Kamianets-Podilskyi as its administrative centre. Whereas most of Podolia was reconquered by the *Rzeczpospolita* quickly after the onset of the Sixteen Years' War, the Ottoman garrison of Kamianets-Podilskyi successfully held all the sieges, so that in 1698 the fortress remained firmly in Ottoman hands. For the Ottoman 'Province of Ḳamaniçe', *see* Dariusz Kołodziejczyk, *Podole pod panowaniem tureckim: Ejalet Kamieniecki 1672–1699* (Warsaw: Polczek 1994).

north of Belgrade, and the adjustment of the frontier in Bosnia to the Ottoman favour. Yet, as the negotiations proceeded, it became clear that the Porte could be content with less. Thus, as the Imperial side was concerned, these were the maximum Ottoman demands.

In the case of Venice, though, things played out differently. The formulation that the Republic would have to evacuate or demolish some fortresses in order to draw the new limits in fashion 'suitable to the Victorious Border' (*serḥādd-ı manṣūreye münāsib*),[89] was too vague and as subsequent events revealed, this formulation was explicitly destined to conceal the greater demands that the Porte would impose at Carlowitz on what it perceived as the weakest member of the alliance. Totally absent from the Ottoman proposals was Muscovy.[90] It is not clear why the Ottomans decided to exclude the tsar from the peace negotiations. His bellicose attitude, well known to the Ottoman administration, might have been a consideration. We will return to this issue later.

There remained the problem of Colyer. Despite his promise 'as a gentleman', Paget left the Dutch entirely in the dark about these first peace overtures. In the letter to his superiors, he tried to justify himself. 'I have not conferr[e]d with the Dutch Ambassr. about these proceedings 1st. because he has not (as I know) offer[e]d his offices here […] 2dy. Because he is not here; 3dy. because the Discours with the Vesier, and the Transactions upon it, were accidentall and suddain, and I had not time nor convenience to advice with him'.[91] Colyer didn't forgive Paget for this behaviour. Later, during the peace congress, Count Luigi Marsigli would report some rumours from a source of his in the mediators' camp: 'Milord Paget wanted from the start to exclude the Dutch from this mediation […] he worked in Holland to acquire from his king the necessary orders for this exclusion, and equally, he operated secretly with the Turks in order that they call him [to Adrianople]'.[92] Whether or not those rumours were true – and most evidence suggests they partly were – they overtly reveal both the problematic relationship between the two mediators, which would continue for many more months and the desire of Paget to establish himself as the mediator par excellence, acquiring all the symbolic capital of a peace broker for himself and his principal.

---

89 *Taʾrīḫ-i ṣulḥ-nāme*, fol. 21^{b}.

90 The Ottoman 'peace proposals' dated ġurre-i Ş[abān] A.H. 1109 (12 February 1698) in ibid., fol. 20^{b}–21^{b}.

91 Ibid., fol. 8^{r}.

92 ÖStA, HHStA, Türkei I, Turcica Box 168, Folder 1 (November 1698, 1st half), fol. 241^{r}, Marsigli to Kinsky, 28 October 1698.

And so, with the handing over of the Ottoman letter and peace proposals destined for the English King and the de facto Ottoman acceptance of the latter's mediation, the first stage of this 'Theatre de la Paix' was completed. Yet, whether the 'play' would continue or not was still uncertain. 'Notwithstanding talks of Peace', wrote Paget, 'all is preparing for to carry on the war with all possible rigour; [...] and every thing looks angrily but we can not see their hearts'.[93] The ball was now in the other court. What would Vienna's response be?

---

93 TNA, SP 97/21, fol. 8r, Paget to Shrewsbury, 23 January 1697 (1698) (J.C.).

Narration Part II: a Mistrust Caused by Distance

For one to understand the long duration of the Preliminaries and the relatively slow exchange of information compared to today's standards, the parameter of distance is of paramount significance. Although postal services had developed considerably by the late seventeenth century compared to earlier periods, connecting large parts of the European continent, a considerable amount of time was still needed for messages to be delivered.[1] To give but a few examples, Paget's first letter to Kinsky, to inform him about the peace inclinations of the Ottoman Court, was sent from Adrianople on 29 December 1697 (J.C.) and reached Vienna on 3 February 1698.[2] A second letter sent by Paget on 22 January 1698 (J.C.), 'per expressum', was only received by Kinsky on 26 February.[3] To this, we would need to add the time needed to deliberate on the content of letters, make decisions, prepare the reply, and then send the letter back with all the extra time it could take to reach its destination.

In late January, Paget's secretary Georg Philipp Schreyer parted from Adrianople with the Ottoman letters and peace proposals destined for the English King. After passing through Vienna on 26 February, he reached England by the first fortnight of March.[4] Schreyer would continue for the next months to act as the indefatigable middleman, carrying letters and information several times between the mediators and the Ottoman side on the one hand and Vienna on the other. He is one of those actors whose role might have been discreet but quite crucial to the advancement of the negotiations. It would be a mistake to consider him as a mere courier. Instead, he was a negotiator in his own right, providing the necessary interpretation of Paget's letters and trying to influence the Imperial ministers in favour of peace. Paget praised him

1 For the early modern European postal network, *see* Nikolaus Schobesberger, Paul Arblaster, Mario Infelise, André Belo, Noah Moxham, Carmen Espejo and Joad Raymond, 'European Postal Networks', in Joad Raymond and Noah Moxham (eds.), *News Networks in Early Modern Europe* (Leiden/Boston: Brill 2016) 17–63. More specifically, for the Ottoman case, Colin Heywood, 'Two Firmans of Muṣṭafā II on the Reorganisation of the Ottoman Courier System (1108/1696)'. *Acta Orientalia Academiae Scientiarum Hungaricae* 54/4 (2001), 485–96. As for the Austrian Habsburgs at the beginning of the eighteenth century, *see* Andreas Helmedach, *Das Verkehrssystem als Modernisierungsfaktor. Straßen, Post, Fuhrwesen und Reisen nach Triest und Fiume vom Beginn des 18. Jahrhunderts bis zum Eisenbahnzeitalter* (Munich: R. Oldenbourg 2002) 47–67.

2 ÖStA, HHStA, Türkei I, Turcica Box 164, Folder 5 (1697), fol. 61v.

3 ÖStA, HHStA, Türkei I, Turcica Box 165, Folder 1 (January–March 1698), fol. 2v.

4 ÖStA, HHStA, Türkei I, Turcica Box 165, Folder 2 (April 1698), fol. 44r; Heywood, 'English Diplomacy', 260. Note that the dates provided by Heywood follow the Julian Calendar.

 | DOI:10.1163/9789004458499_006

in a letter to Kinsky, assuring the latter that he could show absolute trust in Schreyer because of his loyalty and dedication – as much as Paget's – to the conclusion of this affair.[5]

The first news from the Ottoman Court reached Vienna, as we saw, in early February 1698. On 13 February, a 'Deputation' (*Deputation in Turcicis*), formed by some of the most trusted ministers of the emperor, convened to discuss the new situation.[6] As was the custom, a report of the meeting was prepared for Leopold I, who, after reading it, replied to Kinsky,

> Dear Kinsky. I am sending you back the first relation of the conference on the letters of Paget, which I approve in its entirety [...] not only can you respond to Paget, but you can [also] communicate to the Venetian ambassador and to Poland the things that you think could be communicated to them.[7]

The first reception was positive. In his reply to Paget, the Imperial minister stated that if the Ottomans declared their intentions and they would 'be brought to reason' regarding the affairs of the emperor, then the latter would 'use his credit' and would employ 'all the offices' possible to convince all his allies to show 'a similar moderation', to acquire a knowledge of their intentions and to make them 'agreeable' and 'practicable' towards peace.[8] And yet Kinsky still had doubts. 'I confess to Your Lordship [...] that [despite] everything you did the honour to report to me about the thinking of the Turks for the peace [...] I doubt, not without good reason, the good faith of the [...] answer the grand vizier gave to you'.[9] And he issued a warning: 'But I know that they are deceiving themselves if they believe that they will make us dormant regarding the preparations for the war with such actions[10] [...] because I am assuring you that the effects will correspond to the words I give you on that'.[11]

5 ÖStA, HHStA, Türkei I, Turcica Box 165, Folder 3 (May 1698), fol. 18^{v}, Paget to Kinsky, 9 May 1698 (J.C.).

6 ÖStA, HHStA, Türkei I, Turcica Box 165, Folder 1 (January-March 1698), fol. 10^{r}–20^{r}, relation of the members of the 'Turkish Deputation' to Leopold I, 13 February 1698.

7 Ibid., fol. 18^{r}, Leopold I to Kinsky (s.d. but probably February 1698).

8 Ibid., fol. 23^{r}, Kinsky to Paget, 19 February 1698.

9 Ibid.

10 We need to remember that in pre-modern times, due to weather conditions and the inability to surpass them, wars normally ceased during winter and recommenced in spring. Usually, during this de facto period of rest, the belligerents made all necessary preparations for the upcoming resuming of the fighting: Parvev, *Habsburgs and Ottomans*, 43.

11 Kinsky to Paget, 19 February 1698, fol. 23^{r-v}.

Last but not least, it had to be made crystal clear to the Ottoman side that the emperor would not enter negotiations without his allies. 'He is very religious in his engaged faith and too envious of his glory to go back on his word to them', Kinsky declared.[12] Practically, that meant that yet another congress, the second during the Sixteen Years' War, would have to be convened with the participation of all warring parties to put an end to the fighting.

Truly, a crucial issue during the meetings of the Imperial ministers was finding the best way to share information with all the other allies regarding the peace negotiations.[13] The Imperial ministers agreed that the emperor was obliged 'ex religione foedus' not to withhold anything from the other members of the Holy League.[14] Thus, the strategy that the Imperial side adopted throughout the Preliminaries was one in which, on the one hand, it attempted to convince its allies of the need to make peace – or rather to coerce them to agree to concede to it by a series of *faits accomplis* – but on the other, it was careful, ostensibly, as the emperor himself made clear to his ministers, 'not to negotiate contrary to the alliance'.[15]

So, a few weeks after this first meeting of the 'Deputation' and following the instructions of the emperor, Kinsky sent a letter to the Polish King and Elector of Saxony, August II (r. 1697–1706, 1709–33).[16] He notified him of the letter Paget sent him on 29 December regarding the changing of humour at the Ottoman Court and that the ambassador was going to 'penetrate their sentiments' and report back on them.

> Yet because, since then, he hasn't given any detail nor written me any more letter, I suppose that [either] his suppositions were wrong or the Turks changed their designs [...] In any case, I can assure Your Majesty

12 Ibid., fol. 24^{r}.

13 For instance, ÖStA, HHStA, Türkei I, Turcica Box 165, Folder 1 (January–March 1698), fol. 10^{v}, relation of the members of the 'Turkish Deputation' to Leopold I, 13 February 1698.

14 ÖStA, HHStA, Türkei I, Turcica Box 165, Folder 2 (April 1698), fol. 50^{v}–52^{v}, relation of the members of the 'Turkish Deputation' to Leopold I, 15 April 1698.

15 Ibid., fol. 41^{r}, Imperial resolution, 15 April 1698. This evidence fully contradicts a narrative that was put forward by the Polish and Muscovite sides at the time – still taken at face value by part of the contemporary literature – that the Habsburgs supposedly hid the peace negotiations from their allies and thus betrayed them. *See*, for example, Guskov, 'Uchastie Rossii'.

16 Another one was also sent to the Imperial resident ambassador at the Polish Court, Sedlnitzky, with instructions to inform Aleksei Nikitin, the Muscovite resident ambassador there about the peace overtures of the Porte: ÖStA, HHStA, Türkei I, Turcica Box 165, Folder 1 (January–March 1698), fol. 37^{r}–38^{r}, Kinsky to Sedlnitzky, 2 March 1698. And Sedlnitzky's reply dated 25 March 1698, in ibid., fol. 54^{r}–57^{r}.

> that nothing is to be done without communication with You, and that here we don't rest to prepare ourselves as well as possible to wage the imminent campaign.[17]

In fact, Paget had already written and sent a couple of letters, which, of course, Kinsky had yet to receive. His mistrust of the Ottoman intentions was caused largely by distance. The Porte would later experience similar sentiments. The analogous rhetoric voiced by both sides at the state of the peacemaking process could not remain unnoticed. On the one hand, both professed a desire for peace, yet on the other hand, simultaneously, they propagated their readiness to pursue the war with impeccable preparations.

At last, by late February, the details of the 'Adrianople Conferences' were fully known to Kinsky. On 1 March, he wrote back to Paget, informing him of his reception of the ambassador's letter dated 22 January 1698. The Imperial government was willing to enter preliminary discussions for peace.[18] One day later, he dispatched a novel missive to the Polish King. Paget's secretary had been in Vienna on his way to England to deliver the Ottoman propositions of peace to the English King. The latter would then hand them out to the emperor and his allies. 'Verily, I am not able, Sire, to understand the reason for this detour taken by the Turks', Kinsky said. Doubts and second thoughts surfaced once more,

> I suspect that one of the three following motives: because the Turks pretend to want peace in order to oppose us, to make us dormant, and thus slow down the preparations for the next campaign, or they tried through this way of acting to not appear as the ones proposing [peace] by engaging more in the affair the English King, or [lastly] the latter's ambassador wanted to provide his services in this matter, both for the same reason and for notifying the king his Master in writing of all things related to peace […].[19]

Of the three guesses Kinsky made, at least the second was indeed correct. Hence, by early March 1698, the two main rivals of the war, the Ottoman sultan and the Habsburg emperor, had agreed, in principle, to reach the threshold

---

17 ÖStA, HHStA, Türkei I, Turcica Box 165, Folder 1 (January–March 1698), fol. 27^{r-v}, Kinsky to August II, 23 February 1698.

18 ÖStA, HHStA, Türkei I, Turcica Box 165, Folder 1 (January–March 1698), fol. 35^{r}–36^{r}, Kinsky to Paget, 1 March 1698.

19 Ibid. fol. 39^{r-v}, Kinsky to August II, 2 March 1698.

of peace. Nevertheless, as Kinsky wrote to the Imperial resident ambassador at the Polish Court, 'still everything remains uncertain and confused'.[20] Many issues were left on the table. What would be the Imperial response to the 'supposed' Ottoman proposals? How would the other allies of the coalition react? Would they incline as well towards peace? Upon which principles would the foundation of peace have to be established?

20 Ibid., fol. 37^v, Kinsky to Sedlnitzky, 2 March 1698.

Narration Part III: Laying Down the Foundation of Peace

1 First Scene: Adrianople

In late March 1698, Lord Paget wrote once again to Count Kinsky. He assured the Imperial minister of the solid basis for his mediation on the Ottoman side.[1] Nonetheless, other aspiring intermediaries were also making their moves. The grand vizier, Paget writes, had 'resolutely rejected the mediation offers which the French ambassador proposed to him in the name of his king, before my arrival here [in Adrianople]'.[2] What were the French up to?

The signing of the Treaty of Ryswick caused colossal disappointment and bitterness toward the French among the Ottoman administration. It was interpreted as a massive betrayal of the informal military alliance between the two powers against the common enemy, the Habsburg emperor. The French tried hard to justify to the Porte this option of abandoning their allies. One of the arguments they came up with was that they could now be in a position to offer their mediation services to terminate the war in the East. As Rāmī Meḥmed narrates, after the announcement by the French ambassador of the news of the Treaty of Ryswick, 'a trustworthy French nobleman' (*muʿtemed Franca beg-zādesi*) who was accompanying the Ottoman troops visited the grand vizier.[3] If we are to rely on Paget, that should have happened before the Englishman arrived at the Ottoman government's seat, somewhere at the beginning of December 1697.

The 'trustworthy' Frenchman, most probably the Marquis de Ferriol,[4] addressed the following question to the vizier: 'don't you want to make peace as well? If yes, could our king act as mediator?'[5] ʿAmcazāde replied dismissively. 'They [the French] abandoned our companionship in war. There is thus no need for their mediation in peace'.[6] Instead of trying to act as a reconciler, the

---

1 ÖStA, HHStA, Türkei I, Turcica Box 165, Folder 1 (January–March 1698), fol. 48^{r}, Paget to Kinsky, 13/23 March 1698.

2 Ibid.

3 *Taʾrīḫ-i ṣulḥ-nāme*, fol. 33^{a}.

4 Future French ambassador at the Porte (from 1699), Ferriol, was sent as a special envoy by Louis XIV in 1692 to accompany the Ottoman army: Bérenger, 'La politique ottomane de la France', 46–7.

5 *Taʾrīḫ-i ṣulḥ-nāme*, fol. 33^{a}.

6 Ibid.

 | DOI:10.1163/9789004458499_007

French King should have attempted to justify the dishonourable treaty he had just signed with the Holy Roman Emperor.[7] Moreover, how could he constitute a reliable mediator for both sides when he had only recently re-established his friendship with Leopold I?[8] The vizier's answer reveals the extent of Ottoman discontent with their former allies, and a certain disillusionment regarding the French might and grandeur caused by the way the Ottoman side interpreted the Treaty of Ryswick as disadvantageous for the *Roi Soleil*. Finally, the vizier correctly assessed that the Imperials would not accept the mediation of a king who, a few months earlier, was – and continued to be – their arch-rival. As for Louis XIV, seeking to place himself as a mediator between the sultan and the emperor was absolutely congruent with his self-image as the arbiter of the affairs of Europe.[9] And at some point, it indeed appeared that he was about to acquire the mediator's role because, despite the clear negative answer of the vizier, there were still others inside the Ottoman establishment for whom the French figured as more reliable mediators than the English.

In March 1698, when the peace negotiations were already well underway, the *Defterdār*, the head of the Ottoman financial administration, approached the French resident ambassador Châteauneuf to inquire about a possible French interposition. Following the same Ottoman strategy of 'not appearing to be the one to make the first move', there was not to be an official request from the sultan since 'it would be against the dignity of this empire, and even against their law to demand peace'.[10] Châteauneuf immediately informed Louis XIV, who took this offer so seriously as to send a special envoy to Vienna, the Marquis de Villars, to notify the Imperial government of this Ottoman sollicitation.[11] We shall later encounter the ramifications of Villars' mission in the Imperial capital.

Why did the *Defterdār* put forward such a proposal, though? Could it have been made on his own initiative? Was he acting under the directives of some alleged pro-war 'faction-leader'? Was the grand vizier privy to this proposal?

---

7 Ibid. For the Ottoman interpretation of the French-Imperial Treaty of Ryswick, *see* Poulios, 'From the Palace of Ryswick'.

8 *Ta'rīḫ-i ṣulḥ-nāme*, fol. 33[a].

9 For the image of the *Roi Soleil* as arbiter of Europe, *see* Christoph Kampmann, *Arbiter und Friedensstiftung: Die Auseinandersetzung um den politischen Schiedrichter im Europa der Früher Neuzeit* (Paderborn/Munich/Vienna/Zurich: Ferdinand Schöningh 2001) 199–41; Kinga Maria Kantorska, 'Les médiations françaises auprès des couronnes du nord au XVIIe siècle. Les tentatives d'arbitrage.', in Lucien Bély (ed.), *L'invention de la diplomatie. Moyen Age-Temps Modernes*, (Paris: PUF 1998) 225–34.

10 Quoted in Bérenger, 'La politique ottomane de la France', 50.

11 Ibid.

For Jean Bérenger, this was a manifestation of Ottoman distrust of William III and a fear of the terms the Ottomans would have to accept under English mediation.[12] Certainly, some on the Ottoman side were growing both wary and weary of the fact that, after nearly two months since the beginning of the negotiations with Paget, no positive sign had yet come from the allies. As we shall see, the Englishman understood this growing suspicion and took immediate action. Furthermore, it is equally probable that some elements inside the Ottoman Court still believed that the French, as mediators, could guarantee more favourable terms for the Ottoman side.

Understanding that something more concrete was needed to calm the Ottoman suspicions and preserve the peace-oriented mood at the Ottoman Court, Paget advised Kinsky to send him a letter that he could show to ʿAmcazāde, and from which it would clearly appear that the emperor wanted peace. Regarding its content, it had to be 'the project of a proposition, explaining the *uti possidetis*, how you understand it'.[13] It should also be 'firm in substance (but circumstantiated in a manner that will not startle these people when showing the letter to the vizier)'.[14] In the same missive, the Imperial minister had to point out to Paget that the emperor was not willing to relinquish anything that was rightfully his and had been conquered by force of his arms and that the *uti possidetis* was to be absolute, without any reserve or exception.[15] Furthermore, it was to be suggested that deputies could be appointed to adjust the new limits and to discuss on-site some possible demolitions that could further solidify the peace settlement. 'It appears to me that such a letter could only do good', Paget would conclude.[16]

Around the same time, news of the ongoing peace negotiations finally reached Colyer in Constantinople. Despite his constant mediating efforts during the previous decade, the Dutchman had been deliberately sidelined up to this point by Paget. Still, after the initial unpleasant surprise and feelings of enmity towards the Englishman that he might have experienced, he quickly made certain moves to re-enter the central stage. The first was to send a letter to the grand vizier, informing him of what was happening around him without his knowledge and offering again his mediation in the name of the States General of the United Provinces.[17] He was probably counting on the fact

12 Ibid.

13 ÖStA, HHStA, Türkei I, Turcica Box 165, Folder 1 (January–March 1698), fol. 49^{r}, Paget to Kinsky, 13/23 March 1698.

14 Ibid., fol. 52^{r}. Paget to Kinsky, 24 March 1698 (J.C.).

15 Paget to Kinsky, 13/23 March 1698, fol 49^{r}.

16 Ibid.

17 The Ottoman translation of the letter in *Taʾrīḫ-i ṣulḥ-nāme*, fol. 22^{a}–23^{a}.

that it would have been difficult for the Ottoman side to reject something that it had always accepted in the past. And he was proved to be correct. Having his letter reached Adrianople, the Ottoman leadership seemed almost obliged to accept his request. Following Rāmī Meḥmed, '[it was thought] that it is not appropriate for the States General to be left aside and to embark this time on the road of peace only with the English ambassador, without the presence of their ambassador here, having they made efforts in this affair since the beginning'.[18] Or, as he would state elsewhere for the Dutch, 'they were the first to act as mediators in the matter of peace'.[19] As a matter of fact, this statement was not precisely true.[20] Still, it reveals the extent to which the Dutch had imposed themselves on the Ottoman imaginary as mediators par excellence.

However, there were ulterior motives for bringing Colyer back to the game, which Rāmī would only indirectly reveal later in his narrative. As we saw in the case of the French, the Ottomans were eager to have a mediator who could be trusted to further their interests. Colyer, a native of Constantinople, who had spent much of his life in the Ottoman capital, was the ideal candidate for the job. And indeed, as we shall later encounter, contrary to Paget, he was much closer to the Ottoman officials than to Kinsky.

So ʿAmcazāde replied positively to the Dutchman. The Ottoman government accepted his mediation offer.[21] Yet that did not suffice for Colyer. He wanted to be where the events were unfolding and decisions were taken, not to act as a mediator from a distance. He wrote again to the grand vizier, requesting permission to travel to Adrianople, which he was granted.[22] Now that he had secured the approval of one side, he had to do the same with that of the Christian allies. On 1 April 1698, he wrote to Kinsky. He tried to create a *fait accompli* for the imperial minister. The Ottomans had already acknowledged him as a mediator, an affirmation he backed with concrete evidence by attaching a translation of the vizier's letter to him.[23] Yet, Colyer's letter would finally reach Kinsky more than a month later. In another dispatch to the Dutchman on 12 April 1698, the Bohemian Chancellor, still ignoring that Colyer was in the current of the latest developments, would not utter a single word about the peace negotiations.[24]

18 Ibid., fol. 22^{a}.

19 Ibid.

20 *See* above, Prelude, 26.

21 The copy of the letter from the grand vizier to Colyer in *Ta'rīḫ-i ṣulḥ-nāme*, fol. 23^{a-b}.

22 Ibid., fol. 23^{b}–24^{a}.

23 ÖStA, HHStA, Türkei I, Turcica Box 165, Folder 2 (April 1698), fol. 1^{r-v}, Colyer to Kinsky, 1 April 1698.

24 Ibid., fol. 9^{r}–10^{r}, Kinsky to Colyer, 12 April 1698.

2 Second Scene: Vienna

On 12 April 1698, the copies of the translation of the Ottoman proposals and letters finally arrived in Vienna from London, accompanied by official mediation offers from the English King and the States General of Holland.[25] After another meeting of the 'Turkish Deputation' to discuss their content, the Imperial side deliberated on communicating them to the other allies immediately.[26] The first to receive them was the Venetian resident ambassador in Vienna, Carlo Ruzzini.[27] The latter was indeed the only representative of the allies present at this moment at the Imperial Court. Yet, it is also true that the Serenissima, as both Paget and Kinsky believed and the Venetian sources confirmed, was the only one of the emperor's allies to be equally eager for a peace settlement as he.[28] From this point until the congress's opening, the emperor and Venice would form their own pro-peace block inside the alliance, pushing forward with the negotiations against the much more hesitant, if not openly hostile, Polish-Lithuanian Commonwealth and Muscovy.

The two allies had to coordinate their moves and response to the Ottoman proposals, so a meeting was held on 18 April 1698 in Kinsky's residence in the presence of the Venetian ambassador.[29] The minister started by saying that he had already communicated the letters that arrived from England to Ruzzini. Even if the Ottoman propositions did not mention the Muscovites, the fact that the Porte made the first move was positive and was not to be ignored. And he emphatically added 'that the time did not permit to wait for the reports of all the allies, while the Turk appeared to want to do fast what he wanted to do, that is before the [upcoming] campaign [season]'.[30] Then Ruzzini took the floor. The Venetian was in accord with Kinsky's view. 'It would be suitable to

25 ÖStA, HHStA, Türkei I, Turcica Box 165, Folder 2 (April 1698), fol. 44^{r}, relation of the members of the 'Turkish Deputation' to Leopold I, 17 April 1698. The copies of the letters in ibid. fol. 15^{r}–23^{v}.

26 The relation to the emperor concerning this meeting of the 'Turkish Deputation' in ibid., fol. 44^{r}–53^{v}. For the need to communicate the letters to the other allies, ibid., fol. 51^{r}–52^{v}. The Imperial resolution confirming the ministers' deliberations in ibid., fol. 41^{r}.

27 In the meeting of the 'Turkish Deputation', it was agreed to invite Ruzzini to a joint session to have his opinion on the Ottoman proposals and the *modus agendi* from now on: Ibid., fol. 51^{r-v}.

28 For the Imperial side's belief that Venice would be the easiest to accept a peace treaty on the Ottoman conditions, see ibid. For the readiness of the Republic to make peace, *see Narratio*, fol. 3^{r}.

29 The protocol of the meeting is found in ÖStA, HHStA, Türkei I, Turcica Box 165, Folder 2 (April 1698), fol. 54^{r}–57^{v}.

30 Ibid., fol. 54^{r}.

procure the congress before the campaign [season] and then discuss there the *uti possidetis* of the Muscovites if it was not to be obtained sooner'.[31] We should notice once again the preoccupation with achieving a swift resolution of the conflict in order to avoid the extra financial burden that another campaign season would have brought. Kinsky would then also stress 'that the Maritime Powers were making every effort so that the present occasion to embrace peace would not be skipped'.[32] Presenting the Imperial side as somehow enormously pressed by England and the United Provinces to come to the peace table would serve him as a constant justification in his later communication with the Poles and the Muscovites.

Then it was the turn of Count Kaunitz, another influential member of the 'Turkish Deputation' to express his opinion. He remarked that although the Muscovites were also allies and could not be left out of the prospective peace, it would be hard to convince the tsar to partake in the negotiations 'while he was nurturing vast designs and was bragging that he wanted to assault Constantinople'.[33] Perhaps, he could be persuaded by the King of England to embrace peace if he was still in London, on his 'Grand Embassy'.[34] 'In any way (declared Kinsky again) we must demonstrate a disposition towards peace and towards the mediation of the [...] King of Britain, all the more because, from a letter of Lord Paget, it became known how the King of France offered his mediation to the Turks and that the latter rejected it'.[35]

Ruzzini agreed with Kaunitz on the need to inform the Muscovites of the negotiation. He opined that what the Ottomans cared about most was the loss of Azov and that the Muscovites would not enter peace negotiations if they were to return it to the Ottomans.[36] Kinsky retorted that the emperor, being very 'religious' in his alliances, would communicate everything to his confederates. It was still not certain that peace was to be restored. They would not conclude anything, but they would only negotiate, communicating to the Muscovites the peace propositions and thus not violating the laws of the

31 Ibid.

32 Ibid., fol. 55r.

33 Ibid. The grandiose plan of the tsar to capture the Ottoman capital itself was presented again by Nikitin, the Muscovite resident ambassador in Warsaw, to his Imperial colleague Sedlnitzky, during a meeting they had to discuss the peace negotiations in March 1698: ÖStA, HHStA, Türkei I, Turcica Box 165, Folder 1 (January–March 1698), fol. 56r, Sedlnitzky to Kinsky, 25 March 1698.

34 ÖStA, HHStA, Türkei I, Turcica Box 165, Folder 2 (April 1698), fol. 55r. For Peter I's 'Grand Embassy', *see* in more detail below.

35 Ibid., fol. 55r.

36 Ibid.

alliance.[37] And there, he put forward what Paget had advised. They should send a letter to the Englishman stating they were willing to participate in a peace congress but not without the Muscovites.[38] Ruzzini concorded, only adding that the *uti possidetis* had to be well defined for the Serenissima.[39]

The conference ended with Kinsky being optimistic. It would not be difficult to agree on the *uti possidetis* for the emperor and his allies, he opined, without limitations and exceptions. Once this was approved, a congress would only serve to treat the minor points remaining. Presently, there was no ambassador of the Polish King in Vienna, but all the letters from the mediators were also communicated to him. They were waiting for his answer.[40]

This meeting is highly significant because it reveals the strategies adopted and the dilemmas faced by the two allies, the Imperials and Venice. On the one hand, their own interest was to speed up the peace negotiations, but on the other, they had to avoid alienating their other two less peace-inclined allies. A balance had to be struck between pressing forward with the peace talks and appearing simultaneously to fully respect the alliance treaties. Yet the apparent not entirely 'allied feelings' the Imperials nurtured towards the tsar and his 'vast designs' as well as the dismissal of the Poles and their war contribution – Kinsky would remark at the same meeting that their conquests in Moldavia 'are not of consideration'[41] – would not help in this respect. It was clear that the allied front was anything but united.

Venice seemed satisfied for the moment. Surely there was a problem with the English mediation because the Serenissima had not yet recognised William III as King of England. Still, as Ruzzini later claims in his *Relazione Finale*, the negotiation having reached such a point, the Republic had to concede and accept the mediation of the 'Maritime Powers' and, thus, the legitimacy of William.[42] Much more interesting is the picture that Ruzzini provides in the same relation as to how the Ottoman proposals appeared to him. With the experience of the congress and the negative alterations that this brought to the Venetian aspirations, the ambassador presents himself as grasping from the beginning what was to follow. 'I could then foresee what, after the course of months, during the final decisions of the [peace] negotiation, would in fact

37 Ibid.

38 Ibid., fol. 56ʳ. In fact, the letter had already been drafted during an earlier meeting of the 'Turkish Deputation': *See* ibid., fol. 45ᵛ, 46ʳ.

39 Ibid., fol. 56ʳ.

40 Ibid., fol. 56ᵛ–57ʳ.

41 Ibid., fol. 56ᵛ. Or according to Ruzzini, 'its [the Commonwealth's] *uti possidetis* is not a big thing' (*il suo, Uti possidetis non è gran cosa*): Ibid.

42 Ruzzini, *Relazione*, 352.

occur'.[43] It appeared to him that the Imperials 'were giving hope to the Turks' (*far sperar à Turchi*) by conceding to demolitions 'and other various facilitations, to attain the benefit of peace'.[44] On the other hand, the propositions of the Ottomans regarding Venice appeared 'obscure, prone to artifice, and interpretation when the need would have presented to explain them further'.[45] Even more, since, in his letter to the English King, the grand vizier stated that the *uti possidetis stricto sensu* 'was contrary to the honour of the empire' (*era contrario al decoro dell'Imperio*).[46] For this reason, as a precaution, Ruzzini claims that it was he who added that the *uti possidetis* should be accepted without exception, limitation or reserve.[47] If that wasn't followed in the end, the Turks' always present 'violence and bad faith' was to be blamed.[48] And yet, as one observes in the Imperial protocol of the April meeting, apart from his insistence – it is true – for a strict observance of the *uti possidetis* for Venice, he didn't voice any other objection whatsoever. Either he kept these thoughts to himself, or by the time he was composing his relation, he was trying to project onto it realisations that only occurred to him much later.

Nonetheless, the main thrust of this critical April meeting was the 'will-for-peace demonstrating' letter that Kinsky would send to Paget – an important detail: not to the two mediators together – who could also present it then to the Ottoman ministers. Like most such solemn documents, it would have to be composed in Latin, the still higher lingua franca of 'diplomacy' during this period. It was the 'famous' so-called 'Kinsky Letter' – although not drafted exclusively by the Bohemian Chancellor – which would catalytically influence the course of the negotiations up to the congress and would cause much controversy and conflicting interpretations among its various participants during it.

In that letter, written on 24 April 1698, Kinsky, faithfully following Paget's exhortations, laid down his thoughts on the would-be foundation precept on territorial matters of the upcoming congress. The *uti possidetis* was defined as 'an uninterrupted, retained with respect and customary used principle' between the ancestors of the two emperors, an idea that, as we saw, was

43 Ibid., 351.

44 Ibid.

45 Ibid.

46 Ibid.

47 In fact, this expression was already present in the draft of the letter during the earlier meeting of the 'Turkish Deputation' on 17 April: ÖStA, HHStA, Türkei I, Turcica Box 165, Folder 2 (April 1698), fol. 45^{v}, relation of the 'Turkish Deputation' to Leopold I, 17 April 1698.

48 Ruzzini, *Relazione*, 351.

equally shared by the Ottomans.[49] According to the Imperial minister, the emperor and the Venetians were ready to participate in a peace congress based on this maxim. In this congress, then, there could be a further negotiation 'of all those [issues] which either concern the borders or even the obligation, and only for the common convenience, of reciprocal evacuation or demolition of some minor places in Hungary or elsewhere'.[50] It was this very sentence that would later act as the epicentre of controversy. Because the Imperial side, as Ruzzini rightly perceived it – even ex post facto – with this evacuation/demolition clause 'for the common convenience', was, in fact, attenuating the full force of the *uti possidetis*, and he was 'giving hope to the Turks' that they could use this clause to their advantage. Even so, Kinsky believed that his proposals guaranteed that an 'honest and secure peace with the Ottoman Porte' could be concluded.[51]

Besides this 'ostensible letter' which was written – again Paget's influence manifests itself – in a rather mild and moderate tone, Kinsky sent on the same day two other private and, one could guess, non-ostensible ones to the mediators. Contrary to his letter in Latin, the phraseology the Bohemian Chancellor used in those other letters – written in French and Italian, respectively – was far more aggressive and uncompromising. Let's remember this detail because it will serve our narration later on. The content of both letters is roughly the same, so we should take the one addressed to Lord Paget as an example. Kinsky dispelled right from the start every hope that the Ottomans might nurture concerning the issue of Transylvania. The emperor would not even consider abandoning it. For him, this was a matter of honour and interest. Paget should make that clear to the Ottomans and not encourage them on the subject. Whatever the Ottomans may claim, Transylvania always belonged to the Habsburgs, the legitimate Kings of Hungary. They were thus in rightful possession of it, and they were resolute 'to rather go to every extreme [rather] than make a concession on this point'.[52]

49 ÖStA, HHStA, Türkei I, Turcica Box 165, Folder 2 (April 1698), fol. 85r, Kinsky to Paget, 24 April 1698.

50 Ibid., fol. 85r.

51 Ibid., fol. 86r.

52 ÖStA, HHStA, Türkei I, Turcica Box 165, Folder 2 (April 1698), fol. 90v, Kinsky to Paget (Copy), 24 April 1698. In the meeting of the 'Turkish Deputation', besides the arguments against ceding to the Ottoman demand on Transylvania based on the 'law of conquest', dynastic legitimacy, and *ratione status*, another consideration was that agreeing to the Ottoman proposal and thus violating the principle of an absolute *uti possidetis* would be dishonourable to the emperor and his victorious armies. This was especially significant because the Ottomans had offered an 'illimitatum et nulli exceptioni subjectum

On the allies now, the Venetians would accept the *uti possidetis* without difficulty. The Poles constituted a problem, though, because of the 'small shanties' (*petites biscoques*) they held in Moldavia and 'because their king is strongly armed, by having, I assure Your Lordship, thirty-nine thousand Germans in his service, besides the local militia, of the sort that the Turks could well suffer damage if they do not forestall it with a reasonable moderation'.[53] This threat was substantiated in a later letter to the two mediators where Kinsky attached a list of the forces of the King of Poland, 'which is not at all bragging but [something] founded in pure reality'.[54] This list should put the 'Turks' to thinking, because it seemed that in the future, 'they will not be able to have it so easily with Poland as they had in the past'.[55] In the same letter, August II is also described as a 'warrior genius, avid for glory and strongly armed'.[56] Of course, despite such arguments regarding the Commonwealth – the same Kinsky who had dismissed the Polish capabilities – reality would be played out differently on the field, as the coming months would soon reveal. Lastly, concerning Muscovy, the Bohemian Chancellor was again reassuring: 'We are in alliance, yes, but not so strict as the one with Poland and the Venetians'.[57] An arrangement could be found. Finally, he would also make clear to Paget that 'if the Turks wish not the aforementioned simple acceptance of the *uti possidetis*, it would be highly futile to talk of a congress'.[58] As for the massive Ottoman war preparations mentioned by the Englishman in his previous letter, 'Your Excellency can be assured that notwithstanding all [this] appearance of peace, the latter didn't make us dormant here [...] troops would be of no shortage to the emperor'.[59]

uti possidetis' to the Republic of Venice. If Venice was entitled to such a privilege, the emperor's honour demanded that he concede as little as possible: ÖStA, HHStA, Türkei I, Turcica Box 165, Folder 2, fol. 47^{r-v}, relation of the members of the 'Turkish Deputation to Leopold I, 17 April 1698.

53 ÖStA, HHStA, Türkei I, Turcica Box 165, Folder 2 (April 1698), fol. 91^{r-v}, Kinsky to Paget, 24 April 1698.

54 ÖStA, HHStA, Türkei I, Turcica Box 165, Folder 3 (May 1698), fol. 30^{v}, Kinsky to Colyer, 10 May 1698.

55 Ibid.

56 Ibid. Such thoughts don't seem to be mere rhetoric but something that the Imperial ministers may sincerely have believed since during the meeting of the 'Turkish Deputation' the Polish King was described as such: '[...] potenter armiret, famae et gloriae sehr cupidus seye': ÖStA, HHStA, Türkei I, Turcica Box 165, Folder 2 (April 1698), fol. 50^{v}, relation of the members of the 'Turkish Deputation' to Leopold I, 17 April 1698.

57 Kinsky to Colyer, 10 May 1698, fol. 30^{v}.

58 Kinsky to Paget, 24 April 1698, fol. 89^{v}[92^{v}].

59 Ibid., fol. 89^{v} [92^{v}].

Kinsky's strategy, especially regarding the discourse he adopted towards the mediators, was to appear optimistic and peace-leaning but at the same time uncompromising on red-line issues for the imperial side, like Transylvania. The emperor surely wanted peace, but that didn't mean he was prepared to obtain a dishonourable one. The continuation of the war remained on the table. This manifestation of war readiness was utilised to put pressure on the mediators and, thus, on the Ottoman side to accept the allied peace proposals. The bragging about the Polish King's military capabilities also ran in the same vein. Interestingly, this was a game of bluffs and manipulations played by both sides, including the mediators, the bluffers and manipulators par excellence.[60] The main question was who, in the end, would take more seriously, as a reality, the bluff of the other.

Next in the row of Kinsky's addressees was the Polish 'warrior-king'. August II had not yet replied to Kinsky's initial letters of early March. He was probably trying to buy some time to deliberate. The Imperial minister decided to play safe by presenting as the main instigators of peace, not the emperor or even the Ottomans, but the northern Maritimes Powers. 'Your Majesty will understand the eagerness with which the King of England and the States General of Holland wrote to his Imperial Majesty what these powers desire and counsel given the present circumstances in which all Europe finds itself […]'.[61] The emperor could not expose himself to his allies by denying their mediation and thus receive 'the blame and reproaches of everyone'.[62] It was a matter of honour and reputation. Concerning the Ottoman proposals, although 'not being the ones that we would have desired', they still merit consideration. And in the end, negotiating peace is 'what is always the goal of a just and legitimate war'.[63] In any case, preparations for the ongoing campaign to 'assist the negotiations with arms' were well underway.[64]

3 Third Scene: Following Peter I's 'Grand Embassy'

Together with the dispatches to the Polish King, the Imperial side sent all documents related to the peace negotiations that had arrived from England to the

---

60 For the strategies of the mediators, *see* more extensively below in Interlude I.

61 ÖStA, HHStA, Türkei I, Turcica Box 165, Folder 2 (April 1698), fol. 103^{r}, Kinsky to August II, 25 April 1698.

62 Ibid.

63 Ibid., fol. 103^{r-v}.

64 Ibid., fol. 104^{r}.

Muscovite resident ambassador in Warsaw, Aleksei Nikitin, to deliver them to the tsar.[65] This choice was made because the Muscovite monarch was not in Moscow at the time. Since March 1697, Peter had embarked on his famous 'Grand Embassy' in western Europe. It was indeed an exceptional situation since he was travelling incognito as a simple mission member; three ambassadors officially headed the embassy. One of them was Prokopii Bogdanovich Voznitsyn, who would later be appointed as the Muscovite plenipotentiary ambassador to the Carlowitz Congress.[66] The feeling of awkwardness and amazement with which contemporaries met this incognito journey is encapsulated in the way Rāmī Meḥmed chose to narrate it. A narration full of contempt and reproach:

> the present Tsar of Muscovy, a guy named Petros (*Petros nām şaḫṣ*), wasn't stopping his bad-habited actions and was restless. And he added to his other improper deeds yet another unsuitable one. In disguise, together with his chief boyars assigned to the embassy, he left his capital and country [driven by] his passion for wandering and seeing the lands of the Netherlands, England, and Germany.[67]

Of course, apart from the legendary 'passion for wandering' of the young tsar, the embassy had other, more mundane goals as well: the consolidation and strengthening of the anti-Ottoman alliance of the Holy League, of which Muscovy had been an official member since February 1697, as well as the acquisition of technical knowledge and the recruitment of experienced men for the new fleet Peter was dreaming of constructing in the Azov Sea and use for further conquests against the Ottomans.[68] Having such goals in his mind, one could imagine his consternation upon learning from his spies in Vienna, quite early, it seems, about the peace negotiations that had only just commenced between the sultan and the Habsburg emperor.[69]

---

65 Dmitri Guzevich and Irina Guzevich, *Velikoe posol'stvo: Rubezh epokh, ili Nachalo puti, 1697–1698* (Saint Petersburg: Dmitri Bulanin 2008), 104–05.

66 For the 'Grand Embassy', *see* in detail in ibid.

67 *Ta'rīḫ-i ṣulḥ-nāme*, fol. 21b–22a.

68 Guskov, 'Uchastie Rossii', 121–123.

69 D. and I. Guzevich, *Velikoe posol'stvo*, 103–4. According to Sedlnitzky, Nikitin, upon receiving the news of the commencement of the negotiations, sent two letters, one to Moscow and the other to the tsar himself, to inform them of the situation: ÖStA, HHStA, Türkei I, Turcica Box 165, Folder 1 (January–March 1698), fol. 55r, Sedlnitzky to Kinsky, 25 March 1698. Still, in his meeting in May 1698 at the Hague with August II's envoy Christoph Dietrich Bose, he appeared supposedly utterly surprised, as if hearing about the peace negotiations for the first time: Jacek Burdowicz-Nowicki, *Piotr I, August II i Rzeczpospolita 1697–1706* (Krakow: Arcana 2010) 121.

Muscovy had officially entered the Holy League only months before by signing a three-year offensive alliance against the sultan's domains. Besides Azov, taken from the Ottomans in 1696, no other significant deed had been accomplished since then.[70] Now that the tsar was making such an effort to construct a whole new fleet to deploy in the fight against the 'Busurmans', the news of peace negotiations came as an unpleasant surprise. In the beginning, Peter appears not to have fully grasped the seriousness of the situation.[71] Rāmī Meḥmed, who seems quite well-informed, paints in his turn a picture of an indecisive tsar striving to shift his course of action. As he writes,

> during this period, he [Peter] visited the seat of the English King, London. Upon his arrival in the mentioned-above city and in the capital of the Netherlands, the town (sic!) of the Hague, the issue of this peace was spoken with him a lot. [And] sometimes he was persistent in his obstinacy, sometimes he was influenced by the suggestions of his friends.[72]

Rāmī's narration provides many interesting details, but at the same time, leaves many crucial points unanswered. With whom did Peter discuss the issue of peace, with his English and Dutch hosts or solely with his chief companions? Did the latter, or some of the latter, press him to accept making peace, perhaps stressing that Muscovy could be left alone to continue the war against the Ottomans? Whatever thoughts or illusions Peter might have nurtured, things became more evident to him when, by late May 1698, he had the papers sent by Nikitin in his hands.[73] The discovery that the foundation of the upcoming peace treaty was to be the *uti possidetis* finally revealed to the tsar the gravity of the circumstances and convinced him that peace had absolutely to be prevented. This principle was simply unacceptable for the Muscovites. Their main war goal, capturing the Kerch peninsula and opening the Black Sea to the new Muscovite fleet, still remained in their realm of dreams.[74]

His indignation further increased as he officially learned that England and the United Provinces, the two countries in which he had spent the last months, were to act as peace mediators. Whether or not they had actually hidden the negotiations from him, Peter perceived that in their desire to end the war in

70 Tatiana Bazarova, 'The Treaty of Carlowitz and Its Impact on Russian–Ottoman Relations, 1700–1710', in Heywood and Parvev, *The Treaties of Carlowitz (1699)*, 237–8.

71 D. and I. Guzevich, *Velikoe posol'stvo*, 103–5.

72 S.K., Esad Efendi, n. 2241, fol. 14a.

73 D. and I. Guzevich, *Velikoe posol'stvo*, 105; Bazarova, 'The Treaty of Carlowitz', 238.

74 Ibid.

the east for their own interests, they didn't care at all about the interests of Muscovy. This antipathy and enmity that Peter developed towards the two Maritime Powers he had hitherto so admired would result in his later firm refusal to accept them as mediators in the upcoming congress. It was to be his revenge against their 'betrayal'.

However, there was another ruler who was equally disillusioned as the tsar by the prospect of imminent peace based on *uti possidetis*. During his stay in the Hague in May 1698, Peter held meetings with August II's envoy there, Christoph Dietrich von Bose. He aspired to win the new Polish King to the Muscovite orbit,[75] and their present alignment of interests seemed the perfect way to achieve that. He promised Bose close cooperation with his principal, especially on the next big station of his journey. Because, in the current state of affairs, the tsar finally decided that the best he could do was to head with his embassy to Vienna and try personally to convince the emperor and his ministers of the rightfulness of the Muscovite cause for the continuation of the war.[76] The 'Grand Embassy' had already received an invitation to visit the Imperial capital from Leopold back in December 1697.[77] But what back then seemed to be a visit that would further consolidate the alliance between the two monarchs had now become an emergency mission to rescue it from utterly collapsing.[78]

4 Fourth Scene: Adrianople

Back in Adrianople, Colyer reached the seat of the Ottoman government on 28 April to officially kick off his mediation services. The trust placed in him by the Ottoman administration was revealed by the fact that soon after his arrival, he was admitted incognito at night by the grand vizier and other chief ministers of the Porte to be informed of the present state of the negotiations.[79] On 10 May, the English secretary, Schreyer, finally returned after three months of absence, bringing with him the new mediation credentials and instructions

75 For this issue, *see* the comprehensive study of Burdowicz-Nowicki, *Piotr I*.

76 Ibid., 122.

77 D. and I. Guzevich, *Velikoe posol'stvo*, 103. In March 1698, Nikitin told Sedlnitzky that the tsar agreed to head to Vienna with his 'Grand Embassy' and stay there for some time: ÖStA, HHStA, Türkei I, Turcica Box 165, Folder 1 (January–March 1698), fol. 55^r, Sedlnitzky to Kinsky, 25 March 1698.

78 Guskov, 'Uchastie Rossii', 123.

79 Hora Siccama, 'De Vrede van Carlowitz', 137–8.

for Paget and Colyer as well as the letters (*kāğıdlar*) from Count Kinsky.[80] The mediators' credentials (*ruḫṣat-nāme*) were then delivered to the vizier, who then gave an audience to the two ambassadors 'of nearly two hours', according to Paget.[81] There 'Amcazāde told them that he was satisfied with the credentials, but the 'essence of the matter [of peace]' (*āṣl-ı maṣlaḥat*) resting with the emperor, he also demanded if the latter sent them full powers to negotiate with the Porte in his name and if he was satisfied with the delivered Ottoman terms.[82] Paget repeated the main points of Kinsky's 'ostensible' letter. The answers the two ambassadors gave, though, didn't appear convincing enough for the Ottoman officials, who wanted written proof.

'In order to obtain knowledge of the [true] essence and the degree [of progression] of the intended matter',[83] they demanded that the two mediators hand over the letters sent to them by Kinsky. "They didn't hide them" (*ṣaḳlamayub*), Rāmī admitted.[84] Yet, whereas Paget presented to the Ottomans the 'ostensible' missive of the Bohemian Chancellor, Colyer gave them his 'private' one. This move of his almost brought the peace negotiations to the brink of collapse because the Dutchman also rushed through to deliver his dispatches first. The Ottomans reacted with consternation. 'Truly, the tenor of this letter being full of pride, no answer was given to the ambassadors for a few days. And such impolite expressions caused great sadness.'[85] Then it came Paget's turn. The Englishman had a new series of meetings with Mavrocordatos, three in number, in which he employed the familiar strategy of 'role switching' to win once again the Ottoman Grand Dragoman's trust:

> After I had shown reticence for some time, I finally (and as if to confide [to him]) showed him the Latin letter of Your Lordship, the one it supposed to be shown [not the private one], which he read with great attention, and he asked to confide it to him for a day in order to consider it better. I did that, but not without declaring to him that what I was doing was not an obligation but a way to show him, in giving him this satisfaction, how I was pretending to treat honestly with him.[86]

80 Ibid.; *Ta'rīḫ-i ṣulḥ-nāme*, fol. 24ª.
81 ÖStA, HHStA, Türkei I, Turcica Box 165, Folder 3 (May 1698), fol. 16ᵛ, Paget to Kinsky, 9 May 1698 (J.C.).
82 *Ta'rīḫ-i ṣulḥ-nāme*, fol. 27ᵇ.
83 Ibid., fol. 28ª.
84 Ibid.
85 Ibid., fol. 29ª.
86 ÖStA, HHStA, Türkei I, Turcica Box 165, Folder 3 (May 1698), fol. 17ᵛ, Paget to Kinsky, 9 May 1698 (J.C.).

Upon reading the second letter, the Ottomans observed the variance between them.[87] They chose to ascribe it to a deliberate move by the mediators. 'It was understood that they intended it as such: let firstly the letter of the Dutch ambassador be given [to them] and see what they say. Because the missive to the English ambassador was both favourable in its contents and mild in its form'.[88] In this incident, it is paramount to observe the significance of a single letter's writing style in influencing the recipient's decisions. There were certain normative expectations in the manner appropriate to address your interlocutor, namely, to be polite and mild. Paget acutely sensed this need when he had advised Kinsky to draft his letter precisely this way.

Despite the Ottoman interpretation, the 'two letters incident' reveals more about the rift and rivalry between the two mediators than their cooperation. It also manifests the consequences of Kinsky's hitherto sidelining of Colyer in favour of Paget. His 'ostensible' Latin letter was addressed solely to the Englishman, not the two mediators together. Colyer was thus unable to hide his private letter since he didn't have another one to present. The two of them could also have coordinated their moves. Still, it appears that such coordination was impossible since Paget possibly resented the presence of Colyer, and the latter was probably still holding a grudge against the Englishman for keeping him in the dark throughout the previous months. One cannot also rule out the idea that Colyer took this step to gain the Ottomans' trust (he delivered his letter first) or even to embarrass Paget by revealing his duplicity to the Ottomans.

The negotiations were ultimately saved because the Porte, eager to make peace, was willing to forget the first letter and stick to the second, more promising one instead. Although, as Rāmī Meḥmed later confessed, 'to be honest, in the letter of Count Kinsky also, there were some ambiguous expressions whose meaning [...] was not elucidated',[89] the Ottoman side viewed the 'demolition and evacuation clause' as a promising field for future exploitation. Mavrocordatos revisited Paget and appeared satisfied with the letter's contents. In his view, the emperor and Venice clearly wanted peace, whereas the meaning of some sentences implied that the *uti possidetis* could also be applied to the Polish-Lithuanian Commonwealth and even Muscovy if the latter truly wanted an accommodation. Thus, the foundation of peace could, at

87 *Taʾrīḫ-i ṣulḥ-nāme*, fol. 30[b].

88 Ibid.

89 *Taʾrīḫ-i ṣulḥ-nāme*, fol. 86[a].

last, be laid. Paget disagreed on this last point, however.[90] Muscovy would have to be included in it as well.

A new *dīvān* was convened to decide what to reply to the mediators.[91] The next day, Mavrocordatos returned to Paget with the response of the grand vizier:

> The emperor's answer regarding the foundation of peace became known. A new response was needed because, being his ally, the Tsar of Moscow is also to be included in the peace. This matter would have required reflection. Nonetheless, for the subjects' mercy's sake, it is possible to obtain the Imperial approval to make peace with the Tsar of Moscow if it would apply to the latter the same foundation upon which peace is to be made with the other allies. Yet, first things first, as before, you must be given full powers (*ruḫsat-ı külliye*) [to negotiate on the emperor's behalf]. If indeed there is no objection to the cessation of the shedding of human blood, then let it henceforth come to an end.[92]

Demanding *plein-pouvoir* for the mediators to negotiate the basis upon which the peace negotiations were to be established was a clever move. The Ottomans were hoping to win over the two ambassadors and achieve a much more favourable interpretation of the *uti possidetis*, which the emperor would then be constrained to accept. Mavrocordatos further expanded on 'Amcazāde's words, stating that by agreeing to include Muscovy in the negotiations, the Porte had manifested its disposition to stop the bloodshed. If the emperor, though, didn't send full negotiating powers to the mediators to agree on the 'foundations' of the prospective peace talks, 'the world would see who is blocking the progress of the negotiations and on whom henceforth the desolations that will ensue are to be blamed'.[93]

It is paramount here to observe the progress of the peacemaking process as a series of signs and countersigns emitted by the various parties, which revealed their disposition and willingness to negotiate. When one side took a step and showed readiness to advance the peacemaking process, it expected the other side to do the same. A failure to generate a countersign could be interpreted as evidence that a party did not seriously want to make peace. As 'Amcazāde

90 ÖStA, HHStA, Türkei I, Turcica Box 165, Folder 3 (May 1698), fol. 18r, Paget to Kinsky, 9 May 1698 (J.C.).

91 *Ta'rīḫ-i ṣulḥ-nāme*, fol. 31a.

92 ÖStA, HHStA, Türkei I, Turcica Box 164, Folder 5 (1697) fol. 5(?)r.

93 ÖStA, HHStA, Türkei I, Turcica Box 165, Folder 3 (May 1698), fol. 18r–v, Paget to Kinsky, 9 May 1698 (J.C.).

stated to the mediators, 'the emperor didn't send you full power credentials, but opted to delay the matter with the display of obstacles'.[94] Besides its possible ulterior motives, the Ottoman request that the two mediators be explicitly empowered by the emperor and his allies to negotiate the Peace Foundation is not to be considered a mere formality. It was an essential step via which the peace negotiations would have exited the, until then, unofficial sphere restricted to the exchange of private letters. The emperor and his confederates would have officially declared their intention to make peace. From the Ottoman point of view, that was a fair countersign to match the positive peace signs they had already emitted to the Christian allies.

On the other hand, the references to an unspecified 'World' who, acting as a moral judge, would condemn the party responsible for refusing to make peace and thus continuing the devastations of war, cannot remain unnoticed. It was a rhetorical scheme used by both sides in almost all peace negotiations throughout the war, and it was designed to put pressure on the opponent to agree to sit at the negotiation table or to lay the blame on him for the failure to consummate the peace talks. In the domain of ideas, it demonstrated a supra-cultural – at least discursive – appraisal of peace and an equally supra-cultural condemnation of war. It also reveals an interesting perception of the 'Theatre of Peace'. According to this perception, the actors participating in the 'peace play' were not supposed to act alone in an empty theatre but in front of an audience, 'the World', which most probably was comprised of the other members of the 'Society of Princes'. This audience didn't remain solely in the role of a spectator, but somehow directly intervened during the play, applauding or criticising the actors on how well they performed. A failure to act the way the audience expected from a given actor – namely, to be a sincere peacemaker – and the latter would suffer a blow to his theatrical prestige and reputation as a performer. As Paget wrote to Count Kinsky, if the Ottomans rejected the Imperial proposals, 'the world will see that His Imperial Majesty and His allies did, on their part, what was required in order to procure peace, and the woes and desolations of the war will henceforth be blamed on the Turks'.[95]

4.1 *The Grand Vizier in Real and Imagined Troubles*

After that second round of negotiations in Adrianople, the two mediators wrote together, this time, back to Vienna. They asked Kinsky for full powers to lay down the basic (territorial possession-related) principles upon which peace was to be negotiated. If that didn't materialise, the Porte was unwilling

94 *Taʾrīḫ-i ṣulḥ-nāme*, fol. 31ᵃ.

95 ÖStA, HHStA, Türkei I, Turcica Box 165, Folder 3 (May 1698), fol. 17ᵛ, Paget to Kinsky, 9 May 1698 (J.C.).

to open its cards further.[96] They also requested 'clear and positive orders' from the emperor on how to proceed.[97] And to make sure that the Imperial ministers would get the message, they added the following: 'presently, we see the Turks entirely disposed to desire peace seriously and with all their hearts. Still, if they start to suspect that we are fooling them with back-and-forths and irresolutions, they could change their will, and then we would have difficulty recalling and bringing them back to reason'.[98] Once again, Schreyer took the way to the Imperial capital.[99]

During the same period, the French ambassador, Châteauneuf, renewed his efforts to interfere in the negotiations. Failed in his mediation attempt, he tried this time to derail the talks. He approached the grand vizier and presented him with the situation in western Europe and the imminent war that was about to break out over the Spanish succession.[100] He recommended that the sultan should exploit this situation. When the new conflict commences, and the emperor is occupied in the west, 'opportunities will open to take revenge from him'.[101] The grand vizier, while 'respecting the ancient friendship with France [...] didn't give importance to such empty and proofless arguments'.[102] And so, this second French attempt to re-enter the frame failed once more.

A unique glimpse into the mind of ʿAmcazāde by this point and his clear determination to terminate the war and bring peace to the Ottoman dominions is provided by a letter he wrote to the sultan's mother shortly after the departure of Paget's secretary for Vienna.[103] The vizier informed her of the letters that had recently arrived from the Habsburg capital. They were submitted to the sultan, together with the clarifications of the mediators. As for their content, it

> shows that they profoundly seek peace [...] And now, a favourable reply to the conclusion of the matter was given, and [the mediators'] messengers were sent back [to Vienna]. The [mediating] ambassadors claim that with God's help, a reply will come in a month. Well now, if it's not a month, then be it forty days.[104]

96 Ibid., fol. 34^{r-v}, Paget/Colyer to Kinsky, 19 May 1698.
97 Ibid.
98 Ibid., fol. 34^{v}.
99 *Taʾrīḫ-i ṣulḥ-nāme*, fol. 32^{a}.
100 Ibid., fol. 33^{b}.
101 Ibid.
102 Ibid.
103 DABOA, TS. MA.e 523,15, Hüseyn Paşa to the Vālide Sulṭān, second half of May 1698.
104 Ibid.

He goes on to express the wish that God would grant the subjects 'tranquillity and repose' (*āsāyış u istirāḥat*) during the reign of the sultan after so many years of continuous wars that depleted the treasury and exhausted the troops. After securing the approval of the padishah, no obstacle remains to the speedy completion of the affair. And yet, God's will was still unknown. If He did not decree that 'his servants should be at rest' (*ḳullarınıñ rāḥat olmaları*), then 'apparently the fires of war would have to bright again in many places'.[105] His presentation of the situation reveals a general – though in some places reserved – optimism and a desire to conclude the affair as soon as possible. On the other hand, his constant reference to 'tranquillity and repose', the central axis of his pro-peace policy, points to a more profound conviction for their necessity than mere normative rhetoric.

Another crucial issue that surfaces in the letter is the desire of the sultan to embark again on a campaign at the head of his troops. Of course, the last time he was on the battlefield, he was forced to witness the near annihilation of his armies at the Battle of Zenta. Still, that disaster doesn't seem to have deterred Muṣṭafā II from seeking a revanche or at least trying to repair his sultanic prestige by leading his armies again in person. His chief ministers thought otherwise, though. ʿAmcazāde claims that it was deemed better that the sultan remained in his seat of government. Such a decision has nothing to do with a lack of campaign preparation. 'We are not weak, and yet Your Highness knows the state of all the troops due to the prolongation of campaigns. It's an army tired and impatient with them'.[106] One could perhaps grasp a hint here of a possible rebellion of the troops. It was not an unfounded scenario. As we have already seen, the army, after a series of defeats, had rebelled again while on campaign in 1687 and then marched on the Ottoman capital to depose Meḥmed IV, Muṣṭafā's father. The danger that such a situation would repeat itself was genuine.

Nonetheless, conversing with Colyer in early July 1698, the grand vizier would provide a different explanation. He confided to the Dutchman that it took him 'unbelievable efforts' (*ongelooffelijke moeijte*) to convince the sultan to acquiesce in a peace that would leave the 'enemies in possession of so many provinces' (*vijanden het bezit van soo veel Provintiën*). If the Christian allies continued attacking the Ottoman positions, the sultan might be infuriated and could change his mind again.[107] That's why it was thought more advisable to keep him distant from the front line by arguing that his presence in a

105 Ibid.

106 Ibid.

107 Quoted in Hora Siccama, 'De Vrede van Carlowitz', 142.

campaign would entail enormous costs that the treasury was not able to meet.[108] Yet, such words were more destined to pressure the mediators to convince the allies to agree on a general armistice during the peace negotiations and stop their attacks than to convey the truth.

In a text written in the letter's margin, ʿAmcazāde gets more intimate. 'If we have friends, we have enemies too. God knows, they accuse your servant of negligence and fault even if an affair is good, and many words are said about me. I entreat for your protection. Do not remove it from me'.[109] This alarming tone, full of sentiment, provides a unique look behind the scenes of Ottoman high politics of the time. Although it leaves unclear if the vizier was criticised for his peacemaking initiatives or his policies in general, it demonstrates that he didn't feel utterly secure in his position. He needed urgent support from an influential individual inside the court, even more so since he would soon have to depart from the seat of government and march with the troops to Belgrade.[110] His enemies could have exploited his absence to bring about his downfall. Still, he leaves nebulous the issue of who his enemies are. Perhaps that would have been more evident for the *vālide*. He was optimistic, though, because the sultan's mother could see 'our respect and demand [for us] with the army and the rest of the people'.[111]

Although ʿAmcazāde remained in his position, these tribulations inside the Ottoman élite gave rise to a bunch of fanciful rumours – the seventeenth-century 'fake news' – which could travel far and wide, be taken quite seriously and even receive thorough examinations by important decision-makers. In a letter dated 22 May 1698, the Venetian ambassador in Vienna, Carlo Ruzzini, informed Count Kinsky, 'that via the route of Belgrade, news has been received of profound changes in the government of the Porte, with the death of the mufti and the grand vizier'.[112] The Bohemian Chancellor considered it to be so important that after two days, he wrote to General Rabbutin, one of the commanders of the Imperial forces on the Hungarian front, to ask him if he was able to confirm it.[113] In the meantime, novel elements were added to the 'news': 'There is a strong rumour running here of great changes at the Ottoman Porte, according to which the grand vizier is strangled, and the grand mufti deposed and

108 Ibid.

109 DABOA, TS. MA.e 523,15, Hüseyn Paşa to the Vālide Sulṭān, second half of May 1698.

110 'For the sake of the True Faith, I am embarking on the road of Holy War. It is my wish that God entrusts my life to you', ibid.

111 Ibid.

112 ÖStA, HHStA, Türkei I, Turcica Box 165, Folder 3 (May 1698), fol., 48^{r-v}, Ruzzini to Kinsky, 22 May 1698.

113 Ibid., fol. 60^{r-v}, Kinsky to Rabbutin, 24 May 1698.

chased'.[114] Nevertheless, there were other more pressing issues than rumours to occupy Kinsky's mind. 'We are waiting here for the great Tsar of Muscovy, personally mixed among his Grand Embassy headed towards this court. A visit not ordinary at all, but now very much in the tsar's style, which will not fail to cause reciprocal embarrassment'.[115]

5 Fifth Scene: Warsaw

The stance Muscovy would adopt in the peace negotiations was one problem for the Imperial government. The other was what position the Polish-Lithuanian Commonwealth would take. August II's primary preoccupation upon ascending to the Polish throne in 1697 was to stabilise his authority in the Commonwealth and secure the succession for his offspring. He believed that he could achieve both through military successes in the war against the Ottomans.[116] To secure his election, he had already pledged to recuperate with his German forces the Commonwealth lands lost to the Ottomans in 1672 and especially Kamianets-Podilskyi.[117] He nurtured more personal territorial desires, however. Just like King Jan III Sobieski (r. 1676–96) before him, he planned to conquer limitrophe territories and turn them into patrimonial dominions. In this way, the Commonwealth's magnates would have to choose a member of his family in order not to sever ties with the newly acquired lands.[118] For that reason, he fixed his eyes upon the Danubian Principalities and attempted to build close ties with their local élites.[119] Yet, by the spring of 1698, none of those goals had been accomplished. Kamianets-Podilskyi had not fallen, nor had Moldavia and Wallachia been conquered. He was also in possession of a Saxon standing army, twenty thousand men strong, which he desperately desired to keep in place.[120] That explains why the first letters Kinsky sent to the Polish King were reciprocated with silence. August simply had no concrete interest in peace.

Nonetheless, following the Bohemian Chancellor's advice, he chose to hide the information he received from Vienna from the grandees of his realm, many of whom looked favourably upon a peace settlement with the Porte.

114 Ibid.
115 Ibid., fol. 60^{v}.
116 Burdowicz-Nowicki, *Piotr I*, 114–5.
117 Ibid., 115.
118 Ibid.
119 Ibid., 115–6.
120 Ibid., 117–8.

For instance, the Grand Hetman, Stanisław Jabłonowski, was one of them. In April 1698, perhaps still unaware of the details of the already kicked-off negotiations, he was suggesting that the Commonwealth's proposals could be conveyed to the Porte via the French ambassador in Constantinople or the Crimean Tatars, as they had been several times earlier during the Sixteen Years' War.[121] He also disapproved, as did the majority of the Commowealth's élite, of August II's plans to acquire the Danubian Principalities, forwarding instead a concentrated effort to recuperate Kamianets-Podilskyi, a move which he believed would put the Polish side in a better bargaining position in the negotiations.[122]

It was in that general climate that August received the dispatches from Vienna containing the Ottoman peace proposals on 30 April.[123] As was to be expected, the latter's reaction to the peacemaking process was not a positive one. He bitterly remarked that the emperor had significantly advanced the negotiations, but had already spent much money, 'to the ruin of his land and people', on preparations for the next campaign season. Hence, he could not comprehend the necessity of peace talks or the sending of his plenipotentiaries to Vienna to participate in them.[124]

After receiving the peace proposals, August realised that he had to act quickly. He immediately dispatched a Saxon confidant of his, Christoph Dietrich von Bose, to the United Provinces and England. His mission was to convince the two Maritime Powers that his master's interests rested in the continuation of war and not in peace and that the Ottoman peace proposals were not advantageous for the Commonwealth, as to obtain credit for the king to finance his war effort.[125] August might have had an army, but money was needed to keep him up and running. Bose's first stop was the Hague, where he met with the Grand Pensionary of Holland, Anthoine Heinsius (d. 1720). To his dismay, Heinsius's reply was straightforward and even somewhat cynical. 'It was necessary to quicken peace in the east', declared the grand pensionary,

> so that after the death of the King of Spain, who apparently will not live for much longer, the House of Austria and its allies can focus on the succession and impede a French involvement in it. He also expressed his

121 Marek Wagner, *Stanisław Jabłonowski. Politik i dowódca*, vol. 2 (Połomia: Inforteditions 2020) 260.

122 Ibid., 260.

123 ÖStA, HHStA, Türkei I, Turcica Box 165, Folder 4 (June 1698), fol. 4r, Sedlnitzky to Leopold I, 1 June 1698.

124 Ibid., fol. 5r.

125 Burdowicz-Nowicki, *Piotr I*, 122–3.

> hope that Your Majesty would resolve to skip a few formalities and even sacrifice Her proper interests for the good of Europe until a better occasion [presents itself].[126]

Disheartened, the envoy informed the king that he was waiting for the first good wind to sail to England and risk his chances with William III.[127]

If he was hoping to achieve something better at the English Court, he would have been equally disappointed. With the Spanish succession also dominating minds there, nobody cared about the interests of August II or the Commonwealth. So much was the desire to disengage the emperor from his 'Turkish War' that it was thought in London that peace in the east could be achieved even before the beginning of July.[128] In his audience with William III, the latter repeated to the Saxon diplomat the usual refrain of the absolute necessity of reconciling the emperor with the sultan for the greater good of Europe. And although he acknowledged that the Commonwealth 'would acquire very little profit from these [Ottoman] conditions of peace', he advised August to think not as King of Poland but as Elector of Saxony and an important member of the Holy Roman Empire. And the greatest enemy of the empire was not Muṣṭafā II but Louis XIV, who, with his ever-growing power, was putting the 'liberty of Europe in danger' (*la liberté de l'Europe en danger*).[129] Greatly disillusioned by the reigning climate dominant in both Maritime Powers, Bose gave the following advice to his principal: 'Your majesty would rather achieve Her aim by remonstrances at the Imperial Court and by a more close alliance with the tsar rather than by longer negotiations in this country'.[130]

And truly, given the situation, the need for the two monarchs, Peter and August, to coordinate their moves appeared urgent. The king had probably long entertained such a prospect since, during his stay at the Hague, Bose also held talks with the tsar. Failing to acquire any credit from Dutch bankers for his master, he hoped for Muscovite financial assistance as well.[131] In his meeting with Peter, the Saxon inquired whether the latter was willing to continue the war against the Ottomans jointly with August II in case the Imperials and the Venetians made a separate peace. The tsar replied positively, in general terms, declaring that he was going to prevent the Imperial plans for peace

126 AGAD, AKW, 1/3/0/33/78, teczka 497 nr. 825, fol. 4, Bose to August II, May 1698 (?).
127 Ibid., fol. 5.
128 AGAD, AKW, 1/3/0/33/78/ teczka 494 nr. 819, fol. 2, Bose to August II, 19 May 1698.
129 Ibid., fol. 7–8.
130 Ibid., fol. 8–9.
131 Burdowicz-Nowicki, *Piotr I*, 122–3, 127.

during his forthcoming trip to Vienna and proposed that the Polish King dispatch an envoy of his there to coordinate together their moves. These imprecise words, followed by no concrete engagement, didn't impress Bose as much as the Muscovite financial capabilities, but still, it was something compared to the total indifference he encountered from the two mediating powers.[132] Thus, all in all, apart from vague promises of close cooperation by the tsar, Bose's mission in western Europe yielded relatively meagre results.[133]

Besides his personal diplomacy, August was compelled to consult at some point the Commonwealth's constitutional bodies. During his audience with the Imperial resident ambassador, the king declared that he would request the opinion of the Polish Senate. Sedlnitzky was not content with this prospect. The matter was urgent, and deliberations had to be taken quickly. That was not the time to show institutional conformity. Still, under the king's insistence, he agreed, provided that the issue would be carefully presented to the Polish magnates.[134] The next days were spent with Sedlnitzky trying with 'various persuasions' (*durch unterschiedlische persuahovia*) to secure the support of as many members of the senate as possible.[135]

The body was conveyed in late May.[136] There was strong opposition to the prospective peace terms, especially by the Palatine of Marienburg – very close to the king[137] – and his supporters, who, according to Sedlnitzky, made a 'relative noise' (*zimblichen Bruit*) during the session.[138] As in the case of Muscovy, the *uti possidetis* principle was unacceptable to most of the Polish grandees since it would mean that Kamianets, their main war goal, would remain in Ottoman hands.[139] Neither was the recuperation of the Podolian fortress with its walls demolished, as the Ottomans were proposing, acceptable. Apart from being a question of prestige to recuperate the fortress intact, there was also a question of security. As Bose stated to William III, a demolished Kamianets would mean that 'Ukraine and Podolia, which are the most

132 Ibid., 122–3.

133 News of Bose's mission and the talks he had with Peter I reached Sedlnitzky, who communicated it back to Vienna: ÖStA, HHStA, Türkei I, Turcica Box 165, Folder 4 (June 1698), fol. 5v–6r, Sedlnitzky to Leopold I, 1 June 1698; Ibid., fol. 60r–v, Sedlnitzky to Kinsky, 19 June 1698.

134 Sedlnitzky to Leopold I, 1 June 1698, fol. 4r.

135 Ibid., fol. 6r.

136 Wagner, *Stanisław Jabłonowski*, 261; Burdowicz-Nowicki, *Piotr I*, 123.

137 Following Sedlnitzky, the king trusted the Palatine in everything: Sedlnitzky to Leopold I, 1 June 1698, fol. 7r.

138 Ibid., fol. 6v–7r.

139 Serwański, 'Dyplomacja polska', 17.

beautiful Polish provinces, would not be cultivated again, and they would be at every moment exposed to the raids and invasions of the Tatars'.[140]

Finally, Sedlnitzky's 'lobbying' played off. Despite the decision to dispatch letters of protest to William III of England and the emperor, the senate also approved sending the Bishop of Kyiv, Jan Gomolinski, as *Magnum Oratorem seu Commissarium* to the Imperial Court to learn more about the peace negotiations.[141] In his letter to Leopold I, the king actually went one step further, declaring that Gomolinski was to be followed by an *Extraordinarium Ablegatum* to partake in the talks.[142] It appeared as if he had already slowly begun to change his mind.

6 Sixth Scene: Vienna

In Vienna, despite demonstrations of hostility to peace emanating from Warsaw and the Muscovite Tsar, the Imperial side was determined not to further delay the advancement of the negotiations. The arrival of the letters of the mediators from Adrianople at the beginning of June acted as an additional catalyst. Paget made himself quite clear to Kinsky:

> I hope that the difficulties which could be put forward by those who prefer their interest instead of the general one will not be able to hinder the accomplishment of such a good work. Yet, as the plan of those who don't desire peace is to delay the negotiation, our concern could not be any other than to advance it. For this reason, I beg Your Lordship to press things vigorously.[143]

The Bohemian Chancellor grasped the message. He immediately wrote to the Venetian ambassador Carlo Ruzzini:

> I think it's high time for an expedient of a declaration which is to be made by us, which by avoiding the difficulties of a full power given [to the mediators], it will safeguard our decorum, it will conserve our liberty

140 AGAD, AKW, 1/3/0/33/78/ teczka 494 nr. 819, fol. 5, Bose to August II, 19 May 1698.

141 Wagner, *Stanisław Jabłonowski*, 261; Burdowicz-Nowicki, *Piotr I*, 123; ÖStA, HHStA, Türkei I, Turcica Box 165, Folder 3 (May 1698), fol. 71r, August II to Leopold I, 31 May 1698.

142 Ibid.

143 ÖStA, HHStA, Türkei I, Turcica Box 165, Folder 4 (June 1698), fol. 56r, Paget to Kinsky, 19 June 1698 (J.C.).

> of negotiating in the congress, and it will serve more in fully reassuring the Turks of the foundation of *uti possidetis*, accepted by us.[144]

And expanding more on its content, he added, "I think that it should be only worded with general expressions in order to be able later to apply it during the congress in each case according to everyone's and all the participating allies' convenience".[145]

So, the Imperials didn't take the Ottoman bait. Instead of the allies being the ones receiving and agreeing to the general contouring of a peace foundation negotiated without their active participation by empowering the mediators to negotiate and sign a preliminary instrument, Kinsky and Ruzzini chose to advance a step further and issue one of their own. This move was designed to throw the ball back to the Ottoman side and force it to acquiesce to a formal document explaining the foundation of peace conceived and drafted by the allies (or at least some of them) and not by the mediators and the Ottomans.

Immediately after, Kinsky and Ruzzini received from their principals full power to accept and sign the Foundation of Peace,[146] and on 23 June, the members of the 'Turkish Deputation' met in the residence of the Venetian ambassador. At the top of the agenda were three items: 1) the instrument to be sent to the Ottomans, 2) what was to be replied to the Polish King as well as 3) what was to be written to Paget and Colyer concerning the time and place of the upcoming congress.[147] Kinsky remained firm in his conviction that the instrument had to be as general as possible. Thus, they should nominate the venue of the congress preferred by them solely to Paget, not to the Ottomans.[148]

A cardinal preoccupation of the meeting was whether there should be a general armistice for the duration of the congress.[149] In contrast to modern principles, most of the seventeenth-century multilateral peace congresses were taking place amidst war. The military operations of the various participants continued normally. That meant that every significant setback or victory of either side during the congress could significantly impact the negotiations.[150] We will return to this issue later. For the moment, according to the conference protocol kept by Ruzzini's secretary, the Imperial ministers were divided on the

144 Ibid., fol. 27ʳ, Kinsky to Ruzzini, 7 June 1698.
145 Ibid., fol. 71ʳ, Kinsky to Ruzzini, 22 June 1698.
146 Ibid., fol. 79ʳ–80ᵛ.
147 ÖStA, HHStA, Türkei I, Turcica Box 165, Folder 4 (June 1698), fol. 100ᵛ, relation of the members of the 'Turkish Deputation' to Leopold I, 23 June 1698.
148 BNM, Ms.it.VII 399 (8625), fol. 64ʳ, protocol of the 23rd of June meeting.
149 Ibid., fol. 65ʳ.
150 Croxton, *Westphalia*, 176–83; Köhler, *Strategie und Symbolik*, 120–1.

subject. At the same time, their main preoccupation seems to have revolved around the effect a general armistice would have on the duration of the peace negotiations – Kinsky, for instance, argued that the emperor would not accept an armistice because it could cause a delay to the conclusion of peace.[151]

On the other hand, in the relation submitted to the emperor after the meeting, the chief issue appears to have been different – albeit related. Out of pride, the Ottomans had never asked before for a general armistice, and probably they would neither do it this time.[152] Hence, if the emperor and Venice were to request it, it would seem that they were unsure of their present military strength.[153] In which case, the Ottomans might demand more, thus prolonging the peace negotiations. Ultimately, Ruzzini fully concurred with the Imperial ministers' arguments,[154] and Leopold was also of the same mind.[155] No general armistice was to be mentioned.

And so, in this way, the Instrument of the Foundation of Peace (*Fundamentum Pacis*) was signed. It contained the essence of "Kinsky's letter". Nonetheless, it created a series of significant problems which would later surface, especially during the congress. While it was signed in the name of the emperor and the Republic of Venice, it also included their two other allies, the Polish-Lithuanian Commonwealth and Muscovy, without the latter signing or even agreeing to it. Ruzzini, exonerating himself, provides the following reasons why the Imperial ministers took that decision:

> the distance between [the different] locations; the absence of their [the Polish and Muscovite] ministers at the [Imperial] Court; the apprehension to urge a reply to the Porte, in order to keep the [Ottoman] inclination [towards peace] warm, and the danger, that if they entered into negotiations on this with those princes, the latter would bring it to a

151 BNM, Ms.it.VII 399 (8625), fol 65^r, protocol of the 23rd of June meeting.

152 In this case there seems to have been a manipulation or purposeful omittance of information since, in fact, during the Failed Vienna Congress (in which Kinsky himself participated) the Ottomans did propose a general armistice for a specific time period, in order, so they claimed, to facilitate the successful conclusion of the negotiations: *Cerîde-i Takrirât*, 43. Of course, given the recent Imperial advances in the Balkans and those of Venice in southern Greece, such a general armistice would have greatly favoured the Ottoman side.

153 ÖStA, HHStA, Türkei I, Turcica Box 165, Folder 4 (June 1698), fol., 106^v–107^r, relation of the members of the 'Turkish Deputation' to Leopold I, 23 June 1698.

154 Ibid., fol. 107^{r-v}. In another meeting on 30 June, Ruzzini even expressed his satisfaction with the decision of the emperor not to propose a general armistice: Ibid., fol. 123^r, relation of the members of the 'Turkish Deputation' to Leopold I, 30 June 1698.

155 Ibid., fol. 108^v, Imperial resolution, 23 June (?) 1698.

> standstill, and they would disturb it with difficulties streaming from their ostentatiously bellicose spirit.[156]

Despite the declarations of the emperor and his ministers that they should negotiate by abiding by the letter to their obligations towards their allies, the signing of the Instrument was destined as a clear *fait accompli* for both the Commonwealth and Muscovy without necessarily taking into consideration the interests of those two powers.[157] Such moves only made the split inside the alliance more pronounced. As for the future ramifications of the Instrument of the Foundation of Peace during the congress itself, it created a series of major issues since both the Polish and the Muscovite plenipotentiaries would not accept it, arguing that it was not signed by them, so they were not to abide by its stipulations. Nonetheless, the Imperial and Venetian side was currently facing a more urgent matter. The tsar was already in Vienna, and they had to plan their moves as best as possible on how to communicate with him.

•••

By the end of June 1698, the peace negotiations had significantly advanced. In less than six months – an impressively short amount of time compared to other seventeenth-century preliminary peace discussions – three of the principal belligerents, the Ottomans, the Habsburg emperor and Venice, agreed on the basis of the future treaty and the need for a peace congress under the mediation of the two maritime powers of England and the Netherlands. Even though nobody was fully satisfied with the proposals made by the others and many paramount issues remained nebulous, everyone was willing to disregard them for the moment and leave them to be solved later in the congress. Much of the credit for the progress of this successful negotiation should go to Lord Paget. He was the one behind every significant step of the peacemaking process. He adroitly manipulated both sides, convincing them of the sincerity of their opponents' peace sentiments. He immediately grasped what was needed in order to further the negotiations by suggesting to Count Kinsky that he write

156 Ruzzini, *Relazione*, 352.

157 In fact, during another joint meeting with the Venetian ambassador on 30 June, the two allies decided to communicate with the tsar, who was actually present in Vienna, only after Shreyer had been dispatched with the Instrument back to Paget. In this way, they could present the situation to him as 'truly resolved' (*als würkhlich resolviert*) and not as something still in the process of negotiation: ÖStA, HHStA, Türkei I, Turcica Box 165, Folder 4 (June 1698), fol. 123r–124r, relation of the members of the 'Turkish Deputation' to Leopold I, 30 June 1698.

a letter to convince the Ottomans that the Christian allies' desire for peace was genuine and by pressing the Imperial minister to act quickly by bypassing the obstacles thrown at the negotiations by the Polish-Lithuanian Commonwealth and Muscovy. Even so, the road to peace was anything but secure. The tsar and the Polish King would have to accept the fait accompli presented to them by their allies. And what if they wouldn't? The Ottoman side's reaction to the allied Instrument of the Peace Foundation was not predictable. They only expected full powers for the mediators to discuss further and agree to it. It would seem as much like a done deal to them as to the emperor's allies. Various other essential issues, such as the congress venue, remained undetermined. The last phase of the preliminaries would be all about them.

Interlude 1: Mediation

> The role of the mediator is one of the most difficult for an ambassador to uphold and mediation one of the most unpleasant tasks.
>
> ABRAHAM DE WICQUEFORT (d. 1682)[1]

∴

One of the most notable characteristics of the seventeenth-century peacemaking processes was the use by the opposing parties of a mediator – or mediators – who acted as facilitators and promoters of the negotiations. In spite of the fact that the existing literature on mediation in the early modern period is quite vast,[2] most of it focuses exclusively on the western part of the European continent:[3] such a spatial – and cultural – restriction results in misunderstandings and essential omissions. One of those misinterpretations is that the role of mediation in peace congresses diminished from the late seventeenth century.[4] However, the case of Carlowitz is particularly important since it lucidly illustrates that far from being moribund, mediation remained a vital emblem of the peacemaking process, which could advance it, influence it, and shape it in a catalytic way.[5] In addition, despite some minor variations –

1 Abraham de Wicquefort, *L'ambassadeur et ses fonctions*, vol. 2 (Cologne: Pierre Marteau 1690) 114.

2 *See*, among others, Markus Laufs and Christian Wenzel, 'Conflict Management in the Early Modern Period: Mediating and Safeguarding Treaties', in Goetze and Oetzel (eds.), *Early Modern European Diplomacy*, 707–23; Markus Laufs, *In viam pacis. Praktiken niederländischer und päpstlicher Friedens-vermittlung auf den Kongressen von Münster (1643–1649) und Nimwegen (1676–1679)* (Göttingen: Vandenhoeck & Ruprecht 2022); Christian Schneider, "'Types' of Peacemakers: Exploring the Authority and Self-Perception of the Early Modern Papacy", in Stephen Cummins and Laura Kounine (eds.), *Cultures of Conflict Resolution in Early Modern Europe* (London: Routledge 2016) 77–103; Michael Rohrschneider, 'Friedensvermittlung und Schiedsgerichtsbarkeit', in Dingel et al., *Handbuch Frieden*, 473–90; Heinz Duchhardt, 'Arbitration, Mediation oder Bons Offices? Die englische Friedensvermittlung in Nijmegen 1676–1679', in Heinz Duchhardt, *Studien zur Friedensvermittlung in der Frühen Neuzeit* (Wiesbaden: Franz Steiner 1979) 23–88.

3 A notable exception, in spatial terms at least, is Kantorska, 'Les médiations françaises'.

4 Duchhardt, 'Arbitration,', 88; Rohrschneider, 'Friedensvermittlung', 481–2.

5 In his comprehensive and illuminating study on mediation practices during the Congresses of Westphalia and Nijmegen, Markus Laufs dedicates a brief section to the role of mediation during the Congresses of Carlowitz and Passarowitz (1718): Laufs, *In viam pacis*, 512–7.

 | DOI:10.1163/9789004458499_008

which further reinforce its pluralistic nature – mediation was a supra-cultural practice with a common vocabulary and recognised characteristics in an area that stretched from the British Isles and the Iberian Peninsula to the Euphrates and the Russian steppes.[6]

We will start by discussing the practice's origins and providing a definition after separating it from similar concepts we encounter in the same period. Then, the development of the idea of mediation in the seventeenth century and the mediating attempts to end the Sixteen Years' War prior to the Carlowitz negotiations will be briefly touched upon. We will continue with the main tasks and strategies adopted by the mediators, the opposing parties' various attempts to win them over to their side and the accusations of mediation partisanship. Subsequently, we will turn our focus to self-fashioning and the material and symbolic capital a mediator could aspire to acquire from his position. The interlude will conclude with the multiple forms of 'mediation' practised during the Carlowitz Congress.

1 Mediation, Arbitration, Bons Offices

The concept of mediation is not an invention of the Early Modern Period, nor restricted to a particular cultural sphere. It goes far back in time, and one could label it as a universally acknowledged conflict resolution practice.[7] As with other conflict management mechanisms – such as the *uti possidetis* – mediation appears to be transferred from the level of interpersonal accommodation to an inter-polity one.[8] Thus, it reveals the persistence of a way of thinking, quite old, which equated war and peace between polities with legal strife and its resolution between two individuals. Both in Roman-Christian and Islamic legal traditions, there were two main paths that private individuals could follow to resolve a conflict. The first would be to bring it before the court and be subjected to a judge's verdict, an *arbiter* or *ḥākim* whose decision was imposed

---

Although he relies mostly on secondary literature, Laufs argues that the examples these two congresses offer necessitate a re-evaluation of the thesis concerning the diminishing role of mediation in multilateral diplomatic gatherings from the end of the seventeenth century: Ibid., 518.

6 Laufs reaches a similar conclusion, though he offers little further elaboration on the topic: Ibid., 517.

7 Rohrschneider, 'Friedensvermittlung', 473, fn. 2.

8 Konrad Repgen, 'Friedensvermittlung und Friedensvermittler beim Westfälischen Frieden', in Franz Bosbach and Christoph Kampmann (eds.), *Dreissigjährige Krieg und Westfälischer Friede: Studien und Quellen* (Paderborn: Ferdinand Schöningh 2015) 946; Schneider, "'Types' of Peacemakers", 78.

on the opposing parties, binding them to accept it.[9] The second would be to solve their differences without appealing to the judgment of a higher authority. In this case, the parties would resort to a third individual – or individuals – trusted or respected by both, who, without the power to issue a verdict, would count on the goodwill of both parties to help them reach an amicable settlement. This third person was called *arbitrator/amicabilis compositor* (later mediator) or *mutavassıṭ*.[10] Characteristically, in Islamic Law, the amicable settlement by mediation (*tavassuṭ*) bears the same name as one of the principal late seventeenth-century Ottoman words for peace between polities, *ṣulḥ*.[11] Hence, it is from these already established legal patterns that inter-polity conflict resolution with resort to a third party originated. Nevertheless, the above-made distinction brings us to a cardinal issue. Before attempting to define mediation and the mediator in the seventeenth-century peacemaking mechanisms, we should first specify what they are not by separating them – as possible as this might be – from similar concepts and processes.

One such process is arbitration, which is subjecting the resolution of strife between two rulers to a higher authority recognised by both and abiding by its decisions.[12] Arbitration played a much more significant and longer-lasting role in peace settlements in Latin Christendom than in the Islamic world. That could perhaps be explained by the fact that in contrast to the Pope or the Holy Roman Emperor, the Caliph – who embodied, *grosso modo*, the factions of the latter two combined – lost his actual power quite early on. It resulted in the establishment of several independent dynasties, which considered themselves 'sovereign'. Such a diverse historical process could account for the fact that even well into the seventeenth century, there was still no clear differentiation between mediation and arbitration – contrary to the Muslim case – in the Christian European *ius gentium* treatises.[13]

Accordingly, the proliferation in the Latin Christian world of the concept of mediation to the detriment of arbitration – at least from the late Middle Ages onwards – could not be seen separately from the gradually diminishing role and prestige of the Roman Pontiff and the Holy Roman Emperor and the rise of the concept of the sovereign ruler (then state). The recourse to mediation,

---

9 Repgen, 'Friedensvermittlung', 946; Aida Othman, 'And Ṣulḥ is best: Amicable Settlement and Dispute Resolution in Islamic Law' (Ph.D. thesis, Harvard University 2009).

10 Repgen,'Friedensvermittlung', 946; Othman, 'And Ṣulḥ is best', 34, 233.

11 Ibid. Accordingly, in order to speak of an accord between two polities, the Ottomans used the expression, *ıṣlāḥ-ı ẕātu'l-beyn*, which literally means 'a reconciling between two persons': *Ta'rīḫ-i ṣulḥ-nāme*, fol. 19ᵇ.

12 Schneider, "'Types' of Peacemakers", 78; Rohrschneider, 'Friedensvermittlung', 475.

13 Duchhardt, 'Arbitration', 54. On the difficulty to differentiate between the various forms of 'mediation' and 'arbitration', *see* Rohrschneider, 'Friedensvermittlung', 476.

rather than arbitration, meant that the members of the 'Society of Princes' recognised no higher authority apart from their own. During the Carlowitz Congress, when the Ottoman plenipotentiaries demanded that the Imperial ones pressure the Venetian ambassador to agree to the terms the Ottomans proposed to him, the latter would reply that 'the allies are independent sovereigns. We cannot impose laws upon them. Only services (*Uffizii*) we can employ to route them'.[14] However, arbitration was not totally extinguished. The Pope might have ceased to be the Arbiter of Christendom par excellence, but others continued to aspire to such a role throughout the seventeenth century, Louis XIV being a notable example.[15] Negotiating parties were still willing to subject themselves to the arbitration of a third party – concerning mainly some particular set of issues – even in multilateral peace congresses.[16]

1.1 *Bons Offices*

The 'services' mentioned by the Imperial plenipotentiaries, employed to 'guide' their allies, introduce us to another form of interposition: the *bons offices* (good services) or *ḥüsn saʿī* in Ottoman Turkish.[17] Seventeenth-century contemporaries used *bons offices* and mediation so interchangeably that it is extremely hard to define the actual differences between them.[18] The interpretations provided by some notable scholars describe 'good services' as a reduced and unofficial form of mediation, restricting itself to the technical or organizational preparations of the negotiations and the facilitation of communication between the different parties.[19] Nevertheless, as we shall see, those tasks were precisely the same as those that a mediator was supposed to perform. So, such interpretations while partly accurate, do not appear to cover the whole, highly perplexed picture.

It would be better to define *bons offices* in three ways: First, as a stratagem to deprive an aspiring mediating party of exercising significant influence during the negotiations, without alienating it completely, though. Such a stratagem

14 ÖStA, HHstA, Türkei I, Turcica Box 170, Protocollum, fol. 105.

15 Kantorska, 'Les médiations françaises'.

16 *See*, for instance, Duchhardt, 'Arbitration', 84.

17 *Cerîde-i Takrirât*, 45.

18 We even often encounter them together – as *bons offices* somehow define the assistance offered by a mediator – such as in a phrase from Rāmī's relation 'mutavassıṭlarıñ ḥüsn saʿīleriyle tefvīż olunmuş-idi' (*Taʾrīḫ-i ṣulḥ-nāme*, fol. 80ª) or in a letter from the Ottoman side delivered to the Imperials during the congress 'via the good services of the mediators' (*honestis officiis D[omi]norum Mediatorum*): ÖStA, HHStA, Türkei I, Turcica Box 168, Folder 1 (November 1698, 1st half), fol. 146ʳ.

19 Laufs and Wenzel, 'Conflict Management', 709–10; Duchhardt, 'Arbitration', 54–5, 87.

was triggered mainly by the belief that the prospective mediator, if it were accorded such a role, would not serve the interests of one of the principal negotiating sides. For instance, the main reason behind the Imperial choice to deny Hop the title of mediator in 1689 and thus the chance to become – as the Imperial ministers claimed – the 'padrone of the negotiation' (*Padrone des negotij*) was ingrained in the belief that he would not favour the Imperial designs but those of ... Venice! So, he would have to implicate himself in the talks as little as possible, and the *bons offices* were regarded as the best means to achieve that, without offending the United-Provinces, one of the emperor's main allies against France.[20]

Second, *bons offices* could be seen as an expedient used when, again, one of the leading participants in a negotiation did not desire to accord the interposing party any form of a particular distinctive ceremonial position. Such a way of thinking could be a direct byproduct of the blurred boundaries between arbitration and mediation in Christian Europe. Although the mediator didn't impose any binding decision on the main participants of the peace talks, he could still claim a unique ceremonial position resembling that of an arbiter.[21] It is in this particular context that one should place the remark made by the first Ottoman plenipotentiary, Zülfikār Efendi, during the peace congress in Vienna in 1689. 'And they (the Imperials) didn't consent to the mediation of the Dutch Republic because the Christians confuse mediation with arbitration, and whoever acts as mediator has the precedence. But being, in reality, no difference between simple mediation and *bons offices* [...]', the Ottomans also agreed to this arrangement.[22] During the opening phase of the Congress of Nijmegen (1676–79), the Imperial side would once more refuse to recognise the English King's interposition as mediation but solely as *bons offices*. The French plenipotentiaries would try to console the English by repeating what Zülfikār had said, that there was no real difference between the two concepts. And yet, for the infuriated Charles II (r. 1660–85), this simple change in words amounted to a loss of honour and reputation.[23] Thus, in such cases, 'good services' were considered a lesser form of mediation, but only in terms of prestige and not the actual tasks involved.

---

20 Slottman, *Ferenc II Rákóczi*, 79, fn. 29. Quite intriguingly, neither the Ottoman plenipotentiaries were satisfied with Hop's services – they considered him too pro-Imperial. Still, they too agreed to accept his *bons offices* in order not to perturbate their relations with the United Provinces, exactly just like the Austrian Habsburgs: *Cerîde-i Takrirât*, 101.

21 That was what the English tried without success to do during the Congress of Nijmegen: Duchhardt, 'Arbitration', 42–55.

22 *Cerîde-i Takrirât*, 45.

23 Duchhardt, 'Arbitration', 54–5.

A third way to understand *bons offices* – which is connected in a way to the previous one – would be as an informal mediation that often can take place in parallel with a formal one. In seventeenth-century sources, such informal mediation is also referred to as *interposition*.[24] The latter didn't seem to differ much in substance from a mediation proper, apart from its unofficial character.[25] However, except for a truly unique case,[26] the term *interposition* rarely appears in the primary material pertaining to the Congress of Carlowitz. While this was not always the norm, mediators were typically granted credentials by both sides, formally recognising their role. In contrast, those who practised *bons offices* (or *interposition*) alongside an acknowledged mediator undertook this service with the tacit consent of the participants but without formal recognition. As a result, they could not claim any official status. However, their role in negotiations could, at times, equal or even surpass that of the official mediator – contrary to the views of the Imperials in 1689. I emphasise the word *alongside* because, in the absence of an official mediator, even those performing *bons offices* could be granted, it seems, formal credentials by the negotiating parties.[27] Such was the case with Jacob Hop in 1689.[28]

The above-painted puzzled terrain demonstrates that any definition of mediation in the seventeenth-century peacemaking process must be tentative; early modern contemporaries were, in fact, more flexible.[29] So, as mediation, one could define a particular, non-institutionalised form of conflict resolution between two or more polities that agree to resort to a third party or parties accepted officially by both to facilitate the negotiations between them. The mediator does 'not take any binding decision but exerts a varying degree of

24 Laufs and Wenzel, 'Conflict Management', 709–10.

25 Ibid.

26 Refer below, 119.

27 Contrary to what Laufs and Wenzel sustain in their article, defining *bons offices* as "a third party's own initiative to facilitate conflict resolution without being officially approved by the rival parties": Laufs and Wenzel, 'Conflict Management', 709–10.

28 *Cerîde-i Takrirât*, 45–6. Interestingly, the form of the Ottoman credentials given to Hop bore a strong resemblance to those issued by the Porte for mediators officially recognised by her. Compare, for instance, Hop's credentials with the ones given in 1685 to the Transylvanian Prince Mihály Apafi, recognising him as mediator, in Ahmet Kırış, 'Hicrî 1096 (1684–1685) Yılına Dair bir Münşeat Mecmuası ve Değerlendirilmesi' (MA dissertation, Fatih Sultan Mehmet Vakıf University 2017) 98. Such a comparison confirms Zülfikār Efendi's comment that the Ottomans didn't differentiate much between the two concepts.

29 Laufs, *In viam pacis*, 82–5; Rohrschneider, 'Friedensvermittlung', 476.

influence on the disputants'.[30] Lastly, the office of mediation is accompanied by a certain prestige and recognition.

2 The Evolution and Proliferation of Peacemaking by Mediation in the Seventeenth Century

By the end of the seventeenth century, mediation had established itself as a dominant supra-cultural element of the inter-polity peacemaking process. Already during the negotiations at Zsitvatorok in 1606 between the Ottomans and the Austrian Habsburgs, a Hungarian delegation played the role of the mediator between the two parties.[31] The special spatial arrangement to manifest the Hungarians' mediating position, as well as the tasks, typical of that of a mediator, that they performed, suggest that the concept was not novel to the participants.[32] However, the fact that the Hungarian interposition didn't receive a particular mention in the final texts of the treaty could perhaps denote the still embryotic and quasi 'informal' state of the practice at this stage – apart, of course, from other possible reasons the two negotiating parties might have for not acknowledging it.[33]

With the negotiations in Westphalia to end the Thirty Years' War, mediation entered the frame of multilateral peace congresses as one of their essential ingredients.[34] All the major peace conferences of the seventeenth century thereafter took place under a mediator or mediator's auspices. The practice

30 Schneider, "'Types' of Peacemakers", 81; Laufs and Wenzel, 'Conflict Management', 709; Rohrschneider, 'Friedensvermittlung', 474–5.

31 *See* G. Bayerle, 'The Compromise at Zsitvatorok'. *Archivum Ottomanicum* 6 (1980), 12. It was pointed out to me by Gábor Kármán that, in this case, it would be better to speak of a Hungarian and not of a Transylvanian mediation since István Bocskai (d. 1606), whose representatives acted as both mediators and negotiating party (sic!), secured a place in the peace talks as head of the rebellious Hungarian Estates by which it was elected as Prince of Hungary. *See* also, Kármán, 'A Third Party'.

32 Ibid., 12–17. For the Ottoman case, the first – to my knowledge – recorded case of a *bons offices*-like informal interposition of a foreign power in a conflict between the Porte and another polity is that of France during the Ottoman-Venetian negotiation in 1573 to terminate the Cyprus War (1570–3): Işıksel, "Barbaro's Glass Ball". Nonetheless, many scholars still stick to the wrong assumption that the Ottoman Porte adopted mediation as a diplomatic practice only from the end of the seventeenth century. *See*, for instance, Hilal Ciftci, 'Mediation as a Diplomatic Tool in Ottoman Capitulations'. *Codrul Cosminului* 28/1 (2022), 29–54.

33 *See* the translation of different texts of the Peace Instruments and the absence of any reference to mediation in Bayerle, 'The Compromise', 24–28 (the originals in ibid., 42–53).

34 Laufs, *In viam pacis*; Repgen, 'Friedensvermittlung'.

became gradually more formalised and acquired some common characteristics based on precedent. That doesn't mean that peace treaties via mediation became a universal rule. The Treaty of Pyrenees in 1659 between France and Spain, or the Truce of Andrusovo in 1667 between the Polish Lithuanian Commonwealth and Muscovy, were negotiated directly by the opposing parties without recourse to mediation.[35]

In addition, the mediator's role could be undertaken not only by 'sovereign' polities but equally by a ruler's nominal vassals, like the German Electors, in western and central Europe.[36] Similarly, in the south-eastern part of the continent, tributaries or vassals of the sultan, such as the Prince of Transylvania, the Crimean Khan, or the Princes of Moldavia and Wallachia, would often interpose to facilitate the peace negotiations between the Ottomans and their Christian neighbours during the seventeenth century.[37] One such example was the official appointment by the Ottomans in 1685 of the Transylvanian Prince Mihály Apafi to mediate an end to the hostilities between the Porte and the Habsburg emperor.[38]

Three reasons could explain this surge in the recourse to mediation in the seventeenth century. Firstly, it appears that mediation was mostly needed when the participants were immersed in prolonged conflicts with no clear victory achieved by either side. It is no coincidence that mediation in Ottoman–Habsburg negotiations first appeared at Zsitvatorok.[39] The peace treaty came after a thirteen-year conflict (1593–1606) between the two sides, which practically ended in a stalemate.[40] The same could be said about the Thirty Years' War, although the Franco–Spanish conflict (1632–59) evades such a generalisation. Secondly, the multiplication of third parties' interposition in conflicts ranging

35 Daniel Séré (ed.), *La paix des Pyrénées. Vingt-quatre ans de négociations entre la France et l'Espagne (1635–1659)* (Paris: Honoré Champion 2007); Zbigniew Wójcik, *Traktat Andruszowski 1667 i jego geneza* (Warsaw 1959).

36 Laufs, *In viam pacis*, 29, fn. 57.

37 This particularly interesting topic is still under-researched. Some first attempts at a systematic study have recently been undertaken in the framework of the ERC Project *Smallst –The Diplomacy of Small States in Early Modern South-eastern Europe* (ERC CoG 101043451), headed by Gábor Kármán.

38 Poulios, 'Αναζητώντας την ειρήνη'.

39 There was already an unsuccessful attempt to end the conflict via French mediation in 1603: József Zachar, 'Der "Lange Krieg" zwischen dem Osmanischen Reich und dem Habsburgerreich: Von der Kriegserklärung bis zum Friedensabschluss 1593–1606', in János Barta, Manfred Jatzlauk and Klára Papp (eds.), *„Einingkeit und Frieden Sollen auf Seiten jeder Partei sein". Die Friedensschlüsse von Wien (23. 06. 1606) und Zsitvatorok (15. 11. 1606)* (Debrecen: Institute of History, University of Debrecen 2007) 240.

40 For a concise narration of the events of the 'Long Turkish War', *see* ibid.

from the Rhine to the Danube and from the Mediterranean to the Baltic reveals the growing interconnection of events taking place in all those regions and the geographically widening interests of certain powers. For instance, the Treaties of Oliva-Copenhagen, signed in 1660, which ended the so-called Second Northern War (1655–60), were negotiated via mediation from France (in Oliva and Copenhagen) and England and the United Provinces (Copenhagen). The three powers intervened to bring an end to the conflict due to their political and commercial stakes in the Baltic region.[41] Similarly, behind the mediating attempts of England and the United Provinces to end the Sixteen Years' War, one encounters primarily the urge to disengage the Habsburg emperor from his conflict in the east to be able to commit all his forces west in the struggle against France.

Lastly, it would not be farfetched to claim that the constant recourse to mediation during the second half of the seventeenth century created a specific 'vogue'. Having a mediator in the peace negotiations was probably seen as a 'must', an indispensable element of the process. *Pace* the views of many scholars, this 'vogue' of peace treaties by mediation did not fade after the end of the seventeenth century.[42] Most of the peace treaties signed by the Ottomans and their neighbours in the eighteenth century were negotiated via mediators.[43] Not only that, but the Ottomans themselves, for the first time, proposed their own mediation in an inter-Christian conflict, although their offer was rejected.[44] Such facts reveal the tenacity of the practice and could not be overlooked in any general discussion of inter-polity mediation during the early modern period.

3 Mediators and Mediating Undertakings during the Sixteen Years' War

We should place the constant mediating initiatives by various third powers to end the Sixteen Years' War in this frame of historical developments. As we saw, the first officially recognised mediator (at least from the Ottoman side) was the Transylvanian Prince, Apafi. Yet, due to his later actions, which were

41 Kantorska, 'Les médiations françaises'.

42 Duchhardt, 'Arbitration', 88; Rohrschneider, 'Friedensvermittlung', 481–2.

43 Ciftci, 'Mediation'; Rohrschneider, 'Friedensvermittlung', 480–2. Despite the fact that Rohrschneider acknowledges this unabated use of mediation, he still doesn't seem to take it into consideration due to the misleading assumption that it took place on the 'fringes of Europe'.

44 Ibid., 481.

seen as a betrayal by the Ottoman side, and the conquest and annexation of the Principality of Transylvania by the Habsburgs during the late 1680s and early 1690s, a particular *damnatio memoriae* was imposed by both sides upon his mediation attempt. On the other hand, the Crimean Khan tried many times throughout the conflict to mediate between the Ottomans and the Polish-Lithuanian Commonwealth, despite being an active participant in the war himself, and the French also periodically attempted to offer their interposition.[45] Still, the constant efforts from the late 1680s of the two maritime powers of England and the United Provinces to end the conflict would earn them the fame of mediators par excellence.[46] The extent to which such sentiments were manifested, especially on the Ottoman side, is fully revealed by a tantalising passage from the chronicler Üsküdarī Abdullāh Efendi. He narrates as such the reactions of what one might, with many caveats, call 'the Ottoman public opinion' surrounding the news of the imminent arrival to the Ottoman domains of the ambassador of the English King, Conrad van Heemskerck, in late 1692, to act as a mediator in a new round of peace negotiations:[47]

> It acquired fame among the ordinary people that in the age of the late Sulṭān Süleymān Ḫān, the cosmocrator [...] the English King was engaged in the peace treaty made between the King of Vienna and [...] the late Sulṭān Süleymān Ḫān. And it's widespread among the common people that in the time of the aforementioned cosmocrator of the age, [the English King] sent an ambassador to the Porte and acted as mediator in that peace treaty. And yet, this interpreter of events (he refers to himself) had seen many times the works of historians [of the past]. It is not written in them that the above-mentioned peace treaty found completion in this way. [...] They narrated all the wars of Sulṭān Süleymān Ḫān extensively, but they didn't mention a treaty in which the English King acted as a mediator.[48]

Despite the quite intriguing revelation that issues regarding peace negotiations were discussed and debated among the 'common people', of equal importance

45 Bérenger, 'La politique ottomane'; Aleksandra Skrzypietz, 'Zabiegi posła francuskiego o odrębny pokój polsko-turecki w latach 1693–1697' in Czamanskiej and Szulca, *Traktaty Karlowickie*, 95–100.

46 Dutch *bons offices*, 1689–90 and combined Anglo-Dutch mediation, 1691–3.

47 Although a Dutchman himself, Van Heemskerck was encouraged by the English King William III to take over the English affairs in the Ottoman Empire, which provoked a strong reaction by the English 'nation' there: Heywood, 'An Anglo-Dutch dispute', 74.

48 Üsküdarî, *Vâkı'ât-ı Rûz-Merre*, vol. 4, 90.

is the attempt to project an English mediation back in time to surround it with an aura of 'antiquity' and thus legitimisation. Finally, such tenets would provoke Üsküdarī to resort to his historical knowledge based on past chronicles – an interesting practice we shall later encounter again – to refute what he sees as historically baseless allegations.[49]

4 Smooth the Negotiation but Do Not Intervene in It? The (Fluid) Position and Duties of a Mediator

What mediation entailed was not fixed from the outset. Its tasks and roles were continuously evolving as the practice disseminated and experience accumulated, and they were also subjected to the particular circumstances of every singular peace negotiation.[50] Thus the following analysis would more mirror the situation at the end of the seventeenth century, the time of the Carlowitz Peace Congress, when mediation possessed some, more or less, already standardised features.

One of the cardinal roles of a mediator was facilitating communication between the opposing parties.[51] The role of Lord Paget during the preliminary phase of the Carlowitz Congress was paramount in this respect. He and his secretary – and Colyer, later, to a lesser extent – acted as the essential go-betweens via whom the two sides indirectly communed. Furthermore, during the peace congress, all the non-face-to-face communication between the Ottoman and the allied delegations would equally occur through the mediators. In addition, it was one of the cardinal functions of a mediator to transmit the peace proposals of one side to the other. In 1693, in his first mediation attempt, Lord Paget came from Vienna to Adrianople carrying with him the Holy League's peace terms. In this respect, the choice of the Ottoman government in January 1698 to send its proposals to the English King first, who then would pass them over to the Christian allies, was a very clever one. Although Kinsky saw it as an odd move, it hit two birds with one stone: it was the standard practice, and it simultaneously saved the Ottomans ostensibly from appearing as the ones to request peace. Furthermore, the mediators were not only acting

49 Quite engrossingly, when it finally became known that the ambassador of the English King was actually a Dutchman, 'public opinion' shifted immediately, ascribing such a centuries-long mediating role to the Dutch 'nation' (*millet-i Flemenk*) instead: Ibid., 183.

50 Rohrschneider, 'Friedensvermittlung', 476.

51 Ibid., 475.

as the principal carriers of messages but also the foremost purveyors of news concerning the developments taking place on each side of the main negotiating parties.[52]

Apart from facilitating the communication between the negotiating sides, a mediator also occupied himself with the smooth unfolding of bilateral talks or a congress. Westphalia was perhaps a milestone in setting specific precedents in this respect,[53] but similar solutions were already in circulation. During the negotiations at Zsitvatorok, the Hungarian 'mediators' occupied themselves with arranging the order of the visits between the Ottoman and the Imperial delegations, as well as with ensuring the safety of the participants.[54] By 1698, the scope of mediators' organisational tasks was enhanced. Apart from the order of the first and last visits – a pretty crucial point in ceremonial matters – and the security of the congress, the mediators, after consultation with the main participants, regulated the passports essential for the plenipotentiaries to arrive at the location of the gathering, the circumference of the location's venue, the size of the retinue each delegation could have, the comings and goings between the different camps and last but not least, the general ceremonial arrangements of the congress.[55] To this end, they enacted a General Regulation which every participant was bound to follow.[56] As much as this feature resembles arbitration, the General Regulation, although issued in the name of the mediators, was chiefly negotiated and subjected to scrutiny by the main participants.[57]

The papal nuncio at the Congress of Westphalia, Fabio Chigi, once compared the mediator's services to those of a notary because he was acting as the guarantor of the validity and keeper of the most important documents issued by the different parties during the negotiations.[58] The originals of the Foundation of the Peace Instrument during the Carlowitz preliminaries stayed near the mediators for safeguarding, as well as the drafts made of the treaties during the congress before their signing.[59] The main reason behind such an arrangement was the fear of an attempt by one party to induce changes to the

---

52 For instance, *Taʾrīḫ-i ṣulḥ-nāme*, fol. 49^b^–50^a^.

53 Repgen, 'Friedensvermittlung', 944–5.

54 Bayerle, 'The Compromise', 12.

55 *See*, for instance: ÖStA, HHStA, Türkei I, Turcica Box 166, Folder 3 (September 1698, 2nd half), fol. 152^v^–155^v^, Kinsky to Paget, 27 September 1698; ibid., fol. 15^r–v^, Paget/Colyer to the Imperial plenipotentiaries, 8/18 September 1698.

56 Köhler, *Strategie und Symbolik*, 137–8. For the specific regulation for the Carlowitz Congress, refer below to Act II, Interlude II.

57 *See* below, Act II, Narration Part I.

58 Repgen, 'Friedensvermittlung', 943.

59 *Taʾrīḫ-i ṣulḥ-nāme*, fol. 41^b^, 71^a^.

agreed text. On the other hand, the exchange of the credentials of the plenipotentiaries of each side was also effectuated via the mediators who, this way, vouched for their genuineness.[60]

Even so, presenting mediation as mere communication-organisation assistance in the negotiations amounts only to half the actual picture. Of course, a usual mediator's refrain was that he didn't decide anything but only facilitated the parties to reach a decision. When during the Carlowitz Congress, the Muscovite ambassador Prokopii Voznitsyn attempted to persuade the two mediators of the soundness of his claims, they responded to him that it was not their business to decide anything. That was the plenipotentiaries' responsibility. Theirs was to provide counsel and transmit the proposals of one side to the other.[61] Yet, primarily through his 'counsels', a mediator could supersede his supposed 'neutral' stance and directly intervene in the peacemaking process. Changing roles between *ministre public* and *honnête homme* was one strategy, and we have already shown how it was used to its full extent by Paget to provide advice – that generally, he shouldn't have to – to the Ottoman side. In the same vein, he was counselling Count Kinsky in their private correspondence. The influence his recommendations had on the leading participants has already been discussed and was paramount to the advancement of the negotiations.

Another characteristic strategy of the mediators was manipulation. Paget and Colyer tried in their face-to-face meetings and correspondence with the two sides to always paint a positive picture, deliberately exaggerating some facts or downplaying others in an effort to convince the two parties of the sincerity of each other's peaceful feelings. On the other hand, when they perceived a slowdown in the peacemaking process, they were quick to react by sounding the alarm of an imminent collapse of the talks. In a letter to Kinsky on 16 September 1698, Paget tried to press the Bohemian Chancellor to expedite the departure from Vienna of the allied plenipotentiaries by evoking a supposed change of mood in the Ottoman camp.[62] Peace was necessary to the Ottomans, but Paget had to convince Kinsky that it wasn't, so the Imperials should hurry up before it was too late.

The mediators exercised considerable influence during the congress, not so much during the conferences themselves, where they usually acted as moderators without intervening much, but in their private meetings with the different delegations, operating in the backscenes of the talks. As Ruzzini

60 Ibid., fol. 70^{a-b}; ÖStA, HHStA, Türkei I, Turcica Box 170, Diarium et Cerimoniale Tractatus Pacis Carlovicensis Annis 1698 et 1699 (henceforth Diarium et Cerimoniale), fol. 17–18.

61 *Pamiatniki*, 273–4.

62 ÖStA, HHStA, Türkei I, Turcica Box 166, Folder 3 (September 1698, 2nd half), fol. 4^{v}, Paget to Kinsky, 6/16 September 1698.

characteristically says about Lord Paget, the latter wanted 'to retain for himself the arcana of the negotiations (*l'arcano del negotio*)'.[63] For instance, when the Ottomans finally dropped their demand on Transylvania at the beginning of the congress, they followed a suggestion from the mediators.[64] A similar illustrative example occurred after the initial agreement on key topics of the negotiation between the Ottoman delegation and the Imperial side. Then, the government in Vienna pressed its plenipotentiaries for some amendments. The mediators advised against such action because it could jeopardise the whole negotiations, according to them. As Count Leopold Schlik, the second Imperial plenipotentiary, reported to Count Kinsky, the mediators told them,

> that they would absolutely council us not to make this attempt ourselves, but they intended to make one from their side in order to penetrate the last reserves [of the Ottomans] and tell us once and for all what we will have to hope for or fear. In their view, already approved by experience on many points, it would be better for one to press on and obtain more by pursuing the correction of the articles simply and without affectation, rather than by making such forceful demands, which place him [...] in thousands and thousands of scruples.[65]

Some interventions of the mediators in the decision-making during the course of the congress were less supple, though. When the issue of the future status of the Republic of Ragusa was discussed and the Imperial side voiced the demand that the small city-state should be placed under the emperor's protection. Lord Paget, in a rare intervention, said, 'that they have [the Ragusans] an agent or a resident at the Porte who is the greatest enemy of His Imperial Majesty. As for his customs, he is more Turk than Christian', thus actively supporting the Ottoman position that Ragusa should remain a tributary of the Porte.[66] Far more importantly, in late December 1698-early January 1699, when the congress was stalled due to the intransigence of Venice to concede to some of the Ottoman demands, Paget, breaking his 'period of silence' in his correspondence with Kinsky, wrote to the Bohemian Chancellor defending the Ottoman positions vehemently and demanding that the emperor put pressure on the Republic of Saint Mark to accept them.[67]

---

63 Ruzzini, *Relazione*, 375.

64 *Taʾrīḫ-i ṣulḥ-nāme*, fol. 80[a].

65 ÖStA, HHStA, Türkei I, Turcica Box 169, Folder 1 (December 1698, 1st half), fol. 197[r–v], Schlik to Kinsky, 12 December 1698.

66 ÖStA, HHStA, Türkei I, Turcica Box 170, Protocollum, fol. 68–69.

67 ÖStA, HHStA, Türkei I, Turcica Box 169, Folder 2 (December 1698, 2nd half), fol. 178[r]–179[v], Paget to Kinsky, 20/30 December 1698.

5 Efforts to Win Over the Mediators and Complaints of Their 'Partisanship'

As the mediators occupied such a cardinal position in the negotiations, winning their favour and support was one of the top priorities of the different parties. According to the instructions given to the Polish plenipotentiary ambassador at Carlowitz, Stanisław Małachowski, one of his main goals to achieve the king's and Commonwealth's objectives was to 'not [...] omit to seek the full friendship and favour of the ambassadors of the mediating powers and primarily, to employ every means in his power to render them favourable to our side'.[68] A little before the commencement of the congress, Count Kinsky, writing to Lord Paget, would state that,

> His Imperial Majesty, my Lord and Master [...] has ordered me to assure you that his extreme confidence towards your person continues always. He hopes to gain all the advantages through you, which may depend on your affection towards His Imperial Majesty and the reputation that your merits had acquired with the Porte's ministers.[69]

On the Ottoman side of the equation, according to Rāmī Meḥmed, while the mediators and the Ottoman plenipotentiaries were staying close to Belgrade, waiting for the allied delegations to arrive at the frontier, a relation of 'friendship and affection' (*ülfet ü ünsiyyet ve meveddet ü muḥabbet*) was developed between them.[70] It was a 'friendship' based on ulterior motives, of course. As the same Rāmī would declare triumphally,

> the English ambassador showed [at first] some enmity, but his sentiments and his predisposition towards the matter [of peace according to the Ottoman interests] were [ultimately] won over. As for the Dutch ambassador, being raised in Istanbul, his devotion to the Exalted State's side was [duly] expected.[71]

However, if such 'amity' was deemed insufficient, certain insinuations/indirect threats could also be used. Before their departure from the Ottoman camp near Belgrade for the congress venue, the two mediators had a last audience with

68 Gorkowski, *Compendium legationis*, 23ʳ.

69 ÖStA, HHStA, Türkei I, Turcica Box 166, Folder 3 (September 1698, 2nd half), fol. 10ʳ, Kinsky to Paget, 17 September 1698.

70 *Ta'rīḫ-i ṣulḥ-nāme*, fol. 49ᵃ.

71 Ibid.

the grand vizier. The speech the latter gave to them was transcribed as it was supposedly delivered (*ʿaynı ile*), in order to be preserved (*ḥıfẓ olunmak içün*) for posterity.[72] In it, ʿAmcazāde gave an interesting advice/warning to Paget and Colyer. "In some intended matters beneficial for both sides, do not be obstinate and opposing. You know that the Islamic states are greater in numbers than the Christian ones. Their emperors' honour is great".[73] Could this be an indirect allusion to the commercial interests the two powers had from the Mediterranean to the Indonesian archipelago, which, still closely depended upon the goodwill of the dominant Muslim rulers there, would be harmed if the two powers decided to favour their coreligionists and thus acquire a 'bad name' in the Islamic world?

The attempts of the different parties to convince the mediators of the justice of their arguments and secure their support for them continued unabetted throughout the congress.[74] One of the key reasons behind the difficult position the Venetian plenipotentiary Ruzzini found himself in at Carlowitz was his failure to win the mediators to his side. In his *Relazione,* he excused his mishandlings by accusing the mediators of partisanship. They desired to be impartial.

> Appearing though to them less difficult to overcome the allied claims than repel the Turkish ones, they were maintaining their offices towards the first with such an insistence, that it sometimes seemed that [these offices] were inspired of too much partiality towards the second [...] Thus, many came to form an opinion, surmising that the residence of the same mediators close to the Ottomans, the fact that they were hosted, sustained, and honoured by the latter with unusual signs of esteem, could have fomented in their hearts some liking towards the interests of the Porte.[75]

Ruzzini was not the only one to think this way. Voznitsyn, the Muscovite plenipotentiary, would also accuse the mediators in his missives to his superiors and in his own post-congress relation of backing the Ottoman side and remaining silent during the conference without a word of support for him.[76] During one

72 Ibid., fol. 67ᵇ.

73 Ibid.

74 ÖStA, HHStA, Türkei I, Turcica Box 169, Folder 1 (December 1698, 1st half), fol. 196ʳ–197ᵛ, Schlik to Kinsky, 12 December 1698.

75 Ruzzini, *Relazione*, 375.

76 *Pamiatniki*, 259, 299, 317.

conference, greatly irritated by, as he perceived it, Paget's prejudicial handling towards him, he would even declare openly to Colyer 'that his companion is damaging our [the Muscovite] affairs instead of mediating and conciliating'.[77] Of course, Paget's behaviour should not have surprised him since he had refused to accept him and Colyer as mediators for a long time.[78]

Dissatisfaction with Paget and Colyer is also documented in the Imperial camp. In a letter to Kinsky dated 8 November 1698, Count Schlik informed him that, 'I forgot to say to Your Excellency that one can think of placing the mediators closer and closer to the Turks'.[79] Such thinking originated from the fact that it appeared to him that they spoke 'with great eagerness in favour of the proposal' of the Ottoman side to retain Transylvania in its ante bellum status.[80] Such accusations would prompt the Bohemian Chancellor to complain about this 'foiblesse de la Mediation' to the Dutch resident ambassador at the Viennese Court, Hop.[81] However, later on, showing how quickly feelings and perceptions could change according to the moment, following the mediators' abetment of the Imperial delegation on some of its demands, Schlik declared that 'after what lately happened, they cannot be suspected of partiality'.[82]

There is no doubt that there could be a grain of truth to all these allegations. Besides the interests of the mediating powers that would drive them to please one participant more than the other, as in the case of the Republic of Venice and the Ottomans, personal sympathies created by the background of the mediators themselves could have also played a role. For instance, Colyer spent much of his early and adult life in the Ottoman capital, thus creating fears or hopes, according to the side on which one was found, that he would not act impartially.[83]

Finally, religious differences also played a part in creating suspicions regarding the mediators. For instance, during the Congress of Nijmegen, the Imperials were reticent to accept an English mediation due to Protestantism,[84]

---

77 Quoted in Bogoslovskii, *Petr I*, 415.

78 Refer below to Act II, Narration Part I.

79 ÖStA, HHStA, Türkei I, Turcica Box 168, Folder 1 (November 1698, 1st half), fol. 171^v, Schlik to Kinsky, 8 November 1698.

80 Ibid.

81 ÖStA, HHStA, Türkei I, Turcica Box 168, Folder 2 (November 1698, 2nd half), fol. 219^r, Kinsky to Schlik, 25 November 1698.

82 ÖStA, HHStA, Türkei I, Turcica Box 169, Folder 1 (December 1698, 1st half), fol. 197^v–198^r, Schlik to Kinsky, 12 December 1698.

83 For the somewhat obscure early life of Colyer in Constantinople, where his father was also an ambassador of the United Provinces, *see* Hora Siccama, 'De Vrede van Carlowitz', 44, fn. 2.

84 Duchhardt, 'Arbitration', 29.

and in 1698, despite being allies with the English and the Dutch for nearly a decade, similar considerations regarding religion still held their sway. In the first meeting of the Imperial 'Turkish Deputation' in February 1698 to discuss the peace negotiations, the suspicion was uttered that the maritime powers, being Protestant, were deliberately forwarding peace in order to halt the victorious advance of the Imperial troops and thus hinder the 'further propagation of the Catholic religion and the oppression of the Reformed one [Lutherans and Calvinists]'.[85]

6 An Impartial Peacemaker: the Self-Fashioning of a Mediator

A mediator's typical self-fashioning was based on two pillars: his non-partisanship and his desire for peace. He typically presented himself as a well-wisher of both sides with a genuine desire to see his two 'friends' terminate their fighting. As Lord Paget stated during his first audience with the grand vizier in December 1697, 'the King of England, my master, being a well-wisher of the Exalted State and a friend of the German Emperor', was deeply engrieved (*ziyādesiyle müte'ellim olmaġla*) by the spilling of human blood caused by the war between the two sides.[86] Colyer would similarly write to Count Kinsky that the Dutch mediation had no other scope than to bring relief to 'the innocent subjects' of the warring parties, and bring an end to 'one so long and bloody war'.[87] Such 'explosions' of peacemaking feelings were quite typical of the language used by the mediators in their letters addressed to the principal decision-makers of each negotiating party. In a dispatch to Kinsky, after urging the imperial minister to speed up the pace of the congress, Paget would add, 'I employ Your Lordship to pardon me if I take the liberty to speak to you too frankly of my feelings. The desire to see this rude, savage war end [...] made me do it'.[88] In another letter, he would declare characteristically: 'I passionately desire peace'.[89]

---

85 ÖStA, HHStA, Türkei I, Turcica Box 165, Folder 1 (January–March 1698), fol. 11ᵛ, relation of the members of the 'Turkish Deputation' to Leopold I, 13 February 1698.

86 *Ta'rīḫ-i ṣulḥ-nāme*, fol. 17ᵃ.

87 ÖStA, HHStA, Türkei I, Turcica Box 165, Folder 2 (April 1698), fol. 1ʳ⁻ᵛ, Colyer to Kinsky, 1 April 1698.

88 ÖStA, HHStA, Türkei I, Turcica Box 166, Folder 1 (August 1698), fol. 95ᵛ, Paget to Kinsky, 12 August 1698 (J.C.).

89 ÖStA, HHStA, Türkei I, Turcica Box 166, Folder 3 (September 1698, 2nd half), fol. 19ᵛ, Paget to Kinsky, 22 September 1698 (J.C.).

7 The Tangible Material and Symbolic Benefits of a Mediator

However, despite this idealised self-portrayal, the passionate desire for peace was not what would primarily drive an early modern ruler to seek to acquire the role of the mediator. Much more 'mundane' – and certainly less noble – considerations were at play, as we have already seen. As the disillusioned Christoph Dietrich von Bose aptly framed it to August II, after the failure of his mission in the Hague and London, 'we have to regard them not as mediators, but as parties that in this affair have their particular concerns and designs'.[90] But there was more besides the northern maritime powers' desire to 'save Europe' from the omnipotence of Louis XIV. In his farewell speech to the mediators, the grand vizier told them, 'your king has been an old friend of the Exalted State. Besides the fact that hitherto between [us] there has not been any kind of grievance or anything else left unresolved, now, [our] friendship has substantially increased with your fine services. God willing, this sincere amity will bear many fruits'.[91] Those fruits alluded to the concrete material benefits that the English and the Dutch could undoubtedly expect for their services.

Besides the tangible prerogatives, the image of the peacemaker could bring considerable symbolic capital to a ruler, namely an enhancement of his reputation and even his position in the pyramid of the 'Society of Princes'.[92] England is a paradigmatic example. Charles II's mediation at the Congress of Nijmegen aimed, among other things, to secure glory, reputation and a prominent place for his crown in continental politics.[93] The attempt to ensure ceremonial precedence for his ambassadors at the congress went in the same direction. Such an attempt to overturn the 'ceremonial hierarchy' was vigorously rejected by the Imperials, however.[94] More than twenty years later, William III's desire to act as arbiter in the continent's affairs may have played a similar role in his attempt to mediate the conflict between the Holy League allies and the Ottoman Sultan. As Ruzzini claims in his *Relazione*, one driving force behind the mediators' efforts to achieve peace was to secure glory for their principals.[95]

In parallel, the mediator's office was accompanied by considerable material and symbolic capital not just for the ruler but also for his representatives in the 'negotiation arena'. Count Schlik would suggest a 'reconnaissance' to the

---

90 AGAD, AKW, 1/3/0/33/78/ teczka 494 nr. 819, fol. 8, Bose to August II, 19 May 1698.

91 *Ta'rīḫ-i ṣulḥ-nāme*, fol. 67^{b}.

92 Köhler, *Strategie und Symbolik*, 118.

93 Duchhardt, 'Arbitration', 30.

94 Ibid., 44–55.

95 Ruzzini, *Relazione*, 375.

mediators in a letter to Count Kinsky on 31 January 1698 after the congress's termination.[96] What this 'reconnaissance' entailed could be judged by the material and immaterial 'gifts' Colyer received from the different parties for his services. As to the first, 'from the Austrians he received a portrait of the emperor, studded in diamonds; the Polish government sent Colijer two silver decanters and an elaborately worked fireguard mounted on a tripod; and Venice gave him a silver-gilded cooling vessel decorated with the lion of Saint Mark'.[97] Of equal – perhaps even greater – significance were the immaterial benefits: two Imperial diplomas that made him Count of the Kingdom of Hungary (the first) and Count of the Holy Roman Empire (the second).[98] Hence, as a ruler/mediator could ascend the 'Society of Princes' ladder, Colyer advanced his position in the societal pyramid by becoming a nobleman. For the Ottomans, their esteem towards the Dutchman was so great that they would employ his mediating services again during the Congress of Passarowitz in 1718.[99]

8 The Various Types of Mediation at the Carlowitz Congress

A particularity, not just of the Carlowitz but of other seventeenth-century peace congresses, is the presence of multiple forms of 'mediation' alongside the official one, which could even sometimes overshadow it. That was a by-product of the process of the congresses, which, despite their theoretically multilateral character, consisted of bilateral talks, developed independently one from the other. In this way, a member of an allied coalition could conclude its negotiation with the coalition's opponent before the other members of the alliance. Typically, in such cases, the aforementioned member attempted to act as an 'informal' mediator between its confederates and its former enemy. Examples abound. During the Peace Congress of Westphalia, the Dutch, after reaching an agreement with Spain, attempted without success to reconcile the latter with France, despite the parallel presence of Venetian and Papal mediators.[100] Additionally, in the Congress of Nijmegen, the United Provinces, after yet again finishing their business first by concluding a treaty with France, performed an

96 ÖStA, HHStA, Türkei I, Turcica Box 171, Folder 2 (January 1699, 2nd half), fol. 246^{v}, Schlik to Kinsky, 31 January 1699.

97 Maurits H. van den Boogert, 'The Spoils of Peace: What the Dutch Got Out of Carlowitz', in Heywood and Parvev, *The Treaties of Carlowitz*, 56–72, 61.

98 Ibid.

99 Hüseyin Onur Ercan, *Pasarofça Antlaşması 1718. Diplomasi ve Barış* (Ankara: Türk Tarih Kurumu 2022) 140–2.

100 Laufs, *In viam pacis*, 214–26.

'informal mediation' between Louis XIV and the other members of the coalition against him, much to the dismay of the official English mediators.[101]

Carlowitz was not going to be an exception to what had by then become almost a norm. The Imperial delegation reached a general agreement with the Ottomans early on in the congress and undertook *bons offices* to help their other allies reach a peace settlement with the sultan's ambassadors as well. For instance, in one session between the Ottoman and the Habsburg delegations, following a discussion apropos the matters of the allies, Count Schlik stated that 'we inquire about those issues to be able to use [our] services (*fare i Uffizij*)'.[102] It seems that they indeed made use of them quite efficiently since 'the 9 December [the Polish ambassador] [...] came the same evening to thank the Imperial embassy for the good and efficient services (*dei buoni Uffizij ed efficaci*) passed in favour of Poland, which made her obtain very favourable conditions with the restitution of Kamianets in its current state'.[103]

If the Imperial involvement in the negotiations between the Commonwealth and the Ottomans could be defined as *bons offices*, the case with Venice was far more perplexing. It also started at the level of 'good services' with the Imperials trying to 'mediate' between Ruzzini and the Ottoman plenipotentiaries so that a common ground could be found. However, time passed, and with no agreement on the horizon, the Ottoman delegation demanded something unprecedented: that the Imperials be equally present during the Ottoman–Venetian sessions. As Mavrocordatos said to them during the first of these joint conferences in early January 1699, 'we hope [...] that they [the Imperials] will not hold themselves as mere spectators, but will act, and contribute with their reflections and services (*ufficij*) for the conciliation and settlement of the differences'.[104] The Imperial ambassadors explicitly referred to their new role as *Interposition*.[105] And thus, something truly bizarre happened, as the Venetian and Ottoman delegations discussed in the presence of both formal and informal mediators! Soon, though, the Imperial involvement passed the level of simple *interposition*. During the last phase of the congress, they undertook to negotiate the peace terms for the Republic alone, without the presence of Ruzzini, and agreed with the Ottomans on the terms without the ambassador's open full consent. It was again a situation without precedent, which

101 Duchhardt, 'Arbitration', 73–4.

102 ÖStA, HHStA, Türkei I, Turcica Box 170, Protocollum, fol. 64.

103 Ibid., fol. 117.

104 BNM, Ms.it.VII 399 (8625), fol. 298^r^, protocol of the joint Ottoman-Imperial-Venetian conference on 4 January 1698.

105 For instance, ÖStA, HHStA, Türkei I, Turcica Box 171, Folder 1 (January 1699, 1st half), fol. 91^v^, Imperial plenipotentiaries to Leopold I, 5 January 1699.

evades any form of definition in the field of mediation. It could be considered a form of arbitration – undoubtedly from the Venetian standpoint – but then again, the Serenissima was theoretically given the option to refuse the agreed terms.[106]

Thus, whereas in the preliminaries, the 'mediation landscape' was clear, it became more complex during the 'Carlowitz-phase' of the negotiations. After the initial stage of the congress, two parallel mediations, an official and an unofficial one, were in operation, each having a pivotal role in the peace talks. Interestingly, these two interpositions didn't seem to clash with one another, as in previous congresses, but rather coexist in a symbiotic and complementary relationship, which, in the end, proved beneficial for the successful outcome of the talks. Lastly, the Imperial delegation assumed yet another 'mediating' role, this time not related to the negotiations of their allies per se but the strife aroused among them apropos the ceremonial. When spirits rose high between the Muscovite and the Commonwealth ambassador over precedence in the allied camp, the emperor's ambassadors undertook to calm the two sides, an interposition that the second Imperial ambassador Count Schlik described in his journal of the congress as 'mediation' (*ihre Mediation anerbiethen lassen*).[107] Evidently, 'mediation' was a pretty fluid concept that could be applied to any form of reconciliation with the involvement of a third party.

---

106 Refer below to Act IV, Narration Part II.

107 ÖStA, HHStA, Türkei I, Turcica Box 170, Diarium et Cerimoniale, fol. 9. The same applied to a similar later strife between the Polish and the Venetian ambassador: Ibid., fol. 11.

Narration Part IV: on the Way to the Congress

1 Quarrel among the Mediators

Although by the beginning of July 1698 the peace negotiations had matured significantly, the arrival of summer, the primary campaign season at the time, obliged all sides to resume their military preparations in earnest. Fears about the allies' next moves, especially from the least peace-loving ones, Muscovy and the Commonwealth, were intense on the Ottoman side.[1] Such uncertainty about the course the affairs would take obliged decision-makers, at least in rhetoric, to appear prepared for all possible alternatives. And, while the option of the sultan once more leading his troops to the frontier was discarded, Ḥüseyin Paşa was the one to take this task upon himself. Around late May, he departed from Adrianople to Belgrade, accompanied by the Crimean Khan and the two mediators.[2]

Relations between Paget and Colyer hardly improved. The Englishman was simply not willing to give the Dutch mediator an equal role to his in the 'Theatre of Peace'.[3] In May, the Dutchman requested that this time, his brother should to be sent to Vienna with the letters for the Imperial ministers and not Paget's secretary, but the Englishman rejected it.[4] A new point of friction came to the surface as the two mediators followed the Ottoman army towards the frontier. The kernel of the quarrel was the placement of their tents in the Ottoman camp. It was not a mere squabble. As we shall often encounter in our narration, spatial arrangements were one of the most cardinal elements of symbolic communication, conveying explicit messages regarding power relations between the various actors.

Paget claimed that Colyer, a representative of a republic, could not place his tent on an equal level as that of his, an ambassador of a king. Such a claim would visualise Paget's pretensions that he was the one leading the mediation. An intervention of the grand vizier was needed to prevent a direct split between the two men. ʿAmcazāde came up with a compromise solution. The

---

1 *Taʾrīḫ-i ṣulḥ-nāme*, fol. 34ᵃ.

2 Abdülkadir Özcan (ed.), *Anonim Osmanli Tarihi, 1099–1116 (1688–1704)* (Ankara: Printing House of the Turkish Historical Society 2000) 134 (henceforth *Anonim Osmanli Tarihi*); Silāḥdār, *Nusretnâme*, 474.

3 'As if he was jealous and could not tolerate anything being suggested or worked out by me', Colyer would later remark. Quoted in Hora Siccoma, 'De Vrede van Carlowitz', 144, fn. 1.

4 ÖStA, HHStA, Türkei I, Turcica Box 167, Folder 2 (October 1698, 2nd half), fol. 241ʳ, Marsigli to Kinsky, 28 October 1698.

 | DOI:10.1163/9789004458499_009

tents of the two mediators would be placed at an equal distance from his, conserving thus their parity, but Paget's, as representative of a crowned head, would be put at the right side of that of the vizier's.[5] After that clash, Paget and Colyer appeared to have finally reached a modus vivendi. In late July, Colyer wrote back to the Hague that his past misunderstandings with the Englishman were resolved and that the two were now in each other's confidence.[6] Count Marsigli later attributed this rapprochement to the poor health of Lord Paget and the strict orders for a reconciliation from their principals.[7] The circumstances may have also played a role in uniting the two mediators since the negotiations were now entering their most crucial phase.

2 The Ottoman Response to the Imperial-Venetian Instrument of the Foundation of Peace

In the middle of July, Lord Paget's secretary returned from Vienna with the Instrument of the Foundation of Peace and Kinsky's letters to the mediators. According to Rāmī, as Schreyer passed through Belgrade and the Ottoman military camps and during the rest of his itinerary, he was 'greatly impressed by the number of the troops'.[8] It was a successful mise en scene to impress the mediators – and through them, indirectly, the Christian allies – as we can judge by what Paget would later describe to the Imperial minister about the reorganisation he had seen of the Ottoman army.

In his letter to the English ambassador, Kinsky initially tried to justify the long time it had taken him to reply. The allied answer was delayed by the need to reach an agreement with Venice. Now, though, they were sending the 'Instrument of our declaration' (*l'instrument de nôtre Declaration*), which the mediators could use.[9] This Instrument was accepted only by the Imperials and Venice. Regarding the *Rzeczpospolita*, its king, through his letters to the emperor and Kinsky, 'doesn't oppose to a congress, but he does not declare himself on the acceptance or rejection of the uti possidetis'.[10] As for Muscovy,

5 Hora Siccama, 'De Vrede van Carlowitz', 144, fn. 1.
6 Ibid.
7 ÖStA, HHStA, Türkei I, Turcica Box 167, Folder 2 (October 1698, 2nd half), fol. 241^{r}, Marsigli to Kinsky, 28 October 1698.
8 *Ta'rīḫ-i ṣulḥ-nāme*, fol. 34^{b}.
9 ÖStA, HHStA, Türkei I, Turcica Box 165, Folder 5 (July 1698), fol. 8^{r-v}, Kinsky to Paget, 3 July 1698.
10 Ibid., fol. 8^{r} (9^{r}).

the tsar 'is present here for six or seven days now', and they would negotiate with him.[11] Regarding the demarcation of the new borders, a principal matter of discussion for the upcoming congress, there was no question that the emperor and Venice would leave it to commissioners appointed for this task after the talks. 'For good reasons', they desired 'that all this [the demarcation of the borders] should be, in general, and in particular, defined, agreed and concluded in this congress'.[12] Nonetheless, when it came to the *uti possidetis*, the minister's view revealed – as always – some ambiguity: 'The fruit of this peace [...] depends not on the mutual acceptance of the uti possidetis, but on the regulation of this principle of the uti posssidetis, through which the [two] empires should be really divided by determined borders, stipulated not only *en gros*, but also in detail'.[13]

Finally, there was the question of the general armistice: 'It would be useless to speak about an armistice to be made during this campaign or the congress because the emperor and Venice would not accept it, either for their interests or for the opposition Poland and Muscovy could make'.[14] The issue of the Commonwealth and Muscovy as opposers of an armistice was not discussed in the joint Imperial–Venetian meetings in June. Still, it appears to act later as one of the fundamental ostensible reasons for not consenting to it. The Imperial side could legitimately claim – as it, in fact, did – that Muscovy, as much as the Commonwealth, would have ample time to gain more land on the road to the congress and thus quench their territorial ambitions.

After receiving the letters and documents from Vienna, the mediators informed Mavrocordatos about them. They said that the emperor and Venice had appointed Count Kinsky and Carlo Ruzzini as 'plenipotentiaries' (*meʾẕūn u muraḫḫaṣ*) to negotiate peace. And the latter, jointly (*ittifaḳla*) drafted, signed and sealed – to be valid (*maʿmūlun-bih olmaḳ üzere*) – an Instrument (*temessük*) containing what was to act as a Foundation of Peace (*esās-i ṣulḥ*) regarding the point of discussion number one: territorial matters. If the grand vizier accepted the content of this Instrument, then the Ottoman side should also appoint plenipotentiaries and provide them with one similar in content.[15]

11 Ibid.

12 Ibid., fol. 8^{v} (9^{v}). He reiterated the same to Paget in another letter dated 16 July 1698: ÖStA, HHStA, Türkei I, Turcica Box 165, Folder 5 (July 1698), fol. 111^{v}.

13 Ibid. fol. 111^{r-v}.

14 Ibid., fol. 9^{r-v} (10^{r-v}), Kinsky to Paget, 3 July 1698.

15 *Taʾrīḫ-i ṣulḥ-nāme*, fol. 34^{b}. I deliberately chose to reiterate the information I have already given, adding the Ottoman terms to show the common vocabulary and diplomatic practices used by the two sides.

As always in the peacemaking process, every major step taken by one side should be reciprocated by the other. Mavrocordatos read the documents 'repeatedly' (*mükerrer oḳuyub*), translated them and then forwarded them to ʿAmcazāde.[16]

The sending of the Instrument of the Foundation of Peace by the two allies came as a huge surprise to the Ottoman leadership. The Ottomans had only expected full powers from the mediators to negotiate the peace preliminaries. Now the allies seemed to have pushed the process one step further. 'The ministers of the Exalted State and especially His Excellency the grand vizier hesitated a lot'.[17] The crux of the matter remained, as always, the exception of Transylvania from the principle of *uti possidetis*. Now the Ottomans seemed to have been surpassed by circumstances. The negotiations had reached such a point that either they would agree on an *uti possidetis* without exceptions, issue an instrument similar to the allies and march to a peace congress, or they would refuse to do so, and the whole affair would collapse.[18]

In the end, the usual refrain of thinking – the number of the enemies, the incessant campaigns 'for fifty, sixty years now' exhausting the subjects, the restoration of internal order, the maxim of 'peace is good' (*eṣ-ṣulḥu ḫayrun*), etc. – prevalent in the minds of most Ottoman statesmen since the beginning of the negotiations, won the day.[19] For this decision, a catalytic role was played by what the Ottoman side referred to as the 'second article' (*ikinci mādde*) of the Instrument concerning the willingness of the allies to discuss the evacuation, demolition or permutation of some places from which "with God's help a profitable outcome [may] be attained".[20] Of course, as with the previous letter written by Count Kinsky, the Instrument was described as 'vague and not detailed' (*müb-hem ve mücmel*).[21] However, since time was pressing, the grand vizier thought that he would either have to accept it and the road to the congress would be opened, or the negotiations by distance would have to continue, something that could postpone the whole affair. For this reason, Rāmī later recounted, 'it didn't appear a big deal [back then] to accept this vague and not detailed Instrument'.[22] Finally, there was also the acute reading the Ottoman leadership was making of the broader geopolitical situation in Europe at the time. There was ample chance that the Imperial side would, in

16 Ibid., fol. 35[a].
17 Ibid., fol. 38[a].
18 Ibid., fol. 38[a].
19 Ibid.
20 Ibid., fol. 38[b].
21 Ibid., fol. 86[a].
22 Ibid., fol. 86[a].

the end, concede to a less vigorous interpretation of the *uti possidetis* due to the imminent death of the Spanish King Carlos II and the prospective struggle for his succession.[23]

And so, following a parallel to the process on the allied side, the sultan appointed, after the recommendation of the grand vizier, Rāmī Meḥmed (d. 1708), a senior bureaucrat,[24] and Alexandros Mavrocordatos, the 'usual suspect', as his plenipotentiary ambassadors to the upcoming peace congress, and then under orders from Ḥüseyin Paşa, the two ambassadors issued and signed an Instrument, dated 13 Muḥarrem A.H. 1110 (22 July 1698), and handed it over to the mediators.[25] The choice of the plenipotentiaries will be further discussed in Interlude III. However, it should be noted that, contrary to the established literature,[26] it was not the first time the Porte appointed a high-ranking member of the *ḫācegān* (the 'bureaucrats') as its chief representative in peace negotiations, the first actually being Zülfikār Efendi in 1688.[27] As for the Ottoman instrument's content, as Paget referred later to Kinsky, '(although they don't abide by the same words, having wished to follow in their declaration the style and manner of [this] country) they want, and intend the same thing'.[28] Crucially, the Ottoman plenipotentiaries declared the Porte's consent to a peace congress and accepted – officially for the time – the *uti possidetis* principle, 'without exceptions' (*bilā istisnā*), as a basis of the peace negotiations.[29]

It appears, however, that the Instrument created some further misunderstandings. According to Paget, the Ottomans seemed to have inferred from it that the *uti possidetis* would be valid for all the Christian allies and not only for Venice and the emperor.[30]

---

23 In a conversation he had in early July 1698 with the Ragusan consul at the Ottoman Court, Luca Barka, the *Şeyhü'l-islām* Feyzüllāh Efendi (d. 1703) – the highest legal-religious authority in the empire and one of the most influential members of the Ottoman government at the time – expressed his certainty that there would be a war over the inheritance of the Spanish Habsburgs: Jovan Radonić (ed.), *Acta et Diplomata Ragusina*, vol. 4, part 2 (Belgrade 1942) 476.

24 He was the head of the Ottoman Chancery, or in Ottoman terms, the *Re'isü'l-küttāb*. For Rāmī's biography, *see* Abou-El-Haj, 'The Reisülküttab', 25–31 and Recep Ahıshalı 'Râmi Mehmed Paşa', in TDVİA, vol. 34 (Istanbul: Turkish Religious Foundation 2007) 449–51.

25 *Taʾrīḫ-i ṣulḥ-nāme*, fol. 39^{b}–40^{b}.

26 *See*, for instance, Abou-El-Haj, 'The Reisülküttab', 20.

27 *See* above, Prelude, 26.

28 ÖStA, HHStA, Türkei I, Turcica Box 165, Folder 5 (July 1698), fol. 126^{r}, Paget to Kinsky 14/24 July 1698.

29 *Taʾrīḫ-i ṣulḥ-nāme*, fol. 40^{a}.

30 That would indeed be the case during the congress.

> Nonetheless, because they hardly posed any difficulties in that [matter], nor they demanded any explication, I considered myself disobliged of discussing it [...] as to not worry them with difficulties which [really] don't exist [...] provided that those powers [the Commonwealth and Muscovy] will find themselves obliged to conform [to the Foundation of Peace], or better, to take measures which could not but be advantageous to the Porte.[31]

The issuing of an Ottoman Instrument of the Foundation of Peace and the sultan's appointment of plenipotentiaries was another landmark in the preliminary phase of the Carlowitz Congress and a critical step in the peacemaking process. Yet, as we have already seen, every move towards peace made by one side was not only reciprocated by the other but was equally advanced by it a bit further. So, to demonstrate the Ottoman desire to conclude the negotiations as soon as possible and to put pressure on the allied side towards this direction, on 24 July 1698, the two Ottoman plenipotentiaries and the mediators left the Ottoman camp in Sofia and headed towards the frontier.[32]

Still, before departing for their journey to Belgrade as well as en route to it, the four ambassadors had to resolve a cardinal issue: the prospective venue in which the congress would take place. Finding a commonly agreed venue to stage the negotiations was always a bone of contention for seventeenth-century peace congresses.[33] Staging the talks at the court of one of the principal belligerents was not a preferred option, since it would imply a diminution of the honour of the other participants and would bring the hosted delegates directly vis-à-vis the whole administrative apparatus of the host.[34] The example of the Failed Vienna Congress proved how disadvantageous it was for the Ottoman plenipotentiaries to negotiate in the Imperial capital, being kept in semi-captivity with little access to information and always at the mercy of their hosts. Hence, the congress venue had to demonstrate parity and guarantee the participants' safety.

The most common solution applied to such types of multilateral 'diplomatic' gatherings prior to Carlowitz was for them to take place in a neutral or – nominally neutral – territory.[35] For example, the city of Nijmegen and its

31 ÖStA, HHStA, Türkei I, Turcica Box 165, Folder 5 (July 1698), fol. 125ᵛ–126ʳ, Paget to Kinsky, 14/24 July 1698.

32 *Ta'rīḫ-i ṣulḥ-nāme*, op. cit., fol. 43ᵃ.

33 For instance, for the Congress of Nijmegen, *see* Duchhardt, 'Arbitration', 32–3.

34 Köhler, *Strategie und Symbolik*, 117.

35 Ibid., 116–8.

environs, although part of the United Provinces, was temporarily neutralised for the duration of the peace negotiations (1676–79); that is, it became practically an independent city-state in which the States General could not exercise their sovereignty.[36] Furthermore, an armistice was declared in a specific area surrounding the city to ensure the safety of the congress participants.[37]

If peace negotiations didn't occur in an urban setting, then another widespread practice was for two sides to negotiate at their respective frontier, in a no-man's-land or the middle of a river. Such negotiation venues go back centuries, yet by the 1600s, they were always accompanied by a specific 'choreography of peace' that aimed to neutralise any precedence of either side, insisting instead on their equality.[38] The Peace Treaty of the Pyrenees between France and Spain in 1659, negotiated on the Île des Faisans, in the river Bidassoa at the Franco–Spanish frontier[39] or the Peace of Zsitvatorok in 1606 (Figure 3), which was treated at the mouth of the river Žitava (hung. Zsitva), in modern-day southern Slovakia, form some notable examples of such a practice.

However, when the issue of the venue of the prospective congress was first discussed among the Imperial ministers in June 1698, the frontier option was not deemed convenient due to three main reasons. The first was the possible extreme weather conditions in autumn and winter that would make the stay of the different delegations extremely difficult. The second was again nature-related. If the congress were to take place at the frontier, the two delegations, the Ottoman and the allied, would have to stay in different places and meet halfway between the two.[40] In autumn and winter, the days get shorter, so with all the necessary comings and goings, little time would be left for actual negotiations. As for the third and final reason, this had to do with the problem of supplying the different delegations with adequate provisions. Considering all those issues, the Imperial ministers and Ruzzini agreed to propose to Paget as a possible place for the congress, 'for a start' (*anfänglich*), the Imperial capital, Vienna.[41]

36 Duchhardt, 'Arbitration', 41; For Münster and Osnabrück during the Congress of Westphalia, *see* Croxton, *Westphalia*, 132.

37 Duchhardt, 'Arbitration', 41–2.

38 Kolçak, 'A History of Learned Courtesy'; Thomas Rahn, 'Grenz-Situationen des Zeremoniells in der Frühen Neuzeit', in Markus Bauer and Thomas Rahn (eds.), *Die Grenze. Begriff und Inszenierung* (Berlin: Akademie Verlag 1997) 177–206.

39 Ibid., 181–6.

40 The options discussed were either an area between Belgrade and Petrovaradin or between Szeged and Ṭemeşvar: ÖStA, HHStA, Türkei I, Turcica Box 165, Folder 4 (June 1698), fol. 106r, relation of the members of the 'Turkish Deputation to Leopold I, 23 June 1698.

41 Ibid., fol. 105r–106v. Another venue proposed was Debrecen in Hungary: Ibid., fol. 106v.

FIGURE 3 Unknown painter. The Negotiations at Zsitvatorok EN.WIKIPEDIA.ORG/WIKI/LONG_TURKISH_WAR#/MEDIA/FILE:PEACE_NEGOTIATIONS_IN_ZSITVATOROK_1606.JPG (PUBLIC DOMAIN)

Kinsky justified this choice of the allies by resorting to historical precedents: 'There are a thousand reasons which would oblige the Turks not to refuse Vienna. Because this famous Truce of 1606,[42] 1610[43] and all the rest of the peace treaties during this century were concluded and always negotiated in the territory of the Roman Emperors'.[44] And yet, from their part, the Ottomans equally had 'a thousand reasons' to reject the allied suggestions. Not least among them was the Porte's strong desire not to let her enemies perceive her as weak or as

42 He refers here to the Peace of Zsitvatorok (1606).

43 Maybe this is a reference to the negotiations for the ratification of the Treaty of Zsitvatorok that took place in the Ottoman capital in 1610 or the ones in 1615 that indeed took place in Vienna: Bayerle, 'The Compromise', 28; Radu Dipratu and Viorel Panaite, 'A Forgotten Capitulation ('ahdname): The Commercial Privileges Granted by Sultan Ahmed I to Emperor Matthias in 1617'. *Revue des Études Sud-Est Européennes* 58/1–4 (2020), 56–58.

44 ÖStA, HHStA, Türkei I, Turcica Box 165, Folder 5 (July 1698), fol. 9r (10r), Kinsky to Paget, 3 July 1698.

being the one suing for peace, and also not wishing to give them absolute control of the choice of the congress venue as had happened in 1689–90.

Thus, in their first meeting with the mediators, Rāmī and Mavrocordatos made it clear that in choosing a site for the talks, 'the honour and reputation of both sides need to be respected to the utmost'.[45] That meant that the Ottoman side would not accept negotiating on Habsburg soil and, least of all, in the emperor's capital. Thus, Paget would have to convey to Kinsky that 'we have used every resort at our disposal to induce these messieurs to espouse a moving of the negotiation to Vienna, but they declared resolutely right from the start that they would only negotiate in a neutral place, without crossing the frontiers by any means'.[46]

Nonetheless, the 'neutral place' that the Ottomans proposed, in return, happened to be on their side of the frontier. They presented as a choice Slankamen – in modern-day northern Serbia – 'or a more convenient place in its environs',[47] and Paget lamented that, 'given this, it would require that the mediators camp and rest in their tents, where they will be subjected to the incommodities of the air, the cold, rain, snow and bad weather'.[48] Nonetheless, he didn't give up, and raised the issue again with the Ottoman plenipotentiaries while on the way to Belgrade. This time he made use of the whole panoply of the allies' arguments: the previous negotiations, the lousy weather, the lack of provisions and the threat posed by bandits.[49]

According to Rāmī, the sultan's ambassadors realised that Paget was playing the Imperials' game. For them, there was no problem in holding a congress in the open. 'Our tents are as pleasant as a [house] chamber', they declared.[50] But if there was a need to build extra chambers, plenty of forests and carpenters were nearby. As for the provisions, there was no need to worry about them either. The Exalted State would provide everything for the maintenance of the delegations.[51] For the security of the assembled, the Ottomans seemed to be quite well informed, with similar precedents in other multilateral congresses. They proposed a ceasefire that would have to be implemented around the

45 *Taʾrīḫ-i ṣulḥ-nāme*, fol. 41^{b}.

46 ÖStA, HHStA, Türkei I, Turcica Box 165, Folder 5 (July 1698), fol. 126^{r}, Paget to Kinsky, 14/24 July 1698.

47 *Taʾrīḫ-i ṣulḥ-nāme*, fol. 41^{b}–42^{a}; ÖStA, HHStA, Türkei I, Turcica Box 165, Folder 5 (July 1698), fol. 126^{r}, Paget to Kinsky, 14/24 July 1698.

48 Ibid., fol. 126^{r}.

49 *Taʾrīḫ-i ṣulḥ-nāme*, fol. 43^{b}–44^{a}.

50 Ibid., fol. 44^{a}.

51 Ibid.

congress venue so 'that the delegates are not preoccupied with the annoying sound of canons and firearms' but with 'pleasant sounds'.[52]

However, the most intriguing proposal the Ottoman delegation made regarded the would-be spatial arrangement of the congress participants. They suggested that the camps of the two sides should stand opposite one another and that that of the mediators should be placed in the centre to symbolise their office (*tavassuṭuñuz ḥasebiyle orṭa yerde ḳorulur*).[53] In this way, it would be much easier for them to supervise the comings and goings of the ambassadors of both sides and to announce and present the terms proposed by the different participants.[54] Such spatial arrangement was not novel but was based on similar precedents, a further indication that the Ottoman plenipotentiaries had studied them extensively. It was followed, for instance, at the negotiations at Zsitvatorok in 1606, where the camp of the Hungarian mediators was placed in the middle, at an equal distance between the Habsburg and the Ottoman camps.[55] In addition, positioning the mediators in the centre in order to highlight their office was becoming the norm in seventeenth-century peace congresses as well. For instance, the Peace Treaty of Copenhagen, signed in 1660 between Sweden and Denmark under the joint mediation of France, England, and the United Provinces, took place in tents and wooden houses (as was to be the case at Carlowitz) built outside the city. The tents of the mediators were set up in the middle, between those of the principal belligerents.[56]

Besides this general positioning of the different delegations and the mediators, another cardinal point of consideration was the common place where the plenipotentiaries would meet to negotiate. The Ottomans declared that they were ready to provide a big, ornamented tent which would be divided into three parts. The middle part would be reserved for the mediators, and each side of the tent for the plenipotentiaries of the opposing parties. The different parts would be divided by heavy curtains (*perdeler ile ayrılub*); the meetings would take place, when needed, in the middle section of the tent.[57] Thus, the micro spatial arrangement of the sessions would mirror the macro one between the different delegations. "In this way, everyone's place being clear, and the venue of the negotiations being also fixed, the honour befitted each side is respected".[58] They again justified their proposal on the grounds of past examples,

52 Ibid., fol. 41^{b}–42^{a}.
53 Ibid., fol. 44^{a}.
54 Ibid., fol. 44^{a-b}.
55 Bayerle, 'The Compromise', 12.
56 Kantorska, 'Les médiations françaises', 233.
57 *Ta'rīḫ-i ṣulḥ-nāme*, fol. 44^{b}.
58 Ibid., fol. 44^{b}.

> we know that also in previous times when such difficult matters arose between kingdoms and states, negotiations were conducted in two-gated palaces, built in a commonly [agreed] venue, and the conferences were taking place in a chamber in the middle [of the palace]. And often, in common rivers, peace was negotiated in this way: on an island, with the delegates meeting each other [by coming to it] in synchronised moves.[59]

These are genuinely fascinating statements. They reveal that the Ottoman ambassadors had studied not only the ceremonial of previous Ottoman–Habsburg treaties[60] but also those between Christian states. One can clearly see that the primary reference here is none other than the Treaty of the Pyrenees (1659), where indeed a two-gated 'palace' was built on the Île des Faisans, containing two chambers for the different delegations and one in the middle for the peace talks, and where every move of the two delegations to the island had to be synchronised.[61] Moreover, it is of paramount significance to point out the Ottoman preoccupation, prevalent generally in this period, with avoiding ceremonial disputes by resorting to carefully orchestrated moves of the different delegations or trying to come up with some other expedients. 'It is recorded in our chronicles that when the delegates of the Exalted State and the emperor were to meet each other, in order to avoid conflicts over ceremonial, they boarded on ships, and as their vessels came side by side, the negotiations and signing of peace took place in the middle of the Danube'.[62] Such previously practised ceremonial and spatial arrangements were perceived as a customary law. So in Ottoman thinking, it was of paramount importance (*ehem-i mühimmātdan olduġu*) that such a method, having been followed by past generations and successfully safeguarded the honour and reputation of both parties, should be applied this time as well.[63] One thing was to be cleared up, though: 'there was no possibility of compromising the position of the honour of the Exalted State by any kind of move or act'.[64]

---

59 Ibid., fol 44^{b}.

60 For instance, during the Imperial-Ottoman peace negotiations at Szőny in 1627, a two-gate barn was erected to house the talks: Kármán, 'A Third Party'.

61 Rahn, 'Grenz-Situationen', 181–6.

62 *Ta'rīḫ-i ṣulḥ-nāme*, fol. 44^{b}. I was not able to find out in which treaty Rāmī is referring to here.

63 Ibid.

64 Ibid.

3 The Tsar in Vienna and the Developments in the Allied Camp

With their agreement on the Foundation of Peace as drafted by the Imperials and Venice, and the appointment and sending to the frontier of their plenipotentiaries, the Ottomans may have taken the peacemaking process one step further. Nonetheless, the next major scene of the Preliminaries would be played out in Vienna, where the Imperial ministers would attempt to convince the Muscovite Tsar and the Polish-Lithuanian Commonwealth to participate in the upcoming multilateral gathering. This new round of inter-allied negotiations – encompassing most of July and August 1698 – as well as the slow deliberation pace of the Imperial administration, would cause further delays to the start of the congress.

Under the command of Leopold I, it was to Count Kinsky that the heavy task fell to explain to the Muscovite ruler that practically his allies had already agreed to make peace without consulting him. Peter complained that even though the emperor, undoubtedly, had his own good reasons to reconcile with the Porte, he could have at least informed his trusted allies of his inclinations more promptly. That was not strictly true, and Kinsky replied that his master had hitherto sent anything coming from 'Turkey' to his allies in time. He dispatched the relevant documents to the Muscovite resident in the Commonwealth back on 25 April. If those papers didn't reach the tsar, it was not the emperor's fault.[65]

Next on the menu was the principle acting as the Foundation of Peace. Peter didn't hide his dissatisfaction with the *uti possidetis*. Using a rhetoric parallel to the one employed by the Polish King, he complained that he had spent millions on his new fleet, which he could use to make new conquests, 'so everything went for nothing' (*so alle verlohren giengen*). 'Consequently, his Tsarist Majesty could not be content with the Turkish proposal', but encouraged the emperor 'to postpone peace, until he and the King of Poland had made their conquests and could also be satisfied with such uti possidetis'.[66] He had specific arguments for this. Leopold was right to worry about the situation in Spain. However, that was not a reason to precipitate peace but rather to keep his armies strong. In the present circumstances, he was not to be afraid of the 'Turks' anyway. If a war in the west broke out, it would be much easier to conclude peace in the east because it would become more difficult for the French to assist the 'perennial enemy' (*Erbfeind*).[67]

65 ÖStA, HHStA, Türkei I, Turcica Box 165, Folder 5 (July 1698), fol. 45^{r-v}, Kinsky to Leopold I, 5 July 1698.

66 Ibid., fol. 45^{v}.

67 Ibid., fol. 45^{v}–46^{r}.

Kinsky replied that he would convey all these points to the emperor. However, the tsar should pay attention to the fact that peace was not yet certain; all sides had first to accept the Foundation of Peace.

> But should the Turks concede to the uti possidetis for His Imperial Majesty and all the allies, Your Imperial Majesty could not do more than to push things toward a [peace] congress, and thus to accept a secure and honourable peace requested by the [Holy] Roman Empire as well as by Spain, England and Holland, indeed by all Christendom.[68]

As far as spending was concerned, the emperor had given away millions and millions on this war over the past fifteen years. Besides, until the congress commenced, there was still much time. Maybe the tsar could secure territorial gains that would make the *uti possidetis* more satisfactory to him.[69] Nonetheless, if someone were to reflect on the future progress of the war and the possible negative consequences of peace,

> so would be to consider first and foremost that the outcome of every war is uncertain. Because, despite the good progress made [in war] by someone, God has often decided otherwise [and] instead of the desired advantage, He brings destruction and ruin [...] to the ones that bear no shame to assume the responsibility of continuing a useless blood-shedding [instead of accepting] a proposed honourable and decent peace.[70]

Kinsky's reply could be considered a typical example of a combination of arguing and bargaining, where the evocation of pro-peace moral principles goes hand in hand with the promise of prospective territorial gains, all aiming to convince one's interlocutor. The tsar insisted, though, on knowing which were those powers, allies of the emperor, who demanded that he make peace. Kinsky replied as previously. Then Peter revealed his antipathy for the northern Maritime Powers. England and Holland, he said, are not to be trusted. In the last war against France, they had hurried toward peace as well, leaving the emperor alone in the cold. 'These are not people for someone to rely upon because the only thing they care for is their commercial interests (*dem Utili Ihres Commercij*)'.[71]

---

68 Ibid., fol. 46^{v}–47^{r}.
69 Ibid., fol. 47^{r-v}.
70 Ibid., fol. 47^{v}.
71 Ibid., fol. 48^{r}.

The meeting with Kinsky should have made plainly evident to the tsar that his chances of persuading the Imperials to continue the war were indeed slim. The Bohemian Chancellor presented him with an ultimatum – the Commonwealth would receive another later. The young autocrat would be further disappointed by Leopold, since in their personal encounter, although full of pleasantries, little mention of the affairs of war and peace was made.[72]

While in Vienna, besides his meetings with the Imperial ministers and the emperor himself, Peter also held talks with the representative of the King of Poland. Honouring the promise made earlier on his behalf by Bose, August II dispatched to Austria another of his closest Saxon advisors, Hans Carl von Carlowitz (d. 1714), to assist the tsar in his negotiations with the Habsburg side and further coordinate their next moves.[73] August had already accepted the inevitability of a peace congress, but had the following suggestion to make to his ally. Since it couldn't be avoided, they should commonly propose that it should be held in the territory of the Commonwealth so that they could control its course more effectively.[74] Peter also agreed that the congress was, alas, inescapable, and in his *tête-à-tête* with von Carlowitz, he suggested that the Polish ambassadors be Saxons, and thus entirely dependent on the king's will, so that the two delegations could cooperate closely with one another.[75] Probably he had already conceived of the idea to sabotage the work of the congress – his revenge for the Imperial 'treachery' – and he suspected – correctly as it turned out – that a Polish delegate(s), acting also on behalf of the Commonwealth and not solely the king, and probably more in favour to peace, could counter-sabotage those plans of his.[76] Von Carlowitz argued that a Saxon-comprised Polish embassy would not be at all welcomed by the Commonwealth's magnates. As for his master's proposal for the congress venue, he received no comment from the tsar.[77] For the second time, what Peter gave to August II was vague promises.

The tsar's stay in Vienna ended somewhat abruptly. Having received news of an uprising in Moscow during the spring, Peter rushed to return to his capital, cancelling his planned visit to Venice.[78] However, before he departed from Austria, on July 29, he appointed one of his Great Ambassadors,

72 Guskov, 'Uchastie Rossii', 123.

73 Wagner, *Stanisław Jabłonowski*, 261; Burdowicz-Nowicki, *Piotr I*, 123.

74 Ibid.

75 Ibid., 124.

76 Ibid., 127–8.

77 Ibid., 124.

78 Guskov, 'Uchastie Rossii', 125; Bazarova, 'The Treaty of Carlowitz', 238.

Prokopii Bogdanovich Voznitsyn, as his plenipotentiary ambassador to the future congress.[79]

Voznitsyn's task was not an easy one. The tsar left him with unspecified instructions to do everything possible to derail the negotiations.[80] Things became even worse for him because Schreyer arrived in Vienna at the beginning of August with the news of the Ottoman consent to the Foundation of Peace; the congress was getting close indeed. In any case, the Muscovite ambassador started his tenure by engaging in a propaganda campaign of advertising to the Imperials the supposed recent successes of the Muscovite arms against the 'common enemy'.[81] The tsar had to appear victorious so that his claims that the allies would benefit from a continuation of the hostilities would be supported not merely by words but equally by facts.

On 9 August, he had his first conference with the Imperial ministers.[82] Voznitsyn repeated the colossal war preparations made by his master and the latter's dissatisfaction with the prospect of peace.[83] Still, despite all that, the tsar didn't desire the breaking up of the alliance, so he ultimately decided to participate in the congress. Nonetheless, Voznitsyn requested that the allies present joint peace conditions to the Ottomans and that they negotiate at the congress *en bloc* and not separately, just like in the first phase of the previous Failed Vienna Congress.[84] This probably constituted a delaying tactic, since the Imperials (as it turned out) would not agree to it. However, such ulterior motives do not diminish the originality of the proposal – especially since it came from a supposed 'outsider' in multilateral diplomacy. Moreover, such a request made sense from the Muscovite point of view. It would allow the tsar's representative to have a strong say in the drafting of the allied demands, something that was denied to Muscovy by the Imperials up to this point and would deprive the Ottomans of the opportunity to play with the diverse interests of the Holy League members and thus 'divide and conquer them'.

79 Guskov, 'Uchastie Rossii', 124.

80 Ibid., 125.

81 *See*, for instance, a Latin translation of a letter to the tsar, dated 15 July 1698, communicated by the Muscovite ambassador, in which there is a narration of alleged recent Muscovite military successes: ÖStA, HHStA, Türkei I, Turcica Box 165, Folder 5 (July 1698), fol. 108^{r}.

82 ÖStA, HHStA, Türkei I, Turcica Box 166, Folder 1 (August 1698), fol. 136^{r}–143^{v}, protocol of the conference between Voznitsyn and the Imperial ministers, 9 August 1698.

83 Bogoslovskii, *Petr I*, 348. In a visit paid to Ruzzini in early September, Voznitsyn reiterated the same arguments to the Venetian, combined with a series of complaints against the Imperials, in an attempt to win him to his side: Ibid., 356–8.

84 Ibid., 349.

The way the congress would play out would vindicate Voznitsyn's concerns, but the Imperials were unwilling to concede to his demands. They countered that a common principle was applied to all the allies, that of *uti possidetis*, which guaranteed the territorial gains made during the war. Each one of them should then make separate requests to the Ottomans, requests that the other alliance members would solicit. Presenting the Ottomans with a new set of demands would only delay the starting of the congress – but that was Voznitsyn's main goal all along. In addition, the emperor didn't intend to engage himself beforehand on which territories to demand from the Ottomans, since the continuation of hostilities made that still an open process. If the Imperial armies captured more territory before the peace congress commenced, then the Imperial side's demands would automatically increase.[85]

Furthermore, Voznitsyn appears to have been well-versed in the unique format of the Failed Vienna Congress, but his pioneering proposal of a joint allied negotiating stance lacked strong precedent, or in any case, was not the precedent that the Imperial side wanted to follow, just like back in 1689. The Habsburg ministers rather pointed out to the Muscovite ambassador the example of the recent negotiations at Ryswick, where each member of the anti-French alliance negotiated and signed separate agreements with the *Roi Soleil*.[86] Faced with such determination from the Imperial side to conclude peace as soon as possible, Voznitsyn had to lie low for the moment.[87] He would resume his efforts to delay or sabotage the negotiations during the opening phase of the congress.

Around the same time as Voznitsyn's ambassadorial appointment, the extraordinary Polish envoy Jan Gomolinski also arrived at the Imperial capital. His main goal was to promote 'the pleasant memories of the Holy Alliance'.[88] He was soon to find out that the Imperials shared other, not entirely pleasant memories, though. Gomolinski's written statement handed to the ministers of the emperor didn't help in this respect. He voiced strong grievances that Vienna did not promptly inform the king and the Commonwealth of the peace negotiations, which provoked the outrage of the members of the 'Turkish Deputation'.[89] As for the peace proposals, he stated right from the beginning

---

85 Ibid.

86 Ibid., 350.

87 However, he was still nurturing hopes that the negotiations would finally fail: Ibid., 358–9.

88 Gorkowski, *Compendium legationis*, 2^r.

89 ÖStA, HHStA, Türkei I, Turcica Box 166, Folder 1 (August 1698), fol. 66^v–67^r, relation of the members of the 'Turkish Deputation' to Leopold I, 8 August 1698.

that his polity would never agree to a negotiation in which Kamianets-Podilskyi would have to be demolished.[90]

The extraordinary envoy had his own conference with the Imperial ministers on 5 August.[91] It did not go well. As he confided immediately afterwards to Voznitsyn, with whom he met to coordinate their moves, the *uti possidetis* would leave the Commonwealth with practically nothing. Furthermore, he was subjected to the reproaches of the Imperial ministers. They told him that the *Rzeczpospolita*'s contribution to the war effort was not of consideration. They and the Venetians alone had borne the brunt of the fighting while the Poles were quarrelling among themselves, succumbing to French schemes.[92] In the end, they presented him with a brusque ultimatum: the Polish King should send his plenipotentiaries to the location where the congress would take place by 15 September. Otherwise, the emperor would not be responsible for what a failure to appear might entail.[93] Under those circumstances, the two ambassadors needed to work closely and present a united front against the other two allies. Voznitsyn reassured him that he had his full backing and that the tsar was not a fervent supporter of peace either.[94]

When the news of Gomolinski's negotiations in Vienna, together with the Imperial ultimatum, reached the Polish Diet, convened at Lviv on August 20, it caused a tremendous storm of anti-Habsburg rage and indignation among the Polish magnates.[95] Some hardliners even advocated an occupation of Silesia in retaliation for this betrayal of the alliance.[96] A possible continuation of the war was also discussed, but as all the other allies well understood, if the 'locomotive' of the alliance, the emperor, quit the fighting, their chances of success standing alone against the Ottomans would be significantly reduced. It was the Imperial forces who, by keeping the most significant part of the Ottoman armies occupied on the Hungarian front, allowed the other allies to achieve their own conquests. In the end, the Diet participants voted for a small-scale military operation, mainly against the Tatars, and to dispatch letters of protest against Leopold I to the Pope.[97] Last but not least – succumbing to the Habsburg ultimatum – on 25 August, the Voivode of Poznan, Wladyslaw

---

90 Ibid., fol. 14^{v}, Gomolinski's peace proposals to the Imperial ministers, 5 August 1698.

91 Ibid., fol. 17^{r-v}, protocol of the conference between Gomolinski and the Imperial ministers, 5 August 1698.

92 *Pamiatniki*, 39–40.

93 Gorkowski, *Compendium legationis*, 2^{r}.

94 *Pamiatniki*, 40.

95 Wagner, *Stanisław Jabłonowski*, 263.

96 Ibid., 263–4; Burdowicz-Nowicki, *Piotr I*, 129.

97 Serwański, 'Dyplomacja polska', 20.

Małachowski, was appointed the *Rzeczpospolita*'s Great and Plenipotentiary Ambassador to the peace congress.[98] On 3 September, he departed from Lviv for the Habsburg–Ottoman frontier in Hungary, where the congress would finally take place.[99]

Apart from the Commonwealth's apparent weakness in pursuing alone the fighting against the Ottomans, another major cause in accepting participation in the peace congress was the changes in the king's policy priorities. As we have seen, those alterations had probably been made in late May 1698. A further catalyst for August II's reorientation was his personal encounter with Peter I. After his hasty departure from Vienna, the tsar chose to return to his homeland via the Commonwealth, which aroused great anxiety in the Imperial resident ambassador in Warsaw, Sedlniztsky.[100] It was evident that Peter wanted to meet with August to discuss their next moves face-to-face. The reunion took place in Rava from 10 to 13 August 1698. During their secret negotiations there, the two monarchs decided to turn their attention to the north and form an anti-Swedish alliance. Peter also made clear to the Polish King that he could not continue the war without the Imperials and the Venetians. He also informed him that he appointed Voznitsyn as a plenipotentiary ambassador with instructions to sabotage the peace talks and obtained from him the promise – which was not ultimately kept[101] – that August would send a Saxon as representative of the Commonwealth to the upcoming congress. As for Muscovite military and financial assistance in the king's plans to conquer Moldavia, that was not forthcoming.[102] Thus, with no support from any of his other allies, all that was left for August II was to try to gain as much as possible out of the ongoing peace talks.

Hence, with a combination of *faits accomplis* and indirect intimidation, carefully presented as a persuasive argument, Muscovy and the Commonwealth finally acquiesced *nolens volens* to participate in the peace congress.

---

98 Wagner, *Stanisław Jabłonowski*, 264. It should be noted that the decision to send a separate delegate to the peace congress, apart from Gomolinski's mission to Vienna, was taken by the Senate back in May 1698. *See* above, 94.

99 Gorkowski, *Compendium legationis*, 3^{r}.

100 ÖStA, HHStA, Türkei I, Turcica Box 166, Folder 1 (August 1698), fol. 5^{r}–11^{r}, Sedlniztsky to Kinsky, 9 August 1698.

101 When he learned about the appointment of Małachowski, Peter declared to August II's Saxon representative in Moscow, von Carlowitz, that had he known it in advance, he would never have instructed Voznitsyn to cooperate with him: Burdowicz-Nowicki, *Piotr I*, 127, fn. 47.

102 Ibid., 127–8. It is probable that both the Imperials and the Muscovites were not viewing positively August's expansionist plans in Moldavia and were eager to see them fail: Ibid., 128.

Nonetheless, that didn't mean they fully accepted the *uti possidetis* principle, as Kinsky himself would have to admit.[103] Despite an effort to preserve a façade of unity, the Holy League was almost in tatters since not only was there a strong resentment against the Habsburgs, but the two blocks inside the alliance held their separate secret talks, and each of them fomented its own plans based exclusively upon their unique interests. The negotiations in Vienna made plain, once again, that the Imperials were the maestro leading the allied orchestra.

4 Searching in the Archives

Schreyer arrived in Vienna with the news of the Ottoman acceptance of the Foundation of Peace on 3 August.[104] So crucial was his mission this time that he covered the distance between the Ottoman camp in Sofia and the Imperial capital in only nine days![105] The Habsburg ministers were, in general, satisfied with the Ottoman instrument. Parity with the sultan should be achieved at all levels, so it was decided to send two high-ranking officials as plenipotentiaries to the congress.[106] Concerning the venue of the latter, against the solid Ottoman insistence that it should take place at the frontier, the ministers decided that making peace was more important than insisting on the option of Vienna. The Ottomans could have it their way.[107] The border area in the environs of Slankamen would be the location of the peace negotiations. As for the time of the convening of the congress, a deadline for assembling the allied delegations was given of 15 September.[108] However, yet another point was discussed during the meeting that merits special attention.

In his 24 July letter, Paget requested that Kinsky instruct him regarding 'which formalities we must observe in the congress'.[109] These 'formalities' probably concerned the ceremonial regulations as well as the procedure

103 ÖStA, HHStA, Türkei I, Turcica Box 166, Folder 2 (September 1698, 1st half), fol. 6^{r-v} (4^{r-v}), Kinsky to Paget, 1 September 1698.

104 ÖStA, HHStA, Türkei I, Turcica Box 166, Folder 1 (August 1698), fol. 53^{v}, relation of the members of the 'Turkish Deputation' to Leopold I, 8 August 1698.

105 He departed from Sofia on 24 July.

106 Relation of the members of the 'Turkish Deputation' to Leopold I, 8 August 1698, fol. 51^{v}–52^{v}.

107 Ibid., fol. 62^{r-v}.

108 Ibid., fol. 62^{v}–63^{r}.

109 ÖStA, HHStA, Türkei I, Turcica Box 165, Folder 5 (July 1698), fol. 126^{v}, Paget to Kinsky, 14/24 July 1698.

of the assembly. Nonetheless, whereas the Ottoman side – by resorting to chronicles – seemed to have acquired sufficient knowledge, even on intra-Christian precedents, and had already put forward some proposals to the mediators, the Imperial ministers informed the emperor that no reply could be given to Paget 'due to lack of sufficient information'.[110] One had to check the Imperial, the Austrian and the War Council archives in order to find something. They had already checked the Imperial one, 'but there is nothing to be found' there.[111] Under those circumstances, the best option would be to consider the papers relative to previous treaties concluded with the Ottomans – such as those of 1623[112] and 1649[113] – which surely would have been kept somewhere in the *Hofkriegsrat*'s archive.[114]

There are two quite interesting observations that could be drawn from this imbroglio in which the Imperial ministers found themselves concerning the 'formalities' of the upcoming congress. The first concerns the strengths and weaknesses of the early modern archive. By the late seventeenth century, archival materials (and historical works) constituted one of the primary sources for decision-makers and plenipotentiary ambassadors in peace negotiations.[115] However, as the above example reveals, they sometimes lacked the scrupulous systematisation and categorisation of later centuries, so crucial information could be utterly lost or could be quite difficult to retrieve when needed.[116] The second observation is related to the precedents that the Imperial ministers thought useful to check. This was to be a multilateral peace congress, and yet, instead of searching for inspiration in previous examples of such types of negotiations, the main point of reference were the Habsburg–Ottoman bilateral peace negotiations – and not even ones such as Zsitvatorok or Vienna (1689–90), that would have been the closest examples for the present congress.

Such a way of thinking, one might suggest, reveals that for the Imperial ministers, there were different 'formalities' to be observed when negotiating between Christians than when negotiating with the 'Infidels'. But if attention is paid to later Imperial declarations evoking specific precedents practised in

110 ÖStA, HHStA, Türkei I, Turcica Box 166, Folder 1 (August 1698), fol., 63ʳ, relation of the members of the 'Turkish Deputation' to Leopold I, 8 August 1698.

111 Ibid.

112 There was no such treaty concluded in 1623. Perhaps they refer to that of Gyarmat, signed in 1625: Sándor Papp, 'Az Oszmán Birodalom, a Magyar Királyság és a Habsburg Monarchia kapcsolattörténetea békekötések tükrében'. *Aetas* 33/4 (2018), 97.

113 Ibid.

114 Relation of the members of the 'Turkish Deputation' to Leopold I, 8 August 1698, fol., 63ʳ.

115 Laufs, *In viam pacis*, 148–53.

116 Ibid., 150.

inter-Christian congresses[117] – some of them especially selected to fit Vienna's interests[118] – it becomes evident that what is expressed here is the perplexity of combining the 'formalities' of a multilateral congress with the 'formalities' of the essential bilateral character of the negotiations that would take place in it. These were two different things. The first encompassed the totality of the participants, but the second was subject to rules based on what was practised in previous Ottoman–Habsburg treaties.[119]

5 The Final French 'Mediation Gambit'

As all these developments were taking place, suddenly, in the middle of August, an extraordinary ambassador of the French King, the Marquis of Villar, arrived at the Imperial capital. He declared to Kinsky that his mission was the result of an Ottoman demand for the mediation of his Master in the peace negotiations. The Marquis also wished to inquire whether the Imperial side would acquiesce to such a role for Louis XIV. He even assured Kinsky that in such a case, the French King would search in every possible way to further the interests of Christendom in general and those of the emperor in particular. Kinsky politely refused, arguing that the Foundation of Peace had already been agreed upon under the mediation of the King of England and the States General of the United Provinces.[120] A few days later, he wrote angrily to Paget. 'I don't know if the Turks really wanted this interposition (*cett'éntremise*), but if they did that without the knowledge of the accepted mediators and if they agreed to that, that's too much. I leave it to Your Lordship's care to penetrate [to the truth of the matter]'.[121]

117 *See*, for instance, ÖStA, HHStA, Türkei I, Turcica Box 166, Folder 3 (September 1698, 2nd half), fol. 155^{r-v}, Kinsky to Paget, 17 September 1698.

118 For instance, as the Imperial side was unwilling to be held 'captive' by Muscovy and Poland-Lithuania during the negotiations (*see* below, Act III, Narration Part I), it had every reason not to invoke the precedent of multilateral sessions taking place in Vienna in 1689. Instead, as we saw, when Voznitsyn proposed such a multilateral format, the Imperial ministers chose to bring up instead the 'most recent example' of the bilateral discussions at the Congress of Ryswick. Ironically, those same bilateral discussions had not favoured the Imperial at that time since it was forced to sign a peace treaty with France after all its main allies had already concluded accords with Louis XIV: Bély, *Les relations internationales*, 371.

119 Refer below to Act II, Interlude II.

120 ÖStA, HHStA, Türkei I, Turcica Box 166, Folder 1 (August 1698), fol. 176^{v}–177^{r}, Kinsky to Paget, 20 August 1698.

121 Ibid., fol. 177^{r}.

Kinsky's fears of a possible French intervention were further exacerbated by the news that the French ambassador was about to arrive at the Ottoman camp at Belgrade.[122] He wrote to General Nehem with clear instructions: 'We await the certainty of the arrival of the French ambassador in Belgrade, and whether or not he will go to the congress'.[123] And so, the ramifications of the *Defterdār*'s initiative back in March were fully played out. When Paget communicated this news from Vienna to the Ottoman plenipotentiaries, the latter deliberately avoided revealing anything- if they knew of the March initiative at all – and they categorically stated that they were not searching for new mediators now that the negotiations had reached such a mature point.[124] So, Paget tried to calm Kinsky. The ambassador of France had made a similar proposal to the Ottoman Court, but was not listened to, and since then, he has kept silent. 'But he tried to cause difficulties to the negotiation, as much as he could, and he employed all the means that one could imagine in order to reach that goal'.[125] As for the extraordinary French envoy to the Viennese Court, his aim might be 'to delay the treaty or to acquire news about its progress'.[126]

6 Apprehension on the Ottoman Side: Prevarications in Vienna

On 10 and 11 August, Paget and then Colyer moved towards Belgrade to be closer to where the congress would take place. The Ottoman plenipotentiaries stayed somewhat behind, waiting for tidings from the allied side.[127] Finally, the 'Hermes' of the negotiations, Schreyer, was back from Vienna. Thus, the mediators could inform the sultan's ambassadors of the recent events in the Imperial capital: the nomination of Voznytsin as Muscovite plenipotentiary and the imminent arrival of the Polish ablegate Gomolinski.[128]

Despite the understanding of the fact that 'in negotiations that concern the interests of many, one could not move without the agreement of all', as Kinsky

122 ÖStA, HHStA, Türkei I, Turcica Box 166, Folder 1 (August 1698), fol. 93^{r}, Nehem to Kinsky, 14 August 1698.

123 Ibid., fol. 166^{r}, Kinsky to Nehem, 20 August 1698.

124 *Taʾrīḫ-i ṣulḥ-nāme*, fol. 58^{b}–59^{a}.

125 ÖStA, HHStA, Türkei I, Turcica Box 166, Folder 1 (August 1698), fol. 241^{r}. Paget to Kinsky, 28 August 1698 (J.C.).

126 Ibid.

127 *Taʾrīḫ-i ṣulḥ-nāme*, fol. 45^{a}.

128 Ibid., fol. 49^{b}–50^{a}.

would write later to Paget,[129] the delaying of the start of the congress began to cause some apprehension to many on the Ottoman side. As the Imperial general Nehem wrote to Kinsky in late August, exaggerating perhaps a bit but still conveying a general feeling: 'The enemies were only speaking – for a few days now – of an assured peace, but since they are seeing that this much desired affair is not terminating as quickly as they would have fancied it, they are once more assuming their natural arrogance and the vizier has forbidden any talk of peace on penalty of death'.[130] What caused the delay on the allied side?

The distance between the different members of the Holy League was one reason.[131] Yet, in reality, that was a minor cause of delay. The major one appears to be the slow pace of the Imperial decision-making process. Much time was consumed in discussing the best way to arrange the new border with the Ottomans, and members of the military, as well as the chief participants of the 'Turkish Deputation', were invited to put their views into writing and submit them to the emperor.

Furthermore, the issue of whom to nominate as plenipotentiaries to the congress was not solved until the beginning of September. At first, there was a rumour – because no evidence is found in the archives – that Count Kinsky would be one of the two to be appointed to this task. Even the mediators sent a letter congratulating him on his nomination by the emperor as 'ambassador and plenipotentiary' to the upcoming congress.[132] However, they would later inform the Ottoman ambassadors that the Bohemian Chancellor had become severely ill and could not fulfil his appointed mission[133] – something that seems strange since Kinsky regularly participated in the "Turkish Deputation's" meetings throughout this period. When Voznitsyn also inquired about the issue, the Vice Chancellor of the Holy Roman Empire, Count Kaunitz, replied that no decision had been taken yet and that they were still looking for the best options, adding that many candidates were dissuaded by old age and other reasons. There was no one willing to accept the commission.[134] Of course, travelling to the frontier and spending the autumn and winter days in tents would

129 ÖStA, HHStA, Türkei I, Turcica Box 166, Folder 3 (September 1698, 2nd half), fol. 9^{r-v}, Kinsky to Paget, 17 September 1698.

130 ÖStA, HHStA, Türkei I, Turcica Box 166, Folder 1 (August 1698), fol. 224^{r-v}, Nehem to Kinsky, 27 August 1698.

131 ÖStA, HHStA, Türkei I, Turcica Box 166, Folder 3 (September 1698, 2nd half), fol. 9^{r-v}, Kinsky to Paget, 17 September 1698.

132 ÖStA, HHStA, Türkei I, Turcica Box 166, Folder 1 (August 1698), fol. 85^{r}, Paget and Colyer to Kinsky, 12 August 1698.

133 *Taʾrīḫ-i ṣulḥ-nāme*, fol. 57^{b}.

134 Bogoslovskii, *Petr I*, 351.

not have appealed to many, and maybe Kinsky excused himself by hiding behind his old age and weak health. At last, on 3 September, after a selection process that unfortunately could not be followed,[135] the President of the Aulic Council (*Hofratspresident*), Count Wolfgang von Öttingen and the General, Count Leopold Schlik, were appointed by Leopold I as his plenipotentiaries to the peace congress.[136]

Nonetheless, despite the nomination of its representatives, the delays on the Imperial side were unending. The necessary funds had to be allocated by the treasury for their travel and stay at the congress, a process that didn't go with much speed, judging from the constant plaidoyers of the Imperial ministers to the emperor to resolve the matter.[137] Others were asking for financial assistance as well; Voznitsyn pled in his turn for aid to cover the costs of the journey and receive protection along the way.[138] Most ironically, although it was the Imperial side that fixed the deadline for the departure of the ambassadors on 15 September and forced it upon all the other allies, the deadline passed and, as is to be attested by a meeting of the Imperial ministers on 21 September, the departure of the ambassadors had to be further postponed because their instructions were not yet ready.[139] The dominant view was 'that it is worthier to err in time than in substance'.[140]

This extremely slow movement of the Habsburg 'deliberation machine' was starting to cause suspicion and distrust on the Ottoman side. News had reached the vizier's camp that the allied delegations were about to leave Vienna for Petrovaradin on 15 September. 'But in the meantime, many days passed, and gossip was starting to spread in the [Ottoman] Imperial army because no news was received concerning the arrival [there] of the allied plenipotentiaries'.[141]

---

135 According to the available evidence, the issue of the prospective plenipotentiaries to be sent to the congress was only discussed once, during a meeting on 8 August: ÖStA, HHStA, Türkei I, Turcica Box 166. Folder 1 (August 1698), fol. 51^{v}–52^{r}, relation of the members of the 'Turkish Deputation' to Leopold I, 8 August 1698.

136 *See* their respective letters of appointment in ÖStA, HHStA, Türkei I, Turcica Box 166, Folder 2 (September 1698, 1st half), fol. 31^{r-v}, 37^{r}–38^{r}. It is interesting to note that none of them was mentioned as possible candidates during the 8 August meeting: *See* fn. above. For the possible reasons behind their selection, refer below to Act II, Interlude III.

137 For example, ÖStA, HHStA, Türkei I, Turcica Box 166, Folder 1 (August 1698), fol. 232^{v}.

138 Bogoslovskii, *Petr I*, 351. He finally received 1,000 guilders from the emperor's treasury: Guskov, 'Uchastie Rossii', 125.

139 ÖStA, HHStA, Türkei I, Turcica Box 166, Folder 3 (September 1698, 2nd half), fol. 41^{v}, relation of the members of the 'Turkish Deputation' to Leopold I, 21 September 1698.

140 Ibid., fol. 152^{v}, Kinsky to Paget, 27 September 1698. The same argument was repeated in the meeting of the Imperial ministers on 21 September: Ibid., fol. 41^{v}–42^{r}.

141 *Ta'rīḫ-i ṣulḥ-nāme*, fol. 62^{b}.

The most 'innocent' explanation was that they could have been delayed a few days because of the distance between Vienna and the frontier.[142] Of course, such reasoning stemmed from none other than Paget.[143]

And yet, his arguments didn't appear convincing to the Ottomans. There were more 'sinister' explanations for this procrastination. There was a reason behind the Ottoman request – only to the mediators, though – of a general armistice: the logical fear – valid as it turned out – that the allies would profit from the continuation of hostilities to try to capture more land. As Rāmī sustains, by taking advantage of the peace in the west, the Imperials could move more forces to the Hungarian front and attempt to seize more fortresses. Besides, the Foundation of Peace itself stipulated that everything one held at present remained in one's hands. And so,

> the enemies of the [Exalted] State increased the strength of their forces and caused more difficulties than in other years by thinking, on the one hand, this is the year of peace, let us appear strong to our enemies. Let it not make it evident that our desire for peace stems from weakness and exhaustion. And on the other hand, if we attack together on every side of the Islamic Dominions, perhaps, by conquering a castle or a province, during the peace negotiations, we would have crowned our peace with victory besides what we already possess.[144]

Rāmī supports his allegations by painting a picture where all the enemies were simultaneously attacking the sultan's lands: the Imperials tried to advance upon Ṭemeşvar, the Venetians brought their fleet out in the Aegean, the Poles marched upon Kamianets, and the Muscovites along with the Cossacks tried to capture some fortresses close to Crimea.[145]

The chief Ottoman ambassador's thoughts were, by and large, sound. In a letter of his written from Buda on 23 September 1698 to Karol Stanisław Radziwiłł (d. 1719), Grand Chancellor of Lithuania, Stanisław Małachowski strongly opined that the only way the Commonwealth could redress the great dissatisfaction of the Imperial Court towards it was to obtain some military

142 Ibid.

143 ÖStA, HHStA, Türkei I, Turcica Box 166, Folder 3 (September 1698, 2nd half), fol. 4^{v}, Paget to Kinsky, 6/16 September 1698.

144 *Taʾrīḫ-i ṣulḥ-nāme*, fol. 62^{b}–63^{a}. Such allegations were also voiced by the grand vizier during a meeting he had with Colyer in early October 1698: ÖStA, HHStA, Türkei I, Turcica Box 167, Folder 2 (October 1698, 2nd half), fol. 30^{r-v}, extrait d'une lettre du S[ignio]r Colyer ecrite del'armée Ottomanne devant Belgrade le 10 d'Octobre 1698.

145 *Taʾrīḫ-i ṣulḥ-nāme*, fol. 63^{a}.

success at the last moment, 'and at least block Kamianets so tight that we can claim and pretend that it's ours and [if that is achieved] we could easier bargain [for] the rest'.[146] Turning all focus upon the Podolian fortress was also what most of the hetmans were proposing to the king for his prospective campaign in early autumn.[147] Yet the king, having by now other plans in his mind, was not enthusiastic at all about it.[148] 'We spent two weeks [now] in Leopoli [Lviv] without knowing where the king wants to lead his army', reported the Polish bishop, statesman and savant Andrzej Chryzostom Załuski (d. 1711) to a friend of his in a letter dated 26 August 1698.[149] Some advised an expedition to Moldavia, others one towards Kamianets, and thus they didn't permit a decisive resolution. Finally, it was decided that the army would move on 1 September towards the river Dniester.[150] The expedition turned into a complete fiasco. The supposed 'nightmare' of the Ottomans, the German troops of the king, were driven out not by the sultan's armies but by the local Ruthenian peasants, infuriated by the burden imposed on them to feed the Saxon soldiers.[151] If that humiliation wasn't enough, internal struggles led to a real battle between the Polish and the Saxon troops, and the latter had to withdraw from Moldavia and Podolia, ending any hope of capturing Kamianets.[152] Still, the strategy of backing the negotiations at the congress by appearing militarily resilient was not something that only the allies were after, as Rāmī would have us believe. Quite the contrary.

In early September, the Governor (*vālī*) of Bosnia, Daltaban Muṣṭafā Paşa, received an order from the sultan. After being informed of the ongoing peace negotiations, the agreement reached on the Instrument of the Foundation of Peace and the imminent arrival of ambassadors from each side to the frontier for the congress, he was to pay special attention to the fact that during the peace negotiations, no general armistice (*terk-i cidāl*) was agreed and thus the war would continue.

---

146 AGAD, Archiwum Warszawskie Radziwiłłów, 1/354/0/5/9200, fol. 32, Małachowski to Radziwiłł, 23 September 1698. I sincerely thank my colleague Jan Blonski for helping me translate this passage.

147 Wagner, *Stanisław Jabłonowski*, 264.

148 Burdowicz-Nowicki, *Piotr I*, 130.

149 Andrzej Chryzostom Załuski, *Epistolae Historico-Familiares*, vol. 2 (Brunsbergae [Braniewo]: Typis Mandatus 1711) 603.

150 Ibid.

151 Kołodziejczyk, 'The Treaty of Carlowitz', 204–5.

152 Burdowicz-Nowicki, *Piotr I*, 130.

> Now, upon the arrival of my noble order, [...] you should take care to adequately prepare [the defences of] the Bosnia frontier this auspicious year and [to assure] that the soldiers would show [the appropriate] courage against the enemy. It is of paramount significance that, especially during the peace [congress], we should make every zealous effort to show courage and strength towards the enemy and not let them think that we are weak and exhausted.[153]

And somewhat more emphatically: 'God willing [...] the matter of peace is also getting very close, and it will soon be completed. [Only] thirty, forty days of difficulty remain. In this period, we should not show weakness to the enemy'.[154] Muṣṭafā Paşa appears to have taken the message on board since he would later score some victories over the Venetians in Bosnia.[155] It was based on such accomplishments, Rāmī claims, that 'we met and discussed in this congress with the plenipotentiaries of the four [allied] states with our faces clean'.[156]

7 The Arrangement of the Final Details

However, there remained the question of the exact location where the talks were to take place and the fixing of the 'formalities'. The main points as presented by the mediators were: the security of those present, the circumference of the congress venue, the number of the retinue of each delegation, and how to dispose of things so as to avoid communication between the camps of the two sides, from which inconveniences could arise.[157] Perhaps the archival research on past 'formalities' bore few results since Kinsky would inform the Englishman that, for the most part, 'they would have to be adjusted in situ' by the mediators.[158] He also agreed with the Ottomans' suggestions – and with the by-then-established congress practice – of the need to declare 'by mutual convention' a 'neutrality' around the location of the congress for the security of its participants. He also gave Paget a little tip about how many guards the

153 DABOA, A.DVNS.MHM.d 110, fol. 485.
154 Ibid.
155 Refer below to Act II, Narration Part I.
156 *Ta'rīḫ-i ṣulḥ-nāme*, fol. 74^{a-b}.
157 Ibid.
158 ÖStA, HHStA, Türkei I, Turcica Box 166, Folder 3 (September 1698, 2nd half), fol. 152^{v}, Kinsky to Paget, 27 September 1698.

mediators should possess. They had to keep them in small numbers since they 'are usually quicker with their hands than with their heads'.[159]

As for the congress venue, although at the beginning of August, the Imperials had conceded to the Ottoman demand that it was to take place somewhere around the area of Slankamen, they tried one last time to persuade the mediators of the need to transfer it, if not to Vienna, at least to Debrecen.[160] In the end, though, the 'Turks' were not persuaded, and the congress would ultimately be convened in the area between the Ottoman fortress of Belgrade and the Imperial one of Petrovaradin. At last, on 25 September, the Imperial and Venetian plenipotentiaries set out from Vienna to the Hungarian frontier.[161] The Republic had long since appointed Carlo Ruzzini, the man who had successfully negotiated the preliminaries all those months before, as its plenipotentiary ambassador.[162] Voznitsyn departed separately on 30 September, whereas the Commonwealth delegate, Małachovski, was already on the road.[163] The stage for the congress was finally ready.

• • •

And so, a process that started in December 1697 was brought to a conclusion after nearly ten months of continuous negotiations. The Preliminaries set the whole stage for the 'Theatre of Peace', being simultaneously one of its most important constituents. One cannot adequately follow the next part of our play without knowledge of its first Act. An open-ended one, it was, full of contradictions, and uncertainties, of multiple actors with varied and conflicting interests and ideas as to the possible end the play might have. Nonetheless, the key protagonists, pushed by their desires, by *faits accomplis* and constantly fearing what the reaction from the audience, the 'World', could have been regarding the sincerity of their acting, finally decided that the play should go on.

---

159 Ibid., fol. 153^{r-v}.

160 Ibid., fol. 42^{v}, relation of the members of the 'Turkish Deputation' to Leopold I, 21 September 1698.

161 *Narratio*, fol. 4^{r}.

162 His plenipotentiary powers are dated 16 August 1698: BNM, Ms.it.VII 399(8625), fol. 178^{v}.

163 Guskov, 'Uchastie Rossii', 126; Gorkowski, *Compendium legationis*, 2^{r}.

ACT II

The Congress Begins (October–Middle November 1698)

At the start of the affair, [its] immaturity is certain.

RĀMĪ MEḤMED to the Grand Vizier ʿAmcazāde Ḥüseyin Paşa

Dramatis Personae

The Protagonists

ALEXANDROS MAVROCORDATOS: Second Ottoman plenipotentiary ambassador.
CARLO RUZZINI: Plenipotentiary ambassador of the Republic of Venice.
COUNT LEOPOLD SCHLIK: Second Imperial plenipotentiary ambassador.
COUNT LUIGI MARSIGLI: Special adviser of the Imperial embassy on matters of border-making.
COUNT WOLFGANG VON ÖTTINGEN: First Imperial plenipotentiary ambassador.
JACOB COLYER: The Dutch mediator at the congress.
LORD WILLIAM PAGET: The English mediator at the congress.
PETR POSTNIKOV: Chief secretary of the Muscovite delegation and primary interpreter of Prokopii Bogdanovich Voznitsyn.
PROKOPII BOGDANOVICH VOZNITSYN: Great and plenipotentiary ambassador of Muscovy.
RĀMĪ MEḤMED: First Ottoman plenipotentiary ambassador.
STANISŁAW MAŁACHOWSKI: Great and plenipotentiary ambassador of the Polish-Lithuanian Commonwealth.

Second Roles

GIANBATTISTA NICOLOSI: Secretary of the Venetian embassy.
ISRAEL CONEGLIANO: Carlo Ruzzini's personal physician.

 | DOI:10.1163/9789004458499_010

In contrast to modern diplomatic practice, early modern congresses didn't usually have a launching ceremony which would clearly mark their beginning.[1] Instead, the opening of a congress constituted an entire phase of its own, ranging from a couple of weeks to several years, which consisted of specific steps – the *praeparatoria*, as Count Kinsky referred to them[2] – adopted first in situ and gradually formalised through tradition and practice. These steps included the official arrival of the ambassadors at the congress venue, the declaration of an armistice around the area of the negotiations, the drafting and publishing of the regulation of the congress by the mediators and the exchange of full power credentials between the negotiating parties.[3] Yet, besides these formal frontstage proceedings, the initial phase of the Congress of Carlowitz had an even livelier backstage wherein the various actors were trying to approach, gain confidence and even win over to their cause those personalities in the allied, the enemy, or the mediators' camp that they thought essential for the advancement of their interests, as well as entering into secret negotiations with the opposing party to inquire of its intentions beforehand. Unlike earlier seventeenth-century congresses, the initial phase at Carlowitz was relatively short, lasting less than a month. Nonetheless, it carried extreme importance in setting the stage for the official conferences. It also witnessed some of the fiercest ceremonial disputes of the entire congress, which could have led to its failure even before the start of the official talks between its various participants.

1 For the opening ceremony of the Westphalian Peace Congress, *see* May, *Repräsentation und Statuspolitik*, 101–2. Note, though, that this ceremony involved only the Catholic powers.

2 ÖStA, HHStA, Türkei I, Turcica Box 168, Folder 1 (November 1698, 1st half), fol. 1^r, Kinsky to Öttingen, 1 November 1698.

3 Brunert and Oetzel, 'Verhandlungstechniken', 456–60; Bosbach, 'Vefahrensordnungen', 107, 109–10.

Narration Part I: the Arrival of the Delegations

1 'We Have Gathered Here in the Plain of Carlowitz'

Writing to his friend, the Orthodox Patriarch of Jerusalem Dositheos, on 30 October 1698 (J.C.), Mavrocordatos informed him of the arrival of the different delegations at the designated area the congress was to take place: 'We have gathered here in the Plain of Carlowitz, we, the Imperial [Ottoman] [ambassadors], and those of the Caesar and Muscovy and Poland and Venice. The start goes well. We hope for an equally good ending and [one that] will come soon'.[1] Among the allied plenipotentiaries, the first to arrive at the 'determined gathering place, Futog (Futak)'[2] (in modern-day Northern Serbia), was the Venetian on 13 October, followed on the 15th by the Imperials and the Muscovite. The last to turn up was the plenipotentiary of the Polish-Lithuanian Commonwealth on the 16th.[3] The allied ambassadors followed a mixed itinerary, travelling on land and sailing down the Danube in boats.[4] A journey not without perils, passing through a land devastated by the prolonged war, where bandits roamed the countryside, preying on everyone not wise enough to be adequately escorted.[5]

As soon as the different allied delegations reached the congress venue, the rifts between them – rifts created during the Preliminaries – quickly resurfaced. The actual division of the Holy League into an Imperial/Venetian and a Commonwealth/Muscovite 'party' was perfectly reflected in their spatial segregation during the first days after their arrival. Whereas the first stayed at Futog, the others headed for Petrovaradin, accusing the former of a violation of the convention that had been previously agreed between them, according to which they would all have gathered at Petrovaradin.[6] Voznitsyn went one step further, suspecting that the Imperials were staying apart from each other to make it easier for them to conduct secret negotiations with the Ottomans

1 Th. Livadas, *Ἀλεξάνδρου Μαυροκορδάτου τοῦ ἐξ Ἀπορρήτων Ἐπιστολαί Ρ'* (Trieste: Austrian Lloyd Publishing House 1879) 177.

2 ÖStA, HHStA, Türkei I, Turcica Box 170, Diarium et Cerimoniale, fol. 1.

3 Ibid., fol. 1–2. According to the Anonymous Venetian, though, Ruzzini arrived on the 14th: *Narratio*, fol. 7^{v}–8^{r}.

4 Ibid., fol. 4^{r-v}; Bogoslovskii, *Petr I*, 362–4.

5 The Muscovite plenipotentiary, Prokopij Voznitsyn, provides a vivid picture of the desolation in Hungary and of the danger posed by the roaming bandits in his letters to Peter I: Ibid.

6 As Małachowski claimed, 'contra convetionem, quia hic Petervaradini jungi debebamus': Załuski, *Epistolae*, 676.

 | DOI:10.1163/9789004458499_011

through the mediators.[7] His and Małachowski's moves were no less suspicious, however. According to the second Imperial plenipotentiary, Count Schlik, the Pole headed to Petrovaradin only after he had inquired about the whereabouts of the Muscovite.[8] The two of them had already met briefly along the way at Buda, where Małachowski delivered to Voznitsyn a letter from the tsar written in early August during his passage through the Commonwealth on his way home. In that letter, Peter urged his representative to work closely with the ambassadors of the Polish King, who, back then, were supposed to be Saxon Germans[9] and a similar need for close cooperation with the tsar's plenipotentiary was also expressed in the instructions given to Małachowski.[10] Although Voznitsyn was disappointed to find out that the Commonwealth's representative was finally a … Pole,[11] he dissimulated his feelings and assured Małachowski that in the upcoming congress, they would have perfect collaboration in everything.[12] Things did not turn out that way, however.

Instead of strengthening their bond, their joint stay in Petrovaradin resulted in a considerable deterioration in their relations. The main point of contention revolved around questions of ceremonial precedence, which we shall discuss in further detail.[13] Speaking of the ceremonial, the initial choice of Voznitsyn not to send compliments to the second Imperial plenipotentiary Count Schlik and the delay of Małachowski to do the same with the Imperial and Venetian embassies after his arrival only exacerbated the climate of enmity among the allies.[14] The chain of perceived insults and mutual suspicions didn't end there. There was the issue of a letter sent by Małachowski to the mediators and which was secretly communicated by Paget to the Imperial plenipotentiaries, 'filled with innumerable insolences, in a formalistic style, on the issue of peace'.[15] There was also the case of two Poles, who, according to Count Schlik, requested permission to visit the Ottoman camp and their moves in Petrovaradin were

7 Bogoslovskii, *Petr I*, 366. Equally, Małachowski earlier suspected that one of the main reasons behind the delay of the Imperial embassy from Vienna was the Habsburg bargaining with the Porte over the fortresses of Belgrade and Țemeşvar 'per secretam viam': AGAD, *Archiwum Warszawskie Radziwiłłów*, 1/354/0/5/9200, fol. 32, Małachowski to Radziwiłł, 23 September 1698.

8 ÖStA, HHStA, Türkei I, Turcica Box 170, Diarium et Cerimoniale, fol. 2.

9 Bogoslovskii, *Petr I*, 361, 363.

10 Sałuski, *Epistolae*, 630.

11 Bogoslovskii, *Petr I*, 363.

12 Gorskowski, *Compendium Legationis*, 6ᵛ–7ʳ.

13 Refer below to the Interlude on the ceremonial.

14 ÖStA, HHStA, Türkei I, Turcica Box 167, Folder 2 (October 1698, 2nd half), fol. 62ᵛ–63ʳ, Schlik to Kinsky, 18 October 1698.

15 ÖStA, HHStA, Türkei I, Turcica Box 167, Folder 2 (October 1698, 2nd half), fol. 129ᵛ, Schlik to Kinsky, 22 October 1698.

monitored up until the arrival there of the Commonwealth's ambassador.[16] 'It appears, my lord', Schlik reported pessimistically to Kinsky, 'that we will hardly find common ground either with the Poles or with the Muscovites'.[17]

2 'All Is Quiet around Carlowitz'

After the advent of the various delegations, the next crucial step in this opening phase was promulgating an armistice around the venue of the talks. It was not deprived of strategic concerns for the principal two belligerents, being closely related to the continuing military operations.[18]

The Ottoman side (and the mediators) wanted the armistice to include land and water (rivers).[19] They even rushed to proclaim this on 15 October in Belgrade, ahead of the Imperials, to press them further to accept it as they intended.[20] Schreyer, Paget's secretary, also made clear to the Imperial embassy that only after a similar proclamation by the Imperial side would the mediators and the Ottoman plenipotentiaries cross the river Sava.[21] The Imperials had some reservations about extending the armistice to water. Still, as Count Schlik bluntly confessed to Kinsky, 'our fleets, a pure comedy, are better to entertain than to make conquests'.[22] So, it was deemed preferential not to block the 'big affair' (*la grosse afaire*) for a 'triviality' (*pour une bagatelle*).[23] Thus, the Imperial side promulgated the armistice on the 17th at Petrovaradin.[24] It covered an area from Zemun, near Belgrade in the south, up to Petrovaradin in the north, and an equal distance between the rivers Sava and Danube.[25] The insistence of the Ottomans on its immediate implementation is revealed by

---

16 Ibid., fol. 60^{r-v}, Schlik to Kinsky, 18 October 1698. For these Polish visits to the Ottoman camp, *see also* below, Act III, Narration Part II.

17 Schlik to Kinsky 18 October 1698, fol. 62^{v}.

18 In their relation to the emperor, the Imperial plenipotentiaries stated that the Ottomans had promulgated the armistice in order to stall the Imperial military operations and to gain some advantages in the issue of border-making: ÖStA, HHStA, Türkei I, Turcica Box 167, Folder 2 (October 1698, 2nd half), fol. 65^{v}–66^{r}, Imperial plenipotentiaries to Leopold I, 18 October 1698.

19 Ibid., fol. 61^{r}, Schlik to Kinsky 18 October 1698.

20 Imperial plenipotentiaries to Leopold I, 18 October 1698, fol. 65^{r-v}.

21 Ibid., fol. 65^{v}.

22 Schlik to Kinsky 18 October 1698, fol. 61^{v}.

23 Ibid.

24 ÖStA, HHStA, Türkei I, Turcica Box 170, Diarium et Cerimoniale, fol. 2–3; *Narratio*, fol. 8^{r}.

25 Imperial plenipotentiaries to Leopld I, 18 October 1698, fol. 65^{r-v}. The author of the so-called 'Anonymous Ottoman History' mentions a distance by land of fourteen hours (*Karlofça'dan kara tarafindan ondört sâ'at*): *Anonim Osmanlı Tarihi*, 135.

the fact that the sultan's plenipotentiaries didn't want to move from Belgrade before the Imperial fleet retired from the river Temeş.[26] If only they had been aware of Schlik's remarks.

Beyond the armistice zone, though, military operations didn't cease, regardless of the peace congress – as was the seventeenth-century norm – and continued to exercise their influence on the ongoing negotiations in various ways. One of the most common was using military victories – or alleged victories – as another weapon in the talks, a form of 'psychological warfare' combined with manipulating information to intimidate and dishearten the opposing party. One prominent example in this initial phase of the congress concerns a naval victory claimed by the Ottomans over the Venetians between the Aegean islands of Chios and Mytilini on 20 September 1698.[27]

The grand vizier, then in Belgrade together with the mediators, was quick to deliberately let the latter know the news by handing them a letter he had received from his deputy (*ḳāʾim-maḳām*) in Adrianople. Not surprisingly, as was ʿAmcazāde's intention all along, a translation of this missive, forwarded by Colyer, reached the Imperial side.[28] At the same time, and as the allied ambassadors came to the frontier, the Ottomans organised huge celebrations in Belgrade to strengthen the psychological effect upon their opponents.[29] It seems that they achieved their purpose. Count Luigi Marsigli, the 'border advisor' of the Imperial embassy, reported agitation in the Venetian delegation after the news (*tutto è agitato*),[30] whereas Count Schlik wrote that 'the Venetian ambassador is greatly alarmed because of the naval defeat [...]'.[31] The Venetians quickly engaged in a 'counter-propaganda' campaign, trying to downplay the battle or present another, favourable version of the events.[32] Nonetheless, not long after the reports on this naval confrontation in the Aegean, alarming for the Serenissima, news reached the congress from yet another theatre of the war, Bosnia.

26 Ibid.

27 ÖStA, HHStA, Türkei I, Turcica Box 167, Folder 2 (October 1698, 2nd half), fol. 46^{r}, Marsigli to Kinsky: 16 October 1698; Defterdar, *Zübde-i Vekayiât*, 646–647; Uzunçarsılı, *Osmanlı Tarihi*, 579.

28 ÖStA, HHStA, Türkei I, Turcica Box 167, Folder 2 (October 1698, 2nd half), fol. 30^{r-v}, extrait d'une lettre du S[igno]r Colyer ecrite del'armée Ottomanne devant Belgrade le 10 d'Octobre 1698. *See* the copy of the *ḳāʾim-maḳām*'s letter in Italian in ibid., fol. 31^{r-v}.

29 Marsigli to Kinsky: 16 October 1698, fol. 46^{r}; *Narratio*, fol. 16^{r}.

30 Marsigli to Kinsky: 16 October 1698, fol. 46^{r}.

31 ÖStA, HHStA, Türkei I, Turcica Box 167. Folder 2 (October 1698, 2nd half), fol. 58^{v}, Schlik to Kinsky, 18 October 1698.

32 According to the Anonymous Venetian, the news proved false (*Narratio*, fol. 16^{r-v}), whereas Ruzzini sustains that the naval battle was terminated 'indecisively' (*con sorte dubia*): Ruzzini, *Relazione*, 372.

We saw how the Ottoman administration exhorted Daltaban Muṣṭafā Paşa to present a strong face against the Exalted State's opponents. The latter appears to have followed his orders to the letter and had been able to achieve some military successes over the Republic of Saint Mark.[33] He immediately notified the Ottoman plenipotentiaries of his allegedly 'great victories' (*grossen Victori*).[34] Following 'Amcazāde's tactics, Rāmī handed a copy of the letter to the English mediator to forward to the allies.[35] 'It spread like an epic tale between them' (*mābeylerinde destān eylemiş*), the Ottoman plenipotentiary proudly concludes.[36] Ruzzini had to admit in his *Relazione Finale* that those defeats 'could not have arrived at a worse moment, fomenting the difficulties and increasing the unfavourable conditions of the already difficult negotiation'.[37] He was right. Empowered by these victories on the war front, the Ottoman plenipotentiaries would come down hard on what seemed now to be the weakest member of the Holy League.

Continuing military operations on the various war fronts were not the only variables that could significantly affect the negotiations. Events taking place in other parts of the European continent could also exert a substantial impact on them. Most of the *Rzeczpospolita*'s magnates resented the way peace talks with the Porte had been pursued by the Imperials to that point and agreed willy-nilly to send a plenipotentiary ambassador to the congress. However, whatever reluctance they might have had regarding the necessity to terminate the southern war quickly evaporated when, in early November 1698, the Brandenburg forces of Elector Frederic III captured the city of Elbląg (Elbing) in what then constituted the Duchy of Prussia.[38] The background of the events is highly gripping. In a further *coup de force* of 'personal diplomacy', August II had secretly agreed well beforehand with the Elector to undertake the attack in return for a certain sum of money (150.000 Thalers). The main reason behind this move seems to have been to allow the king to strengthen his authority inside his realm by stirring anti-Prussian feelings among the grandees and to provide a *raison d'être* for keeping his Saxon troops active inside the Commonwealth.[39] If that was

33 Defterdar, *Zübde-i Vekayiât*, 648–9.

34 ÖStA, HHStA, Türkei I, Turcica Box 170, Diarium et Cerimoniale, fol. 23–24.

35 *Ta'rīḫ-i ṣulḥnāme*, fol. 74[b].

36 Ibid.

37 Ruzzini, *Relazione Finale*, 372.

38 Under the treaty of 1656, the Elector of Brandenburg acquired some rights over the city if the Commonwealth ever failed to address payment of a debt to him of 400.000 Thalers, raised to face the needs of the Second Northern War (1655–60): Burdowicz-Nowicki, *Piotr I*, 155–6; Robert I. Frost, *The Northern Wars. War, State and Society in Northeastern Europe, 1558–1721* (Harlow (UK)/New York: Longman 2000) 228.

39 Burdowicz-Nowicki, *Piotr I*, 109, 157.

indeed his purpose, it was crowned with complete success. The Elector's moves stirred great uproar inside the *Rzeczpospolita*, as the magnates called for immediate action against Brandenburg.[40] Their attention moved from the south to the north, and under the real risk of a two-front war, peace with the Porte now seemed even more imperative. 'The news of Elbląg unsettles this Polish grandee [Małachowski]', Marsigli reported to the Bohemian Chancellor, 'as he fears that his king will not have an agreement with the Elector of Brandenburg'.[41] How did Małachowski respond to this novel situation? We shall leave that for later.

3 The First Ceremonial Visits

The mediators finally crossed the river Sava on 19 October, followed by the Ottoman plenipotentiaries three days later on the 22nd.[42] The following period (until 2 November) was dominated by the practice of notifications and mutual ceremonial visits between the allied ambassadors and the mediators, and the mediators and the Ottomans, so-called by the latter as 'ceremony of comings and goings' (*āmed şüd merasimi*).[43] These first visits and counter visits mirrored the reception ceremony for an ambassador at a foreign court and, since the time of Westphalia, constituted an indispensable feature of the opening phase of a congress.[44] The Ottoman side, eager to commence talks at the earliest time possible, tended to view them as an unavoidable 'evil'. 'The ceremony of comings and goings apart from the fact of being [a] necessary [part of] the ceremonial, it causes a loss of time', Rāmī explained to 'Amcazāde.[45] However, the main reason those visits and counter visits lasted so long had nothing to do with the slow pace of the practice itself but instead with the strife that had

40 Wagner, *Stanisław Jabłonowski*, 269.

41 ÖStA, HHStA, Türkei I, Turcica Box 168, Folder 1 (November 1698, 1st half), fol. 254v, Marsigli to Kinsky, 12 November 1698.

42 *Ta'rīḫ-i ṣulḥnāme*, fol. 70a; ÖStA, HHstA, Türkei I, Turcica Box 170, Diarium et Cerimoniale, fol. 4–5; ÖStA, HHstA, Türkei I, Turcica Box 167, Folder 2 (October 1698, 2nd half), fol. 120r, Imperial plenipotentiaries to Leopold I, 22 October 1698.

43 *Ta'rīḫ-i ṣulḥnāme*, fol. 70a; *Narratio*, fol. 11a, 14b; ÖStA, HHStA, Türkei I, Turcica Box 170, Diarium et Cerimoniale, fol. 3v–4r (of the separate journal regarding the ceremonial).

44 Brunert and Oetzel, 'Verhandlungstechniken', 459. Rāmī also testifies their established character by referring to them in his relation as 'old ceremony' (*merāsim-i ḳadīm*) or 'old customs' (*resm-i ḳadīmleri*): *Ta'rīḫ-i ṣulḥnāme*, fol. 75a.

45 Ibid.

broken out again on the allied side.[46] Those 'chimerical obstinacies' (*pontiglij chimerici*), as Count Marsigli designated them,[47] were caused mainly, once again, by questions of precedence and the place the various ambassadors were to occupy in the allied encampment. It required the mediation and pressure of the Imperial embassy and the transferring of the allied embassies to a new camp, designed explicitly by Marsigli to erase any form of precedence, to effectively surmount all these differences between them for the negotiations to ultimately start.[48]

The ceremonial dissent between the members of the Holy League was carefully observed by the Ottomans, who must have viewed this Christian 'civil war' with satisfaction.[49] 'In this preliminary phase', wrote Rāmī Meḥmed,

> [in which] so many state representatives came together, they have not been able to remove the ceremonial [disputes] between them yet. Each one of them, with his obstinacy, some time passed in order to find stability between them in these circumstances [...] Although they appear allies, in reality, there was a complete disagreement between them on the question of honours.[50]

4 The Exchange of the Plenipotentiaries' Credentials

When the ceremonial disputes between the allies slightly abated, the negotiations could be further advanced by exchanging the plenipotentiaries' credentials (29–30 October).[51] Following the example set at Rijswijk, the mutual handing over was effectuated via the mediators to avoid another round of visits and the ceremonial questions that might have emerged from them.[52] There was also a novelty, though. As the Christian coalition leader, the Imperial side undertook to assemble all the other allied plenipotentiary credentials

46 We will deal with these disputes in depth in Interlude II below.

47 ÖStA, HHStA, Türkei I, Turcica Box 167, Folder 2 (October 1698, 2nd half), fol. 176ʳ, Marsigli to Kinsky, 25 October 1698.

48 Ibid., fol. 176ʳ–177ʳ.

49 The expression is used by Count Schlik to describe the Muscovite-Commonwealth struggles over precedence: ÖStA, HHStA, Türkei I, Turcica Box 167, Folder 2 (October 1698, 2nd half), fol. 159ʳ, Schlik to Kinsky, 25 October 1698.

50 *Ta'rīḫ-i ṣulḥnāme*, fol. 72ᵃ.

51 ÖStA, HHStA, Türkei I, Turcica Box 170, Diarium et Cerimoniale, fol. 17–19.

52 Brunert and Oetzel, 'Verhandlungstechniken', 459.

and hand them over to the mediators.[53] This exchange was not considered a mere formality but an essential step in establishing trust between the opposing delegations.[54] For instance, after receiving the Imperial full powers, the Ottomans expressed dissatisfaction with them because there was no explicit mention of the Foundation of Peace (*uti possidetis*) or the 'Kinsky letter'. It was only after a categorical reply from the Imperial embassy that they were fully committed to both that the issue was put to rest.[55]

Yet, not even did this phase manage to pass without significant perturbations. Voznitsyn refused to recognise the mediators by submitting to them his credentials, claiming that he had no such decree by the tsar.[56] In all probability, combined with Peter's dissatisfaction with the northern Maritime Powers, it was one of his moves deliberately designed to sabotage the congress. In the end, though, he backed off and delivered his full powers 'when one expected it the least', as Count Schlik remarked.[57] However, he later changed his mind once again and, approaching the Imperials, expressed his wish to negotiate directly with the Ottomans 'without any mediation' (*ohne weitherer mittlung*). 'Good words had little result', commented the second Habsburg ambassador, 'and, in a nutshell, one could truly believe that this man had transformed into a wild beast (*Unbändiges thier*)'.[58] Such erratic comportment, the result of balancing two seemingly conflicting goals to undermine the talks, but equally not leave his master alone in war if his sabotage didn't work,[59] already had earned Voznitysn, by this stage, the reputation of the 'enemy of peace' as he himself narrates in one of his letters to the tsar:

> Also, the Turks, coming to my camp, ask: Who is standing there? They say – the ambassador of Muscovy. They reply – the one who doesn't want to make peace? My people say: Who told you that? They [again]: the

53 ÖStA, HHStA, Türkei I, Turcica Box 170, Diarium et Cerimoniale, fol. 17–18.

54 *Ta'rīḥ-i ṣulḥnāme*, fol. 75ª.

55 ÖStA, HHStA, Türkei I, Turcica Box 167, Folder 2 (October 1698, 2nd half), fol. 277ᵛ–278ʳ, Imperial plenipotentiaries to Leopold I, 30 October 1698.

56 Bogoslovskii, *Petr I*, 389; ÖStA, HHStA, Türkei I, Turcica Box 170, Diarium et Cerimoniale, fol. 17–18. According to Count Schlik, the mediators were also resolute at first not to have any transactions (*de n'avoir aucun commerce*) with those of the allies that were not recognised them as such or hadn't signed the Foundation of Peace but were dissuaded by the Imperial delegation: ÖStA, HHStA, Türkei I, Turcica Box 167, Folder 2 (October 1698, 2nd half), fol. 208ᵛ, Schlik to Kinsky, 30 October 1698.

57 Ibid., fol. 207ᵛ. It would not be the last time Voznitsyn would be accused by his allies of inconsistency in his behaviour as we shall later see.

58 ÖStA, HHStA, Türkei I, Turcica Box 170, Diarium et Cerimoniale, fol. 27–28.

59 These two principal aims would dominate the Muscovite's actions throughout the congress.

> Germans told us. Mine: The Germans are lying. If you want to drink and eat, go to the tents! They answer: When you don't want to make peace, there is no appetite for eating and drinking.[60]

The personal animosity Voznitsyn managed to earn among the Imperials and the mediators in this initial phase of the congress would deprive him of crucial support from both when he later needed it.[61]

5 The Drafting of the Congress Regulation

During this entire period, the Ottoman side was trying to accelerate the talks without appearing desperate to achieve peace by any means. As Rāmī explained in one of his reports (*ḳa'ime*) to the grand vizier, negotiation 'cannot be done in haste. It needs composure and careful thinking. [Because] let us suppose that our side shows great desire for a speedy conclusion [of the affair], our devotion and desire will load upon us, its weight will increase, and our haste will not create benefits, but perhaps can lead to many damages'.[62] However, despite all that effort, the Ottoman apprehension for a speedy conclusion of the congress was too obvious to be hidden. 'The Turks press much for a speed-up of the affair', the Imperial ambassadors reported on 30 October in their relation to the emperor.[63] Not only did they insist on speeding up the construction of a conference house 'but they also reminded the mediators already this morning that they want to start reflecting in time about the manner and order of the negotiation'.[64] And thus began the process for the final step of this initial chapter of the congress, the drafting of its regulation (3–6 November).[65]

Such a regulation – 'to ease the negotiation' (*teshīl-i mükāleme içün*), as Rāmī Meḥmed claimed[66] – had become a standardised practice since the Congress of Nijmegen.[67] Its main points concerned ceremonial and security questions and, more significantly, the *modus tractandi* to be followed.[68] In

60 Quoted in Bogoslovskii, *Petr I*, 390–1.
61 Ibid., 399–400.
62 *Ta'rīḫ-i ṣulḥnāme*, fol. 74ᵃ.
63 HHstA, Türkei I, Turcica Box 167, Folder 2 (October 1698, 2nd half), fol. 299ʳ, Imperial plenipotentiaries to Leopold I, 30 October 1698.
64 Ibid.
65 ÖStA, HHStA, Türkei I, Turcica Box 168, Folder 1 (November 1698, 1st half), fol. 151ʳ–153ʳ; Box 170, Diarium et cerimoniale, fol. 25.
66 *Ta'rīḫ-i ṣulḥnāme*, fol. 70ᵇ.
67 Brunert and Oetzel, 'Verhandlungstechniken', 457, fn. 7.
68 ÖStA, HHStA, Türkei I, Turcica Box 170, Diarium et cerimoniale, fol. 25.

order to agree on the final text, published in the name of the mediators, strenuous negotiations had to precede it; negotiations conducted mainly by the two principal belligerents, the Ottomans and the Imperials. The sultan's embassy made the first proposals on the *manière de négocier*.[69] It proposed starting the talks with the emperor since the latter stood higher among the Christian princes.[70] Contrary to what the Ottomans had advocated in the Failed Vienna Congress ten years earlier, each party would negotiate independently of the other, and whoever finished first would sign their Peace Instrument.[71] That was an apparent attempt to separate the allies and also revealed a strategy, correctly assessed by Ruzzini, that the Ottomans wanted to deal first with their strongest opponent and then use the precedents these discussions would create to impose them on the other allies as well.[72] Of course, since most early modern congresses were based on bilateral norms and each member of an alliance could sign its Peace Instrument with the common enemy[ies] independent of the others,[73] the Ottomans had a solid case to make.

As was expected, the Imperials found the Ottoman proposals unacceptable. It was not that they were against a bilateral mode for the talks in principle. They also favoured such an arrangement to conserve their freedom of movement against possible attempts by the Poles or the Muscovites to undermine the negotiations.[74] They differentiated, however, between the independent progression of each other's talks and the final joint signing of the Peace Instruments by all the allies, which would conserve and demonstrate the unity of the Holy League. This point was considered so delicate that it took three days of continuous exchange of proposals and counterproposals between the Ottoman and the Imperial delegation for the two sides to reach an agreement on the text's

69 ÖStA, HHStA, Türkei I, Turcica Box 167, Folder 2 (October 1698, 2nd half), fol. 209r, Schlik to Kinsky, 30 October 1698.

70 'Cum Romanorum Imperator Christianorum Principum sit maximus ante alios': ibid., fol. 307r.

71 Ibid.

72 Ruzzini, *Relazione*, 355.

73 For instance, at Ryswick, the United Provinces, Spain, and England signed their treaties with France on 20/21 September 1697 and the emperor on 30 October of the same year: Bély, *Les relations internationales*, 371.

74 For example, in the relation to the emperor after a meeting of the 'Turkish Deputation' on 21 September 1698 it was suggested that 'Your Imperial Majesty's interest can be better advanced if the allies were not to negotiate together. Instead, [...] each one of them must take care of his own affairs separately': ÖStA, HHStA, Türkei I, Turcica Box 166, Folder 2 (September 1698, 1st half), fol. 45v, relation of the members of the 'Turkish Deputation to Leopold I, 21 September 1698.

final form.[75] This final form was a compromise between the positions of the two parties. Its main articles concerned the suspension of all ceremonial regulations throughout the congress to facilitate the negotiations; the stipulation that each party was free to advance its own negotiation independently from the others with the explicit provision, though, that even if one lagged in its negotiation, it must still be included in the final peace settlement;[76] the condition that the drafts of the peace instruments would be delivered to the mediators for safe keeping to avoid alterations in their content and lastly, that none of the plenipotentiaries could negotiate contrary to the full powers he possessed or attempt to delay or disturb the congress.[77] Commenting on the last two provisions, Carlo Ruzzini contended that the first was deemed necessary by the Imperials 'as a barrier against the bad faith and inconsistency of the Turks'.[78] The second, on the other hand, was considered paramount in order 'to moderate the designs of Poland and Muscovy, so that the major interests of the two allies (emperor and Venice) that they did fight the war would not be sacrificed because of the fantasies of the other two, who didn't, and who now ensured to realise them upon uncertain hopes'.[79]

If we are to believe the Venetian ambassador, the drafting of the regulations was kept secret by the Imperials and the mediators.[80] After perfecting it, they forwarded it to the other allies, signed in the name of Paget and Colyer, where, 'strangely, it was referring to a common consensus, without having it either requested or obtained'.[81] In their relation to the emperor, though, the Imperial ambassadors claimed that they had forwarded drafts of the regulation to the other allies 'before it assumed its final form'.[82] Irrespective of which version

75 All the different stages of this process in ÖStA, HHStA, Türkei I, Turcica Box 168, Folder 1 (November 1698, 1st half), fol. 151ʳ–153ʳ.

76 Ibid., fol. 153ʳ.

77 A copy of the regulation in ibid., fol. 144ʳ–145ᵛ. The Ottoman translation in *Taʾrīḫ-i ṣulḥnāme*, fol. 70ᵇ–72ᵃ.

78 Ruzzini, *Relazione*, 353. Indeed, such a stipulation was missing from the Ottoman proposals [ÖStA, HHStA, Türkei I, Turcica Box 167, Folder 2 (October 1698, 2nd half), fol. 307ʳ]. Still, contrary to Ruzzini's claims, 'bad faith' in peace negotiations seems not to have known religious or ethnic boundaries and so, such safe keeping was a long-established practice between Christians as well: Laufs, *In viam pacis*, 134.

79 Ruzzini, *Relazione*, 353.

80 Ibid.

81 Ibid., 354.

82 ÖStA, HHStA, Türkei I, Turcica Box 168, Folder 1 (November 1698, 1st half), fol. 134ʳ, Imperial plenipotentiaries to Leopold I, 8 November 1698.

of the events truly transpired,[83] a new torrent of dissent swept through the allied encampment. Voznitsyn, always ready to attest yet another proof of the 'German duplicity', was furious. He addressed the Imperials 'with somewhat strong expressions' (*mit etwas starken expressionen*), and he declared that he wanted neither to accept nor to read those points.[84] He and Małachowski declared their intention to leave, but the Imperials convinced them that such a method was mainly adopted to facilitate their negotiation. They also placated the Venetians by declaring that those regulations were merely a warning to the other two allies, that they were not compulsory and that everyone could proceed as they saw fit regardless of them. Ruzzini posthumously admitted that he, too, conceded because the Venetian affairs had not yet been thrown in jeopardy.[85] He would only later realise what a mistake he had made.

The Congress Regulation's importance for the ensuing peace talks is quite significant, despite the intentional efforts of the Imperials to disparage it. The diversity of interests prevalent among the Christian allies considerably weakened their collective bargaining position, as each of them, the Habsburgs first and foremost, followed their own particular agenda. With all his secret machinations to blow up the congress, Voznitsyn was perhaps right to press for a united allied negotiation with the Ottomans, because the strictly bilateral character of the talks, although prevalent in almost all previous seventeenth-century congresses, appeared, in the end, to have immensely favoured the Ottoman side,[86] as it had favoured the French side during the Congress of Nijmegen.[87] Rāmī Meḥmed was thus totally justified in expressing his contentment. 'God almighty willing, from now on, we will come together, and we should negotiate separately with each one. Each and every one focusing on their own affairs, there is no need to consult with the others'.[88]

---

83 From the Imperial ambassador's relation to Leopold I, it appears that at least Małachowski was privy to the regulations' drafts: Ibid. fol. 134^{r-v}.

84 ÖStA, HHStA, Türkei I, Turcica Box 170, Diarium et Cerimoniale, fol. 26.

85 Ruzzini, *Relazione*, 354.

86 *See* the bitter post-factum realisation of this by the Anonymous Venetian: *Narratio*, fol. 26^{r-v}.

87 Köhler, *Strategie und Symbolik*, 134–58.

88 *Ta'rīḫ-i ṣulḥnāme*, fol. 72^{b}.

Interlude II: the Ceremonial

> A nice invention of Satan to ruin the human race.
>
> JOHANN RUDOLF WETTSTEIN, ambassador of the Swiss Confederation at the Congress of Westphalia on the ceremonial[1]

∴

On 18 September 1698, while waiting for the arrival of the allied plenipotentiaries at the frontier, General Nehem, the commander of the Imperial forces at Petrovaradin, dispatched a letter to Count Kinsky asking for instructions on an issue he deemed to be outside his field of expertise:

> I am finding myself very embarrassed because I have not yet been ordered with which ceremonies and distinction I should receive the afore-mentioned ambassadors. As Your Lordship knows that it is not the job of a soldier to regulate those sorts of things, I hope that you will not find it inappropriate that I dare taking the liberty of asking for instruction from Your Lordship so that I make neither more nor less [than is needed].[2]

Roughly a month earlier, as the mediators were close to Belgrade, the Ottoman plenipotentiaries, perhaps responding to an equal appeal for instructions or maybe anticipating it, wrote a letter to the commander of the Ottoman forces there, ʿAlī Paşa, with guidelines regarding the 'reception of the ambassadors' (*ėlçileriñ istiḳbāl*) and the ceremonial (*merāsim*) to be observed in it:[3]

> They are ambassadors. Your Excellency knows that when [ambassadors] come to the Seat of Government [The Sublime Porte], they are received according to the [sultanic] law by the Aga of the halberdiers of the sultans' guard accompanied by many of his men, and the Agas of the first and second janissary cavalry units with their men. In the present circumstances,

1 Quoted in May, *Repräsentation und Statuspolitik*, 177.
2 ÖStA, HHStA, Türkei I, Turcica Box 166, Folder 3 (September 1698, 2nd half), fol. 29v–30r, Nehem to Kinsky, 18 September 1698.
3 *Taʾrīḫ-i ṣulḥnāme*, fol. 45a–46b.

 | DOI:10.1163/9789004458499_012

> you may appoint [some of] your own men to act as substitutes for the Aga of the halberdiers and the Agas of the janissary cavalry units.[4]

Still, they advised, ʿAlī Paşa should be careful because there were some critical distinctions to make: "England's [ambassador] is [one sent by] a kingdom, and the Netherlands' [one by] a republic (*cümhūr*). An ambassador of a king receives greater honours than the one of a republic" (*ḳral ėlçisi cümhūr ėlçisinden iʿtibārludur*).[5] These interesting parallel cases testify to the importance attached during the late seventeenth century to the theme of this Interlude: the ceremonial.

The preponderant role of the ceremonial in the early modern period in terms of symbolic communication, representation, and (re)production of a hierarchical societal order, mirrored in the early modern 'Society of Princes', has gained wide currency in the scholarship during the last two decades.[6] Nonetheless, its implications for the early modern peace congresses, or the latter as instances of cardinal importance for its further development and codification, are only recently starting to attract the attention of researchers and scholars.[7] Usually, Carlowitz does not figure in their analysis. And yet, an examination of the ceremonial regulations and disputes of this congress can significantly contribute to a better understanding of the phenomenon's *longue durée* evolution, complement the insights based on other western European congresses, and even challenge some of the conclusions drawn by focusing exclusively on these 'usual suspects'. The Carlowitz case not only reveals that powers with supposedly diametrically 'different' ceremonial traditions actually shared much more in common than it is usually thought, but it also demonstrates that questions regarding the ceremonial and precedence, far from receding to the background in the late seventeenth century, continued to dominate the minds of the congress participants and could create severe hindrances to the negotiations.

In this interlude, we will address specific ceremonial-related topics proceeding from the general to the more particular. After a brief sketch of what constitutes the 'diplomatic ceremonial' and an unavoidable yet essential venture into terminology, we will deal with its specific evolution in seventeenth-century peace congresses. Such an overture is crucial for understanding the interplay between precedence and innovation that formed the basis of the Carlowitz

4 Ibid., fol. 46[a].
5 Ibid., fol. 46[b].
6 An extensive bibliographical survey in May, *Repräsentation und Statuspolitik*, 18–25.
7 May's monograph is paramount in this respect.

ceremonial. The early modern hierarchical conception of political entities standing right in the centre of the symbolic representation of the congress participants is of the essence to touch upon how each of them configured it and where each placed himself and the others in it. Closely affiliated are the occasions where and the means through which the particular status stemming from one's perceived place in such a stratified inter-polity 'society' was overtly manifested. This status display was tightly bound to the ambassador, the direct representative of his principal's dignity. Even so, what happened in delegations comprising more than one ambassador? Was their ceremonial position equal, or were there internal stratifications? Entering into the core section of the interlude, we will examine the multiple forms via which the ceremonial made its appearance during and after the end of the talks. The final parts will be dedicated to some of the most important ceremonial disputes that occurred during the congress and their actual significance for the negotiation process. Were they solely ceremonial-related, or could they have also been instrumentalised for other goals?

1 What Is the Ceremonial?

The ceremonial consists of performative acts with a strongly ritual character, based on a repertoire of specific gestures, signs, symbols and words recognisable to all the participants of a particular social occasion, which aimed 1) to project or (re)create a specific social order between them,[8] 2) to signal the inception or abruption of a social relationship,[9] and 3) to reflect a particular social role.[10] As such, it is not a phenomenon strictly restricted to the early modern period but reaches back well into antiquity. One could even claim that, with varying degrees and expressions, it is encountered even in contemporary societies.[11] In relations between polities of the pre-modern period, it was mainly expressed

8 Niels F. May, 'Zeremoniell', in Dingel et al., *Handbuch Frieden*, 609–25, 610.

9 Matthias Köhler, 'Höflichkeit, Strategie und Kommunikation. Friedensverhandlungen an der Wende vom 17. Zum 18. Jahrhundert', in Gisela Engel, Brita Rang and Susanne Scholz (eds.), *Konjunkturen der Höflichkeit in der Frühen Neuzeit* (Frankfurt: Klostermann 2009) 379–98.

10 Sylvio Hermann De Franceschi, 'La négociation à l'épreuve des mœurs, de la moralité et des caractères. Jalons pour une étude de la science morale des diplomates à l'époque moderne'. *Histoire, économie & société* 33/2 (2014), 17–33.

11 Hennings, *Russia*, 15.

during the reception of foreign embassies at various courts[12] or during encounters between potentates or their representatives.[13] It encapsulated multiple issues, ranging – in a peace congress, for instance – from the official entry of the ambassadors to the congress location and the order of visits between them, to the spatial arrangement of the conference venue and the language, written and oral, the actors used during the talks.[14] The ceremonial was the by-product and outright expression of a hierarchical society in which personal honour, glory and status were considered primordial ideals and values, vested with extreme symbolic capital.[15] As such, ceremonial honours and the strife over them were not superfluous Baroque vanities but real power struggles over the position of an actor on the scene of the 'theatre' of early modern princely society.[16]

2 Terminology

There has been a long terminological debate among scholars regarding the differences and similarities between 'ceremonial' and 'ritual', where the dividing line lies between the two, and whether it is more correct to privilege the use of one or the other.[17] I have opted to refer to those performative (and ritualistic) acts of symbolic communication during the congress as 'ceremonial', not least because that is actually how the primary sources mainly refer to them. Because, in contrast to some scholarly views, which sustain that the term was not actually in use until the early eighteenth century,[18] it was in fact widely utilised by the Carlowitz participants, attesting to a longer, previous dissemination of the word. Thus, Małachowski speaks of 'finalising the ceremonial'

12 *See* among others, Gojko Barjamovic, 'Propaganda and practice in Assyrian and Persian imperial culture', in Peter Fibiger Bang and Dariusz Kolodziejczyk (eds.), *Universal Empire. A Comparative Approach to Imperial Culture and Representation in Eurasian History* (Cambridge: Cambridge University Press 2012) 43–59; Alexander Beihammer, Stavroula Constantinou, and Maria G. Parani (eds.), *Court Ceremonies and Rituals of Power in Byzantium and the Medieval Mediterranean. Comparative Perspectives* (Leiden/Boston: Brill 2013); Peter Burschel and Christine Vogel (eds.), *Die Audienz. Ritualisierter Kulturkontakt in der Früher Neuzeit* (Cologne/Weimar/Vienna: Böhlau 2014).

13 Rahn, 'Grenz-Situationen'.

14 May, 'Zeremoniell', 610.

15 Jennings, *Russia*, 12, 15–17.

16 Ibid., 18–9.

17 May, *Repräsentation und Statuspolitik*, 37–45.

18 Ibid., 36. In a later article of his, though, May nuanced this position. Whereas he initially spoke of the term 'ceremonial' in general, he later refined it to 'diplomatic ceremonial': May, 'Zeremoniell', 610.

(*ceremonialium concludendorum*),[19] whereas the unknown Venetian author of the *Narratio conventus caroloviciani*, very attentive to ceremonial regulations, explicitly used the word *cerimoniale* when referring to them.[20] In other instances, though, like in the congress journal kept by the second Imperial ambassador Count Schlik, 'ceremonial' often alternates with the more 'traditional' term of 'ceremony'.[21] Yet, the word also appears to possess some fluidity. Sometimes, it could even be employed to denote the *manier de négocier* of someone. For instance, in a letter to Ruzzini, Count Kinsky would respond to the Venetian's lamentations about what he perceived as an Ottoman violation of the Foundation of Peace, reminding him that 'in the ceremonial (*nell' ceremoniale*), one has to do with people who, apart from their own concepts, badly formed too, they understand neither reason nor temperament'.[22]

Speaking about the Ottoman 'concepts' to refer to the ceremonial, one encounters two principal terms: *merāsim* and *tekellüf*.[23] Both are direct equivalents of the Christian European 'ceremony'.[24] Regarding the first, one of its primary meanings – it possesses many – is, interestingly, that of a sign which is what the ceremonial mainly consists of.[25] As for *tekellüf*, besides its translation as *cerimoniae*, it also carries the meanings of annoyance, discomfort, and dissimulation (or simulation, *simulatio* in Latin).[26] So, it perfectly summarises the performative nature of the ceremonial as much as the feelings of disquiet ceremonial regulations could sometimes cause to seventeenth-century contemporaries, as the epigraph at the beginning of this Interlude attests.

---

19 Załuski, *Epistolae*, 676.

20 For example, 'quando al cerimoniale bisognò alterare il primo concerto': *Narratio*, fol. 17[r].

21 For instance, ÖStA, HHStA, Türkei I, Turcica Box 170, Diarium et Cerimoniale, fol. 21 (*mit beobachtung aller gewönlichen Ceremonien*) and fol. 85 (*das ceremoniale widerumb von vorenen angefangen*). For the use of the term 'ceremony' *see* May, *Repräsentation und Statuspolitik*. 36.

22 ÖStA, HHStA, Turcica Box 168, Folder 2 (November 1698, 2nd half), fol. 156[r], Kinsky to Ruzzini, 22 November 1698.

23 *See*, for instance, *Taʾrīḫ-i ṣulḥnāme*, fol. 71[a], 72[b], 75[a].

24 Meninski, *Thesaurus*, 1346. Thus, since in the Christian sources, 'ceremony' and 'ceremonial' are used interchangeably as synonyms, I also translate *merāsim* and *tekellüf* in both ways.

25 Thus, on one occasion, the Ottoman plenipotentiaries would speak of 'the signs of peace and friendship' (*dostluḳ ve barışıḳlıḳ merāsimi*): *Taʾrīḫ-i ṣulḥnāme*, fol. 115[a]. For the multiple meanings of the word, *see* Meninski, *Thesaurus*, 4544–5.

26 Ibid., 1346.

3 Ceremonial Regulations in Seventeenth-Century Peace Congresses Prior to Carlowitz

The first Ottoman ambassador in Vienna in 1688, Zülfikār Efendi, once stated that 'in the meeting ceremony [between ambassadors and the potentate they were sent to] the rule is generosity. It's not an occasion [to create] animosity'.[27] This was surely not how most 1680s contemporaries, including Zülfikār himself, approached the matter.[28] Ceremonial questions were highly prone to creating quarrels, and during the seventeenth century, peace congresses became a privileged milieu for ceremonial strife.[29] This was natural because there was an unprecedented concentration of representatives of various powers, something that made the congress an arena par excellence for them to affirm or safeguard the claimed status of their principals or to contest that of others. As Ruzzini mentions in his *Relazione*, 'I amplified with abundance the expenditures, in order to make shine [...] in front of so many nations the dignity of the royal representation (*il decoro della Reggia Rappresentanza*)'.[30]

Of course, royal courts were also places where multiple ambassadors might find themselves together. Nonetheless, contrary to established, strict court ceremonial protocol, congresses were typically held in neutral territory where no one could claim precedence. In addition, there was no master of ceremonies to arbitrate the disputes, although this role was gradually taken up by the mediators or other congress participants who attempted to act as conciliators.[31] In the beginning, ceremonial questions in peace congresses were neither formalised nor standardised, which left room for multiple interpretations of specific signs. The formalisation and standardisation of those signs came only gradually.[32] The accumulated experience from earlier congresses played a crucial role in this regard, combined with a good deal of *ad hoc* decisions and improvisations.[33] Westphalia usually acted as an arch-example – although it was instead the congresses of Nijmegen and Ryswick which were mostly mentioned by the Carlowitz participants.[34] Interestingly, the more ceremonial

27 *Cerîde-i Takrirât*, 30.
28 As his strong litigation with the Imperial ministers for the ceremonial treatment of the Ottoman embassy clearly attests: Ibid., 29–32.
29 May, *Repräsentation und Statuspolitik*, 13.
30 Ruzzini, *Relazione*, 378.
31 May, *Repräsentation und Statuspolitik*, 13–4.
32 May, 'Zeremoniell', 620–1.
33 Ibid., 618.
34 *See* below.

questions gained importance, the more they were viewed as an impediment to the negotiations and efforts were made to extenuate their unwanted side effects.[35] For instance, the official arrival and entry to the venue of the talks of the diverse embassies was a momentous occasion, designed to present the might and power of a ruler in the eyes of all the congress parties. Since such ceremonial entries often generated huge quarrels between various powers during the Congress of Westphalia, great efforts were made to curtail them in the following congresses.[36]

Such an attempt to mitigate ceremonial strife by limiting or nullifying the ceremonial itself led some scholars to argue that congresses were the prime venues in which the pre-modern hierarchical conception of polities gave way to the modern conception that was based on the equality between them.[37] The Congress of Carlowitz attests that at the turn of the eighteenth century, that was still not the case. As shall be discussed in detail below, despite the official suspension of all ceremonial during the duration of the negotiations and the strenuous efforts to reduce as much as possible any claim of precedence, the hierarchical conception of the *Société des Princes* was still dominating the minds of the participants, who tried at every possible instance to affirm their position at the expense of their main antagonists. At best, just like the concept of *incognito*, suspending the ceremonial was considered more like a necessary performative convention in which actors ostensibly agreed to temporarily relinquish their ceremonial role only to resume it after the 'play' was over.[38] Yet, Carlowitz, by being the first congress to revoke all ceremonial and precedence – officially at least – did help, by setting yet another precedent, just like its predecessors and antecessors, to advance the slow process of ceremonial equality that would be further developed during the eighteenth and nineteenth centuries.

35 May, 'Zeremoniell', 612.

36 Ibid., 621.

37 Bély, 'Négocier la paix', 185. From his part, May argues that during the seventeenth century, the ceremonial transformed from a constructor and projector of a hierarchical order of polities to a system that expressed the participation to a club of recognised negotiating partners: May, 'Zeremoniell', 615.

38 For the early modern concept of *incognito* and its conventional character in order to avoid ceremonial conflicts, *see* Emmanuel Lemee, 'The Language of Incognito in Late-Seventeenth Century Diplomacy'. *Legatio* 4 (2020), 15–36.

4 The Pioneering Ceremonial Ordering of the Carlowitz Congress

Concerning ceremonial regulations, the Carlowitz Congress constitutes a truly unique case. On the one hand, its participants came from diplomatic cultures that were not similar in every respect. So, for instance, the representation of a ruler through the title of his delegate and the respective honours the latter was entailed to receive based on it, while a significant point of contention in western Europe[39] was absent from the diplomatic vocabulary of Muscovy or the Ottoman Empire, where all representatives of the tsar and the sultan, irrespective of their rank, were thought to represent their master's honour and dignity[40] – although, by 1698, this was also seemingly changing.[41] Still, the ceremonial vocabulary of signs must be shared for anyone to understand and interpret it.[42] Carlowitz proves the existence of such a common ceremonial lexicon cutting across cultural lines. The necessity of the first and last visits, spatial arrangements, large retinue, ostentatious clothing, and sumptuous parades as expressions of power were primarily similar and comprehensible to all participants. If we take, for instance, the Ottoman case, the one supposedly considered the most alien to the western European paradigm, we will encounter equivalent terms for 'ceremony' / 'ceremonial' (*merāsim/tekellüf*), precedence (*taṣaddür ü taḳaddüm*)[43] or the mutual visits, named the 'ceremony of comings and goings' (*āmed şüd merāsimi*),[44] strikingly resembling the term *ceremonie des visites* that one encounters in Christian sources.[45] Hence, the ceremonial observed at the Carlowitz Congress, far from being obstructed

39 In western Europe, there was a distinction between the *potestas* and *dignitas* of a ruler. The first was represented via the title of 'plenipotentiary', while the second was embodied in that of 'ambassador'. By the late seventeenth century, these two roles were combined under the title 'ambassador plenipotentiary'. Furthermore, with the gradual stabilisation of a hierarchy of representation, each delegate was ceremonially treated according to his rank. For an extensive analysis of the subject, *see* May, *Repräsentation und Statuspolitik*, 53–73, and Jennings, *Russia*, 90–111.

40 Ibid., 104–5. For the Ottoman case, a notable late seventeenth-century example is the embassy to Vienna in 1688, where the Ottoman delegates were initially treated by the Imperial side as ablegates (second-rank diplomatic representatives) and not as ambassadors. This provoked the rage of Zülfikār Efendi, who declared that 'the showing of respect to us is a showing of respect to our lord, his Highness the Padishah': *Cerîde-i Takrirât*, 30.

41 *See* below, Interlude III.

42 Hennings, *Russia*, 22.

43 *Ta'rīḫ-i ṣulḥnāme*, fol. 71ª.

44 Ibid., fol. 75ª.

45 ÖStA, HHStA, Türkei I, Turcica Box 171, Folder 2 (January 1699, 2nd half), fol. 246ʳ, Schlik to Kinsky, 31 January 1699.

by supposedly insurmountable cultural differences, was an amalgam of previously applied practices and ad hoc decisions just like any of its predecessors.

Therefore, to understand the Carlowitz ceremonial arrangements, we need to remember – as always – the dual nature of the early modern congresses as both multilateral and bilateral negotiation venues. This meant that the participants' ceremonial norms were not based only on earlier peace congresses but also on previous bilateral peace talks between them.[46] Fundamental to the Ottoman–Imperial ceremonial regulations was the Treaty of Zsitvatorok.[47] On the other hand, Voznitsyn based his pretensions of precedence over Małachowski on arrangements made in previous Moscovite–Commonwealth encounters. For instance, as he claimed, in all past negotiations between the two sides, the Commonwealth representatives were the first to greet those of the tsar; their meetings always took place in the Muscovite territory, a mile from the Polish-Lithuanian border.[48]

Nonetheless, references to previous congresses, those of Nijmegen and Ryswick, frequently made an appearance[49] and exerted considerable influence on the General Congress Regulation. The issuing of such a document in the name of the mediators was a practice that was first initiated at the Congress of Nijmegen and then continued at Ryswick. While in the first, as we saw, an effort was made to curtail the ostentatiousness of the official entrances of the different delegations to the congress venue, in the second, it mainly concerned the arrangements of ceremonial visits, which were abolished entirely. Carlowitz, whilst building on the experience of such precedents, introduced some critical novel elements. As in Ryswick, its first article dealt with the ceremonial. Following its example, all regulations regarding the visits between the ambassadors and between the ambassadors and the mediators were lifted, and anyone could visit all others freely, 'without pomp' (*ullâ pompa*) and with a small retinue. However, it didn't stop there, and by going a step further, it removed all ceremonial and precedence during the conferences. 'Everything, except the time order of the completion of [one's] negotiation, shall be treated and considered in an equal manner (*perinde aequaliter*)'. It is this novelty of ostensibly a complete removal of the ceremonial for the duration of a peace congress that makes the Carlowitz Congress unique and could perhaps later have served as a model for that of Utrecht in 1713, where the ceremonial would

46 May, *Repräsentation und Statuspolitik*, 84–8.

47 Kármán, 'A Third Party'; Kolçak, 'A History of Learned Courtesy'.

48 Bogoslovskii, *Petr I*, 367.

49 *See*, for instance, ÖStA, HHStA, Türkei I, Turcica Box 166, Folder 3 (September 1698, 2nd half), fol. 141^r, 142^r, Instructio pro Legatis Plenipotentiarijs Caes[are]is.

also be kept at bay throughout the talks. Last but not least, the parallel 'internal regulation' between the allies, adopted after the strife between them, to suppress any form of precedence among them in their encampment, is to be considered as yet another originality.[50]

5 The Carlowitz Participants' Hierarchical Conception of the 'Society of Polities'

It formed a common understanding between the contemporaries of the Carlowitz Congress that the 'Society of Polities' was a profoundly stratified one, going back centuries, even ordained as such by God himself.[51] However, despite this basic agreement, there were different competing versions of how the pyramid of the different polities was structured and which place each of its constituents should occupy. The composition of the status pyramid of the early modern 'Society of Princes' was not unambiguous and did not always rely on 'real power' measurements, such as the military might of a ruler.[52] To provide an illustrative example, while the Ottomans justified their claimed position on the top of the hierarchical ladder because of their long history, their military achievements, or the size of their dominions, they placed the Polish-Lithuanian Commonwealth higher than Muscovy, despite the greater esteem they appeared to hold for the Muscovite military machine. But let us examine more closely the different configurations each of the congress members had of his and the other participants' position in the pecking order of early modern polities and how those configurations directly impacted their ceremonial pretensions.

5.1 *The Polish-Lithuanian Commonwealth*

The Polish-Lithuanian conception of the hierarchy of the 'Society of Princes' was vividly expressed by Stanislaw Małachowski during a meeting he had with the Muscovite secretary-cum-interpreter Petr Postnikov. Justifying his king's superiority over the tsar, the Polish ambassador stated that 'it is known that the emperor presides over all; after [him] they follow the kings; between them,

50 Bogoslovskii, *Petr I*, 380.

51 Hennings, *Russia*, 19.

52 Ibid., 14–5. However, in his book *Theatrum Ceremoniale*, published in 1719/20, J.C. Lünig would sustain that the factual basis of precedence is 'preponderant might': Ibid., 20. Also, another late seventeenth-century author of an *ius praecedentiae* treatise, Balthasar Sigismund von Stosch, would place the Muscovite Tsar on an equal order with the Holy Roman Emperor because of his many territories and immense wealth: Ibid., 46–7.

there is no distinction of order; then other powerful princes and dukes follow the kings'.[53] The bottom line of this exposition was that the 'Grand Duke of Muscovy' could not be placed on an equal footing with a crowned head.[54] Małachowski's configuration of the order of polities follows the classical ranking system of the Christian powers at the Papal Court in Rome.[55] Nonetheless, there is one crucial difference. It considers all kings, besides the emperor, irrespective of their power and might, as equals. On the other hand, it is precisely this superiority of the crown heads over grand dukes or republics that would closely guide Małachowski's ceremonial pretensions against the other two allies, Muscovy and Venice, namely that he was entitled to the second place of honour right after the Imperials.

5.2 *Muscovy*

The place Muscovy occupied in the early modern states' pecking order was strongly debatable.[56] For many western and central Europeans, it was not clear if the tsar should be included in the hierarchy of Christian [or civilised] rulers at all.[57] Yet in practice, by the second half of the seventeenth century, Muscovy formed an integral part of the Christian European community of polities.[58] The tsar's representatives were received as ambassadors of a royal head, despite his common title of *magnus dux moscoviae*, and Muscovy was oftentimes placed at some courts even higher than other principal Christian European kingdoms.[59] Not everyone was ready to accord the tsar such honours, yet, nor did his title remain undisputed. Muscovy's official participation for the first time in a Christian coalition, as much as in a multilateral peace congress, was seen as a unique opportunity to raise its status inside the hierarchical system of political entities.[60] Like Małachowski, Voznitsyn didn't question the emperor's precedence. However, either because of the instructions

53 Sałuski, *Epistolae*, 677.

54 Ibid.

55 May, *Repräsentation und Statuspolitik*, 70–1.

56 Hennings, *Russia*, 44–63.

57 Ibid., 30–1.

58 Ibid., 99–100.

59 Ibid., 99.

60 Iskra Schwarcz's assertion that after the inclusion of Muscovy to the Holy League, its desire to improve its status through ceremonial receded doesn't seem to be confirmed by Voznitsyn's behaviour at Carlowitz: Iskra Schwarcz, 'Die kaiserlichen Gesandten und das diplomatische Zeremoniell am Moskauer Hof in der zweiten Hälfe des 17. Jahrhunderts', in Ralph Kauz, Giorgio Rota and Jan Paul Niederkorn (eds.), *Diplomatisches Zeremoniell in Europa und im Mittleren Osten in der frühen Neuzeit* (Vienna: Verlag der Österreichischen Akademie der Wissenschaften 2009) 265–86.

he had or due to his own personal conviction, he was determined to assert Muscovy's superiority primarily over the Polish-Lithuanian Commonwealth (and secondarily over Venice), a claim that would lead to some of the fiercest ceremonial disputes during the congress.[61]

5.3 *Venice*

Similar to Muscovy, Venice's position in the early modern ceremonial was an equally ambiguous one. Although a republic, its main aim was to acquire an equal status to that of a kingdom,[62] a claim based principally on its previous possession of some 'ancient' *Regna* (Cyprus, Crete, etc.) and its current possession of the Morea peninsula, which was also baptised as a kingdom (*Regno di Morea*).[63] During the Congress of Westphalia, the Serenissima held a prominent position, mostly thanks to its role as a mediator.[64] At Carlowitz, it had two primary ceremonial goals. The first was not to appear inferior in the projection of status compared to the other allies. As Ruzzini mentions in his final relation, he strove to uphold 'the image of the public dignity' (*la figura della publica dignità*) by making sure that his 'most numerous entourage' (*il mio numerosissimo seguito*) and his other equipage were not inferior to any other ambassador of the Holy League.[65] The second goal was to supersede or equal Muscovy in the ceremonial of precedence.[66] This implies that, for Venice, the tsar was not considered a crown head, so, in contrast to the Imperials or the Commonwealth, it would have been easier to challenge his ceremonial place and status. Ruzzini brags that he was able not only to not 'overtly cede no rank to the Muscovite ambassador' but to maintain as equal and, at times,

---

61 Bogoslovskii, *Petr I*, 367.

62 Note here that Ruzzini speaks in his relation of a 'Reggia Rappresentanza': Ruzzini, *Relazione*, 378.

63 Olga Katsiardi-Hering, 'Κτηματογραφικοὶ χάρτες τοῦ « Regno di Morea » ἤ αὐτοκρατορικοὶ χάρτες; Εἰσαγωγή', in Olga Katsiardi-Hering (ed.), *Βενετικοὶ χάρτες τῆς Πελοποννήσου τέλη 17ου–ἀρχὲς 18ου αἰῶνα. Ἀπὸ τὴ συλλογὴ τοῦ Πολεμικοῦ Ἀρχείου τῆς Αὐστρίας* (Athens: National Bank of Greece Cultural Foundation 2018) 26. In the Venetian governmental parlance, a *Regno* could literally designate a former 'kingdom' but also a spatially autonomous administrative unit (ibid). Thus, it probably acted as a close synonym of *stato*, which had, among other meanings, that of a province of a polity: Sashalmi Endre, 'Tulajdonosi Dinaszticizmus és Államfogalom a 17. Századi Oroszországban'. *Századok* 138/3 (2004), 893, fn. 2.

64 May, *Repräsentation und Statuspolitik*, 179–93.

65 Ruzzini, *Relazione*, 378.

66 As the Venetian ambassador claimed in a discussion he had with Count Marsigli: ÖStA, HHStA, Türkei I, Turcica Box 167, Folder 2 (October 1698, 2nd half), fol. 45v, Marsigli to Kinsky: 16 October 1698.

even superior. As proof, he provides the order of his visits with Voznitsyn and the mediators.[67]

5.4 *The Emperor*

Despite the increased calling into questioning by various powers, such as France, during the second half of the seventeenth century, of the preeminent ceremonial position of the emperor inside the Christian 'Society of Princes',[68] for the Imperial side, the supreme place of the Habsburgs among the Christian allies and their equal status vis-à-vis the Ottoman Sultan was something that was taken for granted; something that should and could not be compromised in any way.[69] As clearly stated in the instructions given to the two Imperial plenipotentiaries, 'our [ambassadors'] precedence was never subject to any controversy'.[70] Similarly, in the last meeting of the 'Turkish Deputation', prior to the dispatching of the embassy, when matters involving the ceremonial (*circa ceremoniale*) were discussed, it was pointed out that between the Christian powers, 'Your Imperial Majesty's embassy enjoys precedence in all places except when the mediators or the allies' ambassadors pay them a visit'.[71]

Notwithstanding, there was fear of an effort to usurp this prominent place by none other than the mediators, an anxiety derived from analogous attempts in the past. In the imperial instructions, the two previous congresses of Nijmegen and Ryswick were evoked, where the mediators had already tried to assert their precedence over the other participants. 'We fear that the present mediators would claim the same', the emperor concluded.[72] In such a case, the Imperial plenipotentiaries were instructed to avoid any prejudice to his established ceremonial position by all means.[73]

Regarding the rest of the allies, it is of paramount importance to note that in the Imperial instructions, it was stated that '[in a case of a precedence struggle between the allies] the Grand Duke of Muscovy is to be supported, because he

67 Ruzzini, *Relazione*, 378.

68 May, *Repräsentation und Statuspolitik*, 115–20.

69 For the Imperial efforts to safeguard their preponderant ceremonial position during the early modern period, *see* Regina Dauser '„Dann ob Uns gleich die Kayserliche Würdeanklebet" – Der kaiserliche Vorrang bei Friedensverhandlungen und in Friedensverträgen des 17. und 18. Jahrhunderts', in Schmidt-Voges et al., *Pax Perpetua*, 305–26.

70 ÖStA, HHStA, Türkei I, Turcica Box 166, Folder 3 (September 1698, 2nd half), fol. 141^{r}, Instructio pro Legatis Plenipotentiarijs Caes[are]is.

71 ÖStA, HHStA, Türkei I, Turcica Box 166, Folder 2 (September 1698, 1st half), fol. 44^{r}, relation of the members of the 'Turkish Deputation' to Leopold I, 21 September 1698.

72 Ibid., Instructio pro Legatis Plenipotentiarijs Caes[are]is, fol. 141^{r}.

73 Ibid.

is called tsar by all, and he is in possession of many kingdoms and dominions by hereditary right'.[74] This assertion could be considered genuinely revelatory of the success of the Muscovite diplomacy to upgrade the tsar's status and of the growing importance of Muscovy in the European power arena. Still, the emperor thought that his ambassadors were better off not to involve themselves in such controversies and instead leave such 'hot potatoes' to be taken out of the fire by the mediators.[75]

5.5 *The Ottomans*

The Ottoman conception of the *Société des Princes* was not static but rather evolved according to the situation, the novel configurations of power and its relations with foreign rulers. Starting with the Ottoman position in the pyramid, the seventeenth century constitutes a major turning point. In contrast to the absolute superiority of the padishah over all other potentates, expressed in the second half of the sixteenth century, the Ottomans, beginning with the Treaty of Zsitvatorok in 1606, had to acknowledge ceremonial equality with the Habsburg emperor. It was a gradual but steady process, mainly expressed through carefully choreographed manifestations of equal status, constantly evolving over the course of the century, such as the reciprocal exchange of embassies after the ratification of peace treaties or of gifts of equal value.[76] By the time of the Carlowitz Treaties, such practices had become so established that the bureaucrat and historian Muṣṭafā Naʿīmā would refer to them as 'ancient custom' (*de'b-i kadîm*).[77] Issues remained, though, as one could aptly infer from discussions during the congress between the Ottoman and Imperial delegations concerning complaints of unequal treatment of former embassies and disputations over the rank of the ambassadors.[78]

Turning now to the rest of the members of the 'Society of Princes' (the Christian ones), it is clear that they were perceived as inferior to the Ottoman autocrat, as the Habsburg emperor considered all other Christian rulers to be so with respect to himself. But what of their classification? As we have already seen, similarly to Christian Europe, there was a distinction of honours between crown heads and republics. Lacking a late seventeenth-century chancery manual similar to the compilation by the prominent bureaucrat of the sixteenth

74 Ibid., fol. 142r–v.

75 Ibid.

76 Kolçak, 'A History of Learned Courtesy'; Mahmut Halef Cevrioğlu, 'Ottoman Ceremonial Embassies of the First Half of the Seventeenth Century: The Selection of the Ambassador Rıdvan Agha (1633)'. *Austrian History Yearbook* (2024), 1–17.

77 *Târih-i Na'îmâ*, 47.

78 For instance, ÖStA, HHStA,Türkei I, Turcica Box 170, Protocollum, fol. 91.

century, Ferīdūn Beg, *Münşeʾatü's-Selāṭīn* (Correspondence of Sultans),[79] the only way to infer the position of each of the Holy League powers in the Ottoman-conceived political community is via the order by which the allies are mentioned in the official correspondence, both internal and external.

Following those sources, the Ottomans appear to have ranked the four Holy League members in the following sequence: first came the Habsburg emperor, followed by the Polish-Lithuanian Commonwealth, then by the Tsar of Muscovy and lastly by Venice.[80] Of course, of importance here is the placement of the Commonwealth higher than its eastern neighbour. We could assume that, at least at this point, this was probably the result of the lengthier (peaceful) relations between the two powers. How such an order had to be officially upheld, even when it was not in practice, is revealed by the ensuing telling example. It so happened that the Ottomans had a conference first with Voznitsyn and then with Małaschowski. Yet, in his account, Rāmī felt obliged to reinstate the broken Ottoman hierarchy of polities by altering the events and putting *ex post facto* the Exalted State's plenipotentiaries negotiating with the Commonwealth prior to Muscovy.[81]

6 Status Projection Instances and Means

The perceived position of a polity in such a hierarchical princely community was accompanied by a particular status which had to be projected to the other members of this 'City of Opinion' in order to be vindicated. The projection of one's status was effectuated on various occasions and in many different ways and means. Large entourages, sumptuous clothes, carriages, tents and horses were all considered signs of ceremonial grandeur. Perfect occasions to display them were presented by the first visits as well as the first conferences between the various delegations. As the anonymous Venetian author of an account of the congress stated, 'on this occasion everyone presented his retinue with the greatest pomp and decorum'.[82] Describing Voznitsyn's setting off for his first conference in his journal, Count Schlik – typically finding nothing good to say about the Muscovite – remarked that the latter departed from the allied camp

79 Dimitris Kastritsis, 'Ferīdūn Beg's *Münşeʾatü's-Selāṭīn* ('Correspondence of Sultans') and Late Sixteenth-Century Ottoman Views of the Political World', in Dimiter Angelov, Yota Batsaki and Sahar Bazzaz (eds.), *Imperial Geographies in Byzantine and Ottoman Space* (Cambridge, Massachusetts/London: Harvard University Press 2013) 91–110.

80 *See*, for instance, *Taʾrīḫ-i ṣulḥnāme*, fol. 40ᵃ; DABOA, A.DVNS.MHM.d. 110, fol. 485.

81 *Taʾrīḫ-i ṣulḥnāme*, fol. 102ᵃ, 108ᵃ.

82 *Narratio*, fol. 11ʳ.

'accompanied by his entire household in a splendid attire'.[83] Since all the ceremonial was discarded for the rest of the congress, the next occassions for the different embassies to show off were the farewell visits, a literal competition for captivating the senses, where the guests tried to impress their hosts with their large and pompous retinue and the hosts tried to amaze them with their sumptuous and lavish hospitality. No wonder such occasions occupied considerable space in the relations or other accounts of the congress.[84]

On the other hand, failure to meet the standards of such visual exposition of status could lead the other participants, especially the ones vying for the same position, to doubt their place in the hierarchy and render it easier for each to justify any attempt to claim another's place. The best example in this respect is the Polish ambassador Stanislav Małachowski. The latter, believing that he had to be at the congress venue in late September, moved quickly along the way and so landed at Carlowitz with the smallest retinue among the participants.[85] Unfortunately for him, this penury of means of ceremonial display didn't appear congruent with the status he claimed and led to derision by the other ambassadors. Ruzzini, for instance, asserts that 'his excessively restricted retinue [was] inferior to the decorum of the congress'.[86] He also maintained that one of Malachowski's reasons for leaving the conference as quickly as possible was because he wanted 'to get rid of a representation he sustained with little dignity'.[87] Voznitsyn, Małachowski's ceremonial arch-rival, was also quick to notice and record, with great satisfaction, one might assume, the poor entourage of the Pole. When the latter arrived in Petrovaradin, the Muscovite spotted the small number of ships (only three) and personnel, adding with malignant pleasure that Malachowski went straight to a local tavern in search of men upon disembarking his vessel.[88] On another occasion, he wrote even more pointedly, 'he came here with no horses, no carriages, no tents, no carts except for one tent which I don't know whom he begged here [to get]. It seems to me that he is causing trouble just to mask his own disgrace'.[89] The Commonwealth's plenipotentiary had indeed so few carriages that to make his ceremonial entry to the allied encampment, he had to be provided

83 ÖStA, HHStA, Türkei I, Turcica Box 170, Diarium et Cerimoniale, fol. 36.
84 For instance, *Narratio*, fol. 49^{v}–57^{r}.
85 Ibid., fol. 13^{r}.
86 Ruzzini, *Relazione*, 378.
87 Ibid., 362.
88 Bogoslovskii, *Petr I*, 365.
89 Quoted in ibid., 375.

with some by the Imperial embassy. 'We both gave him our less-good carriages', the Imperial ambassadors added, magnifying in this way Małachowski's humiliation.[90]

7 The (Disputed) Ceremonial Equality of the Principal Members of an Embassy

The dignity, honour and grandeur of a potentate during a congress were represented, sustained and defended by his ambassador. Yet, in delegations comprised of more than one delegate, often belonging to different social strata, it was frequently debated and highly disputed whether or not all the principal members of an embassy were entitled to the same honours or if they could only be claimed by its 'leader'.[91] During the Carlowitz Congress, this problem mainly concerned the Ottoman and Imperial embassies, the only ones to consist of two members. In the Ottoman case, there seems to be a double-sided reality. On the one hand, the two delegates bore the same title of plenipotentiary ambassador (*me'ẕūn u muraḫḫaṣ ėlçi*), so they ostensibly expected that they would receive the same honours and be viewed as one. On the other hand, there were implicit signs that distinguished them, such as the size of their retinue[92] or the place in which they sat during the conferences, Rami on the right and Mavrocordatos on the left.[93] What the unknown author of the 'Anonymous Ottoman History' says about the Imperial embassy may suggest that there could have been an internal stratification. According to him the latter had a 'Great and an Inferior, two ambassadors' (*bir büyük bir küçük iki elçi*).[94] Thus, he was probably mirroring in the Imperial delegation an Ottoman reality.[95]

Surely, that was not how the Habsburg side viewed the situation. As clearly mentioned in the Imperial instructions, both ambassadors were to receive the same honours; they bore the same (ceremonial) character/title (*esse ipsos pari*

90 ÖStA, HHStA, Türkei I, Turcica Box 170, Diarium et Cerimoniale, fol. 10r (of the separate journal regarding the ceremonial).

91 May, *Repräsentation und Statuspolitik*, 144–73.

92 According to the Anonymous Venetian, the retinue of Mavrocordatos was somewhat inferior to that of Rami: *Narratio*, fol. 11v.

93 Ibid., 19r. However, the same held true for the Imperial embassy, where, ostensibly, there was also no distinction between the two ambassadors.

94 *Anonim Osmanlı Tarihi*, 135.

95 Still, in the full powers given by the grand vizier to the two ambassadors, there is no mention of a *büyük* and *küçük ėlçi*: *Ta'rīḫ-i ṣulḥnāme*, fol. 39a–b.

caractere instructos) and were 'one body which by no means could be separated' (*unum corpus quod nullatenus separari possit*).[96] As the instructions continued, such clarification was deemed essential in order to avoid uncertainties that led to misunderstandings and ceremonial disputes during previous congresses (Nijmegen, Ryswick).[97] Still, misunderstandings were not evaded in the end. Voznitsyn, upon his arrival at Petrovaradin, sent one of his interpreters to compliment Ruzzini and Count Öttingen, but not Count Schlik, which was viewed as a tremendous personal affront by the latter.[98]

One should also add here the unclarified ceremonial position of Count Marsigli. He was accompanying the Imperial delegation without an official (ceremonial) title (*ohne Caracter*) but as a mere consultant (*Rath*) of the embassy on the issue of borders.[99] However, because of his noble status and crucial role in the negotiations, he aspired to higher honours. Such aspirations brought him on a collision course with the two Imperial ambassadors, especially with Count Schlik. Dissent between the two *protégées* of Kinsky[100] – perhaps a competition between them for the latter's favours might not have been irrelevant – first arose over Marsigli's request to visit the mediators, a demand that Schlik rejected on the grounds that the Ottomans knew the *Bolognese*[101] only with his fake identity as secretary of Lord Paget during his secret mission to the Ottoman capital back in the early 1690s.[102] The second issue was related to the military honours Marsigli received as a colonel, namely an escort and a tambourine. Schlik suggested that the *Bolognese*, as a member of the embassy, was not required to keep the ceremonial privileges attached to his military standing, especially the tambourine, which the latter perceived as a direct insult to his character and as an effort to demote him ceremonially.[103]

96 ÖStA, HHStA, Türkei I, Turcica Box 166, Folder 3 (September 1698, 2nd half), fol. 142ʳ, Instructio pro Legatis Plenipotentiarijs Caes[are]is.

97 Ibid. For such disputes, *see* extensively May, *Repräsentation und Statuspolitik*, 144–73.

98 ÖStA, HHStA, Türkei I, Turcica Box 167, Folder 2 (October 1698, 2nd half), fol. 62ᵛ, Schlik to Kinsky, 18 October 1698.

99 ÖStA, HHStA, Türkei I, Turcica Box 166, Folder 1 (August 1698), fol. 53ʳ, relation of the members of the 'Turkish Deputation' to Leopold I, 8 August 1698.

100 For the relations of patronage both Schlik and Marsigli had with Kinsky, refer below to Interludes III and V.

101 I will often refer to Count Marsigli as the *Bolognese* since he was a native of Bologna.

102 *See* below.

103 He voiced all these grievances in a *foglietto* 'to be read by Signor Count Kinsky alone': ÖStA, HHStA, Türkei I, Turcica Box 168, Folder 1 (November 1698, 1st half), fol. 227ʳ–230ʳ, Marsigli to Kinsky, s.d. (probably early November 1698).

8 The Ceremonial Forms Retained during the Talks

Despite the official abolition of the major ceremonial exigencies for the duration of the negotiations, such as precedence, this didn't mean they were utterly absent from the talks. They retained their presence through forms that would potentially provoke less discord. For example, during the conferences – especially the first ones – the ceremonial was mainly manifested through a certain kind of behaviour based primarily on politeness and the projection of the plenipotentiaries' role as *ministre public*, what Sylvio Hermann De Franceschi refers to as 'conversation ritual'.[104]

The beginning of the talks marked the start of a social relationship between the two negotiating parties. It was thus important that each side give the other signs of its respect and disposition towards a successful outcome.[105] Rāmī Meḥmed speaks of them as the 'familiar intercourse ceremony/signs' (*merāsim-i ülfet*).[106] The latter consisted mainly of initial speeches in which each ambassador complimented his interlocutors and expressed his sovereign's inclination towards peace and his wish for a speedy and successful outcome of the negotiations.[107] During their first conference with the Ottomans, the Imperial plenipotentiaries expressed, first and foremost, 'the good intention that they had to conclude here a holy work [peace]'.[108] The Ottomans, for their part, replied that 'there is no probability' that their interlocutors 'will witness [from them] anything other than sincerity and goodwill'.[109] Such speeches were not mere formalities. They could be interpreted or misinterpreted by the participants as cardinal signs of the degree of one's credibility in desiring peace.[110] As evidence for Venice's intentions of not wanting to conclude a treaty, Mavrocordatos recorded that 'once during a ceremonial speech' (*una volta in espressione Uffitiosa*)[111] – probably during the first conference – Ruzzini told him equivocally that 'peace would have been made' (*che la Pace si*

104 De Franceschi, 'La négociation', 32.

105 Köhler, 'Höflichkeit', 380, 385, 386–8.

106 *Ta'rīḫ-i ṣulḥnāme*, fol. 102ª. Here, the word *merāsim* could be translated as both ceremony/ceremonial and signs.

107 Köhler, 'Höflichkeit', 386–8.

108 ÖStA, HHStA, Türkei I, Turcica Box 170, Protocollum, fol. 8.

109 *Ta'rīḫ-i ṣulḥnāme*, fol. 81ª.

110 Köhler, 'Höflichkeit'.

111 The term *uffitiosa* does not appear to mean 'unofficial', as in modern Italian. Instead, the Anonymous Venetian uses its noun form, *uffitiosità*, as a synonym for *cerimonie*. For instance, *Narratio*, fol. 53ᵛ.

sarebbe fatta) instead of saying – one may guess – more explicitly and affirmatively that peace 'will be made'.[112]

Besides the initial meetings between the various embassies, polite manifestations during the negotiations could often be interpreted as a cardinal sign of the disposition of a party to make concessions. In the Imperial delegation's efforts to convince them to return the fortress of Kamianets-Podilskyi along with its fortifications to the Commonwealth, the Ottoman plenipotentiaries replied 'with so good [and] friendly a manner, that not only the mediators but also we ourselves hope that the place is probably to be received intact after all'.[113] Similarly, acts of impoliteness during the meetings, such as outbursts of anger, were not only spontaneous feelings but performative expressions of the will of one party to terminate, temporarily or permanently, any relationship with the other.[114] Proverbial in this respect were the outbreaks of rage of the 'Efendi',[115] Rāmī Meḥmed, which were considered so worth remembering as to find a place in the protocols kept by the secretaries of the allied embassies.[116]

Keeping note of unusual sentimental outbursts also stemmed from a normative expectation from a *ministre public* to behave and converse in a specific manner.[117] One important characteristic of such behaviour was the simulated voice, the ambassador speaking politely and calmly, conveying a 'friendly and supple spirit' (*esprit laint et souple*) as François de Callières stated in his famous treatise 'On the manner to negotiate with sovereigns'.[118] That this was indeed the case is illustrated by some extreme occasions when the ambassadors were forced to abandon their role-dictated 'ceremonial manners'.

In one instance, during the last Ottoman–Venetian conferences, in which the Imperials also actively participated, the Venetian ambassador Carlo Ruzzini, disappointed by the lack of support from the Habsburg delegation for his claims, 'spoke loudly without simulation and with clear annoyance, declared that the Republic was betrayed in good faith. Count Schlik got equally upset [and] there was almost a risk of some indecorous [incident]'.[119] The following example attests to how such changes could sometimes be made on purpose

112 Ibid., fol. 40ᵛ.

113 ÖStA, HHStA, Türkei I, Turcica Box 168, Folder 2 (November 1698, 2nd half), fol. 174ᵛ, Imperial plenipotentiaries to Leopold I, 23 November 1698.

114 Köhler, 'Höflichkeit", 390–2.

115 In the Christian sources, Rāmī is mainly referred to as 'the Efendi' from the Ottoman short version of his official title, *Re'is Efendi*.

116 *See*, for example, ÖStA, HHStA, Türkei I, Turcica Box 170, Protocollum, fol. 20; BNM, Ms.it.VII 399 (8625), fol. 302ʳ, Alcuni discorsi delle Conferenze raccolti dal Nicolosi.

117 De Franceschi, 'La négociation'.

118 Köhler, 'Höflichkeit', 384.

119 *Narratio*, fol. 35ʳ.

to send appropriate signals to one's interlocutor. Early on in the congress, the issue of Transylvania became once more the focus of the Ottoman–Imperial negotiations, and the demands of the Ottoman side were also assisted by the mediators. In a meeting with the latter, the Imperial ambassadors chose to manifest their strong disagreement and firmness on the matter 'by even speaking a little loud' (*iusques à parler même un peu haut*). Count Schlik defended his abandoning of the *ministre public* ceremonial composure, arguing that 'there are meetings in which one should be arrogant, and there is no better way to get rid of a quarrelsome individual than by forcing him to make a choice'.[120]

There were also moments when the plenipotentiaries proposed a change of roles, from *ministre public* to *honnête homme*, to discourse more 'confidentially'. So, towards the end of the first Ottoman–Imperial conference, Mavrocordatos forwarded to his interlocutors 'that from now on all ceremonial be lifted and that one discusses with every familiarity, [and] with the utmost confidentiality, so to say'.[121] Similarly, before their last conference with Voznitsyn, the Ottoman plenipotentiaries decided to discuss with him 'confidentially/with out ceremonial' (*bī-tekellüf*).[122] It is hard to assess, nonetheless, if this 'familiar discourse' was no more than yet another intentional 'ceremonial script', a strategy through the performance of different roles, to gain the trust and to penetrate the 'true intentions' of one's opponent via a simulation of confidentiality.

Apart from 'ceremonies/signs of friendship' that attested one's goodwill and inclination towards peace during the conferences, we should further add the case of some extraordinary visits during the talks – remember that all ceremonial visits were officially suspended – which were meant to produce a similar result. On 22 November 1698, after the first round of the Ottoman-Imperial negotiations drew to an end, a large Ottoman delegation headed by 'two Efendis, as they were called, or secretaries' came to visit the Imperial embassy on behalf of their principals to inquire about the ambassadors' health and condition. The Imperials replied by sending some of the noblemen in their suite to the Ottoman camp the next day. As they noted in their journal of the congress ceremonial, this Ottoman initiative was not a belated official notification of arrival but, as they later learned, it was designed to be interpreted as a sign of the Ottoman desire for peace (*Verspürten fridens anscheinung*) at a time where the negotiation was still hanging on the balance.[123]

120 ÖStA, HHStA, Türkei I, Turcica Box 168, Folder 1 (November 1698, 1st half), fol. 284^{v}–285^{r}, Schlik to Kinsky, 13 November 1698.
121 ÖStA, HHStA, Türkei I, Turcica Box 170, Protocollum, fol. 15.
122 *Taʾrīḫ-i ṣulḥnāme*, fol. 118^{a}.
123 ÖStA, HHStA, Türkei I, Turcica Box 170, Diarium et Cerimoniale, fol. 14^{v}–15^{r} (of the separate journal regarding the ceremonial).

9 The Ceremonial of the Signing of the Instruments of the Peace Treaties

With the termination of the talks, the signing ceremonies were the next primary instance for ceremonial regulations to make their reappearance. Besides being another occasion for status display for the various embassies, arriving in the Conference House with all their retinue and dressed as sumptuously as possible,[124] they also followed carefully choreographed moves and speeches.[125] At the same time, certain contentious elements had to be regulated well in advance. For example, in one of the last Ottoman-Imperial conferences, while discussing the details of the signing ceremony, it was commonly agreed that 'the tables will be arranged in such a manner as to avoid arguing over precedence'.[126] Nevertheless, despite such a strict ceremonial, there was still space for some improvisations on the spot. During the Ottoman–Muscovite signing ceremony, Mavrocordatos suggested, with Voznitsy's consent, that it should be through the mediators that the exchange of Peace Instruments should occur. The mediators refused and allowed the two parties to exchange them by themselves.[127] Finally, the signing ceremonies – and the farewell visits – contained their own panoply of 'traditional' ceremonial signs of reconciliation and friendship,[128] such as the hugging,[129] the 'kiss of peace',[130] and the exchange of gifts.[131]

124 In the before-hand agreement of the ceremonial regulations for the signing of the Ottoman–Imperial, Ottoman–Commonwealth and Ottoman–Venetian treaties on 26 January 1699, it was stated that apart from the military guard of each embassy, the latter would have to arrive at the Conference House 'with carriages and retinue as magnificent as they can'(*con treno ed equipaggio più magnifico che si può*): ÖStA, HHStA, Türkei I, Turcica Box 171, Folder 2 (January 1699, 2nd half), fol. 133^{r}, Nota dell Corcordato nella coferenza li 23 Genaio 1699.

125 *See* for instance, *Narratio*, fol. 44^{r-v}.

126 ÖStA, HHStA, Türkei I, Turcica 168/1, fol. 326^{v}, protocol of the conference held on 23 January 1699.

127 Bogoslovskii, *Petr I*, 428.

128 For those long-established signs of reconciliation, *see* Nicolas Offenstadt, *Faire la Paix au Moyen Âge* (Paris: Odile Jacob 2007) 185–226.

129 *Narratio*, fol. 41^{v}, 44^{v}.

130 The Imperial protocol described the *osculum pacis* during the signing ceremony in the following manner: "si diedero gli ambaciadori l'osculum Pacis baciandosi l'un l'altro sopra ambe le guancie con grandissima tenerezza di modo che si traspirava una perfetta allegria delle nationi ivi presenti": ÖStA, HHStA, Türkei I, Turcica Box 170, Protocollum, fol. 203.

131 *Narratio*, fol. 49^{r-v}.

10 The Farewell Visits

The last significant ceremonial moments of the congress were the farewell visits between the different embassies. Since the negotiations were practically over, the suspension of all ceremonial precedence was automatically lifted.[132] The greatest problem arose from regulating the order of visits between the Ottomans and the Imperials, especially who would be the first to receive the other.[133] Already on the day after the signing of the treaties, Count Öttingen organised a banquet in his 'house' to which he invited all the other ambassadors, including the Ottomans. The latter refused to attend until the ceremonial regulations between the two embassies were fixed.[134] The matter was paramount since each side was trying to assert its preeminence despite the ostensible ceremonial equality. According to Count Schlik, the Imperial embassy would have preferred that the Ottomans be the first to visit them or that such farewell visits would not have taken place at all.[135] Ultimately, under pressure from Ruzzini to keep the 'Turks' a little longer by any means possible and the threat of the Ottomans to leave without the 'habitual [signs of] friendship',[136] the order was fixed with the help of the mediators, according to the following arrangement: the Ottomans would be the first to receive the Imperials because they, in the beginning, were the last to arrive at the congress venue.[137] Then the Ottomans would repay the visit but, under the pretext of their departure (*à titolo di partenza e di congedo*), would revisit the Imperials, and the latter would reciprocate.[138] With this scheme, the ceremonial balance between the two was upheld, and any claim of precedence was seemingly nullified. Seemingly, because each side could interpret the arrangement in a way that would fit their own pretensions.

Indeed, in the final pages of his congress account, Rāmī Meḥmed alludes that only two reciprocal visits, not four, were made, giving thus the impression that the Ottoman side won the 'battle of precedence' over its main ceremonial antagonist.[139] It is a fine example of how ambassadorial relations were 'constructed' in a certain way to provide a particular version of events favourable to their writer and, intentionally or unintentionally, to create false

132 ÖStA, HHStA, Türkei I, Turcica Box 170, Diarium et Cerimoniale, fol. 85.
133 *Narratio*, fol. 49^{v}.
134 Ibid., 48^{v}.
135 Diarium et Cerimoniale, fol. 85.
136 Ibid.
137 Ibid.
138 *Narratio*, fol. 49^{v}.
139 *Ta'rīḫ-i ṣulḥnāme*, fol. 127^{b}–128^{a}.

precedents.[140] It would be tantalising to see if, during the subsequent major Ottoman–Habsburg diplomatic encounter, the Congress of Passarowitz in 1718, the Ottoman embassy demanded that it receive the Imperials' first visit, basing its assertion upon the Carlowitz precedent, or rather Rāmī's version of it.

Besides the issues related to precedence, restricted only to delicate 'ceremonial relations' of certain parties, farewell visits generally bore another type of symbolism. They served as a capstone in the edifice of peace and signalled a novel relationship of mutual friendship between the erstwhile enemies. It is perhaps no wonder that the only allied ambassador not to have exchanged farewell visits in person with the Ottomans was Carlo Ruzzini, despite the former expressing their wish to meet with the latter and 'have the opportunity to practice with him the same manifestations of friendship and respect'.[141] In the end, Ruzzini sent his nephew to the Ottomans, and they repaid his visit by sending their secretaries to the Venetian.[142] By turning down the Ottoman visit request, the Venetian ambassador was thus refusing to perform the signs of reconciliation, not having been able to agree with the Ottoman delegation – his allies only signing a provisionary Peace Instrument in the Republic's name.[143]

11 Ceremonial Strife during the Congress: a Short Prelude

According to Niels May, 'ceremonial conflicts resulted primarily from the antagonism between two persons for the same position in a linear conceived order'.[144] Such disputes were normally anticipated in advance, as the instructions to the Imperial plenipotentiaries illustrate, and possible arrangements were proposed to avoid them.[145] Nonetheless, Carlowitz, like all the previous congresses, didn't manage to stay immune to ceremonial strife. The fiercest and longest-lasting conflict was between the Polish-Lithuanian Commonwealth and Muscovy. Lesser but no less disruptive in the short term was a Polish–Venetian quarrel over the place of their ambassadors' tents in

140 For the ambassadorial letters and relations as 'constructed' narratives, refer to Interlude III below.

141 *Narratio*, fol. 53^{r}.

142 Ibid., fol. 55^{r}–56^{r}.

143 *See* extensively Act IV, Narration Part II and III below.

144 May, *Repräsentation und Statuspolitik*, 70.

145 ÖStA, HHStA, Türkei I, Turcica Box 166, Folder 3 (September 1698, 2nd half), fol. 142^{r-v}, Instructio pro Legatis Plenipotentiarijs Caes[are]is. However, they only dealt with possible strife among the emperor's allies; the Imperial position remaining, of course, uncontested.

the allies' encampment as well as a controversy over the order in which each allied plenipotentiary would enter into talks with the Ottomans. Before examining them all in detail, a key observation is of the essence. Not all ceremonial disputes led to a confrontation. In most cases, compromises could be and were found.[146] Take, for instance, the Ottoman–Imperial case, which was as prone to conflict as the Commonwealth–Muscovite one. Similarly, while experiencing status quarrels during the preliminaries, the two mediators seem to have reached an accommodation by the time of the beginning of the congress,[147] and no ceremonial strife came from them throughout its course. As we shall further discuss below, such a constatation indicates that ceremonial clashes were as much related to status affirmation and defence of honour as to personal temperament, antipathies and negotiation strategies.

12 'Worse than a Fight of Cats and Mice': the Fierce Muscovite–Commonwealth Ceremonial Dispute

That Voznitsyn was extremely sensitive (perhaps having such orders from Peter I) in ceremonial and status-display is clearly illustrated in his conduct during his stay in Vienna right after the tsar's departure. Not only did he demand that his new title be immediately made known, but also that he should have an immediate audience with the emperor.[148] The Muscovite plenipotentiary also asked that his conference with the Imperial ministers take place in the Imperial palace, where he should receive an appropriate welcome upon his arrival.[149] A dispute followed over the point of the audience and the conference venue, with each side providing precedents to support its claims. In the end, Voznitsyn had to back down from his audience request and the Imperials from their demands over the place of the conference.[150] However, this ceremonial quarrel between Voznitsyn and the Imperials was only an appetiser. The main dish was soon to follow.

As we have seen, the orders he had from the tsar were to collaborate closely with the representatives of the Polish King. Nonetheless, Voznitsyn didn't

146 May, *Repräsentation und Statuspolitik*, 110–5.

147 ÖStA, HHStA, Türkei I, Turcica Box 168, Folder 1 (November 1698, 1st half), fol. 239^{v}, Marsigli to Kinsky, 1 November 1698.

148 Such a request formed a normative feature of the seventeenth-century Muscovite ambassadorial instructions on ceremonial matters: Hennings, *Russia*, 106.

149 He also pretended that he should ride to the emperor's palace on an Imperial carriage, a demand that was eventually granted: Bogoslovskii, *Petr I*, 347.

150 Ibid.

appear enthusiastic about the Poles. Perhaps he held some old grudges against them from when he was Moscow's resident ambassador in Warsaw. Curiously, though, during the first meeting between the two plenipotentiaries at Buda, no ceremonial issues occurred. Could it have been that their meeting was conducted under the guise of incognito because they had yet to arrive at the congress venue? In any case, for Voznitsyn, a precedent seems to have been established since, as he later claimed, it was Małachowski who first sent him a compliment and then visited him.[151] According to the Commonwealth's ambassador, the origins of the dispute lay in Vienna when the Imperial chancery issued an 'almost doubtful passport' (*incerto quasi passaporto*) in which, in the place where the names of the allies were mentioned, that of Muscovy was placed ahead of that of the Commonwealth, which Voznitsyn interpreted as a clear sign 'certifying the issue of precedence with me' (*mecum de praecedentia certaret*) in his favour.[152]

Be that as it may, the next scene of the drama was to unfold at Petrovaradin, where the two plenipotentiaries found themselves together. When Małachowski arrived at the fortress, Voznitsyn invited the Pole to visit him for dinner, thus making use of his alleged precedence (*de praetensa praecedentia*) although Małachowski in reaching there last – one wonders if this was done deliberately by him – was expecting to be visited first, 'as the custom would have it' (*si id moris foret*).[153] Voznitsyn sent his secretary, Posnikov, to apologise by saying that while he wanted to visit the Pole, his legs didn't permit him to. He would certainly do it after he had recovered.[154] Yet, Posnikov's visit, instead of improving the situation, made matters still worse. 'This secretary spoke Latin, and he didn't refer to the Duke of Muscovy in any other way than "our king", also entering into a discussion about the parity between kings'.[155] Małachowski felt the need to remind Posnikov of the 'correct' interpretation of the order of the 'Society of Princes'.[156] The tsar was no king but merely Grand Duke of Muscovy. It was Ivan IV who assumed this title by himself without achieving universal recognition of it.[157] Voznitsyn saw such words as a direct affront to

151 Ibid., 361, 367.

152 Sałuski, *Epistolae*, 677.

153 Ibid. In the Muscovite version, there is a different unfolding of events with a desperate Małachowski trying to secure a first visit to him by Voznitsyn: Bogoslovskii, *Petr I*, 370.

154 In Voznitsyn's relation, it is rather Małachowski who, after being informed about the Muscovite ceremonial pretensions, invited Posnikov to discuss the matter with him: Ibid., 368–9.

155 Sałuski, *Epistolae*, 677.

156 *See* above.

157 Bogoslovskii, *Petr I*, 368–9.

the tsar's honour and demanded an official apology from Małachowski.[158] The latter decided to utilise the familiar trope of *traduttore tradittore,* blaming Posnikov and accusing him of falsely informing the ambassador about what he genuinely said. And acting carefully, as he says, he offered his excuses.[159]

Such symbolic moves, though, could be interpreted in many ways according to each side's intention of reading them. Thus, whereas for the Pole, it was a cautiously designed act to keep on good terms with Voznitsyn, the latter interpreted it and also conveyed it to his principal as a significant victory by depicting the Polish nobles sent by Małachowski to apologise as imploring the ambassador's forgiveness and bowing low to him upon their departure.[160] Małachowski was quite aware of the ambiguity of the signals he sent. 'I don't know, though, how this claim [the Muscovite precedence pretensions] could be laid to rest because, in such delicate matters, where no middle way should be accepted, it's difficult to act without confirming this very pretence of his'.[161]

The turbulent cohabitation between the two men at Petrovaradin culminated in an open fight between their servants for the place each one was to occupy in the allied encampment. There are diverging accounts of how the events unfolded, with each side providing its own version. If we follow Voznitsyn, upon his arrival at the congress venue and having seen in Vienna a draft made by Count Öttingen of a plan for the places to be occupied in the allied encampment, he sent a letter to the Imperial delegation. In this, he claimed a superior position over the Commonwealth, on the right side or immediately after the imperial tent (if the tents were arranged in a row). He also supplied several arguments to support his pretensions, including the Buda precedent and the fact that the tsar's forces were assisting the allies better in concluding the current treaty.[162] The Imperial side replied that the plan Voznitsyn had seen was obsolete, as they had decided that everyone should choose their place freely with no precedence since the venue of the congress was neutral.[163]

As Count Schlik recounts, Voznytsin had misinterpreted these words of the Imperial embassy. He understood 'that, there [concerning the places in the encampment] it is secretly insinuated to him, that it was only up to his cleverness to win a good spot, [so] he rushed, raced into' it in order to occupy the

158 Ibid.; Sałuski, *Epistolae*, 677. According to Małachowski, Voznitsyn complained that the Pole was trying 'to make his lord inferior to the King of Poland and he exaggerated it a lot': Ibid.

159 Ibid.

160 Bogoslovskii, *Petr I*, 368–9.

161 Sałuski, *Epistolae*, 677.

162 Bogoslovskii, *Petr I*, 367.

163 Ibid., 367–8; *Narratio*, fol. 9^r^.

best position.[164] Unfortunately, he only arrived second.[165] Małachowski was quicker, and sending his servants there first, he planted his tents in a place 'deemed better'.[166] When Voznitsyn finally came over, seeing the Poles occupying a position 'that appeared to him more conspicuous', he decided to amend this prejudice by chasing them away, bringing down the Polish tents and planting his own instead.[167] 'From this emergency, as from a tiny spark, a great fire was about to arise because the Pole was meditating to drive away the Muscovite by force in every way [possible] and [thus] compensate for the alleged damage [to his honour]'.[168] An open conflict was avoided at the last moment, with Małachowski retiring to his boat and refusing to return to shore for twelve days, 'insisting for the glory of the king and the honour of the nation (*pro gloria Regis & honore gentis*)'.[169] Count Schlik sarcastically remarked that 'cats and mice would be more likely to agree than these two gentlemen'.[170] Still, this strife over precedence was damaging to the allied cause, and the Imperial side decided to intervene by offering its mediation.[171] Count Marsigli assumed the role of the conciliator. When he visited Voznitsyn, the latter feigned ignorance.[172] He stated, though, thus indirectly admitting the episode, that if such an incident had indeed occurred, he would agree to an Imperial mediation as long as the honour of his principal was not impaired.[173] Ultimately, the mediators' request for a transfer of both camps for the delegations to be closer to one another gave the Imperials a perfect opportunity to terminate the conflict by arranging a new encampment in a square form, with no apparent

164 ÖStA, HHStA, Türkei I, Turcica Box 170, Diarium et Cerimoniale, fol. 7–8.

165 There is some uncertainty about the correct version of the story. In his journal, Count Schlik claims that Voznitsyn won the race and arrived first (ibid.). However, in his report to the emperor, he states that Małachowski was the first to send 'someone from his people' to secure the place on the right of the Imperials, with Voznitsyn arriving later: ÖStA, HHStA, Türkei I, Turcica Box 167, Folder 2 (October 1698, 2nd half), fol. 146$^{r–v}$, Imperial plenipotentiaries to Leopold I, 25 October 1698). Małachowski's account, too, is unclear on this point (Sałuski, *Epistolae*, 677). Nevertheless, since the second version also appears in the *Narratio*, I have chosen to adopt it here.

166 *Narratio*, fol. 9^{v}.

167 Ibid.

168 Ibid.

169 Sałuski, *Epistolae*, 677.

170 ÖStA, HHStA, Türkei I, Turcica Box 167, Folder 2 (October 1698, 2nd half), fol. 207$^{r–v}$, Schlik to Kinsky, 30 October 1698.

171 ÖStA, HHStA, Türkei I, Turcica Box 170, Diarium et Cerimoniale, fol. 10.

172 He also later repeated to the Imperial ambassadors that he didn't have any quarrel with Malachowski: Bogoslovskii, *Petr I*, 375; ÖStA, HHStA, Türkei I, Turcica Box 167, Folder 2 (October 1698, 2nd half), fol. 146^{v}, Imperial plenipotentiaries to Leopold I, 25 October 1698.

173 Bogoslovskii, *Petr I*, 371.

precedence, placing themselves and the Venetians between the Poles and the Muscovites to 'avoid any agitation between their servants'.[174]

The 'tents episode' marked one of the most violent ceremonial disputes of the Carlowitz congress, revealing, with its severity, how vital status questions continued to be considered for the seventeenth-century *fin de siècle*. Not did it mark the end of the Muscovite–Commonwealth precedence dispute sequel, although both sides tacitly decided to avoid another open confrontation. Fast forwarding from the beginning to the end of the congress, Voznitsyn chose to sign his agreement with the Ottomans ahead of all other allies on 24 January 1699. His decision was primarily prompted, as he sustains in his final report, from a desire to avoid the ceremonial disputes with Małachowski that might have occurred both during the signing of the peace instruments as well as in the joint banquet that was to take place afterwards at Lord Paget's tent, even though he was informed that no precedence would be observed in the latter.[175] He excused his absence from the banquet by feigning illness. He followed the same strategy during the farewell visits by leaving the allied camp with the excuse of embarking on a religious pilgrimage to the Orthodox monasteries in the vicinity and returning only after Małachowski's departure.[176]

Summarising, the Commonwealth–Muscovite ceremonial disputes bear some interesting parallels with the Franco–Spanish ones, especially during the Congress of Westphalia.[177] Both entailed a power desperate to preserve and safeguard the status it had acquired during the sixteenth and the first half of the seventeenth centuries against another which attempted through its own perception of grandeur to dethrone it and supersede it in that position. In addition, both disputes culminated in acts of physical violence (fights between servants). They also led to a deliberate refusal of one of the two protagonists to appear together in common gatherings to avoid the perpetuation of the quarrel and thus stick to an unclear status quo, which could be interpreted differently by either side.

13 The 'Tents Incident' No. 2

Following the friction between Voznitsyn and Małachowski over the placement of their tents in the allied encampment and the transferring of the latter to a novel location, an effort was made to definitely erase any form of precedence

174 ÖStA, HHStA, Türkei I, Turcica Box 170, Diarium et Cerimoniale, fol. 10.

175 Bogoslovskii, *Petr I*, 424–5.

176 *Narratio*, fol. 49^{r}.

177 May, *Repräsentation und Statuspolitik*, 94–110.

there. The spatial square-form arrangement of the new camp by Count Marsigli was one step towards this goal. The signing of a document in which all allies agreed that there was not to be a first, second, third or fourth place between them was another.[178] Yet, despite all those attempts by the Imperial side, altering the precedence-oriented way of thinking of the Holy League members turned out to be simply impossible. Ruzzini hailed the placement of his tent right opposite that of the Imperials as a great symbolic victory.[179] Alas, Małachowski, finally persuaded to come on shore, had a similar understanding of the symbolic importance of the Venetian's assigned location. As Rāmī Meḥmed vividly depicts his supposed thoughts, "how is it that I, being an ambassador of a king, am assigned a place to the left of the emperor's ambassadors and the Venetian ambassador opposite to them? This cannot be tolerated in any way".[180] He decided to take matters into his own hands and correct this perceived injustice through a highly provocative move. Following Schlik's account of events, after the Imperials, the Venetians and the Muscovites had taken their assigned place in the camp, some of Małachowski's servants came with a 'ragged tent' (*mit einen zerlumpten zeltan*) and placed it 'fifty of sixty steps' (*50 oder 60 schritt*) in front of Ruzzini's.[181]

This move sparked a novel row of disputes, and the Imperials had to step in again by sending Count Marsigli to the Commonwealth's ambassador to resolve the issue. Ultimately, after eight days of 'so many laborious and distressful talks' (*nach so villen mühesamben undt verdrüslichen abhandlungen*) Małachowski had to withdraw his tent and place it in the original space reserved for him.[182] Interestingly – but perhaps not surprisingly – in the letters to his principals, he passes this episode in complete silence, and only claims that 'I took my place side by side with the Imperials'.[183] Voznitsy's behaviour during the Commonwealth–Venetian quarrel is also intriguing. It seems that the Muscovite, all eager to once again see Małachowski embarrassed and defeated, tried to foment Ruzzini into more drastic action against the Pole.

---

178 Voznitsyn claimed that this was only a stratagem to sweeten the pill for Małachowski so that he would finally leave his ship and agree to take his designated place. He refused to sign it, though, because his name was placed below that of the Pole: Bogoslovskii, *Petr I*, 380.

179 Ruzzini, *Relazione*, 379. Similarly, Voznitsyn didn't fail to mention that he took the right side to the Imperials while Małachowski took the left – that being, of course, a matter of perspective: Bogoslovskii, *Petr I*, 376.

180 *Ta'rīḫ-i ṣulḥnāme*, fol. 73ᵃ.

181 ÖStA, HHStA, Türkei I, Turcica Box 170, Diarium et Cerimoniale, fol. 10–11.

182 Ibid., fol. 22.

183 Załuski, *Epistolae*, 677.

As Schlik furthermore relates, visiting the Venetian more than once the day after the incident, Voznitsyn expressed his wonder 'that he [Ruzzini] could tolerate [having] the Polish tent in front of his face, and offered him all his servants as an aid, if he wanted to remove it by force'.[184] Ruzzini chose not to follow the Muscovite's violence-escalatory suggestions and instead opted for restraint. The 'tents episode n. 2', despite not assuming the violence of its prequel, reveals once again how, despite the strenuous attempts to curtail and limit the disruptive effects of ceremonial precedence, the latter continue to pervade the minds of the congress participants and influence their actions to a considerable extent.

14 Who Is to Sit First at the Table with the Ottomans?

The final chapter of the 'ceremonial precedence play' evolved around the order by which each of the allies was to negotiate with the Ottomans. Regardless of the declared suspension of any form of preeminence for the duration of the talks, each ambassador was determined to claim the best position in the order of the conferences since the latter, far from being innocuous, would act as a mirror of the hierarchy of honour and prestige between them. Despite professing equality, the Imperials were not willing to relinquish their 'privilege' of being the first to negotiate, and the Ottomans favoured this option for their own strategic reasons. Ruzzini, for his part, stated to Count Marsigli that he didn't want to stay behind the Muscovites. The latter had, of course, to compete with the Poles for primacy.

Although the Imperial instructions clearly ordained that the matter of the order of the conferences was to be left to be solved by the mediators and the Ottomans and that the Imperial side should not meddle in such a thorny issue, Voznitsyn claimed that the Habsburg delegation's secretary had presented him with a draft plan in which the conference sequence was supposed to be as such: the first to negotiate would have been the Imperials, followed by the Commonwealth, the Venetians and the Muscovites. Of course, his placement at the end of the row came as a huge symbolic blow to the ambassador of the tsar after the victories he thought he had scored over Małachowski. 'And the Great and Plenipotentiary Ambassador said: why is it so that the Polish and the Venetians precede him?'.[185] He was given the answer that this order was arranged according to the order with which each ally had joined the Holy

184 ÖStA, HHStA, Türkei I, Turcica Box 170, Diarium et Cerimoniale, fol. 11.

185 Quoted in Bogoslovskii, *Petr I*, 389.

League. Voznitsyn counter-stated that this should have been based on a different principle, that of the dignity of the sovereigns.[186]

It is possible that this scheme, ostensibly contrary to the Imperial instructions, was solely conceived to placate Małachowski. It was a mere façade, however. During the last of the four initial conferences with the Ottomans, the Imperial plenipotentiaries fully implemented their instructions by leaving the matter of whom to negotiate after them to their interlocutors. Nonetheless, at the same time, they privileged the Venetians because of the latter's acceptance of the Foundation of Peace and the geographical proximity of their frontier to the Imperial one. The Ottomans tactfully retorted that, although the crown heads always precede, they would leave the matter to be decided among the three allies themselves. Finally, it was only via the intervention of Lord Paget that it was decided that Venice would follow the order of conferences based on the two arguments the Imperial side presented.[187] And thus, inadvertently, the Imperial side influenced the order of meetings without seemingly contradicting its instructions.[188]

This arrangement was a fresh blow to Małachowski,

> I protested against this placement after [Venice], mentioning that my principal, the most serine king, should precede the others for reasons based on law and precedent. And this also would surely convince [them] because it was Poland, ahead of all the allies, that made common cause with the emperor against the Turks.[189]

He protested in vain. Ultimately, he could not even receive the satisfaction of preceding Voznitsyn, the Muscovite having succeeded in negotiating before him.[190] In an effort to avoid that, he suggested they could decide the order by

186 Ibid.

187 ÖStA, HHStA, Türkei I, Turcica Box 170, Protocollum, fol. 42–43. In his account of the congress, Rāmī, while admitting that it was not Venice's place to negotiate after the Imperials (*Venedik èlçisi yeri değil iken*), sustains that this arrangement was made because of the suspension of all ceremonial and precedence claims according to the Congress Regulation: *Taʾrīḫ-i ṣulḥnāme*, fol. 102[a].

188 Ruzzini fully understood that, and in a letter to Kinsky, he felt the need to express his gratitude to the Imperial embassy for placing him directly after them in the negotiations: ÖStA, HHStA, Türkei I, Turcica Box 168, Folder 2 (November 1698, 2nd half), fol. 154[r], Ruzzini to Kinsky, 22 November 1698.

189 Saluski, *Epistolae*, 677.

190 According to Schlik, Voznitsyn was notified by the mediators that the Ottomans wanted to negotiate with him next: ÖStA, HHStA, Türkei I, Turcica Box 170, Diarium et Cerimoniale, fol. 36. Yet, as we saw, in his relation, Rāmī placed him after Małachowski.

drawing lots. Voznitsyn, of course, refused.[191] If Małachowski was the clear loser of this last precedence contest between the allies, the winner was undoubtedly Ruzzini, who celebrated his achievement in his *Relazione Finale*.[192] Fate had it, though, that he would be the last to complete his negotiation.

15 'Faked' Ceremonial Disputes?

It should have been clear by now that struggles over the ceremonial were not a bunch of illogical trivialities. They were fights over matters such as honour, status, dignity, and grandeur, notions that all the Carlowitz participants very much held dear. Nonetheless, that didn't stop them from complaining about the disruptions ceremonial regulations were causing for the negotiations, of suspecting ulterior motives behind the precedence quarrels or of instrumentalising symbolic communication for strategic purposes during the talks.

Rāmī Meḥmed asserted, concerning the Muscovite–Commonwealth strife, that 'the Polish and Muscovite ambassadors were not coming out of their ships and wasted time with the pretext of the ceremonial dispute between them'.[193] He appears suspicious of the sincerity of the dispute and implies that it was a deliberate dilatory tactic. In a similar vein, the Imperial embassy also began to suspect that the ceremonial conflicts triggered by Małachowski might solely be an effort 'to perturbate the congress'.[194] Eager not to let the Venetian ambassador agitate things ahead of the arranged 26 January signing ceremony, the Imperial embassy chose to deprive him of his biggest supporter by then, Voznitsyn. They did that by convincing the latter not only not to wait further for Ruzzini to complete his negotiation by himself but also by fully capitalising upon the Muscovite–Commonwealth ceremonial strife, they also subtly forced him to sign his treaty ahead of all the others. As Count Schlik communicated to Kinsky, 'the chain [of signings] began to unroll itself from Muscovy, who, driven by a motive of rivalry, [against the Pole], that we had adroitly insinuated to him, made his, the day before yesterday'.[195] Ruzzini, in his turn, pressed for a revival of the ceremonial (*ricambiarsi le ufficiosità*) between the Imperials and the Ottomans after the end of the talks in order to keep the latter longer in

191 *Patmiatniki*, 245.

192 Ruzzini, *Relazione*, 379.

193 *Ta'rīḫ-i ṣulḥnāme*, fol. 72^{b}.

194 ÖStA, HHStA, Türkei I, Turcica Box 167, Folder 2 (October 1698, 2nd half), fol. 273^{r-v}, Imperial plenipotentiaries to Leopold I, 30 October 1698.

195 ÖStA, HHStA, Türkei I, Turcica Box 171, Folder 2 (January 1699, 2nd half), fol. 181^{r}, Schlik to Kinsky, 26 January 1699.

the congress venue so that he could receive the appropriate instructions from Venice to sign his treaty as well.[196]

Do all these instances prove that ceremonial regulations and precedence fights were mere smokescreens? It doesn't appear to be the case. The Imperial ambassadors successfully influenced Voznitsyn only because his ceremonial disputes with Małachowski were factual and did actually matter to both of them. And although he indeed had orders from the tsar to disturb the congress with every possible means, there is no clue in his letters or his final report that this purpose alone drove his dissensus with the Commonwealth plenipotentiary. Lastly, Rāmī may have resented and questioned the sincerity of the Voznitsyn vs Małachowski ceremonial duel. Still, when it came to the defence of the honour of the Exalted State, he didn't seem to have any reservations whatsoever in quarrelling. Before the erection of a wooden edifice, the sultan provided a tent to house the conferences. "And also, this one, how much dispute [was made] for the setting up of the negotiations' tent", the Ottoman plenipotentiary relates. 'They said it was given by the Exalted State, and, at last, at this point, they all allied in opposing it. Being a matter pertaining to the safeguarding of the honour of the State and [thus] requiring serious attention, we persisted as well and disputed'.[197]

Hence, as banal as it may appear, the best course would be to opt for a middle ground. Ceremonial regulations and precedence disputes did matter; that's why they could sometimes be instrumentalised. In his seminal monograph on the Congress of Nijmegen, Matthias Köhler convincingly suggested that instead of separating symbolic communication from the actors' strategic concerns, we should regard them as complementing one another.[198] Precedence disputes could be used to slow down a congress without losing their symbolic content. The participants would rather hit two birds with one stone. In the case of Voznitsyn, he had indeed managed to delay the start of the negotiations – if that was his aim – and achieved a symbolic victory over his main 'ceremonial rival'. Lastly, a specific behaviour ascribed to certain ceremonial roles or occasions could be used to convey direct and indirect messages regarding the course of the negotiation or particular issues relating to them. In such instances, ceremonial signs were not empty of meaning. They were the principal means by which to effectuate a strategy.

---

196 Ruzzini, *Relazione*, 365. *See* also ÖStA, HHStA, Türkei I, Turcica Box 171, Folder 2 (January 1699, 2nd half), fol. 246^{r}, Schlik to Kinsky, 31 January 1699.

197 *Ta'rīḫ-i ṣulḥnāme*, fol. 73^{b}.

198 Köhler, *Strategie und Symbolik*.

Narration Part II: the *Arcana Congressus*

One of the most interesting aspects of the first phase of the congress were the offstage negotiations that were taking place among certain delegations as well as the attempts of various individuals from all sides to approach, gain the trust, acquire information, or even win over to their cause more and less prominent players between their opponents, their allies, or the mediators. Such moves were chiefly facilitated by a certain relaxation of the comings and goings between the different camps during the first weeks of the congress. A relaxation that was greatly restricted, though, after the promulgation of the Regulation by the mediators.[1]

Arcane negotiations were the direct byproduct of the disunion among the Christian confederates. Some of them, mainly the Polish-Lithuanian Commonwealth and Muscovy, feeling betrayed by the emperor and Venice, decided to take matters into their own hands and enter into discussion directly with the Ottomans behind the backs of their allies, paying them, thus, one may say, with the same coin. The crux of these informal talks was twofold. On the one hand, to explore the intentions of the opposing party, and on the other, to try to strike a deal even before the commencement of the official conferences. These negotiations were indeed kept so covert that for some of them, either there is no spur in the official documents – even of those of parties directly involved – or, for others, there are only hints and suspicions. As bearers of secret written and oral messages between the various embassies, 'backstage' characters were utilised, individuals usually trusted by both parties who performed the double role of courier and unofficial negotiator.

1 The Secret Negotiations between Voznitsyn and the Ottoman Delegation

The most well-known secret talks were conducted between the Muscovite and the Ottoman plenipotentiaries, something we only know thanks to Russian sources. They were so skillfully kept hidden that, if not for the relation of Voznitzyn, no trace of them would have been preserved. It appears that the order for such dealings came directly from the tsar.[2] However, a significant parameter greatly assisted Voznitsyn in his goal. He and Mavrocordatos were

1 D. and I. Guzevich, *Velikoe posol'stvo*, 130.

2 Bogoslovskii, *Petr I*, 384.

 DOI:10.1163/9789004458499_013

old acquaintances, their relationship going back to 1681 when the Muscovite had been sent to the Ottoman capital to ratify the Ottoman–Muscovite Peace Treaty of Bakhchisarai.[3] As the Ottoman plenipotentiary writes to the Patriarch of Jerusalem, Dositheos, 'The ambassador of Muscovy is [our] common friend,[4] Procopii Bogdanovich. [Having with him] a very good relationship, Divine Providence brought us again now, as in the past, to discuss the affairs of peace together'.[5] Considering that knowledge of such relations between ambassadors could influence the choice of a delegate for a specific mission,[6] it would be interesting to pose the question whether this prior acquaintance with Mavrocordatos had not played a significant role in Voznitsyn's appointment. Being also co-religionists – both Orthodox Christians – the tsar's representative could perfectly utilise such a double friendship/religious affiliation with the Ottoman ambassador to his own advantage and attempt to surprise the 'treacherous Germans' by turning their weapons against them.[7]

To avoid attracting attention, Voznitzyn initiated his secret correspondence with Mavrocordatos by sending to the Ottoman camp a monk of the Serbian Patriarchate of Pec named Gregory, disguised as a layman. The latter carried a letter from the ambassador drafted in Greek by his secretary, Posnikov, to his Ottoman colleague – another way to create proximity. In this letter, Voznitsyn attempted right from the start to procure Mavrocordatos's confidence by reminding him of their long friendship and expressing his ardent wish to engage with him in separate 'underground' talks.[8]

Most likely, Mavrocordatos wanted to weigh his options or to secure Rāmī Meḥmed's approval, and he didn't reply immediately. That caused great apprehension for Voznitsyn, who sent Father Gregory again to the Ottoman camp with yet another letter. This time he got his awaited reply. The Ottomans agreed to proceed to talks. From this point on, the crucial link between the two

3 Ibid., 382; *Ta'rīḫ-i ṣulḥnāme*, fol. 108ᵃ.

4 Voznitsyn's close relationship with Dositheos is evidenced by the gift of expensive sables, which Voznitsyn later sent to the Patriarch through Mavrocordatos, as well as by a secret ciphered letter dispatched to him after the end of the congress. In the letter, the ambassador asked Dositheos for advice and information on whether Muscovy should pursue the war or seek a peace settlement with the Ottoman Empire: Bogoslovskii, *Petr I*, 438.

5 Livadas, *Μαυροκορδάτου Ἐπιστολαί*, 177. Encountering in congresses old acquaintances from previous negotiations or embassies was not something unusual for various early modern ambassadors. *See* Köhler, *Strategie und Symbolik*, 127.

6 Ibid., 128.

7 He himself admits this in a letter to the tsar describing the secret negotiations with Mavrocordatos: Bogoslovskii, *Petr I*, 382.

8 Ibid., 383–4.

ambassadors was taken up by the secretary-cum-interpreter of the Muscovite embassy, Petr Posnikov, 'his [Voznitsyn's] confidant' (*maḥrem ādamısı*), as Rāmī calls him.[9] We will deal later in more detail with Posnikov's intriguing personality. Suffice it to say, his knowledge of Greek and his doctorate in medicine from the University of Padua, where the latter also studied for a time, clearly created a climate of trust between the two delegations. The pretext for Posnikov's visits would have been the ceremonial exchanges of compliments between the two ambassadors. As Mavrocordatos framed it, 'what a strange thing: the English and the Dutch send compliments to one another every day. So why don't we, as Orthodox Christians and friends, do the same?'.[10]

Three meetings between Postnikov and Mavrocordatos ensued, whereas Rāmī Meḥmed participated as well in the fourth and last one.[11] Nonetheless, despite all those discussions and the quite friendly climate between the two sides, fomented by personal relations and common faith (at least in the case of Mavrocordatos), both parties did not manage to come to an agreement. The Muscovite propositions of a short truce (one or one and a half years) during which the most severe issues between the two sides would be further discussed didn't meet the approval of the Ottoman side, who wanted a long-term truce/armistice or peace with duration and a discussion of all the significant issues immediately.[12] And so, there was little chance that Voznitsyn would succeed, as he wished, to secure a separate agreement between the two sides before the commencing of the congress and thus, as he said, deprive 'the Germans' of the pleasure to claim that it was they who had reconciled the sultan and the tsar.[13] Against Postnikov's arguments that it would be best for the Ottomans to conclude a truce/armistice with the tsar now and resume the war with the other Holy League members, trying to secure better terms after the Muscovite withdrawal, Mavrocordatos made clear to him that the Porte was honouring its commitments.[14] The Ottoman side didn't desire to resume the war adventure on some vague promises of the tsar. Lastly, not even Voznitsyn's attempt to bypass the mediators was crowned with success. The Ottomans

9 *Ta'rīḥ-i ṣulḥnāme*, fol. 119[b].

10 Quoted in Bogoslovskii, *Petr I*, 385.

11 A detailed narration in ibid., 385–9.

12 Ironically enough, it is this Muscovite proposition that would be adopted in the end.

13 Bogoslovskii, *Petr I*, 387.

14 Ibid. Postnikov even told Mavrocordatos that the tsar was willing to help the Ottomans and thus avenge the Germans for their betrayal: Ibid., 385–6.

didn't wish to compromise the latter's trust, something they greatly needed for their talks with the other allies, especially with the Imperials.[15]

Failing to convince Mavrocordatos with the force of his arguments, Voznitsyn resorted to other means. He promised him a hefty reward from the tsar for his services and tried to bribe him on the spot with sables and money, but again to no avail.[16] However, gifts were exchanged many times between the two embassies as a sign of mutual friendship and goodwill.[17] As Voznitsyn wrote to Peter I on these reciprocal back-and-forths, 'they ride from me to them and from them to me, going around the camps, by the steppe, and [thus] visible to no one'.[18]

Despite their failure to produce concrete results, the secret Ottoman–Muscovite negotiations disclose a broad canvas of cardinal characteristics of the early modern *manière de négocier*: The crucial role of some less-well-known yet important go-betweens, members or not of an embassy, in performing delicate tasks and even acting as negotiators themselves; the cardinality of exploiting personal relations or religious affiliations to gain the trust of the opposite party; the weapon of 'gifts' used to 'purchase' the services of a member of the opposing party, and, last but not least, that on certain occasions, the 'Theatre of the Congress' was indeed transformed into an actual stage. In the Ottoman–Muscovite case, both parties were aware of the other's position well before their official meetings. And yet, during those intercourses, they *acted* as if they were utterly ignorant of them. Thus, it is challenging to ascertain which times they meant what they were saying during the conferences and which times they were solely performing in front of the mediators, the 'audience', who would have no awareness of this performance, taking their words at face value.[19]

15 Ibid., 388.

16 Ibid., 387.

17 Bogoslovskii, *Petr I*, 388.

18 Quoted in ibid.

19 A similar opinion is also voiced by Andrei Guskov in his article on the Muscovite participation at the congress: Guskov, 'Uchastie Rossii', 133, fn. 64. A perfect example is the final conference between the two delegations on 10/20 December – a true *haut niveau* theatrical performance – where both sides seemingly discussed for the first time matters that had already been agreed upon through secret communications three days earlier: Bogoslovskii, *Petr I*, 412–4. Similarly, while narrating the same conference, Rāmī Meḥmed acknowledges that Voznitsyn had no authority to consent to the demolition or evacuation of fortresses. Yet, during the meeting, he portrays the Ottomans as entirely unaware of such a limitation: *Ta'rīḥ-i ṣulḥnāme*, fol. 118[a–b].

2 Polish Secret Dealings

Voznitsyn was not the only one of the allies to engage in offstage dealings with the Ottoman side before the start of the official meetings. From indirect references and allusions, it becomes evident that the Commonwealth was doing precisely the same. Already in the instructions given to Małachowsky, it was plainly and clearly stated that the plenipotentiary should try to win over important Ottoman dignitaries, in any way possible:

> As in every negotiation, it is generally an established rule that in order to gain safely and efficiently [what one wants], he needs to purchase the favour of many, [our ambassador] needs to pay great diligence to how to win by every means the secret assistance and help for our side with the ministers of the Porte of the Tatar Han, Count Thököly, the Interpreter Mavrocordatos and any other he might deem of value.[20]

Małachowski faithfully followed his instructions, and during his brief stay in Buda, he dispatched two letters to Selīm Giray and Thököly pleading for their assistance in the upcoming negotiations.[21] His constituted a clumsier move than that of Voznytsin, though. It didn't remain unobserved by the other allies and aroused suspicions. We have already encountered the two mysterious Poles attempting to reach the Ottoman camp before the ambassador's arrival, their moves closely monitored by the Imperial side. We can now reveal the identity of one of them. He was no other than the ambassador's secretary, Andrzej Gorkowski. The latter was not only to deliver his principal's letters but also to expose in detail what Małachowski could not put in writing.[22] We do not know what those oral instructions were. Still, it is plausible that, with these moves, the Polish side sought Selīm Giray's support for its claims regarding the fortress of Kamianets-Podilskyi. We will return to this matter in due course. Gorkowski and his companion were sent by Małachowski under the pretext of buying horses from the Ottoman camp. However, both the letters and their carriers were intercepted by Imperial troops en route and returned to the Polish ambassador by the commander of the Habsburg forces, Prince Eugene of Savoy, thereby exposing the Pole's attempted secret dealings.[23]

20 Gorkowski, *Compedium Legationis*, 23^{r}.

21 The copies of the two letters in ibid., 5^{v}–6^{r}.

22 Ibid.

23 Ruzzini, *Relazione*, 353; ÖStA, HHStA, Türkei I, Turcica Box 167, Folder 2 (October 1698, 2nd half), fol. 130^{r}, Schlik to Kinsky, 22 October 1698. Ibid., 6^{r}; [...].

Besides obtaining the support of key actors in the Ottoman decision-making apparatus, the Commonwealth plenipotentiary was also instructed, as we have already encountered, to cultivate his relations with the mediators in order to gain their backing. However, primarily, he was to establish friendship and confidence with the Muscovite ambassador, 'who's working together [with us], could render easier the negotiation […] for the Republic'.[24] As has been shown, that didn't go exactly according to plan.

3 Venetian Anxieties

Another of our congress protagonists who attempted to read the Ottoman intentions in advance was Carlo Ruzzini. 'The Venetian ambassador is very indulgent but very apprehensive at the same time', Count Schlik reported to Kinsky.[25] Driven perhaps by his anxiety, he indirectly approached the Ottoman delegation via a letter written by his Jewish doctor addressed to Mavrocordatos. But who was this doctor? Israel Conegliano undoubtedly personifies what historian Nathalie Rothman labels a 'trans-imperial subject', that is, an individual who could move easily between two (or more) polities and make a career in both by winning the trust of powerful individuals on either side of the borders.[26] Israel was born in Padua somewhere in the middle of the seventeenth century. After completing his medical studies and practising his profession for a couple of years in Venice, he left the city of the lagoons for the banks of the Bosporus. There, due to his medical skills, he won the favour of Sultan Meḥmed IV and the Grand Vizier Ḳara Muṣṭafā Paşa, who even dispatched him back to the Serenissima in 1681 to consult with other prominent physicians there on how to cure the illness of the sultan's son-in-law. It is highly probable that during the same period, Conegliano met with Mavrocordatos. Not only did both share the same profession, but also the same patronage networks. Seeing his growing influence among high-ranking members of the Ottoman élite, the Venetian resident ambassadors in Constantinople recommended that he be employed in the embassy's personnel. In 1682, Israel became the physician of the Serenissima's legation, and he for a brief period even exercised the functions of a *chargé d'affaires*. After the start of the Sixteen

24 Gorkowski, *Compedium Legationis*, 23^{r}.

25 ÖStA, HHStA, Türkei I, Turcica Box 167, Folder 2 (October 1698, 2nd half), fol. 208^{r}, Schlik to Kinsky, 30 October 1698.

26 Nathalie E. Rothman, *Brokering Empire. Trans-Imperial Subjects between Venice and Istanbul* [Ithaca (USA)/London: Cornell University Press 2012].

Years' War, Conegliano remained in the Ottoman capital under French protection, performing the role of an informant for the senate. However, in 1693, he was arrested for espionage. His possession of solid connections in the Porte, though, secured his release, although he was constrained to leave Constantinople and return to Venice, where he was awarded Venetian citizenship for his services to the Republic.[27]

Thus, it is highly plausible that his old Ottoman connections, especially with Mavrocordatos, played a significant role in Ruzzini's choice to include him in his embassy as his personal doctor.[28] Coneglianos's letter to the Ottoman plenipotentiary was reportedly delivered by a certain Count Onigo, who had in the past been taken captive during the Ottoman reconquest of the island of Chios.[29] We encounter yet again, as in the secret Ottoman–Muscovite negotiations, these otherwise obscure personalities, these second-role actors, who at specific points during the play find themselves in the spotlight, aiding in the progression of the plot. Yet, even more significantly, Postnikov and Conegliano's cases illustrate how personal, professional and academic affinities could be adroitly used to facilitate diplomatic communication. What Israel's missive contained is unknown. Still, when Mavrocordatos read it, he supposedly said, 'good, good. When the time comes, we will see what is to happen'.[30] If we judge by the way the Ottoman–Venetian negotiations' drama continued, this exchange didn't seem to have borne much fruit. Still, in the short term, it seems to have raised Ruzzini's hopes, since he appears to have demanded, just like Voznitsyn, to enter immediately into talks with the Ottomans, "without anyone's interposition" (*sans l'entremise de qui ce soit*), a demand that was rejected, though.[31]

27 David Kaufmann, *Dr. Israel Conegliano und seine Verdienste und die Republik Venedig bis nach dem Frieden von Carlowitz* (Vienna: Carl Konegen 1895); Ekkehard Eickhoff, 'Die Selbstbehauptung Venedigs gegen das Osmanische Reich: Strategien und Agenten', in Strohmeyer and Spannenberger, *Frieden und Konfliktmanagement*, 139.

28 Ruzzini, *Relazione*, 444.

29 In contrast to the Ottoman-Muscovite secret talks, Ruzzini's overtures did not go unnoticed by Lord Paget, who then reported them to the Imperial embassy: ÖStA, HHStA, Türkei I, Turcica Box 167, Folder 2 (October 1698, 2nd half), fol. 208^{r}, Schlik to Kinsky, 30 October 1698.

30 Ibid., fol. 208^{r-v}.

31 ÖStA, HHStA, Türkei I, Turcica Box 168, Folder 2 (November 1698, 2nd half), fol. 43^{v}–44^{r}, Schlik to Kinsky, 5 November 1698. Curiously enough, this information is not to be encountered either in Ruzzini's *Relazione Finale* or that of the Anonymous Venetian.

4 Count Marsigli's Moves

Count Marsigli's efforts to establish confidence and friendly relations between all allied ambassadors, the mediators and members of their entourage are of extreme significance. His primary goal seems to be acquiring information, which he duly reported back to his patron, Count Kinsky.[32] He was aided in this task by the significant position he held in the Imperial embassy as an advisor in matters related to the issue of borders, which, by being unofficial, allowed him to present himself at the same time as a non-partisan, objective observer. Early in the congress, he had an 'extensive' (*per estensum*) conversation with Paget's secretary, Schreyer, to inquire about the Ottoman disposition towards peace and the possible Ottoman secret designs.[33] From a friend passing through the mediators' camp, he acquired information about the turbulent relationship between Paget and Colyer and the current status quo at the Ottoman Court.[34]

His next targets were the Polish and the Muscovite ambassadors.

> I am waiting with impatience, he wrote to Kinsky, to camp close to the Muscovite and the Pole. The latter being the same who was with Prince Louis in the year 1691,[35] we already know each other, and the same will soon happen with the Muscovite. [My goal is] to get an idea of them using as leverage that I have information regarding their possible interests in this congress.[36]

In the following letter, he would brag about his success: 'The Muscovite shows courteous subtleties towards me and confidence', as did Małachowski.[37]

---

32 For his patronage relationship with Kinsky, *see* Mónika F. Molnár, 'Luigi Ferdinando Marsigli e gli Ottomani. La frontiera asburgico-ottomana dopo la pace di Carlowitz', in Raffaella Gherardi (ed.), *La politica, la scienza, le armi. Luigi Ferdinando Marsili e la construzione della frontiera dell' Impero e dell' Europa* (Bologna: Cooperativa Libraria Universitaria Editrice Bologna 2010) 151; Ruzzini, *Relazione*, 378.

33 ÖStA, HHStA, Türkei I, Turcica Box 167, Folder 2 (October 1698, 2nd half), fol. 97^{r-v}, Marsigli to Kinsky, 22 October 1698.

34 ÖStA, HHStA, Türkei I, Turcica Box 168, Folder 1 (November 1698, 1st half), fol. 241^{r}–242^{r}, Marsigli to Kinsky, 28 October 1698.

35 Marsigli refers here to the mission Malachowski undertook in 1691 to the Imperial camp in Hungary for the then-peace negotiations with the Ottomans. The *Bolognese* was also present there, on his way to the Ottoman capital for the same negotiations, disguised as secretary of Lord Paget: Molnár, 'Luigi Ferdinando Marsigli', 150.

36 Marsigli to Kinsky, 22 October 1698, fol. 100^{r}.

37 ÖStA, HHStA, Türkei I, Turcica Box 167, Folder 2 (October 1698, 2nd half), fol. 178^{r}, Marsigli to Kinsky, 25 October 1698.

But as Marsigli attempted to use his uncertain status for his 'overtures of confidence', his interlocutors, aware of his instrumental position – although Marsigli could well have exaggerated it – tried to do precisely the same on their part. Their primary aim was to convince him of the justice of their territorial pretensions. They attempted to do it not only by words – Malachowski, for instance, claimed that the Commonwealth forces were in control of 3/4 of Moldavia and that Kamianets-Podilskyi was just about to fall, both untrue[38] – but by maps as well, trying to influence the *Bolognese* with his own weapon, 'the science of borders'.[39] The most eager to enlist his support was none other than Ruzzini.[40] 'Yesterday morning', reported Marsigli to Kinsky, 'I was honoured with a visit in my tent of monsieur the Venetian ambassador, who implored me to be always willing to aid in the service of his Republic in the upcoming negotiation […]'.[41] Ruzzini was followed in this gaining-confidence-visits by the secretary of the Venetian embassy, Gian Battista Nicolosi. 'Many times, I was visited by this secretary Nicolosi', Marsigli again related with an expression of contempt, 'in order to request for help in their negotiation'.[42] The Venetian went so far in his 'confessions' – something that later would not turn out in favour of the Serenissima – as to confide to Marsigli that Venice didn't have the men to secure the full possession of some mountains outside the Morea (Peloponesse) she so much desired.[43]

5 And the Mediators …

In this dissimulation play, one should not forget to pay a special tribute to the mediators. We have already encountered Lord Paget communicating secretly (*a confidenment communiqué*) to the Imperial plenipotentiaries the letter Małachowski wrote to the mediators denouncing the Peace Foundation of *uti possidetis* as well as the secret dealings of Ruzzini with the Ottomans.[44]

38 ÖStA, HHStA, Türkei I, Turcica Box 168, Folder 1 (November 1698, 1st half), fol. 252^{v}, Marsigli to Kinsky, 12 November 1698.

39 Ibid., fol. 246^{r} and fol. 223^{r}, Marsigli to Kinsky, s.d. (probably early November 1698).

40 That Ruzzini felt it necessary to include Marsigli in his description of the Imperial ambassadors, although he was not one, but only an assistant (*assistente*), attests to the importance he placed in him: Ruzzini, *Relazione*, 377–8.

41 ÖStA, HHStA, Türkei I, Turcica Box 167, Folder 2 (October 1698, 2nd half), fol. 45^{r}, Marsigli to Kinsky: 16 October 1698.

42 Ibid., fol. 177^{v}, Marsigli to Kinsky, 25 October 1698.

43 Ibid., fol. 178^{r}.

44 ÖStA, HHStA, Türkei I, Turcica Box 167, Folder 2 (October 1698, 2nd half), fol. 129^{r-v}, Schlik to Kinsky, 22 October 1698.

In their discourse, the mediators didn't change much from the preliminary phase. Theirs was, yet again, a careful manipulation of both sides, based on a selective, supposedly 'confidential' disclosure of information, to ensure the negotiations' success. For instance, during the first visit paid to them by the Imperial plenipotentiaries, the mediators assured them 'that the dispositions for peace were never before so good as they are now'.[45] Yet, they add, it should happen as soon as possible because of the very precarious position of the grand vizier. 'Collier told me', Schlik reported to Count Kinsky, 'that he [the vizier] was very attached to peace, but if the negotiations go on for long, firmness would succumb to politics'.[46]

Despite the seeds of truth in the insecurity of the grand vizier's position, it is clear that the mediators were capitalising on the European Christian prejudices about the Ottoman governmental system, notably the constant alterations of viziers, the 'ancient costumes' (*anciennes coutumes*) as Schlik referred to them, to exert pressure on the Imperial side to conclude the negotiations swiftly and urged the other allies to do the same as well. As the contents of Count Schlik's or Marsigli's letters – anxiously reporting to Kinsky menacing rumours on the imminent downfall of ʿAmcazāde and alleged French schemes at the Ottoman Court[47] – demonstrate, the mediators were perfectly successful in their goal.

6 The Spy

Lastly, we should not fail to mention an interesting yet obscure case of espionage that took place at the beginning of the congress. It involved a particular person named Lagnasco (or Lagnasque, as Count Schlik refers to him).[48] It is unclear from the sources for whom this Lagnasco worked, but it is evident that the Imperial side feared that he might try to mingle with the congress and damage the Imperial interests, so we could assume he might have been a French agent.[49] A missive from Count Kinsky to the second Imperial plenipotentiary provides some tantalising insight into this secret world of spies and

45 Ibid., fol. 208^{v}, Schlik to Kinsky, 30 October 1698.

46 Ibid., fol. 210^{v}.

47 *See*, for example, ibid., fol. 210^{r-v}; ÖStA, HHStA, Türkei I, Turcica Box 168, Folder 1 (November 1698, 1st half), fol. 44^{v}–45^{r}, Schlik to Kinsky, 5 November 1698; ibid., fol. 236^{r}, Marsigli to Kinsky, s.d. (probably early November 1698).

48 ÖStA, HHStA, Türkei I, Turcica Box 167, Folder 2 (October 1698, 2nd half), fol. 60^{v}, Schlik to Kinsky, 18 October 1698.

49 Ibid.

how authorities dealt with them. Speaking of Lagnasco, the Imperial minister noted that 'he is dangerous, and if we can't turn him into a double agent under a promise of accommodation, it would be essential to get rid of him by any means, [and] even if we cannot do it another way, we must instigate a quarrel with one of the emperor's officers'.[50] Unfortunately, the way the story ended and the fate of Lagnasco remain unknown.

•••

And thus, the congress's first and highly eventful phase drew to a close. It was now high time for the official negotiations to commence. As Rāmī reported back to ʿAmcazāde, 'presently, there is to be a struggle between [us] and the German plenipotentiaries on the article we decided [to negotiate] first, [namely] that of Transylvania'.[51] Nonetheless, before watching how this 'struggle' unfolded, we will turn our attention to its protagonists, the plenipotentiaries.

---

50 Ibid., fol. 151^{r}, Kinsky to Schlik, 25 October 1698.

51 *Taʾrīḫ-i ṣulḥnāme*, fol. 74^{b}.

Interlude III: Being a Plenipotentiary Ambassador

> Nine distinguished ambassadors gathered in this place [Carlowitz] […] handpicked men, each one of them, all wanting to protect [the interests of] their own states.
>
> The unknown author of the so-called *Anonymous Ottoman History*[1]

∴

One could justifiably argue that the protocol of the congress kept by the secretary of the Imperial embassy, Johannes Till, resembles a script of a theatrical play: constantly alternating scenes (conferences); small interludes when the narrator intervenes to comment on the plot directly and the actors' script in the form of dialogue. Every play has its protagonists, however. So, the second page, after the one containing its title and central theme – *Protocollum Actorum in Congressu et Conferentijs Tratactum Pacis* […] – is devoted to them, the *dramatis personae*: 'Nomina DD. Mediatorum & utriusque partis Plenipotentiariorum'.[2] For the Carlowitz contemporaries, thus, there was no doubt who the cardinal actors of the *Théâtre de la Paix* were.

Nonetheless, recent trends in early modern diplomatic history have tended to move away from what they perceived as a 'traditional topic' of 'great personalities', to go 'beyond the ambassador',[3] and to focus instead on somewhat lesser-known characters of diplomacy, like the those we encountered in the previous Narration section.[4] However, as much as such a decentralisation can open up new vistas and highlight the critical role of personalities previously neglected by the historiography, a reconstruction of an early modern peace congress that leaves out a detailed analysis of what it was like to be a plenipotentiary ambassador, would deprive the reader of a crucial element in the understanding of the broader late-seventeenth-century diplomatic culture. Because, not only were persons like Count Schlik, Rāmī Meḥmed or Voznitsyn

1 *Anonim Osmanlı Tarihi*, 135.

2 ÖStA, HHStA, Türkei I, Turcica Box 170, Protocollum, fol. 1.

3 Maurits Ebben and Louis Sicking (eds.), *Beyond Ambassadors. Consuls, Missionaries, and Spies in Premodern Diplomacy* (Leiden/Boston: Brill 2021).

4 Ibid. and Birgit Tremml-Werner and Dorothée Goetze, 'A Multitude of Actors in Early Modern Diplomacy'. *Journal of Early Modern History* 23 (2019), 407–22.

 | DOI:10.1163/9789004458499_014

the undisputed leaders of their respective embassies and the primary negotiators during the conferences, but it is also mainly through their accounts, being those letters or relations, that we gather the majority of information regarding the congress. Hence, they shape our perspective of it catalytically.[5] It is usually thanks to and via them that we even get a glimpse of the lesser yet indispensable actors of the play. And even when we possess an account written by one of those minor actors, it is again the plenipotentiaries, their moves and actions that form the kernel of the narrative.[6]

Besides, far from being historiographically 'exhausted', thanks to the so-called 'New Diplomatic History', the study of the office of the ambassador in the early modern age has acquired a new dynamic over the past twenty years. Instead of focusing on narrating the stories of 'great men', a younger generation of historians, influenced by sociology and cultural anthropology, has begun to focus more on the ambassadors' social environment, their multiple roles and modes of self-presentation/self-fashioning. Such studies have manifested the richness and manifoldness of the 'early modern ambassador phenomenon' and the potential of the topic to reveal much more thrilling insights into the workings of the early modern diplomatic practices in the future.[7] Hence, for all those reasons, our analysis has to pass necessarily through the ambassadors before going beyond them.

We shall start by briefly clarifying the terminology. We will proceed with some general profile characteristics of the Carlowitz ambassadors, followed by a discussion of the most important traits a plenipotentiary should possess according to the congress contemporaries. Then, we will address the essential preparation for the negotiations an ambassador had to go through before the congress before turning our attention to the critical issues of his multiplicity of roles, identities and interests, the symbolic and material capital he would aspire to win from the peace negotiations, his daily life and tasks during the congress as well as his self-presentation and self-portrayal towards the other participants as well as through the dispatches to his principals. Lastly, we will attempt to come up with an answer to the thorny question of how actually plenipotentiary the plenipotentiaries were.

---

5 Köhler, *Strategie und Symbolik*, 121.

6 One of the best examples is the *Narratio*.

7 The bibliographical list is enormous, and we will encounter many vital works in the following pages. Here I should limit myself to one of the most recent contributions: Cristina Bravo Lozano and Antonio Álvares-Ossorio Alvariño (eds.), *Los embajadores. Representantes de la soberanía, garantes del equilibrio, 1659–1748* (Madrid: Marcial Pons Historia 2021).

1 Clarifying the Terms

If we were to find a title with which all the main characters of this interlude could identify themselves, that would undoubtedly be that of the plenipotentiary ambassador or just plenipotentiary. These were terms which, with minor alterations – for example, the Muscovites and the Poles added the word 'great' in front of ambassador – were used by all sides to designate their delegates.[8] In western and central Europe, the title 'plenipotentiary ambassador' combined in the individual bearing it the two principal attributes of a ruler, that of *potestas* and that of *majestas*.[9] Normally, only a delegate with the title of an 'ambassador' (*legatus, ambasciatore, Bottschafter, ministre* etc.) could receive *honores regii*,[10] although that was highly contested for the greater part of the seventeenth century, leading to numerous ceremonial quarrels.[11] In south-eastern and eastern Europe, the rule was that the different 'diplomatic ranks' mirrored the social status of the delegate and the importance of his mission[12] while all of them equally encompassing the *majestas* of the ruler.[13] So, for example, in the Moscovite system, *posly* (plural of *posol*) were first-ranking 'diplomats', but that didn't give them any higher representational character than the second-ranking *poslanniki* (envoys).[14] In the Ottoman case,

---

8 For the evolution of the term 'plenipotentiary' and 'plenipotentiary ambassador' in the western European context, *see* May, *Repräsentation und Statuspolitik*, 58–62. Hitherto there is no detailed study shedding light on the origins and evolution of the Ottoman term *meʾẕūn u muraḫḫaṣ* (or simply *muraḫḫaṣ*), or when it was first associated with an ambassadorial dignity. The earliest reference to the term that I was able to find is in a letter from the Grand Vizier Ḳara Muṣṭafā Paşa to the Governor of Buda, Uzun İbrāḥīm Paşa (d. 1683), possibly dated early 1683. There, the grand vizier declared that if there was an attempt by the Habsburg side to initiate peace negotiations, the governor would engage in them as the plenipotentiary of the Porte (*Devlet-i aliyye tarafindan mükâleme-i sulha murahhas ve me'zûnsuz*): Abdülkadir Şeker, 'Nuruosmaniye Kütüphanesi 4297 numaralı Münşeât Mecmuası (1672–1705) inceleme-metin' (MA dissertation, Kocaeli University 2024) 151. Although İbrāḥīm Paşa would not enter the talks as an ambassador but rather in his capacity as governor, it nonetheless appears that the term has been already established in the last quarter of the seventeenth century to define the extent of authority Ottoman representatives were supposed to possess in peace negotiations as *Stellvertreters* (deputies) of the sultanic power. Unfortunately, I couldn't trace the roots and evolution of the Russian term *polnomochnyi posol* (plenipotentiary ambassador).

9 *See* above, 164, fn. 39.

10 Hennings, *Russia*, 97; May, *Repräsentation und Statuspolitik*, 54–67.

11 Köhler, *Strategie und Symbolik*, 108–9.

12 Something that is held, though, equally true for western and central Europe: *See* ibid.

13 *See* above, Interlude II.

14 Hennings, *Russia*, 102–7.

ėlçi was a generic term employed for all kinds of delegates, and the difference in rank was revealed by the word preceding it.[15]

However, it seems that from the last quarter of the seventeenth century, a move towards a unified cross-cultural 'diplomatic vocabulary' regarded the appellation of the various delegates during peace negotiations was taking place across the European continent, mainly out of the practical exigencies to minimise conflicts over titles before the start of the official negotiations. The 'plenipotentiary ambassador' made its appearance already during the Failed Vienna Congress[16] before being redeployed again at Ryswick[17] and, of course, unanimously during Carlowitz. And although it is still unclear if the Ottoman (*büyük*) *ėlçi* and the Muscovite *posol* had acquired by that time the same representative attributes as the western and central European *ambassadeur*, since no strife concerning the official titles occurred (contrary to 1689), it seems that in 1698, by a 'plenipotentiary ambassador', all participants understood or thought that they understood the same thing.

If the appellation 'ambassador' might have held different connotations for the various late-seventeenth-century contemporaries, that of 'plenipotentiary' would have been crystal-clear to all. By designating its representative(s) as such, each side demonstrated its total commitment to the peace process and its readiness to discuss and resolve all issues in situ with its opponent or opponents. That's why much attention was paid by each party to that particular title during the exchange of their credentials in order, as Rāmī puts it, for a 'perfect trust' (*iʿtimād-i küllī*) to be reached between the two.[18]

15 For instance, *büyük ėlçi* (Great Ambassador, the highest rank), *orṭa ėlçi* (internuncio/ablegate) and *küçük ėlçi* (envoy/ablegate). Yet, at the Ottoman Porte, similarly to the European Christian courts, these three ranks of delegates were expected to be treated differently ceremonially. *See*, for instance, *Cerîde-i Takrirât*, 29–30.

16 Mavrocordatos referred to himself as *minister plenipotentiarius* (*see* above, Prelude), and most of the other participants of the Failed Vienna Congress did the same: Hurmuzaki, *Documente*, vol. 5, part 1, 230–1, 245. And although at the beginning, the Imperial side didn't concede to grant the Ottoman delegation the *honores regii* by simply referring to them as plenipotentiary ablegates (ibid., 239), the situation was clarified after the grand vizier supplied them with full powers where they were clearly designated as *ministri plenipotentiarii*: Ibid., 294.

17 Köhler, *Strategie und Symbolik*, 108–9.

18 *Taʾrīḫ-i ṣulḥnāme*, fol. 75[a]. For the attention paid to the titles found in the full powers, *see* also ÖStA, HHStA, Türkei I, Turcica Box 167, Folder 2 (October 1698, 2nd half), fol. 278[v], Imperial plenipotentiaries to Leopold I, 30 October 1698.

2 The Portraits of the Carlowitz Plenipotentiaries

Let us focus now on a general portrait of the plenipotentiaries, their age, education, social status, and previous experience in negotiations. The average age of the Carlowitz participants was forty-nine, very close to that of other congresses such as Nijmegen (fifty-one years).[19] The Imperial embassy comprised the youngest and the oldest participant, Count Schlik, thirty-five years old in 1698 and Count Öttingen, aged seventy-two. A significant proportion (Rāmī, Ruzzini, Colyer) were in their forties or near forties (Małachowski, aged thirty-nine). As for their education, except for Mavrocordatos, who seems to be the only one who held a doctorate, surprisingly little is known. From the clues we have, though, most of them appear to have possessed a considerable degree of erudition, which either duly received the attention of the other participants or was wittingly or unwittingly demonstrated during the conferences or in the dispatches to their principals.[20]

Coming now to the social background, in the early modern period, the general rule was that an ambassador came from the nobility. The higher his place on the social ladder, the greater the manifestation of a sovereign's disposition towards peace.[21] Carlowitz does not differ from this principle. Paget, Öttingen, Małachowski and Ruzzini were high-ranking nobles in their respective polities, although others like Schlik and Voznitsyn belonged instead to the middle and lower nobility, respectively. On the other hand, representatives of republics, such as the Netherlands, were, in general, not nobles, but they aspired through their participation in a congress to acquire a noble title.[22] The Dutch mediator, Colyer, is quite an illustrative example. Belonging to what one might refer to as the *bourgeoisie*, he rose socially by acquiring a noble title from the emperor after the end of the congress in recompense for his mediating services.[23]

---

19 Köhler, *Strategie und Symbolik*, 123.

20 'Credite me certò folium recitare Sybillae' (Believe me, I'm really reciting [to you] a Leaf of the Sybil) Count Schlik assured Kinsky in one of his letters with this slightly altered verse from Juvenal: ÖStA, HHStA, Türkei I, Turcica Box 169, Folder 2 (December 1698, 2nd half), fol. 42^{v}, Schlik to Kinsky, 14 December 1698. The original verse could be found in Juvenal, *Satires*, ed. and trans. Susanna Morton Braund, Loeb Classical Library, vol. 91 (Cambridge, MA: Harvard University Press 2004) 334.

21 Hillard von Thiessen, 'Diplomatie vom *type ancient*. Überlegungen zu einem Idealtypus des frühneuzeitlichen Gesandtschaftswesen' in Christian Windler and Hillard von Thiessen (eds.), *Akteure der Außenbeziehungen. Netzwerke und Interkulturalität im historischen Wandel* (Cologne/Weimar/Vienna: Böhlau 2010) 488–9; May, *Repräsentation und Statuspolitik*, 127.

22 Thiessen, 'Diplomatie', 495–7; May, *Repräsentation und Statuspolitik*, 157–62.

23 *See* above, Act I, Interlude I.

Nonetheless, at Carlowitz, one of the main participants' social order was not nobility-based. We speak, of course, of the Ottomans. In their case, a plenipotentiary's social standing didn't stem from his family's status – although during the late seventeenth century, that was becoming increasingly debatable – but rather from the office and position he held in the government or palace machinery. Hence, Rāmī Meḥmed's prestige and authority were primarily based on the crucial inside the Ottoman bureaucracy office he was entitled to, that of the *Re'isü'l-küttāb* (the head of scribes).[24] Such different conceptions of prestige and social standing often caused misunderstandings. For instance, during the negotiations, Count Schlik complained that the Ottoman ambassador in Vienna in 1665, after the Treaty of Vasvár, Ḳara Meḥmed Paşa, a *müteferriḳa*,[25] was not equal in social rank with the then Habsburg ambassador Count Leslie. Mavrocordatos replied that 'Müteferriḳa [...] is a very sublime rank.[26] He didn't lack the dignity and this kind of nobility that the sultanas have'.[27] The employment of words such as 'dignity' and 'nobility' to culturally translate a different social reality is very interesting, as is the comparison of the *müteferriḳa*'s social standing to that of the female members of the Ottoman dynasty.

Speaking of Mavrocordatos, his case presents a far greater complexity since it is impregnated by true cultural hybridity. His 'international' standing was

24 For this office, gradually rising in importance from the second half of the seventeenth-century, *see* Abou-E-Haj, 'The Reisülküttab', 31–53 and Recep Ahıshalı, 'Reîsükküttâb', TDVİA, vol. 34 (Istanbul: Turkish Religious Foundation 2007) 546–9, where also the rather meagre bibliography on the subject can be found. A detailed study on the origins of the involvement of the *Re'isü'l-küttāb* with foreign affairs, a path that would lead him to occupy in the eighteenth century the unofficial role of a 'secretary of state', is still a research desideratum.

25 Persons in the service of the sultan, the grand vizier and other magnates: Mehmet Zeki Pakalın, *Tarih Deyimleri ve Terimleri Sözlüğü*, vol. 2 (İstanbul: Devlet Kitapları 1971) 637–8.

26 Ahead of the embassy, Meḥmed Ağa was granted' the honorific title of *Beylerbey* (Governor) of Rumelia and thus the rank of pasha to increase his social status: Güneş Işıksel, "Yirmisekiz Çelebi Mehmed Fransa'da: Güzergâh, Toplumsal Algı, Diplomatik Pratikler ve de 'Lale Devri'". *Doğu Batı Düşünce Dergisi* 85 (2018), 110. Such an elevation of dignity through honorary offices was a common Ottoman practice. Narrating the dispatching of a certain Meḥmed Bey, a *defter emīni* (a high-ranking financial branch bureaucrat) as ambassador to the Persian Shah around the time of the Carlowitz treaties, Defterdār Sarı Meḥmed Paşa stated that he was also given the same title of *Beylerbey* of Rumelia 'to make evident his esteem and honour when he reached the land of the Persians': Defterdar, *Zübde-i Vekayiât*, 637.

27 ÖStA, HHStA, Türkei I, Turcica Box 170, Protocollum, fol. 91. For the Great Embassy of Meḥmed Paşa *see* the detailed recent study of Özgür Kolçak, 'Bir Sefaret Hikâyesi (1665–1666): Kara Mehmed Paşa, Viyana Günleri, Elçilik Heyeti ve Sefaretnamesi'. *Osmanlı Araştırmaları / The Journal of Ottoman Studies* 65 (2025), 95–149.

primarily based on the position of the Chief Interpreter he held at the Porte. Nonetheless, in the Ottoman domestic sphere, Muslim and Greek Orthodox alike, he was already recognised as an informal 'aristocrat'. A dignity primarily expressed via the suffix *-zāde* (of noble lineage) attached to his Ottoman 'surname', *İskerletzāde* (the noble descendant of Skarlatos),[28] as via the Greek word κυρίτζης. The latter constitutes a variation of κύριος (κυρ), lord, which since the Middle Ages has been applied to designate noble or high-ranking government individuals.[29] It also corresponded to the Ottoman title *çelebi* – a title usually attributed to learned individuals and scribes – encountered as an appellation for the Greek Orthodox members of the Ottoman Chancery since the fifteenth century.[30]

Mavrocordatos's participation in the congress provided him with a further chance to raise his social position. He acquired for the occasion the ad hoc title, never used before and specially designed for him, of the 'Confidant of the Exalted State' (*Maḥrem-ı esrār-ı Devlet-ı ʿAliyye*).[31] As Dimitri Cantemir narrates, after the acquisition of this new rank, Mavrocordatos demanded that the Princes of Wallachia and Moldavia address him in their letters, not as 'Your Excellency' (*Excellentissimus*), which was the case up to this point, but as the 'most Illustrious' (*Illustrissimus*), "because this appellation [Excellency] was not accompanied with much honour at the courts of those princes and the

28 Skarlatos was the name of his maternal grandfather. The latter, far from being a 'nobleman', was instead a very rich merchant, acquiring his fame and wealth by supplying the Ottoman Court with cattle: Nestor Camariano. *Alexandre Mavrocordato, le grand drogman: son activité diplomatique, 1673–1709* (Thessaloniki: Institute for Balkan Studies 1970) 9–12.

29 Mavrocordatos's appellation in the official Ottoman documents was 'the chiefest among the notables of the Christian nation, lord Alexandros of the noble lineage of Scarlatos' (*ḳıdvet-i ʿuẓamā-ı āʿyānü'l-milletü'l-mesīḥiyye İskerletzāde Kirici Alekisandire*): *Taʾrīḥ-i ṣulḥnāme*, 39ᵃ. For the title *κυρ* in the Byzantine period, *see* Anastasia Kontogiannopoulou, 'Η προσηγορία *κυρ* στη Βυζαντινή Κοινωνία'. *Βυζαντινά* 32 (2012), 209–26.

30 Julian Raby, 'Mehmed the Conqueror's Greek Scriptorium'. *Dumbarton Oaks Papers* 37 (1983), 25, fn. 55.

31 *Taʾrīḥ-i ṣulḥnāme*, fol. 39ᵃ; For this particular title, *see* Cantemir, *Incrementorum et Decrementorum*, 506. In the full powers of the Imperial delegation, it was translated as 'intimate secretary' (*secretarium intimum*): ÖStA, HHStA, Türkei I, Turcica Box 168, Folder 2 (November 1698, 2nd half), fol. 31ᵛ. A similar case to that of Mavrocordatos is Voznitsyn. Shortly after his appointment as head of the Carlowitz embassy, he was granted the title of 'Duma Counsellor' (*Dumnogo sovetnika*). As with Mavrocordatos, this title was created ad hoc to elevate his status and enhance respect for his position: Bogoslovskii, *Petr I*, 389. However, promotions and the acquisition of new titles before diplomatic congresses were a broader phenomenon. For further discussion, *see* Köhler, *Strategie und Symbolik*, 127–8.

[Orthodox] Patriarchate as the one of the 'most Illustrious'".[32] Having thus achieved recognition of his 'noble' claims inside the Ottoman Dominions, Mavrocordatos went one step further and used his new 'confidant' dignity to impose his aspirations for social status beyond them.

It was a gradual process. For instance, in the curriculum vitae he himself wrote in 1689 for his admission to the Imperial *Academia Leopoldina* in Vienna, he didn't fail to mention that he was born from 'illustrious parents' (*ab Illustribus Parentibus*), adding the crucial detail that his mother Roxandra was first married to a Prince of Wallachia and Moldavia.[33] By 1698, with his new ambassadorial commission, he became even bolder. He deliberately started translating in the official diplomatic documents his Ottoman 'surname', *İskerletzāde*, as 'of the noble lineage of Scarlatos' (*de nobili stirpe Scarlati*), projecting thus his unofficial Ottoman social status to a European level.[34] This 'self-ennoblement', which did not pass unnoticed by the Imperial side, looks as if it was tacitly accepted, at least by the latter, since in the full powers bestowed to its two ambassadors at Carlowitz, Mavrocordatos is also referred to as *Alexandrum ex nobili stirpe de scarlatis*.[35]

Most of the early modern ambassadors were not what, today, one would call carrier diplomats. They would usually hold other offices in their respective polity's administration, court or army and acquire their appointment as plenipotentiaries mainly through patronage relations with the ruler or one of his principal ministers. Their experience in diplomatic affairs would be gained usually in practice.[36] Count Schlik and Öttingen, as well as Rāmī Meḥmed, fall into this category of 'diplomacy novices', with little prior experience in negotiations. According to Ruzzini, Count Schlik owed his position mostly 'to the friendship and connection with Kinsky'[37] while Count Öttingen was chosen because, apparently, no one else wanted to volunteer for the job.[38] The choice

32 Cantemir, *Incrementorum et Decrementorum*, 506.

33 *See* above, Prelude.

34 BNM, Ms.it.VII 399(8625), fol. 124^r copy of the official translation in Latin of the full powers of the Ottoman delegation.

35 ÖStA, HHStA, Türkei I, Turcica Box 168, Folder 2 (November 1698, 2nd half), fol. 31^v. After receiving the Ottoman plenipotentiaries' full-power credentials, the Imperial ambassadors duly noticed in Mavrocordatos's title 'the insertion of the family name' (*cum insertione familia*): ÖStA, HHStA, Türkei I, Turcica Box 167, Folder 2 (October 1698, 2nd half), fol. 278^v, Imperial plenipotentiaries to Leopold I, 30 October 1698.

36 Thiessen, 'Diplomatie', 487–8, 491–2.

37 Ruzzini, *Relazione*, 377. For the patronage relation between Kinsky and Schlik *see* more below.

38 Ibid.

of Rāmī was not irrelevant to his close relations with the grand vizier. Marsigli speaks of him – and Mavrocordatos – as the 'beloved creatures' (*care creature*) of 'Amcazāde.[39]

Still, 'seasoned diplomats' who were dedicating their entire careers to matters related to negotiations or who had considerable prior experience in them were not in short supply either. Notable examples of the first category are Alexandros Mavrocordatos – the only ambassador who had participated in all previous peace talks during the Sixteen-Years' War –, the Moscovite Prokopii Voznitsyn, formed since his early years in the famous 'Ambassadorial Chancery' (*Posol'skii prikaz*),[40] and the Dutch Jacob Colyer, who acquired from his father the position of Resident of the Dutch Republic at the Ottoman Porte at the age of twenty-five.[41] In the second category, one might include Lord Paget and Carlo Ruzzini, both of whom had served for many years as resident ambassadors at various major royal courts (notably the Imperial, the Ottoman and the Spanish). As we shall also see, the lack of negotiating experience was becoming reproachable in the eyes of some congress participants.

Finally, one could not avoid touching upon the linguistic capabilities of the Carlowitz plenipotentiaries. Almost all the ambassadors were multilingual, possessing knowledge of at least three foreign languages apart from their maternal ones.[42] The only exception was Voznitsyn, who 'doesn't speak another language than his native [tongue] – which has a great correlation with the Illyrian [Serbo-Croatian] – and always had the interpreter by his side'.[43] Most widespread was the knowledge of Italian and Latin, both languages thus constituting the primary communication vehicle of the peace talks. So, despite established scholarly opinion which sustains – based on a certain geographical region and examples – that by the late seventeenth century, French had entirely replaced Italian and Latin as the principal linguistic means of

39 ÖStA, HHStA, Türkei I, Turcica Box 168, Folder 1 (November 1698, 1st half), fol. 236r, Marsigli to Kinsky, s.d. (probably early November 1698).

40 Bogoslovskii, *Petr I*, 342–3.

41 Hora Siccama, 'De Vrede van Carlowitz', 43–4.

42 *Narratio conventus caraloviciani*, fol. 11r–14r. Multilingualism was a common trait amongst early modern ambassadors : Guido Braun, 'Les problèmes de communication aux congrès internationaux. De Westphalie à Ryswick (1643–1697)' in Dejanirah Couto and Stéphane Péquignot (eds.), *Les langues de la négociation. Approches historiennes* (Rennes: Presses Universitaires de Rennes 2017) 193–9.

43 *Narratio*, fol. 14r.

diplomatic negotiations,[44] the Congress of Carlowitz attests that such a thesis is in serious need of review.[45]

3 The Supra-cultural Traits of an Ambassador

If we were to look for the expected, normative qualities of a plenipotentiary at the twilight of the seventeenth century, the best place to start, apart from the treatises on the 'ideal ambassador'[46] would be their nomination documents. Let us take, for instance, the Imperial side. In his appointment decree of Count Öttingen as plenipotentiary ambassador, Emperor Leopold I justifies the latter's selection because 'of the special most gracious trust [We] bear towards him, and in consideration of his good qualities, experience, and the proven loyalty, zeal and dexterity [he showed] in various Imperial commissions he was previously assigned'.[47] As for Count Schlik, the second Imperial plenipotentiary, his choice was based on 'his good prudence (sic), known experience, excellent qualities and skills'.[48]

How about the Ottoman side? 'Our appointed ambassadors', 'Amcazāde mentioned in his farewell speech to the two mediators, "are prudent, temperate and in [perfect] knowledge of [how to accomplish] the matter in congruence with the Exalted State's honour".[49] In addition, a careful search in Ottoman texts contemporary to the Carlowitz Congress for traits associated with an

44 *See*, for instance, Guido Braun, 'Französisch und Italienisch als Sprachen der Diplomatie auf dem Westfälischen Friedenskongress', in Annette Gerstenberg (ed.), *Verständigung und Diplomatie auf dem Westfälischen Friendenskongress. Historische und sprachwissenschaftliche Zugänge* (Cologne/Weimar/ Vienna: Böhlau 2014) 23–4.

45 Johannes Burkhardt has already shown, using also Carlowitz as one of his primary examples, that the dominant languages of negotiations in south-eastern and eastern Europe followed a different trajectory from the ones in the western part of the continent: Johannes Burkhardt, 'Sprachen des Friedens und was sie verraten. Neue Fragen und Einsichten zu Karlowitz, Baden und „Neustadt"', in Stefan Ehrenpreis et al. (eds.), *Wege der Neuzeit: Festschrift für Heinz Schilling zum 65. Geburtstag* (Berlin: Duncker & Humblot 2007) 503–19.

46 Heidrun R.I. Kugeler, "'Le Parfait Ambassadeur'. The Theory and Practice of Diplomacy in the Century following the Peace of Westphalia" (Ph.D. thesis, University of Oxford 2006).

47 ÖStA, HHStA, Türkei I, Turcica Box 166, Folder 2 (September 1698, 1st half), fol. 35^{r}, Imperial decree, 3 September 1698.

48 Ibid., fol. 31^{r}, Imperial decree, 3 September 1698.

49 *Taʾrīḫ-i ṣulḥ-nāme*, fol. 68^{a}.

ambassador results in words such as *mu'teber* (esteemed)[50] – and its synonym *müte'ayyin*,[51] *mu'temed* (trustworthy)[52] or *müntaḫab* (hand-picked).[53] Thus qualities such as prudence, trust, experience and esteem appear to form a shared picture of what *le parfait ambassadeur* should be. But let's more closely examine some of these commonly shared traits, commencing with the ambassador's experience.

Mavrocordatos's long career in negotiations caught the attention of Ruzzini. 'Because of the long exercise he sustained as an interpreter of the Porte, he possesses enough fame, the portrait of his qualities being displayed before the eyes of the world [...] equipped with experience from the various negotiations he directed'.[54] It was not the same for Count Öttingen, whom the Venetian doesn't seem to have held in high esteem. 'Versed in the affairs of the Empire due to the presidency of the Aulic Council, which he has hold for a long time, but not equally instructed in the other affairs of the world, neither having been trained in commissions outside the court nor even inside, in the most important ones of the ministry'.[55] Ruzzini's comments are particularly significant as they reveal a broader rethinking of the ambassadorial office. This shift, also reflected in late seventeenth-century treatises on the 'ideal ambassador', increasingly emphasised the importance of having more 'professional' ambassadors or negotiators with prior field experience.[56] However, again, as the Venetian plenipotentiary's remarks on his Imperial colleague attest, we are still a long way from a truly professional diplomatic corps.

Another significant attribute of an 'ideal ambassador' continued to be erudition. According to the bureaucrat-cum-historian Muṣṭafā Na'īmā, Rāmī Meḥmed was 'cognizant of the good qualities of the subtle points of the Holy Law and philosophical knowledge and was versed in affirming the certitude of the Muslim tenets'.[57] Ruzzini concorded with the Ottoman historian. To him, Rāmī was 'adorned with [...] information and knowledge superior to the [normal] talent and custom of the Turks'.[58] One of the cardinal marks of eru-

50 Ibid., fol. 50ᵃ; *Cerîde-i Takrirât*, 5.
51 *Anonim Osmanlı Tarihi*, 135.
52 *Ta'rīḫ-i ṣulḥ-nāme*, fol. 39ᵃ, 50ᵃ.
53 *Anonim Osmanlı Tarihi*, 135.
54 Ruzzini, *Relazione*, 376.
55 Ibid., 377. Schlik is equally portrayed by the Venetian as lacking expertise in 'political negotiations' (*maneggi politici*): Ibid.
56 Kugeler, "'Le Parfait Ambassadeur'", 75–7.
57 *Târih-i Na'îmâ*, 47.
58 Ruzzini, *Relazione*, 376.

dition was multilingualism. Combined with more practical needs, the ability to discuss directly with one's interlocutors without interpreters was deemed a vital quality for a plenipotentiary.[59] The Anonymous Venetian indirectly reproached Voznitsyn's complete lack of such a skill.[60] In contrast, Rāmī's knowledge of foreign languages, even 'barbaric' ones, Arabic and Persian, was considered praiseworthy.[61]

Another trait closely related to the command of language(s) was that of eloquence. Despite the scholarly view that by the late seventeenth century, the principal renaissance trait of the ambassador as an orator was receding, an examination of the archival material for the Congress of Carlowitz reveals that eloquence continued to be supra-culturally regarded as a chief attribute for a plenipotentiary although one that shouldn't be used in excess. Besides, convincing one's interlocutor with rational arguments formed one of the major normative expectations of the participants of early modern congresses.[62]

Possessing sublime oratory and persuasion capabilities appears to constitute one of the foremost qualities of an ambassador in the Ottoman mind. Muṣṭafā Naʿīmā described Rāmī Meḥmed, among his other qualities, as 'full of the knowledge of the subtleties of language' (*belîğ-i nüktedân*).[63] Rāmī would try to vindicate such laudatory remarks in his narration of the conferences, a true example of post-factum reconstructed speeches[64] aimed to highlight the strength of the Ottoman arguments and the rhetorical prowess of their composer.[65] However, the Ottomans not only appreciated eloquence among themselves, but they also praised it even when it was encountered among their opponents. Małachowski's rhetorical skills seem to have significantly impressed Rāmī Meḥmed. As he wrote about the Pole, 'he was distinguished among his contemporaries, and a man very competent in arguing, possessing the power of eloquence'.[66]

---

59 Braun, 'Les problèmes de communication', 193–9.

60 *See* above.

61 *Narratio*, fol. 11ʳ.

62 Köhler, 'Argumentieren und Verhandeln', 526–8.

63 *Târih-i Na'imâ*, 47.

64 Compared with the protocols kept by other embassies, it is highly probable that the speeches in Rāmī's account are a reworked version of the protocol kept by the secretary of the Ottoman embassy.

65 A perfect example can be found in *Ta'rīḫ-i ṣulḥ-nāme*, fol. 121ᵃ–122ᵇ, where, after a long oration, the Ottoman plenipotentiaries managed – so the text implies – to convince the Imperial delegation of the justice of their claims and the fallacy of the Venetian positions.

66 Ibid., fol. 102ᵃ.

The plenipotentiaries strove hard to manifest such an oratory power during the conferences. The first occasion was presented in the opening speeches, which closely resembled the solemn address ambassadors usually made during their first audience with the potentate of the court they were sent to for their mission.[67] Nonetheless, it was during the actual negotiations, where the main aim was to win the best-argumentation contest with one's opponent, that the command of rhetoric was needed the most. As Count Schlik recorded in his congress journal on the second Ottoman–Imperial meeting, 'Mister Mavrocordatos made an effort this time to show off his eloquence',[68] only to be effectively 'silenced' though by the 'powerful counterarguments' (*mit knäfftigen gegen Argumenten*) supposedly employed by Schlik.[69] A telling and simultaneously diverting example of the endeavour of the ambassadors to outwit one another rhetorically is encountered in the protocol of the meetings kept by the mediation. On 4 December 1698, there was a conference between the Ottoman and Commonwealth delegations. The main topic of discussion revolved around the question of whether the fortress of Kamianets-Podilskyi would be delivered to the Polish-Lithuanian side empty, without its cannons (the Ottoman position) or precisely in its current state (the Commonwealth position):

> MAVROCORDATOS: When one takes a mistress, he doesn't care how she is [like], but he is satisfied to have her.
>
> MAŁACHOWSKI: The Grand Seigneur wouldn't want to leave her to go naked and ripped. It is up to the honour of the Grand Seigneur to hand her over beautifully ornamented.[70]

No wonder, thus, why Rāmī praised the Pole for his argumentative capabilities. However, the attempt by some plenipotentiaries to display their rhetorical prowess could sometimes be considered by others as detrimental to their negotiation. While narrating to Count Kinsky the events of the first Ottoman–Venetian conference, Schlik remarked that,

---

67 *See*, for example, the first conference between the Ottomans and the Muscovites, which opened with prolix orations by both sides: Bogoslovskii *Petr I*, 395.

68 ÖStA, HHStA, Türkei I, Turcica Box 170, Diarium et Cerimoniale, fol. 33.

69 Ibid. Schlik also claimed that the Imperial embassy's argumentation force was so great that it led the 'Efendi' to leave the conference tent in distress with the excuse to perform his prayers.

70 Paul Cernovodeanu, 'Le journal des travaux du Congrès de Karlowitz'. *Revue des Études Sub- Est Européennes* 19/2 (1981), 336.

> I have strongly begged monsieur the ambassador [Ruzzini] before going to [his] first conference to not enter into any verbosity in [his] discourses [...]. Still, the torrent of his eloquence had carried him away, and with Mavrocordatos also heating up, they quarrelled so fiercely that [in the end] neither the one side nor the other know exactly about.[71]

What feelings Ruzzini's 'logorrhea' could sometimes produce to his interlocutors is perfectly encapsulated in one of Rāmī's remarks. The ever-eloquence-praising Ottoman claims that in one conference with the Venetian, the latter 'extended every speech of his for half an hour. He would cause exhaustion'.[72] To avoid such prolixity fatigue, on other occasions, the ambassadors had to agree from the beginning to cut out superfluous speeches and negotiate to the point with fewer but more precise words.[73]

4 Crash-Courses for Newly Appointed Plenipotentiaries

Although the late seventeenth-century plenipotentiary was normally not a professional negotiator, he needed to prepare for the talks by acquiring essential knowledge that would help him to successfully fulfil his mission. This meant that throughout the journey to the congress venue and before the start of the official conferences, he had to undertake 'crash courses' on several issues, especially those related to border arrangements. For instance, writing to Kinsky on the road to the frontier, Marsigli informed him of the lessons he was delivering to Count Öttingen 'on the so important issue of the borders'.[74] Apparently, they both considered the President of the Aulic Council (and Count Schlik to a lesser extent) to be a total imbecile on the subject.[75] However, Marsigli was happy for Kinsky's 'consolation' to report some progress. 'I find him [Öttingen] increasingly capable in this so vast a matter, where everything is new [to him]'.[76] There appear to be limits to the knowledge on border-making that a plenipotentiary should profess, though. Commenting on Ruzzini's insistence

71 ÖStA, HHStA, Türkei I, Turcica Box 168, Folder 2 (November 1698, 1st half), fol. 164^{v}–165^{r}, Schlik to Kinsky, 23 November 1698.

72 *Ta'rīḫ-i ṣulḥ-nāme*, fol. 124^{a}.

73 Bogoslovskii, *Petr I*, 399.

74 ÖStA, HHStA, Türkei I, Turcica Box 168, Folder 1 (November 1698, 1st half), fol. 233^{v}–234^{r}, Marsigli to Kinsky, 23 September 1698.

75 *See* Kinsky's derogatory comments about Öttigen and Schlik on the issue of borders, as reported by Marsigli in Molnár, 'Luigi Ferdinando Marsigli', 151.

76 Marsigli to Kinsky, 23 September 1698, fol. 233^{v}–234^{r}.

in arranging all border issues at the congress and not resorting to special commissaries for this work afterwards, Count Schlik noted that the Venetian wanted 'to oblige the Efendi and his companion to learn to distinguish, by themselves, mountains, fountains and roads with names that make them laugh'.[77]

Besides border-related issues, some of the most important documents a plenipotentiary needed to consider before the commencement of a congress were those of past treaties. First and foremost, the emperor instructed his ambassadors to carefully study all the previous seventeenth-century Habsburg–Ottoman peace agreements, documents related to the former negotiations to end the war back in 1691, and all the important ones produced during the talks' preliminary phase.[78] Similarly, Rāmī Meḥmed states in his relation that during their journey to the frontier, the Ottoman plenipotentiaries 'restricted themselves to acquiring a perfect knowledge of the terms of the past peace treaties'.[79]

Apart from the clear indication such a practice provides for supporting an argument of a positivist construction of a 'law of nations' through precedent, its main aim was to acquaint the plenipotentiary with the main subjects of his negotiation and provide him with the necessary arguments that he would later use during the conferences to back his proposals. To support its claim in favour of the return of the Principality of Transylvania to its status ante bellum, the Ottoman delegation referred to a similar clause found in the Ottoman–Imperial Treaty of Vasvár (1664).[80] Similarly, when the Imperial embassy proposed that a 'desert', a no-man's-land, be established between the rivers Bega and Tisza to avoid mutual incursion in the territories of the two

77 ÖStA, HHStA, Türkei I, Turcica Box 168, Folder 2 (November 1698, 2nd half), fol. 166^{v}–167^{r}, Schlik to Kinsky, 23 November 1698.

78 "Deinde pro Legatorum Nrorum informatione et directione adjungi iussimus [...] # 2do aliquot Tractatus pacis: nempe Sitvatorokiensem, Viennensem, Comariensem, Thyarmathiensem, Szoniensem et postremum de anno 1664 cum Turcis olim initos. Sub # 3^{tio} instructionem anno 1691 dicto Legato Aglico de Paget circa hoc negotium traditam una cum propositionibus et declarationibus ultrò citroque factis [...] et sub 4to, ea omnia qua hoc anno tam ex Turcia huc allata, quam illuc missa atque hoc in negotio actitata sunt": ÖStA, HHStA, Türkei I, Turcica Box 166, Folder 3 (September 1698, 2nd half), fol. 140^{r}, Instructio pro Legatis Plenipotentiarijs Caes[are]is.

79 *Ta'rīḫ-i ṣulḥ-nāme*, fol. 49^{a}. Studying previous agreements appears to be a quite established task for an Ottoman negotiator in the second half of the seventeenth century. For instance, during the peace overtures taking place in 1684–5, the *Ser'asker* (commander in chief) of the Ottoman forces in Hungary Şeytān İbrāhīm Paşa (d. 1685), requested the central administration to dispatch to him copies of the past treaties with the Holy Roman Emperor and the Polish-Lithuanian Commonwealth in order to consult them for the then ongoing peace talks: Poulios, 'Αναζητώντας την ειρήνη', 19.

80 *Ta'rīḫ-i ṣulḥ-nāme*, fol. 76^{b}.

empires, they referred to similar terms from older treaties which the Ottomans had signed with the Safavids and the Polish-Lithuanian Commonwealth.[81] Locating those arguments required a detailed examination of the documents and sufficient preparation in advance, which would have kept the plenipotentiaries occupied for many hours as they were travelling to the congress venue.

5 The Various Social Roles of an Early Modern Ambassador

The latest research paradigm on the early modern ambassador tends to perceive him not as a mere instrument in the service of his principal but as a person embodying in himself a variety of roles in the *ancien régime* society; someone who, through the defence of his principal's interests was trying to advance in parallel (or sometimes mainly) his own. He was a link in a greater chain of patronage, a 'give me to give you' relationship, in which he acted both as the 'patronee' – so to say – of a ruler or minister and as patron of his own family and clan.[82] As Matthias Köhler deftly presented it, in the office of the early modern ambassador, there was a constant interplay between macropolitical (the principal's) and micropolitical (the ambassador's) aims and resources, which often, yet not always, complemented one another.[83] To this multiplicity of roles and interests, one should also add yet another, that of identities.

A perfect example of patronage relations between a plenipotentiary and an influential court figure is that of Count Schlik. We have already seen how, according to Ruzzini, the latter secured his nomination as Imperial ambassador to the peace congress primarily thanks to Kinsky's protection. It was also not accidental that both originated from Bohemia, so the Bohemian Chancellor clearly regarded Schlik as 'his own creature' to paraphrase Marsigli's statement for the Ottoman plenipotentiaries. The Imperial ambassador, showing his gratitude (or flattery) towards his patron, even went so far as to call him 'my Lord' (*Monseigneur*) in his first letter from Futog, near the congress venue, a title generally reserved for royalty.[84] Nonetheless, such a frank manifestation of a patron-client relationship was perhaps deemed by the Imperial minister as too risky, so in his reply, he thought it imperative to advise the plenipotentiary 'not to call me "my Lord" because this is a title that doesn't pertain to

81 ÖStA, HHStA, Türkei I, Turcica Box 170, Protocollum, fol. 30.

82 Thiessen, 'Diplomatie', 476–7, 483–7, 492–3; Köhler, *Strategie und Symbolik*, 177–238.

83 Ibid., 213–31.

84 ÖStA, HHStA, Türkei I, Turcica Box 167, Folder 2 (October 1698, 2nd half), fol. 62^{v}, Schlik to Kinsky, 18 October 1698.

me'.[85] Nevertheless, he instructed Schlik to send him special notes, enclosed in his letters, which were only for the minister's eyes.[86] Thus, he seems to have worked not only for the emperor's interests but for Kinsky's as well.

All the same, the benefits of this patronage were not unilateral. In a letter to Kinsky written on 10 December 1698, Schlik thanked the Bohemian Chancellor for arranging for his sister to be admitted as a lady-in-waiting in the empress's suite.[87] It was after the termination of the congress, though, that the Imperial plenipotentiary needed Kinsky's protection the most. In one of his last letters from Carlowitz, Schlik didn't forget to discuss his future with his patron.

> After speaking of others, Your Excellency will permit me to discuss myself as well. It is beyond doubt that in this calm brought by peace, a reduction of troops is to be considered. I beg Your Excellency, after having favoured me, to protect me again from this evil and declare yourself my protector on this issue. You can do it without considering it an infraction of justice because, as of seniority, I have more than twelve [years] behind me [...], and it is eight years now that I am a general.[88]

One could only imagine Schlik's desperation when his patron died less than a month after those lines were written. He appears to have invested his future in more than one protector, however, and luckily for him, peace in the Imperial dominions would not last long. In 1701, the War of the Spanish Succession began. A war during which Schlik would further rise in the Imperial military hierarchy and would ultimately succeed in occupying the same office as his erstwhile benefactor, that of the Chancellor of Bohemia.

No one exemplifies better the multiplicity of roles, interests, and especially identities, and the potential conflict between them, than Alexandros Mavrocordatos, a Christian in the service of a Muslim ruler, trying to secure advantages for the latter against his coreligionists. His unique and unprecedented position did not remain unnoticed by the congress participants.[89] Mavrocordatos was well aware of this apparent contradiction and even appeared tormented by it, as a letter to an unknown recipient in the summer of 1698, after he was appointed Ottoman plenipotentiary to the peace

85 Ibid., fol.150^{r}, Kinsky to Schlik, 25 October 1698.

86 Ibid., fol. 150^{r-v}.

87 ÖStA, HHStA, Türkei I, Turcica Box 169, Folder 2 (December 1698, 2nd half), fol. 119^{r}–120^{r}, Schlik to Kinsky, 10 December 1698.

88 ÖStA, HHStA, Türkei I, Turcica Box 171, Folder 2 (January 1699, 2nd half), fol. 246^{v}–247^{v}, Schlik to Kinsky, 31 January 1699.

89 For instance, *Narratio*, fol. 11^{v}.

congress, suggests. The unspecified addressee had seemingly sent a letter to the Ottoman Grand Dragoman to congratulate him on his nomination. The Ottoman stateman's response went as follows:

> And you truly, friend, by making known to me through letters your delight and rejoicing on the honour given to me by the potentate [the sultan][90] and the happiness this caused to your heart, you indeed present it as something of a great favour towards me. And yet, I am totally anxious and immersed in dread and fear. And whereas, ostensibly, I am meticulously trying to handle well the office given to me, I fear if misled by the zeal towards the potentate, I will go against God, or, due to my devotion to the Lord in Heaven, I will neglect in something the will of the [mundane] lord, provoking [thus] his wrath towards me. Since, in my experience, most of the public offices in polities are precipitous. And even more so, when someone is driven to work for foreigners, he stands in grave danger. Hence, because of all these [thoughts], I am entirely pervaded with fright and fear, and it is not letters of congratulation but rather the prayers of my friends that I [currently] deserve.[91]

This letter is only ostensibly revealing, as perhaps its writer wished it to be. As its recipient is unknown,[92] one cannot ascertain his relationship with Mavrocordatos and, thus, how sincerely the latter disclosed his inner feelings to him.[93] But instead of embarking on a futile research quest to uncover the grand dragoman's genuine thoughts, it would be better to view his seemingly conflicting identities not as opposing but rather as complementing one another to achieve a single end: the defence and advancement of Mavrocordatos's own interests and those of his family.[94]

This crucial element did not remain hidden from his collocutors at the congress. 'I discovered', Count Marsigli reported in a letter to Kinsky about the Wallachian issues, 'that Mavrocordatos aspires in recompense for this embassy

---

90 In Greek texts of the early modern period, the Ottoman Sultan is often called the 'potentate' (ὁ κρατῶν), and the Ottomans, in general, the 'potentates' (οἱ κρατοῦντες).

91 Livadas, *Μαυροκορδάτου Ἐπιστολαί*, 95.

92 We only learn that it was sent from Sofia, where the Ottoman plenipotentiaries, the grand vizier and the mediators, were camping on their way to the frontier.

93 Mavrocordatos faced criticism by some of his contemporary Greek Orthodox literati for his position inside the Ottoman administration: Saracino and Makrides, 'Die Aufnahme', 53, fn. 50.

94 For a similar view regarding the successful accommodation by Mavrocordatos of his different identities and roles, *see* ibid., 41–2, 63–4.

to the Princedom of Wallachia'.[95] The same assertion is repeated by Ruzzini in his *Relazione Finale*, adding that the Ottoman *Maḥrem-i Esrār* desired, through successful negotiation, to advance both his position in the Ottoman establishment and that of his sons.[96] Finally, paying particular attention to the recent titles acquired by Mavrocordatos and the insertion of his family name, the Imperial plenipotentiaries judged that 'he seems very eager to rise much more'.[97]

Perhaps the best illustration of the Ottoman ambassador's harmonisation of identities and their effective use as negotiation strategies is given by his relationship with Voznitsyn, with whom he shared bonds of religion and friendship. During a difficult moment in the Ottoman–Muscovite peace talks, he tried to coerce the tsar's plenipotentiary to accept a peace treaty by sending him his priest. The latter told the Muscovite that Mavrocordatos was in great distress because if there were no treaty between the sultan and the tsar, the Ottomans would persecute the Orthodox under their rule and in their anger, they would execute the patriarch and other high-ranking members of the Orthodox clergy, holding them responsible for the failure of the peace negotiations. No one could verify the validity of such claims. Still, this message seems to have struck a chord in Voznitsyn's heart since he resumed his negotiations with the Ottomans the next day.[98] On other occasions, he provided the Muscovite with 'confidential' information that ultimately served not only the Muscovite but also the Ottoman interests.[99]

Finally, yet importantly, one should not forget when discussing Mavrocordatos his double role as both a diplomat and a renowned scholar.[100] Once more, it

95 ÖStA, HHStA, Türkei I, Turcica Box 168, Folder 1 (November 1698, 1st half), fol. 47ʳ, Marsigli to Kinsky, 5 November 1698. For those aspirations of the Greek-Orthodox Ottoman diplomat, *see* Tudor Dinu, 'Ο Αλέξανδρος Μαυροκορδάτος κατορθώνοντας να δημιουργήσει μία οικεία δυναστεία στις Ρουμανικές Χώρες', in N. Mavrelos et al. (eds.) *Ο Πρώιμος Διαφωτισμός στην Εποχή των Πρώτων Μαυροκορδάτων. Αλέξανδρος ο Εξ Απορρήτων και Νικόλαος* (Athens: Gutenberg 2021) 335–46.

96 Ruzzini, *Relazione*, 376. Verily, his son Nicholas would first succeed him in the office of the grand dragoman, and in 1709, a few days after Mavrocordatos's death, he would rise to the princely seat of Moldavia. Members of the Mavrocordatos family would continue to be nominated at the head of the Danubian Principalities until the end of the eighteenth century: Dinu, 'Ο Αλέξανδρος Μαυροκορδάτος'.

97 ÖStA, HHStA, Türkei I, Turcica Box 167, Folder 2 (October 1698, 2nd half), fol. 278ᵛ, Imperial plenipotentiaries to Leopold I, 30 October 1698.

98 Bogoslovskii, *Petr I* 403–4.

99 Ibid., 409.

100 The epitome of this double self-fashioning is the curriculum vitae he submitted for his admission in the *Leopoldina*: *See* Prelude.

becomes clear that the Greek-Orthodox Ottoman statesman managed to combine them effectively, profiting on the one hand from his diplomatic missions to advance his position in the *Respublica Litteraria* while using, on the other, his scholarly acquaintances as a means to facilitate the negotiations. Concerning the second, we have already seen how the professional and academic association with Petr Postnikov or Israel Conegliano played a vital role in the secret dealings during the first phase of the congress. On the first, though, the best example is Mavrocordatos's efforts and ultimate success in being admitted to the Imperial *Academia Leopoldina* in 1689, during his embassy in Vienna (1688–92).[101] And although his admission may not have been devoid of ulterior motives by the Imperial side, namely, to win him over by honouring him in this way, it constituted a unique networking opportunity and a massive recognition for Mavrocordatos, the scholar.[102]

6 Striving for Partaking in the Glory of Peace

In his 'Ode to Peace' (*Ḳaṣide-i ṣulḥiyye*), celebrating the Carlowitz treaties and their – as the author perceives it – chief architect, the Grand Vizier ʿAmcazāde Ḥüseyin Paşa, the famous Ottoman poet Yūsuf Nābī (d. 1712) would claim for his patron that 'with your world-encapturing measures, peace and tranquillity prevailed/ in the land of the Infidels, that of the Muslims and that of the Persians'.[103] Twenty years earlier, in 1679, a medal for Louis XIV celebrated in astonishingly similar lines the arbitration of the *Roi Soleil* in the conflicts of northern Europe. 'Le Roy […] qui imposa des lois à ces Princes dans le fond du Nord pour devenir pacificateur du Monde'.[104] These examples, drawn from two completely different poetic traditions, manifest how the image of the peacemaker could transcend cultural boundaries, creating a similar artistic vocabulary of power laudation.

Still, the glory of peace was not reserved solely for viziers and kings. During one long conference on Ottoman–Venetian affairs on 4 January 1699, a brief pause was made, and the usual coffee was served. 'Mavrocordatos, drinking it, said: with this arduous negotiation, I don't have an appetite for drinking or

101 Saracino and Makrides, 'Die Aufnahme'.
102 Ibid., 59, 70–1.
103 Ali Fuat Bilkan (ed.), *Nabi Divani*, vol. 1 (Ankara: Akçağ Publishing House 2011) 94, verse 100.
104 Cited in Kantorska, 'Les médiations françaises', 234.

anything else'.[105] Count Schlik replied to this expression of despondency by reminding the Ottoman plenipotentiary that 'the more difficult the negotiations, the more glorious their outcome and the bigger the distinction and merit of the one who handles them'.[106] And verily, a peace congress, and especially a successful one, constituted a unique opportunity for an ambassador to catapult his symbolic capital, fame and thus his career.[107]

As Ruzzini claims in his *Relazione Finale* about Alexandros Mavrocordatos, 'he came to the congress with a scheme to raise himself much higher through the merit and glory of the negotiation'.[108] And the Ottoman ambassador did indeed consider the Carlowitz Congress as the *opus magnum* of his life as the epitaph placed upon his grave, composed by himself proudly proclaimed: 'he who set the treaties and reconciled the Ottomans, the Germans, the Muscovites, the Poles, and the Venetians'.[109] Nonetheless, how the glory of the peacemaker could catalytically influence a plenipotentiary's future after the end of the congress is most clearly manifested by Rāmī Meḥmed's case. In a meteoric rise in power, the latter would occupy, though for little less than a year (December 1702–August 1703), the office of the grand vizier.

7 More and Less Innocent 'Gifts'

Symbolic was not, though, the only kind of capital a plenipotentiary could aspire to obtain through his participation in a peace congress. Greater or lesser material gain could be equally expected. Such gains resulted primarily through various types of 'gifts' offered or exchanged, and promises of money being made before, during or after the end of the congress. Yet, before engaging further in this topic, an essential, brief detour is required to elucidate matters pertaining to the definition of terms.

It would be futile to strictly define which of those offerings, exchanges or transactions constitutes a 'gift' and which a 'bribe'.[110] In every instance, there

105 BNM, Ms.it/VII 399(8625), fol. 301ᵛ, Alcuni discorsi delle Conferenze raccolte dal Nicolosi.
106 Ibid.
107 Köhler, *Strategie und Symbolic*, 196–207.
108 Ruzzini, *Relazione*, 376.
109 Émile Legrand, *Généalogie des Mavrocordato de Constantinople rédigée d'après des documents inédits* (Paris: J. Maisonneuve 1900) 31.
110 Gadi Algazi, 'Introduction. Doing Things with Gifts' in Gadi Algazi, Valentin Groebner and Bernhard Jussen (eds.), *Negotiating the Gift. Pre-Modern Figurations of Exchange* (Göttingen: Vanderhoeck & Ruprecht 2003) 13–14; Hillard von Thiessen, 'Korrupte Gesandte? Konkurriende Normen in der Diplomatie der Frühen Neuzeit', in Niels Grüne

would certainly be cases that elude such a definition.[111] The terms encountered in the sources further obscure rather than clarify the matter. Surely, words like *guadagnare* (in Italian) or *comparare* (in Latin) might denote a case of bribery.[112] Still, in other instances, more neutral terms such as *promesse d'argent* or less clear ones, *largesse*, *liberalité* or *reconnaissance* are also used to describe what, for a modern researcher, appears to be a douceur.[113] Similarly, *regalo* (present) or *regalare* (to give a present) could well designate the lawful, established by tradition, publicly made exchange of gifts during the farewell visits of the different embassies, and be equally utilised in murkier instances where the sender's purpose was to create an obligation to someone, to 'buy' (*guadagnare*) his good will and disposition.[114]

A much more fruitful approach would be to consider 'gifts' as 'not given, fixed entities, but contested constructions of social transactions'.[115] As objects whose meaning was not solely, to some extent, pre-inscribed into the cultural vocabularies of the various participants, but was also often negotiated on the spot.[116] An illustrative case from the Carlowitz Congress is one involving the Muscovite plenipotentiary Voznitsyn and Count Marsigli. We have already seen how the latter attempted to win the former's confidence. Yet, things became more complicated when Voznitsyn, trying perhaps, from his side, to do the same, but with more than words, made him a present consisting of forty sable furs.[117] Marsigli returned the present to Voznitsyn, declaring that it was inappropriate for him to receive it in such a congress.[118] The meaning of

---

and Simona Slanička (eds.), *Korruption. Historische Annäherungen an einer Grundfigur politischer Kommunikation* (Göttingen: Vandenhoeck & Ruprecht 2010) 205–20, 209; Croxton, *Westphalia*, 169.

111 Algazi, 'Introduction', 13–4.

112 Ruzzini, *Relazione*, 376; Saluski, *Epistolae*, 630.

113 ÖStA, HHStA, Türkei I, Turcica Box 168, Folder 1 (November 1698, 1st half), fol. 44^{r}, Schlik to Kinsky, 5 November 1698; ÖStA, HHStA, Türkei I, Turcica Box 171, Folder 2 (January 1699, 2nd half), fol. 246^{v}, Schlik to Kinsky, 31 January 1699; ibid., fol. 206^{r}, Paget to Kinsky, 27 January 1699.

114 See for instance, *Narratio*, fol. 38^{v}, 49^{r}.

115 Algazi, 'Introduction', 10.

116 Ibid., 27.

117 ÖStA, HHStA, Türkei I, Turcica Box 167, Folder 2 (October 1698, 2nd half), fol. 178^{r-v}, Marsigli to Kinsky, 25 October 1698.

118 Ibid., fol. 238^{r}, Marsigli to Kinsky, 1 November 1698. How the receivers of such 'gifts' sometimes had to negotiate their meaning even with themselves, is illustrated by the following interesting detail. In an earlier letter to Kinsky (*see* fn. above), Marsigli implies that he accepted the present, reported it to the Imperial ambassadors and even received their applause for his success in winning Voznitsy's confidence. It is only in the second letter that he completely changes his narrative and declares that he returned the 'gift'.

this exchange had thus to be negotiated between the two men, a negotiation which led to different interpretations of it. On the one hand, for Voznitsyn, his present was nothing more than a sign of goodwill and friendship. For Marsigli, though, it implied an endeavour to win him over by creating a future obligation to him.[119]

This episode, as that of another unsuccessful attempt by Voznitsyn to offer sable furs, this time to the mediators, as a 'gift' 'for the current winter season[120] reveals how widespread such practices were in early modern diplomacy in order to win support and friendly disposition to one's demands.[121] It could even be said that 'gifts' (or 'bribes') were, in paraphrasing Clausewitz, a negotiation through other, more secret means. In his first letter to Kinsky from the congress venue, Count Schlik wrote him the following: 'We expected a secret purse and, speaking as a royal servant of His Majesty, I would deem it absolutely essential. It would be a pity if we have to leave a huge advantage slip [out of our hands] for not being able to pay five hundred ducats'.[122] Such backstage transactions seem to have become such an integral part of the peacemaking process – as the royal instructions given to Małachowski plainly admitted – that certain participants considered them a normative expectation[123] and started suggesting them before any negotiation had even begun. 'Milord [Paget] talked to me again with much eagerness', reported Count Schlik to Kinsky in the early days of the congress,

> about a promise of money in favour of the Turkish plenipotentiaries. And he thinks that it should not be inferior to the one formerly made by Chevalier Hussey.[124] I answered that I have noticed many positive

---

119 For 'gift' as a generator of obligation between individuals in the *ancien régime* courtly culture, *see* Barbara Stollberg-Rilinger, 'Zu moralischen Ökonomie des Schenkens bei Hof (17.–18. Jahrhundert)', in Werner Paravacini (ed.), *Luxus und Integration. Materielle Hofkultur Westeuropas vom 12. bis zum 18. Jahrhundert* (Munich: R. Oldenbourg 2010) 193.

120 Quoted in, D. and I. Guzevich, *Velikoe posol'stvo*, 124. The mediators refused by saying that they could only accept the gift after the successful termination of the negotiations: Bogoslovskii, *Petr I*, 402.

121 From the available archival material, at least seven cases of such 'gifts' (promises of money included) involving all embassies can be detected in the course of the congress.

122 ÖStA, HHStA, Türkei I, Turcica Box 167, Folder 2 (October 1698, 2nd half), fol. 63^{r-v}, Schlik to Kinsky, 18 October 1698.

123 Croxton, *Westphalia*, 169, 171.

124 Sir William Hussey (d. 1691). Appointed English ambassador at the Ottoman Court in 1690, he was charged with the first English mediation attempt to end the Sixteen Years' War, but he suddenly died in Adrianople during his mission: Hora Siccama, 'De Vrede van

> dispositions for that, and especially from the part of Your Excellency, when a coup d'état(sic) would have to be made. He demanded [to know] if I could be sure of that. I replied that typically, since the compensation follows the service, he could give [them?] hope in the meantime, and that I will write to you to be more particularly instructed. Your Excellency is humbly asked to order the embassy on what to do on this matter.[125]

To comprehend such situations, we would have to dissociate our thinking from the modern concept of corruption.[126] We have already discussed how an early modern plenipotentiary possessed various roles and how being a representative of a ruler or member of the administrate apparatus of a polity was only one of them. In this sense, any plenipotentiary was experiencing what the German historian of early modern diplomacy Hillard von Thiessen called a 'competition of norms' (*Normenkonkurrenz*): loyalty to their principals as *ministres publiques* and promotion of their private interests as *galantes hommes*.[127] As in many other aspects of the negotiation, so in that of 'gifts' or 'bribes', the plenipotentiary tried to combine both norms by staying loyal to his duty towards his sovereign, but also profiting materially in the process by making concessions on matters of lesser significance in exchange for a certain remuneration.[128]

Let us take as an example the Ottoman embassy, for which we possess greater archival evidence – not from Ottoman sources, evidently. Making a prosopography of every leading participant at the congress, Ruzzini spoke of Mavrocordatos's search for personal glory from his participation in the negotiations.[129] This quest of his for symbolic capital was, according to the Venetian, the principal reason why 'he could not be tempted by a gain in the major points of the negotiation. Still, in minor points, he would have been able to deliver, and to serve, [if] appropriately won over [with money]'.[130] That this was indeed the case is fully demonstrated by what seems to be one of the biggest bribery attempts during the congress.

Carlowitz', 95–99. The sum he then promised to the Ottoman side amounted to 200.000 florins: Slottman, *Ferenc II Rákóczi*, 187.

125 ÖStA, HHStA, Türkei I, Turcica Box 168, Folder 1 (November 1698, 1st half), fol. 44^{r-v}, Schlik to Kinsky, 5 November 1698.

126 As it is generally approached by Slottman in this otherwise instructive book: Slottman, *Ferenc II Rákóczi*, 186–93.

127 My analysis here is based mostly on Thiessen's, 'Korrupte Gesandte?'.

128 Croxton, *Westphalia*, 171.

129 *See* above.

130 Ruzzini, *Relazione*, 376.

The Imperial side had, as it appears, decided to put into good use its 'secret purse' and attempted a 'coup d'état' to win the vital fortress of Ṭemeşvar. Following Ruzzini, the Imperial plenipotentiaries, 'with letters from Count Kinsky authenticated by two lines, written by the emperor himself, were permitted to present also two hundred thousand florins'.[131] Nonetheless, despite the enormous sum, the Ottomans refused to give in. However, the Imperial Court was at least content to exhibit its financial means to use them on another occasion if it was deemed necessary.[132] Such a necessity came to the fore in the final stages of the congress when the Imperial side endeavoured to prolong it as much as possible to provide time for the Venetian plenipotentiary to receive the appropriate orders from the Venetian Senate and conclude his negotiation.[133] 'The Turks want to be paid for their patience', Schlik reported to Kinsky, adding that 'because after everything they have done and moreover, for what they could [still] do, they don't expect anything more than a gratification from His Imperial Majesty, and the mediators sometimes repeat [that] they want to know from us on what we could commit ourselves effectively'.[134]

Just what were the facilitations that the Ottoman plenipotentiaries offered is not clear. Still, judging from what the Ottoman side managed to achieve during the negotiations, one could suppose that such services mostly had to do with those 'minor points' referred to by Ruzzini, such as consenting to

131 Ibid., 367–8.

132 Ibid., 368. There is an intriguing story behind how Ruzzini obtained this information. In a letter to Count Kinsky, Count Schlik, discussing Ṭemeşvar, refers to a 'secret' (*le secret*) that he and Count Öttingen, along with the Imperial secretary Johannes Till, were striving to keep confidential. However, maintaining it so proved challenging, as Schlik noted: 'there are two Venetian nobles, Onigo and Bartolini, who act as spies for the Republic's ambassador within the household of the Dutch envoy, enjoying his trust and confidence': ÖStA, HHStA, Türkei I, Turcica Box 168, Folder 2 (November 1698, 2nd half), fol. 307^{v}–308^{r}, Schlik to Kinsky, 18 November 1698. Schlik's fears might, in the end, have proven correct since there is much probability that Ruzzini learned the attempted bribe through these two spies of his at Colyer's encampment – the Dutch being, as it appears, privy to the 'secret' as well. In another letter, Schlik does allude that it was Colyer who revealed it: ÖStA, HHStA, Türkei I, Turcica Box 169, Folder 1 (December 1698, 1st half), fol. 126^{r}, Schlik to Kinsky, 10 December 1698.

133 Already at the beginning of the congress, in a letter to Schlik, Count Kinsky declared that 'if it is with our money that any sort of advantage could be procured for the allies, in such a case, we should not spare it, the [most] important being to get out of this war together': ÖStA, HHStA, Türkei I, Turcica Box 168, Folder 1 (November 1698, 1st half), fol. 189^{r}, Kinsky to Schlik, 9 November 1698.

134 ÖStA, HHStA, Türkei I, Turcica Box 171, Folder 2 (January 1699, 2nd half), fol. 122^{r-v}, Schlik to Kinsky, 21 January 1699.

stay in the congress venue for a longer amount of time.[135] Though, in this last case, the Ottoman 'impatience' could well have been faked, which would have amounted to a very clever way of gaining extra money by simulating performing a service. The Ottoman case thus indicates that symbolic and material capital could coexist and complement one another for a plenipotentiary and that the former was often considered far too important to be sacrificed on the altar of the latter.[136]

8 The Daily Routine and Obligations of a Plenipotentiary Ambassador

It is a fairly established opinion in the current scholarship that the primary duties of an early modern ambassador were synopsised in the triptych: representation, information, and negotiation.[137] The daily routine of the plenipotentiaries at Carlowitz mostly vindicates such an argument, although one could, or should, add a fourth cardinal occupation, reporting and relating. Having discussed extensively matters pertaining to representation in Interlude II, we should here instead focus on the other three ambassadorial *métieres*.

The plenipotentiary's everyday routine during the congress was dominated by the conferences he had to attend, his principal duty being to negotiate the peace articles in these encounters. Nonetheless, the number of meetings was not the same for all due to their bilateral character. The Ottomans and the mediators were the busiest in this respect, having to attend every single one throughout the congress. They were followed by the Imperials, the Venetians and the Muscovites. The least frequent conference attendee was Małachowski,

135 One could attempt to make some further hypotheses, such as the Ottoman concession to deliver the fortress of Ḳamianets-Podilskyi to the Commonwealth intact or the agreement to an abolition of the 'pension' the Venetians were obliged to pay to the Porte for the island of Zakynthos (Zante). Nonetheless, without concrete evidence, all such assertions are only mere speculations.

136 We later learn that the sum promised by the Imperial side to the Ottoman plenipotentiaries for their various facilitations during the congress totalled fifty thousand Thalers in gold: Slottman, *Ferenc II Rákóczi*, 195, fn. 11. For the efforts to deliver it to the two ambassadors after the congress and the mysterious and uncertain ending of the affair, *see* ibid., 189–93.

137 Lucien Bély, 'Négocier la paix', 172; Jean-Claude Waquet, 'Introduction', in Stefano Andretta et al. (eds.), *Paroles des Négotiateurs. L'entretien dans la pratique diplomatique de la fin du Moyen Âge à la fin du XIXe siècle* (Rome: École Française de Rome 2010) 3.

who terminated his affairs in just three.[138] Attending the official meetings was not an easy task for the ambassadors. Some could last up to ten consecutive hours, such as the first Ottoman–Venetian one.[139] And, despite some short breaks, usually accompanied by the serving of coffee, the ambassadors had to remain highly attentive to their interlocutor's speech and suggestions and be able to argue effectively throughout the meetings. How important even a momentary lack of vigilance might prove to be in securing an advantage for the opposite side is aptly described by Count Schlik, who boasted in a letter to Kinsky how the Imperial embassy managed to catch off guard the usually very scrupulous Ottomans[140] and thus secure some further territorial gains: 'We caught Mavrocordatos in a moment of carelessness (*à un moment de berger*), and [we] also obtain that the line from [the river] Tisza to Sava will be drawn from the tip of the shore [and] beyond'.[141] Tiredness might not have been the sole cause of such a distraction. An empty stomach could also bring a plenipotentiary to his limits. During one long session on the affairs of Venice, where the evacuation of the fortress of Lepanto (modern-day Nafpaktos in southern Greece) was endlessly debated, Count Schlik protested his hunger with a wordplay: 'This evacuation evacuates our stomachs (*questa evacuazione evacua i nostri stomacchi*). It is 8 o'clock in the evening without [us being able] to have lunch'.[142]

Hypertense conferences could also deprive plenipotentiaries of their rest, oftentimes leading to long nights of anxiety and planning ahead for the next session. After a lively second meeting with the Imperial embassy, Rāmī Meḥmed described the state of the Ottoman delegates in the following manner:

> The plenipotentiaries of the Exalted State didn't find rest in their residences even during the night. Because of such a degree of obstinacy and opposition and the firmness and insistence of their [the Imperials] words, this affair is intoxicated once more [they thought], and they became very sad and worried.[143]

---

138 *See* a detailed diagram of the conferences held at the congress in Act III, Narration Part I, 252, and Act IV, Narration Parts I and II.

139 *Narratio*, 20r.

140 For the usual Ottoman scrupulousness, *see* ÖStA, HHStA, Türkei I, Turcica Box 169, Folder 1 (December 1698, 1st half), fol. 197r–v, Schlik to Kinsky, 12 December 1698.

141 ÖStA, HHStA, Türkei I, Turcica Box 168, Folder 2 (November 1698, 2nd half), fol. 162v, Schlik to Kinsky, 23 November 1698.

142 ÖStA, HHStA, Türkei I, Turcica Box 170, Protocollum, fol. 167.

143 *Taʾrīḫ-i ṣulḥ-nāme*, fol. 89b.

After spending the whole night pondering on and planning their strategy on how to proceed, 'the next day, they came again to the conference tent [full] of anxiety on what was to follow'.[144]

It was only natural that all this tension and exhaustion affected the ambassadors' health. Count Schlik reported on 19 November, not without a tone of mockery, that 'after so many transpired conferences, Herr Reis Efendi, could experience nothing else than a digestion problem (*bewegung der gall*)[145] which made him also so indisposed' that a 'rest day' (*rast-tag*) had to be declared for him to recover.[146] He could not digest, figuratively and literally, the Imperials' forceful arguments, so claimed Schlik. However, such small pauses were often met with a feeling of joy by all plenipotentiaries. As the Imperial ambassador recorded in his journal, 'the 27 [November] was, an acclaimed by all sides, day off'.[147] In other instances, strain and weariness tested some ambassadors' nerves and led to outbursts of anger. 'Here the Efendi [Rāmī] spoke with great vehemence and agitation from what one could understand from his voice and movements while speaking in Turkish', wrote the Venetian secretary Nicolosi in his protocol of a conference on 4 January 1699, 'and it appeared from the gestures and the agreeable voice that Mavrocordatos was attempting to appease and calm him down'.[148]

Apart from the official conferences, the *öffentlichen Zusammenkünften*, as Count Schlik names them,[149] various other 'private meetings' (*in privato*)[150] were taking place among the allied ambassadors or between the latter and the mediators. Their primary aims were to inform the other embassies on the progress of one's negotiation; to solicit support from an ally or the mediators when the talks were at a critical point or encountered difficulties; to attempt to 'penetrate' the motives of one's interlocutors, to influence them or win them over to one's side and lastly, to put pressure on someone to conclude his affairs.[151] For instance, that is how the Anonymous Venetian narrates Ruzzini's moves after his initial conferences with the Ottomans: 'The Venetian ambassador suspended his conferences with the Turks but not with the mediators

144 Ibid.
145 I would like to sincerely express my gratitude to my colleague and early modern medicine connoisseur, Vigdis Evang, for enlightening me about the meaning and symptoms associated with a 'bewegung der gall' during that period.
146 ÖStA, HHStA, Türkei I, Turcica Box 170, Diarium et Cerimoniale, fol. 37.
147 Ibid., fol. 40.
148 BNM, Ms.it.VII 399 (8625), fol. 302r, Alcuni discorsi delle Conferenze raccolte dal Nicolosi.
149 ÖStA, HHStA, Türkei I, Turcica Box 170, Diarium et Cerimoniale, fol. 68.
150 Ibid.
151 ÖStA, HHStA, Türkei I, Turcica Box 170, Diarium et Cerimoniale, fol. 61.

and the allies, and especially with the Imperials, trying to make known to all the strange insistence of the Turks and securing the support of the former (the mediators) […]'.[152]

8.1 *Reporting and Relating*

'As ministers [ambassadors], we are obliged to notify our principals', Mavrocordatos once asserted in a conference.[153] Such a notification constituted a prime occupation of a plenipotentiary during the congress and was effectuated through the drafting and dispatching of letters or relations. In nine days (27 November–December 5), Małachowski sent three missives back to his principals in the Commonwealth.[154] Between 9 December and 2 January, Ruzzini dispatched four to the Venetian Senate.[155] Even Voznitsyn, notwithstanding his being very far away from Moscow, by 12 December 1698, had written seven letters/relations to the tsar and the head of the *Posol'skii prikaz*.[156] Let us delve a bit further, though, in two particular cases, the Imperial and the Ottoman.

The Habsburg delegation's principal-notification system's basis was a dual one. The ambassadors had to regularly inform the emperor through relations, as well as specific ministers, Count Kinsky, first and foremost, through letters. Whereas the relations to Leopold I were ostensibly drafted together and signed by both plenipotentiaries,[157] their correspondence with Kinsky was individually grounded. Such a system allowed the latter to be particularly informed of the negotiations, especially by Schlik, as we discussed earlier. A closer look at some figures regarding the Imperial embassy's correspondence will further illuminate our analysis. From 18 October 1698 until 4 February 1699, twenty-four relations were sent to Emperor Leopold (*see* Table 1).

October, the opening phase of the congress, marked the month with the greatest relative dispatch frequency, since five relations were written in only thirteen days. On the other hand, in concrete numbers, November and January were the months in which the most relations were drafted. This is explained by the fact that during the first, the most critical Imperial–Ottoman negotiations took place. In contrast, the second was dominated by the Imperial efforts to bring to a conclusion the Ottoman–Venetian talks. Regarding now the missives

152 *Narratio*, fol. 23^r.

153 ÖStA, HHStA, Türkei I, Turcica Box 170, Protocollum, fol. 170.

154 Sałuski, *Epistolae*, 676–80. It is not clear, though, to whom these letters, written in Latin, were addressed.

155 *Narratio*, fol. 27^v.

156 D. and I. Guzevich, *Velikoe posol'stvo*, 109.

157 See, for example, ÖStA, HHStA, Türkei I, Turcica Box 167, Folder 2 (October 1698, 2nd half), fol. 117^r, Imperial plenipotentiaries to Leopold I, 22 October 1698.

TABLE 1 Number and relative frequency of the relations to the emperor sent by the Habsburg embassy per month during the congress

Month	Days	Number of relations	Relative frequency
October	13	5	38%
November	30	7	23%
December	31	4	12%
January	31	7	22%
February	4	1	25%

SOURCE: ÖSTA, HHSTA, TÜRKEI I, TURCICA BOXES 167–72

to Kinsky, from 18 October 1698 until 4 February 1699, twenty-seven were dispatched by Count Schlik and sixteen by Count Öttingen.[158] Their relative frequency, as well as their monthly number, closely follows the relations' figures since, in the majority of cases, they were dispatched together.

Besides letters, another means of information for specific Imperial ministers regarding the progress of the negotiations was via a journal, kept by Schlik and routinely dispatched to Vienna along with the regular correspondence. This 'secret journal', as the Bohemian count himself refers to it,[159] appears to have sprung from his own initiative. As he claimed to his patron, 'its composition is particular, different from the one [written] by someone in our chancery [with which] we give prey to the public curiosity, and I am not sending it but to Your Excellency and monsieur Count Kaunitz'.[160] One of the journal's 'particularities' would be to provide the two Imperial ministers with details on the manners (*le detail des manieres*) of the various congress participants.[161] Thus, it is no surprise that its language is far more spontaneous and characterisations of individuals much more abrasive – Voznitsyn, in particular, is portrayed as a 'wild beast' (*unthier*) more than once – a unique example of an expression of

158 For the first Imperial plenipotentiary ambassador, the period ranges between 25 October 1698–4 February 1699, ÖStA, HHStA, Türkei I, Turcica Box 167, Folder 2 (October 1698, 2nd half) – Box 172, Folder 1 (February–March 1699).

159 ÖStA, HHStA, Türkei I, Turcica Box 167, Folder 2 (October 1698, 2nd half), fol. 60^{r}, Schlik to Kinsky, 18 October 1698. The complete journal in ÖStA, HHStA, Türkei I, Turcica Box 170, Diarium et Cerimoniale.

160 ÖStA, HHStA, Türkei I, Turcica Box 168, Folder 1 (November 1698, 1st half), fol. 41^{v}, Schlik to Kinsky, 5 November 1698.

161 Ibid., fol. 41^{v}–42^{r}.

personal antipathies and 'national' and religious biases, as we shall have the chance to further explore in a later section.

Apart from Schlik's 'Secret Journal', the Imperial embassy also kept one devoted explicitly to the ceremonial, attesting to the latter's significance in the minds of the congress participants.[162] It deals only with the periods in which ceremonial regulations were in place, that is, during the initial and closing phases of the congress. It describes extensively, among others, the first and farewell visits of the Imperial embassy, the spatial arrangements of the allied encampment, the ceremonial and spatial composition of the first Ottoman–Imperial conference, and the signing ceremony. Not least, it also constitutes a valuable source for the material culture of the congress.

Passing from the Imperial to the Ottoman side, despite a lack of archival documentation similar to the Habsburgs, combined evidence from the Carlowitz Congress and previous negotiations during the Sixteen Years' War allows for a sufficient reconstruction of the Porte's plenipotentiaries' dispatch practices. The embassy informed quite regularly, as it appears, the grand vizier – not the sultan – of any development in the negotiations through reports/relations (*ḳā'ime*) very similar to the ones of the Imperial delegation. Typically, it was the first ambassador who composed them. From the crossing of the river Save through the commencement of the official conferences, less than a month, four such relatively extensive reports were sent to 'Amcazāde by Rāmī Meḥmed.[163] Unfortunately, in his post-congress account, the Ottoman ambassador did not include copies (*ṣūret*) of similar reports he must have dispatched during the negotiations. However, evidence that he did continue writing them is provided by the last phrase of the relation he lastly included, in which he declares that 'everything that is to be successfully agreed upon will be reported to Your Exalted Presence'.[164] From Count Schlik's journal, we also learn that from the start of the official conferences (13 November) until 25 November, the Ottoman embassy reportedly sent three express posts back to Adrianople.[165]

Furthermore, similarly to other embassies, the reports were accompanied by copies of essential documents issued during the congress, such as the latter's Regulation.[166] Besides the *ḳā'imeler*, there is evidence of more particular

162 ÖStA, HHStA, Türkei I, Turcica Box 170, Diarium et Cerimoniale. Attention! The journal regarding the ceremonial is to be found in a separate document inside the diary.

163 *Ta'rīḫ-i ṣulḥ-nāme*, fol. 68ᵇ–80ᵇ.

164 Ibid., fol. 80ᵇ. *See* also BNM, Ms.it.VII 399(8625), fol. 303ʳ, Alcuni discorsi delle Conferenze raccolte dal Nicolosi, where Mavrocordatos is referring to the Ottoman plenipotentiaries reporting the outcome of the negotiations back to the Porte.

165 ÖStA, HHStA, Türkei I, Turcica Box 170, Diarium et Cerimoniale, fol. 40.

166 *Ta'rīḫ-i ṣulḥ-nāme*, fol. 70ᵇ–72ᵃ.

memoranda concerning the conferences under the names of *cerīde* (journal, memorandum) or *taḳrīr* (report, memorandum).[167] Although not entirely clear what those latter strictly contained, it is clear that they were not the same as the *ḳā'ime*. We could suppose that they might have included the protocol of the meetings, which the embassy's secretary kept.[168] Such a claim is further strengthened by the structure of Rāmī's narration of the conferences, which strongly resembles a reworked form of protocol. In this case, the Ottoman ambassador's parts of relation concerning the congress meetings could well have been a re-composition or compilation of the *cerīde/taḳrīr* he was sending back to ʿAmcazāde throughout their course.[169]

Last but not least, not only the first but also the second plenipotentiary had to report to the grand vizier. While no letter of Mavrocordatos to the latter is included in Rāmī's account, such a practice is evidenced from the Failed Vienna Congress, where the then first Ottoman ambassador Zülfikār Efendi closes his report with these words: 'and another letter of obedience is also written by our colleague İskerletzāde [Mavrocordatos]'.[170]

8.2 *Private Letters*

Letters were not only sent back to the ambassadors' respective principals, but they were also exchanged between them at the congress itself. For instance, during the negotiations, Voznitsyn sent a total of eleven to Mavrocordatos, and the latter dispatched five to the Muscovite in response.[171] The relations between the delegates, as well as the process of the negotiations, dominated their content. In a letter to Małachowski, dated 10 December 1698, Voznitsyn informed him of his negotiation after addressing their personal rivalry and suggested that he should conclude a short armistice with the Ottomans, similar to what Voznitsyn was pondering to do.[172] The fact that a copy of that letter – as well as Małachowski's reply – reached the hands of the Imperial embassy[173] reveals that one of the two deliberately chose to share their content, transforming thus

167 *Cerîde-i Takrirât*, 122, fn. 1477.

168 ÖStA, HHStA, Türkei I, Turcica Box 170, Diarium et Cerimoniale, fol. 14ʳ (of the separate journal regarding the ceremonial); *Narratio*, fol. 19ᵃ.

169 The Imperial side also sent copies of parts of its protocol back to Vienna. *See*, for instance, ÖStA, HHStA, Türkei I, Turcica Box 171, Folder 2 (January 1699, 2nd half), fol. 133ʳ⁻ᵛ, Nota dell Corcordato nella Conferenza li 20 Genaro 1699.

170 *Cerîde-i Takrirât*, 122, fn. 1477.

171 D. and I. Guzevich, *Velikoe posol'stvo*, 130.

172 ÖStA, HHStA, Türkei I, Turcica Box 169, Folder 1 (December 1698, 1st half), fol. 151ʳ⁻ᵛ, Voznitsyn to Małachowski, 10 December 1698.

173 Ibid., fol. 151ᵛ–152ʳ.

the letters' character from 'private' to 'public' to discredit the other, as in previous congresses.[174] And indeed, it appears that sometimes such letters were viewed by third parties, the congress 'public sphere' – and maybe provided them with analogous entertainment – like the libels and counter-libels to be found in late seventeenth-century printed news media.[175] That is how Count Schlik described in his journal another, later exchange of letters between the two 'usual suspects': 'On 21 [December] the Muscovite had again chanted with somewhat ruder notes in a letter of his to the Pole, and the latter replied to him anew in an analogous tone afterwards'.[176]

Of equal significance was the keeping of regular correspondence with powerful individuals at foreign courts, who had a decisive say in the decision-making process to be of paramount significance. The best example is the exchange of letters between Count Kinsky and Carlo Ruzzini. Between 18 October and 30 December, the latter dispatched nine letters to the Bohemian Chancellor, trying to convince him of the Serenissima's just claims and the Ottoman violation of the Peace Foundation.[177] Lastly, one should also consider the 'familiar correspondence' each ambassador kept during the congress with family members, relatives, and friends.[178] Mavrocordatos's letter to Patriarch Dositheos or Małachowski's correspondence with the Grand Chancellor of Lithuania, Karol Stanisław Radziwiłł, are such cases in point.[179] Unfortunately, although such

174 Köhler, 'Argumentieren und Verhandeln', 529. Such an interpretation is further strengthened by the fact that there were other instances where the person who shared a letter with someone wanted to keep it absolutely secret by not allowing his interlocutor to have a copy of it. *See*, for instance, ÖStA, HHStA, Türkei I, Turcica Box 167, Folder 2 (October 1698, 2nd half), fol. 123^{r}, Imperial plenipotentiaries to Leopold I, 22 October 1698.

175 For the printed news media as a novel weapon used by various ambassadors in the broader context of early modern European diplomacy, *see* Helmer J. Helmers, 'Public Diplomacy in Early Modern Europe: Towards a New History of News'. *Media History* 22/3–4 (2016), 401–20.

176 ÖStA, HHStA, Türkei I, Turcica Box 170, Diarium et Cerimoniale, fol. 53.

177 *See* ÖStA, HHStA, Türkei I, Turcica Box 167, Folder 2 (October 1698, 2nd half) – Box 169, Folder 2 (December 1698, 2nd half). An interesting detail: It appears that, like many modern scholars, the Carlowitz contemporaries also struggled to 'decipher' some of the letters sent to them. Ruzzini's handwriting, it seems, was giving Count Kinsky a hard time. So, he had some letters of the Venetian recopied in clear handwriting to pore over them smoothly, doing, unintentionally, a great favour to modern researchers as well. For a telling example, *see* ÖStA, HHStA, Türkei I, Turcica Box 169, Folder 2 (December 1698, 2nd half), fol. 77^{r-v} (the original) and 78^{r-v} (the copy), Ruzzini to Kinsky, 14 December 1698.

178 For the example of the French ambassador at the Congress of Nijmegen, Godefroi Comte d'Estrades, *see* Köhler, *Strategie und Symbolik*, 134, 220–1.

179 Małachowski's 'Carlowitz correspondence' with Radziwiłł is found in AGAD, Archiwum Warszawskie Radziwiłłów, 1/354/0/5/9200, fol. 32–55.

correspondence could be particularly valuable in illuminating many essential aspects of the negotiations,[180] it is not always accessible to the researcher. Besides the fact that it could be scattered into various archival collections, Małachowki's correspondence being such a case,[181] in other instances – in Rāmī's or Voznitsyn's, for example – it possibly could not have survived at all.

8.3 *The Drafting Process*

The drafting of relations and letters was not an easy task. A whole day could be spent preparing them.[182] Often, the work was so arduous that a plenipotentiary would feel the need to openly express his distress and desperation. 'The work of this ordinary [post] really exhausted me', exclaimed Count Schlik in a letter to Kinsky. 'And [visitors from] the allies interrupt me so often that I have to say plainly and with good reason that I'm not myself'.[183] Such constant occupation with diverse issues on a daily basis could oblige a plenipotentiary to draft his dispatches mostly during the night or might even cause him to fail to write some of them on time. 'The continuous distractions that spring up every moment and have reduced me to work mainly at night', lamented Count Schlik again, 'didn't let me finish by the dispatch of our last courier the ordinary journal [the 'Secret Journal' mentioned above]'.[184]

Even when they could be sent on time, there was always a danger that the letters might be opened on the road. For instance, forwarding Małachowski's relations from Carlowitz to an unnamed friend, the prominent Polish bishop Andrzej Chryzostom Załuski reported that 'three came together, not without suspicion that they were detained [on the road]'.[185] That such fears were legitimate is proven by what Kinsky said in a letter to Count Schlik. Speaking about the two Polish nobles wanting to reach the Ottoman camp right before the commencement of the congress, the Imperial minister remarked that, 'it will require watching that sort of people in the congress venue closely, paying attention to their letters'.[186] When the Imperial–Venetian relations started

180 Köhler, *Strategie und Symbolik*.

181 Teresa Zielińska, 'Stanisław Antoni Szczuzuka Jako Referendarz Koronny w Latach 1688–1699'. *Kwartalnik Historyczny Rocznik* 111/3 (2004), 10, fn. 15.

182 ÖStA, HHStA, Türkei I, Turcica Box 170, Diarium et Cermoniale, fol. 58.

183 ÖStA, HHStA, Türkei I, Turcica Box 168, Folder 2 (November 1698, 2nd half), fol. 309^{v}, Schlik to Kinsky18 November 1698.

184 ÖStA, HHStA, Türkei I, Turcica Box 169, Folder 2 (December 1698, 2nd half), fol. 41^{r}, Schlik to Kinsky, 14 December 1698.

185 Załuski, *Epistolae*, 676.

186 ÖStA, HHStA, Türkei I, Turcica Box 167, Folder 2 (October 1698, 2nd half), fol. 151^{r}, Kinsky to Schlik, 25 October 1698.

to deteriorate because of the problems Venice faced in its negotiation with the Ottomans, Count Schlik confidently suggested in a separate billet to the Bohemian Chancellor that 'the rule of good precaution would require that we surveil the traffics of letters of monsieur the ambassador [Ruzzini]'.[187] A common countermeasure against such encroachments on sensitive information was encryption.[188] Another was the 'secret-ostensible letter' stratagem. In this scenario, the 'real' dispatches were meticulously hidden by their carriers, and the latter were also provided with another demonstrable document they could present in case of extreme need. In contrast to the genuine ones, the 'fake' letters were typically filled with general expressions and dissimulated feelings to disclose as little as possible and to beguile their aspiring readers.[189]

9 Ambassadorial Self-Portrayal

The self-portrayal of a plenipotentiary was comprised of two levels. The first was the one towards the other participants of the congress. The second was towards his principals and the 'public opinion' of the court. Starting with the former, one of the essential parts of the role and image of an ambassador was to appear in all instances, even during the most adverse ones for his negotiation, as a sincere peacemaker and peace-lover. Such a self-presentation was not only considered a normative part of their 'script'/persona, but it also was a necessary strategy against possible attempts by their opponents to strip a plenipotentiary of the social capital he possessed with other, third-party participants of a congress (the mediators, his other allies etc.), accusing him of not truly desiring a peace settlement.[190] In a moment of high tension during the first Ottoman–Imperial conferences, Mavrocordatos protested 'with an extraordinary expression' (*con una espressione straordinaria*) that he was not driven in his propositions by any other motive 'than by pure zeal, and by the prospect that he has of a decent peace for which he had been painfully working for

187 ÖStA, HHStA, Türkei I, Turcica Box 168, Folder 2 (November 1698, 2nd half), fol. 236ᵛ, Schlik to Kinsky, 2 December 1698.

188 For an example of such a semi-encrypted letter, *see* BNM, Ms.it.VII 399(8625), fol. 366ʳ–368ʳ, Loredano to Ruzzini, 20 January 1698 (1699). For a similar encryption example for the Muscovite side, Bogoslovkij, *Petr I*, 366.

189 A perfect example of such a practice is encountered during the previous peace negotiations in Vienna (1689–90) with the dispatches sent by the Ottoman embassy to the grand vizier: *Cerîde-i* Takrirât, 123–4.

190 Köhler, 'Argumentieren und Verhandeln', 530.

ten years now'.[191] 'I am declaring as a *cavaliere* [...] that the Republic desires peace', Ruzzini exclaimed when the Ottoman plenipotentiaries doubted the Serenissima's sincerity of peace feelings; the evocation of his noble title acting as a guarantee for the truthfulness of his statement.[192]

Sincerity and candour, the two cardinal attributes of an *honnête homme*, were not restricted to one's sentiments towards peace. They had to ostensibly accompany every action of a plenipotentiary to win the trust of his interlocutors. 'We came to this place with good intentions', the Ottoman ambassadors professed to the Imperial ones, attempting to coax them to their side and discredit the Venetian behaviour. 'You and the Poles and the Muscovites have witnessed our sincerity and truthfulness', they added.[193] They seemed to have achieved their goal since the perfect exemplification of what a failure to live up to the *cavaliere* standards could entail for one's negotiating position is no other than Carlo Ruzzini. For Count Schlik, writing to Kinsky at a time when the Venetian–Ottoman negotiations were at their most critical point, the Venetian was no more than the perfect *contre- honnête homme*: 'everything is nice words, finesse and intrigue, and it appears that he makes secret fun of our generosity'.[194]

The ambassadorial dispatches and relations, during or after a congress, should not be seen as an objective portrayal of the facts, but as a deliberate and careful literary construction, the principal aim of which was to influence the decision-making of their reader, or the reader's view of the plenipotentiary, by presenting the events, and most importantly, the conduct of the negotiator, under a certain favourable light.[195] A quite telling example of such a supra-cultural practice of ambassadorial self-portrayal is provided by two letters, written around the same time, a little before the beginning of the negotiations, by Meḥmed Rāmī, addressed to the grand vizier and by Count Schlik, addressed to the Imperial minister, Kinsky. Both passages try to explain why it hadn't been possible for the actual negotiations to commence. The Ottoman text first:

191 ÖStA, HHStA, Türkei I, Turcica Box 170, Protocollum, fol. 33.

192 Ibid., fol. 157.

193 *Ta'rīḫ-i ṣulḥ-nāme*, fol. 121ª.

194 ÖStA, HHStA, Türkei I, Turcica Box 171, Folder 1 (January 1699, 1st half), fol. 177ᵛ–178ʳ, Schlik to Kinsky, 12 January 1699.

195 For early modern ambassadorial relations as a literary construction, see Waquet, 'Introduction', 6–11.

> In order for our time not to pass in vain, we used all diligence, [thinking] a thousand ways, [on how] to finish the affair as soon as possible in a way that is congruent with the honour of the Exalted State. From our side, there is absolutely no failure in duty, but [...]in this preliminary phase, [in which] so many states' representatives came together, they have not been able to remove the ceremonial [disputes] between them yet. Each one of them, with his own obstinacy, some time passed to find stability between them in these circumstances.[196]

Compare now to the Imperial one:

> We are doing everything in our power to press the negotiations. But the difficulties on the part of our allies and the troubles that it requires us to pass through in order to abate them cost us an infinity of time. Voila, [that is] the reason why we have not been able to advance [our negotiation] at all as well.[197]

The resemblance between the two passages is striking. In both cases, much diligence is put into highlighting the immense efforts of the plenipotentiaries to get the negotiations started; efforts, though, were faced with situations outside their control. They wanted to perform their duty to the utmost; the fault for any failure lay not with them but with others.

The portrayal of themselves as prisoners of circumstance, constrained to choose between lesser evils while always defending the interests of their sovereign as best they could, was a normative self-presentation of the ambassadors in their relations and letters. Justifying the embassy's conduct when demolishing and evacuating all the Imperial-held fortresses in the province of Ṭemeşvar, Schlik maintained that they were done 'for the interest of our master and fatherland (*la patrie*)'.[198] If this concession had not been made, the treaty would not have advanced at all.[199] In their relation to the emperor, still, on the same issue, the two ambassadors would also claim that 'we cannot see how we could have helped ourselves perhaps in a different way on these issues so

196 *Taʾrīḫ-i Ṣulḥ-nāme*, fol. 72ª.

197 ÖStA, HHStA, Türkei I, Turcica Box 168, Folder 1 (November 1698, 1st half), fol. 42ʳ, Schlik to Kinsky, 5 November 1698.

198 ÖStA, HHStA, Türkei I, Turcica Box 169, Folder 1 (December 1698, 1st half), fol. 123ᵛ, Schlik to Kinsky, 10 December 1698.

199 Ibid., and ÖStA, HHStA, Türkei I, Turcica Box 169, Folder 2 (December 1698, 2nd half), fol. 43ᵛ–44ʳ, Schlik to Kinsky, 14 December 1698.

important for the whole of Christendom'.[200] Reporting back to the tsar of his decision to conclude a two-year truce/armistice with the Ottomans, Voznitsyn, after imploring Peter to forgive him, adds:

> It was not possible to prevent them all from making peace and to do that comporting in a certain manner. Also, making peace [together] with the others was [again] not feasible because of great difficulties. Leaving the great monarch alone in war [?], I couldn't dare to do that either. [And so], I opted [...] for a small truce/armistice'.[201]

Another common trope encountered in the ambassadorial dispatches is to depict their writer as moderate, fully equipped with logical and reasonable arguments and his opponents as 'opinionated and unreasonable'. Such negative descriptions of one's adversaries were often accompanied by the appropriate stereotypes attributed to them. 'I have always said and observed myself', Count Schlik said in one of his dispatches to Kinsky, 'that this nation [the 'Turks'] wants what it wants violently, and we have seen such manifestations of it in Vienna itself'.[202] The Ottomans repaid the 'compliments' by portraying the Imperials as obstinate brutes, voicing 'unreasonable demands' (*tekālīf-i ḫām*) and being difficult to be reduced to reason by the just and powerful arguments of the Exalted State's plenipotentiaries.[203] But such characterisations were nothing compared to their portrayal of the Venetian plenipotentiary Carlo Ruzzini:

> In order to arrive at his perverse intent and dull thinking, he uttered a bunch of words so beyond argument [...] as to cause amazement. [...] Grave words do not touch him, and he cannot be convinced by arguments [the ambassadors of the State (*Devlet èlçileri*) thought]. He was a garrulous talker of nonsense.[204]

200 ÖStA, HHStA, Türkei I, Turcica Box 168, Folder 2 (November 1698, 2nd half), fol. 22^{v}, Imperial plenipotentiaries to Leopold I, 17 November 1698.

201 Quoted in D. and I. Guzevich, *Velikoe posol'stvo*, 114. I deeply thank my colleague Lana Martysheva for her help in translating this passage.

202 ÖStA, HHStA, Türkei I, Turcica Box 168, Folder 2 (November 1698, 2nd half), fol. 199^{r-v}, Schlik to Kinsky, 12 December 1698.

203 *Ta'rīḫ-i Ṣulḥ-nāme*, fol. 89^{b}, 92^{b}, 94^{b}.

204 Ibid., fol. 96^{b}.

In a letter to the grand vizier during the opening phase of the congress, Rāmī Meḥmed would declare that 'for the benefit of Muslims, this reconciliation as well is in every respect an actual Holy War (*maʿnen bir cihāddır*)'.[205] The plenipotentiary of the Commonwealth, Małachowski, would compare, for his part, the negotiations to an arena.[206] In both cases, the negotiator assumed the role of a warrior, one who fights not with muskets and swords but with the 'firepower' of his arguments. During the second Ottoman–Imperials conference, Count Schlik said at one point to the Ottoman plenipotentiaries that 'you are trying to take from us with the power of words the places and provinces you couldn't capture with the power of armies'.[207] The fact that a similar expression is repeated two more times in Rāmī's account[208] and that in all three cases, the Ottomans utterly prevailed in their demands attests that the *Reʾisü'l-küttāb* was deliberately attempting to assert his superiority – and consequently that of the Ottoman bureaucracy, the *ḫācegān* – over the military men. He managed with the sole force of his eloquence, as even his interlocutors could attest, to achieve what the Ottoman armies simply could not.

Lastly, sometimes, strong emotional language was utilised in the letters to justify some of the plenipotentiary's conduct and convince the recipient of the sincerity of the writer's feelings and thoughts. Reproached for some of the territorial concessions made to the Ottomans, Count Schlik burst into sentimentalism. 'Rest assured, monsieur, I am humbly begging Your Excellence on that, we would have died of grief if we could have reproached ourselves to have out of light-heartedness gone beyond the order of our instructions'.[209] In a following dispatch, always speaking on the same subject, he declared that 'the discontent that his Imperial Majesty appears to have with our way of acting stroke us and overwhelmed us to the point of despair'.[210]

---

205 Ibid., fol. 74[b].

206 Sałuski, *Epistolae*, 676.

207 *Taʾrīḫ-i Ṣulḥ-nāme*, fol. 89[a]. A similar phrase by Schlik, slighly altered though, was also recorded in the Imperial protocol, 'loro ci levano più con un colpo di penna, che non havrebbero fatto con una battaglia': ÖStA, HHStA, Türkei I, Turcica Box 170, Protocollum, fol. 31.

208 *Taʾrīḫ-i Ṣulḥ-nāme*, fol. 90[b], 93[b].

209 ÖStA, HHStA, Türkei I, Turcica Box 168, Folder 2 (November 1698, 2nd half), fol. 17[r–v], Schlik to Kinsky, 2 December 1698.

210 Ibid., fol. 121[r–v], Schlik to Kinsky, 10 December 1698.

10 How Plenipotentiary Was a Plenipotentiary?

Once, during the last phase of the congress, Małachowski, trying to induce Ruzzini, ever scrupulous not to 'overstep his duty',[211] to make some concessions for the sake of peace, said to him that

> it didn't befit a plenipotentiary ambassador to stay so attached to the instructions [...] and that to wait upon every difficulty for replies from the Senate would prolong the negotiation to eternity. If they had followed the same example, both he and the Muscovite, so distant from their sovereigns, whole years would have passed.[212]

And yet, was that really the case? How plenipotentiary was a plenipotentiary, and how far was his autonomy in the negotiations extended?

The general rule appears to have been that a plenipotentiary typically tried to follow as faithfully as possible the instructions of his principal, which set clear limits to his full powers, to what he was allowed or not allowed to negotiate or to concede. Even Małachowski, lecturing Ruzzini on the plenipotentiary's freedom of manoeuvre, strictly followed his king's supplementary instructions concerning one of the significant points of his negotiation, the territorial settlement with the Ottomans. That notwithstanding, there is more there than meets the eye. The prominent French diplomatic historian of the early modern period, Lucien Bély, once correctly cautioned against seeing the early modern ambassadors as mere 'marionettes' moved exclusively by their principals.[213] Of course, the sources written by the ambassadors themselves, or people from their entourage, commonly portray the actions of the protagonists as constantly conforming to the orders and instructions of their superiors, presenting thus to their 'audience', which usually is no other than the principals themselves, the 'ideal image'.

It becomes evident, though, that the degree of how closely a plenipotentiary would abide by the letter of the instructions given to him in advance, or during, a congress, depended as much upon the specific decision-making mechanisms of each polity as upon his personality and the calculation he made on how much an autonomous action could harm or benefit him back home.

---

211 *Narratio*, fol. 25^r.

212 Ibid., fol. 28^v–29^r.

213 Bély, 'Négocier la paix', 186. A similar view is also voiced by Derek Croxton in his book on the Westphalian Peace Congress: Croxton, *Westphalia*, op. cit., p. 159.

The distance from own's sovereign did not, as one might assume, play such a vital role, as Voznitsy's example will attest. Lastly, the iconography of the 'full powers painting' becomes ever harder to be deciphered since there are instances where one cannot discern if the invocation by a plenipotentiary of a lack of power or instructions on a specific issue was a genuine or faked, a mere strategy to avoid the discussion of a certain topic.

But let us start with the Imperial embassy, the one closer to its principal than the rest. If we look at the archival material, the first impression is that of an embassy regularly monitored by Imperial and ministerial instructions. Such was also the view of other participants of the congress. Speaking about and criticising the territorial concessions made by the Habsburg delegation to the Ottomans during the first conferences between them, the Anonymous Venetian remarked that it was not probable 'that the plenipotentiaries had made a decision without first communicating it to the emperor, and without his permission'.[214] And yet, it appears that these same territorial concessions, while following the general spirit of the Imperial commandments, were mainly decided in situ by the plenipotentiaries themselves, based on their first-hand judgement of the situation.[215] Namely, that if they had not been offered, the negotiations would have collapsed.[216] 'The articles, or better say, conditions that we have obtained are the only ones that were obtainable', Count Schlik assured Kinsky.[217] Both Öttingen and Schlik were strongly criticised by the Viennese Court for some of their decisions,[218] provoking an emotional outburst from the latter, that he would rather die than be reproached for not following his instructions.[219] And yet, although the second imperial plenipotentiary assured Kinsky that everything agreed could be easily undone,[220] in fact, the plenipotentiaries' decisions presented the Imperial Court with a *fait accompli*, since every regression on their already made concessions could jeopardise the whole congress. As we shall see, even though there was often a significant

214 *Narratio*, fol. 18^{v}.

215 As they themselves plainly acknowledge in a relation to the emperor: ÖStA, HHStA, Türkei I, Turcica Box 168, Folder 2 (November 1698, 2nd half), fol. 22^{r-v}, Imperial plenipotentiaries to Leopold I, 17 November 1698.

216 Ibid. and ÖStA, HHStA, Türkei I, Turcica Box 169, Folder 1 (December 1698, 1st half), fol. 17^{v}, Schlik to Kinsky, 2 December 1698.

217 Ibid., fol. 17^{r}.

218 *See*, for instance, ÖStA, HHStA, Türkei I, Turcica Box 168, Folder 2 (November 1698, 2nd half), fol. 215^{r}, Kinsky to Öttingen, 25 November 1698.

219 *See* above.

220 ÖStA, HHStA, Türkei I, Turcica Box 168, Folder 1 (November 1698, 1st half), fol. 306^{v}–307^{r}, Schlik to Kinsky, 13 November 1698.

divergence of opinion between the embassy and the emperor himself on the course to be followed on crucial issues, in the end, it was the view of the former that appears to have been imposed on the latter and not the other way around.

A similar situation of a mixed degree of general conformity and ad hoc autonomy seems to hold equally for the Ottoman delegation, although we don't possess sufficient archival documentation – that would be, first and foremost, the letters with the instructions sent from the grand vizier to the two plenipotentiaries at Carlowitz.[221] Nevertheless, from previous negotiations during the Sixteen Years' War, we know that the central government regularly provided its chief negotiators with general instructions and closely monitored their actions, leaving them, however, a fair degree of free-hand action based on their estimation of the situation on the ground.[222] The evidence we have from the Carlowitz Congress appears to confirm such a picture. So, from the one side, conversing with the Imperials on the Polish issues, Mavrocordatos stated that the Ottoman plenipotentiaries could not disconnect themselves from 'even a hair of the propositions of our emperor'.[223] On another occasion, he also indicated that they had explicit instructions not to agree to a reconstruction of the Imperial fortress of Titel.[224] From the other side, though, it appears that it was they who chose to bring the issue of Transylvania again to the negotiations' table just before their first conferences with the Imperial delegation.[225]

In contrast to such delicate balancing acts of conformity and freedom of movement, other ambassadors chose not to risk playing the acrobats but rather to stick with the security of the former, as they perceived it. In the case of Muscovy, in theory, physical distance should have given the ambassador much more autonomy to act on the spot. Still, because of that same distance, his conduct was strictly and in a very detailed manner regulated in advance through the instructions (*nakazy*) given to him ahead of his mission.[226] However, Voznitsyn, given the exceptionality of the circumstances of his task – the tsar appointing him ambassador during the stay of the 'Grand Embassy' in Vienna – was not provided with the usual detailed written instructions.[227] Contrary to the other plenipotentiaries closer to their principals, he

221 The relation of Rāmī Meḥmed does not include any letter of the grand vizier to the Ottoman delegation for the duration of the congress.

222 Poulios, 'Αναζητώντας την ειρήνη'.

223 ÖStA, HHStA, Turcica Box 170, Protocollum, fol. 63.

224 ÖStA, HHStA, Türkei I, Turcica Box 170, Protocollum, fol. 70.

225 *Ta'rīḫ-i Ṣulḥ-nāme*, fol. 79^{b}.

226 Hennings, *Russia*, 89.

227 D. and I. Guzevich, *Velikoe posol'stvo*, 108–9.

received his first supplementary orders on 21 January 1699, three days before the signing of the Ottoman–Muscovite truce/armistice agreement.[228]

That notwithstanding, Peter's shadow continued to loom large upon him. He vehemently insisted that he couldn't recognise the mediators as such, having not received an explicit order to concede to it from his principal.[229] In addition, he explicitly stated to the head of the *Posol'skij prikaz*, Lev Kirillovich Naryshkin (d. 1705), that he had strict instructions from the tsar to concede nothing to the Ottomans,[230] something that restricted his options significantly, as did his fear of doing something against the tsar's will.[231] Nonetheless, if we examine his actions, in the end, Voznitsyn did possess a certain degree of freedom. He was instructed with several options on how to proceed. Still, the ultimate choice of which of those options he was to follow – not least because of the distance – was in practice left to him and his perception of the actual situation on the ground.

Of course, the epitome of 'the plenipotentiary illusion' was incorporated by Carlo Ruzzini. The Anonymous Venetian reveals that some voices in the Serenissima's camp claimed that the senate should not have sent an ambassador with the name plenipotentiary but without the proper autonomy of movements. And if they didn't feel comfortable entrusting such powers to one person, they should have sent two, just like the Imperials.[232] Besides such real restraints to his full powers caused by the Venetian decision-making mechanism, it appears that the personality of Ruzzini himself, careful not to overstep his mandate in anything and thus face criticism, if not something worse, back in Venice, played an equally important role in his actions.

However, we should always bear in mind that, oftentimes, the claim of a plenipotentiary that they had not been invested with authority on specific matters could be used as a strategy of not conceding to some points raised by the opposite side. An illustrative example is that of Mavrocordatos, who, in trying to avoid the discussion of religion-related topics and especially the Imperial pretensions over the Catholic possession of the Holy Sepulchre, claimed that 'our *ḫaṭṭ-ı şerīf* (the document containing the sultanic orders) of full-power, gives [that to us] only on the issue of borders. It is not licit for us [to negotiate]

228 Ibid., 109.

229 Bogoslovskii, *Petr I*, 389, 392, 400.

230 Ibid., 401, 406.

231 As it is vividly demonstrated in a letter he wrote to him on 11 January 1699 (J.C.): Ibid., 424.

232 *Narratio*, fol. 36^{v}–37^{r}.

other issues'.[233] Doubts about the veracity of such statements were, of course, occupying the minds of the congress participants. Full of indignation about Ruzzini's conduct during the last stages of the congress, utterly incomprehensible to him, Count Schlik deemed it imperative to add in a P.S. of one of his dispatches to Kinsky that 'our secret information, corroborated by many [other] circumstances, reports that the [negotiating] power of the Venetian ambassador is not so limited as he wants us to believe'.[234]

This episode between the Imperials and Venice attests that believing or not to claims of lack of full power strongly depended on the relation of trust gradually built between the two sides and the evolution of their mutual sentiments towards one another as the negotiations progressed. In the antipode of Schlik's mistrust towards Ruzzini, the affinity between Voznitsyn and the Ottoman plenipotentiaries, present from their secret talks before their official conferences and the exchange of presents between them, was manifested in the affirmation by Rāmī that although the Muscovite 'in essence [was] entirely [dedicated] to the affair'[235] he could not finish it because he lacked the necessary full powers on specific issues from his sovereign.[236] It didn't matter whether or not that was the case. The important thing was that Voznitsyn managed to win the trust and convince his Ottoman interlocutors of his sincerity.

•••

The example of the Carlowitz Congress provides a unique occasion to view the phenomenon of the early modern ambassador comparatively, or holistically, beyond the commonly depicted cultural and religious divides encountered in historiography that supposedly led automatically to completely diverse diplomatic cultures. We saw that despite the differences caused by diverse social orders or other cultural particularities – even among an allegedly homogenous 'Christianity' – the basic and essential lines of a plenipotentiary ambassador's portrait were recognisable to all the participants of the congress.

---

233 ÖStA, HHStA, Turcica 170, Protocollum, fol. 79. That this was actually not the case, *see* the copy of the sultanic *ḫaṭṭ-ı şerīf* in *Taʾrīḫ-i Ṣulḥ-nāme*, fol. 38^{b}–39^{a}.

234 ÖStA, HHStA, Türkei I, Turcica Box 171, Folder 1 (January 1699, 1st half), fol. 180^{r}, Schlik to Kinsky (P.S.), 12 January 1699.

235 *Taʾrīḫ-i Ṣulḥ-nāme*, fol. 118^{a}.

236 Ibid.

So, how could one synopsize the typical profile of a late-seventeenth-century plenipotentiary ambassador across cultural and religious divides? Exclusively male and middle-aged, a nobleman or high-ranking bureaucrat, he was typically well-educated, eloquent and multilingual, though not always experienced in negotiations. His nomination often came through strong connections in the patronage networks of his polity's power circles. As much a champion of his own interests as of his principal's, he was driven by the promise of glory, prestige, and upward social mobility that participation in a peace congress could bring. Despite varying levels of influence in decision-making, he was one of the undisputed protagonists of the 'Theatre of Peace', now entering the central and most eventful part of its plot.

ACT III

The Central Phase of the Congress (13 November–20 December 1698)

Peace agreements are contracts in which the parties satisfy one another to reach an agreement.

An argument used by voices in the Venetian camp favouring an accord with the Porte upon the Ottoman terms in January 1699

Dramatis Personae

The Protagonists

ALEXANDROS MAVROCORDATOS: Second Ottoman plenipotentiary ambassador.
CARLO RUZZINI: Plenipotentiary ambassador of the Republic of Venice.
COUNT FRANZ URLICH VON KINSKY: High Chancellor of Bohemia and influential Imperial minister.
COUNT LEOPOLD SCHLIK: Second Imperial plenipotentiary ambassador.
COUNT LUIGI MARSIGLI: Special adviser of the Imperial embassy on matters of border-making.
COUNT WOLFGANG VON ÖTTINGEN: First Imperial plenipotentiary ambassador.
FRANCESCO LOREDANO: Resident Venetian ambassador at the Imperial Court.
JACOB COLYER: The Dutch mediator at the congress.
LORD WILLIAM PAGET: The English mediator at the congress.
PETR POSTNIKOV: Chief secretary of the Muscovite delegation and primary interpreter of Prokopii Bogdanovich Voznitsyn.
PROKOPII BOGDANOVICH VOZNITSYN: Great and plenipotentiary ambassador of Muscovy.
RĀMĪ MEḤMED: First Ottoman plenipotentiary ambassador.
STANISŁAW MAŁACHOWSKI: Great and plenipotentiary ambassador of the Polish-Lithuanian Commonwealth.

Second Roles

ANDRZEJ GORKOWSKI: Stanisław Małachowski's secretary.
GIANBATTISTA NICOLOSI: Secretary of the Venetian embassy.
LEOPOLD I: Holy Roman Emperor.

 | DOI:10.1163/9789004458499_015

The exchange of the first written proposals between the various delegations and the commencement of the official negotiations on 13 November 1698 inaugurated the next phase of the congress that lasted approximately until 20 December 1698. This novel act of the 'Theatre of Peace' was played out on various stages. There was the arch-stage of the 'public talks' where the congress protagonists discussed and debated the dominant issues that separated them, most prominently those regarding territorial arrangements and border making. Outside this central podium, the various participants continued to work in another, less formal arena, where, as in the first phase, they were trying to solicit support from their allies and the mediators. Lastly, there was a third stage, this time outside the congress venue, the Viennese Court. There, Venice desperately searched for assistance in its negotiation with the Ottomans.

This Act would prove catalytic for the general peacemaking process. It opened the road for an effective Ottoman–Imperial agreement and drastically reconfigured the situation and relations inside the allied camp. Around 20 December, the Polish-Lithuanian Commonwealth and Muscovy finished their negotiations with the Ottomans successfully and unexpectedly swiftly. The 'bad apples' of the preliminaries were transformed from vehement enemies of peace to effective peacemakers. The only cacophony in this pro-peace symphony came from the least expected among its soloists. By the end of this phase, there would be a new congress 'outcast' and obstacle to general reconciliation: Venice and its ambassador Carlo Ruzzini.

Narration Part 1: Sur la manière de négocier entre les plénipotentiaires

> [The Turks] wanted only [to negotiate] in viva voce. Not through the mediators, though, but [directly] between the parties interested, constraining them to a debate of discourses and truly long conferences.[1]
>
> CARLO RUZZINI, *Relazione Finale*

∴

The period between early November and late December 1698 constituted one of the busiest periods of the Carlowitz Congress. Twenty-five official conferences were held, eleven between the Ottomans and the Imperials, six between the former and the Muscovites, five with the *Rzeczpospolita*, and three with Venice.[2] It was a truly remarkable number for such a short timespan, not typically seen in previous congresses, and a manifestation of the willingness of the majority of participants to achieve a swift conclusion to their affairs.

1 How to Set About the Congress Negotiations and in Which Mode to Pursue Them?

A common practice of previous seventeenth-century peace congresses was that, after the promulgation of the Congress Regulation, the talks would kick off with an exchange of each participant's written proposals, followed by counterproposals from the other side and so on.[3] The mediators played a crucial role in this exchange of epistles, providing their 'good services' as their carriers and primary informants of each party's positions. Sometimes, the negotiations would take place only in this format, without their leading actors meeting each other in person, not even once, as had happened during the Congress of Westphalia between the French and the Spaniards due to their ceremonial

1 Ruzzini, *Relazione*, 353.
2 *See* Table 2 below.
3 Brunert and Oetzel, 'Verhandlungstechniken', 460.

 | DOI:10.1163/9789004458499_016

disputes.[4] As it is, it was only natural that several participants thought that the same practice of exchanging proposals would also repeat itself this time. Thus, writing to Count Kinsky on 30 October, Count Schlik assessed that the Ottomans would 'give their first strike by the pen'.[5]

He was proved only partially correct. The Ottomans did strike first with the written word, but what they dispatched to the Imperial embassy via the mediators was not their general proposals on every topic they wished to discuss but a renewed claim regarding the future status of the Principality of Transylvania. And so, for roughly a week (7–13 November), 'the affairs of Transylvania were in a great agitation'.[6] And, although the Imperial embassy, in a repetition of the procedure followed in the exchange of full powers, demanded that its allies hand over their written demands to be delivered collectively to the Ottomans through the mediation,[7] the Porte's delegates refused to accept them 'not to commit themselves to the obligation to respond, and in the long exchange of writings', as Ruzzini claims.[8] Which mode then did the Ottomans favour?

A straightforward answer is provided by an examination of the most frequently used Ottoman Turkish words to denote 'diplomatic negotiation' during the last quarter of the seventeenth century, notably the nouns *müẕākere* and *mükāleme* and the verb *söyleşmek*.[9] What all of them share in common is the meaning of a candid discussion between two parties, mainly by using oral arguments.[10] However, the preference for viva voce discussions over written ones had only partially to do with the Ottoman cultural background. For instance, during the Failed Vienna Congress, the Ottoman delegation – in which Mavrocordatos was again the second plenipotentiary – conceded to a hybrid oral and written negotiation form.[11] The unsuccessful result of these talks might have proven to Mavrocordatos the perils of indirect communication.

---

4 May, *Repräsentation und Statuspolitik*, 96, 98.

5 ÖStA, HHStA, Türkei I, Turcica Box 167, Folder 2 (October 1698, 2nd half), fol. 209^r, Schlik to Kinsky, 30 October 1698.

6 ÖStA, HHStA, Türkei I, Turcica Box 168, Folder 1 (November 1698, 1st half), fol. 284^r, Schlik to Kinsky, 13 November 1698. *See* more below.

7 ÖStA, HHStA, Türkei I, Turcica Box 170, Diarium et Cerimoniale, fol. 23.

8 Ruzzini, *Relazione*, 353.

9 *See*, for instance, *Taʾrīḫ-i ṣulḥnāme*, fol. 81^b–82^a.

10 James W. Redhouse, *A Turkish and English Lexicon* (Beirut: Librairie du Liban 1987)1096, 1792, 1952. In his dictionary, Meninski defines *müẕākere* as 'conferire, trattar insieme, discorrere' and *mükāleme* as 'colloquio, dialogo, discorso, conferenza, ragionamento': Meninski, *Thesaurus*, 4531, 4858.

11 *See* above, Prelude.

So, in 1698, the preference for direct discussions was first and foremost a conscious strategy adopted by the Exalted State's embassy.[12]

During the first Imperial–Ottoman conference, the Habsburg delegation suggested exchanging proposals on paper using Paget and Colyer's services. This is how the Ottomans perceived it:

> While we have assembled in a conference negotiation, what are the ulterior motives of their statement to [put] their intentions on paper, the plenipotentiaries of the Exalted State pondered? Ostensibly, needing more guts to debate orally, they brought into writing their unmerited thoughts to embarrass us by blurring our desired issue of evacuations and demolitions. And the sheet of paper they will give [us] should [certainly] not be congruent in any way with the intention of the Exalted State. Or, once it is on the table, the talks are to be based [solely] on it. They thought in this vein, and they show absolutely no desire to [negotiations] by writing.[13]

This passage is quite revealing because it manifests how the use of a negotiation medium was not regarded as innocent or solely a recourse for the smoother process of the talks, but it was also seen as a strategic weapon to influence the topics of the agenda of the discussion and push them in the direction each party desired. Not voicing, of course, publicly these secret thoughts of theirs, the Ottomans resorted to an argument about expediency. 'The Turks proposed [...] to negotiate orally', wrote the Imperial ambassadors in their relation to Leopold I, 'because the exchange of letters would require much time in this so late a season and [one] would have finished more in an hour of viva voce [discussion] as in a good deal of days of a written [one]'.[14]

With the Imperial delegation's consent and the backing of the mediators,[15] the oral format was ultimately imposed, resulting in what Ruzzini described

12 As would have been the French one in Münster, Nijmegen and Utrecht to solely negotiate via written proposals: Brunert and Oetzel, 'Verhandlungstechniken', 460.

13 *Ta'rīḫ-i ṣulḥnāme*, fol. 81[b]–82[a].

14 ÖStA, HHStA, Türkei I, Turcica Box 168, Folder 2 (November 1698, 2nd half), fol. 16[r], Imperial Plenipotentiaries to Leopold I, 17 November 1698. *See* also, *Ta'rīḫ-i ṣulḥnāme*, fol. 82[a].

15 During the first Ottoman–Commonwealth session, when Małachowski expressed his wish to submit his peace proposals in writing and delegate the negotiations to the mediators, Lord Paget intervened and recommended following 'the way that was observed with the others', namely the use of the oral medium: Cernovodeanu, 'Le journal', 327.

as 'a debate of discourses and truly long conferences'.[16] Such a feature strongly differentiated Carlowitz from other, earlier seventeenth-century congresses where the indirect, written form of negotiations was more prevalent. Nonetheless, we should bear in mind that even there, the oral medium was not wholly abandoned and was generally considered a safer way to preserve the secret character of the talks since one's written proposals could easily be leaked to the local press by one's opponent.[17] In the end, despite not stemming entirely from practical reasons, it could justifiably be argued that the format of the negotiations adopted at Carlowitz did contribute significantly to the relatively rapid conclusion of the talks since, ironically, the Ottoman faked argument proved equally sound: '[one] would have finished more in an hour of viva voce [discussion] as in a good deal of days of a written [one]'.

2 The Fate of Transylvania Is Sealed

And verily, the fate of the Principality of Transylvania, a major point of contention between the Ottomans and the Imperials during the Preliminaries, was to be decided relatively quickly in their first two conferences. Rāmī Meḥmed justified to the grand vizier the decision of the plenipotentiaries of the Exalted State to bring the Carpathian principality's status back on the table in the following terms,

> [although] it was plain for all to see that a discussion of Transylvania, while they [the Imperials] didn't have the power to cede even a single small fort, would cause a novel, unpleasant conflict and it was evident that [such a claim] could not be based on the Instrument of the [Foundation of Peace], [it was thought better to mention it] for a hope of profit or rather that if this article was not dropped, something beneficial could have possibly come out of it in the future.[18]

---

16 Ruzzini, *Relazione*, 353. According to the Venetian, although they welcomed such a negotiating mode with open aversion, the other ambassadors had to comply out of necessity (ibid). However, their forced consent didn't prevent them from openly expressing their desire for a change of the peace talks' medium during the conferences. For instance, before a meeting he had with the Ottomans on 10 December 1698, Voznitsyn presented the mediators with some written proposals to be handed over to the Porte's delegation, demanding that the latter replied to them also in writing because, according to him, through this method 'one can better see [one's] intentions and this was often practised [in the past]': Cernovodeanu, 'Le journal', 338.

17 Brunert and Oetzel, 'Verhandlungstechniken", 460.

18 *Ta'rīḥ-i ṣulḥnāme*, fol. 79^{a-b}.

TABLE 2 Official conferences held at the Carlowitz Peace Congress from 13 November to 20 December 1698

November 1698	December 1698
13th: 1st Ottoman–Imperial conference	**1st**: 10th Ottoman–Imperial conference
14th: 2nd Ottoman–Imperial conference	**2nd**: 3rd Muscovite–Ottoman conference
15th: 3rd Ottoman–Imperial conference	**4th**: 3rd Commonwealth–Ottoman conference
16th: 4th Ottoman–Imperial conference	**6th**: 11th Imperial Ottoman conference
17th: 1st Venetian–Ottoman conference	**7th**: 4th Ottoman–Muscovite conference
18th: 2nd Venetian–Ottoman conference	**9th**: 4th Ottoman–Commonwealth conference
19th: 1st Ottoman–Muscovite conference	**10th**: 5th Ottoman–Muscovite conference
21st: 5th Imperial–Ottoman and 1st Ottoman–Commonwealth conferences	**18th**: 5th Ottoman–Commonwealth conference
22nd: 2nd Ottoman–Muscovite conference	**19th**: 6th Ottoman–Muscovite conference
23rd: 6th Imperial–Ottoman conference	
24th: 3rd Ottoman–Venetian conference	
25th: 2nd Ottoman–Commonwealth conference	
26th: 7th Ottoman–Imperial conference	
28th: 8th Ottoman–Imperial conference	
29th: 9th Ottoman–Imperial conference	

SOURCE: ÖSTA, HHSTA, TÜRKEI I, TURCICA BOX 170, PROTOCOLLUM, FOL. 8–119

This demand was masked under the guise of compensation for the 'grief and pain' of the loss of so many provinces (*ḥāsıl olacaḳ te'essüf ü telehhüfü def'*)[19] – a discourse the Ottomans would systematically follow during the negotiations when they demanded territorial compensations – and was met with a vehement reaction by the Imperial embassy. 'These messieurs', commented Schlik in indignation, 'after being the ones to start the war and to cause us all the harm they possibly could, now demand a charity and a small one of a kingdom. I have responded to Milord [Paget], that having shown them no mercy during the war, we don't want to give any quarter in the issue of peace either'.[20] The Ottomans should clearly understand right from the start who had the upper hand here. 'There is no better way to get rid of a quarrelsome individual than to present him with an ultimatum', Schlik added emphatically.[21] Either the Ottomans would abandon their claim, or the congress would be blown up in lightspeed. Faced with such vigorous opposition, the Porte's delegation, also advised by the mediators, was forced eventually to back off. Yet could such a concession have been their main aim all along?

While one could not exclude beforehand the interpretation of the request for Transylvania to return to a status quo ante bellum as a genuine desire to conserve by all possible means a vestige of Ottoman control over the Carpathian Principality, being either a matter of prestige for the sultan and his government, as we have already seen, or as a way to present to the internal 'audience' a 'victorious peace',[22] it would be better to interpret it, similarly to the late Ottomanist Rifaat Abou-El-Haj, as a clever negotiating strategy.[23] De facto not in their hands since the early 1690s, any Ottoman pretension on Transylvania was, at best, chimeric. Yet, it seems that such a demand was not entirely genuine, but rather it was presented as such, in order, after its withdrawal, to be used as leverage for the Ottomans to demand compensation for their 'loss' in other matters crucial to them.[24] 'We have conceded to you on the issue of

19 Ibid.

20 ÖStA, HHStA, Türkei I, Turcica Box 168, Folder 1 (November 1698, 1st half), fol. 170^{r}, Schlik to Kinsky, 8 November 1698.

21 Ibid., fol. 285^{r}, Schlik to Kinsky, 13 November 1698.

22 *See* below, 329.

23 Abou-El-Haj, 'The Reisülküttab', 73, 85–6.

24 The Ottoman delegation pursued the same strategy in its negotiations with Venice concerning the 'compensations' the Exalted State claimed for supposedly 'ceding' the entire Morea peninsula to the Republic, despite not having controlled any part of it since the late 1680s. *See* Mavrocordatos's argumentation in BNM, Ms.it.VII 399(8625), fol. 301^{r}, Alcuni discorsi delle Conferenze raccolti dal Nicolosi.

Transylvania. Now you have to make us a [similar] concession on the matter of the Eyalet [Province] of Temeşvar', the Ottoman ambassadors declared during their second conference with the Imperial delegation.[25]

Faced with these bargaining tactics, the Imperial delegation responded with its own. After attesting the effectiveness of issuing ultimatums, Öttingen and Schlik menaced the Ottomans again, adding, this time, some theatrical elements too, to make clear that they were indeed serious. Thus, as Rāmī relates, after a 'hot' third meeting on 15 November, 'everybody went to their tents, and they [the Imperials] prepared their carriages. And they also uttered that they would not convene [with us] again'.[26] Spirits were finally calmed down with the intervention of the mediators.[27] Yet such demonstrations of bravado were not genuine. Their chief purpose was to put pressure on and show determination to one's opponent while trying at the same time not to lead the situation to the point of no return. Nonetheless, when the emperor was informed of this strategy of his embassy, he disapproved of it. 'And because we don't like to see that our side often mentions an abruption of the negotiations, it would be much better when one or the other difficulty is encountered, due to which the negotiations could cause a bit of tense, [to find] other formalities and use them [instead]'.[28]

Tensions did run high quite often during the conferences, especially when the main theme on the daily agenda happened to be territorial possession and border delimitation. It was no coincidence that in both cases in which the Imperial embassy threatened to leave the talks, it was because of a heated debate over the question of the future dominion over Transylvania and the province of Ṭemeşvar. It is thus high time to dive deeper into what the totality of the congress actors regarded as the crux of their negotiation.

25 *Ta'rīḥ-i ṣulḥnāme*, fol. 88^{b}. Mavrocordatos also pointedly stated that, if not for the 'demolition and evacuation clause' – which, according to Ottoman interpretations, applied only to the Imperials in the Ṭemeşvar district – the Porte 'would not have agreed to abandon Transylvania': ÖStA, HHStA, Türkei I, Turcica Box 170, Protocollum, fol. 21.

26 *Ta'rīḥ-i ṣulḥnāme*, fol. 92^{b}.

27 Ibid.

28 ÖStA, HHStA, Türkei I, Turcica Box 168, Folder 2 (November 1698, 2nd half), fol. 99^{v}–100^{r}, supplementary Imperial instructions to the Carlowitz embassy, 19 November 1698.

At the Negotiating Table I: Territorial Claims, Possession and Border Making

> Good peace depends on good borders.[1]
>
> CARLO RUZZINI

•••

> When one side wants to keep everything and the other to get back everything, a way needs to be found that satisfies both.[2]
>
> ALEXANDROS MAVROCORDATOS

∴

Anima tractatus. That's how Lord Paget characterised the issues of territorial possession and border-making during an Ottoman–Commonwealth conference on 3 December 1698.[3] As 'the most important subject of our whole negotiation', would Count Schlik likewise refer to them in a letter to Kinsky, where he summarised the results of the first four conferences the Habsburg embassy had had with the Ottomans.[4] During the *début* Ottoman–Commonwealth meeting, after Małachowski voiced his 'pretensions', Mavrocordatos explained them to Rāmī Meḥmed and divided them into two categories: 'what concerns the borders and the other small points'.[5] The different delegations could not agree on many things, but they all concurred on one: the centrality that territorial and border arrangements occupied in their negotiating agenda. Thus, any reconstruction of the Carlowitz Congress that leaves out an extensive discussion of this cardinal issue is most certainly doomed to be incomplete.

---

1 ÖStA, HHStA, Türkei I, Turcica Box 168, Folder 1 (November 1698, 1st half), fol. 313^{v}, protocol of the Ottoman–Venetian conference with Imperial interposition on 16 January 1699.

2 Cernovodeanu, 'Le journal', 328.

3 Gorkowski, *Compendium Legationis*, 25^{v}.

4 ÖStA, HHStA, Türkei I, Turcica Box 168, Folder 2 (November 1698, 2nd half), fol. 304^{v}–305^{r}, Schlik to Kinsky, 18 November 1698.

5 Cernovodeanu, 'Le journal', 327.

 | DOI:10.1163/9789004458499_017

This section is comprised of three parts. The first provides an overall, cohesive picture of the territorial claims and aspirations with which each party came to the congress. Many of them have already been referenced a few times before. Still, it is useful to have them again aggregated here so that the following two parts are far more intelligible and easier to follow. The second part then focuses on possession and the various interpretations the actors gave to it according to their territorial aims. Lastly, we will touch upon the issue of borders, their types following the congress contemporaries and the multiple ways through which they were to be determined, marked, and drawn.

1 The Territorial Aspirations of the Participants of the Carlowitz Congress

One could not entirely grasp the arguments, conceptions, and interpretations of the various participants on what constituted a possession and how borders should be drawn without an overview of the territorial aspirations of each and every one of the leading congress actors at the start of the negotiations. It was these aspirations and not the actual situation or geographical premises that mostly dictated which piece of land belonged to whom and which border was the best to adopt.

Let us start with the Venetians, the most ardent defenders of an *uti possidetis* without exceptions and the second – after the Imperials – greatest territorial winners of the Sixteen Years' War.[6] Their territorial interests were concentrated in two principal geographic regions: Dalmatia and southern Greece. Dalmatia became the focus of Venetian expansion in the eastern Mediterranean in the 1670s, with the Serenissima aspiring to acquire a new 'Kingdom' there, to compensate for the loss to the Ottomans of the island of Crete in 1669.[7] The chance to realise this aspiration weighed heavily in the decision of the Republic of Saint Mark to enter the anti-Ottoman Christian alliance in 1684. In the Holy League Treaty, it was clearly stipulated that Venice was free to acquire any

6 For the territorial ambitions with which Venice arrived in the peace congress, *see* also Poumarède, *L'Empire de Venise*, 286–7.

7 Ibid., 126–8. For the long Venetian territorial presence and strategical interests in the eastern shore of the Adriatic, dating back to the Late Middle Ages and lasting until the abrupt ending of the Venetian Republic at the end of the eighteenth century, *see* Egidio Ivetic, 'Venezia e l'Adriatico Orientale: connotazioni di un rapporto (secoli XIV–XVIII)', in Gherardo Ortalli and Oliver Jens Schmitt (eds.), *Der westliche Balkan, der Adriaraum und Venedig (13.–18. Jahrhundert)* (Vienna: Österreichische Akademie der Wissenschaften 2009) 239–60.

Ottoman territory in Dalmatia from the eastern Adriatic coast to the Dinaric Alps.[8] Yet the beginning of the fighting brought a significant alteration in the Venetian strategic objectives as the supporters of a territorial expansion in southern Greece prevailed over those who favoured one in the Dalmatian theatre. Thus, the latter was relegated to a secondary role.[9] Despite that, during the war, the forces of the Serenissima in the area managed to acquire some strategic fortresses, but these territorial acquisitions fell relatively short of achieving the initial Venetian designs concretely. Nonetheless, ahead of the Carlowitz Congress, Dalmatia continued to figure prominently in the Venetian mind. In what was characterised by the Anonymous Venetian as 'one of the principal points which the senate aspired',[10] the Serenissima was convinced – or wanted to appear so – that its war conquests in the eastern Adriatic fully justified a unification of its possessions there, by forming a straight, uninterrupted line,[11] which by cutting off from the rest of sultan's domains its long commercial rival and tributary of the Ottomans, the small Republic of Ragusa, would basically deliver it to the mercy of the Venetians and strangle its economy.[12]

Coming now to southern Greece, the Republic of Saint Mark was determined to safeguard its most significant acquisition during the war, the Morea peninsula, or as the Venetians called it, 'il Regno di Morea'.[13] To achieve that

8 Zdenko Zlatar, *Between the Double Eagle and the Crescent. The Republic of Dubrovnik and the Origins of the Eastern Question* (New York: Columbia University Press 1992) 139, 155.

9 Ibid., 152.

10 *Narratio*, fol. 32^v.

11 According to the Anonymous Venetian, Ruzzini was given some flexibility in the latitude but not in the longitude of this line: Ibid., fol. 33^r.

12 As was rightly predicted by Marsigli: ÖStA, HHStA, Türkei I, Turcica Box 168, Folder 2 (November 1698, 2nd half), fol. 224^v, Marsigli to Kinsky, s.d. (most probably early November 1698). The *Bolognese* argued that the Venetians wanted 'to stop entirely this call-port [for commercial] traffic and render [thus] busier theirs of Spalato and Castel Nuovo (ibid). According to Marsigli, Ruzzini would also repeat the same argument in a meeting the two of them had during the last phase of the congress: Ibid., fol. 274^r, Marsigli to Kinsky, 21 January 1699. For the Venetian plans to incorporate Ragusa, *see* also below, At the Negotiating Table Part II.

13 The greatest part of the Morea peninsula was conquered by a Venetian expeditionary force led by Francesco Morosini (d. 1694) between 1684 and 1687: Eutichia Liata and Kostas Tsiknakis (eds.), *Με την Αρμάδα στο Μοριά 1684–1687. Ανέκδοτο ημερολόγιο με σχέδια* (Athens: Hellenic Research Foundation/Olkos Publishing 1998). The conquest of the Morea was widely celebrated in Venice, heralding the regeneration of the Serenissima's military prowess and glorious imperial past: Anastasia Stouraiti, *War, Communication, and the Politics of Culture in Early Modern Venice* (Cambridge: Cambridge University Press 2023).

aim, a security belt surrounding the 'Kingdom' should be established.[14] This belt included the Gerania mountain range north of the Corinthian Isthmus[15] and complete control of the Corinthian Gulf through the strategic fortresses of Lepanto and Castello di Rumelia (Antirrio).[16] Slightly further north, after the capture of the island of Lefkada in 1684[17] and its strategic dependencies on the mainland, the town-fortresses of Preveza and Vonitsa,[18] the Serenissima achieved complete control over the Ionian Islands and the entrance to the Ambrakian Gulf. If Venice's territorial designs were to be realised in full, they would have created a safe maritime route that was in complete Venetian control, connecting their newly conquered territories with the Ionian islands, the Serenissima's possessions in Dalmatia and ultimately Venice itself.[19]

At the heart of the *Rzeczpospolita*'s designs laid the recuperation of Kamianets-Podilskyi, which its forces had been unable to capture all these sixteen years of war. Claiming the fortress was, of course, incongruent with the *uti possidetis* Foundation of Peace. Still, for the Commonwealth, it constituted a prize of highly symbolic value – as revenge for the 1672–78 defeats – and so it was considered a sine qua non for any agreement with the Exalted State. Of

14 ÖStA, HHStA, Türkei I, Turcica Box 167, Folder 2 (October 1698, 2nd half), fol. 45^{v}, Marsigli to Kinsky, 16 October 1698. Finding the best way of securing their precious newly acquired 'Regno' formed a constant preoccupation of the Venetian authorities, with various solutions being put on the table: Aggeliki Panopoulou, 'Da mar a mar. Μιὰ πρόταση γιὰ τὴν ἄμυνα τῆς περιοχῆς τῆς Κορίνθου στὰ τέλη τοῦ 17ου αἰώνα', in Katsiardi-Hering (ed.), *Βενετικοὶ χάρτες*, 230–9.

15 Marsigli to Kinsky, s.d. (most probably early November 1698), fol. 223$^{r–v}$. The Imperial 'special advisor' sustained, though, that those mountains would not provide any real security to the Republic: Ibid., fol. 223^{v}.

16 ÖStA, HHStA, Türkei I, Turcica Box 171, Folder 1 (January 1699, 1st half), fol. 135^{r}, Marsigli to Kinsky, 3 January 1699. Before its capture by the Venetian forces during the summer of 1687 (together with the Castello di Rumelia), Lepanto had been in the Serenissima's possession from 1407 until 1499: Anastasia Papadia-Lala, *Ο θεσμός των αστικών κοινοτήτων στον ελληνικό χώρο κατά την περίοδο της Βενετοκρατίας (13ος–18ος αι.). Μία συνθετική προσέγγιση* (Venice: Greek Institute of Venice 2008) 219–26.

17 Lefkada was the only one of the Ionian Islands that ever came under Ottoman rule (1485–1684). Apart from a brief Ottoman reconquest (1715–16), it remained under the control of the Republic of Saint Mark until 1797: Ibid., 428–54.

18 Ibid., 455–64, which also includes the relevant bibliography on the two town-fortresses under Venetian rule. For the Venetian presence in western Greece during the Sixteen Years' War, *see* A.P. Archondidis, 'Η βενετοκρατία στη Δυτική Ελλάδα (1684–1699). Συμβολή στην ιστορία της περιοχής του Αμβρακικού κόλπου και της Αιτωλοακαρνανίας' (Ph.D. thesis, Aristotelian University of Thessaloniki 1983).

19 In a letter to the tsar, Voznitsyn pointed out Preveza and Lepanto's cardinal importance for controlling the trade routes and invited Peter to check them on the map himself: Bogoslovskii, *Petr I*, 419.

equal symbolic importance was that the fortress be delivered in its present state, with all its artillery, and not demolished, as the Ottoman side proposed since the 1689–90 negotiations in Vienna. Apart from this cardinal demand, the *Rzeczpospolita* could be contended, at least, with a return to the pre-1672 border with the Ottomans along the river Dniester,[20] abandoning thus the relatively meagre gains it made during the war in northern Moldavia.[21]

Muscovy's principal preoccupation was to secure its most valuable conquest during the war, namely the vital port of Azov, the *point d'entrée* of the tsar to the Black Sea. Yet, without the control of the Kerch peninsula, Peter remained blocked inside the Azov Sea. That's why the Muscovites considered their war aims incomplete and vehemently opposed the peace settlement during the Preliminaries. And despite the recommendations of the Imperial ministers that the ambassadors at the congress should support Muscovy's claims on Kerch,[22] the plenipotentiaries themselves realised how unrealistic an Ottoman concession on this matter was. 'As for the fortress of Kerch, though, [...] the Turks are so unlikely to concede to it, as to an evacuation of Constantinople', they reported to the emperor.[23] In addition, of particular importance to Muscovy was a line of fortresses along the southern part of the Dnieper close to Crimea, captured by the Muscovites in the early 1690s.[24] They had been trying to take possession of the lands in the Lower Dnieper since 1681 and had been building fortresses there since the late 1680s during their first unsuccessful attempts to invade Crimea.[25] The control of this region was probably seen as a possible alternative access to the Black Sea[26] and an effective way to keep the Tatars at

20 AGAD, Archivum Koronne Warszawskie, 1/3/0/33/78 teczka 498 nr. 826, fol. 2, Supplementum Instructionis [...] ad Castra Regia die 5ta Mensis Septembris Anno D. 1698.

21 They included the forts – or 'cloisters' according to the Ottomans and Imperials – of Roman, Neamţ, Botoşani, Târgu Frumos, Cîmpulung, Suceava and Soroka, captured during the various campaigns of King Jan III Sobieski in Moldavia (1684–91): Eduard Baidaus, 'Księstwo Mołdawskie w polityce zagranicznej Polski od zwycięstwa pod Wiedniem do zawarcia pokoju karłowickiego (1683–1699)', in Czamanskiej and Szulca, *Traktaty Karlowickie*, 215–21; Wagner, *Stanisław Jabłonowski*, 70–97; *Ta'rīḫ-i Ṣulḥ-nāme*, fol. 107a.

22 ÖStA, HHStA, Türkei I, Turcica Box 168, Folder 1 (November 1698, 1st half), fol. 100v, relation of the members of the 'Turkish Deputation' to Leopold I, 15 November 1698.

23 ÖStA, HHStA, Türkei I, Turcica Box 168, Folder 2 (November 1698, 2nd half), fol. 133r, Imperial Plenipotentiaries to Leopold I, 22 November 1698.

24 Kirill Kochegarov, "From the 'Eternal Peace' to the Treaty of Carlowitz: Relations between Russia, the Sublime Porte and the Crimean Khanate (1686–1699)", in Heywood and Parvev, *The Treaties of Carlowitz*, 195. Those fortresses were Gazikerman (*Казыкермень*), Doğan (*Тавань*), Arslankerman (*Гарсланкермень*) and Şan-Giray(?) (*Шангирей*) (Bogoslovskii, *Petr I*, 399); In the relation of Rāmī Meḥmed, though, they are named as *Ṭoġan*, *Gāzī Giray*, *Nuṣretkerman* and *Ḳalburun*: *Ta'rīḫ-i ṣulḥnāme*, fol. 109a.

25 Kochegarov, "From the 'Eternal Peace' to the Treaty of Carlowitz", 186, 191.

26 As Ruzzini sustained in his *Relazione*: Ruzzini, *Relazione*, 370.

bay and obstruct their communications with the Ottoman-controlled region of Budjak. What is more, the control of the right bank of the Lower Dnieper also possessed a vital economic significance for the Zaporizhian Cossacks, subjects of the tsar.[27]

The Ottomans were the party that had suffered tremendous territorial losses during the war. The vast majority of Ottoman Hungary was gone, except for the cardinal fortress of Ṭemeşvar; the Venetians had snatched away the Morea, Azov had fallen to the Muscovites, Podolia (Kamianets apart) and western Ukraine to the Commonwealth, the latter managing also to take control of parts of the Principality of Moldavia, the most essential cattle provider, together with Wallachia, of the Ottoman capital. Their dire situation notwithstanding, the Ottomans were determined to safeguard as much as possible, regain what they could and arrange the future borders in a way that could favour possible attempts to recuperate some of the lost territories in the near or longer future.

Regarding the Imperials, their greatest effort was primarily concentrated on acquiring de nouveau complete control over the *Eyālet* (province) of Ṭemeşvar. As for Venice, they were determined to deprive the Serenissima of its 'Morea safety belt' in order to ease a reconquest of the peninsula, retain control over the Corinthian Gulf, and pave the way for their return to Lefkada by striping the Republic of the island's principal bastions in the mainland, Preveza and Vonitsa.[28] In Dalmatia, their principal goal was to conserve by all means the territorial connection between Ragusa and the 'Well Protected Domains' and thus their suzerainty over the small Adriatic republic. Moving north-eastwards, the Ottomans were willing to return a demolished Kamianets-Podilskyi to the Commonwealth and renounce their claims over Podolia and western Ukraine in return for an evacuation of all Polish-held territories in Moldavia. Lastly, concerning the Muscovites, while forced by the circumstances to concede to the loss of Azov, at least temporarily, they centred their attention on the demolition of the Muscovite Dnieper fortresses to deprive the tsar's armies of future bases of operation against the Crimean Khanate and to prevent the disruption of the communications between the latter and the rest of the sultanic dominions.

For the Imperial side, the biggest territorial winner of the sixteen-year conflict, the principal goal was to secure the possession of the new conquests by the arrangement of a border that would have deterred future Ottoman incursions

27 Kochegarov, "From the 'Eternal Peace' to the Treaty of Carlowitz", 192.

28 Already during the previous peace negotiations in 1691, the Ottoman side agreed to an *uti possidetis* treaty basis with the Serenissima, with the only exception, though, that Venice would keep none of its possessions in mainland Greece: Van den H. Boogert, 'The Spoils of Peace', 68.

or invasions and would ensure the control of the commercial traffic along the Danube and its tributaries stemming down from Transylvania. No questioning over the possession of the latter would be allowed, whereas an ambitious claim over Wallachia was ultimately dropped and left to be raised at another time.

Lastly, related to the Imperial designs, an interesting example of the degree to which one member of the Holy League was willing to go to protect its own interest, even at the expense of one of its closest allies, is the instructions given to the two Imperial plenipotentiaries regarding the Venetian border arrangements in Croatia, in what was to be referred to in the eighteenth century as the *Triplex Confinium*, where the Ottoman, Imperial and Venetian territories met one another.[29] The emperor stated categorically that in this issue, his interests should be absolutely safeguarded and not compromised in any way.[30] Some compromises appear to have been made in the end, but where negotiations didn't deliver, brute force did. One could only imagine the Venetian consternation and feeling of impotence, when on 10 June 1699, a few months after the conclusion of peace, Habsburg forces, in a vivid manifestation of unequal power relations, launched a surprise attack on the fortress of Zuonigrad held by … the Serenissima, quickly occupying and retaining it even after the demarcation of the new border.[31]

2 '*Uti Possidetis* Sequel': the Congress Playing Out

The disambiguation of territorial possession – who owned what – went part and parcel with the definition of borders. These two were so inseparable as to be even considered by the participants as one and the same thing.[32] However, whether the discussion of one should precede the other or whether it should be done concurrently was subject to the strategic concerns of the various actors.[33] For instance, since their first conference with the Imperials, the Ottomans strongly persisted, for reasons we will touch upon immediately

---

29 For the *Triplex Confinium* and the bibliography relevant to it, *see* Egidio Ivetic, 'Territori di confine (secoli XV–XVIII)', in Oliver Jens Schmitt and Ermanno Orlando (eds.), *Il Commonwealth veneziano tra il 1204 e la fine della Repubblica. Identità e peculiarità* (Venice: Istituto veneto di scienze, lettere ed arti 2015) 192–3.

30 ÖStA, HHStA, Türkei I, Turcica Box 166, Folder 3 (September 1698, 2nd half), fol. 143^{v}, Instructio pro Legatis Plenipotentairijs Caes[are]is.

31 Maria Pia Pedani, *Dalla frontiera al confine* (Venice: Herder 2002) 49–50.

32 ÖStA, HHStA, Türkei I, Turcica Box 170, Protocollum, fol. 12–13.

33 Abou-El-Haj, 'The Reisülküttab', 74–5.

after, in a combined debate of the two issues at once,[34] and, in the end, they succeeded in passing through with their scheme in both their talks with the Habsburg and the Venetian delegations.[35]

However, if a conjoint discussion of the two topics was possible for the Carlowitz plenipotentiaries, it is undoubtedly not recommendable for a historical study unless the author acknowledges from the outset that his readers are going to be lost in the subsequent maze this option would undoubtedly create. Hence, we will instead opt first to clarify how possession was defined and perceived by the actors before 'closing the frontiers' of this section by examining the late-seventeenth-century border-making ideas and practices. Lastly, to better understand the issue at hand, one should proceed from the general to the specific. The general here is the Foundation of Peace, that of *uti possidetis* – already agreed during the Preliminaries – and the ways each party interprets it. The specific is how these interpretations were subsequently applied to individual cases.

Although the principle of *uti possidetis*/*ʿalā ḥālihi* was seemingly established as the Foundation of Peace during the first Act of the negotiations, the ramifications of the will of most of the participants either to loosely interpret it or to deny it overtly were to be played out in total during the congress. Of all the Holy League allies, only Venice had a real investment in its strict observation. We have already discussed how, while seemingly supporting an *uti possidetis* without exception, the Imperial side was tacitly compromising it by admitting that the current situation on the ground was not enough to secure a clear separation of the territories of the two empires. For the Imperial ministers, such a separation could only be achieved through the mutual evacuation or demolition of certain minor fortresses and the permutation of territories wherever a need arose.

Coming now to the Commonwealth and Muscovy, besides the fact that for them a rigorous application of *uti possidetis* was entirely out the question, they hadn't even signed the preliminary Instrument, and so, even if their allies were equally committed there for themselves, they declared that they were not strictly bound by it. Thus, Voznitsyn told the Imperial delegation, 'that the *uti possidetis* is a good thing [only] when one could add [something more] to it'.[36] He voiced a similar amplification demand to the Ottomans, and

34 *Taʿrīḥ-i ṣulḥnāme*, fol. 86[b].

35 ÖStA, HHStA, Türkei I, Turcica Box 168, Folder 2 (November 1698, 2nd half), fol. 16[v], Imperial plenipotentiaries to Leopold I, 17 November 1698.

36 ÖStA, HHStA, Türkei I, Turcica Box 167, Folder 2 (October 1698, 2nd half), fol. 207[v]–208[r], Schlik to Kinsky, 30 October 1698.

when Mavrocordatos mentioned the demolition/evacuation clause and the Ottoman interpretation of it, he pleaded ignorance: 'he doesn't know anything about it [...] when this was written, there was no one of them in Vienna'.[37]

When Małachowski declared to the Ottoman delegation during their first session that his sine qua non-demand was the return of the fortress of Kamianets, 'without tricks and with all the canons and [other] war devices inside it',[38] Mavrocordatos was quick to notice that such a proposal ran contrary to the established Foundation of Peace, since the Podolian fortress was still in the hands of the Ottomans. The Commonwealth's ambassador then recoursed to an analogous to the, as we shall see, Ottoman interpretation stratagem of the preliminary agreement:

> To that, I responded that I don't wish to enter into the question of the Foundation of Peace laid down because I don't oppose it. However, this Foundation cannot strictly bind me because we were not there when it was decided [...] Nonetheless, if we are to accept it rigidly, wasn't there mention of the evacuation of some fortresses? I consider that [to apply] for our part in favour of Kamianets.[39]

It is essential to keep in mind this general imbroglio with the Foundation of Peace and the different meanings each side gave to it to better grasp the particular interpretation adopted by the Ottoman plenipotentiaries and how they were successful in fully imposing it upon the main territorial winners among their adversaries, the Imperials and the Venetians. Because, contrary to the narrative of the actors that were primarily affected by it – mainly the Venetians – a narrative, which is uncritically reproduced in modern scholarship as well,[40] the Ottomans were not the only ones to break the motto of pacta sunt servanda; they were simply following in the footsteps of all the other participants. As Count Schlik would bluntly confess in one of his letters to Kinsky, 'as it is the case with this negotiation, as with all [juridical?/peace?] processes of [this] world (*comme de tous les procéz du monde*), [...] [the different] parties interpret the sense of the Instrument in their favour'.[41]

37 Cernovodeanu, 'Le journal', 328.

38 Saluski, *Epistolae*, 678.

39 Ibid.

40 A notable example is O'Quinn, who refers to the Ottoman interpretation of the *uti possidetis* as 'an act of political and legal mistranslation that enabled the Ottomans to retain their own self-image in a seemingly post-Westphalian situation': O'Quinn, *Engaging the Ottoman Empire*, 40–1.

41 ÖStA, HHStA, Türkei I, Turcica Box 169, Folder 1 (December 1698, 1st half), fol. 125ʳ, Schlik to Kinsky, 10 December 1698.

In Act I, we extensively discussed how the Ottoman side agreed to sign the Preliminary Agreement only to gain time and advance the negotiations, leaving its actual clarification for the congress itself. A peace agreement on an *uti possidetis* basis, without exceptions, was not in the Ottomans' interests and was considered a dishonourable result for the sultan.[42] A possible loophole for profit could be found, though, in the 'evacuation/demolition clause' in the letter sent to the mediators by Kinsky back in spring. Of course, the letter was quite clear in this matter – 'citra [without] obligationem, et solius *communis convenientiae* causa, per evacuationem, aut demolitionem *reciprocam*'[43] – and the Ottomans realised very well that their arguments would not be so potent.[44] Still, they decided to press forward and try to impose their own exegesis on the Peace Foundation.

Their basic strategy was not to reject it altogether – how could that be? They had signed it themselves – but to break it down into two parts. The first part, the *uti possidetis* per se, was to be applied to the allied side. The second part, though, the 'demolition/evacuation clause', was to be interpreted solely in favour of the Porte, 'under the title of sweetening the pill and satisfying the [Ottoman] Empire. A small compensation for all those losses they had to ratify with [this] peace'.[45] This was the sultan's guarantee for an honourable agreement, without which he would never have consented to sit at the peace table.[46] Because according to the Ottoman ambassadors, every deal had to be based on moderation (*iʿtidāl*), on a win-win basis. 'In such beneficial matters', they later declared to Voznitsyn, 'the two sides use, by showing moderation, to meet themselves in the middle, and it is known that agreement is not made when one wants to reclaim all that was taken from him and the other [on the contrary] desires to retain everything'.[47]

However, that was only the general concept. The Ottomans further explained what such an interpretation meant in practice by skilfully using the main argument and preoccupation of their opponents, the need for a secure and clear border that would remove future disputes,[48] as a justification for their

42 *Taʿrīḫ-i ṣulḥnāme*, fol. 84ᵇ.

43 ÖStA, HHStA, Türkei I, Turcica Box 165, Folder 2 (April 1698), fol. 85ʳ Kinsky to Paget, 24 April 1698 (emphasis mine).

44 *Taʿrīḫ-i ṣulḥnāme*, fol. 86ᵇ.

45 Ruzzini, *Relazione*, 355.

46 *Taʿrīḫ-i ṣulḥnāme*, 85ᵃ⁻ᵇ.

47 Ibid., fol. 118ᵇ.

48 For instance, according to Ruzzini, 'peace agreements depend on the [clear] distinction of states and borders for the tranquility of all subjects': BNM, Ms.it.VII 399(8625), fol. 299ᵛ, Alcuni discorsi delle Conferenze raccolti dal Nicolosi.

territorial pretensions. As the anonymous author of the *Narratio* explains, Mavrocordatos

> then distinguished between the actual possessions and those that could have certain] consequences. And on the nature of dominion, [he] implied that as what was owned [by someone] at the moment would have to be retained in full rights, equally, for the future. [On the other hand], a possession that was supposedly offensive and could cause suspicions had to be corrected and moderated.[49]

Naturally, all those 'offensive' possessions did not belong to the Ottomans but to the allies. Discussing the issue of the Imperial-held fortified positions in the province of Ṭemeşvar, Mavrocordatos stated that 'these small places are like thorns that prevent the tranquillity [of the borders] [...] common convenience should be for the common good, that is [the one] of peace'.[50] Demanding from Ruzzini the evacuation of the fortress of Lepanto and the demolition of that of Preveza, he again reasoned that it had to be done 'for the security of the subjects and for removing the reasons for novel offences that could perturbate the peace'.[51] Similar 'security concerns' were also voiced regarding the Muscovite-held fortresses on the Lower Dnieper. The latter, the Ottomans claim, could act as strongholds for the Cossacks to conduct raids in the Ottoman and Crimean territories.[52]

It is not clear who inside the Ottoman administration came up with this elaborate scheme – although for the Anonymous Venetian, the mastermind behind this stratagem was none other than Mavrocordatos.[53] Ruzzini mostly agrees, adding that the Ottoman plenipotentiaries forwarded this interpretation 'to present [as] glorious their conduct to the Porte', and to advance, especially Mavrocordatos, their position and interests inside the Ottoman élite.[54] The Ottoman plenipotentiaries were thinking of glory indeed, but not for themselves, at least as they sustained. Narrating the sultan's ambassadors' inner thoughts regarding the absolute need to regain the totality of the province of Ṭemeşvar, Rāmī Meḥmed claims that only then 'a praiseworthy

49 *Narratio*, fol. 17^{v}.

50 ÖStA, HHStA, Türkei I, Turcica Box 170, Protocollum, fol. 23.

51 BNM, Ms.it.VII 399(8625), fol. 294^{r}, Alcuni discorsi delle Conferenze raccolti dal Nicolosi.

52 Bogoslovskii, *Petr I*, 397.

53 *Narratio*, fol. 17^{v}.

54 Ruzzini, *Relazione*, 355.

delimitation of the borders and peace suitable to the glory of the [Exalted] State and beneficial to [its] subjects will be made'.[55]

However, broadening our chronological perspective and placing the Ottoman ambassadors' interpretation of the Peace Instrument in the context of the peace negotiations that took place throughout the Sixteen Years' War, it becomes quite evident that it was pretty much consistent with the Ottoman goals all along. That is an 'honourable peace' in which the Porte would regain some of its losses and would not exit any talks as the indisputably defeated party.[56]

With that said, there is a tantalising hypothesis from where the Ottoman plenipotentiaries could have possibly taken the inspiration for the 'demolition/ evacuation clause' to be uniquely applied to the allied side. We show at the beginning of the narration regarding the congress preliminaries that the Porte was perfectly aware of the terms of the Imperial-French agreement at Ryswick, a copy of which was also translated into Ottoman Turkish.[57] According to the treaty, the Kingdom of France could retain Alsace with the vital city of Strasbourg. Still, in compensation for that loss, the Holy Roman Emperor demanded and achieved the evacuation or demolition of all the French-held fortresses east of the river Rhine.[58] The parallels here are more than striking. It appears as if the Ottoman side drew some more profound conclusions from what Rāmī himself described as 'disreputable' terms for the French.[59] Namely: to try to use the same tool applied by Leopold I in his treaty with the King of France to compensate for the loss of Alsace to save the Ottoman 'reputation' against the loss of much of Ottoman Hungary and the Morea peninsula.[60]

Nonetheless, as clever a stratagem as it may have been, it all depended upon whether or not the other side would accept the Ottoman exegesis of the Foundation of Peace. The first Imperial reaction was pretty much as expected. Through the 'malicious behaviour of the Turks' (*il doloso procedere de Turchi*), the Preliminary Agreement was manifestly violated, Marsigli protested to Count Kinsky in a letter sent on 17 November 1698.[61] Since when were the

55 *Taʾrīḫ-i ṣulḥnāme*, fol. 91ª.
56 *See* Prelude and Poulios, 'Αναζητώντας την ειρήνη'.
57 *See* above, Act I, Narration Part I.
58 Poulios, 'From the Palace of Ryswick',119–20; Peter Sahlins, 'Natural Frontiers Revisited: France's Boundaries since the Seventeenth Century'. *The American Historical Review* 95/5 (1990), 1434.
59 Poulios, 'From the Palace of Ryswick', 119–20.
60 Ibid.
61 ÖStA, HHStA, Türkei I, Turcica Box 168, Folder 1 (November 1698, 1st half), fol. 218ʳ, Marsigli to Kinsky 17 November 1698.

winners the only ones obliged to demolish and evacuate fortresses, Count Schlik rhetorically asked his Ottoman interlocutors, adding pointedly that 'in the previous peace agreements demolitions were made by the losing side'.[62] Obviously, the situation was not so clear-cut this time, and the Imperials desperately needed peace as much as the Ottomans. Hence, despite this strong reaction of the Habsburg delegation, the Porte's plenipotentiaries remained firm and conditioned any peace agreement on the acceptance of their definition of the Foundation of Peace. In doing so, they gave the Imperial ambassadors a dose of their own 'bargaining medicine': a take-it-or-leave-it option. Since the emperor was determined to make peace, Öttingen and Schlik had no choice but to accept it.[63]

The same applied to another tactic put into use by the ambassadors of the Porte, referring to the method of proceeding with the discussion of territorial possession and border-making. According to them, there was no point in debating the matters concerning other regions before there was an accord on the specific case the discussion had started with.[64] As they stated to the Imperials during their first conference,

> the most appropriate thing [to do] is this: to start by [breaking] the frontier [into] small parts, and to discuss, little by little, each one of them. [Afterwards], if by God's favour, we reach an agreement, we decide together on the [format] of the relative article, and we also put it into writing.[65]

Agreed with little difficulty by the Imperials, this method proved particularly detrimental to Ruzzini and his negotiating effort.[66] By deliberately not opening to him from the outset all their papers on the issue of the borders, the Ottomans were only promising that if he made concessions to their demands

62 ÖStA, HHStA, Türkei I, Turcica 170, Protocollum, fol. 26.

63 In justifying their decision to concede to the Ottoman demands on one-sided demolitions and evacuations in the Ṭemeşvar region, the Imperial embassy claimed that it was the only way to secure peace and not slow down the negotiations, which would have given a very bad example to the other, 'recalcitrant allies' (*den renitenten Allijrten*), most likely Muscovy and the Commonwealth: ÖStA, HHStA, Türkei I, Turcica Box 168, Folder 2 (November 1698, 2nd half), fol. 22^{r-v}, Imperial plenipotentiaries to Leopold I, 17 November 1698.

64 *Narratio*, fol. 22^{r-v}.

65 *Taʾrīḫ-i ṣulḥnāme*, fol. 83^{b}.

66 As the Venetian resident ambassador at the Imperial Court, Francesco Loredano quickly perceived, characterising it as 'rigorous and disadvantageous' (*rigoroso e svantaggioso*): BNM, Ms.it.VII 399(8625), fol. 320^{r}, Loredano to Ruzzini, (?) November 1698.

regarding mainland Greece, they were willing to facilitate the Venetians in Dalmatia without specifying what those facilitations might be.[67]

The Imperial ambassadors' agreement with this method and the Ottoman interpretation of the Foundation of Peace was a massive success for the Porte's delegation and a turning point for the peace negotiations. The Anonymous Venetian fully understood its consequences. Because these 'points were of common interest and although they appeared preliminary, they were essential and fundamental. And once agreed for the emperor, they could, at least as precedent, prejudice [also] the others'.[68] And he was correct. To convince Ruzzini to make the concessions they demanded, the Ottomans made due reference to the example of the Imperials 'who dash to satisfy the Porte in the concessions and demolitions of many places in the frontier'.[69]

In the end, the Ottomans were not only successful in imposing their agenda in practice, but it also appears that their very enemies also adopted their discourse of 'moderation' in peace agreements to justify the compromises they were forced to make. When, in January 1699, the Ottoman–Venetian negotiation hung in the balance, pro-peace voices in the Serenissima's camp were pushing Ruzzini to agree to the Ottoman terms because they contended that, among other arguments, 'peace agreements are contracts in which the parties satisfy one another to reach an agreement'.[70] With the hindsight of the outcome of the negotiations, and trying to justify its poor results for his *Patria*, Ruzzini himself would argue in his *Relazione Finale* that one of the main lessons to be drawn from the Carlowitz Congress was that, after a long war, the victorious party could not demand a complete submission of the losing one without leaving it with the appearance of some advantage to counterbalance the vast losses it had suffered.[71]

However, not every negotiation at Carlowitz was conducted on the *uti possidetis* principle. The Ottoman–Commonwealth agreement was finally based on territorial permutation, a further victory for the Porte since that was its

67 *Narratio*, fol. 22^{r-v}. Ali Yaycıoğlu's argument that this Ottoman method had an epistemological underpinning, the 'inductive method' (going from the particular to the general), while quite interesting and one meriting further discussion, cannot be firmly anchored in the sources, all the more since he ties it with a supposedly more 'humanitarian' Ottoman approach regarding border-making, which is highly debatable: Yaycıoğlu, 'Ottoman Arguments', 71–2.

68 *Narratio*, fol. 18^{r}.

69 Ibid., fol. 22^{r}. The Ottomans would repeat that Imperial precedent in their meeting with Małachowski as well: *Taʿrīḥ-i ṣulḥnāme*, fol. 107^{a-b}.

70 *Narratio*, fol. 37^{r}.

71 Ruzzini, *Relazione*, 367.

principal aim all along. However, the Ottomans could not impose their negotiating techniques on all Holy League members. One managed to refute them effectively: Prokopii Voznitsyn. Despite all the efforts of the sultan's ambassadors to convince or press him to accept the 'demolition/evacuation clause' as they intended it, the Muscovite remained adamant, stoutly declaring that he was only to abide by the *uti possidetis* in its strict sense, those being the orders he had had from the tsar.[72] Here, we could vividly see how the imposition of the Ottoman interpretation of the Foundation of Peace was very much connected either to the lack of alternatives of some participants (the Imperials) or to unequal power relations and lack of allied support for others (Venice). Ruzzini didn't present different arguments from the ones Voznitysn did. Yet, despite the significant military successes of the Republic of Saint Mark during the last war, and the rather meagre Muscovite accomplishments, the respect each of the two commanded with their Ottoman interlocutors, a respect based on the size and the real or imagined military capabilities of their respective polities, differed substantially.[73]

3 Who Possesses What?

The 'correct' sense of the Foundation of Peace was not the only one to be interpreted according to the designs of each participant. What constituted an effective possession in the first place was equally debatable, and arguments were tailored to fit concrete interests. From the discussions among the plenipotentiaries, we can discern three main rationales that could justify territorial possession. Most of the time, each participant would not stick exclusively to only one, but they would apply them all (or most of them) interchangeably whenever they suited them the most. Still, before entering into more details, a brief clarification should be made regarding a critical feature of territorial control shared by the totality of congress actors: the fortress.

During the late seventeenth century, a territory was not considered occupied by a polity simply because the latter possessed its land surface. Following Małachowski, 'a province is effectively controlled by fortresses'.[74] The term fortress is, of course, quite a broad one. Following Palmira Brummett, we could define it as a 'stronghold [...] a place built of wood, earth and stone (ranging from an outpost to a city) that serves to garrison troops and to defend and

72 Cernovodeanu, 'Le journal', 328.

73 For the Ottoman dismissive comments about Venice, *see* below Narration Part II.

74 *Taʿrīḫ-i ṣulḥnāme*, fol. 103[b].

celebrate the limits and resources of sovereign space'.[75] A fortress didn't stand alone but instead acted as a nucleus with a territorial periphery. Thus, whoever controlled it, automatically possessed its dependent area as well, the latter supposedly already known via the internal demarcations of a state's territory.[76] This was quite an old perception, going back at least to the Middle Ages.[77] After this essential elucidation, let us return to the three rationales determining territorial ownership.

1. *Whoever controls the most important stronghold in a province, or its capital, also possesses its dependencies, and so the entire area.*
   In this argument, the central and most significant nucleus of an entire province is its strongest fortress, which, by being such, overshadows all the other smaller ones, that is, the less major forts, which are considered as no more than its satellites.[78] Such a rationale was put forward mainly by the Ottoman side regarding the provinces of Ṭemeşvar and Podolia since, in both cases, they were in control of their key fortresses (Ṭemeşvar and Kamianets) but nearly nothing else around them.
2. *Whoever controls the majority of the fortresses in a province, and so the greatest part of its territory, controls the province itself.*
   This affirmation is the exact opposite of the previous one. Here, every fortress acts as an independent unit regardless of its size and importance. Evidently, such a claim was advanced by the Imperials and the Commonwealth to counter the above Ottoman pretensions in both Ṭemeşvar and Podolia, respectively. As Małachowski characteristically stated, 'it is not Podolia that pertains to Kamianets, but Kamianets that lies in the extremes of Podolia. As an accessory, it follows the main body [of the land]'.[79] Repudiating the Ottoman claims to the totality of the Ṭemeşvar province, the Imperial delegation replied that: 'All the province belongs to us [....] There is only one fortress in your hands [but] we possess ten with all their accompanying lands'.[80] In their turn, the Ottomans

75 Palmira Brummett, 'The Fortress: Defining and Mapping the Ottoman Frontier in the Sixteenth and Seventeenth Centuries', in A.C.S. Peacock (ed.), *The Frontiers of the Ottoman World* (Oxford: OUP/British Academy 2009) 33.

76 Cernovodeanu, 'Le journal', 352; *Taʿrīḫ-i ṣulḥnāme*, fol. 94[a], 104[b].

77 *See*, for instance, Ronnie Ellenblum, 'Were there Borders and Borderlines in the Middle Ages? The Example of the Latin Kingdom of Jerusalem', in David Abulafia and Nora Berend (eds.), *Medieval Frontiers. Concepts and Practices* (London/New York: Routledge 2016)105–20,116.

78 *Taʿrīḫ-i ṣulḥnāme*, fol. 88[a].

79 Sałuski, *Epistolae*, 679.

80 *Taʿrīḫ-i ṣulḥnāme*, fol. 87[b].

made equal use of the same argument to refute Małachowski's allegations of complete Polish control of the Principality of Moldavia.[81]

3. *A region is controlled by whomever its inhabitants pay taxes to and acknowledge as sovereign.*
With this rationale, we move from possession over structures and land to jurisdiction over people. Yet, despite some scholarly views that argue that, in the pre-modern period, princes perceived their authority as strictly jurisdictional and not territorial, in this case, the two are combined since the second is conditioned upon the first. Ruzzini frequently used this argument to prove the veracity of the effective Venetian possessions in mainland Greece outside the Morea peninsula. He claimed, for instance, for the Serenissima the chain of mountains beyond the Corinthian Isthmus because, as he declared, the few towns and inhabitants of the region were paying 'the usual contributions' (*le solite contributioni*) to and recognising the authority of the Republic of Saint Mark.[82] An analogous rationale was also repeated regarding a piece of land right opposite the island of Lefkada,[83] as well as over the area surrounding the fortress of Lepanto.[84] Similarly, to whom the Principality of Moldavia paid taxes and owned allegiance was transformed into a battleground between the Ottomans and Małachowski, with the latter alleging that 'we collect taxes from the Moldavians, so Moldavia is all in our hands'[85] and the former rejecting it by contending that they were actually the ones receiving levies from the Principality's inhabitants.[86]

It is remarkable that such an argumentation connecting jurisdiction over people and control over the territory they lived in was not encountered exclusively in the Congress of Carlowitz. Nearly ten years before it, thousands of miles away to the east, the Qing empire and Muscovy were negotiating at Nerchinsk, in faraway Siberia.[87] Identically to the participants of Carlowitz, the central theme on the agenda between the two delegations was the arrangement of a

81 Ibid., fol. 104ᵇ.
82 *Narratio*, fol. 21ʳ.
83 Ibid., fol. 21ᵛ.
84 *Taʿrīḥ-i ṣulḥnāme*, fol. 99b.
85 Ibid., fol. 104ᵃ.
86 Ibid., fol. 104ᵇ.
87 For the Treaty of Nerchinsk (1689), *see*, among others: Helena Jaskov, 'The Negotiated Geography of the Treaty of Nerchinsk (1689) and the Role of the Jesuits'. *Late Imperial China* 40/2 (2019), 45–88; Peter C. Perdue, 'Boundaries and Trade in the Early Modern World: Negotiations at Nerchinsk and Beijing'. *Eighteenth-Century Studies*, 43/3 (2010),

border between them. Still, they could not agree on where to draw the borderline because, again, just like at Carlowitz, both claimed possession of specific territories based on the alleged allegiance of the nomadic people living in the area, from whom both sides sustained that they were receiving tribute.[88] This small example attests that in the early modern period, specific ideas could be shared over vast geographical spaces and cultural zones, without necessarily the different polities that practised them ever having entered into 'diplomatic talks' before with one another.

3.1 *Rivers*

All the above arguments of the different congress participants were primarily concerned with the possession of land. But what about that of rivers? There are no fortresses in the water (the river islands apart), nor can fish pay tribute and acknowledge the sovereignty of anyone. So, how could such a case be resolved?

The control of the rivers was generally one of the issues with the most potential to cause strife in a negotiation.[89] Rivers were valuable for three principal reasons: 1) for their resources, 2) as cardinal trade arteries, and 3) as strategic assets in the event of a war, blocking or securing easy access for one's troops to the opposing shore.[90] Two primary such river-related matters were propped up during the Carlowitz talks. The first concerned the mastery over the Lower Dnieper, hotly debated between Muscovy, Crimea and the Ottomans since the early 1680s. The tsar was anxious to safeguard the Zaporizhian Cossacks' uninhibited access to the river's resources (and later his own to the Black Sea). According to the ratification document of the Treaty of Bahçeseray (1681), the Cossacks were given such a right but with the obligation to pay tariffs to the sultan and the Crimean Khan.[91] The capturing of the four Ottoman fortresses

---

341–56; Joseph Sebes, S. J., *The Jesuits and the Sino-Russian Treaty of Nerchinsk (1689). The Diary of Thomas Pereira, S. J.* (Rome: Institutum Historicum S.I. 1961).

88 Perdue, 'Boundaries and Trade', 348; Jaskov, 'Negotiated Geography', 52, fn. 26.

89 Reinhard Schneider, 'Lineare Grenzen – Von Frühen zum Späten Mittelalter' in Wolfgang Haubrichs and Reinhard Schneider (eds.), *Grenzen und Grenzregionen* (Saarland: Saarbrücken 1994) 54; Jovan Pešalj, 'The Distinctiveness of the Habsburg-Ottoman Border in the Eighteenth Century', in Maria Baramova, Grigor Boykov and Ivan Parvev (eds.), *Bordering Early Modern Europe* (Wiesbaden: Harrassowitz 2015), 32, fn. 50.

90 Olga Katsiardi-Hering, 'Δούναβης: Ποτάμι πολέμων καὶ εἰρήνης – Γέφυρα ψυχῶν καὶ εἰδῶν (18ος – μέσα 19ου αἰ.)' in *Σκεῦος εἰς Τιμήν. Ἀφιερωματικὸς τόμος ἐπὶ τῇ συμπληρώσει 25ετίας ἀπὸ τῆς εἰς Ἐπίσκοπον χειροτονίας καὶ 20ετίας ἀπὸ τῆς ἐνθρονίσεως τοῦ Μητροπολίτου Αὐστρίας καὶ Ἐξάρχου Οὐγγαρίας καὶ Μεσευρώπης κ. Μιχαὴλ* (Athens 2011), 405–19.

91 Kirill Kochegarov, 'The Moscow Uprising of 1682. Relations between Russia, the Crimean Khanate, and the Polish-Lithuanian Commonwealth', in Denise Klein (ed.), *The Crimean Khanate between East and West (15th–18th Century)* (Wiesbaden: Harrassowitz 2012) 60–1.

on the western bank of the river during the campaigns of Peter I in the 1690s served precisely the purpose of definitely solving the problem by bringing the waterway under Muscovy's sole possession. That's why Voznitsyn was so reluctant to demolish them, and the Ottomans were equally eager to get rid of them and reclaim their lost access to the river without the need to be the ones to pay tariffs to the Muscovites now.[92]

The second most important river-control-related matter of the congress was the one pertaining to the grip over the rivers Tisza and Mureş flowing down from Transylvania and into the Danube. Following the Imperial instructions, the navigation of both rivers was 'of the highest significance' (*von höchster importanz*) and was to be reserved only for the emperor, leaving the 'Turks' no access to them whatsoever.[93] Such a blockage would be achieved through a formation of a no-man's-land, ranging a mile or less, applied only to the Ottoman side of the banks of the two rivers.[94] According to Leopold I, if the Porte was left with access to both waterways, 'it will only act as a means to obstruct our [people], to foment rebellions in both the Kingdom of Hungary as in Transylvania and to make difficult the communication between the former and the latter in the future'.[95]

When the Imperial embassy attempted to implement the emperor's instructions, they were met with vigorous Ottoman resistance. The Ottoman argumentation was grounded on 'humanitarian' considerations:[96] 'Why should the people living in these open spaces be deprived of the benefits of the rivers? Are they going to stay without water? [...] Are they not going to eat fish? [...] Then, are they supposed to eat their fish without bread? Surely [you know] that close to the rivers there are [normally] windmills'.[97] And Mavrocordatos also felt the need to remind his interlocutors that the free navigation of rivers and use of their resources by the neighbouring populations was based on the laws both of nature and those of 'nations' (*del dritto di genti* [...] *alle leggi della natura*).[98] 'You care much less about the Mureş river than about the interruption of the

92 Although the Moscovite ambassador assured his Ottoman interlocutors that the tsar would guarantee free access through the river to the Ottoman merchants: Cernovodeanu, 'Le journal', 335.

93 ÖStA, HHstA, Türkei I, Turcica Box 168, Folder 2 (November 1698, 2nd half), fol. 210^{v}–211^{r}, supplementary Imperial instructions to the Carlowitz embassy, 24 November 1698.

94 Ibid., fol. 211^{r-v}.

95 ÖStA, HHStA, Türkei I, Turcica Box 169, Folder 1 (December 1698, 1st half), fol. 66^{v}, supplementary Imperial instructions to the Carlowitz embassy, 5 December 1698.

96 Those pretexts to cover the Ottoman strategic concerns are same times taken at face value by modern scholars. *See* for instance, Yaycıoğlu, 'Ottoman Arguments', 75.

97 *Taʿrīḥ-i ṣulḥnāme*, fol. 93^{a}.

98 ÖStA, HHStA, Türkei I, Turcica Box 170, Protocollum, fol. 30, 31.

crossing of your large tonnage ships coming [down] from Transylvania', the Ottomans also contended,[99] promising, like Voznitsyn – another of those ironic moments during the congress – an uninhibited, free passage to Imperial merchant vessels through both waterways.[100]

We will find out how both the Lower Dnieper and the Tisza and Mureş problems were finally resolved later in our narration. To return, though, to the initial question, it appears that waterways could be claimed as controlled exclusively by one party only if the latter was in effective possession of both their banks or if it could manage to keep its neighbour away from them through the formation of a wasteland in the latter's territory bordering them. And with bordering, we reach the crux of the matter. Because all three rivers discussed above were either close to a border or actually served as the border itself. That's why they constituted such thorny issues for discussion, and hence the fierce debate as to whether or not the waterways per se were to be open to shared use or, inversely, were to be reserved only for one of the two sides confining them. In the case of Ṭemeşvar, the Imperial delegation's consent to the Ottoman demand to evacuate or demolish the fortresses they held on the eastern side of the rivers and to agree to the latter as the new border between the two empires automatically deprived them of their advantage of controlling both banks – and so the waterways themselves – and gave the Ottomans ample opportunity to (re)claim equal rights over the rivers, a 'water condominium'.

Despite the significant problems resulting from their use, rivers steadily occupied a place in the minds of Carlowitz's contemporaries as a 'natural' boundary par excellence. Thus, the time has finally come to address the next central topic of the congress negotiations: border-making.

4 Borders: Some Preliminary Thoughts

It could be said that border (or 'frontier'[101]) arrangements are among the oldest matters negotiated between polities.[102] Borders, to follow Maria Baramova, 'are […] a manifestation of competing territorial claims backed up by military

99 *Taʾrīḫ-i ṣulḥnāme*, fol. 93ª.

100 Ibid.

101 Although historians distinguish between the terms 'border' and 'frontier' (Pedani, *Dalla Frontiera*, 4), I use them interchangeably here, as the participants at Carlowitz did, to refer to both the actual borderline and the – more or less – broader area surrounding it. When referring specifically to a wider, undefined zone between two polities, I will use the term 'frontier'.

102 Max Pfister, 'Grenzbezeichnungen im Italoromanischen und Galloromanischen', in Haubrichs and Schneider, *Grenzen*, 37.

force, though based to some extent on geographical reality'.[103] Border-making, on the other hand, could be understood, at least for the pre-modern period, as 'a set of material practices'[104] unilaterally adopted or mutually agreed upon by two polities to delimit their space and procure its security. As many scholars have rightly pointed out, border-making was not merely imposed from above, but it often had to be negotiated equally from below.[105] Here, though, we will mainly focus on the first part of this interacting relation, while still keeping in mind that whatever the different élites agreed upon during a congress had to subsequently be imposed on or accepted by the people on the ground.

How the conception of borders evolved during the ages is a perennial debate between historians, and various theories have at times been proposed to explain it.[106] For a long period, it remained a Eurocentric concept. Still, in the past two decades, a growing number of studies attempted to deal with the issue on a more 'global' scale, thus shedding more light on its complex character and revealing some interesting parallels in border-making mechanisms in various areas scattered all around the world.[107] Under the traditionally accepted model, in pre-modern times, the notion of borders was somewhat vague, primarily expressed in undetermined zonal areas, the so-called 'frontier', since any concept of sovereignty was centred more on authority over people rather than land.[108] Besides, it was not through artificially drawn lines but

---

103 Maria Baramova, 'Border Theories in Early Modern Europe'. 2010, available at: www.ieg-ego.eu/en/threads/crossroads/border-regions/maria-baramova-border-theories-in-early-modern-europe.

104 Lisa Hellman and Edmond Smith, 'Borders before Nations: Encounters in the Akan and Dzungar Borderlands, 1450–1750'. *Journal of Early Modern History* 27/5 (2023), 423.

105 Ibid.

106 *See*, among the copious literature: Schneider, 'Lineare Grenzen'; Daniel Power, 'A. Frontiers: Terms, Concepts, and the Historians of Medieval and Early Modern Europe', in Daniel Power and Naomi Standen (eds.), *Frontiers in Question. Eurasian Borderlands, 700–1700* (New York: Palgrave Macmillan 1999) 1–12; Sahlins, 'Natural Frontiers'; Dariusz Kołodziejczyk, 'Between Universalistic Claims and Reality. Ottoman Frontiers in the Early Modern Period', in Christine Woodhead (ed.), *The Ottoman World* (London/New York: Routledge 2012) 205–19; Pešalj, 'The Distinctiveness'; Günter Vogler, 'Borders and Boundaries in Early Modern Europe: Problems and Possibilities', in Steven G. Ellis and Raingard Eßer (eds.), *Frontiers and the Writing of History, 1500–1850* (Hannover: Wehrhahn 2006) 21–38.

107 For example, Hellman and Smith, 'Borders before Nations'; Perdue, 'Boundaries and Trade'; Perdue, 'Boundaries, Maps, and Movement: Chinese, Russian, and Mongolian Empires in Early Modern Central Eurasia'. *International History Review* 20/2 (1998), 263–86; Jaskov, 'Negotiated Geography'.

108 Power, 'A. Frontiers', 5; Sahlins, 'Natural Frontiers', 1427–1428; Baramova, 'Border Theories'; Ellenblum, 'Were there Borders'.

mainly via the possession of fortresses and their surrounding range of control that an area was considered to pertain to one polity or the other.[109] All that changed, so the narrative goes, with the advent of the modern, mainly western European, state, which gradually, from the late Middle Ages, adopted, and then imposed on all others, the linearly conceived and meticulously determined borders we know today.[110] However, as with every historical theory, a model was constructed which didn't consider all the facts or selected only the ones that proved its soundness.[111] For instance, how could one argue based on the 'modern-state border theory' and explain the fact that in the ancient Greek world, 'modern' methods of linear border delimitation between the different city-states were already in place, along with special border commissions to determine it, a whole panoply of words to refer to these processes and even a strong emotional attachment to the border itself?[112]

It is not within the scope of this study to enter a complete discussion of this evidently highly complex and daedal issue – it would require a separate monograph on its own. I should only restrict myself to making the following constatation, drawn from the Carlowitz case as well, which does not constitute a new *longue durée* model for border-making but simply a suggestion to examine it from a different perspective.

Instead of looking at the pre-modern inter-polity territorial delimitations as a linear process 'from the frontier to the border' – to use the title of an otherwise very influential book on the evolution of the Ottoman border conception[113] – that is from a poorly demarcated zonal area between rulerships to a linearly and carefully determined one, we should instead think of them as a highly diversified phenomenon, in which various border-making

109 Ibid., 112–6; Brummett, 'The Fortress', 31.

110 For a brief exposition of the most renowned among these theories, *see* Dariusz Kołodziejczyk, 'Ottoman Frontiers in Eastern Europe', in Norbert Spannenberger and Szabolcs Varga (eds.), *Ein Raum im Wandel. Die osmanisch-habsburgische Grenzregion vom 16. bis zum 18. Jahrhundert* (Stuttgart: Franz Steiner 2014) 25–9.

111 Dariusz Kołodziejczyk, 'Od stanic kresowych do rogatek. Rozwój pojęcia granicy linearnej w Europie Wschodniej'. *Barok: Historia-Literatura-Sztuka* 3/2 (1996), 53–9, 55. Professor Kołodziejczyk's various articles on the nature of the Ottoman frontier were truly instrumental in effectively manifesting the flaws of the 'traditional' border-making theories.

112 Giovanna Daverio Rocchi, 'Systems of Borders in Ancient Greece', in Serena Bianchetti, Michele R. Cataudella and Hans-Joachim Gehrke (eds.), *Brill's Companion to Ancient Geography. The Inhabited World in Greek and Roman Tradition* (Leiden/Boston: Brill 2016) 58–77.

113 Pedani, *Dalla frontiera*.

methods and conceptions co-existed side-by-side with one another,[114] with the actors choosing each time which one to employ. This choice could be based on an array of factors such as the geography of the area,[115] its resources, the density of its population,[116] the specific interests, or not they had to define their territories with each of their neighbours clearly[117] or to frame it in a different way, the lack or the presence of a pressing need to do so. Thus, whereas it was probably in the interests of the medieval Kingdom of Jerusalem and its limitrophe Arab principalities not to form a clear limit between them,[118] this was not the case with the Teutonic Order, which opted instead to distinctly define its territoriality vis-à-vis its neighbouring Slavic polities by establishing with them linear boundaries and also contributing in the process to the spread of the Slavic word *granica* (*Grenzen*) to the rest of the German world.[119] Similarly, while France in the late seventeenth century opted for a more or less 'natural' and linear border with Spain in the Pyrenees, it left its frontier with Flanders and the Holy Roman Empire purposely undefined to further its territorial aspirations in that area.[120] The same holds equally true for the Ottoman–Habsburg border in Hungary until 1683, where it was in the interests of both

114 Power, 'A. Frontiers', 4. Although the author holds onto the rise-of-the-modern-state paradigm: Ibid. 5–6.

115 As the late Maria Pia Pedani rightly pointed out, it would have been really difficult for pre-modern polities to effectively delimit areas such as steppes or deserts: Pedani, *Dalla frontiera*, 17. In their border demarcation of 1705, the Ottoman and the Muscovite commissioners didn't even bother to venture to the Ukrainian steppes to place border marks, restricting themselves to affirm in the final protocol that 'we have confirmed the border by no other signs but this written testimony': Cited in Kołodziejczyk, 'Universalistic claims', 211. However, the Chinese effort to meticulously define the empire's central Asian frontier from the late seventeenth century onwards reveals that steppes could also be tamed if it was deemed imperative: Jaskov, 'Negotiated Geography', 50.

116 Pešalj, 'The Distinctiveness', 28–9.

117 Kołodziejczyk, 'Universalistic claims', 212.

118 *See* Ellenblum, 'Were there Borders'.

119 Schneider, 'Lineare Grenzen', 61–65; Wiesław Długokęcki, 'Die Bildung der Grenze zwischen dem Deutschordensland Preußen und dem Herzogtum Masowien in den Jahren 1343–1422', in Ulrich Knefelkamp and Kristian Bosselmann-Cyran (eds.), *Grenze und Grenzüberschreitung im Mittelalter* (Berlin: Akademie Verlag 2007) 136–51.

120 Vogler, 'Borders', 30. Equally, in the 1680 Ottoman–Commonwealth demarcation, while the western part of the region of Podolia was meticulously demarcated, the eastern one was deliberately left undetermined by the Polish side with the hope that the Ukrainian Cossacks would return in the future under the Commonwealth's jurisdiction because, 'whomever the Cossacks choose, [that ruler] will keep Ukraine as well': Quoted in Kołodziejczyk, 'Universalistic claims', 211.

sides for it to be relatively loose, since both were laying claims to the whole of the country.[121]

Furthermore, examining the border-making procedures commonly accepted by all participants during the Carlowitz Congress, one would be surprised to find out that 'modern', or supposedly 'modern', demarcating methods and conceptions such as territorial sovereignty, linear boundaries and the use of maps to determine boundaries, co-existed, as we saw above, with 'less developed' ones such as feudal and other rights over people or the centrality of the fortress and its own boundaries of territorial control as the chief determinant for one's possession of a given region. Far from being seen as incompatible, all these elements were viewed as complementary to one another.

Apart from these pluralistic practices of territorial delimitation (or not) in the pre-modern era, there is a second general constatation to be made. As was the case with the *uti possidetis* principle or the mediation office, inter-polity border-making bears a strong resemblance to similar agreements between individuals to determine and secure their properties.[122] Such a strong correlation is revealed by the common vocabulary used in both cases, attesting to a transfer of terms from a smaller to a greater level to describe a similar practice. A telling example is the Latin word *finis*, primarily encountered in its plural form *fines* (or a later variation, *confines*), which originated in the early Roman period as a term to denote the signs dividing private properties before its meaning was amplified to include the signs delimiting polities and finally the borders between them while at the same time was in equal usage for similar affairs regarding individuals.[123]

Border-making had more than just a small and a large scale. It had quite an extensive medium scale as well. Just as private individuals were demarcating their properties and polities delimiting theirs, different administrative units, seigneuries, cities and even villages inside a political entity also possessed

121 Pešalj, 'The Distinctiveness', 30. Although loose doesn't mean completely 'open', as Kołodziejczyk again rightly points out: Kołodziejczyk, 'Ottoman Frontiers', 29–30.

122 Merio Scattola, 'Die Grenze der Neuzeit. Ihr Begriff in der juristischen und politischen Literatur der Antike und Frühmoderne', in Bauer and Rahn, *Die Grenze*, 37–72, 37–41; Schneider, 'Lineare Grenzen', 45–6, 59.

123 Pfister, 'Grenzbezeichnungen', 37–9. However, we should be careful because such an evolutionary theory for terms such as *limis* does not take into account the fact that other words, such as the Greek one ὅρος, had a double reference as private and polity boundary already in Antiquity: Daverio Rocchi, 'Systems of Borders', 63. Hence, we should perhaps consider moving the possible time of the transferring of such terms from an individual to an inter-polity setting further backwards and not in the late Roman Period and early Middle Ages as Scattola and Pfister sustain: 'Die Grenze der Neuzeit', 41; 'Grenzbezeichnungen', 37–9.

their respective boundaries, which were determined in similar ways and methods and were referred to with the same vocabulary as the other two cases.[124] There is no clearer exemplification of such similarly conceived multi-level boundary-making than the Ottoman case. As we shall see, when the Ottomans were speaking about the borderline between two polities, they normally used the term *ḥudūd*. Yet this same term was also employed to describe the boundary between the empire's different provinces, towns, villages, and private properties. It does not end there, however. The document validating demarcations of territories between states down to private lots bore in all instances the same name, that of *ḥudūdnāme* (or *sınırnāme*), whereas, as in the border agreements between political entities, special 'disengaged' and 'objective' commissioners/inhabitants of a region or local officials,[125] were typically tasked to determine the respective boundaries.[126] After these unavoidable general remarks on such a highly complicated topic, let us zoom right in on the border-making during the Carlowitz Congress.

5 The Terms

A useful place to start would be an examination of the terms the Carlowitz actors employed to refer to territorial delimitation. They would reveal much, both about the participants' conception of borders or 'frontiers', as to the degree these conceptions were shared or differed among them. At first glance, we encounter a real litany of words, many of them being used for centuries before the congress took place, such as *confinia*, *limites*, *gränitzen*,[127] *ḥudūd*, *sınur* (from the Greek *σύνορον*),[128] *serḥadd*, *confins*, *frontières*,[129] *frontiera*, *termini* and *granica*.[130] The task to determine their exact meaning grows ever

124 Schneider, 'Lineare Grenzen', 59; Katsiardi-Hering, 'Κτηματογραφικοὶ χάρτες', 30–1.

125 Normally, those officials were the local judges, the *ḳāḍıs*, who, interestingly, were also frequently employed as commissioners in border arrangements with limitrophe polities: Pedani, *Dalla Frontiera*, 43.

126 Mübahat S. Kütükoğlu, 'Hududnâme', in TDVİA, vol. 18 (Istanbul: Turkish Religious Foundation 1998) 303–4.

127 On the origins and semantic development of the word *Grenze*, *see* Schneider, 'Lineare Grenzen', 60–5; Power, 'A. Frontiers', 7.

128 For the meaning of *ḥudūd/sınır*, *see* Pedani, *Dalla* Frontiera', 12–3; Kołodziejczyk, 'Ottoman Frontiers', 206.

129 For the evolution and semantic alterations of the word *limiti* and *frontiè*re, *see* Pfister, 'Grenzbezeichnungen', 42–4.

130 *Granica* appears to have been the most common word used by the Muscovites to refer to borders/frontiers/boundaries during this period: *See*, for instance, *Pamiatniki*, 97,

more complex since, most of the time, either they were used interchangeably by the participants[131] or, if we are to consider late seventeenth-century dictionaries as a reliable source, they appear to have quite diverse, and, according to modern historians, contradictory meanings. Take, for instance, the Ottoman word *serḥadd*, of Arabic origin, which most contemporary scholars would translate as 'frontier'.[132] Meninski, though, in this famous Ottoman dictionary, published nearly twenty years before the Congress of Carlowitz, defines the word as follows: 'Extremitas termini aut confinii, confinium, confinia, fines, limes, limites. Gränzen. Estremità dei confini, confine, frontiere, termine, limite. Frontieres, confins, bornes'.[133] What are we to make out of such chaos?

A careful analysis of the sources and a cautious contextualisation of all the above terms encountered in them demonstrates that the imbroglio modern historians face would be totally incomprehensible to the Carlowitz contemporaries. For them, things would be far easier to understand. Thus, when they spoke of a *frontiera*, *serḥadd* or *gränitzen* they appeared to refer to a linearly conceived boundary dividing two territorial units and to the areas along it, much like we would use the words border or frontier today. So, expressions like *luoghi confinarij*,[134] *luochi alla frontiera*[135] or *fortezze alle frontiere*[136] could be interpreted, following and expanding a bit Meninski's translation of the Ottoman word *serḥadd* when it was referring to a fortress, as 'defensive

205, 230, 299. In Latin, it appears to have been normally translated as *confinia* or *limites*. Compare, for instance, the Russian text of the fourth article in Voznitsy's peace proposals (ibid., 205) with its Latin translation in ÖStA, HHStA, Türkei I, Turcica Box 169, Folder 1 (December 1698, 1st half), fol. 191ᵛ.

131 *See*, for instance, ÖStA, HHStA, Türkei I, Turcica Box 168, Folder 2 (November 1698, 2nd half), fol. 134ʳ, Imperial plenipotentiaries to Leopold I, Carlowitz 22 November 1698, where in just a single folio, the Imperial ambassadors speak about the borders using the semi-Germanized expression *das punctum Confiniorum*, followed little after by the term *limites* and then by that of *gränitzen*. Equally, Philip Georg Schreyer, the famous secretary of Paget, in the protocol of the conferences he kept, normally alternates between the words *confins* and *frontières* to obviously refer to the same thing: Cernovodeanu, 'Le journal', 327. The same also applies to Paget himself. For example, ÖStA, HHStA, Türkei I, Turcica Box 166, Folder 1 (August 1698), fol. 95ʳ, Paget to Kinsky, 12 August 1698 (J.C.).

132 Quite intriguingly and perhaps revealing of their own frontier or 'frontier' conceptions, the Ottomans don't seem to have used the Arabic word *Ṯaġr*, which, according to the late Maria Pedani, was used to describe an undetermined zone between two dominions: Pedani, *Dalla Frontiera*, 5–7.

133 Meninski, *Thesaurus*, 2587. The term *ḥudūd*, on the other hand, is translated as 'termini, limites, fines, confinia': Ibid., 1735.

134 ÖStA, HHStA, Türkei I, Turcica Box 170, Protocollum, fol. 132.

135 *Narratio*, fol. 22ʳ.

136 Ibid., fol. 18ʳ.

spot[s] / [or areas in general] situated on the entrance [of a territory], or on the borders, facing the boundaries of others, foes or friends'.[137] Long story short, by the time of the Peace Congress of Carlowitz, the prevalent mode of thinking among its participants was that of linear, settled borders and not of fluid zonal 'frontiers'.

That this was indeed the case is further proved by the expressions applying to the practice of border demarcation. The Ottomans typically used phrases like *ḳaṭʿ-ı ḥudūd*,[138] the actual translation of which would be to intersect, to cut the border, or *taʿyīn-i sınur*, the determination of the boundary.[139] In Italian, we encounter phrases such as 'the distinction of borders' (*la distintione de limiti*),[140] whereas, in German, we meet with 'the separation of borders' (*gräniz-scheidung*).[141] The concept of thinking that unites them all is that a boundary should be clearly and meticulously defined. Lastly, in the Imperial sources, we often encounter another interesting idea, that of the borders as a system (*das Systema seiner völligen gränitzen*).[142] Although it is not entirely clear what it actually implies, we could hypothesise that in a period in which philosophers like Descartes perceived the universe as a mechanical conglomerate, some found that this concept could equally apply to the boundaries between political units, the different parts of which, we might suppose, just like the various elements of the cosmos, would have to be arranged in such a way as to guarantee harmony and security to the whole, that is, to the territorial state.

6 'Natural' and Artificial Boundaries

At the twilight of the seventeenth century, two were the most prevalent border categories that the actors used as a guide to determine and construct a 'boundary system'. 'Regarding the issue of borders', the Ottoman ambassadors claimed during the first conference with the Imperials, 'in some places they are

137 'Locus praesidiarius in primo aditu situs, seu limitaneus, confinis alteri sive hostem sive amicum respiciat': Meninski, *Thesaurus*, 2587.

138 *Taʿrīḫ-i ṣulḥnāme*, fol. 82[b].

139 Ibid., 96[a].

140 ÖStA, HHStA, Türkei I, Turcica Box 170, Protocollum, fol. 10.

141 ÖStA, HHStA, Türkei I, Turcica Box 170, Diarium et Cerimoniale, fol. 84.

142 ÖStA, HHStA, Türkei I, Turcica Box 168, Folder 2 (November 1698, 2nd half), fol. 228[r], Imperial Plenipotentiaries to Leopold I, 27 November 1698; ÖStA, HHStA, Türkei I, Turcica Box 171, Folder 1 (January 1699, 1st half), fol. 91[v], Imperial plenipotentiaries to Leopold I, Carlowitz 5 January 1699.

[already] placed by God [...] in places where this is not the case, [the limits] can be determined between us'.[143] Similarly, following the Imperial ministers, borders could be 'natural' (*die natural limites*) or 'artificial and civil' (*die artificial= und Civil=limiten*).[144] Prominent features of the first category were mountains, rivers or forests.[145] As for the second, the different parties had to agree on specific markers. During one of the ultimate Ottoman–Imperial sessions on 13 January, Count Schlik asked Mavrocordatos how the border lines should be made, 'if they are to be guarded by soldiers or how [else]'.[146] Mavrocordatos replied that usually they were made 'with manifested signs. One does not at all mean by that a wall or a palisade, but a stone here, a ditch there, according to the morphology of each location'.[147]

Stones and stone mounds, ditches or even artificially planted forests were quite old boundary markers.[148] Not directly related to Carlowitz, but still of extreme interest as yet another manifestation of the presence of analogous border-making practices across broader geographical areas in the early modern period, are some intriguing cases of quite peculiar border marks from the seventeenth century. In these instances, specific posts engraved with the articles of a peace treaty or a demarcation act would be placed as border signs, acting as lasting monuments of the agreement, not in some distant archive but on the very ground their signatories had delimited. Thus, according to the famous seventeenth-century Ottoman traveller Evliya Çelebi, along the Ottoman-Safavid frontier, posts were erected containing the stipulations of the demarcation protocol (*ḥudūdnāme*) drafted after the Treaty of Zuhab (1639) between the two powers.[149] One of the articles of the peace agreement between Muscovy and the Qing Empire at Nerchinsk (1689) specified that '... this present treaty, with all its articles, shall be engraved in the Chinese,

143 *Taʿrīḥ-i ṣulḥnāme*, fol. 82ᵃ.

144 ÖStA, HHStA, Türkei I, Turcica Box 168, Folder 1 (November 1698, 1st half), fol. 102ʳ⁻ᵛ, relation of the members of the 'Turkish Deputation' to Leopold I, 15 November 1698.

145 Ibid., fol. 4ʳ, anonymous relation on the issue of the future borders with the Ottoman Porte; *Taʿrīḥ-i ṣulḥnāme*, fol. 82ᵇ.

146 Cernovodeanu, 'Le journal', 347.

147 Ibid. According to Schlik, the traditional way with those ditches was that both parties were to make their own, leaving a piece of land in between. Mavrocordatos also pointed out that specific mention should be made in the peace articles that whoever attempted to remove the marks or fill up the ditches would receive a grave punishment: Ibid.

148 Daverio Rocchi, 'Systems of Borders', 66.

149 Selim Güngörürler, 'The belated consummation of the Ottoman – Safavid peace of Zuhab, 1639–1643'. *Archivum Ottomanicum* 37 (2020), 38, fn. 9.

Russian and Latin languages, upon stones, which shall be placed as everlasting monuments on the frontiers of the two Empires'.[150]

6.1 *The Controversy*

The various actors of the congress could have easily concurred with Count Schlik that 'natural borders' (*limiti naturali*) are already made (*sono fatti*), the artificial ones (*limiti artificiali*) are to be made (*sono* [...] *da fare*).[151] Nonetheless, which were those 'natural borders' and how the artificial ones were to be determined were matters of great controversy, primarily depending, just like almost everything else in the plenipotentiaries' argumentations, on the interests of their respective polities.[152]

6.2 *'Natural Boundaries'*

Let's start with the so-called 'natural boundaries'. Following the logic of the Carlowitz contemporaries, those limits were placed by no greater authority than God himself since time immemorial and were allegedly well-known to everyone.[153] 'God himself placed the limit between us and Wallachia [Moldavia] on the river Dniester', the Polish commissioners would sustain in the Ottoman–Commonwealth delimitation act following the Carlowitz Treaties in 1703.[154] Yet, as Reinhard Schneider had justifiably noted, in reality, there are no 'natural borders' because the latter must be defined as such in a negotiation. So, in this respect, they do not differ much from artificial ones. Instead of 'natural', it would be better to refer to them as 'nature-favoured borders' (*Naturgünstigten Grenzen*), the German historian would add.[155]

Such a 'natural boundaries mirage', where the different parties interpreted the will of God according to their own agenda, is displayed in all its force in the Ottoman–Venetian debate of where the Almighty or Nature placed the frontier of the Morea peninsula. Preoccupied with achieving the maximum

150 Quoted in Sebes, S. J., *The Jesuits*, 151. These monuments containing an abbreviated version of the treaty were erected in 1690: Ibid.

151 ÖStA, HHStA, Türkei I, Turcica Box 170, Protocollum, fol. 10.

152 In his otherwise quite thought-provoking recent study, Ali Yaycıoğlu attempts to portray the border-making issues at Carlowitz as a struggle between two diametrically opposing views: a Christian (Imperial/Venetian) technocratic one based solely on maps and an Ottoman 'humanitarian' which rejects outright the use of maps, relies only on mixed border commissions and takes into consideration the local residents' needs: Yaycıoğlu, 'Ottoman Arguments'. As the subsequent analysis would demonstrate, though, things were actually much more complex than the picture Yaycıoğlu presents.

153 *Taʿrīḥ-i ṣulḥnāme*, fol. 82ª.

154 Quoted in Kołodziejczyk, 'Od stanic kresowych', 57.

155 Schneider, 'Lineare Grenzen', 54.

level of security for their newly acquired possession, as soon as they conquered the region, the Venetians, inspired by similar unsuccessful undertakings during Antiquity, were seriously considering opening a channel in the Isthmus – the 'pietra di scandalo' as the *Provveditore Generale* of the Morea, Giacomo Corner, referred to in a Relazione of his in 1691[156] – thus creating an artificial 'physical' boundary themselves.[157] Nonetheless, this colossal project was finally discarded as too costly.[158] After discussing many alternatives,[159] in the end, they opined that the 'physical' and safer (for them) limit of the 'Regno' was the chain of the Gerania mountains west of the Corinthian Isthmus. As Francesco Loredano, resident Venetian ambassador at the Imperial Court, declared to Count Kinsky, 'the natural and necessary border of the Morea […] is the line of mountains […] that closes the first access to the strait [the Isthmus], established by nature as a barrier and real division for this kingdom'.[160]

That was far different from how the Ottoman side viewed the situation. The Porte's ambassadors counterargued – Rāmī, in particular, claimed at first to have an intimate knowledge of the region[161] – that those mountains were outside the 'kingdom'. As a matter of fact, they declared that the Isthmus was its actual 'natural' boundary. An affirmation based on geographical and historical arguments:

> It is on the Isthmus that the peninsula shrinks the most, and where the two seas of Aegina and Lepanto come the closest to one another, and where during ancient times the Romans desired to dig [a channel for] the communication and the natural boundary of the kingdom was actually at the foot of the mountains of Corinth, where was constructed in the past the Examilion[162] Wall'.[163]

156 Panopoulou, 'Da mar a mar', 229–30.

157 Ibid., 234–6.

158 Ibid., 237.

159 Chrysa Maltezou, 'Βενετσιάνικες εκθέσεις για την οχύρωση του ισθμού της Κορίνθου στα τέλη του 17ου αιώνα' in *Πρακτικά Α Διεθνούς Συνεδρίου Πελοποννησιακών Σπουδών, Σπάρτη 7–14 Σεπτ. 1975*, vol. 3 (Athens 1976–8) 269–76.

160 ÖStA, HHStA, Türkei I, Turcica Box 171, Folder 1 (January 1699, 1st half), fol. 113^{r}, Loredano to Kinsky, 7 January 1698. Interestingly, nowadays, the area in question belongs, administratively, to the Regional Unit of Corinth, thus forming part of the Peloponnese. The Venetians would have surely felt vindicated.

161 *Narratio*, fol. 21^{r}.

162 Meaning 'six miles' in Greek, the Examillion was a wall constructed in Late Antiquity and reconstructed and reused various times until the late Middle Ages: Panopoulou, 'Da mar a mar', 235.

163 *Narratio*, fol. 21^{r-v}.

Another example of an interest-oriented interpretation of 'physical' borders during the congress is provided by the Imperial–Ottoman clash over which such frontier constituted the more suitable one for the province of Ṭemeşvar. The Ottomans, wanting to recover the whole area, argued that the province was 'naturally' limited by the rivers Mureş and Tisza.[164] 'The province of Ṭemeşvar is a region which found its limits [naturally] by the grace of God', they claimed.[165] Au contraire, wanting to exclude, as we saw, the Ottomans from these two rivers, the Imperials upheld that it was instead the river Bega (*Yeñi Ṣuyu*) that 'makes a good border' (*güzel sınur olur*).[166] In the end, in both the Morea and the Ṭemeşvar cases, it was not because of the force of God or Nature but due to the rather mundane calculations of the Imperials and the weakness of the Venetians that the Porte's ambassadors were successful in imposing an 'Ottoman-favoured natural boundary'.

6.3 *Artificial Boundaries*

If agreeing on a 'natural border' was so arduous, deciding on the 'artificial one' often created even more vehement debates. Surely, not all 'man-made' boundaries would have to be discussed in situ. Some have already been determined. 'Transylvania is to remain separated from the lands surrounding it, Podolia, Moldavia, and Wallachia, with the borders subscribed [to it], since the days of old', the Imperial plenipotentiaries assured Leopold I, 'and as Colonel Marsigly informed us, based on his observations, from Podolia as far as the Iron Gate all boundaries are sufficiently known […]'.[167] Still, as they continued, 'from there until the river Mureş their status is unknown […] neither us nor the Turks know the actual ancient limits'.[168] There were also other instances where the question was not to locate an old boundary but to demarcate a brand new one.

In such cases, two central and interrelated controversial questions arose: 1) when those boundaries were to be determined and 2) by whom. Evidently, each party had a different answer to meet its designs. One was that the plenipotentiaries would agree on a general border framework during the congress, leaving the definitive and detailed distinction to special commissioners appointed by both sides sometime after the end of the talks. The appointment

164 *Taʿrīḫ-i ṣulḥnāme*, fol. 87ᵃ.

165 Ibid., fol. 92ᵃ.

166 Ibid., 91ᵃ.

167 ÖStA, HHStA, Türkei I, Turcica Box 168, Folder 2 (November 1698, 2nd half), fol. 134ʳ⁻ᵛ, Imperial plenipotentiaries to Leopold I, 22 November 1698.

168 Ibid.

of border commissions was an ancient practice going back to Antiquity[169] and was also generally followed in other major seventeenth-century peace treaties or congresses.[170] The staunchest supporter of commissioners as the most qualified persons to arrange the frontiers after the congress was the Ottoman side. 'In the past, a certain method regarding the borders was established,' argued Mavrocordatos, 'but [their] particular definition was consistently consigned to deputy commissioners of both parties [...] men of expertise, of old age, with wisdom and dispassionate, who determine them in situ with signs, by raising mounds or in other ways'.[171] This was a practice adopted 'in similar negotiations everywhere in the world', he added.[172]

The leading justification for the imperative need to resort to such 'men of expertise' was, as we encountered before, that it was unlikely that an ambassador would be knowledgeable of the geographical particularities of each location. 'It's impossible [for] the plenipotentiaries, of the one and the other side equally, to know the local conditions of every border mountain, forest, river, land or sign', the Imperial delegation claimed in a relation it sent to Leopold I.[173] Mavrocordatos complained along similar lines about the difficulty of determining the Ottoman–Muscovite border at the congress. The Ottomans requested from Voznitsyn that the new boundary should be instead determined by commissioners (*che si determini i confini per commissarij*), because, allegedly, they knew nothing of the geography of the region (*che non sappiamo noi ne conosciamo niente*).[174] It is hard, though, to take such statements at face value since the ambassadors' knowledge of the different regions and their topography often seemed to miraculously appear and disappear whenever it suited them. Rāmī Meḥmed may have claimed intimate knowledge of the Morea, but in another instance, Mavrocordatos declared that 'the Efendi does not know, nor has [even] seen the Examilion'.[175] When asked in his turn by the second Ottoman ambassador if he knew if those mountains he

169 Daverio Rocchi, 'Systems of Borders', 63–4. For an example from the Early Middle Ages, *see* also Ellenblum, 'Were there Borders', 112.

170 Sahlins, 'Natural Frontiers', 1434–5. For the use of commissaries to determine the border in previous peace treaties between the Ottomans and their Christian neighbours, *see* Pedani, *Dalla frontiera*, 42–4.

171 ÖStA, HHStA, Türkei I, Turcica Box 170, Protocollum, fol. 9–10.

172 Ibid., fol. 11.

173 ÖStA, HHStA, Türkei I, Turcica Box 168, Folder 2 (November 1698, 2nd half), fol. 132ᵛ, Imperial plenipotentiaries to Leopold I, 22 November 1698.

174 ÖStA, HHStA, Türkei I, Turcica Box 170, Protocollum, fol. 107.

175 BNM, Ms.it.VII 399(8625), fol. 300ᵛ, Alcuni discorsi delle Conferenze raccolti dal Nicolosi.

claimed west of the Isthmus formed part of the Morea or not, Ruzzini would also profess complete ignorance.[176]

At the other end of the equation stood Venice. In a letter to Kinsky, Count Schlik described Ruzzini as 'a sworn enemy of commissioners, the name of which he doesn't want to hear [at all]'.[177] As Ruzzini himself 'confided' to Count Marsigli in one of their first Carlowitz meetings, he had explicit orders from the Senate not to conclude any agreement 'if the borders were not [clearly] expressed' (*se bene non erano espresso li limiti*) during the congress.[178] This apprehension of the Serenissima stemmed from the Venetians' unpleasant memories of previous similar occasions with the Ottomans. They feared a repetition of what happened during the last peace they had signed with the Porte, that of Candia in 1669, 'where the agreement was concluded without a precise demarcation of borders, which was left to a future commission'.[179] There, however, so Ruzzini claimed, Venice was forced to cede half the territory she was entitled to according to the peace treaty.[180]

The Imperial stance was more complex. During the Failed Vienna Congress, the Habsburg side was the first to suggest that special commissioners make the demarcation of the future borders.[181] In 1698, the emperor and his ministers had changed their minds, it seems, and Kinsky reiterated in a letter to Schlik before the start of the official conferences that, regarding the distinction of boundaries, the anticipated Ottoman request that the latter should be determined by commissioners after the congress could not be met. On this point, the ambassadors had to stick 'to the letter' of their instructions, achieving a clear definition of the frontiers in the congress venue either by themselves or, as Marsigli suggested, by dispatching commissioners to inspect the areas in question during the course of the talks.[182] However, the two plenipotentiaries didn't share the same views as their principals or those of their 'special adviser'.

176 Cernovodeanu, 'Le journal', 343.

177 ÖStA, HHStA, Türkei I, Turcica Box 168, Folder 2 (November 1698, 2nd half), fol. 247^{r}, Schlik to Kinsky, 27 November 1698.

178 ÖStA, HHStA, Türkei I, Turcica Box 167, Folder 2 (October 1698, 2nd half), fol. 45^{v}, Marsigli to Kinsky, 16 October 1698.

179 Ibid., fol. 46^{r}.

180 Ibid. *See* also, ibid., fol. 98^{r}, Marsigli to Kinsky, 22 October 1698, where the Imperial 'special advisor' presented the Ottoman–Venetian border arrangement after the Candia War (1642–69) as a warning precedent testifying to the Ottoman 'malice' in frontier demarcations.

181 *Cerîde-i Takrirât*, 59.

182 ÖStA, HHStA, Türkei I, Turcica Box 167, Folder 2 (October 1698, 2nd half), fol. 195^{r-v}, Kinsky to Schlik, 29 October 1698; ÖStA, HHStA, Türkei I, Turcica Box 168, Folder 1 (November 1698, 1st half), fol. 218^{v}, Marsigli to Kinsky, 17 November 1698.

For them, the Ottoman demand for commissioners appeared entirely justifiable and well-founded. And so, in yet another instance of a plenipotentiary imposing his own line on his court, they agreed, fairly quickly, to follow the 'old method' proposed by the Porte during their first session with the representatives of the Exalted State,[183] consequently dooming any Venetian hope for a non-repetition of 1669.

7 Border-Making Tools

Despite the proclamations of the different ambassadors that they didn't possess adequate knowledge of the geography of the various regions they were called upon to demarcate, the reality is that they had at their disposal multiple tools to assist them in such a work. These tools fulfilled a double purpose, both as an information source and as evidence to be used to counter the opposing side's arguments. Leaving aside the 'special border advisers' with whom we will deal in Interlude V, two such instruments were mainly utilised by the congress participants: maps and archival material.

7.1 *Maps*

Cartography and its perfection were considered for a long time an appanage of western and central Europe and a proof of the seventeenth-century European 'scientific revolution'.[184] However, older and more novel studies demonstrate that preoccupations with mapping and visually representing 'territoriality'[185] and state control were geographically widely shared from Louis XIV (1643–1715) to Meḥmed IV (1648–87), the Kangxi Emperor (1654–1722) and even nomadic polities in Central Asia.[186] Contrary to the previous 'mimicking Europe' narrative, so these studies sustain, extra-European cartography was actually more of an adoption of certain foreign elements combined with local traditions, resulting in an original synthesis.[187] Such a 'global' seventeenth-century

183 See ÖStA, HHStA, Türkei I, Turcica Box 170, Protocollum, fol. 8–18.

184 Perdue, 'Boundaries', 272–3.

185 The concept of 'human territoriality', as defined by Robert Sack, refers to the strategies adopted by political authorities aiming at controlling, ordering and mastering a space and what lies in it. For the concept and the relevant to it bibliography, *see* Katsiardi-Hering, 'Κτηματογραφικοὶ χάρτες', 24–5.

186 Gottfried Hagen, 'Afterword: Ottoman Understanding of the World in the Seventeenth Century', in Robert Dankoff, *An Ottoman Mentality. The World of Evliya Çelebi* (Leiden/Boston: Brill 2006) 227–32; Hellman and Smith, 'Borders before Nations'.

187 Ibid.; Hagen, 'Afterword', 232; Jaskov, 'Negotiated Geography'.

'cartography mania', brought maps to the forefront as devices to be employed in a boundary-making diplomatic negotiation. Hence, it's only natural to find them everywhere at Carlowitz.

Together with their propositions, the Imperial embassy handed over to the mediators 'a bicolouredly composed map [showing] the division of borders'.[188] According to Marsigli, the Venetians did precisely the same, presenting to Paget and Colyer two maps showing their claimed boundaries regarding the Corinthian Isthmus and Dalmatia and also followed by notes (*con tutte l'annotationi*).[189] A much more intriguing case is that of Voznitsyn. Following the *Bolognese*, the Muscovite had with him an Ottoman-made map of the Black Sea, which he acquired while he was in the Ottoman capital in 1681 to conclude a peace agreement between the tsar and the sultan.[190] As for its accuracy, 'the same ambassador [...] during his journey to the Porte has visited many places on the shores of Asia [and] confirmed it to be good'.[191] Later, he made a copy of that same map for the mediators to inform them about the four Dnieper fortresses, the most challenging issue of the Ottoman–Muscovite talks.[192] Finally, if we also believe Count Schlik, the Ottomans had provided to the mediators and the Imperials a map of the Ottoman–Venetian borders in Dalmatia, as they conceived them, to similarly support their positions.[193]

In all the above cases, maps are presented as a neutral and unbiased representation of reality. Yet, in fact, they are only utilised as yet another weapon to advance the interests of those who commissioned them. As Helena Jaskov correctly observes, 'even though maps may seem to rely on a universally understandable language of signs, they are in fact "repositories of ways of seeing". Rather than being objective representations of the territory, they offer a selective, interested view of it'.[194] Even Marsigli, the ardent proponent of such 'scientific' methods to determine a border, inadvertently confessed their partiality when he related to the emperor how, as chief border commissioner of the Imperial side after the congress, he used the astrolabe, which he described to

188 ÖStA, HHStA, Türkei I, Turcica Box 168, Folder 1 (November 1698, 1st half), fol. 36v, Imperial plenipotentiaries to Leopold I, 5 November 1698.

189 ÖStA, HHStA, Türkei I, Turcica Box 168, Folder 2 (November 1698, 2nd half), fol. 223r, Marsigli to Kinsky, s.d. (most probably early November 1698).

190 ÖStA, HHStA, Türkei I, Turcica Box 168, Folder 1 (November 1698, 1st half), fol. 246r, Marsigli to Kinsky, 12 November 1698.

191 Ibid.

192 Bogoslovskii, *Petr I*, 408.

193 ÖStA, HHStA,Türkei I, Turcica Box 170, Diarium et Cerimoniale, fol. 70.

194 Jaskov, 'Negotiated Geography', 66.

his Ottoman colleague as 'precise and infallible' (*giusto e infallibile*), to draw a borderline 'advantageous to Your majesty' (*tirata a vantaggio della Maestà Vostra*).[195]

Hence, the choice of whether or not to determine a boundary by using a map was often not a question of 'backwardness' and 'progress' but one of pure interest. It is in this vein that one should interpret the following episode. During one of the last conferences of the congress regarding the affairs of Venice, Mavrocordatos complained to Count Schlik that 'never before the distinction of borders was made by using geographical maps but through commissaries. We will make everything clear, but [we will not take upon ourselves] even the job of geographers (*l'Uffizio de geographici*)'.[196] To this assertion, the Imperial plenipotentiary replied, drawing on his military experience, that 'it will never be a shame for an ambassador to know geography in imitation of the army leaders'.[197] Before rushing to conclusions, we should bear in mind that Mavrocordatos's statement was purposely false. The Porte had indeed established borders before by using maps.[198] And the sultan's plenipotentiaries debated with Ruzzini on the issues of Dalmatia based upon them.[199] Besides, Mavorcordatos could hardly justify the stereotype of the 'ignorant Turk', being instead an individual highly versed in contemporary scientific affairs.

7.2 *Archival Material*

If cartography was the visual boundary-determining instrument, archival material was the written one. Writing to Kinsky about the borders of Transylvania, Count Marsigli would recommend him,

> to write to General Rabutin[200] to search in the archives of the Transylvanian government, or in the Capitolo of Alba Julia, where there are the documents of its ancient borders with Wallachia and Moldavia[201] and for

195 Quoted in Raffaella Gherardi, 'Scienza e governo della frontiera: il problema dei confini balcanici e danubiani nella pace di Carlowitz'. *Il Pensiero Politico* 32/3 (1999), 327.

196 ÖStA, HHStA,Türkei I, Turcica Box 168, Folder 1 (November 1698, 1st half), fol. 323ᵛ, protocol of the conference on 22 January 1699.

197 Ibid., fol. 325ʳ.

198 Kołodziejczyk, 'Universalistic claims', 211.

199 ÖStA, HHStA,Türkei I, Turcica Box 170, Diarium et Cerimoniale, fol. 70.

200 He is referring here to Jean-Louis de Bussy-Rabutin, commander of the Imperial forces in Transylvania.

201 Marsigli is probably alluding here to the Treaty of Gyulafehérvár (Alba Julia) of 1595, in which the voivodes of Wallachia and Moldavia, Michael the Brave (1558–1601) and Ştefan

> the Banat of Temesvar, the settlement with Bocgiai(sic)[202] [...] where they were stipulated some new boundaries.[203]

Similarly, the Ottoman plenipotentiaries argued that the borders between Transylvania and the *Eyālet* of Ṭemeşvar were sufficiently known through the cadastres made by the financial branch of the Ottoman administration.[204] In addition, to determine the new border in Bosnia and Croatia, they principally relied upon two registers, one made by a certain Ömer Efendi, a scribe (*dīvān efendisi*) in the service of a previous governor of Bosnia, Şahin Meḥmed Paşa, and a second made under the supervision of another governor of the same province, Aḥmed Paşa.[205]

8 No-Man's-Land and the Issue of Fortresses

The Carlowitz participants never failed to declare that their primary preoccupation was the security of the new boundaries. One way to achieve that was to draw the borderline in places considered safer, just like the Venetians with the Gerania mountains west of the Corinthian Isthmus. Another method, though, was to declare a no-man's-land in a particular zone around the designated natural or artificial limit. This was quite a common practice. The Ottoman–Muscovite Treaty of Bakhchisarai (1681) stipulated such an uninhabited zone on both sides of the river Dnieper, the official boundary between the two polities.[206] In a similar fashion, the Qing delegation at Nerchinsk promised

Răzvan (d. 1595), respectively, swore allegiance to the Transylvanian prince Sigismund Báthory (1573–1613) at the start of the 'Long Turkish War' (1593–1606). I am deeply grateful to Gábor Kármán for providing this information, as well as the details in the following note.

202 Marsigli is likely referring to the appointment document (*berāt*) of Ákos Barcsai (r. 1658–60), who was placed on the Transylvanian throne by the Grand Vizier Köprülü Mehmed Paşa in 1658, following the deposition of György II Rákóczi (r. 1648–58). During this time, several Transylvanian fortresses were incorporated into the *Eyālet* (province) of Ṭemeşvar, thus altering its previous boundaries.

203 ÖStA, HHStA, Türkei I, Turcica Box 168, Folder 1 (November 1698, 1st half), fol. 47^r–50^r, Marsigli to Kinsky, 5 November 1698.

204 *Taʿrīḥ-i ṣulḥnāme*, fol. 87^a.

205 Ibid., fol. 95^b–96^a. For the use of land surveys to determine boundaries as an alternative to maps, *see* also Pešalj, 'The Distinctiveness', 25–6 and Kołodziejczyk, 'Universalistic Claims', 208.

206 Kočegarov, 'The Moscow Uprising', 60–1; Kołodziejczyk, 'Od stanic kresowych', 55.

the Muscovites that it would enforce a wasteland between the Argun and Amur rivers.[207]

At Carlowitz, the Imperials demanded a similar arrangement in the Ṭemeşvar province to exclude the Ottomans from the Mureş and Tisza. The Porte, they reasoned, had frequently applied such methods in previous treaties with Poland-Lithuania and Persia to prevent incursions.[208] Mavrocordatos denied, of course, any such precedent, adding that such a stipulation would be "against the religion and one's conscience".[209] 'The scope of peace is to render prosperous and populous the lands and to avert [any] damages [that could affect] the procreation of the human race. One cannot create a wasteland without offending God', he claimed.[210] So, yet another border-making method was adopted or denied *à la carte* ...

No-man's-land meant not only no habitation in it but specifically, and most importantly, no presence of fortresses. Following the terms of the Treaty of Bakhchisarai, its two signatories, the Ottoman Empire and Muscovy, were not allowed to colonise or erect new fortifications (*palankas*) along hundreds of miles from the banks of the Dnieper, ranging from Kyiv to Zaporozhe.[211] Forts were an arch feature of a pre-modern frontier. A complex system of fortifications dominated the Habsburg–Ottoman boundaries' landscape in Hungary and Croatia for most of the sixteenth and seventeenth centuries.[212] Frontier forts or fortresses were multi-factional. They delimited one's domains and assured control over their surrounding territory; they were defensive points against external or internal enemies, acting equally, though as a basis for incursions into enemy territory.[213] Hence, the erection of new fortifications along the frontier or the reconstruction of those that had previously been agreed to be demolished by one party could be seen by the other as a sign of hostility and a prelude to war. As Thomas Hobbes was writing in Paris during the Congress of Westphalia, '[I]n all times, Kings, and persons of Soveraigne authority [...] are in continuall jealousies, and in the state and posture of Gladiators; having

207 Perdue, 'Boundaries', 351.

208 ÖStA, HHStA, Türkei I, Turcica Box 170, Protocollum, fol. 30. Apparently, they haven't studied the subject so thoroughly since they failed to mention the most recent Ottoman–Muscovite example.

209 Ibid.

210 Ibid., fol. 29.

211 Kołodziejczyk, 'Od stanic kresowych', 55.

212 Pešalj, 'The Distinctiveness', 22–3.

213 On frontier fortresses, see Pedani, *Dalla frontiera*, 46–49; Brummett, 'The Fortress'.

their weapons pointing [...] on one another; that is their Forts, Garrisons, and Guns upon the Frontiers of their Kingdoms'.[214]

Starting from the argumentation basis that 'if [our] predecessors mixed up the territories and [so] they couldn't permit [one] to fortify the borderlands, now that everything is clearer, good intentions are to be doubted less',[215] the Ottomans demanded a mutual commitment by both sides that no new fortifications would be built along the agreed border, nor could those that had been demolished be reconstructed. "It's not fair that one is permitted to fenestrate his house [while] obliging his neighbour to leave his [own] open", they reasoned,[216] and they finally got their way.[217] A similar demand was also made to the Muscovites. The Porte's ambassadors suggested a prohibition of any new fortification on the borders, valid for both sides, for the duration of the two-year armistice/truce between them, under the logic that any such novel fortification could create suspicions and disturb the smooth process of the peace negotiations that were to take place during that time.[218] Faced, though, with Voznitsy's adamant stance, they were obliged to withdraw the claim.[219]

The Ottomans might have deemed it unjust to leave their 'house' without windows, but they did not have the same scruples regarding that of the weakest, in their view, among their western neighbours. After seeing a copy of the agreed articles (*capitoli*) between the Ottomans and the Imperials, Loredano commented that "the one on the fortifications appeared to me suspicious, and I wouldn't like Mavrocordatos [...] to make a precedent here as well, impeding us to construct new stone fortifications in the Straight [the Isthmus]".[220] He could well have been a seer. As Marsigli commented,

> with so great and passionate a debate, the Turks can see clearly and know well now, where a middling prince [Venice] wants to place the defence of so vast a conquest [...] against their power, and they are taking great pains to take their precautions in the negotiation to impede him [from doing] that with the prohibition to raise new fortifications in the Isthmus.[221]

---

214 Quoted in Croxton, *Westphalia*, 376.

215 ÖStA, HHStA, Türkei I, Turcica Box 170, Protocollum, fol. 132.

216 Ibid., fol. 71.

217 Ibid., fol. 71–2.

218 Cernovodeanu, 'Le journal', 340.

219 Bogoslovskii, *Petr I*, 416.

220 BNM, Ms.it.VII 399(8625), fol. 341^{r}, Loredano to Ruzzini, 22 December 1698. For the Venetian projects to refortify the Isthmus, *see* Panopoulou, 'Da mar a mar' and Maltezou, 'Βενετσιάνικες εκθέσεις'.

221 ÖStA, HHStA, Türkei I, Turcica Box 171, Folder 1 (January 1699, 1st half), fol. 136^{r-v}, Marsigli to Kinsky, 3 January 1699.

All the same, specific stratagems could be employed to avoid such unpleasant surprises during the negotiations. According to Ruzzini, the Imperials were able to secure an exception for the no-new-fortification-on the borders clause of the treaties for the 'most important' (*importantissima*), as he claims, island of Arad in the river Mureş, by resorting to the following trick: in late October 1698, as the congress had just been convened, the Imperial Court realising that it would not be possible to attain in the negotiation 'the general freedom' (*la libertà universale*) to erect novel fortifications in the frontier areas, commanded Prince Eugene of Savoy, the commander of the Habsburg armies on the Hungarian front, to go to the island with a few troops and construct 'at least the skeleton and the first floor of a fortress' which could then pass under the Ottomans' nose as already made.[222]

9 Controlling the Borderlands

Deciding and determining a boundary was one thing. Effectively controlling its adjusted areas was another, however. 'Generally speaking', Count Schlik wrote to Kinsky,

> all the frontier from Croatia to Transylvania is a [total] chaos […]. Thousands and thousands of people command, and no one, to put it this way, obeys. We had armed the people without order, without reason and without knowing why. I will say, in a nutshell, that such a shameful and pitiful situation reigns there that without a lot of diligence and rigour, as well as without replenishing the borders with German troops and sending the rest to plough the land, neither the conquests of His Majesty will give him some profit – there will be no safety and no commerce – nor the peace that we are about to conclude will last.[223]

Further east, in the steppes of Budjak and southern Ukraine, the Porte was to face a similar challenge. Like Count Schlik and the Serbian irregulars, members of the Ottoman élite expressed identical contempt for the way of living of the semi-nomadic Tatar populations there, seeing them often as nothing more than plunderers and troublemakers.[224] Like the Ottoman–Imperial,

222 Ruzzini, *Relazione*, 367.

223 ÖStA, HHStA, Türkei I, Turcica Box 171, Folder 2 (January 1699, 2nd half), fol. 123^v–124^v, Schlik to Kinsky, 21 January 1699.

224 Rifaat Abou-el-Haj, 'The Formal Closure of the Ottoman Frontier in Europe: 1699–1703'. *Journal of the American Oriental Society* 89/3 (1969), 472, fn. 28.

the Exalted-State's boundary with the Commonwealth and Muscovy was in a similar turmoil after sixteen years (some less with Muscovy) of constant fighting and raiding.[225] In parallel to the irregular Hajduks in the Imperial borderlands, the Tatars, who were an asset during war, became a burden during peace. Profiting from a rebellion in Budjak by semi-nomadic populations, the Nogays,[226] nearly a year after the conclusion of the Carlowitz Treaties (1700–01), and partly caused by them, the Porte – and the Crimean Khan – found an opportunity to assert total control in the area.[227] Not only did it order the Nogays 'to plough the land', but it went a step further, attempting to reform their entire social and religious practices[228] in a rare instance, unparalleled in early modern Ottoman history, of what one could label with much circumspection as a case of 'confessionalisation'.

The two previous cases, combined with similar contemporary Muscovite and Qing attempts to control their Siberian and central Asian borderlands effectively manifested, as many scholars have already pointed out, analogous centralisation tendencies, as governments tried to *żabṭ ėtmek* (to master) – as the Ottomans would have framed it – their frontier peripheries and bring order to them after the disorders caused by chronic conflicts.[229] This was a long process, though, that would be completed, if ever, long after the Congress of Carlowitz was over.

---

225 Similar conditions reigned equally along the new borders with Venice in southern mainland Greece, as plainly attested by the many orders from the Ottoman central administration to the local governors, stressing the need to pacify the frontier areas and clear them from the irregular troops – now labelled as bandits (*eşḳıyā*). *See*, for example, Burcu Duzcan, '111 Numaralı Mühimme Defterinin 338.-507. Sayfalarının Transkripsiyonu ve Değerlendirilmesi' (MA dissertation, Artvin Çoruh University, 2019) 153–4. We could suppose that the Venetians were facing similar problems and were following parallel tactics to tackle them as well.

226 Alper Başer, 'Bucak Tatarları (1550–1700)' (Ph.D. thesis, Afyon Kocatepe University, 2010).

227 Although one should be extremely careful with the interpretation of events, since the latter are presented quite differently from the viewpoint of early eighteenth-century Ottoman and Crimean historiographers or chroniclers: Denise Klein, 'Tatar and Ottoman History Writing. The Case of the Nogay Rebellion (1699–1701)', in Klein, *The Crimean Khanate*, 125–46. For the Nogay rebellion, *see* also Başer, 'Bucak Tatarları', 161–7; Abou-el-Haj, 'The Formal Closure', 471–5 and Tóth Hajnalka, 'A karlócai béke és a Krími Kánság'. *Keletkutatás* 2012, 27–9.

228 Abou-el-Haj, 'The Formal Closure', 471–2.

229 Ibid., 475; Hellman and Smith, 'Borders before Nations'; Natalia Królikowska-Jedlińska, 'Designers or Obedient Executors of the Ottoman Northeastern Policy? The Governors of the Caffa and Trabzon Provinces at the Turn of the Seventeenth and Eighteenth Centuries', in Gábor Kármán (ed.), *Tributaries and Peripheries of the Ottoman Empire* (Leiden/Boston: Brill 2020) 292–3.

10 A 'Closing' of the Frontier?

'The Formal Closure of the Ottoman Frontier in Europe: 1699–1703'. That's how the late Ottomanist Rifaat Abou-el-Haj described in an influential article published in 1969 the consequences of the border arrangements following the Carlowitz Treaties.[230] In his view, the Carlowitz Congress was a real milestone, altering definitively by its provisions the landscape of south-central and eastern Europe as much as the very nature of the Ottoman state. Loosely defined and penetrable 'frontier zones', ravaged by constant warfare and skirmishes, were transformed into modern linear, impenetrable boundaries which had to be fully respected, as the last remnants of the Ottoman 'Ġāzī ('Holy Warrior') tradition', the nomadic Tatars of the Ukrainian steppes, would soon to find out quite bitterly.[231] Similarly, according to Jovan Pešalj, the new, post-1699 Ottoman–Imperial border arrangements differed substantially from previous ones between the two empires. 'Violence and peacetime excesses of the past suddenly disappeared', he sustains, adding that the novel boundary was the first genuinely artificial one of the Habsburg Monarchy.[232] Yet, was Carlowitz the watershed Abou-el-Haj, and to a lesser extent Pešalj, assert?[233]

In his various studies regarding the Ottoman boundaries in Eastern Europe, Dariusz Kołodziejczyk effectively disclaimed with undeniable evidence the supposed originality of the Carlowitz border-making and the alleged 'closure of the Ottoman frontier in Europe'.[234] If there was anything new about it, he opined, it would be the cartographical tools used by Count Marsigli to determine the boundaries and his original idea of a sanitary cordon all along them to act as a barrier to future epidemics.[235] And even those features, we should add, were not discussed or effectuated during the congress but after it. Apart from that, the notion of a well-defined linear boundary was not strange at all in southern and eastern Europe, going back to the fifteenth century, if not much

230 Abou-el-Haj, 'The Formal Closure'.

231 Ibid.

232 Pešalj, 'The Distinctiveness', 24.

233 To be fair, unlike other contemporary scholars who more or less uncritically adopt Abou-el-Haj's narrative without consulting the latest bibliography on the subject, such as Baramova's 'Border Theories' and Yaycıoğlu's 'Ottoman Arguments', Pešalj's highly informative study takes a more balanced approach. While acknowledging that Carlowitz was not the watershed once believed, he still emphasises the elements that, according to him, made the post-1699 Ottoman–Habsburg boundary distinct.

234 Equally pioneering was also the monograph of the late Maria Pia Pedani on the Ottoman–Venetian case: Pedani, *Dalla frontiera*.

235 Kołodziejczyk, 'Universalistic Claims', 207.

earlier – as were the methods to determine it – whereas the pre-1699 frontier in Hungary was not so 'rough and vague', as Abou-El-Haj would have us believed.[236]

Thus, if something dominates the Carlowitz Congress's border-making practices, that is continuity and not innovation, something that was continuously stressed in our previous analysis. Let us take only two notable examples. Despite the strenuous attempts, primarily by Venice, the precise demarcation of borders was not effectuated by the plenipotentiaries *in situ congressus* but was left to special commissioners after the peace talks, the traditional, prevailing method in Ottoman–Venetian frontier arrangements since the 1470s.[237] As for the use of maps to support and further the claims of the various parties, Carlowitz was not even there a pioneer. Charts were already used in the Crimean/Ottoman–Muscovite negotiations for the Treaty of Bakhchisarai (1680–81) to determine boundaries[238] and formed the principal tool of border-making during the negotiations between the Qing and the Muscovites at Nerchinsk (1689).[239]

Furthermore, it would be an exaggeration to refer to the post-1699 Imperial–Ottoman border as the first artificial one of the Habsburg Domains. Pešalj himself admits that the boundaries of the Kingdom of Bohemia had been well-known since the ninth century.[240] Weren't those frontiers artificial, determined top-down as well? We have already seen in the case of Transylvania that even such a 'modernist' like Count Marsigli didn't bother to determine the majority of its boundaries since he considered them already well-defined from past centuries. The peace treaty between the Holy Roman Empire and the Kingdom of France signed at Ryswick (1697), stipulated, among other things, that 'His Sacred Imperial Majesty and the Empire cede to His Royal Most Christian Majesty and his successors in the kingdom the city of Strasburg and everything that depends to it on the left bank of the Rhine'.[241] The exact limits of the area delivered to France were not specified because – one might justifiably argue – as in the case of Transylvania, they were sufficiently known a priori, although special commissioners did convene afterwards to clarify the details.[242]

---

236 Ibid., 207–12.

237 Pedani, *Dalla frontiera*, 40–6.

238 Kołodziejczyk, 'Universalistic Claims', 211.

239 Perdue, 'Boundaries', 350; Jaskov, 'Negotiated Geography', 65–6.

240 Pešalj, 'The Distinctiveness', 24.

241 *Traité de paix*, 15.

242 Sahlins, 'Natural Frontiers', 1434–5. We still lack a comprehensive study on the conceptions of borders and the practices of border-making during or after other major seventeenth-century congresses.

At the dawn of the eighteenth century, new artificial borders were, as in the past, mainly discussed when circumstances necessitated them.[243] In the Imperial–Ottoman case, it was the immediate result of the vast territorial reconfiguration brought about by the war in a huge area ranging from modern-day Slovenia and Croatia to Transylvania. That held equally valid for Dalmatia and southern Greece, where new borderlines would have to be drawn between Porte and Venice, as well as in the Azov and Lower Dnieper region between the former and Muscovy. With the Commonwealth, the situation was reversed. Whereas the acquisition of Podolia and western Ukraine by the Ottomans as a result of the 1672–76 wars created the need for a detailed delimitation between the two sides, Carlowitz only brought a return to the old boundary along the river Dniester, which had already been agreed upon between the two sides since the early seventeenth century.[244]

Verily, some clauses were indeed introduced for the first time, such as the provision for creating a special bipartisan commission to investigate and resolve future border disputes in the Ottoman–Imperial agreement.[245] However, that doesn't mean that this brought a radical overnight change in the frontier landscape. We need a detailed study of the immediate post-Carlowitz situation to determine whether or not the new border was far more 'rigid' than the previous one, as Pešalj argues,[246] and the pessimistic comments made by Count Schlik regarding the poor state of the Habsburg border areas don't necessarily point in that direction. The principal issue with the 'close of the frontier' assertions, still in vogue today,[247] is that they usually imply a sudden and abrupt transformation caused primarily and solely by a peace agreement, whereas the actual process could have been far slower and more gradual.

Undoubtedly though, what the case of Carlowitz attests is a similar, 'global' discourse during this period, stressing the need for a polity to have clear, secure boundaries that would minimise, as much as possible, any frictions with its limitrophe political entities, as our analysis of the vocabulary and expressions defining borders and border-making attests. In the official Latin text of the

243 This practice changed only in the late eighteenth century, when even 'well-known boundaries' had to be redefined and redrawn. For example, the Imperial border with Wallachia and Moldavia in Transylvania – previously considered by Marsigli to be adequately registered and thus unnecessary for demarcation – had to be redefined in the 1770s: Pešalj, 'The Distinctiveness', 32.

244 That explains why the demarcation protocol of 1680 is far more detailed than the one of 1703: Kołodziejczyk, 'Universalistic Claims', 209–11.

245 Pešalj, 'The Distinctiveness', 24.

246 Ibid.

247 For instance, Helena Jaskov referred to the situation created by the Treaty of Nerchinsk as 'The Closing of the Manchurian Frontier': Jaskov, 'Negotiated Geography', 51.

Nerchinsk treaty, also approved by the Manchu side, it was stated right in the preamble that the two delegations met 'to determine and to place clearly and evidently the borders between the two empires, namely the Chinese and the Ruthenian [Russian] ones'.[248] As Count Marsigli referred to the emperor in one of his relations to him as chief Imperial border commissioner after the congress, Leopold desired a 'well-ordered and clear border [...] to remove these intermixtures of Your subjects with those of the sultan which always caused incursions and disruptions'.[249] The Ottomans couldn't agree more, supporting in their turn a clearly defined border with the emperor in which 'the subjects will live in tranquillity, without the need any more to obey two masters'; a boundary which would ensure a stable peace.[250]

Linear and clearly defined boundaries were, as we saw, only one of the alternatives for pre-modern polities to arrange their relations with their neighbours. As the seventeenth century drew to a close, it had come, at least discursively, to dominate the landscape. Its hegemony would continue to expand throughout the following decades, leading ultimately to the modern notion of a border and its primal function as a means to control and supervise mobility.[251]

•••

The alleged already-known limits of Transylvania were mainly the ones separating it from the Danubian Principalities, tributaries of the Ottoman Empire, Moldavia and Wallachia. Figuring prominently among the border-making aspirations of the Venetians in Dalmatia was the one to cut off the Republic of Ragusa (Dubrovnik), another Ottoman tributary, from the rest of the 'Well-Protected Dominions' (*Memālik-i Maḥrūse*) of the sultan. In their turn, the Ottomans feared the Muscovite presence in and control of the Lower Dnieper, among others, because of the threat this posed for another polity under their protection in the area, the Crimean Khanate. Time thus to bridge and immerse into yet another principal subject of the Carlowitz negotiation: the control over and the regulation of the relations of the big players with smaller political entities situated at the frontiers between them.

---

248 "[...] ad limites inter utrumque Imperium Sinicut videlicet et Ruthenicum clare ac perspicue determinandos ac constituendos": Quoted in Sebes, S. J., *Jesuits*, 157.

249 Quoted in Gherardi, 'Scienza', 323.

250 *Taʿrīḫ-i ṣulḥnāme*, fol. 86b. Here, the Ottomans are referring to the problem of condominiums in pre-1699 Hungary, where many villages usually had to pay double taxes to the Porte and the Hungarian nobles living in the Habsburg-controlled areas: Pešalj, 'The Distinctiveness', 21–3.

251 Ibid., 30.

At the Negotiating Table II: Smaller South-Eastern European Polities as Discussion Topics during the Congress

> It is neither novelty nor monstrosity that the great princes take under their protection the smaller dominions.[1]
>
> The Anonymous Venetian reporting some of the thoughts expressed in the Venetian camp on the Imperial support for Ragusa

In June 1698, as the peace negotiations between the Imperial and the Ottoman Courts were well underway and the two sides were about to sign the Foundation of Peace, a letter from the Senate of the small republic of Ragusa[2] addressed to Emperor Leopold I, reached the Imperial capital.[3] News of the ongoing talks between the great empires to terminate the long war between them should have relatively quickly reached a city that was considered one of the most significant information hubs of the eastern Mediterranean.[4] Like other minor political entities in south-eastern and eastern Europe, all caught between stronger neighbours and their diverse interests, Ragusa was trying to navigate the turbulent waters created by a protracted conflict which had considerably transformed the territorial configuration of the entire region by attempting to

1 *Narratio*, fol. 37v.

2 Ragusa was the Italianised name of Dubrovnik. Since both appellations were used for the small republic during the period under study, I will employ them interchangeably.

3 Zlatar, *Eagle and Crescent*, 200.

4 Johann Petitjean, *L'intelligence des choses. Une histoire de l'information entre Italie et Méditerranée (XVIe–XVIIe siècles)* (Rome: École Française de Rome 2013) 311–79; Zdravko Šundrica, 'The Intelligence Activities of the Dubrovnik Republic in the Austro-Turkish War, 1737–1739'. *Dubrovnik Annals* 5 (2001), 47–79; Sergio Anselmi, *Venezia, Ragusa, Ancona tra Cinque e Seicento: un momento della storia mercantile del Medio Adriatico* (Ancona:Tip. SITA 1969); Nicolaas H. Biegman, 'Ragusan Spying for the Ottoman Empire'. *Belleten* 106 (1963), 237–55.

 | DOI:10.1163/9789004458499_018

delicately manoeuvre between them, balancing one against the other, to safeguard its existence, privileges, and way of life.[5]

Trying to make the best out of the weakening of the Ottomans and the strengthening of the Imperials, the leadership of the Adriatic republic considered it opportune to solicit Vienna's support for the abolition of the annual tribute it paid to the Porte. They reminded the emperor that 'in the past', taking due notice of the stunning successes of the Imperial armies against 'the common enemy' (*commun nemico*), 'we humbly entreated you to deign to command that in the peace treaty with the Turk, an article be inserted expressing the liberation of this Republic from the tribute it delivers annually to him'.[6] 'Now, that the divine kindness reduces even further the Barbarian in a state [to accept peace] terms dictated by Your Most Serene Imperial and Royal Majesty',[7] the heads of the small republic were voicing the same request again, 'in a more obedient way' (*in più divoto modo*), because, they attested, 'be left after the peace with this weight without [commercial] revenues and traffic, we might not maintain our liberty'.[8] Of course, such words of Christian devotion against the 'common enemy' had not prevented the same Ragusans from successfully petitioning the sultan a few years earlier to suspend their annual payment until the end of the conflict based on similar reasons of the alleged hardship and poverty they were suffering because of the war, neither to strive, at precisely the same time they were appealing to Leopold I, to obtain support in the Porte against their greatest enemy, the Republic of Venice.

As we shall further demonstrate below, the Ragusan case reveals the ability and agility of secondary political entities to effectively manoeuvre between their stronger neighbours, aligning their interests with theirs, attempting to influence their decision-making, and imposing their discourse on them. Nonetheless, it will become evident that the final decisions concerning the issue to whom the Republic should pay – figuratively and literally – its allegiance remained the sole privilege of the 'great princes' and their representatives in the peace congress where Ragusa, as well as all the other south-eastern European middling and small polities, accorded no official representation. Hence, the small could try to harmonise their interests with those of the grand, but ultimately, they could only hope that the latter would feel the need to do

5 Ragusa's delicate 'diplomatic balancing acts' during the Sixteen Years' War are analysed in detail in Zlatar, *The Eagle and Crescent*, 128–207. *See* also Grga Novak, *Borba Dubrovnika za slobodu, 1683–1699* (Zagreb: Archbishopal Printing House 1935).

6 ÖStA, HHStA, Türkei I, Turcica Box 165, Folder 4 (June 1698), fol. 25^{r}, the Ragusan Senate to Leopold I, 6 June 1698.

7 Ibid.

8 Ibid.

the same with theirs. Nonetheless, it was primarily due to this complex and sometimes unbalanced interplay of designs between greater and lesser princes that Ragusa 'exited' the Carlowitz Congress precisely as it had 'entered' it: as Ottoman tributary.

Besides Dubrovnik, we will also examine a case that became as significant as questions of possession and border-making in the Ottoman–Commonwealth and Ottoman–Muscovite negotiations: the Crimean Khanate and the Tatar tribes. Their discussion – and, secondarily, that of Ragusa – offers a unique opportunity to touch upon two interconnected issues addressed by the participants at the Carlowitz Congress: who was considered sovereign, and how the payment of tribute or 'gifts' could undermine such claims. Without delving into the broader historiographical debate – vast enough to warrant a separate study – the discussions at the congress reveal that sovereignty remained for its participants a fluid and malleable concept. This was especially true when applied to secondary entities in the political landscape of south-eastern Europe. However, any payment of tribute by primary powers was vehemently rejected as incompatible with the status of a free and sovereign polity.

1 Ragusan Manoeuvrings

Its territory's geographical position and tiny size meant that Ragusa constantly needed more potent protectors to safeguard its existence against its powerful neighbours, first and foremost the Ottoman Empire, especially since the middle of the fifteenth century, as well as its main commercial competitors, the Venetians.[9] Initially, this role was assumed by the Kingdom of Hungary, to which the Republic paid five hundred Hungarian florins annually in exchange for its protection.[10] However, with the vertiginous Ottoman advance in the Balkans during the late fourteenth and especially during the fifteenth century, Ragusa was forced to adjust to the new political constellation. In 1458, the Republic pledged loyalty and agreed to pay yearly to the sultan 1.500 golden coins, an amount that was fixed in 1481 at 12.500 golden coins and remained stable ever since.[11] In exchange, the Ottoman potentate granted the Ragusans

9 Vesna Miović, 'Diplomatic Relations between the Ottoman Empire and the Republic of Dubrovnik', in Kármán and Kunčević, *European Tributary States*, 187–208, 190.

10 Ibid., 191; ÖStA, HHStA, Türkei I, Turcica Box 166, Folder 1 (August 1698), fol. 132^{r}, Informatio Pro Republica Ragusij.

11 Miović, 'Diplomatic Relations', 187–91; Lovro Kunčević, 'Janus-Faced Sovereignty: The International Status of the Ragusan Republic in the Early Modern Period', in Kunčević and Kármán, *European Tributary States*, 92.

a unilateral pact of privileges (*ʿahdnāme*), the most crucial clause among them being the tariff of just two per cent for their merchants in all his dominions, a truly unique case since even Muslim merchants had to pay higher (three per cent).[12]

This double-protection status continued until 1526, when, after the Battle of Mohács, taking place that year, and the ensuing toppling of the Hungarian Kingdom, Dubrovnik ceased to pay tribute to the subsequent claimants to the crown of Saint Stephen, including, first and foremost, the Habsburgs.[13] This didn't mean, though, that it stopped having other Christian protectors – albeit not becoming their tributary – such as the King of Spain and the Pope,[14] but undoubtedly, the Ottomans remained the main guarantor – and constant threat at the same time – of its existence. Still, it was in the Porte's interest not to annex the small republic but to preserve it and grant it extensive autonomy. Thus, Ragusa's 'legal' status always remained pretty unclear, something that suited both sides.[15] Dubrovnik became a commercial and, most importantly, information mecca, as its élite and merchants quasi-monopolised the intelligence traffic between east and west.[16]

To survive in the arena of inter-polity relations, Ragusan patricians adopted different discourses according to their audiences. Towards the Porte, they presented themselves as faithful and voluntary vassals, also inventing a story according to which their ancestors had the clairvoyance to be among the first to predict the future Ottoman greatness and to send an embassy to Bursa in Asia Minor in the distant fourteenth century to place themselves freely and willingly under the protection of the second Ottoman ruler, Orhan (d. 1362).[17] When now addressing the Christian world, they staged an image of a free entity ever eager to assist its coreligionists against the 'common barbarian enemy'.[18] Nonetheless, there was another normative refrain addressed equally to both the East and the West: the alleged precarity and poverty of the small republic. It was a valuable trick to keep the tribute to the Porte stable, reduce it, or even do away with it if the circumstances permitted, and to arouse feelings of empathy in their interlocutors, be they Muslim or Christian, while at the same

12 Miović, 'Diplomatic Relations', 188; Kunčević, 'Janus-Faced Sovereignty', 94.

13 Miović, 'Diplomatic Relations', 191; Informatio Pro Republica Ragusij, fol. 132r.

14 Miović, 'Diplomatic Relations', 190.

15 Kunčević, 'Janus-Faced Sovereignty'.

16 Ibid.

17 Ibid., 105–6.

18 Lovro Kunčević, 'The Rhetoric of the Frontier of Christendom in the Diplomacy of Renaissance Ragusa (Dubrovnik)'. *Dubrovnik Annals* 17 (2013), 37–68.

time increasing their protective tendencies towards the Adriatic city-state.[19] We should keep all these different rhetorical schemes in mind because they would play a significant role when the future of Ragusa was discussed during the Carlowitz Congress.

The Sixteen Years' War presented Dubrovnik with equally grave perils and unique opportunities. The tiny republic had to maintain a delicate balance between the Imperials and the Ottomans while neutralising the greatest threat to its survival as an autonomous polity during those years, the Republic of Venice.[20] In order to achieve that goal, it simultaneously courted both the Habsburg emperor and the Porte, privileging, according to the unfolding of events, one or the other as the Republic's primary protector against the Venetian menace.[21]

As we have already discussed, the Serenissima entered the Sixteen Years' War with grandiose plans to annex considerable swathes of land in the eastern Adriatic, and Dubrovnik formed part of them. Despite strong objections from some Imperial ministers who considered the area as pertaining to the Austrian Habsburgs' sphere of influence as legitimate Kings of Hungary, in the Holy League Treaty of 1684, the Republic of Saint Mark received a *carte blanche* to conquer Ottoman territories in Dalmatia, and as the Venetians were concerned, Ragusa, a tributary of the Porte, was also there for the taking.[22] The Serenissima's strategy to achieve that aim was first to incorporate the Ottoman-controlled Ragusan hinterland, cut the small republic from the sultan's domains, and then absorb it into its own dominions. So, in 1687, the Venetian forces managed to take the vital fortress of Castel Nuovo (Herceg Novi) south of the Ragusan border and initiate a partial blockade of Ragusa itself.[23] In 1694, they conquered another key Ottoman fort in the northern Ragusan hinterland, that of Gabela.[24]

To counter this existential threat, the leadership of the Adriatic republic turned to Vienna. In 1684, just shortly after the formation of the Holy League, Raffael Vladislavi Gozze was sent to the Imperial capital to place the small republic under the protection of Leopold I.[25] The agreement remained secret

19 Miović, 'Diplomatic Relations', 205.

20 Zlatar, *Eagle and Crescent*, 140–1, 151, 157–61.

21 Ibid., 151.

22 Ibid., 138–40.

23 Ibid., 157–9.

24 Uzunçarşılı, *Osmanlı Tarihi*, 574.

25 Zlatar, *Eagle and Crescent*, 141–9; Jovan Radonić (ed.), *Acta et Diplomata Ragusina*, vol. 4, part 1 (Belgrade 1941) 3–19, 21–39, 43–5; Radovan Samardžić, *Veliki vek Dubrovnika* (Belgrade: Prosveta 1983) 428, 495; ibid., 'Borba Dubrovnika protiv mletačkih pokušaja

until 1686, when, after the fall of Buda to the Imperial armies, it was made public. The emperor claimed, as the legitimate King of Hungary, a de jure resumption of his rights over the city-state, which had fallen into discontinuance after the early sixteenth century.[26] Thus, Ragusa restarted paying Leopold the five hundred florins and agreed to receive a resident representative of the emperor.[27] The pro-Habsburg stance of Ragusa continued unabated as long as Leopold's armies scored one victory after the other against the Ottomans in Hungary and Northern Serbia in the years 1684–90. The Ragusans actively encouraged an Imperial annexation of their hinterland, enlisting support for Vienna among the local populations and countering similar Venetian schemes to win the latter to their side.[28] Moreover, from 1688, they ceased paying the annual tribute to the Ottoman Porte altogether.[29]

Nonetheless, this Ragusan 'Imperial turn', except for a brief period between 1688 and 1690, didn't signal a complete severing of ties with the Exalted State. When in 1686, Raffael di Vladislavo Gozze's brother, Luca, was heading to Austria to put the Republic under formal Imperial tutelage, a parallel mission was dispatched to the Porte to convince the Ottoman government of Ragusa's continuous fidelity,[30] something that would cause huge indignation to the Imperial ambassadors when they discovered it during the Carlowitz Congress.[31] In 1688, Luca Barca was appointed as the first permanent resident consul of the Republic in the Ottoman capital (1688–1709).[32] As the Habsburg

---

da unište njegovu nezavisnost u XVII veku', in *Dubrovačko pomorstvo. U spomen sto godina Nautičke škole u Dubrovniku* (Dubrovnik 1952) 383; J.C. von Engel, *Die Geschichte des Freystaates Ragusa* (Vienna: Anton Doll Publishing House 1807) 249, 334–41. The text of this treaty was published in, Josip Gelcich and Lajos Thallóczy (eds.), *Diplomatarium relationum Reipublicae Ragusanae cum regno Hungariae* (Budapest: Hungarian Academy of Sciences 1887) 686–9.

26 Zlatar, *Eagle and Crescent*, 151, 155, 170–1; ÖStA, HHStA, Türkei I, Turcica Box 166, Folder 1 (August 1698), fol. 132^{r}, Informatio Pro Republica Ragusij.

27 Ibid., fol. 132^{r-v}; Ruzzini, *Relazione*, 360. The first Imperial resident representative was the Neapolitan Colonel Domenico Corradini. He was replaced in 1690 by his compatriot, Baron Don Filippo Saponara: Zlatar, *Eagle and Crescent*, 156, 185.

28 Ibid., 162–81.

29 Ibid., 161.

30 Ibid., 156–7.

31 ÖStA, HHStA, Türkei I, Turcica Box 169, Folder 1 (December 1698, 1st half), fol. 10^{r}, Imperial plenipotentiaries to Leopold I, 2 December 1698.

32 Miović, 'Diplomatic Relations', 192, 196. Although Ragusan envoys to the Ottoman capital sent to deliver the annual tribute, typically fulfilled the role of a resident ambassador during their stay, Barca was the first to be appointed permanently, tasked with handling not only commercial but also political matters. I deeply thank Lovro Kunčević for the information.

plenipotentiaries at Carlowitz sustained in one of their relations to the emperor, Barca, 'a true French spy and pensioner' (*Ein ganzt französicher Spion undt Pensionarius*), was doing everything in his power to undermine Vienna's designs.[33] Despite the Habsburg ambassador's efforts to put all the blame on one individual or the Viennese Court to try to justify the Ragusan stance, it was clear that the Adriatic republic was engaging in double dealings. As the outcome of the war became more uncertain in the early 1690s, the Ragusan patricians reverted to a policy of maintaining the status quo while maximising the benefits of protection from both empires.[34]

That's possibly the reason why, upon the ascension of Muṣṭafā II to the Ottoman throne in 1695, another Ragusan embassy headed by Vladislavo di Marino-Secondo Bucchia[35] came to Adrianople on a delicate mission to justify to the Ottoman authorities the non-payment of the tribute since 1688 and a continuation of its suspension until the end of the war on the grounds of the expenses the Republic made to defend itself against Venice and the interruption of its trade with the rest of the Ottoman Dominions. The sultan conceded, issuing a decree (*ḥaṭṭ-ı şerīf*), which, by clearly stating that after the end of the fighting, Ragusa would resume paying the annual tribute as before, was seen by the Porte as a reconfirmation of Dubrovnik's allegiance to her.[36] Thus, when in summer 1698, Luca Barka was instructed to solicit Ottoman support in the upcoming congress against Venice's territorial pretensions to annex the Ragusan hinterland permanently, cutting its connection with the 'Well-protected Dominions', Mavrocordatos assured him of Ottoman assistance by graphically stating that 'a limb must remain attached to the body'.[37] Nonetheless, that was only one part of the Ragusan strategy. Repeating yet again their favourite seize-every-benefit-you-can double game, the city-state's leadership dispatched, as we saw, a letter to Vienna petitioning its other protector to relieve it from the tribute it paid to the Porte altogether.

---

33 ÖStA, HHStA, Türkei I, Turcica Box 169, Folder 1 (December 1698, 1st half), fol. 10r, Imperial plenipotentiaries to Leopold I, 2 December 1698.

34 Zlatar, *Eagle and Crescent*, 175–202.

35 In Rāmī's account, though, the Ragusan ambassador is named Lazar لاوويوكه, and he didn't come to the Porte upon the ascension of Muṣṭafā II but rather 'a year ago' (*geçen sene*): *Taʿrīḥ-i ṣulḥnāme*, fol. 112a.

36 The full text of the decree can be found in ibid., fols. 112a–113a. Also, ÖStA, HHStA, Türkei I, Turcica Box 170, Protocollum, fol. 68; Zlatar, *Eagle and Crescent*, 194–7.

37 Quoted in ibid., 199. For the long history of relations between the Ottoman Chief Interpreter and the small city-state, *see* Vesna Miović, 'Alexander Mavrocordatos Exaporite, Grand Dragoman and Secret Adviser to the Porte: Dubrovnik's Perspective'. *Dubrovnik Annals* 27 (2023), 121–48.

Eager to formalise through the peace negotiations its factual condominium over the Adriatic city-state, the Viennese Court welcomed the Ragusan supplication all too favourably. An anonymous memorandum, probably written in August 1698, to inform the emperor about his 'legitimate' rights over the Adriatic republic, reveals the manipulation and selective interpretation of historical facts by the different sides to advance their goals.[38] After providing a reconstruction of events that proved the legitimacy of the Imperial claims,[39] the unknown author strived to explain the Republic's ambivalent stance during the war years by arguing that it was only after the Ottomans retook Belgrade in 1691 and the Pasha of Bosnia was threatening to invade the city-state if the latter didn't pay the tribute, that the Ragusans decided to send an ambassador to the Porte to plead for a temporary suspension of it until the end of the hostilities. This was the only way to conserve its existence.[40] And it finally comes to the suggestion that the emperor also adopted in the first instructions to his embassy:[41] the suspension of the Republic's tribute to the Ottomans and a condominium of the city-state by the two empires for the protection of which Ragusa would pay the 'ancient' annual 'pension' (*pensione*) of the five hundred Hungarian gold ducats to both.[42] And thus the Adriatic republic and its future turned out to be one of the key topics in both the Ottoman–Imperial and Ottoman–Venetian talks. The two discussions were deeply interrelated; however, we should start with the former, which chronologically preceded the latter.[43]

It's genuinely intriguing how both the Imperials and the Ottomans presented their arguments on this topic by mainly utilising specific parts of the Ragusan discourse, regardless of whether they were taking them at face value or not. Besides repeating the historical arguments of the anonymous memorandum,[44] which they probably had read on their way to or during the

38 The memorandum was drafted in all probability by Count Luigi Marsigli, in close collaboration with his friend, the *Chargé d'Affaires* of the city-state at the Viennese Court since 1686, Don Giulio Cesare Palazuoli: Ibid., 156, 201.

39 ÖStA, HHStA, Türkei I, Turcica Box 166, Folder 1 (August 1698), fol. 132ʳ, Informatio Pro Republica Ragusij.

40 Ibid., fol. 132ᵛ.

41 ÖStA, HHStA, Türkei I, Turcica Box 166, Folder 3 (September 1698, 2nd half), fol. 145ᵛ, Instructio pro Legatis Plenipotentiarijs Caes[are]is.

42 ÖStA, HHStA, Türkei I, Turcica Box 166, Folder 1 (August 1698), fol. 132ᵛ, Informatio Pro Republica Ragusij.

43 Curiously, in his discussion on the 'Ragusan Question' during the Carlowitz Congress, Zlatar completely omits the fierce Ottoman–Imperial debate over its future status and narrates only the Ottoman–Venetian one: Zlatar, *Eagle and Crescent*, 202–7.

44 *Taʾrīḫ-i ṣulḥnāme*, fol. 111ᵇ.

congress, the Imperial ambassadors also made ample use of the rhetoric of the 'poor and destitute' state of the small republic to advance their request for the abolition of the tribute to the Ottomans. According to the account of Rāmī Meḥmed, they started presenting their pretensions on Ragusa, asserting that during the war, its residents were 'highly oppressed by Venice'.[45] Whereas, to stress Dubrovnik's inability to pay the *ḫarāç* (tribute), they were quick to designate them as 'a bunch of poor folks reduced to misery (*bir alay fuḳarādır żaʿīfü'l-ḥāl oldular*).[46]

If the Habsburg side opted to accentuate Ragusa's misfortune, the Ottomans chose to highlight its liberty. Mavrocordatos cleverly tried to dissociate the protection of Ragusa from the tribute the latter paid to the Porte, claiming that the Adriatic republic 'enjoys the protection of the King of Spain and others', thus implicitly arguing that the Imperial safeguarding was simply not needed.[47] He then also recoursed to history, reminding his interlocutors that the Ragusans, centuries ago, 'were the first to come to Bursa in Asia to seek the protection of the Porte',[48] a complete instrumentalisation of this myth of Ragusan creation played to the full advantage of the Porte. Although the Ragusans were 'seemingly subjects of the Exalted State, their actual condition is better than that of foreigners under protection status'.[49] Finally, he declared, Dubrovnik was a 'free republic' (*une Republique libre*). If it wanted to give some form of 'gift' to the emperor as well, it could certainly do that.[50]

The double-dealings of the small Adriatic city-state also came to the surface with Leopold's ambassadors asserting that 'the Christian Republic of Ragusa' had willingly put itself under the protection of the emperor, so they too had a decisive say regarding its future[51] and the Ottomans retorting by presenting a copy of the sultanic decree given recently to Ragusan envoys as evidence that the city-state desired to continue staying under the protective shadow of the padishah.[52] Regardless of all this interesting argumentation, however, Ragusa's

45 Ibid.

46 Ibid., fol. 113[a].

47 ÖStA, HHStA, Türkei I, Turcica Box 170, Protocollum, fol. 68.

48 Ibid., fol. 69.

49 *Taʾrīḫ-i ṣulḥnāme*, fol. 112[a].

50 Cernovodeanu, 'Le journal', 331.

51 ÖStA, HHStA, Türkei I, Turcica Box 170, Protocollum, fol. 68.

52 Cernovodeanu, 'Le journal', 331; ÖStA, HHStA, Türkei I, Turcica Box 170, Protocollum, fol. 68; *Taʾrīḫ-i ṣulḥnāme*, fol. 112[a]. A copy of the order is also provided in ibid., fol. 112[a–b]. It is also of extreme significance to point out that the Ottomans probably knew well in advance that the Imperials would lay claims on the Adriatic Republic, so that's why 'they brought a copy of the Imperial order as a reserve': Ibid., fol. 112[b].

future, like every other aspect of the congress negotiations, was mainly tied to the specific designs of its participants and their determination and ability to pursue them to the end.

The Ottomans were not willing to do away with either the tribute or their suzerainty over Ragusa.[53] Keeping the tiny republic in its status quo appears to have been one of the principal elements of an honourable peace for the Porte. Thus, its ambassadors were unwilling to concede to anything less than that. In the end, the scale was tipped by a third party since it was Paget's overt support for the Ottoman side that appears to have proved catalytic for the Imperials to finally drop their demands.[54] And so, as Rāmī joyfully proclaims in his account, 'the Ragusans remained as before tributaries (*ḫarāc-güẕārları*) solely of the Exalted State'.[55]

The issue was still considered open, though, at least for the Imperial Court. In the supplementary instructions sent to his embassy at Carlowitz on 1 December 1698, Emperor Leopold mentioned a renewed Ragusan supplication for Imperial backing on the issue of tribute and the threat of Venice. He then ordered his ambassadors to do everything in their power so that nothing would be stipulated about Ragusa in the Ottoman–Venetian treaty and to request from the Ottoman side, 'if possible', a quite generous reduction of the tribute the city-state was paying to the Porte, from 12.500 to just five hundred ducats.[56] While, as we shall immediately see, the two ambassadors successfully implemented the first part of the instruction, they were not able, as it turned out, to obtain the second.

Although Venice had succeeded during the war in seizing some cardinal strongholds in Dubrovnik's hinterland, by 1698, it was clear that its initial goal to cut Ragusa entirely from the rest of the sultan's dominions and strangle its economy, had not been totally achieved, despite the highly instrumentalised

---

53 *Narratio*, fol. 38^{v}.

54 ÖStA, HHStA, Türkei I, Turcica Box 170, Protocollum, fol. 68–69. It is not clear why the English supported a Ragusan status quo. They were probably thinking that this would be more beneficial for their commercial interests in the region. I deeply thank Emeritus Professor Olga Katsiardi-Hering for the suggestion.

55 *Taʿrīḫ-i ṣulḥnāme*, fol. 112^{b}. Although the Imperial-Ragusan agreement of 1684 was not clearly repudiated in the Ottoman–Habsburg Treaty, it was evident that the Habsburg withdrawal from pressing any claims upon Ragusa and the control by the Porte of the city-state's hinterland automatically reimposed a sole Ottoman control over the small republic: Zlatar, *Eagle and Crescent*, 206–7.

56 ÖStA, HHStA, Türkei I, Turcica Box 169, Folder 1 (December 1698, 1st half), fol. 1^{r-v}, supplementary Imperial Instructions, 1 December 1698.

Ragusan lamentations to the Ottoman officials of the contrary.[57] Not only that, but both the Imperials and the Porte were not willing to see the Venetian aspirations realised, undoubtedly, each for their own reasons. The former, as Dubrovnik's proclaimed protectors, had a huge stake in its preservation. It was chiefly a matter of honour. 'You [must] secretly [work]' wrote Kinsky to Öttingen, 'to maintain Ragusa against Venice because a subjugation of the Ragusan to the Venetian Republic cannot be decorous for us either in the present and even less in the future'.[58] The latter, on the other hand, besides similar considerations of prestige, were not at all desiring, after managing to retain their sole tutelage over the city-state, to let Venice cut it off from the rest of the 'Well-protected Dominions' and utterly annex it in the first possible instance.

In the beginning, Ruzzini appeared adamant. According to Count Schlik, the toughest of all the difficult points in the Ottoman–Venetian negotiations regarding the question of possession and border-making in Dalmatia was the Ragusan issue. And, as he graphically recounts, not without some tone of derision, 'if he [Ruzzini] only hears the name [Ragusa] pronounced, he immediately turns mad (*sich also stracks entzündet*)'.[59] 'Thus', he continues, 'one can only reason that besides a great animosity [towards Ragusa], a real interest must also be hidden underneath'.[60] Nonetheless, against the interests of two powerful empires, Venice had no hope, as the Venetian ambassador himself would bitterly acknowledge in his *Relazione Finale*.[61] Hence, the small republic was to remain in its antebellum status – a complete victory for the Ottomans and a half one for the Ragusans. The latter could at least be consoled with the thought that this was a much better situation than being left at the mercy of their 'oldest enemies'.[62]

57 For instance, the Venetians were not able to impose a complete blockade of the city-state: Zlatar, *Eagle and Crescent*, 161.

58 ÖStA, HHStA, Türkei I, Turcica Box 171, Folder 2 (January 1699, 2nd half), fol. 203^{r}, Kinsky to Öttingen, 27 January 1699.

59 ÖStA, HHStA, Türkei I, Turcica Box 170, Diarium et Cerimoniale, fol. 69.

60 Ibid.

61 Ruzzini, *Relazione*, 360.

62 Dubrovnik continued to be an Ottoman vassal polity until the 'typhoon' named Napoleon swept it across in his passing as a political entity in 1806: Kunčević, 'Janus-Faced Sovereignty', 92.

2 What Is to Be Done with the Tatars?

As the last remnant of the once mighty Golden Horn in eastern Europe, the Crimean Khanate occupied a unique place in the early modern 'Society of Princes'. Although they had placed themselves under Ottoman protection since the late fifteenth century, the khans, all stemming from the Giray family, held a prominent position inside the Ottoman establishment and many times pursued their own external policies, which did not always coincide with the goals of the Porte.[63] Besides the frequent relations and embassy exchanges with its Christian neighbours, mainly with the Polish-Lithuanian Commonwealth and Muscovy,[64] the Khanate pursued, primarily during the seventeenth century, a very active foreign policy.[65] From 1628 to 1682, twenty-six Tatar embassies were dispatched only to the Imperial Court in Vienna, although they were never reciprocated.[66]

Of course, such a degree of autonomy was also beneficial for the Porte. The geographical proximity of the khans to Muscovy made them indispensable mediators between the two empires.[67] For instance, it was the Crimean ruler who, in a particularly intriguing case of combining the roles of mediator and *Stellvertreter* (deputy), negotiated the first Ottoman–Muscovite peace treaty in 1681 on behalf of the sultan in his capital, Bakhchisarai.[68] Furthermore, trying,

63 Natalia Królikowska, 'Sovereignty and Subordination in Crimean-Ottoman Relation (Sixteenth–Eighteenth Centuries)', in Kármán and Kunčević, *European Tributary States*, 43–65; Dariusz Kołodziejczyk, 'Das Krimkhanat als Gleichgewichtsfaktor in Osteuropa (17.–18. Jahrhundert)', in Klein, *The Crimean Khanate*, 47–58.

64 For the relations of the Khanate with Poland-Lithuania, the key reference work is Dariusz Kołodziejczyk, *The Crimean Khanate and Poland-Lithuania: International Diplomacy on the European Periphery (15th–18th Century). A Study of Peace Treaties Followed by Annotated Documents* (Leiden/Boston: Brill 2011).

65 Kołodziejczyk, 'Das Krimkhanat'.

66 Christoph Augustynowicz, 'Tatarische Gesandtschaften am Kaiserhof des 17. Jahrhunderts – Protokoll und Alltag', in Marlene Kurz et al. (eds.), *Das Osmanische Reich und die Habsburgermonarchie* (Vienna: Böhlau 2005) 315 (fn. 3), 339.

67 Królikowska–Jedlińska, 'Designers or Obedient Executors?', 293; An intriguing instance occurred during the Sixteen Years' War in 1689, when Khan Selīm I Giray served as an intermediary between the Ottoman Porte and the Safavid Shah. He conveyed a proposal from the Safavid shah to mediate a possible peace agreement between the Ottoman Sultan and the Muscovite Tsar. For more on this episode, *see* Selim Güngörürler, 'Diplomacy and Political Relations between the Ottoman Empire and Safavid Iran, 1639–1722' (Ph.D. thesis, Georgetown University 2016), 256–257.

68 Defterdar, *Zübde-i Vekayiât*, 119; Nikita Moiseevich Zotov, *Stateinyi spisok stol'nika Vasiliia Tiapkina i d'iaka Nikity Zotova, posol'stva v Krym v 1680 godu, dlia zakliucheniia Bakhchisaraiskogo dogovora* (Odessa: Municipal Printing House 1850).

like Ragusa, to defend his interests and oscillate amidst his stronger neighbours, the khans, although belligerents, attempted at various times throughout the Sixteen Years' War to assume a mediating role to terminate the conflict between the Ottomans and the Commonwealth.[69]

Another boost to the international prestige of the Khanate was the regular 'payments' it continued to receive as the successor of the Golden Horde from both the Commonwealth and Muscovy. These 'payments' also constituted a significant part of the khans' treasury – besides the portion stemming from booty, acquired from frequent skirmishes in the neighbouring territories not only during war but during peacetime as well.[70] All these elements ostensibly create a truly complicated picture of the status of the Crimean polity.[71] However, in parallel to Ragusa, the Ottomans, the Christian states and even the khans themselves deliberately kept the issue vague, shifting perspectives on it selectively according to the occasion and their interests of the moment, something that would also be plainly manifested in the negotiations at Carlowitz.

In contrast to Ragusa, the Tatars were active participants of the Sixteen Years' War, fighting alongside the Ottoman troops in Vienna – although the role there of the then Khan Murad Giray was highly dubious – and afterwards in Hungary against the Imperials and in Moldavia, Budjak (southern Bessarabia) and Podolia against the Commonwealth.[72] The situation became even more adverse for the Khanate with the entry of Muscovy into the war in 1689. Now, its core lands were under threat as the tsar's armies attempted, unsuccessfully, to invade the peninsula itself.[73] It is thus not a coincidence that the mediating efforts of the khans to terminate the war with Poland-Lithuania intensified at precisely that period to avoid being overrun by the combined strength of their two northern neighbours.[74]

Attesting the Crimean polity's ambiguous status, while its rulers were directly negotiating a cessation of hostilities with the Commonwealth and the Muscovites,[75] its issues were parallelly discussed in the talks between the big

69 Kołodziejczyk, *The Crimean Khanate*, 193–4.

70 Ahmet Türk, 'Gift Exchange as a Means of Expression of Power: The Case of Crimean-Muscovite Relations'. *Acta Orientalia Academiae Scientiarum Hungaricae* 76, no. 2 (2023), 221–37; Kochegarov, "From the 'Eternal Peace' to the Treaty of Carlowitz", 186; Królikowska, 'Sovereignty and Subordination', 49–52.

71 Ibid.

72 Kołodziejczyk, *The Crimean Khanate*, 190–4.

73 Kochegarov, "From the 'Eternal Peace' to the Treaty of Carlowitz".

74 Kołodziejczyk, *The Crimean Khanate*, 193. They also tried during this period to solicit a French mediation to end the war with the Commonwealth: Ibid., 193, fn. 542.

75 Ibid., 193–4; Kochegarov, "From the 'Eternal Peace' to the Treaty of Carlowitz", 191, 194.

players. For instance, one of the Imperial peace terms during the Failed Vienna Congress (1689–90) was the highly improbable withdrawal of the Tatars behind the river Dnieper and their total evacuation of Budjak and the Principality of Moldavia, a demand that caused a vehement reaction by the then Ottoman plenipotentiaries.[76] As for the *Rzeczpospolita*, it not only demanded war reparations from the Tatars, based on a clause from a treaty between Süleymān the Magnificent (r. 1520–66) and Sigismund II (r. 1548–72) back in the sixteenth century, but also went so far as to request the total relocation of all their populations to other parts of the Ottoman Dominions and the splitting up of their territories between itself and Muscovy.[77]

At Carlowitz now, the matters related to the Crimean Khanate were turned into one of the principal topics of discussion during the Ottoman–Commonwealth and Ottoman–Muscovite talks, mainly because of the determination of both Poland-Lithuania and Muscovy to procure an abolition of the regular 'present'/tribute they paid to the khans[78] and their concerns with the Tatar raids in their respective domains, as with Muscovy's strategy to instrumentalise and exaggerate the 'Tatar threat' to justify and advance its territorial claims in the Black Sea.[79] The demands and complaints put forward by the two allies were so similar that the Ottoman ambassadors suspected a coordinated attempt by Peter I and August II to deliberately raise the Crimean issue, even paying close attention to voice identical arguments;[80] a suspicion, however, that doesn't appear to be validated by the Polish or Muscovite archival material. There were three principal debated issues: 1) how sovereign the khan was, 2) the question of the 'payment'/tribute to him, and 3) the Tatar way of life. Let's deal with them one by one.

After its failed attempt to invade Crimea, Muscovy's chief goal shifted from the incorporation of the peninsula into the tsar's dominions to a gradual transformation of it into a 'vassal-state'.[81] This design could perhaps explain why

76 *Cerîde-i Takrirât*, 58, 61.

77 Ibid., 92–3.

78 The Muscovites had first demanded an annulment of the regular 'payment' to the khans in their negotiations in 1689, but this was not accepted by the Crimeans: Kochegarov, "From the 'Eternal Peace' to the Treaty of Carlowitz", 191–3. Interestingly, the Commonwealth didn't bring up the issue in the 1688–92 talks with the Ottomans in Vienna: *Cerîde-i Takrirât*, 56–60.

79 For the Khanate as a subject of discussion during the Carlowitz congress, *see* also Hajnalka, 'A karlócai béke'. However, the author focuses mainly on the stipulations of the final treaties rather than on the actual debates on Crimea taking place during the congress.

80 *Taʿrīḫ-i ṣulḥnāme*, fol. 113^{b}–114^{a}.

81 Kochegarov, "From the 'Eternal Peace' to the Treaty of Carlowitz". 198.

Voznitsyn attempted from the beginning to separate the Khanate from the Ottoman Empire, treating them as two different political entities. During the first Muscovite–Ottoman session, he immediately asked the Porte's plenipotentiaries if Crimea was to be included in the ongoing peace treaty as well or if it was to negotiate a separate settlement with the tsar.[82] 'We must not confuse the [different] parties; the matters [relating] to the khan and the sultan', he also pointedly declared during another conference[83] while insisting on a separate agreement with the Crimean ruler in which the Porte would commit itself that if a war was to break out between the Khanate and Muscovy, it would not intervene on behalf of the former![84] Nonetheless, such an effort to present the Girays as 'independent' princes did not prevent Voznitsyn from complaining to Rāmī and Mavrocordatos about the inability of the sultan to control the Tatars' transgressions and demanding that in the future, he should hold them at bay.[85]

Interestingly, while it was the Commonwealth with which the khans maintained their stronger relations[86] – Polish embassies were even dispatched to him twice during the congress[87] – contrary to Voznitsyn, Małachowski didn't adopt a discourse of clear separation between the Khanate and the Ottomans. For him, when it came to the abolition of the *pelles Tatarias*, as he referred to the regular 'payment' to the khans,[88] or the topic of the prohibition of Tatar intrusions into Polish territories, the Porte and not the Crimean rulers had the last word.

Even more intriguing is the Ottoman stance. Certainly, the position of the Giray dynasty inside the Exalted State was not the same as that of the Wallachian and Moldavian voivodes, the Kurdish chieftains, or the Georgian princes.[89] At the turn of the eighteenth century, this is proven by the following fact. Somewhere in the second half of the late seventeenth century, a significant reform took place in the Ottoman chancery regarding the keeping and

82 Bogoslovskii, *Petr I*, 397.
83 Cernovodeanu", 'Le journal', 328.
84 Bogoslovskii, *Petr I*, 398.
85 *Ta'rīḥ-i ṣulḥnāme*, fol. 110b.
86 In 1685, to pull the khan out of the conflict, Polish King Jan III Sobieski had even promised him that the Holy League would guarantee his sovereignty: Kołodziejczyk, *The Crimean Khanate*, 191.
87 *See* below, Narration Part II.
88 Sałuski, *Epistolae*, 679.
89 Güneş Işıksel, 'La politique étrangère ottomane dans la seconde moitié du XVIe siècle: le cas du règne de Selîm II (1566–1574)' (Ph.D. thesis, Écoles des Hautes Etudes en Sciences Sociales 2012) 60–71.

division of the sultanic correspondence. Whereas up to this point, orders to various officials inside the Ottoman Dominions were kept together with letters to foreign monarchs, such as the King of France, in the so-called 'Registers of Important Affairs' (*Mühimme Defterleri*),[90] henceforth the external correspondence of the padishah was primarily preserved in a special register called 'the August Letters' one (*Defter-i Hümāyūn defterleri*) while the *mühimme* continued to record only the internal communication of the administration. The interesting thing is that sultanic missives addressed to the Crimean Khan were normally included in the first and not in the second,[91] in contrast to other Ottoman tributaries such as the rulers of the Danubian Principalities.[92] Thus, for the Ottoman administration, the Khanate lay in a grey zone between 'what is inside and what is outside', to use Dariusz Kołodziejczyk's quite pertinent expression to refer to the Ottoman conceptions of what constituted a tributary.[93]

However, even from the early sixteenth century, long before the accentuated subordination of the Khanate to the Porte and its declining influence as an autonomous player in the early modern inter-polity scene, the Ottomans were holding a purposedly ambivalent stance on its status, sometimes claiming that the khans were their vassals and sometimes asserting that Crimea was an independent dominion.[94] To avoid a discussion of the Tatar issues during the failed congress in Vienna (1689–90), Zülfikār and Mavrocordatos sustained that 'although the Tatars are under the protection of the Exalted State, they are a state on an equal footing with it (*Devlet-i 'Aliyye ile beraber koşulmuş bir devlettir*)',[95] adding that the sultan could not command them to leave their lands and relocate elsewhere as that would run contrary to their religion[(sic)] and their honour and sovereignty (*ne dinlerine ve ne 'ırz ve saltanatlarına düşer*).[96] A similar double-language strategy was equally pursued by the Porte's representatives during the Congress of Carlowitz. According to the Imperial plenipotentiaries, to counter Voznitsyn's attempts to separate the two entities,

90 *See*, for instance, DABOA, A.DVNS.MHM.d 60, fol. 271–272.

91 For example, DABOA, A.DVNS.NMH.d/5, fol. 1–2.

92 For instance, in the *Mühimme Defteri* no. 111 which covers the years 1700–1, we encounter various sultanic orders (*ḥükm*) to the two princes but none to the khan: Recep Temel, '111 Numaralı Mühimme Defterinin 168.-337. Sayfalarının Transkripsiyonu ve Değerlendirilmesi' (MA dissertation, Artvin Çoruh University 2019); Duzcan, '111 Numaralı Mühimme Defteri'.

93 Dariusz Kołodziejczyk, 'What is Inside and What is Outside? Tributary States in Ottoman Politics', in Kármán and Kunčević, *The European Tributary States*, 421–32.

94 Ibid., 422.

95 *Cerîde-i Takrirât*, 61.

96 Ibid.

> the Turks replied that the Porte has direct dominion and ownership over Tatary. The Tatars are their subjects, and the khan is only an appointed governor who can be deposed anytime. And he can perhaps fully [negotiate] things regarding neighbouring relations or disputes, but on [matters] of land and territory, he can neither negotiate nor give away anything.[97]

Faced, though, with Małachowski's demand for the repeal of the tribute, they resorted back to the assertion of Crimean 'autonomy'. Mavrocordatos was of the opinion 'to not mention it at all in this treaty with the Porte because it concerns the khan'.[98] He was informed that recently a Commonwealth embassy visited Selīm Giray. Perhaps its purpose was to discuss that very matter.[99] And he added, changing perspectives again, that the only thing the Porte could do was to order the Tatars not to raid the Commonwealth's lands again.[100]

A quite similar 'intentional ambiguity' surrounded also the status of Ragusa during the congress. As we saw, according to the self-portrayal narrative of the city-state, the latter always remained a free polity despite willingly paying tribute to the Ottomans. 'We might not maintain our liberty', the Republic's patricians warned Leopold I as they supplicated him for an abolition of their annual payment to the Porte.[101] The Ottoman delegation skilfully used this rhetoric to combat the Imperial claims on the small city-state. However, referring equally to its citizens as the Porte's 'tributary subjects' (*ḫarāc-güzār reʿāyāsı*) posed apparently no problem. The Venetians naturally held a different view based on their own designs against Dubrovnik. 'Great the chasm between the Venetian Domain, so grand and glorious, and Ragusa, a miserable city, more enslaved than free', argued the Anonymous Venetian, lamenting the Imperial support for the Adriatic city-state.[102] Hence, both Ragusa and the Crimean Khanate were free or dependent, depending on whether or when it suited each side to claim so during the negotiation.

2.1 *No More Tributes!*

The payment of various forms of tribute was a widespread phenomenon in pre-modern relations between polities. Whether such 'payments' or 'gifts' were

---

97 ÖStA, HHStA, Türkei I, Turcica Box 168, Folder 2 (November 1698, 2nd half), fol. 133ᵛ, Imperial plenipotentiaries to Leopold I, 22 November 1698. *See also, Taʿrīḫ-i ṣulḥnāme*, fol. 110ᵃ and Bogoslovskii, *Petr I*, 397–8.

98 Cernovodeanu, 'Le journal', 336.

99 *Taʿrīḫ-i ṣulḥnāme*, fol. 115ᵃ.

100 Cernovodeanu, 'Le journal', 336–7.

101 ÖStA, HHStA, Türkei I, Turcica Box 165, Folder 4 (June 1698), fol. 25ʳ, the Ragusan Senate to Leopold I, 6 June 1698.

102 *Narratio*, fol. 36ʳ.

voluntary or not, they were always grounded, just like sovereignty, on an ambiguity of meaning and interpretation.[103] Thus, whereas when Muscovy or the Commonwealth were baptising the lump sum, they were paying regularly to the Crimean Khanate with less demeaning terms such as 'treasury' (*kazna*) or 'gifts' (*upominki*), the Tatars and the Ottomans would refer to them, among other words, as tribute (*vėrgi*).[104] Such a double-sided reality where different connotations could be used to accommodate both parties could be tolerated under certain circumstances, but not when one side felt powerful enough to do away with such 'payment' obligations completely. The 'tribute issue' popped up quite frequently during the Carlowitz negotiations, not only with regards to Crimea, and it would be appropriate to make a short intermission and refer to these instances to subsequently contextualise the debate on the *pelles Tatarias* better.

Demanding some form of 'payment' to crown or to frame the result to their internal audience as a 'victorious peace' seems to be a strategy that the Ottomans typically adopted in negotiations that were more or less favourable to them.[105] Take, for instance, the example of Poland-Lithuania. The War of Khotin (1620–21), the first direct conflict between the Commonwealth and the 'Exalted State', ended in a draw, with each of the two participants claiming to have won the day. An anonymous Ottoman chronicler thus wrote a *ẓafer-nāme* (a book of victory) to celebrate 'Os̱mān II's (r. 1617–22) alleged triumphs against the Poles, claiming that in the ensuing peace treaty, the latter were even obliged to pay a tribute to the Porte.[106] However, far from being a triumph, 'Os̱mān's

---

103 Birgit Tremml-Werner, Lisa Hellman and Guido van Meersbergen, 'Introduction. Gift and Tribute in Early Modern Diplomacy: Afro-Eurasian Perspectives'. *Diplomatica* 2 (2020), 185–200; Christian Windler, 'Afterword. Gift and Tribute in Early Modern Diplomacy: a Comment'. *Diplomatica* 2 (2020), 291–304.

104 Türk, 'Gift Exchange', 224–228; Królikowska, 'Sovereignty and Subordination', 49–50.

105 Based on my observations from the Carlowitz Congress, this interpretation appears more probable than Kołodziejczyk's, who argues that the tribute served as a way to 'hide' an alliance or eternal peace with the 'infidels' and reconcile it with Islamic Law: Dariusz Kołodziejczyk, 'La res publica polono-lituanienne était-elle le vassal de l'empire ottoman?', in Anna Parzymies (ed.), *Studies in Oriental Art and Culture in Honour of Professor Tadeusz Majda* (Warsaw: Dialog, 2006) 126–7. Consider, for example, the first peace treaty between Muscovy and the Ottoman Empire in 1681, was concluded for twenty years despite Muscovy – like the Commonwealth – paying 'tribute' to the Tatars. Therefore, as we will discuss in detail in Interlude VI, the duration of peace was primarily determined by the participants' interests and customary practices, rather than religious considerations.

106 Kołodziejczyk, 'La res publica polono-lituanienne', 134.

campaign yielded meagre results, and the sultan rushed to conclude peace as soon as he could and then return to Adrianople.

It was primarily to conceal these not-so-glorious exploits and instead present the agreement as a 'victorious one' that in the Ottoman text of the treaty, it was added that the Polish ambassador sent to the Ottoman capital for the confirmation of the treaty was to pay a *pişkeş* (a 'present') which the Ottoman side could easily interpret as a form of tribute.[107] Nonetheless, when in another negotiation taking place in 1634, the Ottomans brought up the issue again, the Commonwealth's representatives vehemently rejected it on the same grounds as at Carlowitz, that Poland-Lithuania was a free polity.[108] The situation changed dramatically, however, when the Porte achieved a clear victory in the first Podolian War (1672). With the Treaty of Buczacz the same year, the Commonwealth was obliged to officially agree to pay annually to the sultan a 'gift' of 22.000 red Zlotys.[109] Still, this stipulation didn't last for long since the war resumed, and in the subsequent Treaty of Żurawno in 1676, which the Poles were able to negotiate from a better ground, the 'gift' clause was abolished.[110]

Just as in 1621, at Carlowitz, the Ottomans made once again plain use of the 'tribute weapon' to achieve terms which they could better 'sell' to the Ottoman internal audience.[111] They did that by aptly attempting to capitalise on the ambiguity words such as 'gift' and 'present' could have. All their efforts, though, were in vain. They could have imposed their interpretation of the *uti possidetis* principle. Still, there were certain limits that their interlocutors were determined not to cross, and even worse for the Ottomans, they were now in a position to bargain from a place of strength. The first negative answer came from the Imperial side.

Despite the Habsburg ambassadors' categorical refusal to discuss any form of Ottoman suzerainty over Transylvania immediately before the start of the official conferences, the Ottomans persisted, bringing up the topic once

---

107 Ibid.

108 Ibid., 135.

109 Marek Wagner, *Wojna polsko-turecka w latach 1672–1676*, vol. 1 (Inforteditions 2009) 288–92.

110 Kołodziejczyk, *The Crimean Khanate*, 189.

111 The significance attached to questions of tribute by the Ottoman internal audience is revealed by an inverse situation in which a sultan was accused of making 'payments' to the 'Infidels'. During the 1703 rebellion that led to the downfall of Muṣṭafā II, some insurgents even accused him of agreeing at Carlowitz to pay tribute to the Holy Roman Emperor for Wallachia and Moldavia! Abou-El-Haj, 'Ottoman Attitudes Toward Peace Making: The Karlowitz Case'. *Der Islam* 51/1 (1974), 137, fn. 16.

again during their second meeting with the Habsburg delegation. This time, they declared, they were willing to acknowledge the emperor's possession of the Carpathian Principality in its 'ancient borders' (*i limiti* [...] *come furono ab antiquo*) but as compensation to the Exalted State for its loss, they only requested 'a yearly voluntary present for Transylvania'.[112] Count Schlik was quick to point out the equivocation of such a 'present' 'that others could call tribute' (*che altri dicessero Tributo*), and he rightly guessed, 'that what you name consolation, you can [easily] misinterpret it as if so great an empire was reduced to a necessity of a small gift or gratification'.[113] The Ottomans had no other option but to withdraw their demand.

However, when they met Ruzzini for the first time, they strove to achieve something similar, this time regarding the Morea. They presented the Venetian with two options: either the Serenissima could keep all its current acquisitions, but 'in return, you will arrange something – call it a present – to be given annually to the Exalted State' for the possession of the peninsula[114] or if not, then she would have to relinquish all its footholds in mainland Greece.[115] There was no question that the Venetian *Cavaliere* would agree to such a 'pension' (*pensione*), so this demand was also discarded.[116] All the same, the Republic of Saint Mark could further be consoled by the fact that the Imperials, trying to procure some tangible benefit for her out of an otherwise not so 'victorious' treaty, requested from the Ottoman side that not only should Venice not pay anything new to them, but also that all the other 'pensions' it was already sending to the Porte should also be annulled.

One of them was the tribute/'payment' the Republic gave annually since the late fifteenth century for the possession of the island of Zakynthos.[117] Despite Mavrocrodatos' argumentation presenting it 'as a small sign of friendship for the many privileges that the Republic enjoys in the [Ottoman] Empire',[118] Count Schlik was categorical. The emperor, he declared, would not

---

112 ÖStA, HHStA, Türkei I, Turcica Box 170, Protocollum, fol. 16. Interestingly, this Ottoman demand of a yearly 'present' for Transylvania is absent from the account of Rāmī Meḥmed: *Taʿrīḥ-i ṣulḥnāme*, fol. 80^{b}–84^{a}.

113 ÖStA, HHStA, Türkei I, Turcica Box 170, Protocollum, fol. 17–18.

114 *Taʿrīḥ-i ṣulḥnāme*, fol. 99^{a}.

115 Ibid.

116 Ruzzini, *Relazione*, 355.

117 Initially, it amounted to 500 ducats; it was raised to 1500 ducats after the 'War of Cyprus' (1570–73) and remained stable until the Carlowitz Treaties: Poumarède, *L'Empire de Venise*, 426–7. The Venetians had already voiced a demand for the abolition of the tribute for Zakynthos during the 1688–92 negotiations in Vienna: *Cerîde-i Takrirât*, 80.

118 ÖStA, HHStA, Türkei I, Turcica Box 170, Protocollum, fol. 198.

let 'a sovereign colleague of his' (*un sovrano suo collegato*) be burdened with a tribute.[119] As for a similar Ottoman request for a 'little sign of peace' regarding the island of Aegina, the Imperial ambassador's answer was again definite: 'The tribute or payment for Aegina to the Ḳapudan Paşa should be lifted. Because it is contra-decorum that a sovereign, as the Republic is, should agree in a peace treaty [to pay] a tribute to a servitor of another sovereign'.[120] The Imperials were not on the same power level as Venice, so the Porte's representatives, deeming it more important to achieve the Exalted State's free access by land to Ragusa, had to assent to both demands.

The question of sovereignty and the indecorous character of paying tribute to a vassal of another polity formed precisely the kernel of the Polish-Lithuanian and Muscovite requisitions for the abolishment of the Tatar *kazna*/*pelles*. As vividly reported by Rāmī, both ambassadors claimed that 'it is clear to the whole world that the Polish and Muscovite states are independent ones (*müstaḳil devlet olduḳları*)'. If they would not give a tribute, disguised as a present (*pīşkeş nāmıyla bir dürlü vėrgü*) to the Ottomans, why should they be tributaries of the Tatars, who are themselves under the protection of the sultan?[121] They used to give the Crimeans a 'gift' (*armaġan*) out of their free will because of the military services they performed for them, but 'they turned this into a customary tribute'.[122] Now, this murky situation had to be clarified once and for all by the explicit (*ṣarāḥaten*) mentioning of the abrogation of the tribute in the text of the treaties.[123]

After a rigorous dispute with both ambassadors on the matter, extending, according to Rāmī, for six to seven hours, 'which not only tired the mediators but also brought the ambassadors of the Exalted State to their limits',[124] things came to a standstill. As in other moments during the congress, the intervention of Paget and Colyer proved catalytic. 'Either you give up the Tatar dispute or forget about peace', they brusquely declared to the Ottomans,[125] reminding them that if they didn't cede, they would only strengthen the bond between the Commonwealth and Muscovy, playing thus once again masterfully with the main concerns of each of the congress participants.[126]

---

119 Ibid.
120 Ibid., fol. 200.
121 *Taʿrīḫ-i ṣulḥnāme*, fol. 114[a].
122 Ibid.
123 Ibid., 114[b].
124 Ibid., fol. 116[a].
125 Ibid.
126 Ibid.

In the meantime, Małachowski[127] succeeded in soliciting the support of the Imperials. Rāmī ridiculed the Pole by presenting him as a crying child rushing to complain to Öttingen and Schlik, imploring them to assist him by reminding them of the decisive role of the Commonwealth during the Siege of Vienna. 'After all these services paid to the emperor, it is now neither proper nor fair for them to pay a tribute', Małachowski supposedly said.[128] As for the Imperials and Venice, not conceding to any form of tribute was also a question of honour. 'What is the possibility that our king, who has at his disposal 30.000 German troops and added the Polish lands to [his own] dominion of Saxony, would ever agree to such a diminishment of honour and reputation?', the Pole asked his Ottoman interlocutors rhetorically.[129] Against such a strong stance and persuaded by the mediators that there was no other way out of it, the Ottomans had, in the end, to back off and accept a middle ground: there would be no explicit mention in the treaties of the Commonwealth's 'gift' to the khan.[130] Still, it would be stated that since Poland-Lithuania was an 'old and independent state' (*ḳādimī ve müstaḳil devlet olmağla*), it was not obliged to give anything to the Ottomans or their vassals.[131] Even framed as such, this agreement practically signalled the end of the *pelles Tatarias* and all other Ottoman tribute pretensions on the *Rzeczpospolita* since the beginning of the seventeenth century.

2.2 *Hard Times for Raiders and Nomads*

However, the tribute was not the only thorny issue between the Khanate and its two northern neighbours. The mode of living of its warriors and the latter's supposed constant raids inside the Commonwealth and Muscovite territories were of equal importance. 'The Tatars are a tribe that cannot be put to rest', both Voznitsyn and Małachowski maintained.[132] Apart from a genuine

---

127 I focus here on the Commonwealth because the issue of the Muscovite *kazna* to the Tatars, along with other significant differences between the tsar and the sultan, was not resolved at Carlowitz but rather in the Peace Treaty of Istanbul in 1700, which ultimately abolished it. *See* Defterdar, *Zübde-i Vekayiât*, 696.

128 *Taʿrīḫ-i ṣulḥnāme*, fol. 116[b].

129 Ibid., fol. 117[a].

130 Writing to Karol Stanisław Radziwiłł, Małackowski argued that it was not possible to explicitly mention the 'gift' to the Tatars in the final text of the agreement because the Ottomans didn't want to irritate them: AGAD, Archiwum Warszawskie Radziwiłłów, 1/354/0/5/9200, fol. 46–47, Małachowski to Radziwiłł, 26 December 1698.

131 *Taʿrīḫ-i ṣulḥnāme*, fol. 117[a–b]; Gorkowski, *Compendium Legationis*, 28[r–v].

132 *Taʿrīḫ-i ṣulḥnāme*, fol. 114[a].

preoccupation with such raids that greatly disturbed the frontier populations, there was clearly some degree of instrumentalisation and exaggeration. For instance, during his first official meeting with the Ottomans, Voznitsyn immediately brought to the table the Tatar issue, claiming that the Crimeans' continuous incursions into Muscovite territory and the inability of the Porte to control them, despite her promises to the contrary, was one of the main reasons that allegedly moved Peter to occupy Azov, a blatant prevarication.[133] He also demanded the fortress of Kerch 'because the Tatars are not efficiently controlled with [sultanic] orders, and they will not stay put [...]. [Yet, if] the above-mentioned fortress [Kerch] comes into our possession, the Tatars will be restrained, and we will be secure from their hostile acts'.[134]

The Ottomans acknowledged that the Tatars were 'an unaccountably large and numerous clan, and their basic occupations revolve around war. And every one of them being accustomed [to such a way of life] from a very young age, they are [truly] bold and warlike tribes'.[135] However, they assured Voznitsyn that 'they will make them live in tranquillity, even force them to work the land [in such a way] that they will not be capable of giving them the minimum trouble'.[136] That this time, they meant their words was quite clearly demonstrated in how they reacted to the rebellion of the Nogays (a Tatar tribe) in Budjak nearly a year after the conclusion of the Carlowtiz Congress.[137]

Natalia Królikowska–Jedlińska places the decisive turning point of the Crimean Khanate's eclipse as a player in the arena of the early modern 'Society of the Princes' at the turn of the eighteenth century, right after the Treaties of Carlowitz.[138] Despite Voznitsy's allegations about the khan's autonomy, the tsar decided to bypass him for the first time and negotiate the Peace Treaty of Istanbul (1700) directly with the Porte.[139] The Girays' prestige was further diminished by the abolition of the tribute from the Commonwealth and Muscovy, and consequently, so were their material resources.[140] The brutal suppression

133 Ibid., fol. 109[b].
134 Ibid.
135 Ibid., fol. 114[b].
136 Cernovodeanu, 'Le journal', 335; Bogoslovskii, *Petr I*, 404.
137 *See* above, 306.
138 Królikowska–Jedlińska, 'Designers or Obedient Executors?', 293.
139 Ibid. However, in a secret letter sent to the Greek Orthodox patriarch of Jerusalem, Dositheos, after the conclusion of the congress, Voznitsyn sought his advice on whether it would be better to negotiate the future peace treaty with the Porte directly in the Ottoman capital or through the mediation of the Crimean Khan (among others): Bogoslovskii, *Petr I*, 438. From the course of events, Dositheos appears to have favoured the first option.
140 Abou-el-Haj, 'The Formal Closure', 472.

of the Budjak rebellion and another in 1702–03 demonstrated that the Porte was determined to take the upper hand in its relations with Crimea and tighten its control over its northern borders. It was precisely during this period, the first decades of the eighteenth century, that Dimitri Cantemir would cite the Khanate among the examples of how the Ottomans could presumably reduce, through the imposition of a tribute, a once free and fertile land into servitude and destitution. Look at the Crimean khans, he warned his readers, 'whose far ancestors in the distant past were given [far] greater privileges from the Turks than the ones their descendants enjoy today'.[141]

141 Cantemir, *Incrementorum et Decrementorum*, 431.

Interlude IV: the Physical and Social Environment of the Congress

> We are in a desolate wilderness, much like being in Nova Zembia [an Arctic Island], where one sees nothing in front of him but snow, ice, and water.
>
> JACOB COLYER, describing the physical environment of the Carlowitz Peace Congress[1]

•••

> During this period, as the weather was [unexpectedly] quite good, a lot of particular visits took place between the Turks and the Christians, also because abandoned for the most part the previous rigidity, the passage […] from one camp to the other was made almost free.
>
> The Anonymous Venetian reporting on the conviviality of the congress at the beginning of January 1699[2]

The Peace Congress of Carlowitz was one of the few such seventeenth-century diplomatic gatherings that did not occur in a city – or near one – but rather in an open field on the frontiers, greatly affected by the ongoing warfare of the past fifteen years. This unusual geographical and physical setting of the congress venue significantly influenced its duration and the speed of decision-making by its participants. Nevertheless, much like all previous gatherings of this nature, the 'desolate wilderness', as described by Colyer, quickly transformed – at least for a few months – into a vibrant social hub, where individuals who spoke various languages, held different religious beliefs, and hailed from diverse cultural backgrounds came together to socialise in the same space. This social interaction would lead to either confirming or reshaping their stereotypes of the

1 Quoted in Hora Siccama, 'De vrede van Carlowitz', 146, fn. 2.
2 *Narratio*, fol. 27ᵛ–28ʳ.

 | DOI:10.1163/9789004458499_019

various 'Others', something that, as we shall see, was not always unrelated to political considerations and personal animosities.

In this interlude, we are thus zooming out for a while from the negotiating table, and are moving with our camera across the northern Serbian field, acquiring a broader perspective of the wider spatial, physical, and social milieu of the congress as it is only through this angle that it can be better understood as a distinctive 'social organism' of its own. In the first section, we will touch upon the geography of the congress venue and the practical reasons that dictated the choice of the Plain of Carlowitz to host it; the adverse weather conditions and the effects they had on the talks and the efforts of the different embassies to transform their surroundings to fit what they considered to be 'decent' living conditions, something that was done primarily through the construction of various structures, the Conference House being one of the most prominent among them.

The opening of the second section will primarily focus on the everyday interactions of the – not so much, as we shall argue – 'silent majority' of participants in this 'Theatre of Peace'. We will examine the role of the private individuals in the ambassadors' suites as an often vociferous 'public opinion', which could even seek to influence the resolutions of the 'big stars' of the congress. Subsequently, we will discuss some principal occasions for social interaction *en masse*, aside from the conferences themselves, that both the plenipotentiaries and the numerous members of their retinue could attend. Lastly, we shall conclude this interlude by examining the perceptions of 'Otherness' – mainly those centred on character and physiological traits – that many participants held for their interlocutors, 'friends' and foes alike.

1 The Practical Choice of the Plain of Carlowitz

We have extensively discussed in Act I how the two sides, despite the initial strong resentment of the allies, finally agreed to stage the talks in a location at the Ottoman–Habsburg border. The next major issue was actually finding the ideal place. The initial plan proposed by the mediators was that the allies would camp near Carlowitz, the Ottomans near Slankamen and the mediators in the vicinity of the monastery of Krušedol, 'an old and miserable Greek cloister, situated almost halfway between Petrovaradin, Carlowitz and Slankamen', as the Imperial ambassadors described it,[3] where the negotiations were also to take place.

3 ÖStA, HHStA, Türkei I, Turcica Box 167, Folder 2 (October 1698, 2nd half), fol. 120r, Imperial Plenipotentiaries to Leopold I, 22 October 1698.

Yet this choice had a variety of drawbacks. One was the lack of water and the rugged terrain. As Rāmī Meḥmed related to the grand vizier, 'the mountain coming from above reaches all the way [down] to the bank of the Danube, and in between, to a distance of three to four hours, one finds [only] difficult places, [full] of valleys, hills, with no water. [In short], there is no proper location [there] to hold the talks'.[4] Another was the relative distance it created between the two sides. Rāmī sustained, with perhaps some exaggeration, that with this initial arrangement, it would have taken three days for an answer to reach the Ottoman camp from that of the allies.[5] Lastly, one should also consider the weather parameter. 'From now on, the weather is not to be trusted', the Porte's chief plenipotentiary related to ʿAmcazāde, '[and] when it will become severe, the difficulty of coming and going will be greater'.[6]

All delegations understood the need for the different camps and the conference venue proper to be located close to a river, as most of their provisions – mainly wood and fodder – would have to be carried from afar since the populations of the nearby villages were entirely destitute due to the conflict and could not support them,[7] but also that the distance between the different encampments would have to be calculated in such a way as to render the communication between them more accessible. So, all sides finally concorded that the most suitable place to camp and hold the negotiations would be the 'Plain of Carlowitz' (*Ḳarloviça ovası*), primarily because of its proximity to the river Danube.[8] If the different plenipotentiaries were there to terminate the war, they would probably have yet another motive to do so because they could see in front of them the desolation brought by the protracted conflict. The unknown Venetian author of an account of the congress does not speak of Carlowitz but of its ruins (*le rovine di Carlowitz*),[9] whereas Ruzzini described the location in which the different camps were erected as 'deserted and ruined' (*siti deserti, e distrutti*).[10] The spatial arrangement was meticulously designed to reflect symmetry and neutralise any form of precedence (Figure 4).

The allies' new camp (Figure 5), 'although in the hills' (*benche in montagna*), was erected on a plane, a nice location (*dilitioso*) with 'perfect air' (*aria perfettissima*), according to its designer, Count Marsigli, towards the Imperial-held

4 *Taʾrīḫ-i ṣulḥnāme*, fol. 68ᵇ–69ᵃ.
5 Ibid., fol. 69ᵇ.
6 Ibid., fol. 69ᵃ.
7 ÖStA, HHStA, Türkei I, Turcica Box 167, Folder 2 (October 1698, 2nd half), fol. 176ʳ, Marsigli to Kinsky, 25 October 1698; *Taʾrīḫ-i ṣulḥnāme*, fol. 69ᵃ⁻ᵇ.
8 *Taʾrīḫ-i ṣulḥnāme*, fol. 69ᵇ.
9 *Narratio*, fol. 10ᵛ.
10 Ruzzini, *Relazione*, 352.

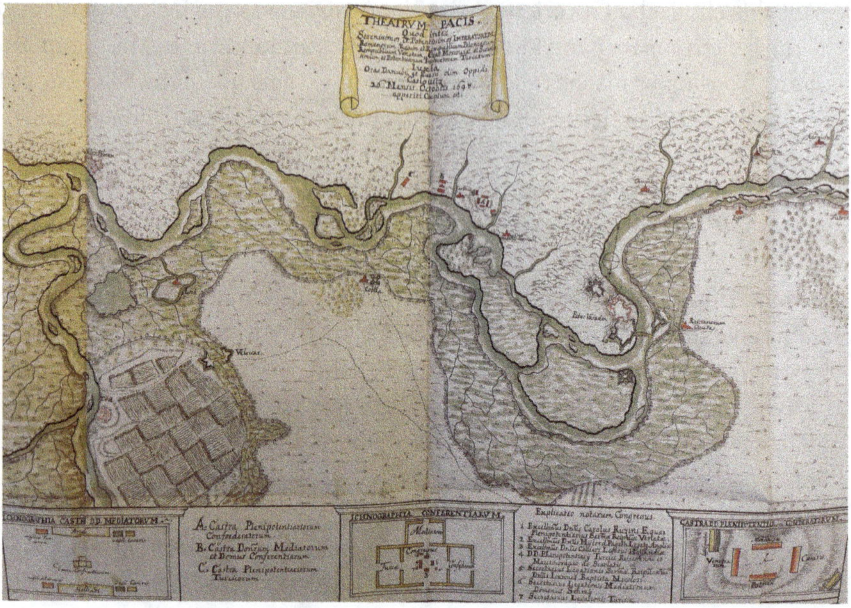

FIGURE 4 *Theatrum Pacis.* The geography and spatial arrangement of the congress venue
BNM, MS. IT VII 381 (7782), C. [1]R. SU CONCESSIONE DEL MINISTERO DELLA CULTURA – BIBLIOTECA NAZIONALE MARCIANA. DIVIETO DI RIPRODUZIONE

fortress of Petrovaradin.[11] The *Bolognese* planned it, as we have already seen, 'in the form of a perfect square [...] according to the usual rules for military encampments in the open field' with no apparent distinction of place.[12] Each one of its four corners was occupied by a delegation. Roads connected the different parts of the encampment, and every tent or edifice was facing the central square where the main guard was also located.[13]

The Ottomans, for their part, occupied the location which was originally to serve as the allied encampment, towards the fortress of Slankamen, which was in Ottoman hands.[14] The camps of the two sides were situated, according to the Imperial embassy, 'not over an hour's distance from each other'.[15] Finally, the mediators were placed in the middle between the two sides, 'at Carlowitz

11 Marsigli to Kinsky, 25 October 1698, fol. 176^{r-v}.

12 Ibid., fol. 176^{v}.

13 ÖStA, HHStA, Türkei I, Turcica Box 170, Diarium et Cerimoniale, fol. 8^{r} (of the separate journal regarding the congress ceremonial).

14 ÖStA, HHStA, Türkei I, Turcica Box 167, Folder 2 (October 1698, 2nd half), fol. 176^{r}, Marsigli to Kinsky, 25 October 1698. The *Bolognese* did not also fail to mention that the allied camp was situated higher (*sopra*) than the Ottoman one (*più basso*): Ibid.

15 Ibid., fol. 147^{v}, Imperial plenipotentiaries to Leopold I, 25 October 1698.

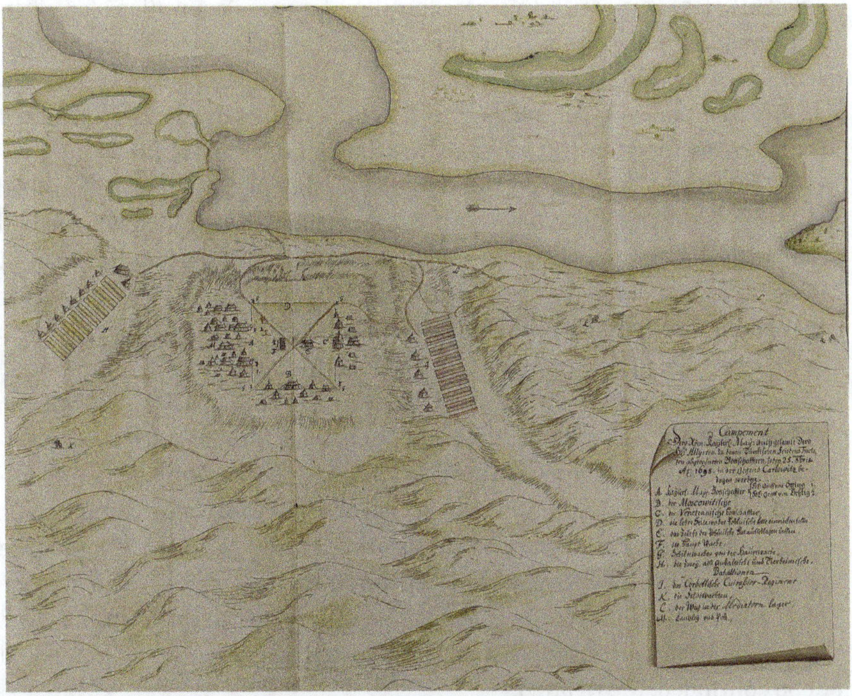

FIGURE 5 Detail of the allied encampment. Since the drawing was made on 25 October 1698, it captured some very interesting details of the situation at the time. With D, one sees the designated place for the Commonwealth's ambassador, towards the Danube, which rests vacant for the moment. E depicts the position of Małachowski's tent in front of that of the Venetian plenipotentiary (C). ÖSTA, HHSTA, SB KARTENSAMMLUNG F, KE 3-7/5-8. ZELTLAGER BEI KARLOWITZ, CAMPEMENT DERO KAYSERL. MAY. AUCH GESAMTE DERO HERRN ALLYRTEN ZU DENEN TÜRCKISCHEN FRIEDENS-TRACTATEN ABGEORDNETEN BOTTSCHAFFTERN, SO DEN 25. OCTOBRIS ANNO 1698 IN DER GEGEND CARLOWITZ BEZOGEN WORDEN

proper' (*nefs-i Ḳarloviça'da*), a quarter of an hour from both.[16] They didn't camp together, 'but each one of them with a relative distance from one another' – to avoid ceremonial disputes on precedence, one might guess.[17] The negotiations were to take place in the area between the mediators' encampments (Figure 4 on the bottom left).[18]

16 *Taʿrīḫ-i ṣulḥnāme*, fol. 69^{b}.

17 ÖStA, HHStA, Türkei I, Turcica Box 167, Folder 2 (October 1698, 2nd half), fol. 121^{r-v}, Imperial plenipotentiaries to Leopold I, 22 October 1698.

18 *Narratio*, fol. 14^{v}.

Nevertheless, even with this new location, far more convenient for external provisioning, the problem of the adequate supply of the different delegations was anything but resolved. Already at the beginning of the congress, the Imperial embassy complained to the emperor about the lack of fodder for the horses, food for the men and other crucial subsistence it was suffering from.[19] Writing to Peter I on 29 October/8 November 1698, Voznitsyn described in his turn his own difficulties in securing provisions. The principal issue had to do with the emptiness of the surrounding lands. He sent a nobleman of his retinue to Belgrade to buy some foodstuffs, but 'here and there, bread is very expensive. To buy a pound of it costs ten golden coins. [There is] also [an extreme scarcity] of animals and firewood because [the area] from Buda to the sea [the Danube] is a barren steppe just like the Dniester, the Dnieper, the Don, and the Volga'.[20] Similar provisioning questions troubled the participants throughout the congress. During its last month, the Ottomans were putting pressure on Ruzzini to conclude his negotiation with them, complaining, among other things, of the lack of 'subsistence for the men and fodder for the horses', something that resulted in desertions from their guard.[21] And if, as we saw, it was hoped that resources could reach the delegations from the river, they would be greatly disappointed since there was another factor that could not be controlled: the weather.[22]

One of the main reasons the Ottomans, as much as the other parties, suffered greatly from a supply scarcity in January 1699 was that the Danube was frozen, making the transfer of basic necessities via the river impossible.[23] In the beginning, things appeared more promising, however. 'During the whole month of October', the Anonymous Venetian relates, "the weather was very soft and [this] was giving hope that [its] alteration shouldn't be very bothersome".[24] However, Mother Nature had other plans. 'During the night of 8 November, a wind blew from the east, so powerful that it uprooted almost every tent and caused damage to all lodgings. Then, on 11, the snow came, and one could sense somewhat rigidly the first cold'.[25] 'What worries us the most, though', wrote

19 ÖStA, HHStA, Türkei I, Turcica Box 167, Folder 2 (October 1698, 2nd half), fol. 301^{v}–302^{r}, Imperial plenipotentiaries to Leopold I, 30 October 1698.

20 Quoted in Bogloslovskij, *Petr I*, 391.

21 Ruzzini, *Relazione*, 362.

22 One of the first scholars to stress the importance of the weather-factor for the unfolding and duration of the negotiations was Ernst Petritsch in his short article on the congress: Petritsch, 'Rijswijk und Karlowitz', 305.

23 Ibid.

24 *Narratio*, fol. 15^{v}.

25 Ibid., fol. 16^{r}.

the Imperial ambassadors to Leopold I on 12 November, 'is the bad weather, which persisted recently in such a strong way, with snow, frost, humidity and cold, that neither man nor horse can resist it anymore'.[26] To avoid a 'complete ruin', the two plenipotentiaries decided to send the most significant part of the militia to Petrovaradin and leave only two hundred men on horse and one hundred on foot to guard the camp. On 10 November, an 'Arab' (*ein Araben*) in the service of Lord Paget 'truly froze to death' (*würklich erfrohren*), and the night of the following day 'various people got sick because of the cold' and so the Ottomans though it wise as well to dispatch a good part of their entourage.[27]

This 'inaugural wave' of lousy weather also contributed to the belated start of the Ottoman–Imperial negotiations – and to the decision to build a conference house – it also caused the first severe disruption in the supply chain. 'Our provisions cannot be delivered any more', lamented the Habsburg ambassadors, 'neither by water, because of the daily tempests, nor by land, because of the unpaved and terrible roads. And those [provisions] we presently have would be sufficient for only eight, ten days [more]'.[28]

Extreme weather conditions could make the life of the participants really miserable. Reporting to Count Kinsky right after the hurricane and heavy snowfall of the beginning of November, Count Schlik wished that 'instead of [being in the middle] of cold and snow we were amid the sweetest amenities'.[29] And he continued narrating his sufferings to his patron: 'This is the reason I write to you so poorly legibly on a very sticky paper. I most humbly ask Your Excellency to pardon me for that. And to also speak the truth, I don't feel well, and I have an extreme fear of getting really sick'.[30] However, others were determined not to stay in the open field and suffer. Immediately after the first bad weather hit, Małachowski and Voznitsyn declared that they would instead move to Petrovaradin, a step that was, in the end, taken only by the former.[31] In describing his departure, Voznitsyn also added a grotesque scene with the Poles dismantling the wooden structures they had built and taking all the materials to the Imperial fortress with them.[32]

---

26 ÖStA, HHStA, Türkei I, Turcica Box 168, Folder 1 (November 1698, 1st half), fol. 200v, Imperial plenipotentiaries to Leopold I, 12 November 1698.

27 Ibid.

28 Ibid., fol. 198r, Imperial plenipotentiaries to Leopold I, 12 November 1698.

29 Ibid., fol. 285r, Schlik to Kinsky, 13 November 1698.

30 Ibid.

31 *Narratio*, fol. 16r.

32 Bogoslovskii, *Petr I*, 392. However, we should note that the Polish option might have been quite logical since, as Voznitsyn himself admits, sufficient wood supplies were almost

The combined problems of supply provisioning and a severe climate exerted a real and significant impact on the duration of the negotiations. As Ruzzini claimed in his *Relazione Finale*, it was clear from those two major issues that the congress couldn't last long.[33] In their relation to Leopold I on 22 November, the Imperial embassy contended that an acceleration of the decision-making process was needed 'because, in so late a season, neither the one nor the other side [can] persevere any longer in the open field'.[34] If the congress were to be transferred to a 'more convenient place', the two ambassadors would greatly welcome it.[35] Similarly, one of the principal reasons behind Małachowski's apprehension to conclude his negotiation as quickly as possible was, according to him, bad weather.[36]

Yet even this apparent physical reality could sometimes be instrumentalised to pressure participants to accelerate or conclude their talks. According to the Anonymous Venetian, when during early December, one of the most crucial phases of the congress, the weather again deteriorated quickly, entering fully into the 'bitter winter' (*il maggior rigore dell' inverno*), 'some truly, and others as an excuse were uttering lamentations and complaints'.[37] The Ottomans, wanting to coerce the allies into a swift agreement, declared that they would retire to Belgrade, 'not desiring, they were saying, to die at Carlowitz'.[38] They successfully repeated the same tactic to further isolate Ruzzini during the last month of the congress, when the Venetian was facing everyone's rage as the chief reason for their continued suffering. Furthermore, without disclaiming the reality of the plight of the ambassadors, one should perhaps take some of their comments with a grain of salt, since it was quasi-normal for congress plenipotentiaries to complain about their surroundings, even if they were much more comfortable than the north Serbian plains. 'Münster, behind the pigsty'. Thus opened the first dispatch to Vienna from Count Maximilian von Trauttmansdorff, the head of the Imperial delegation at the Congress of Westphalia.[39]

---

absent from the vicinity (ibid., 391). In addition, there was always the danger of nearby thieves stealing it from the unguarded constructions.

33 Ruzzini, *Relazione*, 353. Voznitsyn was also of the same opinion: Bogoslovskii, *Petr I*, 406.

34 ÖStA, HHStA, Türkei I, Turcica Box 168, Folder 2 (November 1698, 2nd half), fol. 133r, Imperial plenipotentiaries to Leopold I, 22 November 1698.

35 ÖStA, HHStA, Türkei I, Turcica Box 168, Folder 1 (November 1698, 1st half), fol. 198r, Imperial plenipotentiaries to Leopold I, 12 November 1698.

36 Załuski, *Epistolae*, 679.

37 *Narratio*, fol. 24v.

38 Ibid., fol. 25r.

39 Quoted in Croxton, *Westphalia*, 127.

Still, the example of Carlowitz demonstrates how constraints caused by the climate could seriously affect a pre-modern peace congress, and it is perhaps no coincidence that previous ones, taking place in cities like Westphalia or Nijmegen, lasted for years, while in our case, something less than four months.

2 Transforming the 'Wilderness'

Because of and despite all these adverse conditions, the different embassies tried hard to transform their environment, as much as possible, to meet their needs and offer themselves at least a minimum of amenities. A cardinal role in his transformation was played by the engineers and billeting officers (*ḳonaḳçılar*) of the various delegations, who were sent in advance to assess the ground and erect tents, fences, stables, and other necessary constructions in the different encampments.[40] In the allied and the mediators' camps, wooden houses were built to offer greater protection from the cold.[41] Not for all, though. 'Now, we are all obliged to leave the tents, and to this end, I erected as many [wooden] chambers as possible', reported Colyer, 'because it is always feasible to let my ordinary servants crawl into the earth like moles and mice and cover their huts with reeds'.[42] In Voznitsyn's list of lamentations against the Imperials and the Venetians was added yet another one: they built wooden houses with materials transported from Vienna by water while he had to remain in the tents, enduring 'great hardship and cold'.[43]

Material to construct residences was not the only thing the Habsburg delegation brought with it from the Imperial capital. So that their stomachs would not be 'evacuated' – to use Schlik's simile we encountered above – they transported down the Danube, according to the Muscovite ambassador – secretly jealous, we might guess – whole kitchen apparatuses.[44] Besides eating, another less carnal and more spiritual need of a late-seventeenth-century individual was praying. Since the majority of the Christian ambassadors (Mavrocordatos included) had brought with them a priest to perform religious services or

40 ÖStA, HHStA, Türkei I, Turcica Box 167, Folder 2 (October 1698, 2nd half), fol. 121^{r}, Imperial plenipotentiaries to Leopold I, 22 October 1698; *Taʿrīḫ-i ṣulḥnāme*, fol. 69^{b}.

41 Ruzzini, *Relazione*, 353. But even those could offer only limited security from the forces of nature. According to Schlik, during the great storm of 8 November, not only the tents but also the roofs of some of the wooden edifices were taken away: ÖStA, HHStA, Türkei I, Turcica Box 170, Diarium et Cerimoniale, fol. 27.

42 Quoted in Hora Siccama, 'De Vrede van Carlowitz', 146, fn. 2.

43 Quoted in Bogloslovskij, *Petr I*, 391–2.

44 D. and I. Guzevich, *Velikoe Posol'stvo*, 112.

confessions, one could assume that some form of a small chapel could have been constructed, at least in the allied camp, although we don't have evidence for that. We only know that Voznitsyn was going to Petrovaradin to attend an Orthodox mass there.[45] As for the Muslims, the construction of a small mosque wouldn't be considered so necessary since they could perform their prayers independently of a specific building. Thus, Rāmī Meḥmed interrupted the discussions, interestingly often during a heated debate, to pray.[46] One could plausibly assume that he retired to do so initially in the separate Ottoman tent, and after the construction of the Conference House, in the room reserved for the Porte's ambassadors.

The Ottoman plenipotentiary could live perhaps without a *mescid* (a small mosque), but not without another of the most prominent structures in Ottoman culture. At one point during the initial phase of the congress, he sent Paget's secretary, Schreyer, to the Imperial embassy with a peculiar request. He was asking for permission to take 'some one hundred bricks' (*ein par hundert ziegelstein*) from the 'old ruins' (*alten gemäuer*) in the vicinity and reuse them 'to build a bath on [the bank of] the Danube' ([…] *zu erbauung eines baads an der Donaw*).[47] His request was most probably granted,[48] but unfortunately, we don't have any other information on this quite intriguing *ḥamām*, a telling example of pre-modern material recycling.

The epicentre of this hectic construction activity was the wooden structure to house the congress conferences. Prior to its construction, the talks took place in three tents that were placed in a row: one for the allies, the other for the Ottomans and a third one set in the middle and provided by the sultan, destined for the discussions (Figure 6).[49] The house was constructed at the insistence first of the Imperial embassy, followed subsequently by the other ambassadors, to convene there 'with minor suffering, as they feel less secure [from the weather] under the tents'.[50] Still, apart from weather considerations, the allies also objected to the use of the Ottoman tent for ceremonial reasons because it would have implied that the Ottomans were the hosts and the Holy League members the guests.[51] The same problem was encountered during the

45 Vinzenz Oskar Ludwig, 'Memoiren eines Vergessenen (1691–1716)'. *Jahrbuch des Stiftes Klosterneuburg* 7/1 (1915), 37.

46 *See*, for example, ÖStA, HHStA, Türkei I, Turcica Box 170, Protocollum, fol. 20.

47 ÖStA, HHStA, Türkei I, Turcica Box 170, Diarium et Cerimoniale, fol. 19.

48 Schlik does not specify, but we might guess so; otherwise, he would have mentioned the Imperials' refusal.

49 *Narratio*, fol. 15^{r}; *Taʿrīḥ-i ṣulḥnāme*, fol. 73^{b}.

50 Ibid., fol. 15^{v}–16^{r}.

51 *Taʿrīḥ-i ṣulḥnāme*, fol. 73^{b}; Hora Siccama, 'De Vrede van Carlowitz', 148.

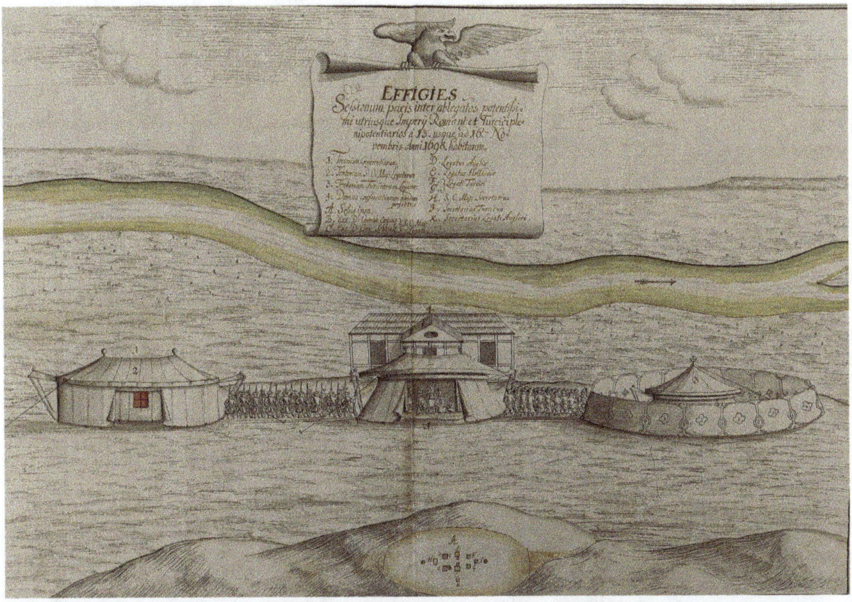

FIGURE 6 A depiction of the three tents that housed the negotiations at the beginning of the congress. Behind the central one, one can see the wooden edifice which will later host them, and which was still under construction at that point.
ÖSTA, HHSTA, SB KARTENSAMMLUNG F, KE 3-7/5. EFFIGIES SESSIONUM PACIS INTER ABLEGATOS POTENTISSIMI UTRIUSQUE IMPERIJ ROMANI ET TURCICI PLENIPOTENTIARIOS A 13. USQUE AD 16. NOVEMBRIS ANNI 1698. HABITARUM

Franco–Spanish negotiations leading to the Treaty of Pyrenees (1659), where, in the beginning, the Spaniards proposed to build themselves the edifice which would lodge the talks, an offer that the French rejected on exactly the same grounds.[52]

However, specific arrangements finally unblocked the deadlock. As in the Spanish-French peace talks of 1659,[53] the Carlowitz Conference House was constructed using an equal amount of materials and workforce by both the Ottoman and Imperial sides to manifest the parity between them.[54] This joint undertaking produced a quite interesting example of 'architectural hybridity'[55]

52 Rahn, 'Grenz-Situationen', 182.

53 Ibid., 182.

54 ÖStA, HHStA, Türkei I, Turcica Box 170, Diarium et Cerimoniale, fol. 24.

55 For the concept of 'hybridity' *see* the succinct work of Peter Burke, *Cultural Hybridity* (Cambridge (UK)/Maiden (US): Polity Press 2009).

FIGURE 7 Detail of the Conference House
GRÜND- UND UMSTÄNDLICHER BERICHT, PAGE NOT NUMBERED

(Figure 7). The relatively harmonious coexistence of western European and Ottoman architectural forms (especially the roof), attests how peace congresses or bilateral talks taking place in the open field could sometimes usher in quite inventive architectonic styles which, by mirroring the tastes of all the participants created a commonly accepted setting of symbolic parity for the negotiations to take place between them. An equally diverse interior complemented the 'hybrid' exterior of the structure, the only difference being that instead of another mixture, each side had its own private space decorated and furnished according to its lifestyle customs, the only area where these traditions co-existed again being the main conference room.[56]

As for the Conference House's overall plan,

> [It] was designed [to have] three compartments and three doors [...] so that the allies, the Turks and the mediators enjoy each one of them an entrance from his side, without an advantage or distinctive prerogative, [and] a room to rest, [with] the central chamber serving for the congress(sic) and the [common] reunions (Figure 8).[57]

In yet another illustrative exemplification of how blueprints adopted in previous congresses could be re-employed, this plan mirrored the Palace of

56 ÖStA, HHStA, Türkei I, Turcica Box 170, Diarium et Cerimoniale, fol. 43.

57 *Narratio*, fol. 14v–15r. *See* also a detailed spatial description of the Conference House in *Taʿrīḫ-i ṣulḥnāme*, fol. 75a–b.

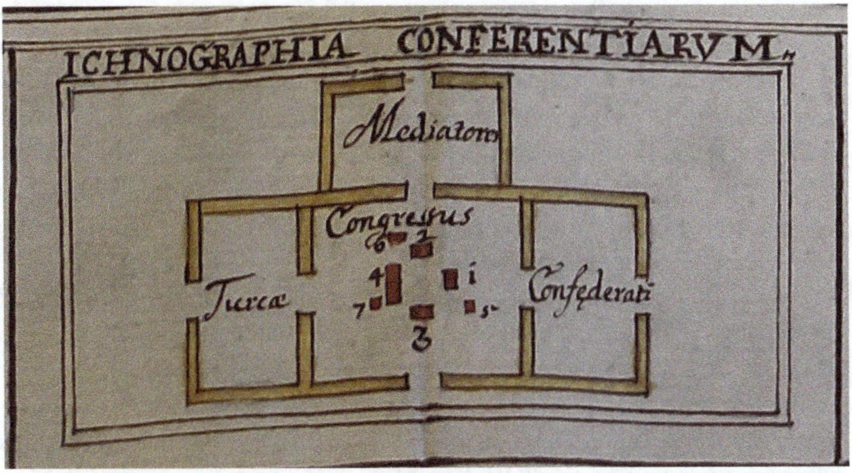

FIGURE 8 Detail of the plan of the Conference House
BNM, MS. IT VII 381 (7782), C. [1]R. SU CONCESSIONE DEL MINISTERO DELLA CULTURA – BIBLIOTECA NAZIONALE MARCIANA. DIVIETO DI RIPRODUZIONE

Ryswick, where the negotiations to terminate the Nine Years' War (1688–97) had taken place only a year prior.[58] There similarly, the French and allied delegations entered the palace from different entrances on each side, whereas the Swedish mediator entered from the middle to avoid questions of precedence. Inside, each embassy had its own apartments facing each other, with the mediator occupying a room in the middle, allowing him thus to communicate and transfer messages with ease from one party to the other while also serving as a common conference chamber if the need arose.[59] The Carlowitz Conference House was finally ready for use by late November 1698.[60]

3 A Multicultural Social Environment

The novel structures erected to facilitate the life of the diverse participants were not the only feature that transformed the Carlowitz area for the nearly four months that the congress lasted. The numerous delegations themselves rendered it its multicultural character and breathed new life into the once semi-deserted terrain. Take, for instance, the allied camp that hosted quite an interesting medley of people coming from nearly all over central, southern, and

58 Van den H. Boogert, 'The Spoils of Peace', 56; Petritsch, 'Rijswijk und Karlowitz', 304–5.
59 Bély, 'Négocier la Paix', 185.
60 ÖStA, HHStA, Türkei I, Turcica Box 170, Diarium et Cerimoniale, fol. 43.

eastern Europe, including Germans, Italians, Poles, and Russians with their distinctive attires and languages, many of whom probably got to know each other in proximity for the first time. An even more tantalising mixture would have been seen in the mediators' encampments where English, Dutch, Germans, Italians, and Ottomans shared the same space. The Ottoman campsite was less varied in this respect, although the probable strong Greek-Orthodox presence due to members of Mavrocordatos's retinue[61] may have equally contributed to its – at least religious – diversity.

The spatial arrangement of the different encampments may have divided the congress participants, but that didn't deter single individuals – or groups of them – from all sides from making frequent trips from one camp to another to socialise, especially during the initial phase of the congress where the movement was relatively uninhibited, assisting thus in parallel the secret negotiations between the various parties.[62] We have already seen the Ottomans visiting the allied camp, meeting with the Christians there and learning from the Germans of the supposed Muscovite aversion towards peace.[63] Nonetheless, this period of inter-camp unrestrained communication did not last long.

A basic concern of all previous congresses was the upkeep of order and the avoidance of violence between the members of the retinue of the different delegations.[64] Such a preoccupation attests to the fact that, as much as such gatherings facilitated unique intercultural exchanges, they were not always peaceful bazaars. People carried with them animosities and prejudices for specific participants, which could easily lead to violence. We should not forget that part of the logic behind the spatial arrangement of the new allied camp was to separate the Poles and the Muscovites in order to avoid further clashes between the servants of the two embassies, such as the one that took place in the first days of the congress.[65] On the other hand, aggressiveness could have equally stemmed from other causes, drunkenness being the chief among them, as we shall see further below.

Being that as it may, such clashes and brawls could escalate, even placing the talks themselves in jeopardy since it was not clear who should bear the responsibility for apprehending and punishing the culprits and satisfying the affronted side. Thus, after the Ottomans voiced strong concerns over possible

61 Although we don't have much evidence for the Carlowitz Congress, during the Failed Vienna one, much of Mavrocordatos's retinue was comprised of Greek subjects of the sultan. *See* Hurmuzaki, *Documente*, vol. 5, part 1, 210.

62 *See* above, Act II, Narration Part II.

63 Act II, Narration Part I.

64 Croxton, *Westphalia*, 131.

65 *See* above, Act II, Interlude III.

incidents between their entourage and the many Germans that were visiting their camp, or even staying there overnight,[66] the mediators declared that 'it was prohibited to anyone to pass from one camp to the other without permission and the latter had to be granted only for reasons relating to the negotiation or [extreme] need',[67] a ban that entered into effect on the evening of 28 October 1698.[68]

The mediators were also the ones to set in their Congress Regulation the rules of social interaction between the members of the different delegations for the duration of the talks. According to them,

> every noble, official, [free] servant and slave present in the retinue and household of all the [...] ambassador plenipotentiaries is obliged during this peace congress to behave everywhere to one another quietly, peacefully and with decent civility, abstaining from all brawls and quarrels, offering mutual help and all [other] kind services instead.[69]

In addition, anyone caught disturbing the peace of the congress would be apprehended, kept in custody for the night and then, the following day, delivered to his master to receive the appropriate punishment.[70] Despite such regulations, 'decent civility' could not consistently be enforced. On the evening of Catholic Christmas Day (according to the Gregorian Calendar), Voznitsyn's chaplain was attacked by a drunk German soldier with a bayonet. To the latter's surprise, though – as much as he could be surprised in that condition – the priest was able to overcome him, take his rifle and force him to flee.[71] Appearances sometimes, it seems, can really deceive.

The ban on unnecessary trips from camp to camp could have limited the chances for ordinary people from both sides to interact, but it didn't erase them completely. Both mediators possessed a mixed honorary and protective guard of Imperial and Ottoman soldiers, mounted and on foot, in equal numbers.[72] Furthermore, waiting outside the conference tent – house subsequently – typically were many officers of the two sides. As the Imperial

66 Ludwig, 'Memoiren', 36.

67 *Narratio*, fol. 10^{v}–11^{r}.

68 Ludwig, 'Memoiren', 36.

69 ÖStA, Türkei I, Turcica Box 168, Folder 1 (November 1698, 1st half), fol. 145^{r}, Projecta ad facilitandas Congressûs Conferentias pro tractandâ Pace.

70 Ibid., fol. 145^{v}.

71 ÖStA, Türkei I, Turcica Box 170, Diarium et Cerimoniale, fol. 55.

72 ÖStA, HHStA, Türkei I, Turcica Box 167, Folder 2 (October 1698, 2nd half), fol. 121^{v}, Imperial plenipotentiaries to Leopold I, 22 October 1698.

ambassadors related in their journal regarding the congress ceremonial, during their first meeting with the Ottomans, the respective entrances to the conference tent were guarded by officers 'who could see everything but hear nothing'.[73]

In their regular contact and long hours of standing by as their masters were deliberating – don't forget that meetings could last up to ten consecutive hours – one could suppose that these soldiers would have the opportunity to discuss and learn things from one another. That this was indeed the case is revealed from a unique Ottoman memorandum in the form of a dialogue between a Christian and an Ottoman officer that supposedly took place during the Congress of Passarowitz (1718) and was subsequently presented to the sultan to advocate for military reforms.[74] Although the author is unknown, this memorandum nonetheless manifests the presence of such everyday exchanges that could have similarly occurred at Carlowitz.

In addition, as the congress entered its final month, and taking advantage of the January Halcyon Days, 'a lot of particular visits took place between the Turks and the Christians, also because abandoned for the most part the previous rigidity, the passage [...] from one camp to the other was made almost free'.[75] However, this renewed opportunity for 'intercultural sociability' was also short-lived. There was the case of a drunk Ottoman brawling with a Muscovite and being injured by the latter, as well as a janissary found dead in a nearby forest, supposedly killed by Serbian bandits. And so, to avoid once again matters of responsibility, the prior restrictions were reintroduced.[76]

4 The Congress's 'Public Opinion'

The common participants of the congress may have had difficulties moving around, but that didn't apply to the circulation of information between them. It was based on such first and second-hand testimonies that they formed their view of specific greater or lesser protagonists of the talks as well as of the progress of the negotiations in general. They constituted thus an informal 'public opinion' of the congress. The incident with the Ottomans visiting the allied camp in its early phase and their refusal to socialise with the Muscovites

73 ÖStA, HHStA, Türkei I, Turcica Box 170, Diarium et Cerimoniale, fol. 14ʳ (of the separate journal regarding the congress ceremonial).

74 Faik R. Unat, 'Ahmed III devrine ait bir ıslahat takriri'. *Tarih Vesikaları* 1 (1941), 107–21.

75 *Narratio*, fol. 27ᵛ–28ʳ.

76 Ibid., fol. 28ʳ.

because of the Imperials describing them as 'enemies of peace' is again an illuminating case at hand.[77] Voznitsyn's steward, in particular, had also acquired such notoriety among the Habsburg retinue that, as Schlik relates, they were calling him *Hassefort* (the Most Hated) to his face.[78]

There is, though, a far more intriguing incident concerning once more the Muscovite ambassador and recounted by him in a letter to the head of the *Posol'ski Prikaz*, Lev Kirillovich Naryshkin, on 25 November/5 December 1698. It appears that by the beginning of December 1698, the perception among the Ottoman ambassadors' retinue of Voznitsyn as an opponent of peace had not been completely eradicated, but it was rather accentuated by the difficulties in reaching the conclusion of an agreement between the two sides. Faced with the extremities of winter weather, which caused many of them to desert or request to leave, they personified their sufferings in the Muscovite, whom they were holding responsible not only for refusing to make peace but also for supposedly preventing all the others from doing so. Therefore, just like the Germans before, they spread those rumours throughout the congress venue.[79] However, as if that weren't enough, they were also considering taking further, more drastic actions:

> They requested their ambassadors to let them all come to me, and to plead with me in tears, to make peace and not inhibit the Germans from doing [the same] so that they can be freed [from this misery]. I think that instead of pleading, they may come and kill me; there is no guard. I am staying in the open field with only about ten men, having sent the rest away to Petrovaradin due to the cold.[80]

We don't know if the Ottomans were finally permitted to protest outside Voznitsyn's tent – the mediators' ban on any unnecessary inter-camp crossing was still in place, and the Muscovite survived their supposed wrath in any case – but this episode is quite unique in revealing how the common participants of the congress could publicly voice their opinion and even attempt to put pressure themselves, from below, on the leading actors with such bold moves.

---

77 *See* above Act II, Narration Part I.

78 ÖStA, HHStA, Türkei I, Turcica Box 167, Folder 2 (October 1698, 2nd half), fol. 63r, Schlik to Kinsky, 18 October 1698.

79 Bogoslovskii, *Petr I*, 406.

80 Quoted in ibid.

5 Instances of *Ensemble* Social Interaction

There were certain instances in which the social interaction of the congress would naturally reach its climax. One of those moments was the signing ceremonies. A mixed crowd of Imperial, Ottoman, Muscovite, English, and Dutch bystanders gathered to watch the Ottoman–Muscovite signing ceremony on 24 January 1699.[81] At the ceremony of 26 January, the crowd was so large 'that the ambassadors [standing] in the middle didn't have almost any space, although with their diverse attires, [they] made up a [unique] spectacle of magnificent commotion'.[82] That was but the beginning. A banquet followed at Paget's lodging. This was the only social occasion that most ambassadors – except Voznitysn – and their retinues found themselves all together during the congress. In contrast to the conferences, the banquet was a unique opportunity for the plenipotentiaries to socialise and converse with one another in a friendly and relatively unofficial climate. For instance, despite their frequent clashes throughout the talks and their failure to reach an agreement, Ruzzini and Rāmī sat next to each other and 'with great familiarity' (*con molta disinvoltura*) shown on the part of the latter, they engaged in a 'cheerful discussion'.[83] However, there was one participant who managed to conquer the central stage. 'No one distinguished himself more than Mavrocordatos, who spoke in many languages, and showed spirit, promptness, and great vivacity in his feelings'.[84] Of course, even in such joyous instances, social stratification had to be upheld. "While the masters' banquet was going on, in the other tents, tables had been prepared for everyone's satisfaction", reported the Anonymous Venetian.[85]

The next day, another feast was organised, this time by the Imperials, yet not with the participation of the Ottomans, due to reasons relating to ceremonial regulations, and Ruzzini, who was disappointed by the terms the Imperials agreed for him, excused himself by stating that he had to prepare his dispatch to the senate. This banquet lasted until late in the evening.[86] As in the day before, there was a separate feast 'for the military and the commoners', which, apart from abundant food and drink (vine was springing out of an artificial fountain), also contained, as the night fell, 'entertainments and games of many sorts' (*luochi di gioia e di giocco di più sorte*).[87]

81 Ibid., 426.
82 ÖStA, HHStA, Türkei I, Turcica Box 170, Diarium et Cerimoniale, fol. 81.
83 *Narratio*, fol. 45ᵛ.
84 Ibid.
85 Ibid.
86 Ibid., fol. 48ᵛ.
87 Ibid., fol. 48ᵛ–49ʳ.

6 The 'Other'

The coming together of so many people from different geographies and cultural environments gave them a unique chance to get in touch – in the mostly peaceful context of the congress – with what each considered the 'Other'. It is evident that most of them already had in mind some pre-constructed conceptions. However, the degree to which they would stick to them or not appears to be mainly connected with the personality of each observer or with the negative or positive impact the 'Others' had on their polity's interests. A notable example of the first case is the Anonymous Venetian, most probably a participant in the congress himself, who, although he often refers to the Ottomans as 'barbarians',[88] equally admits that those at the congress were, in fact, highly well-mannered and educated. We should instead focus here, though, on a case study that not only combines the abovementioned parameters but also reveals some strongly grounded negative perceptions of alterity in the seventeenth century's twilight.

We have already referred briefly, in a previous interlude, to Count Schlik's 'Secret Journal' as the epitome of unfavourable stereotypes of the 'Other'. Now it's time to take a closer look at it. If one goes through the journal, it becomes immediately apparent that the Imperial ambassador particularly dislikes two main ethnic or religious groups: the Jews and the Muscovites. Let us start with the first. Antisemitism had strong roots in Christian Europe since the Middle Ages,[89] and Schlik appears to have had a particular aversion towards the followers of the Mosaic Law. For him, it was unthinkable that he could socialise openly with them. On 16 October, the two Imperial ambassadors and other prominent members of their retinue were invited by Ruzzini to have lunch in his tent. 'It was a bit awkward', he wrote, 'that they and several renowned army officers found themselves sitting together at the table in the company of [the Venetian's] Jewish doctor'.[90] However, for the Habsburg plenipotentiary, Jewishness was not only a religious and social but also a physiognomic trait that could create repugnance even if encountered in a non-Jew. On 22 November, the Ottoman ambassadors sent a delegation to pay a visit to the Imperial plenipotentiaries headed by Rāmī's secretary and Mavrocordatos's

88 *See*, for instance, ibid., fol. 7^{v}, 43^{v}–44^{r}.

89 Thomas Kauffman, *Luther's Jews. A Journey into Antisemitism* (Oxford: Oxford University Press 2017).

90 ÖStA, HHStA, Türkei I, Turcica 170, Diarium et Cerimoniale, fol. 2.

cousin, 'a true Jew-face' (*ein wahrhaft Israelitisches gesicht*), as Schlik commented for the second.[91]

However, those comments were nothing compared to the strong repulsion the Imperial ambassador felt for the Muscovites in general and Voznitsyn in particular. Depictions of Muscovy as a barbarous land and its people as, at best, semi-civilised ran rampant in early modern western and central Europe.[92] But the personal affront he thought he had received from the Muscovite at the beginning of the congress, as much as the diverse interests of the two parties, served only to confirm and exacerbate any such negative pre-conceptions Schlik may have had in his mind. Already in one of his first letters to Kinsky from the congress venue, he complained about 'a fool of a steward' (*une bête de commissaire*) Voznitsyn had, the infamous *Hassefort*, 'who, by fomenting his caprices instead of attenuating them, he will make difficult it for us to work [things] out [with him]'.[93]

We should keep in mind the word *bête* in its principal meaning as 'beast', since this would also be a typical designation the Imperial ambassador would use in his journal to refer to the Muscovite.[94] After the latter failed to advance his negotiation further in his second conference with the Ottomans, Schlik wrote: 'It remains so, [it seems], that it is easier to gut that beast rather than correct it'.[95] The appellation is not random, but it is purposely used to dehumanise Voznitsyn. It could imply that the Muscovites were so barbarous that they looked more like monsters than humans. A similar, but far more nuanced, opinion is provided by Ruzzini when he claimed that the tsar's plenipotentiary 'in his outlook and his negotiation [style] possessed something of the uncultivated and unrefined spirit of the nation'.[96] Such comments further alluded to the fact that a beast always remains a beast even though it has a doctoral degree from a university of the 'civilised world'. Receiving a letter from Voznitsyn on 16 December, Schlik commented that it was delivered to the Imperial ambassadors 'via his Padova doctorate-holder, but [still] with no erudition whatsoever acquired [there], personal doctor', a reference to Petr Postnikov.[97]

---

91 Ibid., fol. 38.

92 *See* Hennings, *Russia*, 25–44.

93 ÖStA, HHStA, Türkei I, Turcica Box 167, Folder 2 (October 1698, 2nd half), fol. 63^r^, Schlik to Kinsky, 18 October 1698.

94 For instance, ÖStA, HHStA, Türkei I, Turcica Box 170, Diarium et Cerimoniale, fol. 28.

95 Ibid., fol. 38.

96 Ruzzini, *Relazione*, 378.

97 ÖStA, HHStA, Türkei I, Turcica Box 170, Diarium et Cerimoniale, fol. 50.

Another 'natural' Russian trait that Schlik also confirmed in his interactions with the Muscovites appears to have been that of inconsistency. Narrating in his 'Secret Journal' the first Ottoman–Muscovite conference, he remarked on Voznitsyn's behaviour that 'it causes amazement, and one cannot almost believe how abruptly and often this man [he at least became a man again] goes from the one extreme to the other',[98] showing such respect for the mediation and the Foundation of Peace when a few days earlier he had vehemently refused to accept them.[99] Similar comments were voiced by the Anonymous Venetian, indignant because the Muscovite abandoned Ruzzini, despite his professing otherwise, in the final stage of the congress. Commenting on Voznitsyn's signing his armistice with the Ottomans on 24 January, he attributed it to the 'usual inconsistency of the nation' (*la solita inconstanza della natione*).[100]

In his comment on the Muscovite's sudden changes of mind that brought him closer to the Imperial stance on peace, Schlik added that 'he should only be fully praised if he continues like that all the way to the end'.[101] The Imperial plenipotentiary might have despised him, but less than a month later, he would feel compelled to applaud him. In a major plot twist of the congress, Voznitsyn, despite being hitherto generally designated as the archenemy of peace, agreed to a two-year truce/armistice with the Ottomans. The path that led him to that decision was not smooth, however. It was a rather complicated process full of backstage manoeuvres and explorations of possible alternatives, as by 20 December 1698, for most of the allies, peace had already been achieved or was close to being so. Not for all, though …

---

98 Ibid., fol. 36–37.

99 Ibid.

100 *Narratio*, fol. 41^{v}.

101 ÖStA, HHStA, Türkei I, Turcica Box 170, Diarium et Cerimoniale, fol. 37.

Narration Part II: Peace Is Ostensibly Drawing Near … at Least for Most

Reporting to his principals at the beginning of December 1698, Małachowski summarised the current state of the negotiations of each Holy League ally: 'The Germans have almost concluded [their] peace articles […] the Muscovite has likewise finished [his] work. The Venetian is expecting a resolution from the Republic on the issue of the demolition of five fortresses on which the Turks don't want in any way to back off'.[1] As for himself, 'We are still working. If only we would be able to get something that would truly be satisfying to us in this negotiation, we [could] terminate it easily, given the continuous extreme weather and my so hasty dispatch [here]'.[2] It appears that he did find the satisfaction he was looking for relatively quickly, since a few days after this missive, he successfully concluded his talks with the Ottomans. But how exactly did the play unfold, and how did the particular stage of the congress at the end of December 1698 come to be formed?

1 The Imperials

Let us commence with the Imperials. After their first round of conferences with the Ottomans, there were mixed feelings about their results. Count Marsigli, the 'special adviser' of the embassy, expressed his disappointment to his patron: 'Finally, Signor Count Kinsky, I am not a minister, and I claim to be a soldier, but the non-observance of the preliminaries, and the Turkish *modus tractandi* make me anticipate little clarity and also security in the peace itself'.[3] Different was the opinion of the actual negotiators. Summarising the discussions with the Ottomans on the issue of possession and border making, Schlik maintained that the general plan for the new Imperial frontiers would not be able to be implemented 'without sacrificing these little locations which are beyond the Mureş and Tisza […] The afore-mentioned huts are of

1 Sałuski, *Epistolae*, 679.
2 Ibid.
3 ÖStA, HHStA, Türkei I, Turcica Box 167, Folder 2 (October 1698, 2nd half), fol. 220r, Marsigli to Kinsky, 17 November 1698.

 | DOI:10.1163/9789004458499_020

no consequence'.[4] He and Öttingen, he claimed, made up somehow for the losses in Ţemeşvar through the area between the Sava and the Drava where they acquired more than they could have expected,[5] meaning the retention of the fortress of Petrovaradin 'with so broad a dependence of land',[6] something that as Count Öttingen wrote to Kinsky 'nobody was [even] allowed to think of when we left Vienna'.[7] Similarly, in Croatia, nearly nothing was lost. As for the border commissions, the work left to them would be minimal since the boundaries would be, for the most part, clearly expressed in the final treaty. Only the issue of the navigation of the rivers remained unsettled.[8]

But even if they had wanted to, they could not have obtained better conditions without risking a total collapse of the negotiations.[9] 'Between the two extremes of leaving things fall into a state where they would not have been possible to fix them [again], meaning the dissolution of the negotiations, and keeping them afloat with conventions that are not at all obligatory, we thought we should prefer the latter', the second Imperial plenipotentiary claimed.[10] As we discussed in a previous section, such declarations contained a major contradiction. On the one hand, the Imperial ambassadors asserted that everything they had agreed to could easily be undone. Still, on the other hand, they maintained that these were the only possible terms, with the only other alternative being a continuation of the war.

However, equally conflicted were the Imperial instructions they were receiving from Vienna. While Leopold I demanded that his ambassadors not concede to specific demands – the clear demarcation of boundaries during the congress, the evacuation/demolition of the forts in the Ţemeşvar region[11] – something that, according to the ambassadors, would not advance the

4 ÖStA, HHStA, Türkei I, Turcica Box 168, Folder 2 (November 1698, 2nd half), fol. 305^{v}, Schlik to Kinsky, 18 November 1698.

5 Ibid.

6 ÖStA, HHStA, Türkei I, Turcica Box 169, Folder 1 (December 1698, 1st half), fol. 4^{v}, Imperial plenipotentiaries to Leopold I, 2 December 1698.

7 Ibid., fol. 200^{v}, Öttingen to Kinsky, 12 December 1698.

8 ÖStA, HHStA, Türkei I, Turcica Box 168, Folder 2 (November 1698, 2nd half), fol. 306^{r-v}, Schlik to Kinsky, 18 November 1698.

9 ÖStA, HHStA, Türkei I, Turcica Box 169, Folder 1 (December 1698, 1st half), fol. 16^{v}–17^{r}, Schlik to Kinsky, 2 December 1698; Ibid., fol. 154^{v}–155^{r}, Imperial plenipotentiaries to Leopold I, 12 December 1698.

10 Ibid., fol. 17^{v}, Schlik to Kinsky, 2 December 1698.

11 ÖStA, HHStA, Türkei I, Turcica Box 168, Folder 2 (November 1698, 2nd half), fol. 209^{v}, 210^{r-v}, supplementary Imperial instructions, 24 November 1698; ÖStA, HHStA, Türkei I, Turcica Box 169, Folder 1 (December 1698, 1st half), fol. 66^{v}–67^{r}, supplementary Imperial instructions, 5 December 1698.

negotiations, he firmly commanded them not to lead the congress to a breaking point, because of the blow that would cause to his reputation in the eyes of the 'whole world' (*der gantzen Welt*).[12]

At the beginning of December, after receiving news of the strong criticism that the articles they had agreed so far with the Ottomans were met with at the court, the Imperial ambassadors decided to dispatch Count Marsigli to Vienna to present to the emperor and his ministers the current state of affairs in person and justify their choices in the matter of boundaries.[13] "We hope that the Imperial Court will be persuaded on the borders' chapter [and] that we did not [agree to] them on a mere caprice", Schlik wrote to Kinsky.[14] At the same time, trying to implement the Imperial orders that demanded essential adjustments to the articles that had already been agreed upon, notably regarding the thorny issue of river navigation, the two ambassadors met on 11 December with the mediators to scout for possibilities of success.[15] Nevertheless, the day before, Schlik had categorically stated to the Bohemian Chancellor, in a rare expression of bravado by the protégé towards his patron, that if this move was to misfire and 'the Efendi gets in his post-horses, as he is meditating for a few days now, we hope that we will be not held responsible for that'.[16]

The result of their meeting with Paget and Colyer was almost predetermined. The mediators strongly advised against any proposal to alter the articles already agreed, lest the Imperial side see the congress collapse like a house of cards.[17] And after they met with the Ottomans, they confirmed that 'they couldn't bend the Turks [to accept] additional concessions other than those they had already made'.[18] 'I begged Your Excellency to consider that it is no more in our power to treat with the Turks as it pleases us', Schlik pointed out the unsettling reality,[19] concluding in this manner: 'As much as I am concerned,

12 ÖStA, HHStA, Türkei I, Turcica Box 168, Folder 2 (November 1698, 2nd half), fol. 99^{v}–100^{r}, supplementary Imperial instructions, 19 November 1698. He reiterated the imperative need for the negotiations not to be aborted for any reason in his next instructions as well: ÖStA, HHStA, Türkei I, Turcica Box 169, Folder 1 (December 1698, 1st half), fol. 72^{v}, supplementary Imperial instructions, 5 December 1698.

13 ÖStA, HHStA, Türkei I, Turcica Box 169, Folder 1 (December 1698, 1st half), fol. 18^{r-v}, Schlik to Kinsky, 2 December 1698.

14 Ibid., fol. 18^{v}.

15 ÖStA, HHStA, Türkei I, Turcica Box 170, Protocollum, fol. 118.

16 ÖStA, HHStA, Türkei I, Turcica Box 169, Folder 1 (December 1698, 1st half), fol. 122^{r-v}, Schlik to Kinsky, 10 December 1698.

17 Ibid., fol. 196^{v}, Schlik to Kinsky, 12 December 1698.

18 ÖStA, HHStA, Türkei I, Turcica Box 169, Folder 2 (December 1698, 2nd half), fol. 98^{r}, Schlik to Kinsky, 20 December 1698.

19 Ibid., fol. 198^{r-v}.

I desire what the Master desires. However, suppose peace is necessary to us, as everyone deems and shouts. In that case, we should not miss this opportunity which probably will present itself again neither so good nor so favourable for many years [to come]'.[20] The ball was now with the Imperial Court for the final decision.

2 Venice

Another primary purpose for the dispatching of Count Marsigli to Vienna was to buy some time for Ruzzini,[21] waiting desperately for instructions to arrive from Venice to lift him out of the impasse in his talks with the Porte's plenipotentiaries. All participants, even the Ottomans, were confident that Venice's negotiation would be terminated relatively easily and swiftly.[22] They were to be deceived. As the second in the row of conferences, the Serenissima's ambassador started his discussions with a significant drawback: the precedent created by all the concessions the Imperials had made to the Exalted State's plenipotentiaries during their initial meetings. As he stated in his *Relazione Finale*, the Ottomans walked out of the first round of negotiation 'greater armed with courage and with false perceptions that they could imitate [the example set by the Imperials] in [their] talks [with] the others'.[23] The Anonymous Venetian would, in its turn, strongly criticise Count Öttingen's behaviour: 'and with great ease Count Öttingen [conceded] to put into paper demolitions, evacuations [and] abandonment of fortresses and lands'.[24]

Rāmī and Mavrocordatos did walk more boldly into their meeting with Ruzzini not only, though, because of what they had achieved in their talks with the Habsburg delegation, but also because of the disregard they manifested for the Republic and its military capabilities. The Ottomans 'finally showed not to especially esteem Venice', the Imperial plenipotentiaries reported to the emperor.[25] This contempt is excellently encapsulated in a passage from Dimitrie Cantemir's history of the 'Rises and Falls of the Ottoman Court'. According to the Moldavian prince, seeing Ruzzini being more rigid and causing much more

20 Ibid., fol. 42ᵛ, Schlik to Kinsky, 14 December 1698.
21 Ruzzini, *Relazione*, 356–7.
22 *Taʿrīḫ-i ṣulḥnāme*, fol. 96ᵃ.
23 Ruzzini, *Relazione*, 355.
24 *Narratio*, fol. 18ʳ.
25 ÖStA, HHStA, Türkei I, Turcica Box 168, Folder 2 (November 1698, 2nd half), fol. 132ᵛ, Imperial plenipotentiaries to Leopold I, 22 November 1698.

trouble to the plenipotentiaries of the Exalted State than the other ambassadors, Rāmī Meḥmed supposedly admonished him with the following words:

> Elçi Beg [lord ambassador] [...] you should not behave so immoderate and boastfully, particularly in front of such an assembly [comprised] of the most dignified ambassadors, all of whom are very well acquainted with the condition of the Republic of Venice and the Ottoman Empire and [can] compare their strengths. Nor could you ever be able to extend so far and wide your fingers, which by nature are so short, unless it occurs [to you], by chance, what a very famous fable of ours recounts.[26]

And he continued narrating to him the ensuing tale, which is so telling as it deserves to be quoted in full:

> It so happened that two most robust and most renowned athletes met once, and in order to contend by using much more force without obstacles, they took off their clothes and descended nude into the arena. In between, as they were competing with one another, a certain pickpocket (*yanḳesici*) [...] creeping secretly along the earth like a snake, stole the vestments of both. Ultimately, the athletes, exhausted by the contest, gave each other the kiss of peace as is the norm. When they went to [find their] clothes, they realised they had been taken by the pickpocket [and so] were forced to conceal their nudity with other garments. After a while, one of them was walking in the market and, seeing the thief wearing the athletic attire, [...] said to him. 'These are not your clothes but mine. When I was facing the other most potent athlete, you acquired them without fighting, secretly, like a cunning fox. However, given the opportunity, let us descend alone in the arena, and then you will truly experience what makes a lion different from a fox, and an athlete from a thief. [Then] we will really find out if you are equally good at fighting as you are at stealing. I am afraid, though, that apart from the clothes you took from me by fraud, you [will end up] giving your own as well'.[27]

Thus, feeling like one of the two robust athletes of the fable – it is pretty evident who the other one was supposed to be – the Ottoman ambassadors descended into the 'negotiation arena' with Ruzzini and presented him with an ultimatum. Either the Serenissima would 'clear' mainland Greece of all its

26 Cantemir, *Incrementorum et Decrementorum*, 506.

27 Ibid.

possessions, or there was no deal at all. However, the 'pickpocket' was far more daring than they had imagined. Ruzzini was equally resolute in holding his ground.[28] After the third Venetian–Ottoman conference on 24 November and finding the Ottomans persisting 'in the same obstinacy', he decided to write back to Venice and wait for the senate's orders on how to proceed.[29] He would have to wait a whole month to ultimately receive a reply.

Still, in the meantime, he lost no time in trying to secure support from his allies, commencing with the strongest. He implored the Imperial ambassadors to demonstrate to the Ottomans the unity of their League by voicing to them loud and robust protestations against the 'unlawful pretences introduced against the possessions of the Most Serene Republic',[30] and later he entreated them to slow down their negotiation.[31] He didn't find favourable ears there, though. The climate had changed considerably during this period in the Imperial camp regarding the erstwhile 'most trusted ally'.

In a letter to Kinsky, dated 22 November, Count Schlik, whereas still supportive towards the Venetian, started to voice criticism mainly about the way Ruzzini wanted to arrange border-making and the strict instructions he got from the Senate.[32] On his next dispatch, on 27 November, he became even more critical: 'The Turks, even if they were the most reasonable in the world, could never give him what he demands, nor with the manner by which he demands it'.[33] His claims to the mountains north of the Morea were based on an imaginary possession; in mainland Greece 'he is inflexible to demolish any of his shanties'.[34] As for Dalmatia, 'he has a map with [its] borders marked by the Senate which cannot be disobeyed in any way'.[35] His stance on border delimitation was equally absurd.

> Sworn enemy of the commissioners, whose name he does not [even] want to hear, he poses as a *conditio sine qua non* that the borders [...]

28 Schlik even claimed that behind the fierce debate between Mavrocordatos and Ruzzini was lurking a personal aversion towards one another: ÖStA, HHStA, Türkei I, Turcica Box 168, Folder 2 (November 1698, 2nd half), fol. 165ᵛ, Schlik to Kinsky, 22 November 1698.

29 *Narratio*, fol. 23ʳ; Ruzzini, *Relazione*, 356.

30 ÖStA, HHStA, Türkei I, Turcica Box 169, Folder 2 (December 1698, 2nd half), fol. 73ᵛ, Ruzzini to Öttingen/Schlik, 12 December 1698.

31 Ibid., fol. 78ᵛ, Ruzzini to Öttingen/Schlik, 18 December 1698.

32 ÖStA, HHStA, Türkei I, Turcica Box 168, Folder 2 (November 1698, 2nd half), fol. 165ᵛ–167ʳ, Schlik to Kinsky, 22 November 1698.

33 Ibid., fol. 246ʳ, Schlik to Kinsky, 27 November 1698.

34 Ibid., fol. 246ᵛ.

35 Ibid.

> should be [clearly] specified and inserted in the [peace] articles [...] naming forests, mountains, streams, fountains with their proper names; a [truly] terrifying litany.[36]

As November ended and the first days of December also passed without news from Venice and with Ruzzini still in his adamant position, this essentially subtle criticism turned into suspicion and annoyance.[37] 'This conduct of the Venetian ambassador makes us suspicious', Schlik confessed to Kinsky. How could the Senate invest its ambassador with such limited powers? How could it prescribe 'inalterable articles in the form of laws for the Ottoman Empire'?[38] Such doubts were further exacerbated and corroborated by a series of other shady coincidences:

> the Jewish doctor who was all his life a pensioner of France;[39] the last encrypted letter Nicolosi received from one of ambassador Chateauneuf's puppets [...]; a word slipped from Nicolosi's mouth that in times of peace the Republic would be obliged, with huge expenses, to maintain four thousand more men to assure its frontiers.[40]

Suspicion and indignation ran both ways, though. The Venetian side correctly perceived that the readiness with which the Habsburg concessions to the Ottomans were made was the result of the emperor's apprehension to conclude a peace treaty with the Ottomans 'whatever the cost' (*ad'ogni costo*), sacrificing the interests of his ally.[41] They also supposed, but wrongly in this instance, that such prejudicial compromises could not have been made simply by the will of the ambassadors without the knowledge of the emperor and the court. And because of the short distance that allowed them to receive instructions in only a few days, 'it was thought that the *modus operandi* of the plenipotentiaries [was based on their] commissions and the disagreement of the court was [only for] appearances'.[42]

36 Ibid., fol. 247^{r}, Schlik to Kinsky, 27 November 1698.

37 ÖStA, HHStA, Türkei I, Turcica Box 168, Folder 2 (November 1698, 2nd half), fol. 236^{r-v}, Schlik to Kinsky, 27 November 1698 (P.S., 2 December 1698).

38 Ibid., fol. 249^{v}.

39 As we mentioned, after the outbreak of the war between Venice and the Ottoman Empire in 1684, Conegliano placed himself under French protection. *See* above, Act II, Narration Part II.

40 Schlik to Kinsky, 27 November 1698, fol. 249^{v}–250^{r}.

41 Ruzzini, *Relazione*, 355.

42 *Narratio*, fol. 18^{v}.

The changing climate in Imperial–Venetian relations was also noticed by Voznitsyn. As he reported in a letter to the tsar, despite the friendly façade they were still trying to maintain, they were holding a secret antipathy towards each other, which, according to him, stemmed from the fear of the Imperials that Venice would become much more powerful, since she had conquered too many territories during the last war.[43] Interestingly, the same argument would be repeated later in the Venetian camp and used by the Ottomans to win over the Habsburg plenipotentiaries during the last phase of the congress.[44]

By the end of December, all his other allies having concluded or been in the process of concluding their affairs, Ruzzini found himself increasingly isolated. As if the Ottoman ultimatum was not enough, the Imperials presented him with an equal one, declaring to him categorically that 'in December the negotiations had either to be dissolved or to be concluded'.[45] Małachowski, who had basically completed his talks, was also pestering Ruzzini to make swift resolutions, sustaining that it was necessary for him to depart as quickly as possible and even offering to leave his Peace Instrument signed in the hands of the mediators until all the others had concluded their talks.[46] And so started the strenuous efforts of Ruzzini, which would continue until the last moment of the congress to keep the Pole at Carlowitz at every cost. Only Voznitsyn, for his own reasons, continued to show strong support for the *Cavaliere*.

This was primarily the outcome of the *modus tractandi* adopted at the beginning of the congress, as the Anonymous Venetian bitterly realised, in a brilliant summary of the situation. Following it, the bilateral character of the talks, in which every one of the allies was negotiating separately with the Ottomans, 'led naturally to one concluding [his talks] before the other, and the Turk free to concede or resist each one as he saw fit'.[47] Fully vindicating Voznitsy's proposals before the start of the talks for a common allied front, it continued that it would be much more efficient if all Holy League members had presented joint proposals to the Ottoman side and promoted them together, 'keeping themselves in a position to dictate the terms to the enemy, rather than to receive them, and by offering him peace, offering him a great good, [while] by threatening him with war, threatening him with an immense

43 Bogoslovskii, *Petr I*, 419.

44 *See* below, Act IV.

45 Ruzzini, *Relazione*, 356.

46 *Narratio*, fol. 24^v–25^r.

47 Ibid., fol. 26^r.

harm, since, both the one and the other would count for all'.[48] Nonetheless, with the current mode,

> it was evident that the door was open to the Turks to separate and divide the allies in the conclusion [of the treaties] as they were [split] during the negotiations, and whoever managed to finish [his own affairs] would not contribute anything other than apparent pressure on his companion. And finally, after some deferment or delay [in signing his agreement], he would not wish to lose the gift of his [good] fortune and the fruit of his efforts.[49]

He couldn't have been more accurate in his analysis. Still, the Venetian position appears to have been undermined not only from the outside but from the inside as well. If we are to believe Count Marsigli, the relations between Ruzzini and the embassy's secretary, Nicolosi, were not ideal, the latter being unhappy with the negotiating method of the former.[50] Not only that but in a conversation he had with the Imperial 'special adviser', asserting his own expertise of the locations claimed by the Republic in the Morea and mainland Greece, he declared that 'Lepanto is a castle of trivial [significance] […] that Preveza did not serve anything more than covering a fishery' and that the Republic would have given them both voluntarily if it had been informed in time about the changes in the preliminary agreement.[51] Naturally, such assertions were far from what Ruzzini professed during the official conferences where he was trying desperately to hold on to both fortresses, and it harmed the Republic's interests in the long term since it disclosed to the Imperial side that the Venetians were not, in fact, as rigid in matters of territorial possession as they were trying to appear.

Hence, by the end of this second phase of the congress, the Venetian position was in great jeopardy, its negotiation not even slightly advanced, even if Ruzzini was desperately trying to conceal this adverse reality.[52] Isolated, despised and suspected by the majority of his allies and the mediators, faced with the Ottoman (and Imperial) contempt and unalterable demands yet unable or unwilling to make any concessions, the Venetian could only hope for the new instructions from the Senate and the support of the Imperial Court.

---

48 Ibid.

49 Ibid., fol. 26v.

50 ÖStA, HHStA, Türkei I, Turcica Box 168, Folder 2 (November 1698, 2nd half), fol. 294v, Marsigli to Kinsky, 28 November 1698.

51 Ibid., fol. 295r.

52 Bogoslovskii, *Petr I*, 419.

3 The Polish-Lithuanian Commonwealth

In the complete antipodes of the *Cavaliere*, Małachowski finalised his agreement on 18 December, after just five conferences with the Ottomans.[53] However, he too encountered some difficulties along the way. Faced with initial Ottoman intransigence on the issues of the return of an intact Kamianets-Podilskyi and the tribute to the Tatars, just like Ruzzini, the Pole started knocking on his allies' 'doors' for help. He was so desperate as to even ask for Voznitsyn's assistance, with the latter claiming that he was willing to help but on condition that the Pole would reconcile with him (offer an apology) for the past disputes they had had.[54] He then visited the Venetian, declaring that he hoped Ruzzini would not finish his negotiation before him, a perfect irony if we consider what ensued next.[55] However, he was much luckier than the Serenissima's plenipotentiary because the Imperials and the mediators were inclined to aid him. It was undoubtedly through their intervention that the Ottomans agreed to alter their stance on the two above-mentioned thorny issues,[56] something that the Pole himself acknowledged when, after his conference on 9 December, he visited his Imperial colleagues to inform them of the felicitous ending of his talks and to sincerely thank them for their valuable assistance, without which it would not have been possible to acquire what he finally got.[57]

Three days later, he wrote to Karol Stanisław Radziwiłł, conveying the satisfactory – as he saw them – results of his negotiation. He managed to acquire the restitution of an intact Kamianets, the restoration to the Commonwealth 'of two broad and fertile provinces, namely Podolia and Ukraine', the abolition of the tribute to the Tatars and an explicit Ottoman promise to prohibit the latter's raids into Polish territories.[58] He also expressed his hope that those

53 ÖStA, HHStA, Türkei I, Turcica Box 170, Diarium et Cerimoniale, fol. 51. Practically, however, he had already ended his negotiation nine days earlier, on 9 December: Ibid., fol. 46–47. In his relation, Gorkowski states wrongly that this conference took place on 10 December: Gorkowski, *Compendium Legationis*, 26^r–v^.

54 Ibid., 24^v^.

55 Ibid., 25^r^.

56 For the critical role of the Imperial embassy on the Kamianets issue, *see* ÖStA, HHStA, Türkei I, Turcica Box 168, Folder 2 (November 1698, 2nd half), fol. 174^v^, Imperial plenipotentiaries to Leopold I, 23 November 1698; ÖStA, HHStA, Türkei I, Turcica Box 169. Folder 1 (December 1698, 1st half), fol. 89^v^, Imperial plenipotentiaries to Leopold I, 9 December 1698. For their equal assistance on the Tatar tribute, Sałuski, *Epistolae*, 679–80.

57 ÖStA, HHStA, Türkei I, Turcica Box 170, Diarium et Cerimoniale, fol. 47.

58 AGAD, Archiwum Warszawskie Radziwiłłów, 1/354/0/5/9200, fol. 39, Małachowski to Radziwiłł, 12 December 1698. I sincerely thank Jan Blonski for assisting me in translating the letter.

terms would be approved back home since – in a manner similar to that of the Imperials – under the present circumstances, 'we couldn't have secured a better peace'.[59] Those circumstances, as he confided to Count Marsigli in a meeting he had with him in early January, were the pressing need the Commonwealth had to disengage itself from the 'tiresome'(*noioso*) war with the Ottomans and to rather focus on the north against Brandenburg, avenging the capture of Elbląg.[60]

Still, when the peace terms were made public in Warsaw after the end of the congress, there was criticism, not satisfaction, and the ambassador was strongly reproached for his conduct.[61] Not having been able to defend himself – he died prematurely shortly after his return to the Commonwealth – this task fell upon the embassy's secretary Andrzej Gorkowski. The latter composed a relation of the congress which told an entirely different reality, favourable to his late master.

Following Gorkowski, to press the Polish ambassador to conclude a treaty, the mediators, using their usual manipulation techniques, declared to him that the Imperials and the Muscovites were about to terminate their affairs. Just like Voznitsyn later did, Malachowski immediately visited the Habsburg plenipotentiaries to corroborate this statement, only to receive a positive reply, which left him, as Gorskowski related, in complete confusion. Also wishing to ascertain if the same applied for Voznitsyn, he curiously dispatched the secretary not to the Muscovite but again to the mediators. Not having received a clear answer from them this time, Gorkowski went with an excuse to Mavrocordatos, where he found the secretary of the Muscovite embassy along with the Imperial interpreter already working together on the translation of the text of the Ottoman–Muscovite truce/armistice from Turkish to Latin. Only then did he arrive at Voznitsyn's tent, where he strongly protested against the violation of the terms of the 'Eternal Peace' (1686) between the

59 Ibid.

60 ÖStA, HHStA, Türkei I, Turcica Box 168, Folder 2 (November 1698, 2nd half), fol. 281r–v, Marsigli to Kinsky, 9 January 1698. For the 'affair of Elbląg', *see* above, Act II, Narration Part I.

61 He was accused, mainly by Jan Gomolinski – the Polish ablegate in Vienna in summer 1698, who probably held personal grudges against Małachowski for 'stealing' from him a position he might have aspired to – as being too lenient with the Ottomans, failing to capitalise on supposed favourable for him occasions and even falling under the influence of Voznitsyn who supposedly was acting in cahoots with the Ottomans to the detriment of the Commonwealth's interests: Włodzimierz Dworzaczek, 'Stanisław Małachowski', in *Polski Słownik Biograficzny*, vol. 19 (Warsaw: Institute of History of the Polish Academy of Sciences 1974) 414–5.

two polities, which prohibited the one from signing a peace agreement with a common enemy without considering the other's interests. It was solely after this 'Muscovite betrayal' that Malachowski decided to accommodate himself with the Ottomans as well.[62]

Gorkowski's relation is a perfect example of a fabricated story which inverted reality[63] – Voznitysn was actually the one to reach the accommodation only after Małachowski's agreement[64] – to exonerate the Polish ambassador, constrained to take the course of action he took, as to equally blame any claim of a violation of the 'Eternal Peace' pact on the part of the Muscovites.

However, criticism of the terms the Commonwealth secured came from other congress participants who also felt betrayed by the Poles. Voznitsyn argued in a letter to the tsar that Małachowski got basically nothing out of his negotiations with the Ottomans, having been tricked and cheated by the Germans.[65] In his *Relazione Finale*, Ruzzini commented, not without a slight tone of sarcasm, that 'it could be said for this kingdom [Poland-Lithuania] that it was generously recompensated for the endeavours of the one year, as memorable as it might have been, [it actually] fought, and the desires of all [its] subsequent campaigns'.[66] Similarly, he found it a bit bizarre that the Ottomans, not having lost Kamianets by force of arms, were ready 'to cede [it] with negotiations willingly'.[67] 'Who fancies to interpret [the events] with the subtlety, very often fallacious, of conjectures', he continued,

> would say that this might have been the prize of inaction, perhaps secretly promised well in advance through the frequent handlings [they] had with the Tatar Khan, rather than believe what the Turks profess, that they desired to disengage themselves from a place not useful to them [and], if anything, quite burdensome, [because] it required three hundred purses per year to maintain its garrison.[68]

62 Gorkowski, *Compendium Legationis*, 25ᵛ–26ʳ.

63 For instance, in his letter to Radziwiłł on 12 December, summarising the results of his already concluded negotiation, Małachowski also informed him that the Venetians and the Muscovites 'had barely advanced anything' by that point: AGAD, Archiwum Warszawskie Radziwiłłów, 1/354/0/5/9200, fol. 39, Małachowski to Radziwiłł, 12 December 1698.

64 *See* below.

65 Bogoslovskii, *Petr I*, 418. Malachowski repaid him with the same coin, arguing in another letter to Radziwiłł that he could not understand what kind of advantage Voznitsyn had secured by concluding a mere two-year truce/armistice: AGAD, Archiwum Warszawskie Radziwiłłów, 1/354/0/5/9200, fol. 44–45, Małachowski to Radziwiłł, 26 December 1698.

66 Ruzzini, *Relazione*, 368.

67 Ibid.

68 Ibid.

Ruzzini's particular reading of these conjectures was, of course, related to the two Polish nobles trying to visit the khan, a little before the beginning of the congress,[69] as much as a second formal embassy that took place during it. According to Schlik's 'Secret Journal', 'it was heard by the Turkish plenipotentiaries that a Polish ambassador met with the Tatar Khan on [the latter's] return journey [to Crimea] through Wallachia and reportedly had with him a large suite. Of which [visit] the one here [Małachowski] appears to be surprised to some extent'.[70] But what was the purpose of these two mysterious encounters?

Writing his autobiography towards the end of the second decade of the eighteenth century, Jan Jabłonowski (d. 1731), voivode of Ruthenia, Crown Chancellor (1706–09) and son of the Grand Hetman Stanisław Jabłonowski, provided the following explanation. Seeing that the fortress of Kamianets could not be taken by force, in a secret meeting in Lviv, presided over by Jabłonowski, the father, it was decided to turn for assistance to the Crimean Khan. According to Jabłonowski junior, Selīm I Giray had a long and friendly history with the Commonwealth, not only secretly assisting the Poles twice in crucial battles, namely those of Żurawno (1676) and during the one of Kahlenberg in 1683, in front of the walls of Vienna (sic!),[71]but also being considered a brother-in-arms with King Jan III Sobieski and the Grand Hetman, since they had fought together against the Swedes and the Muscovites during the Second Northern War (1655–60).[72]

The person sent to Selīm Giray was a captain named Dubrawski. The latter travelled under the pretext of buying horses, but in reality, was there to negotiate the question of the Podolian fortress. He met with the khan, and after declaring to him that without its return to the Commonwealth, there would be no lasting peace between the two sides, he promised him 20.000 Zlotys if he could facilitate that happening, a promise that appears to have been an initiative of the Grand Hetman without the knowledge of the king.

After leaving his meeting with the Crimean ruler, Dubrawski also met with Małachowski, who, by that point, had arrived at Carlowitz and informed him about his negotiations, advising him to also address the khan himself.[73] With that promise of money, Selīm Giray allegedly brought to the attention

69 *See* above Act II, Narration Part II.

70 ÖStA, HHStA, Türkei I, Turcica Box 170, Diarium et Cerimoniale, fol. 46.

71 Actually, Murad (1678–83), not Selīm Giray, was khan during the siege of Vienna.

72 Jan Stanisław Jabłonowski, August Bielowski (ed.), *Pamiętnik Jana Stanisława Jabłonowskiego wojewody ruskiego* (Lviv: National Ossoliński Institute 1862) 73.

73 Thus, Dubrawski's meeting with the khan should have taken place right after or simultaneously with Gorkowski's failed mission to the Ottoman camp.

of the grand vizier the impossibility of a durable peace if the fortress was not returned and convinced him to opt for a restoration of the old border between the two states. When the deal was made known, the Grand Treasurer, Hieronim Lubomirski, refused to pay the sum to the khan, pleading poverty, but then August II intervened by giving it out of his own treasury; only then was Kamianets returned to the Commonwealth.[74]

Jabłonowski's story is undoubtedly an intriguing one, revealing the backstage dealings we discussed earlier between the different actors as much as how the designs of the Crimean rulers often diverged from the Ottoman ones. Indeed, a part of the Khanate's leadership didn't welcome the Ottoman occupation of Podolia. It considered it an Ottoman attempt to restrain Crimean autonomy by meddling with its own sphere of influence and slave reservoir.[75] So, it was most probably in the interests of some of the khans – Selīm Giray was one of them – to see the Porte abandon the area, and they could have played a role in persuading her to take that step.[76] In fact, Selīm Giray had offered his mediation to the Commonwealth to help her recuperate Kamianets and Podolia in a delegation he sent in 1692–93 to the Polish Court to negotiate a peace settlement.[77]

However, Jabłonowski's narrative has many inconsistencies. The most obvious is the chronological one. We know that Selīm Giray was present and spoke in favour of peace during the crucial Ottoman Imperial Council, which took place in January 1698, months before he would receive the Polish representative in his camp near Belgrade. Furthermore, despite the mediating efforts of the khan, the Ottomans had been offering the Podolian fortress to the Commonwealth – demolished – since the negotiations in Vienna in 1689–90.[78] Thus, the Crimean ruler did not need to convince them to do so

74 Bielowski, *Pamiętnik*, 73–5.

75 Królikowska, 'Sovereignty and Subordination', 63; Kołodziejczyk, 'Das Krimkhanat', 52.

76 However, not all Crimeans held the same opinion as demonstrated by the criticism of a junior member of the Giray dynasty, Meḥmed, who, despite being a fervent supporter of a general peace settlement with the Holy League, resented the ceding of Kamienets to the Poles: Uğur Demir, 'Mehmed Giray, Tarih-i Mehmed Giray (1095–1115/1684–1703) (Değerlendirme, Çeviri, Metin)' (MA dissertation, Marmara University, Istanbul 2006) 116–7.

77 AGAD, Archiwum Koronne Warszawskie, 1/3/0/32/64, Folder 5, nr 536, Selīm Giray to Jan III, s.d. (1693); Kołodziejczyk, *The Crimean Khanate*, 193.

78 *Cerîde-i Takrirât*, 105.

in 1698. It also becomes evident that if the Ottomans were finally convinced to return Kamianets to its status quo, that was because of Imperial insistence and – one might guess – money. Finally, in Jabłonowski's account, there is no mention of the second embassy to the Crimean ruler.

A tentative alternative explanation of the course of events would be that, initially, the Poles, likely capitalising on earlier promises, tried to secure the khan's assistance in recuperating the fortress intact by offering him a sum of money, just like Małachowski's instructions plainly stated.[79] Nonetheless, there were other, more Crimean-related topics they were equally eager to discuss with him: the tribute and the Tatar raids. It is probable that the chief purpose of the second embassy was related to exactly these two issues, as the Ottomans themselves alluded to the Polish plenipotentiary.[80] The latter considered the prohibition of the upcoming Tatar incursions so important that he demanded to meet yet another time with the Ottomans on 14 January to request them to keep the Crimeans at bay since the peace agreement was almost ready; only the signing was missing.[81] As for the 20.000 Zlotys, they could have procured, in the end, the khan's aid regarding the canons to be left inside Kamianets, a matter that was left undecided during the congress but was to be discussed when the Polish embassy arrived in the Ottoman capital for the ratification of the treaty.[82]

Hence, Jabłonowski's presentation of events is probably an attempt to highlight the role of his father in recuperating the Podolian fortress with a *coup d'état*, to remember Schlik's pertinent expression for such moves. It wouldn't have sounded particularly flattering to admit that the Ottomans were willing to deliver the fortress themselves or that Małachowski had received Imperial assistance in getting it back intact.

To summarise, although the agreement the Commonwealth's plenipotentiary had managed to secure was not what many would consider the appropriate one back home, with his skilful bargaining and the assistance he received from third parties, he managed to acquire the minimum his instructions commanded from him on territorial issues and to liberate his polity from a humiliating tribute it had paid for centuries.

79 *See* above, Act II, Narration Part II.

80 *Taʿrīḥ-i ṣulḥnāme*, fol. 115ª.

81 Cernovodeanu, 'Le journal', 348–9.

82 Silâhdâr, *Nusretnâme*, 515.

4 Muscovy

For Count Schlik, Voznitsyn, besides being a beast, was also a true actor who was constantly changing roles and characters 'on this theatre [stage]' (*auf disen theatro*), one time appearing as a vehement denier of peace and another as its fervent supporter.[83] Verily, when one tries to understand the process of the Ottoman–Muscovite talks, one should be cautious since it is sometimes really hard to distinguish what from the things that transpired in the official negotiations between the two sides was genuine and what was simply acting.[84]

In addition, it is not entirely clear if Voznitsyn was still attempting with his behaviour to cause the congress to fail or at least to delay its conclusion. In his long final relation, written after the end of the negotiations, he portrays himself as being in constant uncertainty on what to do next, constrained in his moves by external forces, mainly by the determination of his other allies to make peace. However, one should be very cautious about accepting uncritically everything he claims. In the end, one may assume that he was attempting to keep all his options open, just like he was instructed by the tsar,[85] from a dissolution of the congress and a continuation of the war to the signing of a short truce/armistice with the Ottomans, continuously re-evaluating them according to circumstances. Hence the inconsistency he appeared to display in the eyes of the other participants.

After these essential initial remarks, let us follow his manoeuvres a bit more closely. The primary bone of contention between Voznitsyn and the Ottomans was the one regarding the Lower Dnieper fortresses. Just like in the Ottoman–Venetian case, both parties stuck adamantly to their respective positions. After a new series of secret talks with Mavrocordatos brought no result, the Muscovite decided to follow the example of Ruzzini and Małachowski and seek external support. Ironically, he decided to turn to the mediators, whom, in the beginning, he was unwilling to accept. He strived to influence them with words and other means, but to no avail.[86] Then he sent Postnikov to the Imperials only for the latter to get the blunt answer that the Muscovites would not force them to fight another fifty years; the sixteen over which they have already waged war at great expense were more than enough.[87]

---

83 ÖStA, HHStA, Türkei I, Turcica Box 170, Diarium et Cerimoniale, fol. 51.

84 *See* above, Act II, Narration Part II.

85 Bogoslovskii, *Petr I*, 406.

86 Ibid., 402–4.

87 Ibid., 411.

Voznitsyn's mind was tormented by other concerns as well. Like the Poles, he feared a second war front in the north against the Swedes and the Commonwealth, explaining to his fellow 'Grand Ambassador', Fyodor Alekseyevich Golovin, in a letter dated 18/28 November 1698, the need for an immediate alliance with the Elector of Brandenburg and the King of Denmark.

> If we are to remain at war with the Turks, we must keep a close eye on the Poles and the Swedes who are always looking for trouble, and they have set their eyes upon us. For this reason, shall we not make an alliance with the Kurfürst of Brandenburg and the Danish king while there is still time?[88]

Such thoughts are quite revealing of the level of suspicion and antipathy Voznitsyn nurtured towards the Commonwealth and how he was entirely in the dark about the secret arrangement of his master with August II back in August 1698 to coordinate their actions against Sweden.

With the coming of the first winter month and his negotiation finding itself at a standstill, Prokopii Bogdanovich began another round of visits to his allies. 'Around this period', related Rāmī Meḥmed,

> the Muscovite ambassador caused amazement both to the [allied] plenipotentiaries as to the mediators with his various actions. Was it really out of anxiety, was it because he wanted to be informed of their situation, sometimes he visited the Pole and others the Venetian, and he was spending his time with such deferring [moves].[89]

After becoming alarmed by what Mavrocordatos told him 'in confidence' to force him to reach an agreement with the Porte that the other allies would look to their interests and leave him on his own, Voznitysn rushed to the Venetian tents to confirm that information. Ruzzini gave him a mumbling reply, asserting that the 'Turks' might have heard it from someone else, but not from him. When the Muscovite pressed him further, 'he placed his finger in his lips and, after a moment of silence, answered me: [...] the old friendship of His Majesty with the Commonwealth [the Republic of Venice] compelled him to tell me the truth. That, if [all] the others conclude their affairs, it would be impossible for them to remain at war alone'.[90] To this affirmation, Voznitsyn set in motion

88 Quoted in ibid., 403.

89 *Taʾrīḥ-i ṣulḥnāme*, fol. 117^{b}.

90 Quoted in Bogoslovskii, *Petr I*, 410.

a strategy that he would keep applying to his relations with the Venetians until the end of the congress: 'Not alone, with us! I answered. He remained silent and said nothing about it'.[91] Nonetheless, at the end of their conversation, he advised him to beware of the Imperials and the Poles since they were concluding their affairs with the Ottomans.[92]

Armed with this warning, the Great and Plenipotentiary Ambassador turned his eyes on Małachowski, who was truly finishing his business. In a letter he sent to the Pole on 10 December, he reminded him that according to the 'Eternal Peace' between the Commonwealth and Muscovy, one could not conclude a peace agreement with the Ottomans without the other (*secundum eum cum Turcis foedus pacisci*). So, he exhorted him that if presently it wasn't possible for the Commonwealth to wage a full-scale war against the Ottomans, to make at least, just like Voznitsyn, a short truce/armistice of 'one or two years'.[93] The Commonwealth ambassador's reply was categorical. His polity did not desire a brief respite but peace.[94]

Understanding perhaps the danger of leaving his master alone in the war against the Porte, and after sending Postnikov for a new round of informal negotiations with Mavrocordatos,[95] Voznitsyn terminated his negotiation, concluding a two-year truce/armistice with the Ottomans, one day after Małachowski finalised his agreement, on 19 December.[96] Things were to remain in a status quo, and negotiations were to resume during this period for the two sides to reach a long-lasting arrangement.[97] He didn't sign the

91 Ibid.

92 Ibid., 410–1.

93 ÖStA, HHStA, Türkei I, Turcica Box 169, Folder 1 (December 1698, 1st half), fol. 151^{r-v}, Voznitsyn to Małachowski, 10 December 1698. In their meeting in Buda, just before the commencement of the congress, the two ambassadors had declared that the 'pact of the everlasting peace between them [still] resounds': Gorkowski, *Compendium Legationis*, 6^{v}. This was before they clashed over the ceremonial, though.

94 ÖStA, HHStA, Türkei I, Turcica Box 169, Folder 1 (December 1698, 1st half), fol. 152^{r}, Małachowski to Vosnitysn, 11 December. In a letter to Radziwiłł, Małachowski sustained that Voznitsyn's main aim with these missives he sent was to put the blame for the failure of his negotiation on him: AGAD, Archiwum Warszawskie Radziwiłłów, 1/354/0/5/9200, fol. 45–46, Małachowski to Radziwiłł, 26 December 1698.

95 Bogoslovskii, *Petr I*, 412.

96 Cernovodeanu, 'Le journal', 339–341. According to Schlik, Voznitsyn rushed to conclude his affairs after Małachowski finished his own: ÖStA, HHStA, Türkei I, Turcica Box 170, Diarium et Cerimoniale, fol. 51.

97 Ironically, as Voznitsyn diligently followed his master's orders, Peter I had, in the meantime, changed again his mind and was now prepared to negotiate a proper peace with the Ottomans, even at the cost of sacrificing the Dnieper fortresses. To that end, he even dispatched new instructions to his ambassador, but alas, due to the inescapable 'distance

instrument of his agreement, though, out of respect, he claimed, for the alliance, waiting for all his colleagues to finish their affairs.[98] As we have seen, he explained his decision to the tsar, arguing that he had run out of alternatives and thought it to be the only possible and logical option under the circumstances he was facing. He was probably right, but that didn't mean he stopped trying to undermine the congress. How? We shall find out in the next Act.

5 New Rapproachments in the Allied Camp

The cataclysmic changes brought by this second phase of the congress resulted in a major realignment within the allied camp. At the start of the negotiations, there were two distinctive blocs, the Imperial/Venetian and the Commonwealth/Muscovite. The latter was already in tatters before the commencement of the official talks, and the former was, unofficially, steadily collapsing in the ensuing month. At the beginning of December, a new form of informal entente took shape between the two 'black sheep' of the congress. Ruzzini and Voznitsyn were both in need of each other for different reasons. The Venetian, because he was in a desperate search for supporters, and the Muscovite for the same reasons, and because he probably saw a unique chance to undermine the negotiations, counting on the idea that the Imperials wouldn't leave Venice to face the Ottomans alone on the battlefield. This rapprochement did not pass unattended by the other parties. After receiving a letter from Voznitsyn to the Imperial embassy on 13 December, Count Schlik recorded in his 'Secret Journal' that the Muscovite was now acting as a supporter (*Advocaten*) for the Serenissima's interests.[99]

6 The Ottomans

As December drew to a close, no one could be more satisfied with the results of the negotiations so far than the Ottomans. The Porte's plenipotentiaries managed to impose – with Imperial help – a *modus tractandi* that suited them ideally, splitting the allies and watching them afterwards undermining one another as each followed his own interests at the expense of the whole. Taking

factor', they arrived almost a month after the congress was over: Burdowicz-Nowicki, *Piotr I*, 135–7.

98 Bogoslovskii, *Petr I*, 418.

99 ÖStA, HHStA, Türkei I, Turcica Box 170, Diarium et Ceremoniale, fol. 50.

full advantage of the Imperial desire for peace, they also succeeded in forcing their strongest enemies to accept their interpretation of the Foundation of Peace and the method to discuss and define borders. By doing that, they managed to achieve significant territorial gains, notably against the Imperials, the most important of them being the recuperation of the Ṭemeşvar area. 'With the whole Ṭemeşvar province under the possession of the Exalted State', argued Rāmī,

> not only [...] His Majesty, the Emperor of Islam, will again be master of such an extensive and fertile province of Hungary, but also the forces of Islam, having a permanent foot in the province, will not be cut off [completely] from Hungary. Whenever the need arises, they can crisscross the Danube, whose two banks will remain [in our] possession through the two [cardinal] fortresses of Belgrade and Ṭemeşvar.[100]

The Ottomans were also able to effectively secure the former by acquiring a fair amount of territory all the way up to Carlowitz.[101] In Croatia, they also managed to snatch away from the Imperials lands north of the river Una (Tributary of the Save).[102] And, despite the return of Kamianets to the Commonwealth, 'Moldavia, the region acting as the pantry of the Exalted State, was placed again under [its] full control'.[103] Furthermore, in spite of the Imperial desire for 'minor profits' (*bir cezvi'i fā'ide*) on other matters of the negotiations besides the cardinal point of borders,[104] the Ottomans were successful in shattering the Habsburg designs of a condominium over the Republic of Ragusa and in strongly resisting other demands like the question of the ownership of the Christian Holy Sites in Jerusalem, the extradition of Imre Thököly and the prisoner exchange without ransom. They had to make concessions, that's certain. The de facto abolition of the Tatar tribute paid by the Commonwealth, an intact Kamianets and the two-year truce/armistice with Muscovy, to name but the most important. Yet, in the first two cases, they could justifiably claim that this was the only way to make peace, and in the third, a short truce/armistice was better than no agreement at all.

---

100 *Ta'rīḥ-i ṣulḥnāme*, fol. 91[a].

101 Ibid., fol. 93[b]–94[a].

102 Ibid., fol. 94[a]–96[a].

103 Ibid., fol. 117[b]. For the role of the two Danubian Principalities as important provisioners of the Ottoman capital in bread, salt and meat (among others), *see* Traian Stoianovich, 'Conquering Balkan Orthodox Merchant'. *Journal of Economic History* 20/2 (1960), 241.

104 *Ta'rīḥ-i ṣulḥnāme*, fol. 111[b].

Another factor that contributed to the Ottoman success was the ability of the two ambassadors to convince their chief opponents, the Imperials, of the need they supposedly had to conclude the negotiations as soon as possible, thus further neutralising any attempt of the Viennese Court to re-negotiate some of the articles, especially the ones regarding territorial possession and border-making, which had already been agreed. They were, of course, greatly assisted by the manipulating tactics of the mediators playing on familiar Christian European tropes regarding the frequent alterations in the top echelons of the Ottoman government. The 'Ottoman rush', which precluded and excluded any modifications to the status of the talks, accompanied, as a constant refrain, the relations of the Habsburg ambassadors to the emperor as well as Schlik's dispatches to Kinsky.[105]

In a still greater manifestation of how the Ottoman plenipotentiaries managed from initially being the allegedly 'defeated party' to ending up dictating their terms during the congress, at the beginning of December, they declared that being tired of the allies' 'slowness', they demanded an eight-day deadline 'to arrange everything',[106] a demand which the Imperial embassy was successful in avoiding, though.[107] Setting deadlines, requesting swift resolutions and threatening to leave the congress were strategies that the Ottoman embassy would often follow, especially during the last Act of the 'Theater of Peace'.

The question of Venice remained, however. In that matter, the Ottomans were determined not to take any step backwards. 'How the [Ottoman] Empire could tolerate in front of the eyes of the [whole] world to not have been able to obtain from the Republic of Venice [a bunch of] trifles?', Mavrocordatos asked rhetorically,[108] encapsulating all the scorn of the Porte towards the Serenissima. In his view, as that of Rāmī's, the latter was an easy prey which the Ottoman 'lion' could easily devour. And the drama was to intensify. How would it finally play out? We have to demand some patience from our audience.

105 For instance, ÖStA, HHStA, Türkei I, Turcica Box 169, Folder 1 (December 1698, 1st half), fol. 2^{r-v}, Imperial plenipotentiaries to Leopold I, 2 December 1698; Ibid., fol. 122^{r-v}, Schlik to Kinsky, 10 December 1698.

106 Ibid., fol. 2^{v}, Imperial plenipotentiaries to Leopold I, 2 December 1698.

107 Ibid.

108 ÖStA, HHStA, Türkei I, Turcica Box 170, Protocollum, fol. 107.

Interlude V: the Composition of an Embassy

> He had mounted guard, a secretary, a physician, dragomans, six pages, seventy grooms [...] besides [...] other officials necessary to his numerous family.
>
> The Anonymous Venetian speaking of Rāmī Meḥmed's suite[1]

∵

If the ambassadors were the undisputed heads of a congress embassy, it is equally irrefutable that they could not have functioned without other various members that sustained and complemented the head. We reasoned above that to go 'beyond the ambassador', one had to pass first necessarily through him. Having addressed this in a previous interlude, the present discussion will focus on the numerous individuals that formed the plenipotentiaries' retinue and to their multiple roles and tasks, from the ambassadors' relatives and the embassy's secretary down to the simple servants, so crucial for the upkeeping of the 'protagonists', and the guard, so essential for their safety.

1 'The More the Better': the General Structure and Size of a Congress Embassy

The embassy was a heteroclite organism with many composites, 'virtually an entirely self-contained economic unit', as Derek Croxton deftly puts it.[2] In its essence, it resembled an extensive household, and we often encounter the term 'family' to describe the ambassadorial retinue.[3] One of the most basic general traits of this 'family', especially in the case of peace congresses, was its size. As we have already discussed in the interlude regarding the ceremonial, the size of the plenipotentiaries' entourage constituted one of the foremost means of manifestation and projection of one's status and grandeur. For instance, Ruzzini's strenuous efforts to appear with no lesser magnificence than his other colleagues resulted in a suite that numbered as many as eighty-nine

1 *Narratio*, fol. 11^{r-v}.

2 Croxton, *Westphalia*, 135.

3 For instance, *Narratio*, fol. 11^{v}, 43^{v}.

 | DOI:10.1163/9789004458499_021

individuals.[4] Voznitsyn's was also comprised of sixty-two persons,[5] and that of the Imperials numbered at least eighty-four.[6] For the latter, we are fortunate to possess an almost complete list of its members thanks to a diary kept by the embassy's supplies provider, Johann Caspar Anton Hammerschmid.[7]

2 Family Members

The different delegations at Carlowitz were families in the literal sense as well since most ambassadors have brought with them closer or more distant relatives. Paget was accompanied by his brother, who, however, is described by the Anonymous Venetian as 'mentally retarded' (*di mente debole, e legiera*).[8] Colyer also travelled with his brother, Alexander, and young nephew, Pietro de la Fontaine.[9] Ruzzini had in his retinue his nephew, too, Domenico.[10] In Voznitsyn's suite, one encounters two relatives of his, Andrei and Ivan Voznitsyn.[11] Mavrocordatos kept alongside him his cousin, who, apparently, was also performing the role of his private secretary.[12] Although we don't have any evidence, we could justifiably guess that Rāmī could equally have brought with him members of his immediate family. That this could have been the case is inferred from the previous Ottoman embassy in Vienna in 1688, when the then-first plenipotentiary of the Porte, Zülfikār Efendi, was accompanied by Muṣṭafā Beg, his brother's son and ʿAbdī Çelebi, his brother-in-law.[13] The presence of family members is perhaps justified by the need for the ambassadors to have reliable people around them. However, it also presented – especially for young relatives – a unique opportunity for apprenticeship in the intricacies of the *ars tractandi*.

4 Poumarède, *L'Empire de Venise*, 284.
5 Bogoslovskii, *Petr I*, 346–7.
6 Ludwig, 'Memoiren', 26–38.
7 Ibid.
8 *Narratio*, fol. 12r.
9 Ibid.; Horo Siccama, 'De Vrede van Carlowitz', 143, fn. 1. Later, he was joined at the congress venue by yet another nephew, Justinus Constantinus de Hochepied (ibid.).
10 *Narratio*, fol. 11v.
11 Bogoslovskii, *Petr I*, 346–7.
12 ÖStA, HHStA, Türkei I, Turcica Box 170, Diarium et Cerimoniale, fol. 38. He could be identified with Antonaki Kremiti (Antonakis Keremitis?), who also accompanied Mavrocordatos during his 1688–92 embassy in Vienna: Hurmuzaki, *Documente*, vol. 5, part 1, 210. Unfortunately, I couldn't find more information on Kremiti/Keremitis.
13 Ibid.

3 Noblemen

A peace congress was a memorable event worthy of someone claiming that he had participated in it, even as an observer. Noblemen were such a category. Their presence enhanced the magnificence and display of the embassy in general and the ambassador in particular.[14] As with family kin, most of the Carlowitz delegations contained several aristocrats. Together with Ruzzini and his nephew, also travelled the Venetian nobles Almorò Pisani and Francesco Manà Pecovi (?).[15] Voznitsyn was joined by the nobleman Vladimir Borzov, who had arrived in Vienna from Moscow a little before the ambassador's departure for the congress venue with presents for the emperor's court.[16] Paget brought with him 'two English Gentlemen; one from Aleppo, and the other from Tripoli'.[17] The Imperial embassy was accompanied, besides Count Marsigli, by three other nobles: 1) Heinrich Johann Franz von Strattmann (d. 1707),[18] son of the powerful Imperial Chancellor Theodor von Strattmann (d. 1693), 2) Count Sulm,[19] and 3) Otto Ferdinand the Younger, Count Abensperg/Traun (d. 1748).[20]

We should note that noblemen were not always acting as simple bystanders but could perform more obscure roles as well. The case of the two Venetian aristocrats in the retinue of Jacob Colyer, Onigo and Bartolini, who, according to Count Schlik, were acting as spies for Carlo Ruzzini in the Dutch mediator's camp, is quite an illustrative one.[21]

4 The Secretary

Among the most vital components of an embassy was its secretary, one of its most multifarious and multitasking members and also the composer and manager of some of its most cardinal paperwork. His significant position in

14 Croxton, *Westphalia*, 135–6.
15 *Narratio*, fol. 7ᵛ–8ʳ, 13ᵛ.
16 Bogoslovskii, *Petr I*, 347.
17 Quoted in O'Quinn, *Engaging the Ottoman Empire*, 69.
18 Strattmann was also the one to carry the news of the conclusion of the peace treaties to Vienna after the signing ceremony of 26 January 1699: ÖStA, HHStA, Türkei I, Turcica Box 170, Diarium et Cerimoniale, fol. 82.
19 Perhaps Count Karl Theodor Otto zu Salm (d. 1710).
20 Ludwig, 'Memoiren', 26.
21 ÖStA, HHStA, Türkei I, Turcica Box 168, Folder 2 (November 1698, 2nd half), fol. 307ᵛ–308ʳ, Schlik to Kinsky, 18 November 1698. Onigo was also the one to deliver Israel Conegliano's letter to Mavrocordatos during the initial phase of the congress, *see* above, Act II, Narration Part II.

early modern diplomacy has recently attracted increased historiographical attention.[22] Secretaries were usually not members of the aristocracy – at least in nobility-based polities – but, in most cases, well-trained functionaries holding higher or lower positions inside their respective bureaucracies.[23]

Secretary of the Venetian embassy was Gian Battista Nicolosi, also holding the same position in the Venetian Senate, who was not only added to the Carlowitz delegation because of the importance of the congress but also because of his prior knowledge of the geography and topography of the Morea.[24] Count Marsigli describes Nicolosi as a 'solid man' (*omo sodo*) and a 'great friend' of the resident Venetian ambassador at the Imperial Court, Francesco Loredano.[25] Firdevsī Efendi, one of the scribes of the Imperial Council (*Dīvān-ı Hümāyūn*), performed secretarial duties in the Ottoman embassy.[26] Unfortunately, nothing more is known about him.[27] Secretary of the Imperial embassy was Johannes Till, a member of the War Council (*Hofkriegsrat*); the same position was held in the Commonwealth's delegation by Andrzej Gorkowski. Lord Paget's, and de facto mediation's secretary was, of course, the by now famous Georg Philipp Schreyer von Wegmar (d. 1701), of German origin, whose pivotal role as a courier of all the essential messages and liaison between the mediators and the allied side during the phase of the Preliminaries and the first part of the congress we have already discussed.

The Muscovite case is more perplexing. Voznitsyn had six secretaries in total: Postnikov, Volkov, Rodostamov, Larionov, Chencov and Buslaev.[28] The first appears to have held the leading position among them, with the Muscovite plenipotentiary referring to him as the "embassy's secretary" (*sekretar' posol'stva*).[29] Thus, Postnikov was combining two roles, being at the same time the delegation's primary interpreter. Still, since he could not perform both

22 For example, Florian Kühnel and Christine Vogel (eds.), *Zwischen Domestik und Staatsdiener. Botschaftssektretäre in den frühneuzeitlichen Außenbeziehungen* (Cologne/Weimar/Vienna: Böhlau 2021).

23 Florian Kühnel, Christine Vogel, 'Frühneuzeitliche Botschaftssekretäre zwischen Domestik und Staatsdiener', in Kühnel and Vogel, *Domestik und Staatsdiener*, 18–21.

24 *Narratio*, fol. 13^{v}. He accompanied Francesco Marosini during the Venetian conquest of the peninsula: ÖStA, HHStA, Türkei I, Turcica Box 168, Folder 2 (November 1698, 2nd half), fol. 294^{v}–295^{r}, Marsigli to Kinsky, 28 November 1698.

25 Ibid., fol. 294^{v}.

26 Defterdar, *Zübde-i Vekayiât*, 673.

27 However, it is highly probable that he is the same person who, in 1718 – at an old age by that point – was again acting as secretary to the Ottoman delegation during the Peace Congress of Passarowitz: Ercan, *Pasarofça Antlaşması*, 181–2.

28 Bogoslovskii, *Petr I*, 347.

29 *Pamiatniki*, 466.

of them at once during the conferences, the protocol was kept by Mikhail Rodostamov.[30] As for the tasks of the other four, they remain vague.

Like the various plenipotentiaries, a secretary had to possess both specific virtues and knowledge. For instance, in the Imperial decree appointing him as secretary of the Habsburg embassy, Johannes Till was praised for 'his good qualities, dexterity and acquired experience in both political and military matters'.[31] Additionally, secretaries had to be deeply trustworthy as the only individuals apart from the ambassadors to attend both official and unofficial meetings and gain complete knowledge of the proceedings. Most likely, they received extensive training in their respective chanceries, becoming highly skilled in drafting diplomatic documents and mastering diplomatic vocabulary and practices.[32] Nevertheless, as with the plenipotentiaries, current scholarship debates whether the role of the embassy secretary underwent gradual professionalization during the early modern period or remained shaped by ad hoc nominations influenced by patronage.[33] What is certain, however, is that a secretary had to be multitalented to successfully manage the diverse responsibilities assigned during the congress.

One of the principal tasks was to keep the protocol of the conferences.[34] This meant that he needed to have possessed essential skills in that sphere, such as sufficient knowledge of the negotiated matters as much as to have been exceptionally well versed in stenography – although he often re-worked the notes he kept during the meeting after it.[35] 'Next to us', recounted the Imperial ambassadors, describing the spatial arrangement of their first conference with the Ottomans, "sat at a small table the embassy's secretary. In the same way, at another small table behind the English mediator, the English secretary. And

30 Bogoslovskii, *Petr I*, 395.

31 ÖStA, HHStA, Türkei I, Turcica Box 166, Folder 2 (September 1698, 1st half), fol. 26r.

32 For the Venetian case, for instance, *see*, Andrea Zannini, 'Una buracrazia repubblicana. Stato e amministrazione a Venezia tra XVI e XVIII secolo', in Gherardo Ortalli, Oliver Jens Schmitt and Ermanno Orlando (eds.), *Il Commonwealth Veneziano tra 1204 e la fine della Repubblica. Identità e peculiarità* (Venice: Instituto Veneto di Scienze, Lettere ed Arti, 2015) 141–3.

33 Kühnel and Vogel, 'Botschaftssekretäre', 26–8; Hillard von Thiessen, 'Kommentar: Spezialisten und Multitalente. Befunde, Kontroversen und Forschungspespektiven zu Sekretären in der frühneuzeitlichen Diplomatie', in Kühnel and Vogel, *Domestik und Staatsdiener*, 224–40.

34 Maria-Elisabeth Brunert, 'Vom Rapular zum Dictatum. Entstehungsstufen der reichständischen Protokolle', in Gerstenberg, *Verständigung und Diplomatie*, 210.

35 Ibid., 211–3, 215–6.

behind the Turkish embassy(sic) stood, in the beginning, and then seated on the floor, the Turkish secretary, all of them keeping together the protocol".[36]

The various protocols constitute a truly unique source for any early modern congress since they are the only documents through which we can get as close as possible to the original conversations during the meetings, to hear the participants' voices 'live'.[37] Yet, this 'vivacity' provided by them is often an illusory one, since they do not record the participants themselves but rather their words as they were vehiculated through the secretaries' plume, and not all of their arguments and speeches, but only those the latter thought worthy, or appropriate to record. Thus, in a sense, the protocol is similarly 'constructed' the same way the ambassadors' letters or relations are. This is not independent of the fact that, similarly to the latter two, the protocol was customarily sent back to the court to provide the ruler or his chief ministers with a 'vivid' picture of the talks and to act as a 'monument in posterity' of the embassy's good conduct.[38] Ruzzini encapsulated exactly this selective character of the protocol by giving – most probably himself – as a title to a copy of the notes Nicolosi kept during the meetings, the following: 'Some discourses of the conferences collected by Nicolosi. However, not the totality of all the circumstances, argumentations, or conducts'.[39] And yet, despite their apparent partiality and incompleteness, the protocols often include, by the conscious or unconscious choice of their composers, quite intriguing and often entertaining 'congress anecdotes';[40] 'anecdotes' that can reveal exciting aspects and details of the broader culture of the period as of the everyday life during the negotiations that typically other sources do not generally include.[41]

Apart from keeping the protocol, a secretary was often tasked with stylistically perfecting the draft of the different versions of the Peace Instrument or, on

36 ÖStA, HHStA, Türkei I, Turcica Box 170, Diarium et Cerimoniale, fol. 14r (of the separate journal regarding the congress ceremonial).

37 For the issue of protocol keeping in the early modern period in general and in early modern congress in particular (Westphalia), as well as its valuable character and hidden traps for the historian, *see* Brunert, 'Vom Rapular zum Dictatum', 201–23 and eadem, 'Nonverbale Kommunikation als Faktor frühneuzeitlicher Friedensverhandlungen. Eine Untersuchung am Beispiel des Westfälischen Friedenskongresses', in Kampmann et al., *L'art de la paix*, 323.

38 Ibid., 292; Brunert, 'Vom Rapular zum Dictatum', 207–9.

39 BNM, Ms.it VII 399 (2625), fol. 294r, Alcuni discorsi delle Conferenze raccolti dal Nicolosi.

40 Brunert, 'Nonverbale Kommunikation', 293. Remember the exchange between Mavrocordatos and Małachowski on the merits of having a mistress or Schlik's 'stomach evacuation'.

41 For instance, it is mainly through the protocols that we know that coffee was served during the small pauses of the meetings.

other occasions, checking its language instead of the interpreters or together with them.[42] Nor did Secretaries act merely as scribes.[43] Some of them, like Nicolosi, Gorkowski or Postnikov, played a significant role in the negotiations themselves, combining the role of the bearer of their ambassadors' messages with that of a negotiator in their own right.[44] Nicolosi, especially, tried many times in his private conversations with Marsigli to win him over to the Venetian side by sometimes, as we saw, even voicing views that ran contrary to the official ones promoted by Ruzzini, and he actively participated in the crucial for the Serenissima's negotiation 'informal' Imperial–Venetian sessions during the last phase of the congress.[45] Johannes Till was also assigned, besides Marsigli, to reconcile the Poles and the Muscovites during their friction over ceremonial precedence.[46] Secretaries could also represent their masters in courtesy visits. While in Buda, after receiving as guests a group of Polish nobles sent by Małachowski to greet him, Voznitsyn replied by dispatching to the Pole Mikhail Rodostamov together with one of his interpreters, Peter Wolf.[47] They formed quite a numerous social group at the Carlowitz Congress because, apart from the principal secretary related to the embassy as a whole, each ambassador had their private one as well. For example, Ruzzini brought with him 'his usual secretary Colombo',[48] and the same was done by Count Öttingen, who was also accompanied by a personal scribe.[49] This double secretarial presence creates some complex issues for the researcher, however.

Late seventeenth-century treatises on the office of the ambassador – Western European in their majority – made a clear distinction between the private secretary of an ambassador and the secretary of the embassy, the first

42 Cernovodeanu, 'Le journal', 334, 352; ÖStA, HHStA, Türkei I, Turcica Box 170, Diarium et Cerimoniale, fol. 71–72.

43 Kühnel and Vogel, 'Botschaftssekretäre', 21–5; Croxton, *Westphalia*, 157.

44 For example, it was Johannes Till that informed Voznitsyn of the order each of the allies was to negotiate with the Ottomans: Bogoslovskii, *Petr I*, 389. Similarly, as we have seen, the Polish secretary Andrzej Gorkowski was tasked by Małachowski to visit the Moscovite and the Venetian ambassador at the beginning of December 1698 to solicit help for the Commonwealth's negotiations with the Ottomans and gather information on the status of the Muscovite negotiations.

45 ÖStA, HHStA, Türkei I, Turcica Box 168, Folder 1 (November 1698, 1st half), fol. 307^{r}, protocol of the conference held on 7 January 1699.

46 Ludwig, 'Memoiren', 36. He was also the one to deliver the allied plenipotentiaries' credentials to the mediators and receive the Ottoman ones in return: Ibid.

47 Bogoslovskii, *Petr I*, 361. On another occasion, in the last days of the congress, Postnikov and Rodostamov were sent together with gifts to the Ottoman and Imperial ambassadors and the mediators: Ibid., 435.

48 *Narratio*, 13^{v}.

49 Ludwig, 'Memoiren', 38.

being his 'valet', a member of his household, while the second 'his controller', answering only to the prince.[50] The situation in practice appears to have been far more complex, though. For instance, while secretaries like Till and Nicolosi were directly appointed by the Habsburg emperor or the Venetian Senate, respectively, others, like Schreyer, incorporated both functions (private and embassy secretary), and the exact status of others, like Gorkowski or Postnikov, is challenging to determine.[51]

The case of the Ottoman embassy poses a similar problem. Firdevsī Efendi is described as being employed as a scribe in the Imperial Council. Thus, apparently, he was not Rāmī's private secretary.[52] However, there is no mention of him in the latter's relation and in Christian sources. It is not at all clear if the 'secretary of the Efendi', who was often sent on compliment visits to the allied embassies together with Mavrcordatos' cousin, was Firdevsī or someone else.[53] Still, during the discussion between the Ottoman and Imperial delegations regarding the 'protocol' of the exchange of the treaties ratified respectively by the sultan and the emperor, when the Habsburg ambassadors proposed that the person to effectuate it from their side be the embassy's secretary and demanded from the Ottomans to choose a person 'of similar status and title' (*di simile carico e carattere*), Mavrocordatos designated 'our secretary' (*il nostro secretario*), implying thus that Firdevsī Efendi may have indeed enjoyed a position analogous to that of Till or Nicolosi.[54]

5 Interpreters

The topic of early modern interpreters has gained much currency these past two decades, mostly under the influence of the 'New Diplomatic History' as well as the relatively novel trend of 'Early Modern Global Diplomatic History'. Interpreters are portrayed as the 'cultural brokers', the 'go-betweens' and 'trans-imperial subjects' par excellence. The essential bridges that facilitated the intercultural encounters of a 'global early modernity'.[55] However, despite

50 Kühnel and Vogel, 'Botschaftssekretäre', 9–10.

51 Although the fact that the former was tasked (or undertook himself) to write a relation of the negotiations attests that he might have a status similar to the Imperial and Venetian ones.

52 Although Rāmī, as *Re'isü'l-küttāb*, was actually his 'boss'.

53 For instance, ÖStA, HHStA, Türkei I, Turcica Box 170, Diarium et Cerimoniale, fol. 38.

54 ÖStA, HHStA, Türkei I, Turcica Box 170, Protocollum, fol. 197.

55 The existing literature is extensive; here, I provide only a few representative examples: E. Nathalie Rothman, *The Dragoman Renaissance. Diplomatic Interpreters and the Routes*

the growing interest in the topic as well as in that concerning the problems of translation during early modern congresses, apart from a few scattered references here and there, an extensive study on the presence, social and educational background, role, and functions of the interpreters in the latter, remains hitherto a huge research desideratum.[56] Carlowitz is from this point a quite interesting research case study, since despite the relatively minor role most, but not all, of the interpreters finally came to play in the actual negotiations, it nonetheless illustrates their indispensability for the various embassies, an indispensability closely related to the multiple tasks they expected to perform in a peace congress.

Just like secretaries, interpreters were omnipresent at Carlowitz. According to the Anonymous Venetian, almost every embassy had one or more.[57] For some – the Ottoman ones, for instance – we are not given any further information. Let us start by introducing, though, those whom we know relatively well, beginning with the Imperial side. The Habsburg delegation had two interpreters, Johann Adam Lachowitz (or Lachewitz) (d. 1709) and Michael Talmann. Both were direct 'products' of the reorganisation of the Imperial translating service in the second half of the seventeenth century, with the establishment in 1674 of a College of Oriental Languages in Vienna under the supervision of Johann Baptist Podestà and the appointment to the office of the Chief Interpreter of the *Hofkriegsrat* of François de Mesgnien, alias Meninski (d. 1698?), the author of the famous dictionary, *Thesaurus Linguarum Orientalium*, encountered many times throughout these pages.[58] After studying at the College of Oriental Languages, Lachowitz was sent to Constantinople to

of Orientalism (Ithaca/London: Cornell University Press, 2021); Anna Busquets, 'Three Manila-Fujian Diplomatic Encounters: Different Aims and Different Embassies in the Seventeenth Century'. *Journal of Early Modern History* 23 (2019), 442–57; Maartje van Gelder and Tijana Krstić, 'Introduction: Cross-Confessional Diplomacy and Diplomatic Intermediaries in the Early Modern Mediterranean'. *Journal of Early Modern History* 19 (2015), 93–105.

56 Braun, 'Les problèmes de communication', 193–4.

57 *Narratio*, fol. 11^{r}, 12^{r-v}, 13^{v}–14^{r}. No information is provided for the Polish embassy. However, according to Count Schlik, on 14 December, the secretary of the Polish embassy, Andrzej Gorkowski, visited Mavrocordatos 'to work [with him] on the translation of his [peace] articles': ÖStA, HHStA, Türkei I, Turcica Box 170, Diarium et Cerimoniale, fol. 49–50. Did Gorkowski know Ottoman Turkish and, like Postnikov, serve as both embassy secretary and interpreter, or did he bring an interpreter with him whom Schlik does not mention? Unfortunately, as we lack sufficient evidence, this intriguing question cannot be answered.

58 Dóra Kerekes, 'A Császári Tolmácsok a Magyarországi Visszafoglialó Háborúk Idején'. *Századok* 138/5 (2004), 1199–1202.

complete his language training at the Imperial embassy there. He was admitted as a regular interpreter in the Imperial service in 1682. From 1684–87, he was appointed interpreter of the Imperial army in Hungary and followed the troops in their campaigns.[59] He played a crucial role during the 1688–91 Vienna negotiations as the link between the Ottoman embassy and the Imperial government. As for Talmann, he entered the service as an Imperial interpreter in 1691. In 1692–93, he accompanied the Dutch mediator Coenraad van Heemskerck in his embassy to the Ottoman capital for the then-peace talks, and in 1697, he was also appointed interpreter of the army in Hungary.[60]

The Venetian embassy also had two interpreters, Gian Rinaldo Carli and Alvise Fortis, both of whom originated from prominent Levantine dragoman households.[61] As for the first, his family came from Istria. He entered the Venetian service as a 'novice dragoman' (*Giovane di Lingua*) around 1670, and by 1677, he was 'Public Drangoman' (*Dragomano Pubblico*) of the *Provveditore Generale* of Dalmatia. He was transferred to Constantinople at the beginning of the 1680s to help the chief dragoman of the Venetian resident embassy with his work. At some point after the start of the Sixteen Years' War, he returned to Venice. In 1691, he was sent to Vienna to assist the Serenissima's ambassador there with the then ongoing and ultimately failed peace negotiations.[62]

We have left for the end, perhaps, the most prominent among the Carlowitz interpreters, Petr Postnikov. He was born in Moscow in 1676, a son of an official of the *Posol'ski Prikaz*.[63] He received his first letters in the Slavic-Greek-Latin Academy established in Moscow by the Greek Lichoudis brothers, where he took lessons in rhetoric, Greek, Latin, logic and physics.[64] When he graduated, profiting from Peter I's efforts to send gifted young Russians to European universities in order to acquire knowledge of what the tsar regarded as the western European scientific breakthroughs, Postnikov travelled to Italy in the spring of 1692 to continue his studies at the University of Padua.[65] While there, he also learned and perfected his Italian and French.[66]

59 Ibid., 1222–1223; Hajnalka Tóth, 'Harminc év Habsburg-Szolgálatban. Betekintés Johann Adam Lachowitz török tolmács áldozatos munkájába (1678–1709)'. *Fons* 26/1 (2019), 42–54.

60 Kerekes, 'Czászári Tolmácsok', 1226.

61 Miović, 'Diplomatic Relations', 193.

62 G. Paladino, 'Due dragomanni veneti a Costantinopoli (Tommaso Tarsia e Gian Rinaldo Carli)'. *Nuovo Archivio Veneto* 17/33 (1917), 193–198.

63 Iser Steiman, 'P.V. Posnikov: A Russian Pioneer in Physiology'. *Canadian Slavonic Revue/Revue Canadienne des Slavistes* 7 (1965), 65.

64 Natal'ia Nikolaevna Zapol'skaia. 'Postnikov P.V. – vypusknik Slaviano-greko-latinskoi Akademii (novye materialy dlia biografii)'.*Cyrillomethodia-num* 12 (1988), 76–79.

65 Ibid., 81.

66 Ibid., 82.

In 1695, he was awarded a doctorate in Philosophy and Medicine and a year later, he travelled to the Dutch Republic for what could be considered an early modern 'post-doc' at the University of Leiden.[67] During the time he stayed in Italy and then during his journeys in western Europe to perfect his medical knowledge, Postnikov kept a regular correspondence with the tsar, informing him of the situation there.[68] Such an informer's task could be considered a prelude to his latter involvement in diplomatic affairs. Petr Vasil'evich took part in Peter I's 'Grand Embassy' in the double role of interpreter and procurator of medical potions, and in the spring of 1698, on the orders of the tsar, he travelled to Venice to prepare the ground for Peter's journey there, which was not finally effectuated.[69]

Nonetheless, the Muscovite ambassador didn't rely solely on Postnikov's translation services. He brought two other interpreters with him as well: Peter Wolf, probably of German origin, who was also employed for the 'Grand Embassy',[70] and Ivan Zekan, a young Habsburg subject of Slavic origin who had recently entered the Muscovite service in Vienna.[71] Only Postnikov was present at the conferences, however.[72]

As one might plausibly guess, one of the principal and diachronic tasks of an interpreter was to assist his employer during the negotiations, acting as the communication channel between him and his interlocutor. At Carlowitz, this was not, for the most part, necessary, though. 'There was no need for interpreters', explained the anonymous Venetian account, 'thanks to Mavrocordatos speaking Italian perfectly and conversing with the ambassador [Carlo Ruzzini] whenever there was need, explaining then everything in Turkish to his companion the Reis Efendi'.[73] Only Voznitsyn, possessing knowledge of no other language than his own, found himself in constant need to have Postnikov by his side. Hence, the first time the Imperial interpreters were present in a conference was on 30 December 1698,[74] almost two months after the official talks between the sides had begun, and their primary task then was not to participate in the negotiations per se – those they had been essentially concluded by that point – but to assist the two Habsburg plenipotentiaries in a different way.

67 Ibid.
68 Ibid., 83.
69 Ibid., 84.
70 Ibid.
71 Bogoslovskii, *Petr I*, 347.
72 Ibid., 395.
73 *Narratio*, fol. 20^{r-v}.
74 Cernovodeanu, 'Le journal', 341–2.

Not being necessary to act as a communication medium, the majority of the interpreters during the Congress of Carlowitz applied their expertise in the highly important matter of meticulously checking the Ottoman texts of the separate articles or the final Peace Instruments and verifying that their content was similar to the copies in Latin or Italian. Some examples include: on 13 December, after the de facto end of the first and most crucial round of talks between the Imperial and the Ottoman delegations, the latter sent to the former an Ottoman version of the peace articles agreed thus far, and the text was examined by one of the interpreters.[75] After Paget and Mavrocordatos drafted the Latin text of the Ottoman–Muscovite two-year truce/armistice, 'they gave it to Dr. Postnikov. And the doctor read it and said: All is in order'.[76]

Despite Postnikov's translation talents, though, Voznitsyn's embassy was lacking a vital asset: someone who could read Ottoman Turkish. Therefore, to be able to verify the similarity of the Latin and Ottoman text of his agreement with the sultan's plenipotentiaries, he was obliged to hire Lachowitz from the Imperial embassy, who provided a Latin translation of it.[77] It was Lachowitz's translation of the Ottoman original that was subsequently checked against the Latin translation provided earlier by Mavrocordatos.[78] Therefore, Voznitsyn had to rely exclusively on the Imperial interpreter's trustworthiness. He had to request his services again during the signing ceremony to check the Ottoman text once more, while his other two interpreters examined the Ottoman Latin copy of it.[79]

Diligent and minute examination of the peace articles to verify their similar content in the main languages in which they were written was considered of paramount significance for the participants. Hence, the role of interpreters in doing that correctly and trustworthily was pivotal. A slight disparity in the different texts could lead to different interpretations and create serious future problems. Following the secretary of the Imperial embassy, Johannes Till, the last conference between Małachowski and the Ottoman delegation was entirely devoted to the adjustment of 'differences that arose regarding expressions in Turkish made somewhat different from those in Latin'.[80] The Polish side's insistence was justified against the following precedent. As we

75 ÖStA, HHStA, Türkei I, Turcica Box 170, Diarium et Cerimoniale, fol. 49.
76 Quoted in Bogoslovskii, *Petr I*, 415.
77 Ibid., 416.
78 Ibid., 417.
79 Ibid., 426.
80 ÖStA, HHstA, Türkei I, Turcica Box 170, Protocollum, fol. 119.

previously saw, the Commonwealth–Ottoman peace agreement of 1621 was concluded after a war with no clear winner. The Ottoman side benefited from the maze created by the different levels of communication and translation between the representatives of the two sides (during the talks, each sentence had to pass from Polish to Rumanian, then to Greek and finally to Ottoman Turkish and all the other way around) to insert in its own Peace Instrument an article according to which the Commonwealth's ambassador to be sent to the Porte for the confirmation of the treaty was to pay a *pişkeş* (a 'present') or tribute, as the Ottomans might have interpreted it, something that of course was missing from the Polish version of the text.[81]

We should notice, though, that the close examination of the peace articles was often used as a delaying technique by some of the congress participants. For instance, in December 1698, to win time, the Imperial embassy resorted to the stratagem of supposedly fixing the language of the articles to keep the Ottomans in the congress venue without raising their suspicions.[82]

As cardinal a task as the collation of the different texts of the treaties might have been, the interpreters' routine during the congress did not solely revolve around it. Like the secretaries, they were also used to perform certain ceremonial functions (compliment visits) with other embassies instead of the ambassador himself.[83] Interpreters could also be valuable in other everyday instances. Since, as we saw, the wooden house for the congress conferences was jointly built by Ottoman and Imperial masons and workers, one of the two Habsburg interpreters had to accompany the Imperial engineer, Hollstein, to help him communicate with his Ottoman colleagues.[84]

If these were the typical tasks of an interpreter during the Congress of Carlowitz, two genuinely unique examples escape the norm. The first is Petr Postnikov. Because of Voznitsyn's inability to communicate directly with his interlocutors, his role in being the one who primarily conducted the formal and informal negotiations with Mavrocordatos on behalf of his master was catalytic. He also represented the Muscovite ambassador in significant dealings with his other allies. For instance, he was the one who was sent during a critical moment of the negotiations to remind the Imperial ambassadors of their obligations towards Muscovy.[85]

81 Kołodziejczyk, 'La res publica polono-lituanienne', 132–4.

82 ÖStA, HHStA, Türkei I, Turcica Box 170, Diarium et Cerimoniale, fol. 52–53.

83 Bogoslovskii, *Petr I*, 361; *Narratio*, 55ʳ.

84 Ludwig, 'Memoiren', 37.

85 Bogoslovskii, *Petr I*, 411.

The second is Mavrocordatos. Although he held an ambassadorial position, he simultaneously fulfilled the function of 'Chief Interpreter' of the Ottoman embassy. A typical procedure during the conferences would be that the second Ottoman plenipotentiary would listen to the arguments of his interlocutor(s). Then he would report them *de nouveau* to Rāmī Meḥmed in Ottoman Turkish. Then, if the 'Efendi' wanted to intervene directly with a response, this had to pass again through the 'Mavrcordatos medium'.[86] Such a procedure ostensibly gave the second Ottoman plenipotentiary great power in determining what to pass over to his colleague and what to re-transmit to the other side. However, there were certain restrictions since Mavrocordatos was not the only one who could understand and speak Christian European languages and Ottoman Turkish in the conference room. That was also the case for the Dutch mediator Jacob Colyer. In a heated Ottoman–Venetian session with the presence of the Imperial ambassadors in early January 1699, Rāmī became so angry, even shouting, that Mavrocordatos had to use all his persuasive techniques to calm him down. After the meeting, Colyer confided to the Habsburg plenipotentiaries that the second Ottoman ambassador 'had translated not even half of [what the Efendi had really said] against us'.[87] Thus, Mavrocordatos was not free to translate at his whim, and as a juxtaposition of the Ottoman and allied protocols may attest, the messages were conveyed almost accurately.[88]

Besides assuming the de facto role of the interpreter during the talks,[89] the Ottoman ambassador was also the one to translate the agreed articles from Latin into Ottoman Turkish and to diligently examine the languages of the Peace Instruments.[90] His attempt to imitate as faithfully as possible the

86 *See* for instance, BNM, Ms.it.VII 399(8625), fol. 294ᵛ, Alcuni discorsi delle Conferenze raccolti dal Nicolosi.

87 ÖStA, HHStA, Türkei I, Turcica Box 171, Folder 1 (January 1699, 1st half), fol. 88ʳ, Imperial plenipotentiaries to Leopold I, 5 January 1699. In other instances, Rāmī Meḥmed communicated directly with the Dutch in Ottoman Turkish to convey his views to the mediators. For example, in the protocol he kept of one of the Ottoman–Venetian conferences, Nicolosi recorded: "L'Effendi sotto voce discorre col Med[iator]e Olandese in Turco; Il mediatore si lascò per communicar il discorso à Paget": BNM, Ms.it.VII 399(8625), fol. 308ᵛ, Alcuni discorsi delle Conferenze raccolti dal Nicolosi.

88 Compare, for instance, the passages from the first Imperial–Ottoman conference regarding the border-making procedures in ÖStA, HHStA, Türkei I, Turcica Box 170, Protocollum, fol. 9–10 and *Taʿrīḥ-i ṣulḥnāme*, fol. 82ᵃ.

89 Count Schlik assumed a similar role to that of Mavrocordatos because Count Öttingen's meagre knowledge of Italian – the main linguistic medium during the negotiations between them – didn't allow him to directly participate in the discussion: Ruzzini, *Relazione*, 377. However, we don't know if Schlik was also translating the discussions to him or if he could at least sufficiently understand the conversation.

90 Cernovodeanu, 'Le journal', 337; Bogoslovskii, *Petr I*, 426.

Ottoman writing style in his Latin translations, or perhaps the influence one language exerted through the prolonged use of the other, sometimes resulted in derisive comments from some of the other participants. Receiving a second clarification letter from the Ottoman embassy on 9 November 1698 regarding the issue of Transylvania, Schlik commented in his 'Secret Journal': 'One cannot but notice here, that [with] all these concepts filled with phrases from Arabic, Herr Mavrocordatos's Latin look quite similar to the writing style of the Quran'.[91] Equally, after so many years of service as Chief Interpreter of the Porte, Mavrocordatos's writing manner was so well-known as to be immediately recognised. 'While we were reading the draft of the projected articles', Emperor Leopold I notified his ambassadors, 'we [...] noticed they are composed in the style of Mavrocordatos'.[92]

6 Special Advisers

As border-making was one of the most paramount matters for all negotiating parties, and the plenipotentiaries' expertise on the topic was limited, there was a need for 'special advisers' to be included in the embassy who, with their knowledge of the geography of specific regions, would assist the ambassadors in their work. One of the most prominent of these was undoubtedly Count Luigi Marsigli.[93] In his years of Imperial service, the *Bolognese* managed to win a reputation for himself as an authority in matters relating to the geography of the Habsburg–Ottoman frontier as well as for the protection he enjoyed of powerful court individuals, notably Count Kinsky.[94] When the 'Turkish Deputation' discussed in August 1698 the composition of the Imperial embassy to the upcoming congress, Marsigli's carefully constructed self-image and patronage networks paid off. As the ministers' relation to the emperor suggested,

> for the better arrangement of the borders, and consideration of which places Your Imperial Majesty should use, restitute, evacuate, demolish, or exchange, this side's plenipotentiaries [should be] provided with a person

91 ÖStA, HHStA, Türkei I, Turcica Box 170, Diarium et Cerimoniale, fol. 27.

92 ÖStA, HHStA, Türkei I, Turcica Box 168, Folder 2 (November 1698, 2nd half), fol. 214^r, supplementary Imperial instructions, 24 November 1698.

93 For the life and multifaceted interests of the Count, *see* Gherardi, *La politica* and John Stoye, *Marsigli's Europe 1680–1730. The Life and Times of Luigi Ferdinando Marsigli, Soldier and Virtuoso* (New Haven and London: Yale University Press 1994).

94 Ruzzini, *Relazione*, 377.

> versed in geography. And on this point, no one more suitable could be found than Colonel Marsigli, as he is a man of an unprejudiced mind.[95]

Of course, Marsigli's role at the congress was not confined to advising services. Although he did not participate in the official conferences with the Ottomans, only in the 'semi-official' ones between the Imperials and their allies,[96] he used his self-presentation as an 'unprejudicial mind' in issues of boundary-making to gain the confidence of the other allied ambassadors and gather information from them.[97]

His ambiguous position and higher aspirations than those of a simple 'Legationsrat' created tensions between him and the two Imperial ambassadors. Following Ruzzini,

> although the Imperial ambassadors showed an ostensible appreciation towards him and used his services for the connection and credit he had with Kinsky, in reality, they didn't like his assistance at all, and when they were thinking that they didn't have so much his need, then, they were treating him with superiority and little esteem.[98]

The *Bolognese* was well aware of this fact, and he strived hard on the way to the congress to win Öttingen's favour, in the same way he tried to do so later with the other allied ambassadors. 'He places in me not only simple confidence for the services to [our] master but also personal love, and I am not deprived of the hope to win him completely', he optimistically wrote to his patron on 23 September 1698 en route to the frontier.[99] If we are to believe Ruzzini's remarks, however, it appears that the first Imperial plenipotentiary ambassador was very competent in dissimulating his true feelings.

Despite the conflicting relationship between them, it was Marsigli whom the two plenipotentiaries sent to Vienna to convince the Imperial ministers and the emperor about the territorial arrangements they had decided in their

---

95 ÖStA, HHStA, Türkei I, Turcica Box 166, Folder 1 (August 1698), fol. 53^r, relation of the members of the 'Turkish Deputation' to Leopold I, 8 August 1698.

96 Ruzzini, *Relazione*, 377.

97 The Jesuit mediators during the Treaty of Nerchinsk (1689) similarly fashioned themselves as experts in geography and cartography to gain material and symbolic capital from both negotiating parties. In reality, however, they possessed no knowledge whatsoever of northern Siberia: Jaskov, 'Negotiated Geography', 64.

98 Ruzzini, *Relazione*, 378.

99 ÖStA, HHStA, Türkei I, Turcica Box 167, Folder 2 (October 1698, 2nd half), fol. 234^r, Marsigli to Kinsky, 23 September 1698.

conferences with the Ottomans. His services during the negotiations were duly appreciated at the court, which secured him the position of Inspector General of the Imperial Commission to arrange the new Habsburg–Ottoman border after the congress.[100]

Lastly, besides Nicolosi's expertise in the matters relating to the Morea, the Venetian embassy had a second expert, 'Signor Dottor [Lorenzo] Fondra, a man of virtue and experience, that is commissioned by the Public (*dal Publico*) to assist His Excellency in matters pertaining to the borders of Dalmatia', being himself a tax official of the province.[101]

7 Physicians and Priests

Having to endure a months' stay in the open field and some of them being of a certain age by the time of the congress, plenipotentiaries had to safeguard their health. The best way to do that was to have a physician in their entourage to take care of them if their services were needed. Thus, doctors figured prominently in almost every delegation.[102] The only embassy that appears not to have one was that of Muscovy. And despite the presence of Postnikov – to whom Schlik referred as we have seen as Voznitsyn's 'personal physician' – when the latter fell seriously ill in the final days of the congress due to a cerebral stroke, he had to appeal, as he had done with the interpreters, to the Imperial embassy to send him one of their own.[103] How important the presence of doctors turned out to be is manifested by the fact that a significant number of ambassadors were 'visited' by some form of disease or faced serious health issues during the negotiations.

As soon as he arrived at the congress venue, Lord Paget fell ill, and his indisposition was one of the main reasons it was decided to transfer all camps closer to one another since it would be hard for him to move long distances.[104] Already at the beginning of the official talks, Rāmī Meḥmed developed gastric problems that rendered him unable for a few days to attend any meetings. He fell ill for a second time in late January 1699. Following Count Schlik, as he was entering his carriage to attend the joint Ottoman–Imperial–Commonwealth

100 Gherardi, 'Scienza'.
101 *Narratio*, fol. 13^{v}. Fondra is descrided as 'Fiscale di quella Provincia': Ibid., fol. 33^{v} and Ruzzini, *Relazione*, 444.
102 *Narratio*, fol. 8^{v}, 11^{r}, 13^{v}.
103 Bogoslovskii, *Petr* I, 437; *Narratio*, fol. 49^{r}.
104 *Taʿrīḥ-i ṣulḥnāme*, fol. 69^{a}.

conference on 22 January on the issues of Venice, 'he was struck by a fever outburst' (*von einen fieber-access angegriffen worden*) and was obliged to remain in his tent.[105]

More severe was Małachowski's condition. Despite his relatively young age, even for late-seventeenth-century standards (thirty-nine), the Pole's health appears to have been very fragile, which could explain his decision to quickly relocate to Petrovaradin after the first outbreak of lousy weather. Things got worse for him towards the end of the congress. On a joint session with the Imperial, the Polish, and the Ottoman ambassadors on 22 January 1699 on the issues of Venice, he didn't feel well and almost fainted.[106] Writing to Karol Stanisław Radziwiłł the following day, he complained of 'the severe headache that mercilessly tortures me for the third day now', leaving him unable even to compose his letters by himself.[107] These were serious presages. He died some months after his return to the Commonwealth from the congress.

Besides the health of their body, ambassadors were equally preoccupied with that of their soul, bringing with them – the Christian ones – their private chaplains.[108] Nonetheless, physicians and priests were not only looking after their masters' physical and spiritual needs. Just like secretaries and interpreters, they could also perform various delicate tasks since they would not have aroused great suspicions because of their status – especially the priests. Israel Conegliano was secretly communicating with Mavrocordatos, and the latter also used his chaplain to deliver messages and conduct backstage negotiations with Voznitsyn on his behalf.[109] In his turn, the Muscovite had two priests in his entourage to perform different roles. His private one, Ivan, for his spiritual comfort,[110] and Archimandrite Gregory, entrusted with carrying confidential dispatches.[111]

---

105 ÖStA, HHStA, Türkei I, Turcica Box 170, Diarium et Cerimoniale, fol. 76.

106 *Narratio*, fol. 39ᵛ.

107 AGAD, Archiwum Warszawskie Radziwiłłów, 1/354/0/5/9200, fol. 50, Małachowski to Radziwiłł, 23 January 1699. I am deeply grateful to my colleague Jan Bloski for assisting me in translating this letter.

108 *Narratio*, fol. 8ᵛ, 11ʳ, 13ᵛ; Bogoslovskii, *Petr I*, 347; Ludwig, 'Memoiren', 38. Colyer also had with him a Calvinist pastor named Henricus Meerkens or Mierkens: Hora Siccama, 'De Vrede van Carlowitz', 143, fn. 1.

109 Bogoslovskii, *Petr I*, 403, 422.

110 Ibid., 346–7.

111 Gregory was abbot of the Serbian monastery of Rakovica near Belgrade: D. and I. Guzevich, *Velikoe posol'stvo*, 143. Apparently, Voznitsyn had already established contact with the Serbian Orthodox Patriarch, Arsenije III Crnojević (d. 1706), who at this point was residing in the area and was probably willing to assist in the secret talks taking place between the Muscovites and the Ottomans before the start of the official talks: Ibid., 383.

8 Postmen, Cooks, Provisioners, Hajduks, Servants and Others

Speaking of dispatches, an individual whose importance could be said to be as great as the one of the congress 'protagonists' was the postman or *ulaḳ*, in Ottoman-Turkish.[112] How quickly he could travel and how swiftly he could bring the resolutions of the different decision-making centres was of paramount significance for the peacemaking process at the congress venue. The postman had to be very trustworthy since he was carrying extremely sensitive documents and was instructed with their safety on the road. The Imperial embassy, which is the most well-documented, had a postmaster to handle its correspondence and one regular post-carrier – they could be raised to three if the need arose – all of them officers of the Imperial regiments camping around the congress venue.[113]

Another sine qua non component of an embassy was the cook. His presence in each delegation denoted the ambassadors' intense need to make themselves at ease while away from the conforms of their respective homes.[114] The Imperial kitchen personnel included four cooks and six assistants (three girls and three boys) as well as a confectioner so that the two plenipotentiaries, their entourage and their guests could enjoy a proper dessert even in the 'wilderness'.[115] Voznitsyn had equally brought with him five cooks, and the Ottomans had an unspecified number of them as well.[116] Of course, with the cooks and their assistants, one should not forget other essential individuals who were directly involved in earlier stages of this 'food-chain'. One of them was the provisioner, who, due to the scarce resources in the vicinity, had an enormous task to guarantee that the bellies of the members of the various embassies would stay filled.[117] The Imperial one, Johann Caspar Anton Hammerschmid, even left a journal of the embassy's journey all the way from Vienna to Carlowitz as well as of the opening phase of the congress (until 3 November 1698).[118] This journal constitutes a unique source as it provides an account of the events written from the viewpoint of a lesser member of a delegation.

The patriarch also paid a visit to the Imperial ambassadors on 22 October 1698 to discuss with them the affairs of his people: Ludwig, 'Memoiren', 34.

112 *Taʿrīḫ-i ṣulḥnāme*, fol. 120^{b}.

113 Ludwig, 'Memoiren', 38. Ruzzini also had two couriers for his messages: Poumarède, *L'Empire de Venise*, 284.

114 Croxton, *Westphalia*, 137.

115 Ludwig, 'Memoiren', 38.

116 Bogoslovskii, *Petr I*, 347; *Narratio*, fol. 54^{v}.

117 Croxton, *Westphalia*, 137.

118 Ludwig, 'Memoiren'.

An important accessory of almost all the Carlowitz embassies was the famous hajduks, the irregular infantry which thrived in central and south-eastern Europe during the early modern period.[119] Apart from forming traditionally an indispensable part of a nobleman's bodyguard, especially in the Polish-Lithuanian Commonwealth,[120] it appears that with their distinctive attires, they were adding an 'exotic touch' to the ambassadors' entourage, increasing thus its ostentatiousness. For instance, when ceremoniously crossing the river Save to arrive at Carlowitz, Paget, riding on horseback, was accompanied by his two interpreters and 'two Heydukes in their own Country Habit'.[121]

Another 'professional group' that could add ceremonial magnificence and provide entertainment to each delegation were the musicians. The Venetian embassy possessed trumpet players to accompany the ambassador in his official processions, and the Imperial one had four, two of them belonging to Count Strattmann. The Ottomans also had musicians and buffoons in their suite.[122]

At the bottom of the social hierarchy of the embassy, one founds the grooms, pages and other servants who comprised the bulk of its personnel. According to the Anonymous Venetian, the Serenissima's delegation included four pages and 10/50 (?) grooms (*staffieri*), while Rāmī Meḥmed alone had sixty-six of them.[123] Despite their meagre presence in the sources, their role in the upkeeping of the ambassadors and the other embassy members was vital. They exercised a variety of tasks: taking care of the horses and the carriages of the plenipotentiaries, serving their meals, accompanying them on official processions, and increasing their prestige and pomp with their numbers and their ostentatious clothes.

---

119 For instance, Voznitsyn had four of them (Bogoslovskii, *Petr I*, 347) and the Imperials six: Ludwig, 'Memoiren', 38.

120 Richard Brzezinski, *Polish Armies 1569–1696*, vol. 1 (London: Osprey Military Publishing 1987) 21, 39–41.

121 Quoted in O'Quinn, *Engaging the Ottoman Empire*, 69.

122 *Narratio*, fol. 8ᵛ, 52ʳ; Ludwig, 'Memoiren', 38.

123 *Narratio*, fol. 11ʳ, 13ᵛ.

Narration Part III: Meanwhile in Vienna ...

> It stands now in Your Imperial Majesty's [....] high interest [if] it's more beneficial [to make] peace on these conditions or to continue the war. And if [...] with these borders, Your lands are to be considered as sufficiently more safeguarded.
>
> Imperial plenipotentiaries to Leopold I[1]

•••

> I speak, write, make what I know and can do.[2]
>
> FRANCESCO LOREDANO to Carlo Ruzzini

⁘

1 'You Take It, or You Leave It'

When the first news of the results of the negotiations at Carlowitz reached the Imperial Court, they were met with irritation and indignation. The Imperial ministers were furious with the Ottoman interpretation of *uti possidetis*. Kinsky vehemently complained to the Dutch ambassador in Vienna about the 'weakness of the mediation' (*la foiblesse de la Mediation*) and reminded him that one of the latter's primary duties was to guarantee that 'the agreements and covenants are observed' (*ut pacta [et] coventa serventur*). If that was not going to happen and the congress would dissolve, 'it would not be us but they [the mediators] and the Turks who would have torn it apart'.[3]

As for the peace terms, the Imperial plenipotentiaries tried so hard to defend and present as 'glorious'[4] and as the only ones currently obtainable, 'I have only this to say', the Bohemian Chancellor wrote to Count Öttingen. 'If peace is concluded without ensuring free navigation on the Tisza and the Mureş,

---

1 ÖStA, HHstA, Türkei I, Turcica Box 168, Folder 2 (November 1698, 2nd half), fol. 22ᵛ–47ʳ, Imperial plenipotentiaries to Leopold I, 17 November 1698.

2 BNM, Ms.it.VII 399(8625), fol. 340ʳ, Loredano to Ruzzini, 10 December 1698.

3 ÖStA, HHStA, Türkei I, Turcica Box 168, Folder 2 (November 1698, 2nd half), fol. 219ʳ, Kinsky to Schlik, 25 November 1698.

4 Ibid., fol. 180ᵛ, Imperial plenipotentiaries to Leopold I, 23 November 1698.

DOI:10.1163/9789004458499_022

reserved exclusively for the emperor, it is certainly going to be a bad one'.[5] Whereas, in another letter to the Imperial plenipotentiary, he further added that concerning the borders in Slavonia and Croatia it was simply unacceptable that the Ottomans would demand evacuations and demolitions solely from the Imperial side without offering an equivalent in return, adding that according to the 'correct' interpretation of the preliminary agreement any concession was not to be made out of obligation but out of mutual convenience for both parties.[6] Not even the arguments of his plenipotentiaries regarding the 'Turkish stubbornness' seemed to have convinced the emperor, who demanded from them more outstanding efforts to implement his instructions.[7]

Nonetheless, the Imperial Court's insistence on a tougher stance on some negotiation issues, such as the navigation of rivers, apparently could not be harmonised with its simultaneous dire need to end the war and not lead the talks to a breaking point, something that the two plenipotentiaries spared no effort to convey in their dispatches. The negative climate only began to change with the arrival of Count Marsigli in Vienna, where, as we shall later see, he managed, by evoking his authority on matters of border-making, to convince the Imperial ministers and the emperor himself that the stipulated boundaries could result in a 'secure and honourable peace' (*sicher=und reputirlichen Frieden*), to use Kinsky's terms.[8]

However, the emperor continued not to be totally satisfied with the outcome of his ambassadors' negotiation. In a small note to Kinsky, dated 22 December 1698, he expressed the uneasiness the terms proposed by the Ottomans were continuing to cause to his mind as much as his inability to refuse them due to the greater imperative of peace: 'the border question upsets me when I see the Turks not to deploy well the principle of uti possidetis and to demand that I [should] give them back many [lands, fortresses etc.] which actually [translates in]: you take it, or you leave it (*Vogel friß oder stirb*)'.[9] Equivalently exhausted by the protracted conflict, with a new one looming ominously in western Europe and perhaps finally persuaded by his plenipotentiaries that there was no other way out, the emperor could not but grudgingly accept the deal.[10]

---

5 Ibid., fol. 215ʳ, Kinsky to Öttingen, 25 November 1698.

6 ÖStA, HHStA, Türkei I, Turcica Box 169, Folder 1 (December 1698, 1st half), fol. 58ᵛ–59ʳ, Kinsky to Öttingen, 4 December 1698.

7 Ibid., fol. 66ʳ, supplementary Imperial instructions, 5 December 1698.

8 Kinsky to Öttingen, 4 December 1698, fol. 58ᵛ.

9 Quoted in Laszlo and Seewann, *A karlócai béke és Európa*, XLIII.

10 According to the Bavarian resident representative at the Imperial Court, Hannibal Mörmann, even after the end of the congress, many on the Habsburg side claimed

Equally confused was the court's position regarding the process of the negotiation of the other Holy League members, especially Venice. Before the start of the official congress conferences, Kinsky had plainly stated to Count Schlik the indispensability of a 'common march' to peace with the Republic of Saint Mark, pointing out to him that the Imperial side could conclude its own agreement without the Commonwealth and Muscovy, 'but to do it without Venice, things could be more difficult, and they would merit greater consideration'.[11] The imperative for such 'greater consideration' came relatively quickly after the disappointing results of the first Venetian–Ottoman meeting. 'After I saw what the Turks practised with respect to the [implementation?] of the uti possidetis, I predicted that Venice might receive far, far harder [proposals]. And therefore, the good outcome of these negotiations is doubted here', the Bohemian Chancellor claimed in a letter to Count Marsigli.[12]

As the 'Venetian drama' started to unfold, the position of the emperor and his ministers on the matter began to manifest an ambivalence that would become even more enhanced as the congress progressed. The Imperial plenipotentiaries should provide the Serenissima 'with every possible assistance' on its territorial pretensions based upon the *uti possidetis*. However, if Venice was to pretend something *ultra fundamentum pacis* 'out of convenience and to achieve greater security', the two ambassadors had to remind their Venetian colleague of the difficulties to acquire with talks something that the Republic could not conquer through the force of arms (a great irony, since the Ottomans did exactly that), 'extensively explaining to him what concessions from this Foundation we have made for the love of peace, and urging him to advance his negotiation together with us'.[13] Such a statement, ostensibly the main result of the influence of the arguments made in the letters and relations of Marsigli and the plenipotentiaries was, of course, a massive blow to the Serenissima's territorial designs, since it implied that no support was forthcoming for anything that the Imperial side could loosely define, supposedly objectively, as an unjust Venetian demand.

---

that, given the current advantageous Imperial position over the Ottomans, one would have expected better peace terms: BayHStA, Kasten Schwarz 310, fol. 44^{r-v}, Mörmann to Maximillian II Emanuel, 7 February 1699.

11 ÖStA, HHStA, Türkei I, Turcica Box 168, Folder 1 (November 1698, 1st half), fol. 188^{v}, Kinsky to Schlik, 9 November 1698.

12 ÖStA, HHStA, Türkei I, Turcica Box 168, Folder 2 (November 1698, 2nd half), fol. 217^{r}, Kinsky to Marsigli, 25 November 1698.

13 Ibid., fol. 213^{v}–214^{r}, supplementary Imperial instructions, 24 November 1698.

On the other hand, though, the two plenipotentiaries had to appear equally resolute towards the Ottomans and the mediators by making crystal-clear to both of them that there was no way they could conclude a peace treaty without their allies, giving in parallel their best to obtain more advantageous terms for all of them, particularly for Venice.[14] Naturally, considering the above, what those 'better terms' could be was a matter of interpretation, as the last Act of the 'Theatre of Peace' would fully demonstrate.

In their letters to and private conversations with the Venetian officials, the Imperial ministers tried equally to show full support, blaming the Ottomans for violating the principle of *uti possidetis* and advising patience.[15] This was not always a mare façade. 'In essence, it's true that the Turks did not respect the stipulated [principle] [...] neither for his Imperial Majesty nor for the Republic of Venice', Kinsky confessed to Count Öttingen.[16] Similarly, against the bombardment of suspicions and accusations of Schlik against Ruzzini, his patron would first react moderately, replying to him that 'the conduct of the Venetian ambassador is not entirely normal but not equally so abnormal'.[17] However, peace was the ultimate goal and pressure was exercised to make the Republic lower its bargaining price. 'I'm hoping', Kinsky wrote to Ruzzini, 'that the Serenissima Republic won't desire because of this [the alteration of the preliminary agreement], to ruin the congress and make the hope of peace, for the love of which the emperor gives away so much, evaporate'.[18]

To summarise, in its dealings with Venice during the second phase of the congress, the Habsburg Court was chiefly attempting to combine its main interests, which were an effective conclusion of peace and the need not to alienate the Serenissima and lose face in the 'Society of Princes' for leaving its ally alone and violating the pact between them. As Kinsky would reiterate to Count Öttingen in the middle of December, '[I cannot] see how this can end honourably, safely, and also profitably if the emperor should conclude [his agreement] without Venice. Hence, [you should] leave no stone unturned so that the aforementioned Republic could reach together with us the end of the

14 ÖStA, HHStA, Türkei I, Turcica Box 169, Folder 1 (December 1698, 1st half), fol. 69^{r-v}, supplementary Imperial instructions, 5 December 1698.

15 *See*, for instance, ÖStA, HHStA, Türkei I, Turcica Box 168, Folder 2 (November 1698, 2nd half), fol. 156^{r}, Kinsky to Ruzzini, 22 November 1698.

16 Ibid., fol. 169^{v}, Kinsky to Öttingen, 27 December 1698.

17 ÖStA, HHstA, Türkei I, Turcica Box 169, Folder 1 (December 1698, 1st half), fol. 60^{r}, Kinsky to Schlik, 4 December 1698.

18 Ibid., fol. 64^{r-v}, Kinsky to Ruzzini, 4 December 1698.

road'.[19] However, in the end, as was made explicit in a meeting of the 'Turkish Deputation' on 13 December, if things were to 'reach the extremes' (*ad extrema kammen*), there was no doubt that the emperor would have again to prioritise his own designs instead of those of the Republic of Saint Mark.[20] Pursuing this double goal naturally resulted in purposefully different 'internal' and 'external' discourses that were not often left unnoticed by the Venetian side, accentuating its mistrust towards its ally. The effort to accommodate Venice with the Ottomans in an honourable way, as Vienna deemed it, for the former, without compromising the Imperial interests, would accentuate in the last phase of the congress, where the situation was indeed about to reach the extremes.

2 Francesco Loredano at the Imperial Court

After the impasse in Ruzzini's talks with the Ottomans and the great difficulties encountered in obtaining the terms it was hoping for, in late December, the Venetian Senate ordered Francesco Loredano, its resident ambassador in Vienna 'to operate at the [Imperial] Court so that the interests of the Republic be vigorously supported and sustained by the emperor and the benefits of the alliance not be lost with the conclusion of peace'.[21] Thus, a new negotiation' hub, separate from the congress venue geographically but in practice tightly connected with it, was about to emerge.

In reality, Loredano's 'operation' at the Viennese Court had started much earlier, as soon as he got news of the first results of the Ottoman–Venetian negotiations at Carlowitz. 'Really, this is not a good start', he wrote to Ruzzini upon receiving notice of the initial round of the talks.[22] "The preliminary [agreement] is evidently violated, and not even Mavrocordatos's ingenuity can conceal it".[23] His task in convincing the emperor's ministers and Leopold himself to assist the Serenissima was going to be arduous. He had only recently assumed his post to replace Ruzzini. Thus, he did not have enough time to cultivate his relations at Hofburg and build his own networks there.

19 ÖStA, HHStA, Türkei I, Turcica Box 169, Folder 2 (December1698, 2nd half), fol. 39^{r-v}, Kinsky to Öttingen, 14 December 1698.

20 Ibid., fol. 29^{r-v}, relation of the members of the 'Turkish Deputation' to Leopold I, 13 December 1698.

21 *Narratio*, fol. 25^{v}.

22 BNM, Ms.it.VII 399(8625), fol. 320^{r}, Loredano to Ruzzini, (?) November 1698.

23 Ibid.

Nonetheless, he lost no time, attempting to win Count Kinsky because, as he stated, 'I know well that he is the most passionate for peace'.[24] He visited the Bohemian Chancellor in his residence to explain to him the nefarious byproducts of the 'bad faith of the Turks' and the need for a coordinated response of the Imperial plenipotentiaries together with the Venetian one. 'Kinsky showed good disposition in everything [...] and promised [...] to keep me informed', Loredano concluded.[25] Still, the Venetian was not able to obtain an audience from the emperor and was starting to suspect that behind the nice words of his ministers, there might be other, more sinister motives at play.[26]

By the beginning of December, as further news reached the Habsburg capital regarding the progress of the Ottoman–Imperial negotiations, Loredano struggled to convince the members of the 'Turkish Deputation' to instruct their plenipotentiaries at the congress venue to halt their talks and not to resume them until the Ottomans were persuaded to back down from their unjust demands on the Serenissima.[27] As he bitterly realised, everything 'depends on the firmness of the Imperials not to advance their negotiation rather than on the progress of our own'.[28] A few days later, he described his herculean efforts with a tone of exasperation: 'I speak, write, make what I know and can do. Misfortune had it that I couldn't even see the emperor [...], and now, for a couple of days, I am finding myself in bed [...] nailed [down] because of podagra in both legs'.[29] Finally, he was able to secure an audience with Leopold. To his disappointment, though, he found the emperor's responses to his implorations for more firmness to the Ottomans to be 'quite general' (*assai universalli*).[30]

At least his pressure appeared to have produced some results. In a postscript to his instructions to the Carlowitz embassy dated 13 December 1698, Leopold underlined to his plenipotentiaries that in no way were the good relations with the Serenissima to be perturbed and that no move contrary to the stipulations of the Holy League alliance should be made. They were commanded, once again, to do everything in their power so that the Republic would acquire more

---

24 Ibid., fol. 330^{r}, Loredano to Ruzzini, 13 December 1698.

25 BNM, Ms.it.VII 399(8625), fol. 320^{v}, Loredano to Ruzzini, (?) November 1698.

26 Ibid., fol. 322^{r}, Loredano to Ruzzini, 3 December 1698.

27 ÖStA, HHStA, Türkei I, Turcica Box, 169, Folder 2 (December 1698, 2nd half), fol. 35^{r-v}, Loredano to Kinsky, 13 December 1698.

28 BNM, Ms.it.VII 399(8625), fol. 324^{r}, Loredano to Ruzzini, 6 December 1698.

29 Ibid., fol. 340^{r}, Loredano to Ruzzini, 10 December 1698.

30 Ibid., fol. 332^{r-v}, Loredano to Ruzzini, 20 December 1698.

favourable terms and conclude a satisfactory peace agreement together with the Imperials.[31]

The following day, Kinsky decided to write, after a long time, to Lord Paget. Following complains that because of the Ottoman demands in this negotiation, 'the saying of the Gospel "the least became the first and the first became the least" appears to [truly] have found its verification',[32] he quickly passed over to the affairs of Venice, making clear to Paget that although the Ottoman–Imperial negotiation had advanced to a considerable extent, any attempt of the Ottomans to prejudice the Serenissima could cause 'this large ship [of peace] to capsize [even] inside the port itself'.[33] As with other subsequent letters of the Bohemian Chancellor to the English mediator, though, such words were not genuine but basically a bluff. The Imperial side was not contemplating breaking the congress, not least because of Venice. Sending Count Öttingen a copy of another letter of his to Paget later on, he commented that 'you will see [there] me saying what I'm not thinking and thinking what I'm not saying'.[34] He also advised the two plenipotentiaries to adopt the same strategy in their dealings with the Ottomans and the mediators regarding the Republic of Saint Mark.[35] The goal always remained the same: putting pressure on both sides so that an agreement could be reached between them as soon as possible.

Still, the Imperial instructions to the plenipotentiaries at Carlowitz to support with all their strength the Republic of Saint Mark created yet another incongruity of opinion between the court and its congress delegation, since the latter not only, as we saw, totally mistrusted Ruzzini and his principals, but also, strongly opined, that, similarly to any attempt to renegotiate articles it had already agreed with the Ottomans, persistence on a determined backing of Venice could place into peril the whole congress edifice. 'I'm reiterating once more that if His Majesty has decided to hold firm on this issue, we can absolutely count on [the continuation of] war', Schlik assured his patron.[36] Hence,

31 ÖStA, HHStA, Türkei I, Turcica Box 169, Folder 2 (December 1698, 2nd half), fol. 25^{r}, supplementary Imperial instructions (P.S.), 13 December 1698.

32 Ibid., fol. 47^{r}, Kinsky to Paget, 14 December 1698.

33 Ibid., fol. 47^{r-v}.

34 ÖStA, HHStA, Türkei I, Turcica Box 171, Folder 1 (January 1699, 1st half), fol. 240^{r}, Kinsky to Öttingen (copy), 14 January 1699.

35 'Say something different from what [you really] think' (*aliud dicere, aliud cogitare*): ÖStA, HHStA, Türkei I, Turcica Box 169, Folder 2 (December 1698, 2nd half), fol. 169^{v}, Kinsky to Öttingen, 27 December 1698.

36 Ibid., fol. 45^{r}, Schlik to Kinsky, 14 December 1698.

even if Loredano could have convinced Leopold and his ministers, determined not to compromise their interests but equally sensitive to their reputation, to show some resolution, even a faked one, to the Ottomans, would the two Imperial plenipotentiaries obey their commands to the letter and do the same?

•••

The stage is now fully set for the culmination of the drama. Our theatre's curtains are falling as Act III comes to a close. What will the next scene reveal when they are raised again for the grand finale?

ACT IV

The Grand Finale (20 December 1698–5 February 1699)

One could not distinguish between the real and the verisimilar.

CARLO RUZZINI

Dramatis Personae

The Protagonists

ALEXANDROS MAVROCORDATOS: Second Ottoman plenipotentiary ambassador.
CARLO RUZZINI: Plenipotentiary ambassador of the Republic of Venice.
COUNT LEOPOLD SCHLIK: Second Imperial plenipotentiary ambassador.
COUNT LUIGI MARSIGLI: Special adviser of the Imperial embassy on matters of border-making.
COUNT WOLFGANG VON ÖTTINGEN: First Imperial plenipotentiary ambassador.
FRANCESCO LOREDANO: Resident Venetian ambassador at the Imperial Court.
JACOB COLYER: The Dutch mediator at the congress.
LORD WILLIAM PAGET: The English mediator at the congress.
PETR POSTNIKOV: Chief secretary of the Muscovite delegation and primary interpreter of Prokopii Bogdanovich Voznitsyn.
PROKOPII BOGDANOVICH VOZNITSYN: Great and plenipotentiary ambassador of Muscovy.
RĀMĪ MEḤMED: First Ottoman plenipotentiary ambassador.
STANISŁAW MAŁACHOWSKI: Great and plenipotentiary ambassador of the Polish-Lithuanian Commonwealth.

Second Roles

COUNT FRANZ URLICH VON KINSKY: High Chancellor of Bohemia and influential Imperial minister.
GIANBATTISTA NICOLOSI: Secretary of the Venetian embassy.

 | DOI:10.1163/9789004458499_023

The final phase of the congress, roughly from 20 December 1698 until 5 February 1699, when the last plenipotentiaries departed from Carlowitz, was mostly dominated by the affairs of Venice. It was a challenging multi-actor 'poker game' in which, as Ruzzini succinctly framed it, 'one could not distinguish between the real and the verisimilar'.[1] Manipulation, dissimulation, deceit, double-talk, bluffing, and even outright bribery were regularly brought as 'hidden aces' to the table, as the principal players, the Venetians, the Ottomans, the Imperials, and the mediators, were desperately trying to turn the balance of the game to their favour. In that effort, the two ambassadors who had essentially already concluded their affairs, Małachowski and Voznitsyn, suddenly became a catalyst since the way they were going to act, and whom they would support, would determine how the whole play would end. So, may the audience prepare for a climactic finale to our 'Theatre of Peace'.

1 Ruzzini, *Relazione*, 363.

Narration Part I: 'The Ultimate Great Obstacle for Peace'

> In a nutshell, we find ourselves in the nastiest crisis in the world.
>
> COUNT SCHLIK to Kinsky on the Ottoman–Venetian negotiations[1]

...

> We are at this disadvantage without [that being] our fault.
>
> FRANCESCO LOREDANO to Ruzzini[2]

1 Setting the Stage for the Final Act

Writing from Vienna on 21 December, Count Marsigli proudly informed the Imperial delegation at Carlowitz of his achievement in convincing the court to accept the peace articles that the two plenipotentiaries had already agreed with the Ottomans.

> In the conferences [I had here] [...] I demonstrated the deal, its advantages, the reasons why certain things cannot be done, [all] the troubles and circumstances, and in the end, I pulled all the votes to our party [...] On the borders, they are persuaded, contented, and would only have been even more so if the [construction of] windmills [on the bank] of the Mureş was negated to the enemy. As for all the other articles, they were equally approved in their essence.[3]

Despite a feeling that, in specific issues, better terms could have been acquired, with this general consent to the peace agreement by the emperor and its

1 ÖStA, HHStA, Türkei I, Turcica Box 171, Folder 1 (January 1699, 1st half), fol. 30^{r}, Schlik to Kinsky, 2 January 1699.

2 BNM, Ms.it.VII 399(8625), fol. 336^{r-v}, Loredano to Ruzzini, 24 (27?) December 1698.

3 ÖStA, HHStA, Türkei I, Turcica Box 169, Folder 2 (December 1698, 2nd half), fol. 135^{v}, Marsigli to Öttingen/Schlik, 21 December 1698.

 | DOI:10.1163/9789004458499_024

chief ministers, the road to a swift and successful conclusion of the Carlowitz Congress, just a little more than two months after its start, appeared to be, finally, wide open. A major obstacle remained, however. 'All hindrances lie with the Venetians [and] I assure Your Excellences that they have the entire court on their side, and Signor Count Kinsky visited many times this Loredano', the *Bolognese* alerted the delegation.[4]

Marsigli was exaggerating. He was referring, however, to the latest ostensible change of mood – as we saw, positive for the Venetian interests – at the Viennese Court, an impression that Loredano got as well from a new audience he had with the emperor, whose answers were now 'somewhat more definite and precise than the last ones',[5] as from one of the most recent visits he received by Count Kinsky. The latter assured him – if only Loredano knew that he didn't entirely mean what he was saying– that the Imperials would spare no effort to aid the Serenissima and stand stoutly beside her, fully acknowledging – alas, post facto – that the *modus tractandi* adopted in the congress was a huge mistake.[6] Thus assured, for the moment, of the Imperial backing, what worried the Venetian ambassador the most was 'the important mutation' caused primarily by the Ottoman–Muscovite truce/armistice agreement and the similar conclusion of the Polish negotiation. He thus strongly advised Ruzzini to cultivate his relationship with both so that they would not sign their Instruments, focusing specifically on the more uncertain Małachowski: 'Everything depends on the Pole who should be won over with reason or with other means', he said emphatically.[7] His apprehension was most probably magnified by no other than Kinsky, who made use of these developments to exert further pressure on Ruzzini, either by personal letters[8] or via Count Marsigli[9] – who, as we saw, had won the confidence of the Venetians – urging him to speed up his negotiation, since with two Holy League members having concluded their affairs, the game was dramatically altered.

The *Bolognese* returned to Carlowitz from Vienna on 27 December 1698.[10] With him, he brought the novel Imperial instructions to the two plenipotentiaries and letters from Kinsky, commanding them to assist in all possible ways

4 Ibid., fol. 136^{r}.
5 BNM, Ms.it.VII 399(8625), fol. 335^{v}, Loredano to Ruzzini, 24 (27?) December 1698.
6 Ibid., fol. 335^{v}–336^{r}.
7 Ibid., fol. 342^{v}.
8 ÖStA, HHStA, Türkei I, Turcica Box 169, Folder 2 (December 1698, 2nd half), fol. 176^{r}–177^{r}, Kinsky to Ruzzini, 19 December 1698.
9 Ibid., fol. 171^{r}, Kinsky to Marsigli 27 December 1698.
10 ÖStA, HHStA, Türkei I, Turcica Box 170, Diarium et Cerimoniale, fol. 55.

the Serenissima and not sign an agreement, unless concurrently with her.[11] However, in parallel, revealing Kinsky's double-game and double language, the two plenipotentiaries were also to approach Małachowski and find out 'more asking [...] than persuading [him] not to do it (*mehrers quaestionando* [...] *als persuadendo ut non faciat*)' , if the Pole was determined to separately sign the treaty he had already concluded, 'so that [if the worst happens] the break of the alliance would come not from the Imperial but from the Polish side [...] [and] His Imperial Majesty [....]would be [thus] able to justify [his own decision to conclude a separate treaty as well] to the whole world and especially to Venice'.[12]

Öttingen and Schlik were not particularly enthusiastic about the new orders from the court. They constantly warned their principal of the perilous situation he could find himself in if the Imperial side persisted in the matter of the Republic of Saint Mark. With Małachowski and Voznitsyn out of the equation, 'Your Imperial Majesty [will] stay with only just Venice, embroiled even longer in an uncertain war'.[13] Swift resolutions on the issue were imperative because having concluded almost two-thirds of the peace articles, '[...] we can find no pretext any more to head the Turks off the imminent conclusion [of the treaties]'.[14]

However, as much as they didn't concur with Vienna's stance, orders were orders, and Öttingen and Schlik were obliged to implement them, presenting themselves in their relations to Emperor Leopold as doing everything in their power to aid their ally.[15] They were not doing it wholeheartedly, though, as Schlik himself confessed to his patron. Recounting a meeting they had with the Ottomans on 1 January 1699, he described himself and his colleague as being 'constrained to appear eager to obey to the letter the orders of His Majesty and serve in this way our ally'.[16] This unwillingness to genuinely provide complete assistance to the Republic did not remain unnoticed by the Venetians, who once again felt betrayed.[17]

Despite such accusations, however, in the short term, the Ottomans were substantially agitated by this change of tone, even a half-mumbled one, on the

11 *Narratio*, fol. 26ᵛ.
12 ÖStA, HHStA, Türkei I, Turcica Box 169, Folder 2 (December 1698, 2nd half), fol. 90ᵛ, Kinsky to Öttingen, 19 December 1698.
13 Ibid., fol. 96ᵛ, Imperial plenipotentiaries to Leopold I, 20 December 1698.
14 Ibid., fol. 96ᵛ–97ʳ.
15 ÖStA, HHStA, Türkei I, Turcica Box 171, Folder 1 (January 1699, 1st half), fol. 39ᵛ, Imperial plenipotentiaries to Leopold I, 2 January 1699.
16 Ibid., fol. 28ʳ, Schlik to Kinsky, 2 January 1699.
17 *Narratio*, fol. 26ᵛ–27ʳ.

Imperial side. Besides instructions and letters for the two plenipotentiaries, Marsigli carried with him back to Carlowitz the letter of support for Venice that Kinsky addressed to Lord Paget, the one in which he said what he was not thinking and thought what he wasn't saying. His bluff verily hit the mark as both the Ottomans and the mediators took the bait. News of Loredano's rigorous efforts to solicit support among the Imperial decision-makers had also reached the Ottoman delegation. 'The Venetian ambassador in Vienna', Rāmī relates scornfully,

> turned upside down the emperor's court with clamour, shouting a thousand complaints about the Imperial plenipotentiaries – that they negotiated the terms [of the treaty] in haste, and that by agreeing to the evacuation and demolition of so many fortresses, they were the main reason for the arrogant behaviour of the Exalted State's plenipotentiaries.[18]

He managed to bring on board to his cause some monks close to the emperor, and together they persuaded him to dispatch letters to the congress venue ordering his plenipotentiaries to assist the Republic.[19] 'So much so, that a letter also came to the English ambassador from Count Kinsky, which apart from many other rude words wrote that [...] although the vessel of peace entered the port, if not all our allies are not satisfied, then, there is a possibility that it can capsize [even] inside it'.[20]

Rāmī's chief source of information on all these facts was probably none other than the mediators, who also shared the content of Kinsky's letter with their Ottoman counterparts, something that the Bohemian Chancellor should have surely counted upon. It greatly alarmed them both, just as Loredano had rightly predicted in a conversation he had with Kinsky, where he opined that a more potent demonstration of support for the Serenissima and the threat to break the negotiations, if her interests would not be protected, would instil fear in the mediators that 'all their hitherto work and toil is thrown away' and the same would apply to the Ottomans.[21] Contrary, though, to what the Venetian ambassador might have hoped, instead of rendering the mediation and the Porte's delegation more malleable towards the Republic of Saint Mark, Kinsky's letter only strengthened the determination of both to try to deprive Venice of its support either at the Imperial Court or at the congress venue itself.

18 *Taʿrīḥ-i ṣulḥnāme*, fol. 120^{b}.

19 Ibid.

20 Ibid.

21 BNM, Ms. It VII 381 (7782), fol. 336^{r}, Loredano to Ruzzini, 24 (27?) December 1698.

Loredano was correct to assess that the English and the Dutch had a vested interest in the successful conclusion of the congress. What he failed to understand, however, at least at this stage, was that just like Öttingen and Schlik, Paget and Colyer saw Ruzzini as the greatest obstacle to the fulfilment of their goals, and despite the ostensible understanding they showed towards him, leading him to believe that he had their support,[22] in reality, they loathed him as much as the second Imperial plenipotentiary. Characteristically, in his letters to his principals Colyer described him as 'the Venetian rogue/joker' (*Venetiaanschen quandt*).[23]

2 The Unsuccessful Restart of the Ottoman–Venetian Talks

Although at a standstill, in waiting for the return of the courier from Venice, in the last weeks of December 1698, there were renewed attempts by the Imperials and the mediators to set the Republic's affairs again in motion, especially after the positive results of the Ottoman–Commonwealth and Ottoman–Muscovite negotiations. A session between the Imperials and the Ottomans on 22 December 1698 (see Table 3) was exclusively dedicated to the 'interests' of Venice, a prelude to the upcoming direct involvement of Öttingen and Schlik in the Ottoman–Venetian negotiations, first as informal mediators, and then as sole negotiators on the part of the Serenissima. After a lengthy discussion, what the Habsburg plenipotentiaries and the mediators could only secure from the Ottomans was again a general assurance that they were ready to facilitate things in Dalmatia if the Venetian side was willing to accommodate itself with the Ottoman demands regarding the borders of Morea and the abandonment of its possessions in mainland Greece. 'Time, that otherwise softens everything, only made these Turkish heads more unyielding', Schlik commented bitterly in his 'Secret Journal',[24] adding pessimistically on the outcome of the Ottoman–Venetian affairs that 'it is more to wish than hope that this present negotiation can have good results'.[25] This session was followed by equally unsuccessful efforts by the mediators to move the talks between the two sides forward, the Ottomans firmly refusing to meet with Ruzzini if the latter didn't have anything new to put on the table.[26]

---

22 *Narratio*, fol. 25^r.
23 Hora Siccama, *Der Vrede van Carlowitz*, 153.
24 ÖStA, HHStA, Türkei I, Turcica Box 170, Diarium et Cerimoniale, fol. 54.
25 Ibid.
26 Ibid., fol. 55.

TABLE 3 Official conferences held at the Carlowitz Peace Congress from 21 to 31 December 1698

22nd: 12th Ottoman–Imperial conference
23rd: 13th Ottoman–Imperial conference
30th: 14th Ottoman–Imperial conference
31st: 4th Venetian–Ottoman conference

SOURCE: ÖSTA, HHSTA, TÜRKEI I, TURCICA BOX 170, PROTOCOLLUM ET CERIMONIALE, FOL. 53–57

Finally, the long-awaited Venetian courier reached Carlowitz on 28 December.[27] It arrived just on time. Ruzzini was facing difficult times. The Polish and the Muscovite ambassadors, having concluded their affairs, were expressing their desire to leave the congress venue, the former having already sent away his portable equipment,[28] and Mavrocordatos also started to insinuate that the Republic would receive worse terms if it continued to delay the peacemaking process.[29] However, if the Venetian plenipotentiary was hoping that these much-anticipated instructions of the Senate would considerably alleviate his burden, he was mistaken. While they contained facilitations for some of the thorny issues, they commanded the ambassador to stay firm on others – especially on the mountains north of the Peloponnese.[30] Even though nothing good was presaged if the Ottomans were to remain resolute in their position, the same evening, Ruzzini visited the Imperial ambassadors and the mediators to inform them 'that he is now in a state to reassume his negotiation',[31] also declaring that to satisfy the Ottomans, he was even ready to accept some form of disadvantage.[32]

Implementing at the same time Loredano's advice, he successfully managed to persuade Małachowski to delay the signing of his agreement and wait for him to conclude his own negotiation.[33] 'He also turned entirely against us, the

27 Ruzzini, *Relazione*, 357.

28 ÖStA, HHStA, Türkei I, Turcica Box 169, Folder 2 (December 1698, 2nd half), fol. 96v, Imperial plenipotentiaries to Leopold I, 20 December 1698.

29 Ruzzini, *Relazione*, 358.

30 Ibid., 357.

31 ÖStA, HHStA, Türkei I, Turcica Box 170, Diarium et Cerimoniale, fol. 56.

32 *Narratio*, fol. 26v.

33 Ibid., fol. 25r–v. Schlik alludes to a possible bribe, claiming tellingly that 'for a Pole, there is no word that can be kept against the promise of money': ÖStA, HHStA, Türkei I, Turcica Box 172, Folder 1 (February–March 1699), fol. 26v, Schlik to Kinsky, 4 February 1699.

Pole and the Muscovite, who abated their impatience greatly since he implored them so insistently not to sign their treaties ahead of the rest of us',[34] Schlik complained to Kinsky, revealing the henceforth secret Imperial strategy – not so much different from the Ottoman one – to isolate Ruzzini and thus force him to come to an agreement.

Having managed to secure the backing of Małachowski and secondarily of Voznitsyn – who already supported him – and despite the scepticism of the mediators about the chances of a possible agreement even with his novel instructions, the Venetian walked into a conference with the Ottomans on 31 December 1698. The meeting turned out to be another disaster. Both sides remained adamant in their respective positions. Following the relation of the Imperial plenipotentiaries, Rāmī was so enraged by Ruzzini's continued insistence on the mountain range north of the Corinthian Isthmus that he stood up and left the session.[35] As for the Venetian, 'he came immediately to the Imperials to lament his hardship and appealed for help', the Habsburg delegates would recount slightly dismissively.[36] Schlik's ill feelings against the *Cavaliere* were brought once again to the fore: 'Tiring himself infinitely, he causes no lesser fatigue to the others as well', he wrote to Kinsky.[37] He complained that despite the instructions the Imperial ambassadors received from Vienna, they didn't support him with great rigour. That was slander. The mediators and even the Ottomans could attest that that was not true.[38] Yet, he could not seriously think that they were to sacrifice the profit of their master 'for a pure interest of convenience of his'.[39] 'But I would dare to say', Schlik opined, stressing this time the intransigence of both the Venetians and the Ottomans, 'that between these two parties, the most erudite people of Europe would lose their [knowledge] of Latin'.[40] 'In a nutshell', he concluded, 'we find ourselves in the nastier crisis of the world'.[41] To be continued …

34 ÖStA, HHStA, Türkei I, Turcica Box 171, Folder 1 (January 1699, 1st half), fol. 26^{r}, Schlik to Kinsky, 2 January 1699.
35 Ibid., fol. 40^{v}, Imperial plenipotentiaries to Leopold I, 2 January 1699.
36 Ibid.
37 Ibid., fol. 25^{r-v}, Schlik to Kinsky, 2 January 1699.
38 Imperial plenipotentiaries to Leopold I, 2 January 1699, fol. 41^{r-v}.
39 Schlik to Kinsky, 2 January 1699, fol. 25^{v}–26^{r}.
40 Ibid., fol. 28^{r}.
41 Ibid., fol. 30^{r}.

At the Negotiating Table III: Peace or Truce/Armistice? The Duration of the Treaties

'Since the days of old [and] up to that moment', declared the two Ottoman plenipotentiaries to their Imperial counterparts during the Failed Vienna Congress (1689–90),

> between states, peace is made in two ways. Either a part of the conquered lands [during the war] is returned [to their previous owners], and the rest are kept; both sides feel, as much as that is possible, satisfied [and being that way, they conclude] a stable peace and a strong friendship; no form of treachery will surface between them anymore; [amity and union will reign until the day of the resurrection].[1] Or, if they do not desire to renounce [some of their conquests] and make a stable peace, everything stays in its status quo, and as an act of mercy for the subjects, a time-limited reconciliation is stipulated for the cessation of hostilities.[2]

Whatever the Ottomans may have claimed, Count Marsigli held an entirely different opinion on their sincere proclivity towards a 'stable peace'. In one of his letters to Kinsky from Carlowitz, he described them as 'barbarians who declare to make truces, not peace, only to take a breath, and afterwards think [again] of war, which actually means that they reflect on every [possible] way that could facilitate it'.[3] However, his comments acquire a sense of great irony if one considers the fact that, according to Zülfikār Efendi, the Imperial plenipotentiaries categorically stated to the Ottoman delegation that 'our emperor will make again with you a time-limited peace'.[4] The same situation would repeat itself ten years later because 'His Majesty the Emperor still lays claim to many lands of the Ottoman Porte, and therefore, as a Christian potentate, he could not consent to any eternal peace'.[5] 'Barbarians' were everywhere,

1 *Cerîde-i Takrirât*, 73.

2 Ibid., 63.

3 ÖStA, HHStA, Türkei I, Turcica Box 171, Folder 1 (January 1699, 1st half), fol. 137^{v}–138^{r}, Marsigli to Kinsky, 3 January 1699. The topos of the warlike, treacherous 'barbarian' who cannot grasp the true meaning of peace, the latter being for him only a respite from pursuing the fighting anew, is quite old, going back to Roman times: Nicolas Drocourt, *L'autre Empire du Milieu. La diplomatie byzantine* (*VIIe–XIIe siècles*) (Rennes: Presses Universitaires de Rennes, 2023) 43.

4 *Cerîde-i Takrirât*, 65.

5 BayHStA, Kasten Schwarz 310, fol. 42^{r}, Mörmann to Maximilian II Emanuel, 7 February 1699.

 | DOI:10.1163/9789004458499_025

it seems. However, what makes the Ottoman ambassadors' statement genuinely intriguing is not only that it points once again to the presence of shared conceptions of peacemaking developed steadily through a long tradition of relations between polities with dissimilar religious or 'ideological' precepts. As I will try to demonstrate in the following pages, it also manifests – like the Imperial argumentation for not making permanent peace with the Porte – that the type and duration of a reconciliation agreement was not exclusively, or perhaps even primarily, a question of faith – even if the latter was usually brought in to officially justify or legitimize it[6] – but one touching fundamentally upon the interests and strategical concerns of the opposing parties.

And yet, some notable exceptions apart,[7] the majority of the available scholarship tends, just like seventeenth-century contemporaries like Marsigli, to treat the Christian and Muslim peacemaking norms and conceptions as incommensurable, sui generis for each side and determined chiefly by manifestly distinct cultural and religious canons.[8] Following the dominant narrative, these two separate principles only became 'reciprocal' after Christian Europe imposed its own on the rest of the world, starting from the beginning of the eighteenth century.[9] Additionally, whereas Christian European peacemaking tenets are constantly evolving and adapting themselves to new circumstances, the Muslim ones, as with Islamic Law itself, remain quasi-perennial, unsusceptible to any evolution or reinterpretation.[10] It is indeed very hard to understand how the 'international' realities of the eighth, ninth or tenth centuries reflected in classical Islamic 'International' Law, the so-called *Siyar*,

---

6 For a notable Ottoman case, concerning specifically the type and duration of peace treaties with non-Muslim rulers, in which diplomatic practice was subsequently integrated in Islamic Law tradition to acquire legitimization, *see* Poulios, 'From the Palace of Ryswick', 112.

7 Stefan Rohdewald, '„bu sulh u salah mukarrer ve mü'ebbed"/„Pax perpetua"? Polnisch-litaunische Friedensformeln und Allianzen mit Osmanen und Krimtataren bis 1790'. *Zeitschrift für Ostmitteleuropa-Forschung* 65/2 (2016), 167–92.

8 *See*, among many others, Gilles Veinstein, 'Les fondements juridiques de la diplomatie Ottomane en Europe'. *Oriente Moderno, Nuova Serie* 88/2 (2008), 509–22; Maria Pia Pedani Fabris, *La dimora della pace. Considerazioni sulle capitolazioni tra i paesi islamici e l'Europa* (Venice 1996); Viorel Panaite, *Ottoman Law of War and Peace. The Ottoman Empire and its Tribute-Payers from the North of the Danube*, 2nd revised edn (Leiden/Boston: Brill 2019); Randall Lesaffer, Erik-Jan Broers and Johanna Waelkens, 'From Antwerp to Munster (1609/1648). Truce and Peace under the Law of Nations', in Randall Lesaffer (ed.), *The Twelve Years Truce (1609). Peace, Truce, War and Law in the Low Countries at the Turn of the 17th Century* (Leiden/Boston: Brill 2014) 233–55.

9 For instance, Heywood and Parvev, 'Introduction', in Heywood and Parvev, *The Treaties of Carlowitz*; Pedani- Fabris, *La dimora della pace*, 37–8.

10 *See* for instance, Veinstein, 'Les fondements juridiques'.

could have remained the same as those of the seventeenth century.[11] A more fruitful and correct approach would be to consider the Ottomans, as legal historians do with Christian Europe, not as merely repeating what was handed down to them but instead as enriching and re-interpreting it.[12]

As in other matters of early modern diplomatic culture already discussed, complete 'legal incommensurability' is not at all the impression one gets by reading the different sources pertaining to the Carlowitz Congress. But before getting there, since religious doctrine or law allegedly determined the choice of the negotiating parties regarding the type and time span of their agreement, a brief excursus on the role and presence of religion and the degree of impact that religious motivation had on decision-making during the peace talks is of the essence.

1 Religion: the 'X Factor'?

There is no denying of the significant effect religion evidently exercised on policymaking during the late seventeenth century. Christian rulers often consulted with their theologians and private confessors when faced with decisions that were not entirely in line with the precepts of their faith,[13] and Muslim potentates, like the Ottoman sultan, sought the oral and written approval of the leading religious-juridical authorities in their domains in essential

11 A classic by now introduction in classical Islamic 'International' Law is, Majid Khadduri, *War and Peace in the Law of Islam* (Richmond, Virginia: John Hopkins Press 1955). While succinctly presenting the classical definitions of the early medieval Islamic lawmakers, Khadduri's work does not capture their evolution, adaptation and enrichment in the subsequent centuries. Pedani Fabris, *La dimora della pace* and Panaite's, *Ottoman Law*, attempt to integrate Ottoman practice but still take mostly for granted the inalterability of the *Siyar* and its terminology over the centuries. Himlar Kruger's still pioneering study does not unfortunately contain much about the Ottoman jurists' (re)interpretation of key terms such as 'truce' or 'peace': Himlar Kruger, *Fetwa und Siyar: zur internationalrechtlichen Gutachtenpraxis der osmanischen Seyh ul-Islam vom 17. bis 19. Jahrhundert unter besonderer Berucksichtigung des 'Behcet ul-Fetava'* (Wiesbaden: Otto Harrosowitz 1978).

12 For such an approach in Ottoman Islamic Law in general and the Ottoman 'International' Law in particular, *see* Guy Burak, *The Second Formation of Islamic Law. The Hanafi School in the Early Modern Ottoman Empire* (Cambridge: Cambridge University Press 2015) and Nicola Melis, 'Some Observations on the Concept of *dār al-ʿahd* in the Ottoman Context (Sixteenth-Seventeenth Centuries', in Giovanna Calasso and Giuliano Lancioni (eds.), *Dār al-islām / dār al-ḥarb. Territories, People, Identities* (Leiden/Boston: Brill, 2017) 182–202.

13 Croxton, *Westphalia*, 343–51.

matters, peace negotiations included.[14] Issues like the safeguarding of the privileges of specific confessional groups inside multi-religious polities or the question of the custodianship of the Christian Holy Sites in and around Jerusalem figured among the instructions given to the allied ambassadors and in the peace proposal submitted by the latter to the Ottomans[15] and, especially, in the Ottoman–Imperial case, they were extensively debated during the conferences.[16] For Count Schlik, the insertion of the rights of the Church of Rome over the Holy Sepulcher in the final treaty was done primarily because of the emperor's piety[17] and 'to satisfy the Catholic world so that they don't think that His Imperial Majesty didn't think about them but only of his personal interests'.[18] Similarly, the Ottomans raised Islamic Law prohibitions a few times when rejecting particular demands voiced by their interlocutors, although, quite intriguingly, the type and duration of the treaties did not figure among them.[19]

As for the congress plenipotentiaries themselves, their religiosity was manifested in various ways: the presence of priests in their entourage and Rāmī Meḥmed's frequent interruption of the sessions to perform his prayers being some notable examples. Their religious affiliation could even concretely impact their attitude during the negotiations, or at least some contemporaries thought so. According to the Anonymous Venetian, Mavrocordatos's tough stance towards the Serenissima was principally explained because of his hatred of the 'Latins' (the Roman Catholics).[20] 'In the matter of religion […] I sense little good disposition […] predicting that with a Quaker, a Huguenot

14 Pointing out how widespread the issuing of such religious-legal opinions (*fetvā*) was among the broader Ottoman population, Cantemir would argue, perhaps with a bit of an exaggeration, that the 'common people believe that they can do nothing except if it is at once approbated by a fetva': Cantemir, *Incrementorum et Decrementorum*, 444. On the *fetvā* and its textual structure, *see* in detail Panaite, *Ottoman Law*, 13–20.

15 For instance, ÖStA, HHStA, Türkei I, Turcica Box 166, Folder 3 (September 1698, 2nd half), fol. 144^{r}–145^{r}, Instructio pro Legatis Plenipotentiarijs Ces[are]is; Załuski, *Epistolae*, 631; Ms.it VII 399 (8625), fol. 226^{r-v}; Bogoslovskii, *Petr I*, 393–4. For religious issues in the general context of the Ottoman agreements with Christian powers during the early modern period, *see* the recent study of Radu Dipratu, *Regulating Non-Muslim Communities in the Seventeenth-Century Ottoman Empire. Catholics and Capitulations* (London/New York: Routledge 2022).

16 ÖStA, HHStA, Türkei I, Turcica Box 170, Protocollum, fol. 77, 79, 100, 179–180; Cernovodeanu, 'Le journal', 332, 347.

17 ÖStA, HHStA, Türkei I, Turcica Box 170, Protocollum, fol. 77.

18 Ibid., fol. 179.

19 Ibid., fol. 211; *Taʾrīḫ-i ṣulḥ-nāme*, fol. 73^{b}–74^{a}.

20 *Narratio*, fol. 48^{r}.

and a Greek schismatic we will reap minimal benefit', Count Marsigli pessimistically opined to Kinsky, alluding that the Imperial aspirations for the strengthening of Catholicism in the Ottoman Domains were to be blocked by a Protestant/Calvinist/Orthodox front comprised by Paget, Colyer and Mavrocordatos respectively.[21]

Nonetheless, despite Derek Croxton's remarks for the case of the ambassadors during the Westphalian Peace Congress, namely that 'even if they did not want to pursue religious aims through diplomacy, they certainly wanted their diplomacy to be consistent with their religious beliefs',[22] Carlowitz presents a somewhat different reality. Mavrocordatos could be Orthodox and, as such, sympathise with Muscovy.[23] Still, when the latter raised in its peace proposals the issue of its protection of the Ottoman Orthodox subjects of the sultan and the possession by them of the Holy Sites in Jerusalem, the Ottoman negotiator chose to privilege the Porte's interests – not to have outside involvement in internal Ottoman matters clearly expressed in treaties[24] – rather than those of his faith.[25] Similarly, when Colyer, in order to implement the instructions he received from the States General at the Hague, attempted to form a Dutch-Anglo-Ottoman union regarding the protection of the privileges and religious freedom of the Transylvanian Protestants and Calvinists, he would not receive the support of Lord Paget, who probably didn't want to compromise the English alliance with the emperor ahead of an imminent new joint war against France.[26]

As for the Ottomans, in complete knowledge that their propagated image as pious Islamic holy warriors had permeated many of their Christian interlocutors, they adroitly exploited this to reject certain matters in negotiation that were unfavourable to them. For instance, to avoid the stipulation of a wasteland on their bank of the rivers Tisza and Mureş, they pointed out, among other arguments, that it was prohibited by Islamic Law,[27] a bluntly false statement since they had themselves imposed a no-man's-land on Muscovy in

21 ÖStA, HHStA, Türkei I, Turcica Box 168, Folder 1 (November 1698, 1st half), fol. 48^{v}, Marsigli to Kinsky, 5 November 1698.

22 Croxton, *Westphalia*, 348.

23 As Carlo Ruzzini remarked in his *Relazione*: Ruzzini, *Relazione*, 378.

24 Oded Peri, *Christianity under Islam in Jerusalem. The Question of the Holy Sites in Early Ottoman Times* (Brill: Leiden/ Boston/Köln 2001) 149–52.

25 Since at Carlowitz, the two sides didn't finally get to discuss religious matters, Mavrocordatos's stance is clearly manifested in the Ottoman–Muscovite negotiations leading to the Peace Treaty of Constantinople (1700): Nicolas Pissis, *Russland in den politischen Vorstellungen der griechischen Kulturwelt 1645–1725* (Göttingen:Vandenhoeck & Ruprecht 2020) 180.

26 Hora Siccama, 'De Vrede van Carlowitz', 163–6.

27 ÖStA, HHStA, Türkei I, Turcica Box 170, Protocollum, fol. 30.

their territorial settlement concerning their lands in Ukraine only almost two decades before. It hit its mark entirely, however, with Count Schlik declaring that 'since you raise a point about religion to [not] create a wasteland, we will not insist'.[28]

All the above examples illustrate not only the manipulation of religion to achieve one's aims – which attests, however, to its continuous ostensible relevance – but also that when worldly interests clashed with the dictates of Heaven, most of the time the latter had to be accommodated with the former. As the famous Swedish seventeenth-century statesman Axel Oxenstierna framed it, Sweden's entry into the Thirty Years' War 'was not so much a matter of religion, but rather of saving the public condition (*status publicus*), wherein religion is also comprehended'.[29] Tantalisingly, the Hanafi Islamic legal tradition, mainly followed by the Ottomans, accords a significant role to the general good or public interest (*maṣlaḥatu'l-ʿumūm*) – a concept strikingly similar to Oxenstierna's *status publicus* – equipping thus the policymakers with broad freedom to act as they saw fit.[30] Hence, for most of the chief negotiators and their principals, the answer to the question of the consistency of their designs and strategies with their religious beliefs was often quite simple: the latter were served by the former. If the 'public interest' or the 'public condition' favoured a permanent peace with the 'Infidels' or the 'Barbarians', then, for the sake of religion, religious rhetoric had to step aside.

•••

The present section is divided into two parts. The first is dedicated to clarifying the terminology. Which terms did late-seventeenth-century contemporaries use to refer to the different typologies and temporal validity of bilateral agreements that end a state of war, and what meaning did those terms hold for them? As will be argued, similarly to other aspects of the early modern peacemaking process, the vocabulary and conceptions of the various participants at the congress on the matter were not defined by a religious or culturally geographical entity – being either 'Christendom' or 'Islamdom' – nor were they strictly based on a particular 'Law', whether religious or secular. Instead, it appears that they were, for the most part, reciprocally developed through centuries of diplomatic contacts, acquiring a semi-legal status through repeated praxis.

28 Ibid., fol. 31.

29 Quoted in Croxton, *Westphalia*, 346.

30 Melis, 'Some Observations', 191. Hence, it is no coincidence that the peace negotiations are frequently described by the Ottomans as *maṣlaḥat*: *Taʾrīḫ-i ṣulḥnāme*, fol. 20^{a}, 72^{a}, 74^{b}.

Furthermore, contrary to the valuable yet incomplete picture provided by studies that focus mainly on juridical texts[31] or attempt to interpret diplomatic arrangements through a legalistic prism,[32] the 'everyday' language of the protagonists, and even the official texts of the treaties themselves, reveal a far less rigid and extremely fluid terminology. I chose to concentrate largely on the main actors' much more labyrinthine and multifaceted discourses since it is primarily through their interaction that a shared peacemaking vocabulary first came into being before its codification in the different legal treatises.

The second part deals with the question of why the congress participants chose to privilege certain types of agreements with their opponent(s) instead of others and how the different kinds of treaties and their duration were discussed and debated during the talks. The matter is sometimes so puzzling that no clear answers can be provided. Nonetheless, I will suggest that the options favoured were grounded on several parameters, including power relations, territorial disputes (whether they were able to effectively resolve them during the negotiations or not), possible future territorial aspirations or customary practice.

2 Terminology

All participants of the Carlowitz Congress distinguished first and foremost between two principal kinds of agreements based on their duration.[33] On the one hand there was the eternal (*müe'bbed ü mü'ekkid ṣulḥ u ṣalāḥ*,[34] *ewigen*

31 For instance, Pedani-Fabris, *La dimora della pace*; Panaite, *Ottoman Law*.

32 Lesaffer, Broers and Waelkens, 'From Antwerp to Munster'.

33 Such a distinction goes back at least to the early Middle Ages: Jean-Marie Moeglin and Stéphane Péquignot, *Diplomatie et « Relations Internationales » au Moyen Âge (IXe–XVe Siècle)* (Paris: PUF 2017) 542; Drocourt, *L'autre Empire du Milieu*, 73–81; Khadduri, *War and Peace*.

34 *Ta'rīḫ-i ṣulḥnāme*, fol. 109a. In Islamic Law, the term *ṣulḥ* denotes an amicable settlement between individuals: Othman, 'And Ṣulḥ is best'. As many other diplomatic practices originated in interpersonal relations, it was then transferred into a broader frame to designate a short-period truce (up to ten years usually) that a Muslim ruler can sign with a non-Muslim counterpart: Panaite, *Ottoman Law*, 170–2. However, by the late seventeenth century in the Ottoman context, the term had long come to refer more generally to amicable settlements (that is, peace rather than truce) between two rulers and their respective polities: Poulios, 'From the Palace of Ryswick', 111–13. Meninski defines the word as 'componere rem, pacem facere, compositio, pax, conciliatio, conventio, pacificatio, concordia'. As its synonyms, he cites "barışıḳ, barışıḳlıḳ, ṣalāḥ and muṣālaḥa" (*pacificatio, compositio rei aut controversiae, reconciliatio*): Meninski, *Thesaurus*, 2980, 4694. As for the expression *ṣulḥ-i müe'bbed*, the latter is already encountered in official Ottoman documents to

frieden,[35] *vechnyi mir*[36]), or perfect (*Perfetta pace*,[37] *musâlaha-i kâmile*[38]), or positive (*positiva Pace*[39]) peace. The Ottomans referred to it with some additional terms as well, such as 'strong friendship' (*kavî dostluk/ḳavī muḥabbet*)[40] or 'sturdy peace' (*sulh-i müeyyed*).[41] As all these appellations made clear that, not only was this type of treaty supposed to last indefinitely or as long as one of the two signatory rulers was alive,[42] but it also implied that the two negotiating parties had managed to overcome in their talks all, or the majority, of the contentious issues among them and thus they would have been able to establish durable peaceful relations in the future.[43]

If that could not be accomplished, the two warring sides could opt for a time-limited peace or cessation of hostilities. Such types of bilateral treaties were not at all uncommon in the seventeenth century.[44] They normally left

---

designate an eternal peace/friendship concerning the Polish-Lithuanian Commonwealth at the beginning of the seventeenth century: Rohdewald, 'Pax perpetua?', 175. That does not mean, of course, that the expression could not have been used earlier in peace or trade agreements with other Muslim or Christian powers.

35 BayHStA, Kasten Schwarz 310, fol. 42ʳ, Mörmann to Maximilian II Emanuel, 7 February 1699.

36 *Pamiatniki*, 184.

37 ÖStA, HHStA, Türkei I, Turcica Box 171, Folder 2 (January 1699, 2nd half), fol. 275ʳ, Marsigli to Kinsky, 21 January 1699.

38 *Cerîde-i Takrirât*, 74. Manifesting how terms can evolve their meaning throughout the ages and how practices could significantly alter, in classical Islamic Law, the term *muṣālaḥa* was only to be applied to a proper peace among Muslim potentates: Panaite, *Ottoman Law*, 171. By the late seventeenth century, as Zülfikār's relation attests, that was no longer the case.

39 Ruzzini, *Relazione*, 357. Lord Paget uses also the expression 'regular peace' (*Paix reguliere*): ÖStA, HHStA, Türkei I, Turcica Box 164, Folder 5 (1697), fol. 60ᵛ, Paget to Kinsky, 29 December 1697 (J.C.).

40 *Cerîde-i Takrirât*, 63; *Taʾrīḫ-i ṣulḥnāme*, fol. 16^{a-b}, 110^{b}.

41 *Cerîde-i Takrirât*, 116.

42 *See* below.

43 *Cerîde-i Takrirât*, 63, 73; Moeglin and Péquignot, *Diplomatie*, 543; Lesaffer, Broers and Waelkens, 'From Antwerp to Munster', 242–3. Yet, the claim of Christian jurists that an eternal peace 'exhausts the right of the parties to resort to war for the causes the war has been fought over' was more of a wishful thinking – perhaps valid for manifestos of declaration of war – than an actual practice (ibid., 243). In this respect, their Ottoman colleagues were more pragmatic. In a famous *fetvā* justifying the Ottoman conquest of Cyprus in 1570 from the Venetians, the prominent sixteenth-century Ottoman jurist Ebussuud Efendi (d. 1574) claimed that a time-limited (*muvaḳḳit*) or indefinite (*müe'bbed*) peace could be unilaterally broken as long as it didn't serve the interests of the Muslim community: İbrahim Peçevi, *Tarīh-i Peçevi*, vol. 1 (Istanbul H. 1283/1866) 486–7.

44 For instance, in 1629, Sweden and the Polish-Lithuanian Commonwealth signed a six-year Truce at Altmark: Ulf Sundberg, *Svenska freder och stillestånd 1249–1814* (Stockholm:

the postbellum territorial landscape in a status quo, theoretically undecided.[45] This kind of temporal reconciliation was used by the opposing sides in order to eventually conclude a proper or more stable peace.[46] If that was palpable enough, in contrast to perpetual peace, the terminology used in the various languages of the congress's main actors to designate such temporally delimited agreements presents a picture of extreme fluidity and complexity. *Induciae*,[47] *armistitio*,[48] *Stillstandt*,[49] *peremir'e*,[50] *pax inducialis/paix inducielle*,[51] *cessasion d'armes*,[52] *tregua*,[53] *terk-i cidāl u muvādaʿa*,[54] *müddet ile sulh*:[55] all these words are used interchangeably by the different actors, making any clear-cut distinction between them impossible.

For instance, the Ottoman–Muscovite two-year treaty is sometimes described as 'truce',[56] sometimes as 'armistice',[57] denoting that these two terms were mainly synonymous in the late-seventeenth century. However, on

---

Hjalmarson & Högberg 2002) 235–8; Croxton, *Westphalia*, 48. In 1635, it was renewed for another twenty years (ibid., 49). For the more famous Twelve Years Truce (1609) between Spain and the United Provinces, *see* Lesaffer, Broers and Waelkens, 'From Antwerp to Munster'.

45 Something that is perfectly captured by the contemporary to the Congress of Carlowitz German word for such agreements, *Stillstandt: See* below.

46 *Taʿrīḫ-i ṣulḥnāme*, fol. 16^{a-b}, 109^{a}; *Cerîde-i Takrirât*, 63, 74, 120; *Pamiatniki*, 184; Moeglin and Péquignot, *Diplomatie*, 542.

47 ÖStA, HHStA, Türkei I, Turcica Box 166, Folder 3 (September 1698, 2nd half), fol. 139^{r}. The term was already present in the early Middle Ages: Lesaffer, Broers and Waelkens, 'From Antwerp to Munster', 237.

48 ÖStA, HHStA, Türkei I, Turcica Box 168, Folder 2 (November 1698, 2nd half), fol. 275^{r}, Marsigli to Kinsky, 21 January 1699; ÖStA, HHStA, Türkei I, Turcica Box 169, Folder 1 (December 1698, 1st half), fol. 151^{v}, Voznitsyn to Małachowski, 10 December 1698.

49 Ibid., fol. 7^{v}, Imperial plenipotentiaries to Leopold I, 2 December 1698.

50 *Pamiatniki*, 181.

51 Cernovodeanu, 'Le journal', 338.

52 Ibid., 340.

53 ÖStA, HHStA, Türkei I, Turcica Box 170, Protocollum, fol. 119.

54 *Taʿrīḫ-i ṣulḥnāme*, fol. 109^{a}. Or *taʿṭīl-i ḥarb u ḳıtāl* – literally meaning, just like *terk-i cidāl*, a cessation of war (ibid). This reveals again how the Ottomans incorporated new elements into the traditional 'Islamic Law of Nations'. None of these expressions appear in the classical *Siyar*, where it is rather the term *ṣulḥ* that is used in this context: Panaite, *Ottoman Law*, 170–2. The term *muvādaʿa* is more problematic. Whereas Rāmī uses it in this case with its classical Islamic Law meaning of truce (Panaite, *The Ottoman Law*, 171), in other instances, the word is employed as a synonym for peace (*muṣālaḥa u muvādaʿa*): DABAO, A.DVNS.MHM.d, 100, fol. 306. Similarly, Meninski defines it as *quietare, pacem facere*: Meninski, *Thesaurus*, 4998.

55 *Cerîde-i Takrirât*, 63.

56 ÖStA, HHStA, Türkei I, Turcica Box 171, Folder 1 (January 1699, 1st half), fol. 178^{v}, Schlik to Kinsky, 12 January 1699.

57 *Narratio*, fol. 24^{r}.

other occasions, it appears that the Carlowitz participants also distinguished between a 'short truce/armistice' (*breves inducias, petite treve*)[58] and a 'long truce/armistice' (*lunga Tregua, treve longue*)[59] or 'time-limited peace' (*müddet ile sulh, Pax Inducialis*).[60] If we judge from the Ottoman–Muscovite case, the former constituted a treaty without articles, stipulating only a complete cessation of hostilities on a status quo basis for the two sides to proceed with their negotiations and reach an ultimate reconciliation.[61] The latter, though, was a genuine – or very close to a genuine – peace settlement,[62] containing an extensive list of specific articles regulating various spheres of the relations between two polities.[63] The Imperial–Ottoman agreement is a telling example of this category, which one might call 'mixed-type treaties'.

The latter's hybrid nature is perfectly attested by the terminological amalgamation we encounter in the sources concerning them. In his initial instructions to his two plenipotentiaries, Leopold I clearly stated that they would negotiate a 'truce or armistice' (*Inducias seu Armistitium*) with the Ottomans.[64] Nonetheless, a few lines below, he would refer to it as peace (*quo pax ista*),[65]

---

58 ÖStA, HHStA, Türkei I, Turcica Box 169, Folder 1 (December 1698, 1st half), fol. 152r, Małachowski to Voznitsyn, 11 December 1698; Cernovodeanu, 'Le journal', 338. Remember that short truces/armistices were also agreed upon for a specific geographical area to facilitate the convening of a peace congress. *See* Act I.

59 Cernovodeanu, 'Le journal', 338; Ruzzini, *Relazione*, 357.

60 However, as we shall see below, the Ottoman–Imperial agreement is also described as *armistitium, Stillstandt*, or *terk-i cidāl*.

61 *Gründ- und umständlicher Bericht* 29–32. Similarly, the Ottoman–Venetian Provisional Peace Instrument stipulated that from the day it was signed on behalf of the Serenissima by the Imperial and Commonwealth plenipotentiaries, until its formal signing by the Venetian ambassador, a truce/armistice (*terk-i cidāl*) on land and sea would be enforced: Silâhdâr, *Nusretnâme*, 511. These cases challenge the distinction made by Lesaffer, Broers, and Waelkens, who argue that truces 'normally apply to all hostile actions between two belligerents and are generally entered into by the sovereign', whereas armistices 'can be made by battlefield commanders as well as sovereigns and often are limited to certain theatres of war': Lesaffer, Broers, and Waelkens, 'From Antwerp to Münster', 238.

62 As is evidenced by the terms *müddet ile sulh* or *pax inducialis* that are sometimes ascribed to it by the participants.

63 Lesaffer, Broers, and Waelkens, 'From Antwerp to Münster', 243–55; However, Voznitsyn claimed that even a short-term truce/armistice could restore friendly relations on a broader level, mainly through a free and undisturbed resumption of trade: *Pamiatniki*, 185.

64 ÖStA, HHStA, Türkei I, Turcica Box 166, Folder 3 (September 1698, 2nd half), fol. 139r, Instructio pro Legatis Plenipotentiarijs Cas[are]is. Note again the same meaning the two words share, which is further proved by their interchangeability in other parts of the text. For instance, ibid., fol. 148r.

65 Ibid.

and Kinsky would do the same in his various letters to Paget[66] as much as the Ottomans did when speaking of their agreements with the Holy League powers in general.[67] Sometimes, the in-between nature of such settlements was overtly expressed by the plenipotentiaries themselves. Reporting to the Habsburg emperor about the agreed duration of the treaty they had negotiated with their Ottoman counterparts, Öttingen and Schlik would write that 'this peace or truce/armistice is [to last] for twenty-five years'.[68] A similar phraseological duality equally dominated the Ottoman and Latin texts of the Imperial–Ottoman Peace Instruments. Whereas the word peace is encountered in them far more often,[69] interestingly, truce/armistice (*terk-i cidāl*/*armistitium*) is clearly employed in both languages in the article concerning the temporal limitation of the agreement.[70]

3 Temporal Validity of the Agreements

At the dawn of the eighteenth century, treaties in the 'Society of Princes' continued to resemble interpersonal agreements, engaging and binding two rulers and not some abstract political entities.[71] That meant that, if not clearly stated

66 For instance, ÖStA, HHStA, Türkei I, Turcica Box 169, Folder 2 (December 1698, 2nd half), fol. 47r–v, Kinsky to Paget, 14 December 1698. In addition, in the Imperial protocol concerning the discussion of the technicalities of the signing ceremony during one of the last conferences, we encounter the phrase 'the signing of peace' (*la sottoscrittione di Pace*) and not of truce/armistice: ÖStA, HHStA, Türkei I, Turcica Box 171, Folder 2 (January 1698, 2nd half), fol. 133r, Nota dell Concordato nella conferenza li 23 Genaio 1699.

67 *Taʿrīḫ-i ṣulḥnāme*, fol. 127b; DABOA, İE.DH 8–756.

68 ÖStA, HHStA, Türkei I, Turcica Box 169, Folder 1 (December 1698, 1st half), fol. 7v, Imperial plenipotentiaries to Leopold I, 2 December 1698.

69 'İşbu muvâda'a ve musâlaha, bu sulh [ü] salâh ve dostluk ve barışlıklık': Silâhdâr, *Nusretnâme*, 503–4. And in the Latin text, 'Pax ista […] Incipiat verò modo dicta Pax': *Gründ – und umständlicher Bericht*, 22, 24. Interestingly, the term *muvâda'a ve musâlaha* is rendered in Latin as *Armistitium* (ibid, 21), revealing once again the semantic plurality of certain words.

70 Silâhdâr, *Nusretnâme*, 504; *Gründ – und umständlicher Bericht*, 21. However, *see* the Treaty of Vasvár (1664), where, in the same clause of the Ottoman Peace Instrument, the term *mübârek sulh* (holy peace) is used, which was translated in Italian as *benedetta pace*: Özgür Kolçak, 'XVII. Yüzyıl Osmanlı-Habsburg Diplomasi Tarihine bir Katkı: 1664 Vasvar Antlaşması'nın Tasdik Sürecine Dair Yeni Bulgular'. *Dîvân Disiplinlerarası Çalışmalar Dergisi* 22/43 (2017), 69, 72.

71 Lesaffer, Broers and Waelkens, 'From Antwerp to Munster', 239. *See*, for instance, the preambles of the Carlowitz Treaties, where the different potentates are mentioned as the sole contracting parties: *Gründ – und umständlicher Bericht*, 10–11, 25, 29–31. There is only one exception; *see* below.

otherwise, an amicable settlement, being that a peace or truce/armistice[72] was usually valid only as long as its two signatories remained alive or in power.[73] In Western Europe, this practice continued up until the sixteenth century. In the subsequent period, rulers would typically engage in the ratification of a treaty themselves and on behalf of their successors, although the binding of the latter, while widely endorsed, was not axiomatic.[74] However, in the agreements between the Ottoman Empire and its neighbours, be they Muslim or Christian, this method would only be more steadily adopted from the seventeenth-century *fin de siècle*.[75]

Such a divergence could perhaps be explained firstly, from the Ottoman part – with some parallels to Christian European polities – by the internal political structure of the empire. Especially in the fifteenth and sixteenth centuries, the death of a ruling sultan automatically meant a literal, temporary suspension of his 'Dominion'. All acts, treaties and appointments made by him were considered nullified until the enthronement of a new monarch and the establishment of his own rule, his own 'Dominion', with the (re)confirmation, or not, of his antecedent's decisions. With the diminishing role of the sultan in the Ottoman governmental system from the seventeenth century onwards, and the development of a more clear conception of an impersonal 'state' among the members of the Ottoman élite, continuity rather than abruption became steadily and increasingly the norm, and that could not but have an equal impact on the perception regarding treaties with foreign powers.[76] Intriguingly, in the preamble of the Ottoman–Venetian Peace Instrument,

72 Most studies focus primarily on perpetual peace agreements, often overlooking the equally significant issue of long-term truces/armistices and whether these would remain valid if one of the signatories died or was deposed. For example, Moeglin and Péquignot, *Diplomatie*, 538–9; Lesaffer, Broers and Waelkens, 239. While Viorel Panaite provides indirect insights into this matter, his analysis lacks concrete conclusions: Panaite, *Ottoman Law*, 179–84.

73 Ibid.; Rohdewald, 'Pax Perpetua?', 173–174; Randal Lessafer, 'Peace treaties from Lodi to Westphalia', in Randal Lessafer (ed.), *Peace Treaties and International Law in European History. From the Middle Ages to World War One*, (Cambridge/New York: Cambridge University Press 2004) 20–2.

74 Ibid.

75 For instance, in the late seventeenth century, the Safavids still had to send embassies to the Porte upon the ascension to the throne of a new sultan – and not the other way around – to reconfirm or renegotiate the existing peace agreement between the two polities: Selim Güngörünler, 'Fundamentals of Ottoman-Safavid Peacetime Relations, 1639–1722'. *Turkish Historical Review* 9 (2018), 170.

76 Nicos Sigalas, 'Des histoires des sultans à l'histoire de l'État. Une enquête sur le temps du pouvoir ottoman (XVIe–XVIIIe siècles)', in François Georgeon and Frédéric Hitzel (eds.), *Les Ottomans et le temps* (Leiden/Boston: Brill 2012) 99–127.

contrary to the rest, it is not the sultan and the doge but 'the Exalted State' (*Devlet-i ʿAliyye*) and the 'Republic of Venice' (*Venedik cumhūru*) which are mentioned as the two treating parties.[77] The perpetual Ottoman–Commonwealth peace agreement is the first between the two powers to engage the successors of the two ruling monarchs,[78] and a similar stipulation is to be found in the Imperial–Ottoman 'peace with duration/long truce-armistice'.[79]

Nonetheless, one cannot explain such developments solely under the prism of the steady rise of the modern concept of sovereignty or the 'depersonalisation of treaty law'.[80] Such arguments, while correct, cannot entirely explain why the Porte, while committing the ruling sultan's successors in its 1699 peace settlement with Poland-Lithuania or the Habsburg emperor, abstained from doing it before[81] or why a similar stipulation was not present for the Venetians.[82] It appears that for the Ottomans, restricting the duration of a treaty to the lifespan of a ruler could be seen as a concrete and symbolic manifestation of force since it would have implied – at least to them – that they would be the ones to control the progress of their bilateral relations with foreign powers, while the latter would always be the ones supplicating the Porte for a renewal of the agreement between them.[83]

It is thus no coincidence that the single time before 1699 – to my knowledge – that an Ottoman sultan (not universally accepted as such, though) agreed to commit his successors to a peace treaty was in 1403. In that

77 Silâhdâr, *Nusretnâme*, 506. Similarly, in the text of the Treaty of Nerchinsk, it is the *Imperium Sinicum* and *Ruthenicum*, not their rulers, who figure as the main contracting parties: Sebes, S.J, *The Jesuits*, 157.

78 Silâhdâr, *Nusretnâme*, 518.

79 Ibid., 504; *Gründ – und umständlicher Bericht*, 23.

80 An approach that Lesaffer adopts in idem, 'Peace treaties', 20–2.

81 For the Polish-Lithuanian case, *see* Rohdewald, 'Pax Perpetua?', 173. The Ottoman–Imperial Treaty of Vasvár (1664) equally did not contain such a stipulation. Kolçak, 'Osmanlı-Habsburg Diplomasi', 69, 72–73.

82 If fact, the latter had to renew their treaty in 1706 after the accession on the throne of Aḥmed III (r. 1703–30): Özgür Oral, 'Osmanlı-Venedik Diplomatik İlişkileri Tarihine Bir Katkı: 1763 Tarihli Cezayir-Venedik Antlaşması'. Avrasya *İncelemeleri Dergisi/Journal of Eurasian Inquires* 6/2 (2017), 106. The Serenissima would only be able to obtain such a clause regarding the internal, beyond the life of a single ruler, validity of its treaties with the Porte in 1733. Pedani Fabris, *La Dimora della Pace*, 37–8.

83 For instance, in the sultanic *ʿahdnāme* (ratification document) of the Ottoman–Muscovite peace treaty of 1681, valid for twenty years, it was stated that little before the lapse of its duration (one or two years), 'the King of Muscovy (sic!) could petition and implore [my Exalted Porte] for the renewal of peace'. *See* the, in all probabilities, contemporary to the events Greek translation of the Ottoman text in Eudoxiu Humurzaki (ed.), *Documente privitóre la istoria românilor*, vol. 13 (Bucharest 1909) 46–7.

year, Süleymān (I) (d. 1411), one of the sons of Bayezid I (r. 1389–1402) and a contender to the Ottoman throne, signed a peace settlement with a coalition of various Christian powers in the Balkans and the eastern Mediterranean. In it, he declared to uphold friendly relations with them 'fina che seremo viuj e li fiuolj de nostri fiuolj, e che li nostri fiuolij sia cum lor in bona paxe'.[84] Yet, this treaty was concluded in a specific historical conjuncture in which the Ottoman polity was falling apart after the crushing defeat Bayezid I suffered from Timur in the Battle of Ankara (1402). It also contained highly favourable territorial clauses for the Christian princes in an effort by Süleymān to win their support for his claim of sole dominion over the Ottoman Empire.[85] Thus, the slowly shifting balance of power between the Porte and some of its neighbours in the late-seventeenth century also contributed to the gradual loss of the ability to project the strength of a non-engagement of every future sultan on a bilateral agreement with a foreign ruler or polity manifested.[86] Additionally, the relative balance of power among the Christian European rulers could perhaps have been one of the reasons why this commitment-of-successors precept was generally accepted between them earlier.

4 Which Type of Agreement to Pick?

Power balances, strategic concerns (mostly related to territorial matters), the particular interests of each one of the main participants and previous bilateral practice were among the factors that appear to have mainly influenced, with varying degrees, the preference of the type and temporal validity of the various agreements signed during the Carlowitz Congress. Asked by Petr Postnikov during their secret talks before the start of the official conferences about the Ottoman intentions regarding the duration of the treaties with the other Holy League members, Mavrocordatos initially stated that the Porte supposedly intended to propose to all of them a short truce/armistice because to grant

84 Riccardo Predelli (ed.), *Diplomatarium Veneto-Levantorum, sive Acta et Diplomata Res Venetas Graecas atque Levantis Illustrantia*, vol. 2 (1351–1454) (New York: Cambridge University Press 2012) 290.

85 For this period, *see* the now classical study of Dimitris Kastritsis, *The Sons of Bayezid. Empire Building and Representation in the Ottoman Civil War of 1402–13* (Leiden/Boston: Brill 2007).

86 However, we should note that while such a balance of power consideration may explain the Ottoman–Imperial case, it does not allow the same with the one of the Ottoman–Commonwealth, since it cannot be argued that the *Rzeczpospolita* was militarily stronger than the Porte.

one 'for a long period it goes against [the] old customs (*prezhnih obychaev*)'.[87] 'And if they will ask for peace [instead]?', Postnikov wondered.[88] 'If we see that [this] is for the best, why not?' the Ottoman plenipotentiary meaningfully retorted.[89]

4.1 *The Ottoman–Imperial Example*

Mavrocordatos's intriguing assertions provide an excellent background for our analysis. Let us thus delve deeper, case by case, starting from the Ottoman–Imperial one. During the Vienna negotiations (1689–90), the then-Ottoman delegation proposed two possible ways to end the conflict. Either the Imperials would return to the Porte some of their recent conquests in Hungary, in which case, 'a steady peace and a strong friendship' (*müstakirren sulh ve kavî dostluk*) could be reached, or the principle of the *uti possidetis* was to be applied, leading instead to a (long) truce/armistice.[90] Although there was no way Vienna – its armies victorious on the battlefield – could have possibly agreed with the first option, the fact that the Porte, in order to regain some of its lost lands, was even willing to propose eternal peace to one of its greatest enemies is in itself telling. However, the Imperial refusal to consent to such a perpetual agreement was not only prompted by the exuberance of the Ottoman demands. As would happen ten years later at Carlowitz, feeling that they were the ones who now had the upper hand, the Habsburgs, with their declared intentions being to restore the borders of the medieval Kingdom of Hungary,[91] probably wanted to leave open their options for further territorial aggrandisement at the expense of the Porte in the future.

As we have seen, Öttingen and Schlik were instructed to conclude a long truce/armistice with the Ottomans, leaving, it seems, the exact number of years for them to decide.[92] Vienna considered that there were some unresolved matters with its opponent.[93] Ironically, against the background of

---

87 *Pamiatniki*, 186.

88 Ibid.

89 Ibid.

90 *Cerîde-i Takrirât*, 63–4, 73–4.

91 *See* above, Act III, At the Negotiating Table II.

92 This is the impression one gets from what the two ambassadors report on the matter in one of their relations to the emperor: ÖStA, HHStA, Türkei I, Turcica Box 169, Folder 1 (December 1698, 1st half), fol. 7v, Imperial plenipotentiaries to Leopold I, 2 December 1698.

93 BayHStA, Kasten Schwarz 310, fol. 42r, Mörmann to Maximilian II Emanuel, 7 February 1699. As Mörmann's dispatch implies, the Imperial ministers were also trying to cloak their option for a truce/armistice with the Ottomans under the guise of Christianity and the impossibility of a Christian monarch to conclude a permanent peace with the 'Turk'. The

such intentions, Marsigli, in a letter to Count Kinsky before the start of the official conferences, claimed that, apart from agreeing to stipulate clear borders during and not after the congress, the true motives of the Ottomans regarding their commitment to a stable and durable peace with the Imperials would be revealed 'in the issue of the length of the years of the truce/ armistice [they will propose]'.[94] He was to be surprised. At the very first meeting, Rāmī and Mavrocordatos alluded again to a possible 'perpetual friendship' (*ad una amicitia perpetua*) if, this time, the Imperial side agreed to transfer to the Porte an annual 'gift' for its possession of Transylvania.[95] Otherwise, as Rāmī's comments imply regarding the strategic significance the retention of the Ṭemeşvar province had for the Ottoman side, the latter was not at all willing to conclude a proper peace which would officialise the loss of the rest of its former Hungarian territories. The Imperial delegation categorically refused any talk of what it perceived as a concealed Ottoman attempt to present the emperor as the sultan's tributary. So, the debate ultimately centred around the temporal limitation of the agreement. The ensuing discussion, one of several really amusing bazaaresque scenes that took place during the negotiations, transpired according to the Imperial protocol in this way:

> COUNT SCHLIK: Proposes the duration of the truce/armistice for thirty years.
> MAVROCORDATOS: In the former treaties, we always find twenty years. Let's stick to that.[96]
> COUNT SCHLIK: This number of twenty did not bring [good] fortune up to this moment.[97] So, let us take another limit, [one] of thirty years.
> COUNT ÖTTINGEN: Says that twenty years is a small time period.

intriguing detail here is that they primarily evoked their future territorial pretensions as a reason, and then the question of faith: Ibid.

94 ÖStA, HHStA, Türkei I, Turcica Box 167, Folder 2 (October 1698, 2nd half), fol. 97ᵛ, Marsigli to Kinsky, 22 October 1698.

95 ÖStA, HHStA, Türkei I, Turcica Box 170, Protocollum, fol. 16. We must reiterate that such a 'gift'/tribute does not appear to have been proposed as a means to justify or align an eternal peace agreement with Islamic Law. Instead, it was likely intended to reinforce the narrative of a 'victorious peace' for the Ottoman domestic audience. This interpretation is supported by the fact that in 1689, during negotiations in Vienna, as well as at Carlowitz with Muscovy (*see* below), the Ottomans did not associate perpetual peace with any form of payment.

96 Remember Mavrocordatos's statement to Postnikov about following the 'old custom'.

97 Schlik hints at the infelicitous end of the Treaty of Vasvár (1664) – concluded again for twenty years – when the Ottomans opted for war instead of accepting its renewal in 1682.

> MAVROCORDATOS: Says that [an] additional duration [of twenty years] was [to be] provided for the renovation [of the treaty after its expiration].
> COUNT SCHLIK: Let's divide the ten. Make [them] twenty-five.
> EFENDI (Rāmī Meḥmed): Put twenty-two.
> THE MEDIATORS: Let us put twenty-five years, and so the article remains the same [as follows].[98]

To place the Carlowitz agreement in a broader chronological perspective, the duration of the two subsequent Ottoman–Imperial treaties, that of Passarowitz (1718) and that of Belgrade (1739), was twenty-four and twenty-seven years, respectively.[99] It is perhaps no coincidence that the first perpetual peace settlement concluded by the two powers would not occur until 1747.[100] By then, both of them had, by and large, accepted the Danube as their definite border.[101]

4.2 *The Ottoman/Polish-Lithuanian Case*

Such a definite soothing of territorial disputes arrived much earlier between the Ottomans and the *Rzeczpospolita*. The relatively amiable relations and the absence of fighting between the two polities during the sixteenth century probably played a role in Poland-Lithuania being among the Christian powers with which the Ottoman sultans concluded permanent peace agreements – even if those were limited to their lifetime.[102] However, during the seventeenth century, the situation was drastically altered, and the two sides clashed quite often, especially during the last quarter of the century, when the Ottomans sought to impose direct control over the region of Podolia and an indirect one in western Ukraine, both controlled up to that point by the Commonwealth.[103] Still, with the Ottomans willing to renounce their recent conquests of Polish territory and providing that the *Rzeczpospolita* showed readiness to do the same with its claims in Moldavia, most of the issues between them would be solved.

---

98 ÖStA, HHStA, Türkei 1, Turcica Box 170, Protocollum, fol. 81.

99 Panaite, *Ottoman Law*, 181.

100 Veinstein, 'Fondements juridiques', 516.

101 It is important to note that by the late seventeenth century, establishing a clear boundary did not necessarily resolve territorial disputes between the participants unless both parties deemed it in their interest to formally recognise the status quo as permanent.

102 *See* extensively in Rohdewald, 'Pax Perpetua?'.

103 For an overview of the Ottoman–Commonwealth relations during the seventeenth century, *see* Dariusz Kołodziejczyk, *Ottoman-Polish Diplomatic Relations (15th to 18th Centuries). An Annotated Edition of 'Ahdnames and Other Documents* (Leiden: Brill 2000) 129–57.

Thus, contrary to Mavrocordatos's statement to Postnikov, the Porte, following indeed the custom of its bilateral treaties with its northern neighbour, had only one proposal to make: permanent friendship. Already in 1689, the Ottoman plenipotentiaries in Vienna reported to the grand vizier that the then Commonwealth's ambassador had shown inclination to agree on a 'sturdy peace' (*sulh-i müeyyed*) with a return to the old border between the two polities.[104] A decade later, nothing had changed. When Małachowski was urged by Voznitsyn to conclude, like him, a two-year truce/armistice with the Ottomans, the Pole replied categorically that the Republic wanted a proper peace and not a time-limited agreement.[105]

From the mediation's protocol or the Ottoman and Polish accounts, it appears that the two sides did not even enter into a discussion of the issue, possibly because it seemed to them self-evident. The only significant difference, going verily against the previous practice, was the equal validity of the treaty for the successors of the two monarchs ratifying it. Informing the Bavarian Elector Maximilian II Emanuel, Hannibal Mörmann claimed that the Ottoman–Commonwealth treaty was 'eternal' (*Ewig*), adding that this is 'generally not common between the Christians and the Turks'.[106] The main reason for such a choice, according to him, was that with the return by the Ottomans of the fortress of Kamianets, '[Poland] received [back] everything that the Turks possessed from [the said] kingdom', so, contrary to the Imperials, they had no further territorial claims.[107] And despite voices in the Ottoman élite or among the ordinary people, who were not entirely satisfied with some of the terms of the treaty,[108] how the latter indeed mirrored the will of the two polities to definitely settle the century-old disputes between them, is plainly proved by the fact that not only did they never again declare war against one another, but the agreement conserved its full validity and force until the end of the eighteenth century and the disappearance of the Commonwealth as an independent state.[109]

104 *Cerîde-i Takrirât*, 116.

105 *See* above, Act III, Narration Part II.

106 BayHStA, Kasten Schwarz 310, fol. 41^{v}–42^{r}, Mörmann to Maximilian II Emanuel, 7 February 1699. Of course, he would have arrived at a quite different conclusion had he known the full history of the Ottoman–Commonwealth agreements since the sixteenth century.

107 Ibid., fol. 42^{r}.

108 Hora-Siccoma, 'De Vrede van Carlowitz', 174–5.

109 Kołodziejczyk, 'The Treaty of Carlowitz', 208–10.

4.3 *Venice and the Ottomans*

Venice presents in many respects a rather peculiar case, revealing the complexity of effectively deciphering all the motives behind the choice of the type and duration of an inter-polity reconciliation agreement. In a manner similar to Poland-Lithuania, the Serenissima had a centuries-old tradition of concluding perpetual peace agreements with the Ottoman Empire (valid for the reign of a single ruler, however) despite their relations falling relatively short of being perpetually amicable.[110] This long tradition, connected perhaps with the clear Ottoman superiority over the Republic from the late fifteenth century onwards, seems to have created a particular kind of pattern that was to be almost automatically followed in every negotiation between them. In their talks with the Venetian ambassador in Vienna in the late 1680s and early 1690s, the Ottomans argued that they got the impression from the Serenissima's peace terms that the Republic ostensibly desired a 'strong friendship' with the Porte since 'there is no mention [there] of a time-limited peace with the keeping of the conquered [by you] territories'.[111]

Quite interestingly, regarding the Serenissima, in Vienna and Carlowitz, the Ottoman side did not connect the *uti possidetis* principle with a specific type of agreement. When Rāmī and Mavrocordatos presented Ruzzini with two options, namely that either the Republic would keep all its current possessions yet pay a 'present' for the Morea, or relinquish all fortresses in mainland Greece, they did not, as in the case of the Imperials, relate the first to eternal peace and the second to a 'peace with duration'.[112] In fact, the subject of the type and temporal validity of the Ottoman–Venetian treaty was hardly discussed. In his protocol of the conference on 23 January between the Ottomans and the Imperials to agree on the articles of the Venetian peace agreement, Johannes Till would state that 'for the duration of peace, finding nothing explicit in the Venetian [peace] proposals, there is no discussion of a time-limit'.[113]

Hence, the agreement was considered eternal, even if it was not explicitly declared as such,[114] with the crucial element, though, that contrary to the

110 As early as 1419, Sultan Meḥmed I (r. 1414–21) concluded a 'paxe dreta, lial e veriteuele' with the Serenissima, which remained valid for the duration of his reign: Predelli, *Diplomatarium*, 318–19. Not surprisingly, when viewed through the lens of strategic interests shaping the choice of reconciliation agreements, the Serenissima was, during the same period, primarily concluding short truces/armistices (*treuguae*) with the Christian Byzantine Emperor: Ibid., 301, 304, 316–7.

111 *Cerîde-i Takrirât*, 88–9.

112 *Taʾrīḫ-i ṣulḥnāme*, fol. 99[a].

113 ÖStA, HHStA, Türkei I, Turcica Box 170, Protocollum, fol. 200.

114 Ruzzini clearly refers to it as 'Pace perpetua': Ruzzini, *Relazione*, 374.

Ottoman–Imperial or Ottoman-Polish treaty, there was no explicit mention that its validity was also extended to the sultan's successors. The Venetian approach to not mentioning a specific temporal limit could be understood, besides the peacemaking tradition with the Exalted State, as an attempt from the evidently weaker party to guarantee peace for as long as possible. An explanation of the Ottoman stance to restrict the perpetuity of the agreement to the reign of Muṣṭāfā II needs to consider, among possible other motives, not only the feelings of superiority the Ottomans nurtured towards the Serenissima but also the fact that they still had open business with it. Loredano would – acutely, as it turned out – argue that in their present negotiations with Venice, especially regarding the Morea, the Porte had no other purpose than 'to prepare and enhance the ways to effectuate [an invasion], wanting [...] to pave now the road [for it]'.[115] This invasion would indeed come in 1715, as the Venetian predicted. It was only after the Treaty of Passarowitz and the Ottoman reconquest of the southern Greek peninsula, along with all the remaining Aegean islands under Venetian control, that the territorial disputes between the two polities finally came to an end.

4.4 *The Ottoman–Muscovite Case*

If strife over land possession between the Porte and the Republic of Saint Mark had decreased by the end of the second decade of the eighteenth century, that of the Exalted State with Muscovy (later Russia) was only beginning. Their first formal agreement in 1681, dividing Ukraine into two spheres of influence, was concluded for twenty years. However, in 1698, given the vast aspirations of Peter I and his desire, until the very last moment, to continue the war with the Ottomans, any long truce/armistice, let alone perpetual peace, was out of the question. Voznitsyn had already made that clear to his Ottoman counterparts from the outset.[116] The latter held different opinions, however. 'Peace [can] be made in two ways', they declared during the first session, in a manner strongly reminiscent of the 1689 Ottoman–Imperial talks in Vienna. If Muscovy returned Azov to the Ottomans, an 'eternal peace' (*müe'bbed ü mü'ekkid ṣulḥ u ṣalāḥ*) could be established. If not, then with the stipulation of a new border for the Azov region and the evacuation by Muscovy of its fortresses in the Lower Dnieper, the two sides could accord on a (long) 'truce/armistice' (*terk-i*

115 ÖStA, HHStA, Türkei I, Turcica Box 171, Folder 1 (January 1699, 1st half), fol. 115r, Loredano to Kinsky, 7 January 1699.

116 Bogoslovskii, *Petr I*, 385–6.

cidāl u muvādaʿa) for a specific period.[117] 'The merits of the first option are obvious', they continued, 'the second one, a truce and a cessation of hostilities, is not deprived of profits either. Maybe we could work out a way to revive the ancient friendship during this interval'.[118]

There was, of course, no chance that the Muscovite would agree to return Azov to the Ottomans, but he was not even prepared to demolish the Dnieper fortresses. It was better to conclude a two-year truce/armistice, he asserted, because the differences between the two sides were many, making a 'perpetual' or a 'time-limited' peace impossible.[119] 'A one-year(sic) truce/armistice is a way to avoid [dealing with all sorts of problems]. It was practised between frontier lords'[120] not by plenipotentiary ambassadors with absolute authority to discuss, resolve all issues and restore 'a strong friendship' (*ḳavī muḥabbet*) between the two empires, the Ottomans complained.[121] Nevertheless, Voznitsyn would not back down, and the Porte's representatives were left with no other option but to consent too. A quite lengthy truce/armistice (or time-limited peace), lasting for thirty years, was finally agreed upon with the subsequent Treaty of Constantinople (1700).[122] It was not exactly the 'strong friendship' or 'perpetual peace' the two sides ostensibly hoped for at Carlowitz, but still, the Muscovites could at least boast that they secured the exact duration that the Imperials could not. Both sides should have realised, though, that this was a temporary respite. The tsar turned his eyes to the north, and the Porte was hoping to recover after a period of incessant wars.

117 *Taʿrīḫ-i ṣulḥnāme*, fol. 109ª. Mavrcordatos would later define three options: 1) a small truce/armistice (*petite treve*), 2) [eternal] peace (*Paix*), or 3) a long truce/armistice (*treve longue*): Cernovodeanu, 'Le journal', 338. However, he claimed that the Ottomans' intentions were not to negotiate a truce/armistice: Ibid., 340.

118 *Taʿrīḫ-i ṣulḥnāme*, fol. 109ª. The same idea, but with a different timetable was voiced by Voznitsyn, who, in his initial secret negotiations with the Ottomans, proposed a 'truce/armistice for a year, or a year and a half' – which the Ottomans rejected as too short – during which the two parties could work out their differences and conclude an 'eternal peace' (*vechnyi mir*): *Pamiatniki*, 184.

119 *Taʿrīḫ-i ṣulḥnāme*, fol. 110ª; Cernovodeanu, 'Le journal', 340.

120 *Taʿrīḫ-i ṣulḥnāme*, fol. 110ª.

121 Ibid.

122 Kołodziejczyk, *Ottoman-Polish Diplomatic Relations*, 84.

Narration Part II: the Deadline

> We want to know if the Republic desires war or peace [...] we want to know it now!
>
> ALEXANDROS MAVROCORDATOS during a session on 4 January[1]

•••

> [This] month [of January] [...] started with troubles and will probably finish with chagrins.
>
> COUNT SCHLIK reporting to Count Kinsky on 21 January[2]

∴

'The new year 1699 emerged', relates the Anonymous Venetian,

> while things were in the aforementioned [strenuous] stance and the spirits of the Venetians very perplexed and agitated because of the time vainly spent, of the prejudice of the delays that weakened [their] negotiating [position], and of the particular thoughts that everyone made to his private interests and their abandoned, faraway, households.[3]

The Ottoman delegation was also experiencing similar feelings due to the futile passing of days and the inattentiveness to their private affairs back home.[4] Another plenipotentiary who appeared to be even more apprehensive about attending to his public and private interests in his homeland was Małachowski. After remaining, shortly it seems, persuaded by the Venetian to prolong his stay, he started again pestering the *Cavaliere* 'both in conversations and through letters' to hasten the termination of his talks,[5] warning him that

1 ÖStA, HHStA, Türkei I, Turcica Box 170, Protocollum, fol. 153.

2 ÖStA, HHStA, Türkei I, Turcica Box 171, Folder 2 (January 1699, 2nd half), fol. 121ʳ, Schlik to Kinsky, 21 January 1699.

3 *Narratio*, fol. 27ᵛ.

4 ÖStA, HHStA, Türkei I, Turcica Box 170, Protocollum, fol. 123.

5 *Narratio*, fol. 28ᵛ–29ʳ.

 | DOI:10.1163/9789004458499_026

TABLE 4 Official conferences held at the Carlowitz Peace Congress during January 1699

1st: 15th Imperial–Ottoman conference
4th: 1st combined Ottoman–Venetian–Imperial conference
10th: 16th Ottoman–Imperial conference
13th: 17th Ottoman–Imperial conference
14th: 6th Commonwealth–Ottoman conference
15th: 18th Imperial–Ottoman conference
16th: 2nd combined Ottoman–Venetian–Imperial conference
18th: 19th Imperial–Ottoman conference
19th: 20th Ottoman–Imperial conference
22nd: Combined Ottoman–Imperial–Commonwealth conference on the affairs of Venice
23rd: Imperial–Ottoman conference on the affairs of Venice

SOURCES: ÖSTA, HHSTA, TÜRKEI I, TURCICA BOX 170, DIARIUM ET CERIMONIALE, FOL. 58–78; CERNOVODEANU, 'LE JOURNAL'

otherwise, he would sign his agreement and leave, being thus 'the first, to his grief, to give the Turks this great pleasure that they were waiting for, to see the League scattered before the conclusion of peace'.[6]

1 Ruzzini Remains Firm; the Imperials Actively Intervene

After his latest failure to advance his affairs, the *Cavaliere*, ever eager to follow to the letter the rules of the Venetian decision-making playbook, had no other option but to dispatch again a courier to the Senate, stressing 'the extremely pertinacious insistence of the Turks, the rush of the allies [to conclude the congress] and the danger that the interest of the Republic lay upon'.[7] The next conference with the Ottomans he attended took place on 4 January. It was the first one with the simultaneous presence of the Imperial plenipotentiaries after an explicit request by the Ottoman delegation.[8] By that move, the latter hoped, perhaps, to exercise greater constraint upon both allies and especially the Imperials, since any direct involvement of the latter in the Ottoman–Venetian talks increased their responsibility for their success or failure. A thought

6 Ibid., fol. 29^{v}.
7 Ibid., fol. 27^{v}.
8 *Taʿrīḫ-i ṣulḥnāme*, fol. 122^{b}.

equally based, so it seems, on the correct assumption that Vienna would not, in the end, risk putting its interests into jeopardy for the sake of Venice and therefore do everything in its power to make the republic see (the Ottoman) reason. All the same, its unique format with the simultaneous presence of formal and informal mediators was quite unprecedented for a peace congress. The 4 January conference 'lasted from nine in the morning until eight o'clock in the evening. Many things were discussed and debated; many notes were kept on them by the secretaries, but nothing was concluded'.[9] Rāmī and Mavrocordatos also attempted during it to further alienate the Imperial support for Ruzzini by skillfully playing with the general suspicions among the allies, and the mediators of a secret connivance between France and Venice, to cause the congress to fail. 'We are suspecting', Mavrocrodatos said plainly, 'that the Republic does not want peace, perhaps instigated by another part'.[10]

In the end, the Ottoman strategy of tying the Habsburg delegation more tightly to the results of the Venetian negotiation paid off. The Imperials committed themselves to a 'persuasion deadline' (*Eines termini persuasionis*) of five days – the first one to be applied to Venice – during which they promised to undertake strenuous efforts to arrange things with Ruzzini.[11] Hence, the following days passed with both the Habsburg duo and the mediators coercing the Republic's ambassador to accept the Ottoman terms for the Morea and the Greek mainland. Nonetheless, as the anonymous Venetian account maintains, the *Cavaliere* neither could nor wanted to. He couldn't because of his limited plenipotentiary powers that made it imperative for him not to commit to anything without the agreement of the Senate, and he did not want to because, having seen the Ottoman territorial aspirations for the Levant, he had every reason to believe that, despite the Porte's professions to the contrary, its designs for Dalmatia were equally prejudicial for the Serenissima's interests.[12]

The pressure culminated in a semi-official conference between Ruzzini and the Imperial ambassadors on 7 January, which Schlik described in his 'Secret Journal' as 'a long-drawn-out torture' (*nach einer langwirrigen tortur*).[13] The latter played the card of the seemingly pressing need for war preparations if no agreement is reached, reminding his interlocutor that they had already futilely spent 'half of winter without making ready for war, although Poland

9 *Narratio*, fol. 29ᵛ.

10 BNM, Ms.it.VII 399 (8625), fol. 303ʳ, Alcuni discorsi raccolti dal Nicolosi; *Taʿrīḫ-i ṣulḥnāme*, fol. 125ᵃ; Ruzzini, *Relazione*, 359.

11 ÖStA, HHStA, Türkei I, Turcica Box 170, Diarium et Cerimoniale, fol. 60.

12 *Narratio*, fol. 30ᵛ.

13 ÖStA, HHStA, Türkei I, Turcica Box 170, Diarium et Cerimoniale, fol. 61.

and Muscovy appear to be abandoning the League'.[14] He invited him, though, to think carefully about what risks 'he wants to expose Christendom and the emperor to for a trifle'.[15] 'His Imperial Majesty does not want to break [the congress] […] War is a disaster for [our] master', he briskly concluded.[16] However, the *Cavaliere* remained immovable. 'Not even two paces forward' were made, Schlik reported with distress in his *Journal Secret*.[17] 'The mania of this minister [ambassador] cannot be expressed', Count Marsigli, who was also present during the meeting, would also comment in a letter he sent to Kinsky.[18]

Having failed to convince the Venetian with arguments or indirect threats, the Imperial ambassadors turned the focus of their efforts to stripping him of the support of the other two Holy League members, especially the one whom they considered to be Ruzzini's greatest advocate, Prokopii Voznitsyn.

2 Voznitsyn's Moves

During late December 1698 and early January 1699, Prokopii Bogdanovich chose, according to Count Schlik, to follow his own path, autonomous from the other allies. 'The Muscovite handles now his affairs directly with Herr Mavrocordatos, and he is in no further need of any other mediator than his doctor [Postnikov], who finds himself almost daily [in the Ottoman camp]'.[19] The purpose of Postnikov's allegedly 'under the table' (*unter der handt*)[20] novel round of meetings with the Ottoman ambassador 'is surmised to have been', as Schlik recounts, 'the secret drafting of the Instrument of the projecting truce/armistice'.[21] However, that was not how Voznitsyn viewed the situation. For his part, he had valid reasons to desire a direct drafting of his agreement with the Ottomans since he firmly believed that the mediators, and especially Lord Paget, greatly prejudiced him in favour of the Porte when a first version of the text was discussed during the last official Ottoman–Muscovite session.[22]

---

14 ÖStA, HHStA, Türkei I, Turcica Box 168, Folder 1 (November 1698, 1st half), fol. 305^{r}, protocol of the Imperial–Venetian session on 7 January 1699.

15 Ibid., fol. 306^{r}.

16 Ibid., fol., 307^{r}.

17 ÖStA, HHStA, Türkei I, Turcica Box 170, Diarium et Cerimoniale, fol. 61.

18 ÖStA, HHStA, Türkei I, Turcica Box 171, Folder 1 (January 1699, 1st half), fol. 124^{r}, Marsigli to Kinsky, 12 January 1699.

19 ÖStA, HHStA, Türkei I, Turcica Box 170, Diarium et Cerimoniale, fol. 56.

20 ÖStA, HHStA, Türkei I, Turcica Box 171, Folder 1 (January 1699, 1st half), fol. 44^{v}, Imperial plenipotentiaries to Leopold I, 2 January 1699.

21 ÖStA, HHStA, Türkei I, Turcica Box 170, Diarium et Cerimoniale, fol. 56.

22 Bogoslovskii, *Petr I*, 414–7.

One of the favourable terms he was able to secure for his side through this latest direct negotiation with his Ottoman counterparts was that the two-year truce/armistice was to have immediate effect from Old Calendar Christmas Day, even before the signing and exchanging of the Instruments.[23] It was a clever provision. Voznitsyn was able to secure his position by acquiring an immediate termination of hostilities for his master while arguing at the same time that by doing so, he had not actually betrayed his allies since he was waiting to sign his agreement together with them. Not everyone was fooled, however. Following Count Schlik, by the effectuation of the Ottoman–Muscovite truce/armistice on 25 December 1698/4 January 1699, Muscovy was officially partly (*en partie*) no longer a member of the League.[24]

Still, 'the wild beast' had to be tamed, especially regarding the issue of Venice. On 1 January 1699, Count Öttingen visited the Muscovite to congratulate him on the successful termination of his negotiations. To Voznitsyn's declaration that the matter was not over yet since the Venetians had not concluded their affairs and the *Cavaliere* had persuaded him to defer the signing of his Instrument, Öttingen duly replied, 'that he, the Muscovite ambassador, should speak for himself and stick to his own judgement, and he should not listen to those [like the Venetians]. [People] advising him that way are not His Majesty's [the tsar's] friends'.[25] Öttingen, together with Schlik this time, revisited Voznitsyn on 7 January, after the strenuous meeting they had with Ruzzini, asking him to use his friendship with and the leverage he had over the Venetian to induce him to make some concessions. They equally tried to defame the *Cavaliere*, professing, as Voznitsyn claims, that 'he is possessed by some evil spirit, and he is undermining peace on purpose',[26] this 'evil spirit' being none other than the French, as the Imperial ambassadors would clarify, who did everything possible in their power to prevent an agreement between the emperor and the sultan.[27] Meanwhile, their master was obliged to keep his troops in the winter quarters and pay them for no apparent reason. Not everyone was so prepared to continue the war as the tsar, they concluded with a slight sarcasm.[28]

Voznitsyn should have greatly enjoyed this 'civil war' between the two erstwhile close allies. He still held strong grudges against the Imperials for their conduct all along from the Preliminaries towards Muscovy, and having

---

23 *See* more below, Narration Part III.

24 ÖStA, HHStA, Türkei I, Turcica Box 171, Folder 1 (January 1699, 1st half), fol. 179^r, Schlik to Kinsky, 12 January 1699.

25 Quoted in Bogoslovskii, *Petr I*, 420–1.

26 Ibid., 422.

27 Ibid.

28 Ibid., 421.

guaranteed the latter's withdrawal from the conflict, he would probably have been delighted to see the much 'peace-loving Germans' fail to reach an agreement with the Ottomans because of Venice. It would be poetic justice for him, one may say. So, he vehemently continued to ostensibly support the Serenissima and his representative, arguing that rather than pushing him to make concessions, both he and the Imperials should do their best to aid Ruzzini. The latter was not stubborn, as Öttingen and Schlik maintained. 'He concedes to what he can. To what he cannot, how can he concede?'.[29] Furthermore, instead of urging the *Cavaliere* to conclude his affairs, as the Imperials wished him to do, he urged him with letters not to give in to their pressure, adding that they were only terrorising him with the supposed looming departure of the Ottomans from the congress venue for their own profit.[30]

3 Apprehension at the Imperial Court

Back in Vienna, realising the difficulty of the situation, the members of the 'Turkish Deputation' were trying to find ways to deal with the 'Venetian headache' without jeopardising their peace agreement with the Porte and the emperor's reputation by leaving Venice entirely alone. One option was to arrange a time limit during which the Republic could conclude its negotiations in the congress venue. Another was that the Serenissima would sign a truce/armistice with the Ottomans and then continue the peace talks in Vienna or Constantinople. One also had to count the possibility, not at all desirable for the Imperials, that the Republic had already opted to continue the war.[31]

At the same time, Loredano was finding himself in a new series of attempts to get the ear of the Imperial ministers. In continuous letters to Kinsky, he complained about the inefficiency of the latest Imperial instructions, which 'didn't produce any good effect [on the Turks], appearing rather to [only] have been worthy of rendering them more recalcitrant and ferocious'.[32] The Habsburg plenipotentiaries should press the 'Turks' more. In a quite interesting, yet inverted, parallel to the Ottomans' thinking about the Imperials, the Venetian ambassador bet that the latter's uncompromised stance on the Serenissima

29 Quoted in ibid., 422.

30 Ibid., 421.

31 ÖStA, HHStA, Türkei I, Turcica Box 171, Folder 1 (January 1699, 1st half), fol. 146ʳ, relation of the members of the 'Turkish Deputation' to Leopold I, 8 January 1699.

32 Ibid., fol. 114ʳ, Loredano to Kinsky, 7 January 1699.

was mere appearances.[33] What Loredano failed to grasp, though, was that irrespective of whether or not the Ottomans were bluffing, Vienna was not going to risk everything for Venice's sake.

Another who also appeared to have not yet sufficiently weighed the circumstances was the Venetian Senate. Still believing in the force of the preliminary agreement and the false hopes of support coming from the Imperial Court, it dispatched to Carlowitz new resolutions, reaching Ruzzini on 13 January, which basically altered nothing in essence from its previous ones.[34] 'Poor ambassador Ruzzini', Count Marsigli commented in a letter to Kinsky, 'miserable to the point of [arousing] compassion by seeing him so badly supported by the necessary orders from his homeland'.[35]

4 Time Is Running Out

The end of the five-day deadline, the, according to Schlik, 'awaited with pain' (*mit schmerzen erwahrtetne*(sic)) January the 10th, finally arrived.[36] Not being able to move Ruzzini, the Imperial ambassadors took the situation into their own hands and asked the Ottomans for 'a peremptory deadline' (*terminum peremptorium*) of fifteen days to accommodate Venice, after which, irrespective of the results of the Ottoman–Venetian negotiations, the Imperials and the Poles would sign their agreement – Voznitsyn being considered, as we have seen, as having already abandoned the alliance through his actions.[37] This ultimate time limit was another decisive turning point of the congress, opening up the road to its end, and an enormous success for the Ottoman delegation, which, sure now of its agreements with all the other allies, could be almost certain to secure most of its demands on Venice, now officially isolated and under extreme duress.[38]

In their relation to the emperor, the two ambassadors justified their initiative by arguing that they had been left with no other means to keep the Ottomans at Carlowitz. This explanation was also given to a consterned Ruzzini.[39] They

33 Ibid., fol. 115ᵛ.
34 *Narratio*, fol. 31ʳ.
35 ÖStA, HHStA, Türkei I, Turcica Box 171, Folder 2 (January 1699, 2nd half), fol. 187ʳ, Marsigli to Kinsky, 26 January 1699.
36 ÖStA, HHStA, Türkei I, Turcica Box 170, Diarium et Cerimoniale, fol. 62.
37 ÖStA, HHStA, Türkei I, Turcica Box 170, Diarium et Cerimoniale, fol. 64; *Taʿrīḫ-i ṣulḥnāmẹ*, fol. 127ᵃ.
38 *Narratio*, fol. 35ᵛ–36ʳ.
39 Ruzzini, *Relazione*, 358.

had to accord to this deadline – which, ironically, they had proposed – *nolentes volentes*, as they claimed.[40] This novel *fait accompli* of the Imperial embassy was equally *nolentes volentes* accepted in Vienna.[41]

As the drama was greatly intensifying, in a conference on 16 January, the Ottomans finally revealed their plans for Dalmatia, which, as Ruzzini feared, were 'exceedingly disrespectful and prejudicial' and went entirely against the instructions of the Senate.[42] Ruzzini's hands, once more, were tied, as Małachowski reported to Karol Stanisław Radziwiłł.[43] Dissimulating his feelings of frustration against the Imperials, especially on the issue of Ragusa – ironically, such feelings were mutual – and accompanied by Nicolosi, he met with Öttingen and Schlik in a desperate effort to convince them of the just claims of the Serenissima concerning the eastern shore of the Adriatic: all went in vain. In the next combined session with the Ottomans on 18 January, Ruzzini was utterly isolated. Intensely disillusioned by the stance of the Habsburg delegation, the *Cavaliere* could not hold himself any longer and had a robust discoursal *brat de fer* with Schlik.[44] 'And the conference finished at seven thirty in the evening, without concluding anything and without doing anything more than dispute and complain [about] articles that [in the end] were not accepted', Johannes Till laconically wrote in his protocol.[45]

All these developments caused lively internal debates in the Venetian camp, as everyone attempted to 'scrutinise the most profound intentions of princes'.[46] There were two lines of thinking, one condemning the Imperial duplicity, the other trying to exonerate Vienna.[47] 'But the ambassador, listening only to the dictates of prudence and dissimulating what in other contingencies he would not have dissimulated, tried to meet again with the Imperial ambassadors to win them over with dexterity and with reason, or at least not to lose [their support] completely'.[48] Yet, when one of the nobles of his retinue was sent to Count Öttingen to arrange a meeting, he was told that the count was resting, and Schlik equally replied that he could not listen to Ruzzini without his

40 ÖStA, HHStA, Türkei I, Turcica Box 171, Folder 1 (January 1699, 1st half), fol. 170^{v}–171^{r}, Imperial plenipotentiaries to Leopold I, 12 January 1699.

41 Ibid., fol. 9^{v}, supplementary Imperial instructions, 19 January 1699.

42 *Narratio*, fol. 32^{r}, 33^{v}.

43 AGAD, Archiwum Warszawskie Radziwiłłów, 1/354/0/5/9200, fol. 52, Małachowski to Radziwiłł, 23 January 1699.

44 *Narratio*, fol. 35^{r}.

45 ÖStA, HHStA, Türkei I, Turcica Box 170, Protocollum, fol. 197.

46 *Narratio*, fol. 36^{r}.

47 Ibid., fol. 36^{r}–38^{r}.

48 Ibid., fol. 38^{r}.

colleague. The Venetian was fully reaping the consequences of his earlier clash with both.[49] Fed up with what they now clearly perceived as the *Cavaliere*'s duplicity, and with the Ottomans declaring that 'they were not willing to see him (Ruzzini) or negotiate with him' any longer,[50] the Habsburg delegation decided to take a step further and, instead of its so far informal mediation, directly handle the talks with the Ottomans on Venice's behalf without the participation of Ruzzini, another major blow to the latter's – and the Republic's – honour. A draft of the proposed articles was sent with Schreyer to the Venetian, who rejected them, declaring 'that this was not the form to make peace'.[51]

Abandoned by his most trusted allies, the *Cavaliere* turned for aid to Mavrocordatos, sending him 'a lavish present of rose oil and textiles', which the Ottoman plenipotentiary received 'with full courtesy of words' and replied after a few days with a gift of some coffee packages.[52] This 'friendly' exchange, though, did not seemingly usher in any concrete benefit for the Venetian, apart perhaps from the delight of enjoying some good quality Turkish coffee.

Patience with Venice was also running out in Vienna. In a letter to Marsigli on 21 January, Kinsky declared that any failure of the Serenissima to reach an agreement with the Ottomans would rest entirely on her shoulders as to what would subsequently unfold.[53] Finally realising that despite all his efforts, 'the hearths and interests' of the Imperial ministers were impenetrable, Loredano advised his colleague in an encrypted letter dated 20 January 1699 to embrace pragmatism and opt for the lesser evil, that is, to leave the Imperials agree themselves on the conditions for the Serenissima. In their desire to appear to the world as having been able to obtain for her terms that would be 'the least unjust' (*le più meno inique*), they might be able to achieve more than Ruzzini could have hoped to win by himself.[54]

With the deadline of 26 January drawing near and excluded from any direct discussion of his affairs with the Ottomans, Ruzzini was spending his days writing urgent dispatches to Venice and knocking on every door in a despairing effort to solicit backing from his allies and the mediators, assuring them that at any moment a courier could arrive from Venice with the necessary orders to

---

49 Ibid., fol. 38^{r-v}.

50 AGAD, Archiwum Warszawskie Radziwiłłów, 1/354/0/5/9200, fol. 52, Małachowski to Radziwiłł, 23 January 1699.

51 *Narratio* 38^{v}.

52 Ibid., fol. 38^{v}.

53 ÖStA, HHStA, Türkei I, Turcica Box 171, Folder 2 (January 1699, 2nd half), fol. 111^{r}, Kinsky to Marsigli, 21 January 1699.

54 BNM, Ms.it.VII 399 (8625), fol. 367^{r}–368^{r}, Loredano to Ruzzini, 20 January 1698 (1699).

finish his negotiation.[55] His 'social capital' was finding itself at the lowest level, though, as he was almost universally 'designated as the [principal] cause of the sufferings, the difficulties and the perils to the common [allied] advantages'.[56]

Facing the actual risk of leaving the Republic without a treaty, not an ideal situation for Vienna, as we have seen, the Imperial ambassadors took Venice's fate in their hands, and during two quite peculiar 'multilateral' conferences taking place on 22 and 23 January, respectively, the majority of the Ottoman–Venetian peace articles were negotiated and drafted by the Imperials, the Poles, the Ottomans and the mediators.[57] 'Although, openly, the ambassador [Ruzzini] did not want to appear as having a part in it', recounted Count Schlik, the agreed articles were communicated to him secretly (*sous main*).[58] 'He would probably have found another occasion to complain if we had acted by surprise', he mockingly added.[59]

The Imperials decided to bring Małachowski into the game as well, 'to declare vociferously that we are doing that [agreeing on behalf of Venice] as the Holy League [in its entirety]and share', as Schlik cynically admitted, 'the detest that could result out of it'.[60] He was right to think this way since, by agreeing to sign a provisional Venetian Peace Instrument themselves, without Ruzzini's open consent, in order not to separate the Serenissima from the League and the general peace – although giving her a period to ratify it or not, as if it supposedly had a genuine choice[61]– the Imperial ambassadors were significantly infringing upon the sovereignty of the Republic, which, ironically, Schlik so vehemently defended during those same conferences. Nonetheless, as even

55 *Narratio*, fol. 38^{v}.

56 Ruzzini, 'Relazione', 362.

57 ÖStA, HHStA, Türkei I, Turcica Box 170, Diarium et Cerimoniale, fol. 75–78; Nicolosi and Dottor Fondra were simply briefed post factum by Count Marsigli about the results of the two meetings. *Narratio*, fol. 38^{v}.

58 ÖStA, HHStA, Türkei I, Turcica Box 172, Folder 1 (February–March 1699), fol. 27^{r}, Schlik to Kinsky, 4 February 1699.

59 Ibid.

60 ÖStA, HHStA, Türkei I, Turcica Box 171, Folder 2 (January 1699, 2nd half), fol. 181^{v}–182^{r}, Schlik to Kinsky, 26 January 1699.

61 *Narratio*, fol. 38^{v}; The final article of the Ottoman–Imperial Provisional Peace Instrument allowed the Republic to accept or reject it within thirty days. If rejected, a new round of talks would take place in Vienna with the extraordinary Ottoman ambassador, present there as part of the ceremonial arrangements for the formal conclusion of the Ottoman–Habsburg peace. These negotiations, lasting up to six months, would be mediated jointly by Imperial, English, and Dutch representatives but confined to the terms of the Provisional Peace Instrument: Silâhdâr, *Nusretnâme*, 512. This compromise balanced Ottoman inflexibility on territorial matters with the need to give the Serenissima time to agree and avoid exclusion from the general peace settlement.

voices inside the Venetian camp would later suggest, 'it was neither original nor monstrous that the rest of the members of an alliance agreed on behalf of another one of them. Not a long time ago [in the Congress of Ryswick?], peace was arranged in this form for Spain and even for the [Holy Roman] Emperor'.[62] In any case, the interests of Venice were rescued', Schlik assured the Bohemian Chancellor.[63] Małachowski, even without fully participating in the two meetings because of his poor health,[64] was mainly of the same opinion, although also admitting that the *Cavaliere* might not feel entirely satisfied with it.[65] In any case, the Pole was feeling happy to finally be able to leave this 'purgatory', as he referred to his stay at the congress venue.[66]

One by one, all allied plenipotentiaries abandoned Ruzzini. However, the greatest and most surprising betrayal for the *Cavaliere* came from Voznitsyn. For quite some time, the Muscovite was also under pressure from the Ottomans to sign his agreement. On 19 January, Mavorcordatos sent to him his priest to inform him that the Porte's plenipotentiaries had already packed their things and sent them to Belgrade and were about to depart.[67] The following day, it was the turn of Lord Paget, who, in his usual double language, warned the Muscovite that his Instrument had been lying with the mediation for quite some time. If he did not want the 'Turks' to refuse to abide by it any longer, as the 'barbarians' they were, he should instead hurry up and sign it.[68] On 22 and 23 January, Mavrocordatos repeated to Postnikov the need for an immediate exchange of the Instruments, assuring him that the Imperials and the Poles were about to do the same on the 26.[69]

Convinced now that he could do nothing more to impede the successful conclusion of the congress, Voznitsyn has left with no other choice but to sign his agreement.[70] '[My] business here is coming to an end', he wrote to Peter I one day before his signing ceremony.[71] Nonetheless, despite having taken that decision, he and Postnikov continued dissimulating their true intentions to

62 *Narratio*, fol. 48r.
63 ÖStA, HHStA, Türkei I, Turcica Box 171, Folder 2 (January 1699, 2nd half), fol. 181v–182r, Schlik to Kinsky, 26 January 1699.
64 He could only be partly present during the first of the two sessions: ÖStA, HHStA, Türkei I, Turcica Box 170, Diarium et Cerimoniale, fol. 76–77.
65 AGAD, Archiwum Warszawskie Radziwiłłów, 1/354/0/5/9200, fol. 50–55, Małachowski to Radziwiłł, 23 January 1699.
66 Ibid., fol. 50.
67 Bogoslovskii, *Petr* I, 422.
68 Ibid.
69 Ibid., 423.
70 Ibid., 423–4.
71 Quoted in ibid., 423.

Ruzzini. 'He [Voznitsyn] assured the Venetian many times', the Anonymous Venetian bitterly relates,

> not to conclude [peace] if not together [with him], expressing that even if the Turks had given him Constantinople, he would not have made peace without all the others, and showing him a letter written by the hand of his tsar himself, in which he wrote that he did not desire peace at all but rather the continuation of war.[72]

However, for all the categorical declarations of Ruzzini to Postnikov that the rumour the Imperials were spreading that the Venetian peace articles were already agreed and even signed was 'utterly wrong', and despite the doctor appearing to be satisfied with them, 'with the usual inconsistency of the nation, he [Voznitsyn] changed [attitude] in an instant' and on the next day, 24 January, 'with all his suite [and] with the greatest pomp and fanfare went to the Conference [House] and signed his treaty'.[73]

---

72 *Narratio*, fol. 41^{r}. He also advised Ruzzini – as he had done earlier with Małachowski – that if it was not possible for him to conclude a proper peace treaty, he could then opt, just like himself, for a one-year truce/armistice: Bogoslovskii, *Petr I*, 423.

73 *Narratio*, fol. 41$^{r–v}$.

Narration Part III: the Finale

> Done with the battlefield, praise be to God,
> With the arrival of peace, order returned to the World.
>
> YUSUF NĀBĪ (1642–1712), *Ḳaṣide-i ṣulḥiyye* (Ode to Peace)[1]

•••

> Peace in the empire of His Caesarian Majesty.[2]
>
> COUNT MARSIGLI to Count Kinsky on 26 January 1699

1 Reconciliation in Public Display: the Signing Ceremonies

1.1 *Voznitsyn Signs First*

It was the consideration of a variety of factors that led Voznitsyn to his drastic decision to sign his agreement with the Ottomans alone, ahead of all his allies. A probable novel round of ceremonial disputes with Małachowski over precedence figured prominently among them, with the Imperials also diligently fomenting such thoughts in the Muscovite.[3] Besides the obvious fact that they would not allow new strife between the two ambassadors to ruin a ceremony that they envisaged as a strong demonstration of the unity of the Holy League, they would also be quite contented to see Prokopii Bogdanovich, the arch-defender of the Venetians, being the first to abandon them and hence bare the greatest load of the latter's loathing for doing so.

On the other hand, though, Voznitsyn's separate signing ceremony cannot but be seen as the epitome of his behaviour throughout the congress, one that mainly consisted of following an independent path. As we have already discussed, such a stance, as he continuously asserts, was a direct outcome of the rancour he held for various reasons against every one of his allies and the mediators. For the occasion of the signing ceremony, however, he focused

1 Bilkan, *Nabi Divanı*, 85.

2 ÖStA, HHStA, Türkei I, Turcica Box 171, Folder 2 (January 1699, 2nd half), fol. 187r, Marsigli to Kinsky, 26 January 1699.

3 Ibid., Folder 2, fol. 181r, Schlik to Kinsky, 26 January 1699.

 | DOI:10.1163/9789004458499_027

this general acrimony on the Habsburgs and the Poles. Having fulfilled their primary goals at the expense, as he thought, of his (and Venice's), he did not desire to give them the pleasure of being a part of their self-indulgent fiesta. "It seemed improper for me to dance at someone else's wedding", he wrote pointedly.[4]

Such a 'lonely-raider posture' was not welcomed in the Polish camp and was viewed as another outright proof of Muscovy's duplicity and violation of the agreement between the two polities. Andrzej Gorkowski, the secretary of the Commonwealth's embassy, complained that Voznitsyn's decision to sign his agreement ahead of all others was 'against the [alliance] treaties' (*in contrarium Pactorum*).[5] He was sent to the Muscovite by Małachowski, as soon as the latter learned the news, to strongly complain to him that in doing so, he did not appear to care much about the need to manifest the union of the Christian allies, nor about the imperative to wait until the lapsing of the designated deadline for Venice of 26 January. 'He was confused and did not reply to that', Gorkowski relates.[6]

The ceremony occurred at ten o'clock in the morning, on 24 January, at the conference house. Voznitsyn arrived first with the most lavish possible ostentation. The mediators were already there waiting for the ambassadors of the two sides, while around the building, a heterogeneous crowd of bystanders from the Ottoman, Imperial and the mediators' retinue had gathered to watch the event. After the advent of the Ottomans, the ceremony commenced with the customary speeches followed by the last scrutinous checking of the Instruments to corroborate that nothing was added or removed since their handing over for safekeeping to the mediators. Then, on the suggestion of the Porte's plenipotentiaries, all the doors of the house were opened, and the spectators waiting outside were let in to view the signing, sealing, and exchanging of the treaty texts.[7]

The Anonymous Venetian found a cunning way to 'avenge' Voznitsyn's betrayal by inserting in his account of the ceremony 'a ridiculous accident' (*redicolo accidente*), which, interestingly, is nowhere else recorded.

4 Quoted in Bogoslovskii, *Petr I*, 425.

5 Gorkowski, *Compendium*, 31ʳ.

6 Ibid.

7 Bogoslovskii, *Petr I*, 425–7.

> As the capitulations [the treaties][8] were mutually signed in a small table divided in two, which was explicitly placed between them for the occasion, and the documents themselves were exchanged, Mavrocordatos and the Muscovite stood up from their seats intending to embrace one another. [However], as the one was advancing towards the other, thinking that they could support themselves in the small table, the latter was removed by the mediators [...] and the too-weighty Muscovite fell over Mavrocordatos, who pushed by the sudden and unexpected weight receded and they [found themselves] tumbling down [on the floor] one above the other.[9]

With direct reference to Voznitsyn's weight, the latter is transformed into a caricature while the whole ceremony forfeits all its solemnity, becoming a laughable fiasco. Having officially finished his business in the congress, Voznitsyn visited the Imperials the next day and immediately embarked on a brief religious sightseeing trip, a *Kirchfart* as Schlik designates it, to the nearby Serbian churches and monasteries.[10] Not only did he not desire to be part of the Imperial/Commonwealth–Ottoman 'wedding', but he would not even tolerate, it appears, to watch by proxy the 'German-Polish' festive procession accompanying 'bride Peace' to the conference house.

1.2 *26 January 1699: the Grand Ceremony*

Małachowski could accuse the Muscovites of breaking the 'Christian unity' and alliance obligations with their actions. Yet, if we were to believe Count Schlik, he would have immediately followed Voznitsyn and signed his treaty separately as well, if not for the Imperials having prevented and convinced him to do it together with them.[11] A façade of unity between the two founding

8 The term *capitulationi* as used by the author, should not be confused with the better-known trade privileges granted by the Ottoman Porte to various European powers from the sixteenth century onwards. Historically, the word had a much broader meaning, dating back to the Middle Ages, where it referred to any document divided into chapters or articles – such as a peace treaty: Panaite, *Ottoman Law*, 174. Interestingly, the text of the Ottoman–Muscovite truce/armistice does not contain any articles. However, the Anonymous Venetian's use of the term highlights its broader application as a synonym for any bilateral agreement between polities.

9 *Narratio*, fol. 41v–42r.

10 ÖStA, HHStA, Türkei I, Turcica Box 170, Diarium et Cerimoniale, fol. 79.

11 ÖStA, HHStA, Türkei I, Turcica Box 171, Folder 2 (January 1699, 2nd half), fol. 181v, Schlik to Kinsky, 26 January 1699.

powers of the Holy League needed to be kept, and, as in the agreement of the terms for Venice, the responsibility for signing her provisional treaty had to be equally shared. For some unknown reasons, though – probably he wished to dissociate himself from the Ottoman–Venetian agreement – Małachowski changed his mind again at the last moment and expressed a will to sign after the Imperials.[12] It fell on Count Marsigli to bring him back into line. 'During this night and early morning', he recounted to Count Kinsky on 26 January, 'I had to rack my brain on the signing of the Pole, who wanted to perform [it] after the Imperials, against the [previous] agreement. [At the end], it was stipulated that we walk into this jointly'.[13]

Also, a day before the signing ceremony, the Imperial embassy received a peculiar request from the Ottoman camp. Rāmī Meḥmed, quite versed in astrology, it seems, had made a horoscope and kindly asked the Habsburg delegation if the signing of the agreements could take place at precisely eleven forty-five in the morning, 'being then a most propitious conjunction of the stars, which would not present itself again so favourable for a long time to come'.[14]

The 26 January could be astrologically friendly, but that did not apply equally to its weather conditions. 'Arrived the day of the 26', narrates the anonymous Venetian account, 'extremely tough because it snowed abundantly during the night and there was [also] a pesky breeze'.[15] Nonetheless, that did not deter the different delegations from arriving at the conference house with the maximum pomp and retinue.[16] *Au début*, only the ambassadors, together with the mediators, the secretaries and the interpreters, entered it to re-read and check together the articles of the Ottoman–Venetian provisional treaty. To accommodate Rāmī's request, at the time designated by him, this process had to be interrupted.[17] The doors then opened, and everyone who wished could enter and hear Philip Georg Schreyer reading aloud the different Instruments in Latin, a symbolic act marking the transition of the peace articles from the private sphere – between the ambassadors and their principals – to the 'public' one. It is no coincidence that the only agreement that was not read aloud publicly was the Ottoman–Venetian one, since, due to its provisional character and its non-approval by the Republic, it still had to be kept 'secret'. This first publication of the Ottoman–Imperial and Ottoman–Commonwealth

12 ÖStA, HHStA, Türkei I, Turcica Box 170, Diarium et Cerimoniale, fol. 80.

13 ÖStA, HHStA, Türkei I, Turcica Box 171, Folder 2 (January 1699, 2nd half), fol. 189^{r}, Marsigli to Kinsky (P.S.), 26 January 1699.

14 ÖStA, HHStA, Türkei I, Turcica Box 170, Protocollum, fol. 202–203.

15 *Narratio*, fol. 43^{v}.

16 Ibid., fol. 43^{v}–44^{r}.

17 ÖStA, HHStA, Türkei I, Turcica Box 170, Protocollum, fol. 203.

peace agreements was immediately followed by their signing by each party's plenipotentiaries.[18] When they finished, the bystanders had once more to exit so that the proofreading of the Ottoman–Venetian agreement could be terminated.[19]

> The ports were [then] reopened, and after a great number of people from all the four sides had entered, the consignment of the Instruments was made with cordial speeches and expressions for the just renovated friendship [peace], everybody auguring joy for the princes and [their] subjects, and long duration for this holy peace. After the speeches were over, the ambassadors gave the *osculum pacis*, kissing each other on both cheeks with [such an] extreme tenderness that it caused great rejoicing in the nations there present.[20]

What ensued was a universal, cheerful, and tumultuous celebrating polyphony, brilliantly depicted by the Anonymous Venetian:

> Notified, the troops that were stationed and attending [outside the Conference House] with 13 *salve* from every part solemnised the occasion with ceremonial firing, as the clamour of the arquebuses was combined with that of trumpets, tambours and the other military [musical] instruments of the Turks and the [cheering] voices from all encampments and the bystanders.[21]

2 When Is Peace Considered Concluded?

However, did the signing and exchanging of the Peace Instruments between the ambassador plenipotentiaries, together with all the accompanying mutually shared symbolic gestures of reconciliation, render peace actually concluded? Until the Late Middle Ages, it was quite normal for rulers to engage directly in peace talks with other princes or their representatives. In such instances, they immediately ratified the agreement they had negotiated by their signature and seal and usually by swearing an oath in front of the delegates of the other contracting party that acted as a further binding commitment not

18 *Narratio*, fol. 44^r.
19 ÖStA, HHStA, Türkei I, Turcica Box 170, Protocollum, fol. 203.
20 Ibid.
21 *Narratio*, fol. 44^v.

to break the treaty.[22] But from the late fifteenth century, as the presence and unmediated involvement of rulers in negotiations became more and more uncommon, it was the figure of the plenipotentiary who acquired the central role in the peacemaking process. So, in negotiations through plenipotentiaries, the final act of the 'Theatre of Peace' would typically contain two stages. The first was that the two parties' representatives would sign and exchange a Peace Instrument, *temessük*, in Ottoman Turkish,[23] or 'Instrument of Ratification' (*Instrumento di Ratificatione*) or 'provisional ratification' (*Instrumento di prouisionale Ratificatione*), to use Ruzzini's terminology.[24] From the Carlowitz example, it is plainly evident that the congress participants commonly accepted that all fighting between them stopped in this first stage.[25] Thus, the signing of the Peace Instrument meant a de facto restoration of peace. So, in the Ottoman–Imperial Instrument, it is stated that 'the peace, tranquillity and security for the subjects of both empires, really starts from the day of the signing [of the Instruments] and cease after that [...] all fighting between them'.[26]

Yet, in order for the treaties to be considered 'de jure' valid and terminated, they would then have to be reciprocally ratified by the sovereigns themselves after a period agreed between the parties,[27] in order, as Rāmī formulates it, to consolidate the terms stipulated by the delegations during the talks.[28] It was this second stage that officially signalled the end of the peacemaking process.[29]

---

22 Lessafer, 'Peace Treaties', 22–3; Güneş Işıksel, 'Hierarchy and Friendship: Ottoman Practices of Diplomatic Culture and Communication (1290s–1600)'. *The Medieval History Journal* (2019), 5; Panaite, *Ottoman Law*, 189–204.

23 The principal meanings of the word – Meninski defines it as 'obligatione, obligo, scritto obligatorio [...] istromento' (Meninski, *Thesaurus*, 1391) – as an obligation of or proof of payment of a debt, illustrate the tight conceptual connection between an inter-polity agreement and a contract among private individuals. For the term, *see* also Mübahat S. Kütükoğlu, 'Temessük', in TDVIA, vol. 40 (Istanbul: Turkish Religious Foundation 2011) 413–4.

24 Ruzzini, 'Relazione', 366.

25 Although in the Ottoman–Muscovite case, as we saw, such a cessation of hostilities came into effect even well before this step.

26 *Gründ – und umständlicher Bericht*, 24. *See* the Ottoman text, which was reproduced *mot-à-mot* in the sultanic *ʿahdnāme* (ratification document) in Silâhdâr, *Nusretnâme*, 504.

27 Lessafer, 'Peace Treaties', 22; Brunert and Oetzel, 'Verhandlungstechniken', 463; Kołodziejczyk, *Ottoman-Polish Diplomatic Relations*, 47–56; Işıksel, 'Hierarchy and Friendship', 5–6.

28 *Taʿrīḥ-i ṣulḥnāme*, fol. 127^b.

29 Brunert and Oetzel, 'Verhandlungstechniken', 463; Kołodziejczyk, *Ottoman-Polish Diplomatic Relations*, 54–5. There were exceptions, though. For instance, in the Treaty of Nerschinsk (1689), the Muscovite and Qing delegations signed, sealed their Instruments, and swore to observe the treaty, which was enough to bring it into effect: Perdue,

At Carlowitz, this two-step final reconciliation phase was unanimously observed. Yet, the ratification process and its accompanying ceremonial were not the same for every participant; rather, as with the treaties themselves, it was either bilaterally negotiated in situ[30] or followed the established peacemaking custom between two polities.[31] As Mavrocordatos pointedly declared when the issue was discussed during a session with the Imperial delegation, 'we have to follow the usage between the two empires and not stick to the custom [followed by] others'.[32]

The differentiation between a 'provisional' (Peace Instrument) and a 'definite' (Ratification) agreement created opportunities for the various parties to try, in the lapse between the two stages, to alter or renegotiate some of the terms their plenipotentiaries had already agreed during the peace talks. For instance, in the Ottoman–Commonwealth Peace Instrument, it was written that the evacuation of the Polish forces from northern Moldavia and the Ottoman troops from Kamianets-Podilskyi would have to start taking place from the beginning of March 1699.[33] However, the Porte, having some second thoughts about abandoning the fortress, tried to delay its withdrawal by refusing, on some pretexts regarding the form of the Polish king's ratification, to issue the sultanic *ʿahdnāme* (ratification document).[34]

Similarly, Venice attempted to improve the terms it obtained at Carlowitz, sending for that purpose Lorenzo Soranzo as extraordinary ambassador to the Porte to acquire the sultan's ratification. Whereas in the Imperial case, the sultanic *ʿahdnāme* was issued in just thirty days and with Poland-Lithuania and Muscovy in a couple of months, Soranzo was only able to obtain his in 1701.

'Boundaries', 351. However, one could surmise that this was primarily done because of the enormous distance between the capitals of the two empires.

30 The best example of such an ad hoc arrangement is the Ottoman–Imperial case, where after a debate between the two delegations on the matter, it was agreed that the sultanic and Imperial ratification documents were to be exchanged thirty days after the signing of the Instruments via the mediators – who were to remain in Belgrade for that reason –and the respective embassy secretaries at a convenient place near Slankamen: ÖStA, HHStA, Türkei I, Turcica Box 171, Folder 2 (January 1699, 2nd half), fol. 133ʳ, Nota dell Concordato nella conferenza li 23 Genaio 1699.

31 For instance, in the Ottoman–Commonwealth Peace Instrument, it was stated that 'according to the ancient custom' (*muʿtâd-ı kadîm üzre/juxta antiquam consuetudinem*), a Polish ablegate/envoy (*Ablegatus, Küçük èlçi*) would be dispatched 'the soonest possible' (*bir gün evvel/ priùs*) to the Ottoman capital carrying with him the Polish King's ratification of the treaty and bringing back to the Commonwealth the sultan's one: Silâhdâr, *Nusretnâme*, 519; *Gründ – und umständlicher Bericht*, 28.

32 ÖStA, HHStA, Türkei I, Turcica Box 170, Protocollum, fol. 185.

33 *Gründ – und umständlicher Bericht*, 26; Silâhdâr, *Nusretnâme*, 515.

34 Kołodziejczyk, 'The Splendor of Barocco', 674–5.

Most importantly, the final text he received was substantially larger, thirty-three articles instead of just sixteen written in the Carlowitz Peace Instrument.[35]

All the same, the fact that the treaties were negotiated by ambassador plenipotentiaries,[36] who could even agree between them well in advance on the textual form and content of their principals' ratification acts,[37] meant that the latter, while still universally considered an integral part of the peacemaking process, could also sometimes in practice be no more than a simple formality.

3 The Last Days of the Congress

The signing ceremony followed a banquet at Lord Paget's. Despite Venice not yet being de facto at peace with the Porte, the Imperials considered it imperative to invite Ruzzini as well 'to avoid any appearance of a separation [of the allies]'.[38] Contrary to Voznitsyn, choosing once again to abstain due to his ceremonial feud with Małachowski, the Venetian decided to put the League's unity, which he so stoutly defended during the whole of this period, first, and attend together with Nicolosi. It happened that he was seated right next to Rāmī Meḥmed, with whom he had a 'cheerful conversation' (*allegra conversatione*) despite their fierce clashes during the conferences.[39]

Returning that night to his tent from the feast, Ruzzini received orders from the Senate conceding to the Ottomans' demands concerning the mountain range north of the Corinthian Isthmus and the demolition of the Castello di Rumelia. Nevertheless, once again, the principal Venetian decision-makers were unwilling to back down from their initial pretensions in Dalmatia.[40] Commenting on the arrival of this last courier from Venice, the anonymous Venetian account lamented *de nouveau* the partiality and indiscreetness of the Imperial plenipotentiaries towards the Republic. So anxious were they to sign

35 Dipratu, *Non-Muslim Communities*, 79. Interestingly, the Doge had already ratified the treaty in February 1699. Ibid.

36 In bestowing as the sultan's plenipotentiary full powers to the two ambassadors to be sent to the peace congress, the grand vizier clearly stated in his order (*buyuruldu*) that 'whatever you accept will also be accepted by the Exalted State and there will be no chance of [subsequent] dishonesty': *Taʿrīḫ-i ṣulḥnāme*, fol. 39ᵇ.

37 For the Ottoman–Imperial case, *see* ibid., fol. 127ᵇ; Cernovodeanu, 'Le journal', 348; ÖStA, HHStA, Türkei I, Turcica Box 170, Protocollum, fol. 185.

38 ÖStA, HHStA, Türkei I, Turcica Box 170, Diarium et Cerimoniale, fol. 82–83.

39 *Narratio*, fol. 45ʳ⁻ᵛ.

40 Ruzzini, 'Relazione', 365; *Narratio*, fol. 45ᵛ–46ʳ.

their peace, 'that if [only] they had waited for some more hours, they would have been able to justify their decision better'.[41]

Regardless of Schlik's statements that Ruzzini was kept secretly informed of the agreed articles, the *Cavaliere* and people close to him continued to forcefully deny this, claiming instead that despite the many attempts by Nicolosi to acquire them with dexterity (*con desterità*), the ambassador was only able to check them on 27 January, and not in the original Peace Instrument but in a copy of it.[42] Irrespective of where the truth lies, Ruzzini had every reason to want to officially distance himself from terms where 'the decorum of the Republic appeared in some parts to be damaged [and] gravely prejudiced'.[43] One was, of course, the disruption of the much-desired continuous borderline in Dalmatia, to leave the communication between Ragusa and the Ottoman Domains open. Another was the stipulation that if the Republic were not finally to accept the agreed terms, she would face 'a total separation from the perpetual alliance [with the Imperials and the Commonwealth], obliged to wage war all alone'.[44] That was precisely the principal aim of the Ottomans all along, argued the Anonymous Venetian, greatly assisted in that respect by Paget, 'who evidently revealed himself most partial in favour of the Porte' and of the other two allies who were looking after 'more their particular than the common interest'.[45]

The Venetian side had, though, to admit 'that the same articles also included profitable conditions and contained many honourable and advantageous parts'.[46] In the end, besides various other considerations, the *Cavaliere* could equally ease his conscience with the thought that all these developments could not have taken place but with God's will 'and [that] such [was] the destiny of the Republic'.[47] This statement contains a tremendous amount of irony since, for Ruzzini, as for some modern scholars, it is the Ottomans that

41 Ibid., fol. 46r.

42 Ibid., fol. 46r–v.

43 Ibid., fol. 46v. Interestingly enough, if we are to believe Colyer, despite the multiple advantageous articles it contained for the Porte, some on the Ottoman side – just like people at the Imperial Court in Vienna – opined that the two plenipotentiaries could have scored much better and perceived the treaty as disadvantageous: Hora-Siccoma, 'De Vrede van Carlowitz', 174–5.

44 *Narratio*, fol. 47r.

45 Ibid.

46 Ibid., fol. 47r–v. Among others, the safeguarding of the possession of the Morea, the islands of Lefkada and Aegina, and 'almost all the [Venetian] acquisitions in Dalmatia' (*quasi tutti gli acquisti della Dalmatia*): Ibid., fol. 47v.

47 Ibid., fol. 48v.

were (are) stereotypically portrayed as abandoning themselves to fate and 'divine plans'.[48]

In any case, being able to conclude by himself a formal peace agreement with the Ottomans was now, for Ruzzini, a matter pertaining to his honour and reputation. Following Count Marsigli, the Venetian implored him to ask Kinsky not to communicate extensively (*per estensum*) to Loredano the agreed articles for Venice but only to inform him 'that the Republic is included [in the peace] and not abandoned, fearing that he may dispatch a courier to the Senate that could act as a motive to send another person to complete what his honour would require him to conclude inside the deadline of thirty days'.[49] Hoping, as always, to get the necessary instructions from the Senate soon, finally permitting him to do exactly that, he tried to profit from the ceremonies of the farewell visits between the Imperials and the Ottomans, which protracted the latter's stay at the congress venue for some more days. Nothing came, however.[50] He then tried through other expedients to convince the Ottomans to slow their return journey to Belgrade and stay there another three days. In the beginning, that indeed transpired. Yet, reaching the Save, the two plenipotentiaries received news from the Porte to return immediately to Adrianople.[51]

Only on 9 February, with Ruzzini still waiting at Petrovaradin, did the dispatches expected from Venice reach him.[52] Immediately, a messenger was sent to Belgrade to inform the mediators that the ambassador was ready to formally conclude his treaty. Unfortunately, by then, the Ottoman ambassadors were already far away, having departed from there four days previously.[53] Thus, finally, Ruzzini signed the Venetian Peace Instrument, which was then handed over to the mediators in Belgrade by Nicolosi, where it was exchanged with the Ottoman one by the governor of the fortress.[54] It did not turn out exactly as the *Cavaliere* would wish, but he could claim, at least, that his honour was not compromised as he had completed his mission, even belatedly.

---

48 For instance, Ruzzini, 'Relazione', 349; Ethan Menchinger, 'Revisiting "Turkish Fatalism"; Or, Why Ottoman Theology Matters'. *Aca'ib: Occasional Papers on Ottoman Perceptions of the Supernatural* (2022), 9–37.

49 ÖStA, HHStA, Türkei I, Turcica Box 171, Folder 2 (January 1699, 2nd half), fol. 187^{v}–188^{r}, Marsigli to Kinsky, 26 January 1699.

50 *Narratio*, fol. 48^{v}.

51 Ruzzini, 'Relazione', 366.

52 *Narratio*, fol. 57^{v}.

53 Ibid.

54 Ibid., fol. 61^{r}–63^{r}.

The last days of the congress were mainly spent exchanging ceremonial farewell visits between the different delegations. The first to embark on the return journey was, quite expectedly, Małachowski, always impatient to take that step since the conclusion of his affairs. He left the congress venue just a day after the signing ceremony, on 27 January.[55] After staying a few days at Petrovaradin, Voznitsyn departed on 3 February,[56] followed the next day by Count Schlik, the Ottomans and the mediators.[57] The last remaining were Count Öttingen and Ruzzini, quitting their camp on 5 February, 'leaving Carlowitz again deserted, to which the famous congress donated for many months a noble character, and for many centuries an even more noble remembrance'.[58]

55 ÖStA, HHStA, Türkei I, Turcica Box 170, Diarium et Cerimoniale, fol. 83.
56 *Narratio*, fol. 56v.
57 ÖStA, HHStA, Türkei I, Turcica Box 170, Diarium et Cerimoniale, fol. 90–91.
58 *Narratio*, fol. 57r.

Conclusions

Carlowitz is undoubtedly one of the most significant diplomatic gatherings of the seventeenth century. It constituted the first truly multi-religious peace congress of the early modern period and hosted most of the great powers across the European continent. Yet, generally speaking, it does not represent a watershed moment in terms of long-term political history. Indeed, it confirmed the Habsburg Monarchy's territorial expansion into Hungary and the northern Balkans, a development that would significantly influence its existence for centuries to come. However, this *Drang nach Süden* strategy of Vienna had already been initiated during the late 1680s. Nor did Carlowitz signify the beginning of a supposed Ottoman decline. Despite the significant territorial losses mainly suffered in Hungary, the congress could justifiably be considered a 'diplomatic' success for the Porte and proof that the 'Sick Man of Europe' lay, for the moment, in the distant future. Its delegation managed not only to avoid appearing as the defeated party but also to profit from the disunion between the Christian allies, the military weaknesses of Venice and the Polish-Lithuanian Commonwealth, and the desire of the Imperials to end the war as soon as possible. It imposed its agenda on crucial issues such as the congress venue and the interpretation of the Foundation of Peace, and even dictated the terms of its treaty with the Republic of Saint Mark.

And speaking of Venice. Instead of representing a long-lasting regeneration of its maritime empire in the eastern Mediterranean, Carlowitz proved, retrospectively, to be but a mere short interlude of imperial glory.[1] The Morea peninsula, Venice's 'crown jewel' acquisition,[2] was swiftly reconquered by the Ottomans less than twenty years later in the last war between the two polities (1715–18), along with the last remaining Aegean islands under

1 Anastasia Stouraiti argues that the significant Venetian conquests during the Sixteen Years' War should not be judged in light of subsequent events (Stouraiti, *Early Modern Venice*, 3). However, she appears to contradict her own admonition when discussing the Ottomans, claiming that the Treaties of Carlowitz 'marked the beginning of Ottoman decline': Ibid., 2.

2 So determined were the Venetian authorities to retain the peninsula under their possession and effectively exploit its resources that shortly after its conquest, they initiated a colossal cartographical project, mapping most of the regions of the 'Regno' in astonishing detail, launching a land survey which unfortunately did not manage to complete, and introducing a series of administrative and economic reforms: Katsiardi-Hering, *Βενετικοί χάρτες*; Papadia-Lala, *Ο θεσμός των αστικών κοινοτήτων*, 465–500.

 | DOI:10.1163/9789004458499_028

Venetian rule.[3] Moving further east, the congress may have recorded the first Muscovite attempts to get direct access to the Black Sea and to claim the right of protection for the Orthodox subjects of the sultan.[4] Still, since neither of these two goals was achieved, we are still far from the truly new era the later treaty of Küçük Ḳaynarca (1774) would herald. If there is a real political turning point in the Carlowitz Treaties, then it is to be found in the relations between the Ottoman Porte and the *Rzeczpospolita*. They signalled the end of the continuous struggles between them during the 1600s and the beginning of a stable, peaceful relationship that lasted until the Commonwealth was erased from the map at the end of the eighteenth century.

Such an interpretation of the Congress of Carlowitz may seem less appealing to a political history geek who is constantly attentive to locating landmarks. Still, its fascinating aspects lie elsewhere, in the spheres of early modern diplomatic culture and peacemaking norms as well as in the important insights it can offer about the polycentric origins and development of multilateral diplomacy, a key feature of modern international law. Carlowitz, as well as its direct forerunner, the Failed Congress of Vienna (1689–90), manifests how easily this negotiation format was adopted by polities to whom was supposedly 'alien', like the Ottoman Empire. Not only did the Ottomans come up quickly with a word of their own – quite similar in meaning to the western Christian European one – to refer to such gatherings, that of *cem'iyyet*, but they, as well as the other supposed 'peacemaking-by-congress ignorants', the Muscovites, equally favoured – when it suited their goals, of course – quite innovative practices, like the common sessions between all the participants. Because most early modern congresses rested on seemingly contradictory precepts: Although they formed multilateral gatherings, each of their participants was supposed to engage in separate, bilateral talks with their opponent(s) and even conclude their negotiation ahead of their other allies. That meant that congresses were a mixture of ad hoc solutions or accumulated experiences from earlier ones, mainly concerned with ceremonial regulations and the technical aspects of the talks (who was to negotiate first; if one was allowed to progress his negotiations independently from or to sign his Peace Instrument before the other members of his coalition etc.) and peacemaking norms that were slowly developed in the past relations between each one of the participating polities.

3 Dionisios Hatzopoulos, *Ο τελευταίος Βενετο-Οθωμανικός πόλεμος 1714–1718* (Athens: Papadimas 2002).

4 For the latter, see Bogoslovskii, *Petr I*, 393.

Regarding the multilateral aspect, while building on the precedents of Nijmegen (1676–78) and Riswyck (1697), Carlowitz was the first early modern congress in which all ceremonial rules were officially discarded for the duration of the talks, and there was no apparent distinction of order among its participants. Nonetheless, this pioneering solution neither prevented fierce ceremonial disputes from arising between some of the participants – the Muscovite-Commownealth 'duel' being the most notorious – nor did it inhibit the various strenuous efforts of the protagonists to manifest their and their principals' status and grandeur. Thus, far from marking the onset of a novel era in inter-polity relations, Carlowitz instead confirmed how predominantly stratified the late-seventeenth century 'Society of Princes' was and how questions of precedence and the ceremonial manifestations related to them were deeply entrenched in the minds of the congress contemporaries. However, that observation does not diminish the trendsetting effect the adoption of such a regulation had for future diplomatic gatherings, such as that of Utrecht (1713), and for the gradual future adoption of the tenet of equality of status among political entities.

Finally, it should also be remarked that Carlowitz witnessed some quite interesting and rare negotiating formats such as the common Ottoman–Imperial–Venetian sessions or the last two conferences of the congress involving the Ottoman, Imperial and Polish delegations (Małachowski could only attend the first of the two), in which the articles of the Ottoman–Venetian provisional treaty were finalised. Such unusual formats, blending bilateral and multilateral elements, attest to the fact that congresses, such as Carlowitz – often portrayed merely as receptors and replicators of pioneering diplomatic norms and practices taking place elsewhere – were, in fact, intriguing sites of experimentation in multilateral diplomacy.

Turning now to the strictly bilateral level, despite the persistence of some peculiar arrangements based on previous customary diplomatic practices among the diverse negotiating parties, Carlowitz reveals a common repertoire of peacemaking norms and vocabulary that transcended cultural and religious boundaries, resulting from centuries-old encounters between polities in western, central, and eastern Europe.

First and foremost, whether in a strictly bilateral or congress format, peacemaking was primarily viewed as a process that had to traverse distinctive phases, each containing specific requirements. The first was the Preliminaries. There, the different parties typically laid down the Foundation of Peace, accepted the mediation, *bons offices*, or arbitration of a third party(ies) – if one was to be appointed – designated their delegations, and agreed upon the venue for the negotiations. If that phase progressed smoothly and the representatives of the warring parties managed to gather at the designated location, then the second phase began. Firstly, an exchange of the delegates' credentials had to occur so that each side could confirm that their interlocutors possessed sufficient authority to negotiate a treaty. Normally, this would be followed by an equal exchange of each side's written proposals to initiate the talks. The third and most central phase was dominated by negotiation, either viva voce or through written communication, where the two parties discussed their main issues. If the outcome was successful, the final act of the 'theatre of peace' would consist of the signing of a Provisional Peace Instrument, which would then have to be ratified by the respective sovereigns after a period agreed upon by both contracting parties for the agreement between them to be considered 'de jure' valid.

Let us now examine some of the most prominent instances of the basic vocabulary of peacemaking. By the late seventeenth century, major peace treaties, and even more so those discussed in a congress, were expected to be negotiated by representatives bearing the title of 'plenipotentiary ambassador'. The latter combined the two fundamental attributes of a sovereign ruler: his *potestas* and *majestas*. Although it remains debatable whether the representative implications of the term 'ambassador' resonated the same for all, the definition of 'plenipotentiary' as denoting the absolute authority to negotiate the majority of, or at least the most critical items on the agenda, certainly did, and minute attention was paid in the ambassadorial credentials to the precise mentioning of that term.

Furthermore, all Carlowitz participants recognised a distinction between two types of inter-polity reconciliation agreements based on their duration: a time-limitless and a time-limited one. The former could commit or not commit the successors of a ruler, while usually signifying that the two sides had overcome the entirety of the most contentious issues between them. The latter could be extended from a few years to decades, and, in the second case, did not differ at all from the format of an eternal peace treaty, save for its non-eternal character. The choice between the two types was not primarily dictated by religious or cultural precepts but rather by a combination of strategic concerns and customary practice. These strategic concerns primarily related to territorial arrangements. For instance, a truce/armistice was chiefly associated with one based on the status quo post bellum, exemplified by the supra-cultural concept of *uti possidetis* or *ʿalā ḥālihi* in Ottoman Turkish.

After, or concurrently, with determining who owned what, the different possessions of the various polities had to be separated from one another; to be delimited. Instead of the (up to that point) more varied practice, in which a polity could choose to clearly demarcate or not specific parts of its frontiers with limitrophe political entities, for the Carlowitz contemporaries, more or less minute territorial delimitation was a sine qua non. They divided borders into two categories. The natural ones (rivers, mountain ranges etc.) allegedly 'created' already by God or Nature and the artificial ones, which had to be made by humans. To ascertain the latter, they all had to resort to a combination of archival registers, maps, and special commissioners on the ground, with each side promoting one or the other according to which of these methods suited it the most.

Another significant transculturally resonant peacemaking mechanism was mediation. Not only did the Carlowitz Congress participants share long-established conceptions of the role and principal tasks of a mediator, but they had also developed a similar vocabulary to express other forms of interposition like the *bons offices* (or *ḥüsn say*ʿ in Ottoman Turkish). Contrary to the established literature, Carlowitz manifests that mediation still played a cardinal role in peace congresses during the late-seventeenth century. The actions of Paget and Colyer were instrumental in promoting the negotiations during the phase of the Preliminaries, and their stance in the subsequent acts of the 'drama' was equally catalytical. Carlowitz was also one of the few early modern congresses where a formal (English, Dutch) and an informal (Imperial) mediator operated together in harmony and were even both present during conferences between third parties, as the Ottoman–Venetian case plainly attests. That was yet another of its pioneering aspects.

Equally engrossing is the social environment of the Carlowitz Congress. A truly unique multicultural and multireligious assembly in the open, ravaged by the prolonged war, Northern Serbian fields; bringing together with their distinct attire, languages, culinary habits, and music Germans, Poles, Muscovites, Venetians, English and Dutch. Only the Congress of Westphalia could rival such a multi-ethnic concentration. Despite the limitations posed to their socialising by the Congress Regulation, frequent contact between the various encampments was by no means absent. Surely, Carlowitz was not a 'peaceful bazaar'. Prejudices against the various 'Others' ran rampant, resulting, among other consequences, in frequent brawls between – typically – drunken individuals.

To summarise, the case of the Carlowitz Congress invites us to radically rethink our assumptions about early modern norms and practices of peacemaking. It also challenges the effectiveness of the 'Westphalian Paradigm' in explaining the origins and subsequent development of multilateral diplomacy by demonstrating that a sufficient understanding requires us to broaden our geographical scope, look beyond supposedly insurmountable cultural and religious barriers, and abandon any form of centrism. Let us depart for a while from the familiar Westphalian region and the towns of Nijmegen, Ryswick, and

Utrecht. Let us travel east, across the Hungarian plain, following the banks of the Danube, passing through the northern Black Sea region, and even reaching all the way to the distant Siberian steppes where in 1689 the Muscovite and Qing delegations met to 'to determine and to place clearly and evidently the borders between the two empires'. Then we will probably discover that early modern diplomatic norms – the direct prelude to the modern ones – could often be far more supra-cultural than we may initially have thought before embarking on this long journey.

Archival Material

Archiwum Główne Akt Dawnych (AGAD), Warsaw

Archiwum Koronne Warszawskie
1/3/0/33/78, teczka 497 nr. 825
1/3/0/33/78/ teczka 494 nr. 819
1/3/0/32/64 teczka 05 nr 536
Archiwum Warszawskie Radziwiłłów
1/354/0/5/9200

Bayerisches Hof-, Staatsarchiv (BayHStA), Munich

Kasten Schwarz 310

Biblioteca Nazionale Marciana (BNM), Venice

Ms. It VII 381 (7782), Congresso di Carlowitz (1699) e Carte Relative e Missione di Carlo Ruzzini
Ms. It. VII 407(=7594), Narratio conventus caroloviciani, quam dedit quidam a secretis Carolo Ruzzini, veneti cum summa potestate ad eum conventum legati
Ms.It VII 381 (7782)

Devlet Arşivleri Başkanlığı Osmanlı Arşivi (DABOA), Istanbul

Divan-ı Hümayun Sincillatı Mühimme Defteri (A.DVNS.MHM.d) n. 60, 110
Divan-ı Hümayun Sincillatı Name-i Hümayun Defterleri (A.DVNS.NMH.d), n. 5
Topkapı Müzesi Arşivi Evrakı (TS. MA.e), 523,15
İbnülemin Dahiliye (İE. DH), 8–756

Österreichisches Staatsarchiv (ÖStA), Vienna

Haus, Hof-, und Staatsarchiv (HHStA)
Türkei I, Turcica
Box 154, Folder 1 (February 1689)
Box 155, Folder 3 (December 1689)

Box 164, Folder (1697)
Box 165, Folder 1 (January–March 1698); 2 (April 1698); 3 (May 1698); 4 (June 1698); 5 (July 1698)
Box 166, Folder 1 (August 1698); 2 (September 1698, 1st half); 3 (September 1698, 2nd half)
Box 167, Folder 1 (October 1698, 1st half); 2 (October 1698, 2nd half)
Box 168, Folder 1 (November 1698, 1st half); 2 (November 1698, 2nd half)
Box 169, Folder 1 (December 1698, 1st half); 2 (December 1698, 2nd half)
Box 170, Protocollum; Diarium et Cerimoniale Tractatus Pacis Carlovicensis Annis 1698 et 1699
Box 171, Folder 1 (January 1699, 1st hallf); 2 (January 1699, 2nd half)
Box 172, Folder 1 (February–March 1699)
Türkische Urkunden 11 (1689–1718)
SB Kartensammlung F, Ke 3–7/5
SB Kartensammlung F, Ke 3–7/5–8

Süleymaniyye Kütüphanesi (SK), Istanbul

Esad Efendi, n. 2241

The National Archives (TNA), London

SP 97/20
SP 97/21

Topkapı Sarayı Müzesi Kütüphanesi (TSMK), Istanbul

Revan, no. 1311, Ta'rīḫ-i Ṣulḥ-nāme-i ʿAmcazāde Ḥüseyin Paşa

Published Sources

Bilkan, Ali Fuat. *Nabi Divani*, vol. 1. Ankara: Akçağ Publishing House 2011.

Bues, Almut. 'Ein venezianischer Bericht zu den Friedensverhandlungen von Karlowitz 1698/99'. *Münchner Zeitschrift für Balkankunde* 10/11 (1996), 163–243.

Burcu, Duzcan. '111 Numaralı Mühimme Defterinin 338.-507. Sayfalarının Transkripsiyonu ve Değerlendirilmesi'. MA dissertation, Artvin Çoruh University 2019.

Cantemir, Demetrius. *Incrementorum et Decrementorum Aulae Othoman[n]Icae Sive Aliothman[n]Icae Historiae a Prima Gentis Origine Ad Nostra Usque Tempora Deductae Libri Tres*. Timisoara: Amarcord 2001.

Cernovodeanu, Paul. 'Le journal des travaux du Congrès de Karlowitz'. *Revue des Études Sud-Est Européennes* 19/2 (1981), 325–54.

Dapondes, Kaisarios. 'Χρονογράφος'. In Konstantinos Sathas (ed.), *Μεσαιωνική Βιβλιοθήκη*, vol. 3. Venice: Chronos Publishing House 1872.

Defterdar Sarı Mehmet Paşa, Abdülkadir Özcan (ed.). *Zübde-i Vekayiât: Tahlil ve Metin (1066–1116/1656–1704)*. Ankara: Printing House of the Turkish Historical Society 1995.

Demir, Uğur. 'Mehmed Giray, Tarih-i Mehmed Giray (1095–1115/1684–1703) (Değerlendirme, Çeviri, Metin)'. MA dissertation, Marmara University 2006.

Gelcich, Josip and Lajos Thallóczy (eds.). *Diplomatarium relationum Reipublicae Ragusanae cum regno Hungariae*. Budapest: Hungarian Academy of Sciences 1887.

Gorkowski, Andrzej. *Compendium legationis jaśnie wielmożnego* [...] *Stanisława Małachowskiego, woiewody poznańskiego, od* [...] *Krola Imci y stanow Rzeczypospolitey Polskiey ad tractandam pacem z Portą Otomańską deputowanego commissarza* [...] *zebrane przez* [...] *Andrzeia Gorkowskiego* [...]. [Place of publication unknown]: [Publisher unknown], [n.d.].

Gründ- und umständlicher Bericht von denen römisch-kayserlichen wie auch ottomannischen Groß-Bothschafften, wodurch der Friede oder Stillstand zwischen dem allerdurchleuchtigst-großmächtigst- und unüberwindlichstem römischen Kayser Leopoldo Primo und dem Sultan Mustafa Han III. den 26. Januarii 1699. Zu Carlowiz in Sirmien auf 25. Jahre geschlossen und darauff auch denen respective Höffen zu Wienn und Constantinopel bestätiget worden. Vienna: Schönwetter 1702.

Güler, Mustafa (ed.). *Zülfikâr Paşa'nın Viyana Sefâreti ve Esâreti. Cerîde-i Takrirât-ı Zülfikâr Efendi [1099–1103/1688–1692]*. Istanbul: Çamlıca 2008.

Humurzaki, Eudoxiu (ed.). *Documente privitóre la istoria românilor*, vol. 13, Bucharest 1909.

Humurzaki, Eudoxiu (ed.). *Documente privitóre la istoria românilor*, vol. 5, part 1. Bucharest 1885.

Kırış, Ahmet. 'Hicrî 1096 (1684–1685) Yılına Dair bir Münşeat Mecmuası ve Değerlendirilmesi'. MA dissertation, Fatih Sultan Mehmet Vakıf University 2017.

Lielowski, August. *Pamiętnik Jana Stanisława Jabłonowskiego Wojewody Ruskiego*. Lviv: National Ossoliński Institute 1862.

Livadas, Th. *Ἀλεξάνδρου Μαυροκορδάτου τοῦ ἐξ Ἀπορρήτων Ἐπιστολαί Ρ΄*. Trieste: Austrian Lloyd Publishing House 1879.

Ludwig, Vinzenz Oskar. 'Memoiren eines Vergessenen (1691–1716)'. *Jahrbuch des Stiftes Klosterneuburg* 7/1 (1915), 1–68.

Mavrocordatos, Alexandros. 'Πρευσβευτικός πρὸς Γερμανοὺς Λόγος Ὑπὲρ Εἰρήνης'. In *Ἐπιστολάριον ἐκ Διαφόρων Ἐρανισθέν*, 315–40. Constantinople: Patriarchal Printing House 1804.

Mavrocordatos, Alexandros. *Pneumaticum instrumentum circulandi sanguinis, sive de motu, & usu pulmonum dissertatio philosophico-medica*. Bologna: Ferroni 1664.

Meninski, Franciszek. *Thesaurus linguarum orientalium turcicae, arabicae, persicae*. Vienna 1680.

Mercure Historique et Politique, vol. 26 (January–June 1699).

Na'îmâ, Mustafa, Mehmed İpşirli (ed.). *Târih-i Na'îmâ: Ravzatü'l-Hüseyn Fî Hulâsati Ahbâri'l-Hâfikayn*, vol. 1. Ankara: Turkish Historical Association 2007.

Özcan, Abdülkadir (ed.), *Anonim Osmanli Tarihi, 1099–1116 (1688–1704)*. Ankara: Printing House of the Turkish Historical Society 2000.

Pamiatniki diplomaticheskih snoshenij drevney Rossii s derzhavami inostrannymi, vol. 9. Saint Petersburg 1868.

Peçevi, İbrahim. *Tarīh-i Peçevi*, vol. 1. İstanbul A. H. 1283/1866.

Predelli, Riccardo. *Diplomatarium Veneto-Levantorum, sive Acta et Diplomata Res Venetas Graecas atque Levantis Illustrantia*, 2 vol. New York: Cambridge University Press 2012.

Radonić, Jovan (ed.). *Acta et Diplomata Ragusina*, vol. 4, part 1. Belgrade 1941.

Radonić, Jovan (ed.). *Acta et Diplomata Ragusina*, vol. 4, part 2. Belgrade 1942.

Ruzzini, Carlo. 'Relazione del Congresso de Carloviz e dell' Ambasciata di Vienna di Sr. Carlo Ruzini Cavr.'. In *Fontes Rerum Austriacarum*, Diplomataria et Acta, vol. 27, 345–444. Vienna: Imperial and Royal Printing House 1867.

Sebes, Joseph, S.J. *The Jesuits and the Sino-Russian Treaty of Nerchinsk (1689). The Diary of Thomas Pereira, S.J.* Rome: Institutum Historicum S.I. 1961.

Silāḥdār Fındıḳlılı Meḥmed Aga, Mehmet Topal (ed.), *Nusretnâme: inceleme – metin (1106–1133–1695–1721)*. Ankara: Turkish Academy of Sciences 2018.

Silāḥdār Fındıḳlılı Meḥmed Aga. *Silāḥdār Ta'rīḫi*, vol. 2. Istanbul: Orḫaniye Maṭba'ası 1928.

Szita, Laszlo, and Gerhard Seewann (eds.). *A karlócai béke és Európa: dokumentumok a karlócai béke történetéhez 1698–1699*. Pécs: Gálos Nyomdász, 1999.

Şeker, Abdülkadir. 'Nuruosmaniye Kütüphanesi 4297 numaralı Münşeât Mecmuası (1672–1705) inceleme-metin'. MA dissertation, Kocaeli University 2024.

Temel, Recep. '111 Numaralı Mühimme Defterinin 168.-337. Sayfalarının Transkripsiyonu ve Değerlendirilmesi'. MA dissertation, Artvin Çoruh University 2019.

Traité de paix entre l'Empereur, la France, et l'Empire conclu à Rysvvick le trentiéme Octobre 1697. Paris: Frederic Leonard 1697.

Unat, Faik R. 'Ahmed III devrine ait bir ıslahat takriri'. *Tarih Vesikaları* 1 (1941), 107–21.

Üsküdarî Abdullah Efendi, *Vâkı'ât-ı Rûz-Merre*, 4 vols. Ankara: Turkish Academy of Sciences 2017.

Venier, Girolamo. 'Relazione del Nob. Ec. s. Gir^{mo}. Venier C^{r}. fù ambasciator in Germania'. In *Fontes Rerum Austriacarum*, Diplomataria et Acta, vol. 27, 309–44. Vienna: Imperial and Royal Printing House 1867.

Załuski, Andrzej Chryzostom. *Epistolae Historico-Familiares*, vol. 2. Brunsbergae [Braniewo]: Typis Mandatus 1711.

Zotov, Nikita Moiseevich. *Stateinyi spisok stol'nika Vasiliia Tiapkina i d'iaka Nikity Zotova, posol'stva v Krym v 1680 godu, dlia zakliucheniia Bakhchisaraiskogo dogovora*. Odessa: Municipal Printing House 1850.

Bibliography

Abou-El-Haj, Rifa'at. 'The Narcissism of Mustafa II (1695–1703): A Psychohistorical Study'. *Studia Islamica* 40 (1974), 115–31.

Abou-El-Haj, Rifa'at. 'Ottoman Attitudes Toward Peace Making: The Karlowitz Case'. *Der Islam* 51/1 (1974), 131–7.

Abou-El-Haj, Rifa'at. 'The Formal Closure of the Ottoman Frontier in Europe: 1699–1703'. *Journal of the American Oriental Society* 89/3 (1969): 467–75.

Abou-El-Haj, Rifa'at. 'The Reisülküttab and Ottoman Diplomacy at Carlowitz'. Ph.D. thesis, Princeton University 1963.

Ágoston, Gábor. 'Defending and Administering the Frontier: The Case of Ottoman Hungary'. In Christine Woodhead (ed.), *The Ottoman World*, 220–36. London/New York: Routledge 2012.

Ahıshalı, Recep. 'Râmi Mehmed Paşa'. In TDVİA, vol. 34, 449–51. Istanbul: Turkish Religious Foundation 2007.

Ahıshalı, Recep. 'Reîsükküttâb'. In TDVİA, vol. 34, 546–9. Istanbul: Turkish Religious Foundation 2007.

Algazi, Gadi. 'Introduction. Doing Things with Gifts'. In Gadi Algazi, Valentin Groebner, and Bernhard Jussen (eds.), *Negotiating the Gift. Pre-Modern Figurations of Exchange*, 9–27. Göttingen: Vanderhoeck & Ruprecht 2003.

Amsler, Nadine, Henrietta Harrison and Christian Windler. 'Introduction: Eurasian Diplomacies Around 1800: Transformation and Persistence'. *The International History Review* 41/5 (2019), 943–6.

Andretta, Stefano. 'Venise à Karlowitz: Historiographie et Diplomatie'. In Jean Bérenger (ed.), *La paix de Karlowitz 26 Janvier 1699. Les relations entre l'Europe centrale et l'Empire Ottoman*, 133–45. Paris: Honoré Champion 2010.

Anselmi, Sergio. *Venezia, Ragusa, Ancona tra Cinque e Seicento: un momento della storia mercantile del Medio Adriatico*. Ancona: Tip. SITA 1969.

Archondidis, A.P. *Η βενετοκρατία στη Δυτική Ελλάδα (1684–1699). Συμβολή στην ιστορία της περιοχής του Αμβρακικού κόλπου και της Αιτωλοακαρνανίας*. Ph.D. thesis, Aristotelian University of Thessaloniki 1983.

Augustynowicz, Christoph. 'Tatarische Gesandtschaften am Kaiserhof des 17. Jahrhunderts – Protokoll und Alltag'. In Marlene Kurz et al. (eds.), *Das Osmanische Reich und die Habsburgermonarchie*, 315–40. Vienna: Böhlau 2005.

Badel, Laurence and Stanislas Jeannesson. 'Introduction. Une Histoire Globale de la Diplomatie?'. *« Monde(s) »* 5/1 (2014), 7–26.

Baidaus, Eduard. 'Księstwo Mołdawskie w polityce zagranicznej Polski od zwycięstwa pod Wiedniem do zawarcia pokoju karłowickiego (1683–1699)'. In Ilona Czamanska and Witold Szulc (eds.), *Traktaty Karlowickie z 1699 roku i ich następstwa*, 215–21. Poznan: Adam Mickiewicz University Press 2003.

Barjamovic, Gojko. 'Propaganda and practice in Assyrian and Persian imperial culture'. In Peter Fibiger Bang and Dariusz Kolodziejczyk (eds.), *Universal Empire. A Comparative Approach to Imperial Culture and Representation in Eurasian History*, 43–59. Cambridge: Cambridge University Press 2012.

Başer, Alper. 'Bucak Tatarları (1550–1700)'. Ph.D. thesis, Afyon Kocatepe Üniversitesi 2010.

Bayerle, G. 'The Compromise at Zsitvatorok'. *Archivum Ottomanicum* 6 (1980), 5–53.

Bazarova, Tatiana. 'The Treaty of Carlowitz and Its Impact on Russian-Ottoman Relations, 1700–1710'. In Ivan Parvev and Colin Heywood (eds.), *The Treaties of Carlowitz (1699). Antecedents, Course and Consequences*, 236–49. Leiden/Boston: Brill 2020.

Beihammer, Alexander, Stavroula Constantinou, and Maria G. Paran. *Court Ceremonies and Rituals of Power in Byzantium and the Medieval Mediterranean. Comparative Perspectives*. Leiden/Boston: Brill 2013.

Bély, Lucien. 'Négocier la Paix, de Westphalie au Temps des Révolutions'. In Franck Petiteville et al. (eds.), *Négociations Internationales*, 171–98. Paris: Presses de Sciences Po 2013.

Bély, Lucien. *Les relations internationales en Europe, XVIIe–XVIIIe siècle*, 4th edn. Paris: PUF 2007.

Bély, Lucien. *La société des princes. XVIe–XVIIIe siècle*. Paris: Fayard 1999.

Bély, Lucien. 'La médiation diplomatique au XVIIe siècle et au début du XVIIIe siècle'. In *Armées et diplomatie dans l'Europe du XVIIe siècle. Actes du colloque de 1991*, 129–47. Paris: 1992.

Bély, Lucien. *Espions et ambassadeurs au temps de Louis XIV*. Paris: Fayard, 1990.

Benton, Lauren, *They Called It Peace. Worlds of Imperial Violence*. Princeton/Oxford: Princeton University Press 2024.

Benton, Lauren and Adam Clulow. 'Legal encounters and the origins of global law'. In Jerry H. Bentley, Sanjay Subrahmanyam and Merry E. Wiesner-Hanks (eds.), *The Cambridge World History*, vol. 6, part 2, 80–100. Cambridge: Cambridge University Press 2015.

Bérenger, Jean. 'La politique de l'empereur Léopold 1er face à l'Empire Ottoman (1689–1699)'. In Jean Bérenger (ed.), *La paix de Karlowitz 26 Janvier 1699. Les relations entre l'Europe centrale et l'Empire Ottoman*, 9–24. Paris: Honoré Champion 2010.

Bérenger, Jean. 'Conclusions générales'. In Jean Bérenger (ed.), *La paix de Karlowitz 26 Janvier 1699. Les relations entre l'Europe centrale et l'Empire Ottoman*, 235–42. Paris: Honoré Champion 2010.

Bérenger, Jean. 'La politique ottomane de la France de Vienne à Carlowitz (1683–1699)'. In Ilony Czamanskiej and Witolda Szulca (eds.), *Traktaty Karlowickie z 1699 roku i ich następstwa*, 35–53. Poznan: Adam Mickiewicz University Press 2003.

Biegman. Nicolaas H. 'Ragusan Spying for the Ottoman Empire'. *Belleten* 106 (1963), 237–55.

Bogoslovskii, M.M. *Petr I. Materialy dlia biografii*, vol. 3. Moscow: OGIZ 1946.

Boltanski, Luc and Laurent Thévenot. *De la justification: les économies de la grandeur*. Paris: Gallimard 2008.

Bosbach, Franz. 'Verfahrensordnungen und Verhandlungsabläufe auf den Friedenskongressen des 17. Jahrhunderts. Überlegungen zu einer vergleichenden Untersuchung der äusseren Formen frühneuzeitlicher Friedensverhandlungen'. In Christoph Kampmann et al. (eds.). *L'art de la paix. Kongresswesen und Friedensstiftung im Zeitalter des Westfälischen Friedens*, 93–118. Münster: Aschendorff 2011.

Braun, Guido. 'Les problèmes de communication aux congrès internationaux de Westphalie à Ryswick (1643–1697)'. In Dejanirah Couto and Stéphane Péquignot (eds.), *Les langues de la négociation. Approches historiennes*, 191–218. Rennes: Presses Universitaires de Rennes 2017.

Braun, Guido. 'Französisch und Italienisch als Sprachen der Diplomatie auf dem Westfälischen Friedenskongress'. In Annette Gerstenberg (ed.), *Verständigung und Diplomatie auf dem Westfälischen Friedenskongress. Historische und sprachwissenschaftliche Zugänge*, 23–65. Cologne/Weimar/Vienna: Böhlau 2014.

Bravo Lozano, Cristina and Antonio Álvares-Ossorio Alvariño (eds.). *Los embajadores. Representantes de la soberanía, garantes del equilibrio, 1659–1748*. Madrid: Marcial Pons Historia 2021.

Bromley, J.S. (ed.). *The New Cambridge Modern History*, vol. 6, The Rise of Great Britain and Russia, 1688–1715/25. Cambridge: Cambridge University Press 1971.

Brummett, Palmira. 'The Fortress: Defining and Mapping the Ottoman Frontier in the Sixteenth and Seventeenth Centuries'. In A.C.S. Peacock (ed.), *The Frontiers of the Ottoman World*, 31–55. Oxford: OUP/British Academy 2009.

Brunert, Maria-Elisabeth and Lena Oetzel. 'Verhandlungstechniken und -praktiken'. In Irene Dingel et al. (eds.), *Handbuch Frieden im Europa der Frühen Neuzeit / Handbook of Peace in Early Modern Europe*, 455–72. Berlin/Boston: De Gruyter 2020.

Brunert, Maria-Elisabeth. 'Vom Rapular zum Dictatum. Entstehungsstufen der reichständischen Protokolle'. In Annette Gerstenberg (ed.), *Verständigung und Diplomatie auf dem Westfälischen Friedenskongress. Historische und sprachwissenschaftliche Zugänge*, 201–23. Cologne/Weimar/Vienna: Böhlau 2014.

Brunert, Maria-Elisabeth. 'Nonverbale Kommunikation als Faktor frühneuzeitlicher Friedensverhandlungen. Eine Untersuchung am Beispiel des Westfälischen Friedenskongresses'. In Christoph Kampmann et al. (eds.), *L'art de la paix. Kongresswesen und Friedensstiftung im Zeitalter des Westfälischen Friedens*, 281–331. Münster: Aschendorff 2011.

Brzezinski, Richard. *Polish Armies 1569–1696*, vol. 1. London: Osprey Military Publishing 1987.

Burak, Guy. *The Second Formation of Islamic Law. The Hanafi School in the Early Modern Ottoman Empire*. Cambridge: Cambridge University Press 2015.

Burdowicz-Nowicki, Jacek. *Piotr I, August II i Rzeczpospolita 1697–1706*. Krakow: Arcana 2010.

Burke, Peter. *Cultural Hybridity*. Cambridge (UK)/Maiden (US): Polity Press 2009.

Burkhardt, Johannes and Benjamin Durst. 'Friedenskongresse'. In Irene Dingel et al. (eds.), *Handbuch Frieden im Europa der Frühen Neuzeit / Handbook of Peace in Early Modern Europe*, 437–53. Berlin/Boston: De Gruyter 2020.

Burkhardt, Johannes. 'Sprachen des Friedens und was sie verraten. Neue Fragen und Einsichten zu Karlowitz, Baden und „Neustadt"'. In Stefan Ehrenpreis et al. (eds.), *Wege der Neuzeit: Festschrift für Heinz Schilling zum 65. Geburtstag*, 503–19. Berlin: Duncker & Humblot 2007.

Burschel, Peter and Christine Vogel (eds.). *Die Audienz. Ritualisierter Kulturkontakt in der Früher Neuzeit*. Cologne, Weimar, Vienna: Böhlau 2014.

Busquets, Anna. 'Three Manila-Fujian Diplomatic Encounters: Different Aims and Different Embassies in the Seventeenth Century'. *Journal of Early Modern History* 23 (2019), 442–57.

Camariano, Nestor. *Alexandre Mavrocordato, le Grand Drogman, son activité diplomatique 1673–1709*. Thessaloniki: Institute of Balkan Studies 1970.

Ciftci, Hilal. 'Mediation as a Diplomatic Tool in Ottoman Capitulations'. *Codrul Cosminului* 28/1 (2022), 29–54.

Clark, Christopher. *The Sleepwalkers: How Europe Went to War in 1914*. London/New York: Penguin 2013.

Croxton, Derek. *Westphalia. The Last Christian Peace*. New York: Palgrave Macmillan 2013.

Çolak, Songül. 'Zülfikar Paşa'. In TDVİA, vol. 44, 557–9. Istanbul: Turkish Religious Foundation 2013.

Daverio Rocchi, Giovanna. 'Systems of Borders in Ancient Greece'. In Serena Bianchetti, Michele R. Cataudella, and Hans-Joachim Gehrke (eds.), *Brill's Companion to Ancient Geography. The Inhabited World in Greek and Roman Tradition*, 58–77. Leiden/Boston: Brill 2016.

De Bruin, Renger et al. (eds.). *Performances of Peace: Utrecht 1713*. Leiden/Boston: Brill 2015.

De Franceschi, Sylvio Hermann. 'La négociation à l'épreuve des mœurs, de la moralité et des caractères. Jalons pour une étude de la science morale des diplomates à l'époque moderne'. *Histoire, économie & société* 33/2 (2014), 17–33.

Dinu, Tudor. 'Ο Αλέξανδρος Μαυροκορδάτος κατορθώνοντας να δημιουργήσει μία οικεία δυναστεία στις Ρουμανικές Χώρες'. In N. Mavrelos et al. (eds.), *Ο Πρώιμος Διαφωτισμός στην Εποχή των Πρώτων Μαυροκορδάτων. Αλέξανδρος ο Εξ Απορρήτων και Νικόλαος*, 335–46. Athens: Gutenberg 2021.

Dipratu, Radu. *Regulating Non-Muslim Communities in the Seventeenth-Century Ottoman Empire. Catholics and Capitulations*. London and New York: Routledge 2022.

Długokęcki, Wiesław. 'Die Bildung der Grenze zwischen dem Deutschordensland Preußen und dem Herzogtum Masowien in den Jahren 1343–1422'. In Ulrich Knefelkamp and Kristian Bosselmann-Cyran (eds.), *Grenze und Grenzüberschreitung im Mittelalter*, 136–51. Berlin: Akademie Verlag 2007.

Drocourt, Nicolas. *L'autre Empire du Milieu. La diplomatie byzantine (VIIe–XIIe siècles)*. Rennes: Presses Universitaires de Rennes 2023.

Doğan, Güner. *"Venediklü ile dahi sulh oluna". 17. ve 18. Yüzyıllarda Osmanlı-Venedik İlişkileri*. Istanbul: İletişim 2017.

Duchhardt, Heinz. 'Peace Treaties from Westphalia to the Revolutionary Era'. In Randall Lesaffer (ed.), *Peace Treaties and International Law in European History. From the Middle Ages to World War One*, 45–58. Cambridge/New York: Cambridge University Press 2004.

Duchhardt, Heinz et al (eds.). *Der Friede von Rijwick 1697*. Mainz: Philipp von Zabern 1998.

Duchhardt, Heinz. 'Arbitration, Mediation oder Bons Offices? Die englische Friedensvermittlung in Nijmegen 1676–1679'. In Heinz Duchhardt, *Studien zur Friedensvermittlung in der Frühen Neuzeit*, 23–88. Wiesbaden: Franz Steiner Verlag 1979.

Ebben, Maurits and Louis Sicking (eds.). *Beyond Ambassadors. Consuls, Missionaries, and Spies in Premodern Diplomacy*. Leiden/Boston: Brill 2021.

Eickhoff, Ekkehard. 'Die Selbstbehauptung Venedigs gegen das Osmanische Reich: Strategien und Agenten'. In Arno Strohmeyer and Norbert Spannenberger (eds.), *Frieden und Konfliktmanagement in interkulturellen Räumen*, 129–41. Stuttgart: Franz Steiner 2013.

Ellenblum, Ronnie. 'Were there Borders and Borderlines in the Middle Ages? The Example of the Latin Kingdom of Jerusalem'. In David Abulafia and Nora Berend (eds.), *Medieval Frontiers. Concepts and Practices*, 105–20. London and New York: Routledge 2016.

Elliott, J.H. 'Foreign Policy and Domestic Crisis: Spain, 1598–1659'. In J.H. Elliott, *Spain and Its World 1500–1700. Collected Essays*, 114–36. New Haven and London: Yale University Press 1989.

Endre, Sashalmi. 'Tulajdonosi Dinaszticizmus és Államfogalom a 17. Századi Oroszországban'. *Századok* 138/3 (2004), 893–919.

Ercan, Hüseyin Onur. *Pasarofça Antlaşması 1718. Diplomasi ve Barış*. Ankara: Turkish Historical Society 2022.

Fassbender, Bardo and Anne Peters (eds.). *The Oxford Handbook of the History of International Law*. Oxford: Oxford University Press 2012.

Frost, Robert I. *The Northern Wars. War, State and Society in Northeastern Europe, 1558–1721*. Harlow (UK)/New York: Longman 2000.

Gherardi, Raffaella. *La politica, la scienza, le armi. Luigi Ferdinando Marsili e la costruzione della frontiera dell'Impero e dell'Europa*. Bologna: Cooperativa Libraria Universitaria Editrice Bologna 2010.

Gherardi, Raffaella. 'Scienza e governo della frontiera: il problema dei confini balcanici e danubiani nella pace di Carlowitz'. *Il Pensiero Politico* 32/3 (1999), 323–51.

Gleghill Dickison, Joycelyne. *The Congress of Arras 1435. A Study in Medieval Diplomacy*. New York: BIBLO and TANNEN 1972.

Greenblatt, Stephen. *Renaissance Self-Fashioning: From More to Shakespeare*. Chicago/London: University of Chicago Press 1980.

Gounaris, Basil C. "'The Turks are Like Women; quidquid volunt, valde volunt.' Alexandros Mavrocordatos, William Paget, and the Preliminaries of the Karlowitz Treaty (1697/98)". *Südost-Forschungen* 71 (2012), 1–18.

Guskov, Andrei G. 'Uchastie Rossii v Karlovitskom Kongresse (1698–1699 Gody): Russkaja Diplomatija v rannee novoe vremja'. *Novaja i novejshaja istorija* 3 (2018), 119–41.

Guzevich, Dmitri and Irina Guzevich. *Velikoe posol'stvo:Rubezh epokh, ili Nachalo puti, 1697–1698*. Saint Petersburg: Dmitri Bulanin 2008.

Güngörürler, Selim. 'The belated consummation of the Ottoman – Safavid peace of Zuhab, 1639–1643'. *Archivum Ottomanicum* 37 (2020), 35–68.

Güngörürler, Selim. 'Diplomacy and Political Relations between the Ottoman Empire and Safavid Iran, 1639–1722'. Ph.D. thesis, Georgetown University 2016.

Hagen, Gottfried. 'Afterword: Ottoman Understanding of the World in the Seventeenth Century'. In Robert Dankoff (ed.), *An Ottoman Mentality. The World of Evliya Çelebi*, 215–56. Leiden/Boston: Brill 2006.

Hajnalka, Tóth. 'A karlócai béke és a Krími Kánság'. *Keletkutatás* (2012), 19–31.

Hatzopoulos, Dionisios. *Ο τελευταίος Βενετο-Οθωμανικός πόλεμος 1714–1718*. Athens: Papadimas 2002.

Hellman, Lisa, and Edmond Smith. 'Borders before Nations: Encounters in the Akan and Dzungar Borderlands, 1450–1750'. *Journal of Early Modern History* 27/5 (2023), 418–43.

Helmers, Helmer. 'Public Diplomacy in Early Modern Europe: Towards a New History of News'. *Media History* 22/3–4 (2016), 401–20.

Hennings, Jan. *Russia and Courtly Europe. Ritual and the Culture of Diplomacy, 1648–1725*. Cambridge: Cambridge University Press 2016.

Heywood, Colin and Ivan Parvev. 'Introduction'. In Colin Heywood and Ivan Parvev (eds.), *The Treaties of Carlowitz (1699). Antecedents, Course and Consequences*, 1–16. Leiden/Boston: Brill 2020.

Heywood, Colin. '"This Great Work": Lord Paget and the Processes of English Mediating Diplomacy in the Latter Stages of the Sacra Lega War, 1697–1698'. In Colin Heywood and Ivan Parvev (eds.), *The Treaties of Carlowitz (1699). Antecedents, Course and Consequences*, 35–55. Leiden/Boston: Brill 2020.

Heywood, Colin. 'An undiplomatic Anglo-Dutch dispute at the Porte: the quarrel at Edirne between Coenraad van Heemskerck and Lord Paget (1693)'. In Colin Heywood, *The Ottoman World, the Mediterranean and North Africa, 1660–1760*, 56–94. London/New York: Routledge 2016.

Heywood, Colin. 'English Diplomacy Between Austria and the Ottoman Empire in the War of the Sacra Liga, 1684–1699, with Special Reference to the Period 1688–1699'. Ph.D. thesis, University of London 1970.

Hora Siccama, J.H. 'De Vrede van Carlowitz en wat daaraan voorafging'. *Bijdragen voor Vaderlandsche Geschiedenis en Oudheidkunde* IV/VIII (1910), 43–185.

Höbelt, Lothar. 'Die Sackgasse aus dem Zweifrontenkrieg: Die Friedensverhandlungen mit den Osmanen 1689'. *Mitteilungen des Instituts für Österreichische Geschichtsforschung* 97 (1989), 329–80.

Ivetic, Egidio. 'Territori di confine (secoli XV–XVIII)'. In Gherardo Ortalli, Oliver Jens Schmitt and Ermanno Orlando (eds.), *Il Commonwealth veneziano tra il 1204 e la fine della Repubblica. Identità e peculiarità*, 183–201. Venice: Istituto veneto di scienze, lettere ed arti 2015.

Ivetic, Egidio. 'Venezia e l'Adriatico Orientale: connotazioni di un rapporto (secoli XIV–XVIII)'. In Gherardo Ortalli and Oliver Jens Schmitt (eds.), *Der westliche Balkan, der Adriaraum und Venedig (13.–18. Jahrhundert)*, 239–60. Vienna: Österreichische Akademie der Wissenschaften 2009.

Işıksel, Güneş. 'Barbaro's Glass Ball and Soḳollu Meḥmed's Finesse Ottoman-Venetian Peace in 1573'. *Librosdelacorte.es* 26 (2023), 295–311.

Işıksel, Güneş. 'Hierarchy and Friendship: Ottoman Practices of Diplomatic Culture and Communication (1290s–1600)'. *The Medieval History Journal* (2019), 1–20.

Işıksel, Güneş. 'Yirmisekiz Çelebi Mehmed Fransa'da: Güzergâh, Toplumsal Algı, Diplomatik Pratikler und Lâle Devri'. *Doğu Batı* 85 (2018), 99–112.

Işıksel, Güneş. 'La politique étrangère ottomane dans la seconde moitié du XVIe siècle: le cas du règne de Selîm II (1566–1574)'. Ph.D. thesis, Écoles des Hautes Études en Sciences Sociales 2012.

Jablonka, Ivan. *L'histoire est une littérature contemporaine. Manifeste pour les sciences sociales*. Paris: Éditions du Seuil 2014.

Janžekovič, Izidor. 'The Balance of Power from the Thirty Years' War and the Peace of Westphalia (1648) to the War of the Spanish Succession and the Peace of Utrecht'. *History of European Ideas* (2022), 1–19.

Jaskov, Helena. 'The Negotiated Geography of the Treaty of Nerchinsk (1689) and the Role of the Jesuits'. *Late Imperial China* 40/2 (2019), 45–88.

Kampmann, Christoph. 'The Treaty of Westphalia as Peace Settlement and Political Concept. From a German Security System to the Constitution of International Law'.

In Marc Weller, Mark Retter and Andrea Varga (eds.), *International Law and Peace Settlements*, 64–85. Cambridge: Cambridge University Press 2021.

Kampmann, Christoph et al. (eds.). *L'art de la paix. Kongresswesen und Friedensstiftung im Zeitalter des Westfälischen Friedens*. Münster: Aschendorff 2011.

Kampmann, Christoph. 'Der Ehrenvolle Friede als Friedenshidernis: Alte Fragen und neue Ergebnisse zur Mächtepolitik im Dreißigjährigen Krieg'. In Inken Schmidt-Voges, Siegrid Westphal, Volker Arnke and Tobias Bartke (eds.), *Pax perpetua. Neuere Forschungen zum Frieden in der Frühen Neuzeit*, 141–56. Munich: De Druyter Oldenbourg 2010.

Kampmann, Christoph. *Arbiter und Friedensstiftung: Die Auseinandersetzung um den politischen Schiedrichter im Europa der Früher Neuzeit*. Paderborn/Munich/Vienna/Zurich: Ferdinand Schöningh 2001.

Kantorska, Kinga Maria. 'Les médiations françaises auprès des couronnes du nord au XVIIe Siècle. Les tentatives d'arbitrage.' In Lucien Bély (ed.), *L'invention de la diplomatie. Moyen Age – Temps Modernes*, 225–34. Paris: PUF, 1998.

Kármán, Gábor. 'A Third Party: Gábor Bethlen, Prince of Transylvania and the Habsburg – Ottoman Peace Negotiations 1624–1627'. In Rubén González Cuerva and Francesco Caprioli (eds.), *Beyond European Courts. Models of Indirect Diplomacy in Imperial Borderlands* (forthcoming).

Kármán, Gábor. 'King Thököly in Chains: The Fall of the Ottoman Tributary State of Upper Hungary'. In (eds.) *Tributaries and Peripheries of the Ottoman Empire*, 264–89. Leiden/Boston: Brill 2020.

Kastritsis, Dimitris. 'Ferīdūn Beg's Münşe'atü's-Selāṭīn ("Correspondence of Sultans") and Late Sixteenth-Century Ottoman Views of the Political World'. In Dimiter Angelov, Yota Batsaki and Sahar Bazzaz (eds.), *Imperial Geographies in Byzantine and Ottoman Space*, 91–110. Cambridge, Massachusetts/London: Harvard University Press 2013.

Kastritsis, Dimitris. *The Sons of Bayezid. Empire Building and Representation in the Ottoman Civil War of 1402–13*. Leiden/Boston: Brill 2007.

Katsiardi-Hering, Olga (ed.). *Βενετικοὶ χάρτες τῆς Πελοποννήσου τέλη 17ου-ἀρχὲς 18ου αἰῶνα. Ἀπὸ τὴ συλλογὴ τοῦ Πολεμικοῦ Ἀρχείου τῆς Αὐστρίας*. Athens: National Bank of Greece Cultural Foundation 2018.

Katsiardi-Hering, Olga. 'Κτηματογραφικοὶ χάρτες τοῦ « Regno di Morea » ἢ αὐτοκρατορικοὶ χάρτες; Εἰσαγωγή'. In Olga Katsiardi-Hering (ed.), *Βενετικοὶ χάρτες τῆς Πελοποννήσου τέλη 17ου–ἀρχὲς 18ου αἰῶνα. Ἀπὸ τὴ συλλογὴ τοῦ Πολεμικοῦ Ἀρχείου τῆς Αὐστρίας*, 13–57. Athens: National Bank of Greece Cultural Foundation 2018.

Katsiardi-Hering, Olga, 'Δούναβης: Ποτάμι πολέμων καὶ εἰρήνης – Γέφυρα ψυχῶν καὶ εἰδῶν (18ος – μέσα 19ου αἰ.)' in *Σκεῦος εἰς Τιμήν. Ἀφιερωματικὸς τόμος ἐπὶ τῇ συμπληρώσει 25ετίας ἀπὸ τῆς εἰς Ἐπίσκοπον χειροτονίας καὶ 20ετίας ἀπὸ τῆς ἐνθρονίσεως τοῦ Μητροπολίτου Αὐστρίας καὶ Ἐξάρχου Οὐγγαρίας καὶ Μεσευρώπης κ. Μιχαὴλ* (Athens 2011), 405–19.

Kaufmann, David. *Dr. Israel Conegliano und seine Verdienste und die Republik Venedig bis nach dem Frieden von Carlowitz*. Vienna: Carl Konegen 1895.

Kauffman, Thomas. *Luther's Jews. A Journey into Antisemitism*. Oxford: Oxford University Press 2017.

Kerekes, Dóra. 'A Császári Tolmácsok a Magyarországi Visszafoglialó Háborúk Idején'. *Századok* 138/5 (2004), 1189–1228.

Keul, István. *Early Modern Religious Communities in East-Central Europe: Ethnic Diversity, Denominational Plurality, and Corporate Politics in the Principality of Transylvania (1526–1691)*. Leiden/Boston: Brill 2009.

Khadduri, Majid. *War and Peace in the Law of Islam*. Richmond, VA: Johns Hopkins University Press 1955.

Klein, Denise. 'Tatar and Ottoman History Writing. The Case of the Nogay Rebellion (1699–1701)'. In Denise Kein (ed.), *The Crimean Khanate between East and West (15th–18th Century)*, 125–46. Wiesbaden: Harrassowitz 2012.

Kochegarov, Kirill. 'From the "Eternal Peace" to the Treaty of Carlowitz: Relations between Russia, the Sublime Porte and the Crimean Khanate (1686–1699)'. In Colin Heywood and Ivan Parvev (eds.), *The Treaties of Carlowitz (1699): Antecedents, Course and Consequences*, 186–200. Leiden/New York: Brill 2020.

Kochegarov, Kirill. 'The Moscow Uprising of 1682. Relations between Russia, the Crimean Khanate, and the Polish – Lithuanian Commonwealth'. In Denise Klein (ed.), *The Crimean Khanate between East and West (15th–18th Century)*, 59–73. Wiesbaden: Harrassowitz 2012.

Kocić, Marija and Nikola Samardžić. 'Porta na Kongresu u Karlovcu (1698.–1699.): kraj ad hoc diplomatije'. *Historijski Zbornik* 68 (2015), 15–30.

Kolçak, Özgür. 'Bir Sefaret Hikâyesi (1665–1666): Kara Mehmed Paşa, Viyana Günleri, Elçilik Heyeti ve Sefaretnamesi'. *Osmanlı Araştırmaları / The Journal of Ottoman Studies* 65 (2025), 95–149.

Kolçak, Özgür. 'A History of Learned Courtesy: Habsburg-Ottoman Diplomatic Encounters in the 17th Century (1606–83)'. *Turkish Historical Review* 15 (2024), 223–51.

Kolçak, Özgür. 'XVII. Yüzyıl Osmanlı-Habsburg Diplomasi Tarihine bir Katkı: 1664 Vasvar Antlaşması'nın Tasdik Sürecine Dair Yeni Bulgular'. *Dîvân Disiplinlerarası Çalışmalar Dergisi* 22/43 (2017), 25–88.

Kolçak, Özgür. 'Vasvar Antlaşması', in TDVİA, vol. 42, 560–2. Istanbul: Turkish Religious Foundation 2012.

Kołodziejczyk, Dariusz. 'The Treaty of Carlowitz in Polish Memory – a Date Better Forgotten?'. In Colin Heywood and Ivan Parvev (eds.), *The Treaties of Carlowitz (1699). Antecedents, Course and Consequences*, 201–12. Leiden/Boston: Brill 2020.

Kołodziejczyk, Dariusz. 'The Orthodox Exarchate of Little Rus': A Few Remarks on the Ottoman Confessional Policy in the Late Seventeenth Century'. *Archivum Ottomanicum* 33 (2016), 247–55.

Kołodziejczyk, Dariusz. 'Ottoman Frontiers in Eastern Europe'. In Norbert Spannenberger and Szabolcs Varga (eds.), *Ein Raum im Wandel. Die osmanisch-habsburgische Grenzregion vom 16. bis zum 18. Jahrhundert*, 25–37. Stuttgart: Franz Steiner Verlag 2014.

Kołodziejczyk, Dariusz. 'What is inside and what is outside? Tributary States in Ottoman Politics'. In Gábor Kármán and Lovro Kunčević (eds.), *The European Tributary States of the Ottoman Empire in the Sixteenth and Seventeenth Centuries*, 421–32. Leiden/New York: Brill 2013.

Kołodziejczyk, Dariusz. 'Between universalistic claims and reality. Ottoman frontiers in the early modern period'. In Christine Woodhead (ed.), *The Ottoman World*, 205–19. London/New York: Routledge 2012.

Kołodziejczyk, Dariusz. 'Das Krimkhanat als Gleichgewichtsfaktor in Osteuropa (17.–18. Jahrhundert)'. In Denise Klein (ed.), *The Crimean Khanate between East and West (15th–18th Century)*, 47–58. Wiesbaden: Harrassowitz 2012.

Kołodziejczyk, Dariusz. *The Crimean Khanate and Poland – Lithuania: International Diplomacy on the European Periphery (15th–18th Century). A Study of Peace Treaties Followed by Annotated Documents*. Leiden/New York: Brill 2011.

Kołodziejczyk, Dariusz. 'La res publica polono-lituanienne etait-elle le vassal de l'empire ottoman?' In Anna Parzymies (ed.), *Studies in Oriental Art and Culture in Honour of Professor Tadeusz Majda*, 125–36. Warsaw: Dialog 2006.

Kołodziejczyk, Dariusz. 'Native Nobilities and Foreign Absolutism: a Polish – Ottoman case'. *Studia Caroliensia* 3–4 (2004), 303–8.

Kołodziejczyk, Dariusz. 'Between the Splendor of Barocco and Political Pragmatism: The Form and Contents of the Polish-Ottoman Treaty Documents of 1699'. *Oriente Moderno, Nuova serie* 22 (83)/3 (2003), 671–9.

Kołodziejczyk, Dariusz. *Ottoman – Polish Diplomatic Relations (15th to 18th Centuries): An Annotated Edition of 'Ahdnames and Other Documents*. Leiden: Brill 2000.

Kołodziejczyk, Dariusz. 'Od stanic kresowych do rogatek. Rozwój pojęcia granicy linearnej w Europie Wschodniej'. *Barok: Historia-Literatura-Sztuka* 3/2 (1996), 53–9.

Kołodziejczyk, Dariusz. *Podole pod panowaniem tureckim: Ejalet Kamieniecki 1672–1699*. Warsaw 1994.

Kontogiannopoulou, Anastasia. 'Η προσηγορία κυρ στη Βυζαντινή Κοινωνία'. *Βυζαντινά* 32 (2012), 209–26.

Köhler, Matthias. 'Argumentieren und Verhandeln auf dem Kongress von Nimwegen'. In Arndt Brendecke (ed.), *Praktiken der Frühen Neuzeit. Akteure-Handlungen-Artefakte*, 523–35. Cologne/Weimar/Vienna: Böhlau 2015.

Köhler, Matthias. *Strategie und Symbolik. Verhandeln auf dem Kongress von Nimwegen*. Cologne/Weimar/Vienna: Böhlau 2011.

Köhler, Matthias. 'Höflichkeit, Strategie und Kommunikation. Friedensverhandlungen an der Wende vom 17. zum 18. Jahrhundert'. In Gisela Engel, Brita Rang and Susanne

Scholz (eds.), *Konjunkturen der Höflichkeit in der Frühen Neuzeit*, 379–98. Frankfurt: Klostermann 2009.

Krischer, André J. and Hillard von Thiessen. 'Diplomacy in a Global Early Modernity: The Ambiguity of Sov-ereignty'. *The International History Review* 41/5 (2019), 1100–07.

Królikowska–Jedlińska, Natalia. 'Designers or Obedient Executors of the Ottoman Northeastern Policy? The Governors of the Caffa and Trabzon Provinces at the Turn of the Seventeenth and Eighteenth Centuries'. In Gábor Kármán (ed.), *Tributaries and Peripheries of the Ottoman Empire*, 290–301. Leiden/Boston: Brill 2020.

Królikowska–Jedlińska, Natalia. 'Sovereignty and Subordination in Crimean-Ottoman Relation (Sixteenth – Eighteenth Centuries)'. In Gábor Kármán and Lovro Kunčević (eds.), *The European Tributary States of the Ottoman Empire in the Sixteenth and Seventeenth Centuries*, 43–65. Leiden/Boston: Brill 2013.

Kruger, Himlar. *Fetwa und Siyar: zur internationalrechtlichen Gutachtenpraxis der osmanischen Seyh ul-Islam vom 17. bis 19. Jahrhundert unter besonderer Berucksichtigung des 'Behcet ul-Fetava'.* Wiesbaden: Otto Harrosowitz 1978.

Krys'ko, V.B. (ed.). *Slovar' russkogo jazyka XI–XVII vv.*, vol. 29. Moscow: Nauka 2012.

Kunčević, Lovro. 'Janus-Faced Sovereignty: The International Status of the Ragusan Republic in the Early Modern Period'. In [idem] and Gábor Kármán (eds.), *The European Tributary States of the Ottoman Empire in the Sixteenth and Seventeenth Centuries*, 91–121. Leiden/Boston: Brill 2013.

Kunčević, Lovro. 'The Rhetoric of the Frontier of Christendom in the Diplomacy of Renaissance Ragusa (Dubrovnik)'. *Dubrovnik Annals* 17 (2013), 37–68.

Kühnel, Florian, and Christine Vogel. 'Frühneuzeitliche Botschaftssekretäre zwischen Domestik und Staatsdiener'. In Florian Kühnel and Christine Vogel (eds.), *Zwischen Domestik und Staatsdiener. Botschaftssekretäre in den frühneuzeitlichen Außenbeziehungen*, 9–28. Cologne/Weimar/Vienna: Böhlau 2021.

Kütükoğlu, Mübahat S. 'Temessük'. In TDVİA, vol. 40, 413–4. Istanbul: Turkish Religious Foundation 2011.

Kütükoğlu, Mübahat S. 'Hududnâme'. In TDVİA, vol. 18, 303–4. Istanbul: Turkish Religious Foundation 1998.

Laufs, Markus and Christian Wenzel. 'Conflict Management in the Early Modern Period: Mediating and Safeguarding Treaties'. In Dorothée Goetze and Lena Oetzel (eds.), *Early Modern European Diplomacy. A Handbook*, 707-24. Berlin/Boston: De Gruyter 2024.

Laufs, Markus. *In viam pacis. Praktiken niederländischen und päpstlicher Friedensvermittlung auf den Kongressen von Münster (1643–1649) und Nimwegen (1676–1679).* Vandenhoeck & Ruprecht 2022.

Lemee, Emmanuel. 'The Language of Incognito in Late-Seventtenth Century Diplomacy'. *Legatio* 4 (2020), 15–36.

Lesaffer, Randall. 'The Lore and Laws of Peacemaking in Early Modern and Nineteenth-Century European Peace Treaties'. In Marc Weller, Mark Retter and Andrea Varga (eds.), *International Law and Peace Settlements*, 46–63. Cambridge: Cambridge University Press 2021.

Lesaffer, Randall, Erik-Jan Broers, and Johanna Waelkens. 'From Antwerp to Munster (1609/1648). Truce and Peace under the Law of Nations'. In Randall Lesaffer (ed.), *The Twelve Years Truce (1609). Peace, Truce, War and Law in the Low Countries at the Turn of the 17th Century*, 233–55. Leiden/Boston: Brill 2014.

Lesaffer, Randall. 'Peace Treaties and the Formation of International Law'. In Bardo Fassbender and Anne Peters (eds.). *The Oxford Handbook of the History of International Law*, 71–94. Oxford: Oxford University Press 2012.

Lesaffer, Randall. 'Peace treaties from Lodi to Westphalia'. In Randall Lesaffer (ed.), *Peace Treaties and International Law in European History. From the Middle Ages to World War One*, 9–44. Cambridge/New York: Cambridge University Press 2004.

Liata, Eutichia and Kostas Tsiknakis (eds.). *Με τὴν Αρμάδα στὸ Μοριά 1684–1687. Ανέκδοτο ἡμερολόγιο με σχέδια*. Athens: Hellenic Research Foundation/Olkos Publishing 1998.

Lynn, John A. *The Wars of Louis XIV 1667–1714*. Abingdon/New York: Routledge 2013.

Maltezou, Chrysa. 'Βενετσιάνικες εκθέσεις για την οχύρωση του ισθμού της Κορίνθου στα τέλη του 17ου αιώνα'. In *Πρακτικά Α Διεθνούς Συνεδρίου Πελοποννησιακών Σπουδών*, Σπάρτη 7–14 Σεπτ. 1975, vol. 3, 269–76. Athens: 1976–8.

Matveyev, Vladimir. *The Karlowitz Congress and the Debut of Russia's Multilateral Diplomacy (1698–99)*. Leicester 2000.

May, Niels F. 'Zeremoniell'. In Irene Dinkel et al. (eds.), *Handbuch Frieden im Europa der Frühen Neuzeit / Handbook of Peace in Early Modern Europe*, 609–25. Berlin/Boston: De Gruyter 2020.

May, Niels F. *Zwischen fürstlicher Repräsentation und adliger Statuspolitik. Das Kongresszeremoniell bei den westfälischen Friedensverhandlungen*. Stuttgart: Thorbecke 2016.

Melis, Nicola. 'Some Observations on the Concept of dār al-ʿahd in the Ottoman Context (Sixteenth – Seventeenth Centuries)'. In Giovanna Calasso and Giuliano Lancioni (eds.), *Dār al-islām / dār al-ḥarb. Territories, People, Identities*, 182–202. Leiden/Boston: Brill 2017.

Menchinger, Ethan L. 'Revisiting "Turkish Fatalism"; Or, Why Ottoman Theology Matters'. *Aca'ib: Occasional Papers on Ottoman Perceptions of the Supernatural* (2022), 9–37.

Miović, Vesna. 'Alexander Mavrocordatos Exaporite, Grand Dragoman and Secret Adviser to the Porte: Du-brovnik's Perspective'. *Dubrovnik Annals* 27 (2023), 121–48.

Miović, Vesna. 'Diplomatic Relations between the Ottoman Empire and the Republic of Dubrovnik'. In Gábor Kármán and Lovro Kunčević (eds.), *The European Tributary States of the Ottoman Empire in the Sixteenth and Seventeenth Centuries*, 187–208. Leiden/Boston: Brill 2013.

Moeglin, Jean-Marie and Stéphane Péquignot. *Diplomatie et « Relations Internationales » au Moyen Âge (IXe–XVe Siècle)*. Paris: PUF 2017.

Molnár, Mónika F. 'Der Friede von Karlowitz und das Osmanische Reich'. In Arno Strohmeyer and Norbert Spannenberger (eds.), *Frieden und Konfliktmanagement in interkulturellen Räumen*, 197–220. Stuttgart: Franz Steiner 2013.

Molnár, Mónika F. 'Luigi Ferdinando Marsigli e gli Ottomani. La frontiera asburgico-ottomana dopo la pace di Carlowitz'. In Raffaella Gherardi (ed.), *La politica, la scienza, le armi. Luigi Ferdinando Marsili e la costruzione della frontiera dell'Impero e dell'Europa*, 147–72. Bologna: Cooperativa Libraria Universitaria Editrice Bologna 2010.

Molnár, Mónika F. 'The Treaty of Karlowitz in the Venetian sources. Diplomacy and ceremony'. In Hasan Celal Güzel. C. Cem Oğuz and Osman Karatay (eds.), *The Turks*, vol. 3, 405–14. Ankara 2002.

Nessi, Giuseppe. 'Uti possidetis Doctrine'. In Rüdiger Wulfrum (ed.), MPEPIL, vol.10. Oxford: Oxford University Press 2018.

Novak, Grga. *Borba Dubrovnika za slobodu, 1683–1699*. Zagreb: Archbishopal Printing House 1935.

Oetzel, Lena. 'A Diplomatic Sphere of Its Own: Early Modern Peace Congresses'. In Dorothée Goetze and Lena Oetzel (eds.), *Early Modern European Diplomacy. A Handbook*, 465–82. Berlin/Boston: De Gruyter 2024.

Offenstadt, Nicolas. *Faire la Paix au Moyen Âge*. Paris: Odile Jacob 2007.

Oral, Özgür. 'Osmanlı-Venedik Diplomatik İlişkileri Tarihine Bir Katkı: 1763 Tarihli Cezayir-Venedik Antlaşması'. *Avrasya İncelemeleri Dergisi/Journal of Eurasian Inquires* 6/2 (2017), 103–30.

O'Quinn, Daniel. *Engaging the Ottoman Empire. Vexed Mediations 1690–1815*. Philadelphia: University of Pennsylvania Press 2019.

Osborne, Toby. 'Whither Diplomatic History? An Early-Modern Historian's Perspective'. *Diplomatica* 1 (2019), 40–5.

Ostapchuk, Victor. 'Cossack Ukraine in and out of Ottoman Orbit, 1648–1681'. In Gábor Kármán and Lovro Kunčević (eds.), *The European Tributary States of the Ottoman Empire in the Sixteenth and Seventeenth Centuries*, 123–52. Leiden/Boston: Brill 2013.

Othman, Aida. 'And Ṣulḥ is best: Amicable Settlement and Dispute Resolution in Islamic Law'. Ph.D. thesis, Harvard University 2009.

Pakalın, Mehmet Zeki. *Tarih Deyimleri ve Terimleri Sözlüğü*, vol. 2. İstanbul: Devlet Kitapları 1971.

Paladino, G.'Due dragomanni veneti a Costantinopoli (Tommaso Tarsia e Gian Rinaldo Carli)'. *Nuovo Archivio Veneto* 17/33 (1917), 183–200.

Panaite, Viorel. *Ottoman Law of War and Peace. The Ottoman Empire and Its Tribute-Payers from the North of the Danube*, 2nd revised edn. Leiden/Boston: Brill 2019.

Panopoulou, Aggeliki. 'Da mar a mar. Μιὰ πρόταση γιὰ τὴν ἄμυνα τῆς περιοχῆς τῆς Κορίνθου στὰ τέλη τοῦ 17ου αἰώνα'. In Olga Katsiardi-Hering (ed.), *Βενετικοὶ χάρτες τῆς Πελοποννήσου τέλη 17ου–ἀρχὲς 18ου αἰῶνα. Ἀπὸ τὴ συλλογὴ τοῦ Πολεμικοῦ Ἀρχείου τῆς Αὐστρίας*, 229–48. Athens: National Bank of Greece Cultural Foundation 2018.

Papadia-Lala, Anastasia. *Ο θεσμός των αστικών κοινοτήτων στον ελληνικό χώρο κατά την περίοδο της Βενετοκρατίας (13ος–18ος αι.). Μία συνθετική προσέγγιση*. Venice: Hellenic Institute of Venice, 2008.

Papp, Sándor. 'Az Oszmán Birodalom, a Magyar Királyság és a Habsburg Monarchia kapcsolattörténetea békekötések tükrében'. *Aetas* 33/4 (2018), 86–99.

Parvev, Ivan. *Habsburgs and Ottomans between Vienna and Belgrade (1683–1739)*. New York: Columbia University Press 1995.

Pedani-Fabris, Maria Pia. *Dalla frontiera al confine*. Venice: Herder Editrice 2002.

Pedani-Fabris, Maria Pia. *La dimora della pace. Considerazioni sulle capitolazioni tra i paesi islamici e l'Europa*. Venice 1996.

Penskaya, Elena and Joachim Küpper. 'Introduction'. In Elena Penskaya and Joachim Küpper (eds.), *Theater as Metaphor*, 1–8. Berlin/Boston: De Gruyter 2019.

Perdue, Peter C. 'Boundaries and Trade in the Early Modern World: Negotiations at Nerchinsk and Beijing'. *Eighteenth-Century Studies* 43/3 (2010), 341–56.

Perdue, Peter C. 'Boundaries, Maps, and Movement: Chinese, Russian, and Mongolian Empires in Early Modern Central Eurasia'. *International History Review* 20/2 (1998), 263–86.

Peri, Oded. *Christianity under Islam in Jerusalem. The Question of the Holy Sites in Early Ottoman Times*. Leiden/Boston/Köln: Brill 2001.

Pešalj, Jovan. 'The Distinctiveness of the Habsburg-Ottoman Border in the Eighteenth Century'. In Maria Baramova, Grigor Boykov, and Ivan Parvev (eds.), *Bordering Early Modern Europe*, 21–38. Wiesbaden: Harrassowitz 2015.

Petitjean, Johann. *L'Intelligence des choses. Une histoire de l'information entre Italie et Méditerranée (XVIe–XVIIe Siècles)*. Rome: École Française de Rome 2013.

Petritsch, Ernst D. 'Rijswijk und Karlowitz. Wechselwirkungen europäischer Friedenspolitik'. In Heinz Duchhardt et al. (eds.), *Der Friede von Rijwick 1697*, 291–312. Mainz: Philipp von Zabern 1998.

Petritsch, Ernst D. 'Der habsburgisch-osmanische Friedensvertrag des Jahres 1547'. MÖStA 38 (1985), 49–80.

Pfister, Max. 'Grenzbezeichnungen im Italoromanischen und Galloromanischen'. In Wolfgang Haubrichs and Reinhard Schneider (eds.), *Grenzen und Grenzregionen*, 37–50. Saarland: Saarbrücken 1994.

Pissis, Nikolas. *Russland in den politischen Vorstellungen der griechischen Kulturwelt 1645–1725*. Göttingen: Vandenhoeck & Ruprecht 2020.

Poulios, Konstantinos. 'From the Palace of Ryswick to the Sultan's Seraglio: The Ottoman Translation and Interpretation of a Chris-tian European Peace Treaty'. *Legatio* 6 (2022), 99–124.

Poulios, Konstantinos. 'Αναζητώντας την ειρήνη εν μέσω πολέμου. Η οθωμανική διπλωματική δραστηριότητα του έτους 1685 και ο ρόλος του Αλέξανδρου Μαυροκορδάτου'. *Mnimon* 38 (2021), 11–32.

Poumarède, Géraud. *L'Empire de Venise et les Turcs XVIe–XVIIe siècle.* Paris: Classiques Garnier 2020.

Power, Daniel. 'A. Frontiers: Terms, Concepts, and the Historians of Medieval and Early Modern Europe'. In Daniel Power and Naomi Standen (eds.), *Frontiers in Question. Eurasian Borderlands, 700–1700*, 1–12. New York: Palgrave Macmillan 1999.

Raby, Julian. 'Mehmed the Conqueror's Greek Scriptorium'. *Dumbarton Oaks Papers* 37 (1983), 15–34

Rahn, Thomas. 'Grenz-Situationen des Zeremoniells in der Frühen Neuzeit'. In Thomas Rahn and Markus Bauer (eds.), *Die Grenze. Begriff und Inszenierung*, 177–206. Berlin: Akademie Verlag 1997.

Repgen, Konrad. 'Friedensvermittlung und Friedensvermittler beim Westfälischen Frieden'. In Franz Bosbach and Christoph Kampmann (eds.), *Dreissigjähriger Krieg und Westfälischer Friede: Studien und Quellen*, 3rd edn., 939–66. Paderborn: Ferdinand Schöningh 2015.

Rohdewald, Stefan. '„bu sulh u salah mukarrer ve mü'ebbed"/„Pax perpetua"? Polnisch-litaunische Friedensformeln und Allianzen mit Osmanen und Krimtataren bis 1790'. *Zeitschrift für Ostmitteleuropa-Forschung* 65/2 (2016), 167–92.

Rohrschneider, Michael. 'Friedensvermittlung und Schiedsgerichtsbarkeit'. In Volker Arnke et al. (eds.), *Handbuch Frieden Im Europa Der Frühen Neuzeit / Handbook of Peace in Early Modern Europe*, 473–90. Oldenbourg: De Gruyter 2020.

Rohrschneider, Michael. 'Reputation als Leitfaktor in den internationalen Beziehungen der Früher Neuzeit'. *Historische Zeitschrift* 291/2 (2010), 331–52.

Rothman, Nathalie E. *The Dragoman Renaissance. Diplomatic Interpreters and the Routes of Orientalism.* Ithaca/London: Cornell University Press 2021.

Rothman, Nathalie E. *Brokering Empire. Trans-Imperial Subjects between Venice and Istanbul.* Ithaca (USA)/London: Cornell University Press 2012.

Sahlins, Peter. 'Natural Frontiers Revisited: France's Boundaries since the Seventeenth Century'. *The American Historical Review* 95/5 (1990), 1423–51.

Samardžić, Radovan. *Veliki vek Dubrovnika.* Belgrade: Prosveta 1983.

Samardžić, Radovan. 'Borba Dubrovnika protiv mletačkih pokušaja da unište njegovu nezavisnost u XVII veku'. In *Dubrovačko pomorstvo. U spomen sto godina Nautičke škole u Dubrovniku*, Dubrovnik 1952.

Saracino, Stefano and Vasilios N. Makrides. 'Die Aufnahme des Alexandros Mavrocordatos ex Aporriton in die Academia Naturae Curiosorum (1689). Die Quellen aus dem Archiv der Leopoldina'. *Ο Ερανιστής* 30 (2021), 33–114.

Scattola, Merio. 'Die Grenze der Neuzeit. Ihr Begriff in der juristischen und politischen Literatur der Antike und Frühmoderne'. In Thomas Rahn and Markus Bauer (eds.), *Die Grenze. Begriff und Inszenierung*, 37–72. Berlin: Akademie Verlag 1997.

Schneider, Christian. '"Types" of Peacemakers: Exploring the Authority and Self-Perception of the Early Modern Papacy'. In Stephen Cummins and Laura Kounine (eds.), *Cultures of Conflict Resolution in Early Modern Europe*, 77–103. London: Routledge 2016.

Schneider, Reinhard. 'Lineare Grenzen – Von Frühen zum Späten Mittelalter'. In Wolfgang Haubrichs and Reinhard Schneider (eds.), *Grenzen und Grenzregionen*, 51–68. Saarland: Saarbrücken 1994.

Schobesberger, Nikolaus, Paul Arblaster, Mario Infelise, André Belo, Noah Moxham, Carmen Espejo, and Joad Raymond. 'European Postal Networks'. In Joad Raymond and Noah Moxham (eds.), *News Networks in Early Modern Europe*, 17–63. Leiden/Boston: Brill 2016.

Schock, Flemming, Oswald Bauer and Ariane Kolle (eds.). *Dimensionen der Theatrum-Metapher in der Frühen Neuzeit. Ordnung und Repräsentation von Wissen/Dimensions of the Early Modern Theatrum-Metaphor. Order and Representation of Knowledge*. Hannover: Wehrhann 2008.

Schwarcz, Iskra. 'Die kaiserlichen Gesandten und das diplomatische Zeremoniell am Moskauer Hof in der zweiten Hälfe des 17. Jahrhunderts'. In Ralph Kauz, Giorgio Rota, and Jan Paul Niederkorn (eds.), *Diplomatisches Zeremoniell in Europa und im Mittleren Osten in der frühen Neuzeit*, 265–86. Vienna: Verlag der Österreichischen Akademie der Wissenschaften 2009.

Séré, Daniel (ed.). *La paix des Pyrénées. Vingt-quatre ans de négociations entre la France et l'Espagne (1635–1659)*. Paris: Honoré Champion 2007.

Serwatński, Maciej. 'Dyplomacja polska wobec zasady uti possidetis w negocjacjach karłowickich 1698–1699'. In Ilony Czamanskiej and Witolda Szulca (eds.), *Traktaty Karlowickie z 1699 roku i ich następstwa*, 15–24. Poznan: Adam Mickiewicz University Press 2003.

Skrzypietz, Aleksandra. 'Zabiegi posła francuskiego o odrębny pokój polsko-turecki w latach'. In Ilony Czamanskiej and Witolda Szulca (eds.), *Traktaty Karlowickie z 1699 roku i ich następstwa*, 95–100. Poznan: Adam Mickiewicz University Press 2003.

Slottman, William B. *Ferenc II Rákóczi and the Great Powers*. New York: Columbia University Press 1997.

Smiley, Will. *From Slaves to Prisoners of War: The Ottoman Empire, Russia, and International Law*. Oxford: Oxford University Press 2018.

Sowerby, Tracey. 'Early Modern Diplomatic History'. *History Compass* 14/9 (2016), 441–56.

Steiman, Iser. 'P.V. Posnikov: A Russian Pioneer in Physiology'. *Canadian Slavonic Revue/Revue Canadienne des Slavistes* 7 (1965), 63–70.

Stoianovich, Traian. 'Conquering Balkan Orthodox Merchant'. *Journal of Economic History* 20/2 (1960), 234–313.

Stollberg-Rilinger, Barbara. 'Zu moralischen Ökonomie des Schenkens bei Hof (17.–18. Jahrhundert)'. In Werner Paravacini (ed.), *Luxus und Integration. Materielle Hofkultur Westeuropas vom 12. bis zum 18. Jahrhundert*, 187–202. Munich 2010.

Stouraiti, Anastasia. *War, Communication, and the Politics of Culture in Early Modern Venice*. Cambridge: Cambridge University Press 2023.

Stoye, John. *Marsigli's Europe 1680–1730. The Life and Times of Luigi Ferdinando Marsigli, Soldier and Virtuoso*. New Haven and London: Yale University Press 1994.

Strohmeyer, Arno. 'Der Friede von Zsitvatorok 1606 und die Friedensschlüsse der "Türkenkriege"'. In Irene Dingel et al. (eds.), *Handbuch Frieden im Europa der Frühen Neuzeit / Handbook of Peace in Early Modern Europe*, 969–84. Berlin/Boston: De Gruyter 2020.

Šundrica, Zdravko. 'The Intelligence Activities of the Dubrovnik Republic in the Austro-Turkish War, 1737–1739'. *Dubrovnik Annals* 5 (2001), 47–79.

Trédé, Monique. 'Le téâtre comme métaphore au IIe siècle ap. J.-C.: survivances et metamorphoses'. *Comptes rendus des séances de l'Académie des Inscriptions et Belles-Lettres* 146/2 (2002), 581–605.

Tremml-Werner, Birgit, Lisa Hellman and Guido van Meersbergen. 'Introduction. Gift and Tribute in Early Modern Diplomacy: Afro-Eurasian Perspectives'. *Diplomatica* 2 (2020), 185–200.

Tremml-Werner, Birgit and Dorothée Goetze. 'A Multitude of Actors in Early Modern Diplomacy'. *Journal of Early Modern History* 23 (2019), 407–22.

Türk, Ahmet, 'Gift Exchange as a Means of Expression of Power: The Case of Crimean-Muscovite Relations'. *Acta Orientalia Academiae Scientiarum Hungaricae* 76/2 (2023), 221–37.

Tzelepis, Dimitris. *Τὰ 'Ρωμαϊκὰ τοῦ Ἀλέξανδρου Μαυροκορδάτου τοῦ « Ἐξ Ἀπορρήτων »*, vol. 1. Athens: Irodotos 2023.

Uzunçarşılı, İsmail Hakkı. *Osmanlı Tarihi*, 8th edn, vol. 3, part 1. Ankara: Turkish Historical Society 2011.

Van den Boogert, Maurits H. 'The Spoils of Peace: What the Dutch Got Out of Carlowitz'. In Colin Heywood and Ivan Parvev (eds.), *The Treaties of Carlowitz (1699). Antecedents, Course and Consequences*, 56–72. Leiden/Boston: Brill 2020.

Van Gelder, Maartje and Tijana Krstić. 'Introduction: Cross-Confessional Diplomacy and Dip-lomatic Intermediaries in the Early Modern Mediterranean'. *Journal of Early Modern History* 19 (2015), 93–105.

Van Zuijlen van Nijevelt, Robert. *De Vrede van Carlowitz*. Utrecht: J. van Boekhoven Publishing House 1883.

Veinstein, Gilles. 'Les fondements juridiques de la diplomatie Ottomane en Europe'. *Oriente Moderno, Nuova Serie* 88/2 (2008), 509–22.

Vogler, Günter. 'Borders and Boundaries in Early Modern Europe: Problems and Possibilities'. In Steven G. Ellis and Raingard Eßer (eds.). *Frontiers and the Writing of History, 1500–1850*, 21–38. Hannover: Wehrhahn Verlag 2006.

Volkmer, Gerald. *Siebenbürgen zwischen Habsburgermonarchie und Osmanischem Reich. Völkerrechtliche Stellung und Völkerrechtspraxis eines ostmitteleuropäischen Fürstentums 1541–1699*. Munich: De Gruyter Oldenborg 2015.

Von Engel, J.C. *Die Geschichte des Freystaates Ragusa*. Vienna: Anton Doll Publishing House 1807.

Von Thiessen, Hillard. 'Kommentar: Spezialisten und Multitalente. Befunde, Kontroversen und Forschungspespektiven zu Sekretären in der frühneuzeitlichen Diplomatie'. In Florian Kühnel and Christine Vogel (eds.), *Zwischen Domestik und Staatsdiener. Botschaftssektretäre in den frühneuzeitlichen Außenbeziehungen*, 224–240. Cologne/Weimar/Vienna: Böhlau 2021.

Von Thiessen, Hillard. 'Diplomacy in a Changing Political Order: An Actor-Centred View of European Diplomats at the Time of the Spanish Succession'. In Matthias Pohlig and Michael Schaich (eds.), *The War of the Spanish Succession: New Perspectives*, 63–84. Oxford: Oxford University Press 2018.

Von Thiessen, Hillard. 'Diplomatie vom type ancient. Überlegungen zu einem Idealtypus des frühneuzeitlichen Gesandtschaftswesen'. In Hillard von Thiessen and Christian Windler (eds.). *Akteure der Außenbeziehungen. Netzwerke und Interkulturalität im historischen Wandel*, 471–503. Cologne/Weimar/Vienna: Böhlau 2010.

Von Thiessen, Hillard. 'Korrupte Gesandte? Konkurriende Normen in der Diplomatie der Frühen Neuzeit'. In Niels Grüne and Simona Slanička (eds.). *Korruption. Historische Annäherungen an einer Grundfigur politischer Kommunikation*, 205–20. Göttingen: Vandenhoeck & Ruprecht 2010.

Wagner, Marek. *Stanisław Jabłonowski (1634–1702). Polityk i dowódca*, 2 vol. Połomia: In-forteditions 2020.

Wagner, Marek. *Wojna polsko-turecka w latach 1672–1676*, 1 vol. Połomia: Inforteditions 2009.

Waquet, Jean-Claude. 'Introduction'. In Stefano Andretta et al. (eds.). *Paroles des Négotiateurs. L'entretien dans la pratique diplomatique de la fin du Moyen Âge à la fin du XIXe siècle*, 1–26. Rome: École Française de Rome 2010.

Windler, Christian. 'Afterword. Gift and Tribute in Early Modern Diplomacy: a Comment'. *Diplomatica* 2 (2020), 291–304.

Windler, Christian (ed.). *Kongressorte der Frühen Neuzeit im europäischen Vergleich: Der Friede von Baden (1714)*. Cologne/Weimar/Vienna: Böhlau 2016.

Wójcik, Zbigniew. *Traktat Andruszowski 1667 i jego geneza*. Warsaw 1959.

Yaycıoğlu, Ali. 'On the Ottoman Arguments during the Congress of Karlowitz (1699)'. In Kären Wigen (ed.), *Territorial Imaginaries: Beyond the Sovereign Map*, 61–76. Chicago: University of Chicago Press 2025.

Yaycıoğlu, Ali. 'Karlofça ânı: Osmanlı İmparatorluğu 18. yüzyıla nasıl başladı?'. *Tarih ve Toplum Yeni Yaklaşmalar* 18 (2021), 8–56.

Yılmaz, Yasir. 'An Ottoman Peace Attempt at the Habsburg Court during the Ottoman-Holy League War: Zülfikâr Efendi in Vienna, 1688–1693'. MA dissertation, Bilkent University 2008.

Yurdusev, Nuri. 'Karlofça Antlaşması ve Diplomasi Tarihi'. *Çanakkale Araştırmaları Türk Yıllığı Dergisi* 4 (2006), 1–16.

Zachar, József. 'Der "Lange Krieg" zwischen dem Osmanischen Reich und dem Habsburgerreich: Von der Kriegserklärung bis zum Friedensabschluss 1593–1606'. In János Barta, Manfred Jatzlauk and Klára Papp (eds.), *„Einingkeit und Frieden Sollen auf Seiten jeder Partei sein". Die Friedensschlüsse von Wien (23. 06. 1606) und Zsitvatorok (15. 11. 1606)*, 229–44. Debrecen: Institute of History, University of Debrecen 2007.

Zapol'skaia, Natal'ia Nikolaevna. 'Postnikov P.V. – vypusknik Slaviano-greko-latinskoi Akademii (novye materialy dlia biografii)'. *Cyrillomethodia-num* 12 (1988), 75–91.

Zarakol, Ayşe. *Before the West. The Rise and Fall of Eastern World Orders*. Cambridge: Cambridge University Press 2022.

Zielińska, Teresa. 'Stanisław Antoni Szczuka Jako Referendarz Koronny w latach 1688–1699'. *Kwartalnik Historyczny Rocznik* CXI/3 (2004), 5–22.

Zlatar, Zdenko. *Between the Double Eagle and the Crescent. The Republic of Dubrovnik and the Origins of the Eastern Question*. New York: Columbia University Press 1992.

Webpages

Baramova, Maria. 'Border Theories in Early Modern Europe'. 2010, available at: www.ieg-ego.eu/en/threads/crossroads/border-regions/maria-baramova-border-theories-in-early-modern-europe.

University of Chicago, *Logeion: A Digital Dictionary*, 'Congressus', available at: https://logeion.uchicago.edu/congressus.

Index of Names and Places

Academia Caesareo-Leopoldina 27*n*12, 217, 229
Adrianople 45, 49–50, 60, 62, 64, 67, 69, 72, 82, 86, 94, 109, 121, 156, 232*n*124, 240, 317, 329, 458
Aegina (Aegean island) 295, 331, 457*n*46
ʿAmcazāde Köprülü Ḥüseyin Paşa (Ottoman grand vizier) 46, 49, 52, 57–59, 69, 71–72, 83, 85–90, 114, 121, 124–125, 156–158, 208–209, 218–219, 229, 240–241, 337
Andrusovo
  Truce of (1667) 106
Ankara
  Battle of (1402) 429
Apafi, Mihály (Prince of Transylvania) 26, 104*n*28, 106–108
August II (King of Poland and Elector of Saxony) 66–67, 75, 78–79, 80*n*69, 82, 90–95, 98, 117, 132, 134, 137–138, 154, 157, 189, 324, 369, 372, 455
Azov 38, 74, 81, 270–271, 309, 333, 435–436
  Sea of 80, 270

Bakhchisarai (capital of the Crimean Khanate) 322
  Treaty of (1681) 29*n*21, 200, 283, 302–303, 308
Barca, Luca (Ragusan consul) 125*n*23, 316–317
Battle of Zenta (1697) 39, 45, 47, 49, 88
Bayezid I (Ottoman sultan) 429
Bega (river) 224, 296
Belgrade 25, 37, 51, 62, 89, 113, 121–122, 126, 127*n*40, 129, 142, 148, 154*n*7, 155–156, 165, 318, 340, 342, 369, 375, 447, 455*n*30, 458
  Treaty of (1739) 432
Black Sea 15, 35, 59, 81, 270, 283, 300, 324, 461, 465
Bocskai, István (Prince of Transylvania) 13, 105*n*31
Bose, Christoph Dietrich von (Saxon envoy) 80*n*69, 82, 91–93, 117, 134
Bosnia 62, 146–147, 156, 302, 318
Bucchia, Vladislavo (Ragusan envoy) 317
Buczacz
  Treaty of (1672) 329
Budjak (region in the north-western Black Sea coast) 271, 305–306, 323–324, 333–334

Callières, François de (French diplomat and writer) 3, 184
Camilo, Giuseppe (Catholic bishop) 34–35
Candia
  Peace of (1669) 55*n*52, 56, 298–299
  Treaty of. *See* Peace of
  War of (1642–1699) 298*n*179
Cantemir, Dimitrie (Moldavian prince and historian) 45, 49, 216, 334, 359, 419*n*14
Carli, Gian Rinaldo (interpreter in Venetian service) 386
Carlos II (King of Spain) 47, 125
Carlowitz
  Congress of 1–24, passim
  town of 1, 336–337, 339, 375
  Plain of 22, 153, 336–337, 459
  Treaties of 10, 15, 16, 178, 215*n*26, 229, 330*n*117, 333, 460*n*1, 461
Carlowitz, Hans Carl von (Saxon envoy) 134, 138*n*101
Castello di Rumelia (fortress in south-western Greece) 269, 456
Charles II (King of England) 103, 117
Châteauneuf, Pierre-Antoine de (French ambassador) 70, 87
Chios (Aegean island) 28, 34, 38, 156, 205
Colyer, Jacob (Dutch ambassador) 37, 47–49, 62, 71–72, 82–84, 88, 95, 109–118, 121–122, 142, 156, 163, 206–208, 214, 218, 234*n*132, 261, 300, 331, 335, 343, 358, 378–379, 390, 413, 420, 464
Commonwealth. *See* Polish-Lithuanian Commonwealth
Commonwealth-Ottoman Peace Agreement of 1621 328–329, 389
Conegliano, Israel (Jewish doctor in Venetian service) 204–205, 229, 362, 394

Constantinople 28–29, 49, 71–72, 74, 91, 204–205, 270, 385–386, 442, 448
Peace Treaty of (1700) 420*n*25, 436
Copenhagen
Peace Treaty of (1660) 109, 130
Corinthian Gulf 269, 271
Corinthian Isthmus 269, 282, 295, 298, 300, 302, 304, 415, 456
Crimea 145, 270, 283, 368
Crimean Khanate 23, 271, 310, 313, 322–334, 367–370
Croatia 272, 302–303, 305, 309, 357, 375, 398

Dalmatia 267–269, 271, 279, 300–301, 309–310, 315, 321, 361, 386, 393, 413, 439, 444, 456–457
Daltaban Muṣṭafā Paşa (Ottoman governor of Bosnia) 146–147, 157
Danube 8, 20, 51, 107, 131, 153, 155, 272, 284, 337, 339, 340, 343–344, 375, 432, 465
Defterdār Sarı Meḥmed Paşa (Ottoman statesman and chronicler) 46, 215*n*26
Dnieper 270–271, 276, 283, 285, 300, 302–303, 309–310, 324, 340, 371, 435, 436
Dniester 146, 270, 294, 309, 340
Dositheos (Greek-Orthodox Patriarch of Jerusalem) 153, 200, 242, 333*n*139
Dubrawski, – (Polish envoy) 368–369
Dubrovnik. *See* Ragusa

Elbląg (city) 157–158, 366
England 6, 26, 36, 47, 61, 64, 67, 73–74, 79–81, 91–92, 94, 97, 107–108, 117, 130, 133, 162*n*73, 166
King of 37*n*63, 75, 79, 116, 141
Exalted State. *See* Ottoman Empire

Father Gregory (Greek-Orthodox priest in Muscovite service) 200, 394
Ferriol, Charles de (French ambassador) 69
Firdevsī Efendi (Ottoman secretary) 380, 384
Fortis, Alvise (interpreter in Venetian service) 386
France 6, 10, 26, 47–48, 57, 87, 103, 105*n*32, 106–107, 118, 127, 130, 133, 141*n*118, 142, 162*n*73, 177, 288, 362, 420, 439
Kingdom of 277, 308
King of 36, 57, 74, 277, 326. *See also* Louis XIV
Frederic III (Elector of Brandenburg) 157

Gentili, Alberico 13
Gerania (mountain range in southern Greece) 269, 295, 302
German Emperor. *See* Holy Roman Emperor
Gomolinski, Jan (Polish clergyman and envoy) 94, 136–137, 138*n*98, 142, 366*n*61
Gorkowski, Andrzej (Polish secretary) 203, 366, 380, 383–384, 385*n*57, 450
Gozze, Luca (Ragusan envoy) 316
Gozze, Raffael (Ragusan envoy) 315
Grotius, Hugo 13

Habsburg Monarchy 1, 6, 9, 13, 30–39, 54–58, 64–68, 73–79, 94–97, 132–148, 177–178, 181–182, 187–188, 271–272, 305–321, 356–359, 397–404, 409–413, 426–432, 438–440, 442–446, 451–460
Habsburgs. *See* Habsburg Monarchy
Hammerschmid, Johann Caspar Anton (provisioner of the Habsburg embassy) 395
Heinsius, Anthoine (Grand Pensionary of Holland) 91
Heemskerck, Coenraad van (Dutch ambassador) 37, 38n64, 108, 386
Holland. *See* United Provinces
Holy League 1, 2*n*1, 14–15, 25, 30, 34, 36, 66, 80–81, 109, 117, 135, 139, 143, 153, 157, 159, 162, 176, 179, 194, 201, 267, 272, 273, 280, 344, 356, 363, 399, 402, 410, 426, 429, 440, 446, 449, 452
Alliance Treaty of (1684) 31
Holy Roman Emperor 32, 36, 46–47, 51, 57, 70, 101, 116, 174*n*52, 224*n*79, 277, 329*n*111, 447
Holy Roman Empire 36, 92, 118, 133, 143, 288, 308

Hop, Jacob (Dutch ambassador) 30, 32, 103–104, 115
Hungary 25, 35, 51–53, 77, 138, 153*n*5, 206*n*35, 224*n*79, 288, 303, 308, 316, 323, 375, 386, 430, 460
  Kingdom of 118, 284, 313
  Kings of 315–316
  Medieval Kingdom of 15, 430
  Middle 53
  Ottoman 271, 277
  Prince of 105*n*31
  Upper 53

Jabłonowski, Jan (Polish statesman) 368–370
Jabłonowski, Stanisław (Polish grand hetman) 91, 368–370
Jan III Sobieski (Polish King) 90, 270*n*20, 325*n*86, 368
Jerusalem
  Christian Holy Sites in 375, 419–420
  Medieval Kingdom of 288

Kamianets-Podilskyi 61, 90–91, 93, 119, 137, 145–146, 184, 203, 207, 222, 235*n*135, 269, 271, 274, 281, 365–370, 375, 433, 455
Ḳara Muṣṭafā Paşa (Ottoman grand vizier) 36*n*53, 204, 212*n*8
Kaunitz, Dominik Andreas von (Imperial minister) 74, 143, 239
Kerch
  Fortress of 270, 333
  Peninsula 81, 270
Khotin
  War of (1620–21) 328
Kinsky, Franz Ulrich von (Imperial minister) 19*n*59, 31, 38, 47, 50, 53, 56–60, 64–69, 71–79, 83–84, 86, 89–90, 94–97, 109, 111–113, 116, 122–125, 128–129, 132–134, 139, 141–144, 147, 152, 155, 160, 165, 169, 182, 206, 208, 222–223, 226, 234, 238, 242–243, 245, 250, 260, 275, 277, 295, 298, 321, 341, 356–357, 391–392, 397–404, 410–412, 415, 426, 431, 440, 442–443, 445, 452, 458
Kollonitsch, Leopold Karl von (cardinal) 34, 36
Köprülüzāde Fāżıl Muṣṭāfā Paşa (Ottoman grand vizier) 37
Krušedol (Greek-Orthodox monastery) 336
Küçük Ḳaynarca
  Treaty of (1774) 461

Lachowitz, Johann Adam (Habsburg interpreter) 385, 388
Lefkada (Island in the Ionian Sea) 269, 271, 282, 457*n*46
Leopold I (Holy Roman Emperor) 30, 34–35, 47, 53, 65, 70, 132, 134, 137, 144, 219, 238, 261, 277, 296, 310–311, 315–316, 319–320, 327, 357, 397–402, 404, 411, 425
Lepanto (Fortress in south-western Greece) 269, 276, 282, 295, 364
London 73–74, 81, 92, 117
Loredano, Francesco (Venetian ambassador in Vienna) 295, 304, 380, 401–404, 410, 412–414, 435, 442–443, 445, 458
Louis XIV (King of France) 36, 47, 69*n*4, 70, 92, 102, 117, 119, 141, 229, 299

Małachowski, Stanisław (Polish ambassador) 113, 137–138, 145, 154, 158, 164, 168, 173, 174–175, 180–181, 190–198, 203–204, 206–207, 214, 222, 232, 235–236, 238, 241, 248–249, 266, 274, 280–282, 325, 332, 341, 356, 363, 365–368, 370–371, 373, 383, 388, 408, 410–411, 414–415, 433, 437, 444, 446–447, 449–452, 456, 459, 462
Marsigli, Luigi (Italian scholar and military commander in Habsburg service) 46*n*8, 62, 122, 156, 158, 159, 182, 192, 194–195, 206–207, 218, 223, 227, 231–232, 268*n*12, 277, 298, 300–301, 304, 307–308, 310, 318*n*38, 337, 356, 358–359, 364, 366, 379–380, 383, 391–393, 398–399, 409–410, 412, 416–417, 420, 431, 440, 443, 445–446, 452, 458

Mavrocordatos, Alexandros (Ottoman grand dragoman and ambassador) 27–30, 32, 34–35, 46, 49–53, 58, 60–61, 83–85, 119, 123–125, 129, 153, 181, 183, 185–186, 199–205, 213*n*16, 214–218, 220, 222–223, 226–230, 233, 236–238, 241, 244, 251–252, 260, 266, 274, 276, 284, 293, 297, 301, 303–304, 317, 319, 325–327, 343, 348, 352–353, 359, 366, 371–373, 376, 378, 384, 387–391, 394, 401, 414, 419–420, 429–434, 439–440, 445, 447, 451, 455
Meḥmed IV (Ottoman sultan) 25–26, 30, 61*n*88, 88, 204, 299
Meninski, Franciszek (Imperial interpreter and linguist) 3, 32*n*33, 260*n*10, 291, 385, 422*n*34, 424*n*54, 454*n*23
Mesgnien, François de. *See* Franciszek Meninski
Moldavia 28, 38, 52, 61, 75, 78, 90, 106, 138, 146, 207, 216–217, 270–271, 282, 294, 296, 301, 309*n*242, 310, 323–325, 375, 432, 455
  Principality of. *See* Moldavia
Morea. *See* Peloponnese
Moscow 80, 134, 138*n*101, 238, 379, 386
  Slavic-Greek-Latin Academy in 386
Murad Giray (Crimean khan) 323
Mureş (river) 284–285, 296, 301, 305, 356, 409, 420
Muscovy 1, 7, 9, 15, 30*n*25, 62, 73, 78, 80–82, 84–85, 90, 93, 96–98, 106, 121–123, 126, 135, 138, 153, 160, 163, 172, 174–179, 188–203, 251, 258, 270–271, 273, 283–284, 293, 303, 306, 309, 322–334, 354, 371–375, 393, 399, 420, 435–436, 440–441, 450, 455
Muṣṭafā II (Ottoman sultan) 38, 88, 92, 317, 329*n*111, 435

Nābī, Yūsuf (Ottoman poet) 229
Naʿīmā, Muṣṭafā (Ottoman historian and bureaucrat) 4*n*9, 34, 178, 220–221
Naryshkin, Lev Kirillovich (head of the Muscovite 'Ambassadorial Chancery') 252, 351
Nehem, – (Habsburg general) 142–143, 165
Nerchinsk 282–283, 302–303, 308
  Treaty of (1689) 282*n*86, 293, 309–310, 392*n*97, 428*n*77
Nicolosi, Gian Battista (Venetian secretary) 47*n*12, 207, 237, 362, 364, 380, 382–384, 390*n*87, 393, 444, 446*n*57, 456–458
Nikitin, Aleksei (Muscovite ambassador) 66*n*16, 74*n*33, 80–81, 82*n*77
Nijmegen 126, 464
  Congress of 6, 99*n*5, 103, 115, 117–118, 161, 164, 170, 173, 177, 182, 198, 214, 261*n*12, 343, 462
Nine Years' War (1688–97) 2*n*1, 4, 36, 57*n*66, 347

Oliva-Copenhagen
  Congress of 7
  Treaties of 107
ʿOs̱mān II (Ottoman sultan) 328–329
Ottoman Empire 7, 9, 12, 21, 25, 29–30, 38, 54, 60*n*78, 61, 108*n*47, 113, 116–117, 124, 129, 131, 145, 157, 172, 179, 198, 200*n*4, 216, 219, 236, 246–247, 261–262, 269, 275, 277, 299, 303, 306, 310, 313, 316, 319–320, 325–326, 328, 330–331, 359–360, 362, 375–376, 412, 427–429, 434–435, 456*n*36, 461
Ottoman Porte 1, 4, 9, 13, 16, 26, 32, 37–38, 47–50, 52–53, 59–62, 67, 69, 73, 77, 82–86, 89, 91, 96, 104*n*28, 105*n*32, 106, 108, 112, 114, 125–126, 132, 157–158, 165, 201, 203, 205, 216, 218, 220, 275–279, 284, 298–301, 303, 305–306, 309, 312, 314–322, 325–330, 333–334, 369, 372–373, 376, 378, 389, 416–417, 428–431, 433–436, 440, 442, 455–458, 460–461
Öttingen, Wolfgang von (Habsburg ambassador) 144, 182, 187, 191, 214, 217, 219–220, 223, 234*n*132, 239, 250, 265, 278, 321, 332, 357, 359, 383, 397, 400, 403, 411, 413, 426, 430–431, 441–442, 444, 459

Padua 204
University of 201, 386
Paget, William (English ambassador) 37–38, 45, 49–54, 58–67, 69, 71–76, 82–87, 94–95, 97, 109–118, 121–122, 125, 127, 129, 139–142, 147, 154–155, 163, 182, 193, 196, 206–208, 214, 218, 232, 261, 264, 266, 300, 320, 331, 341, 344, 352, 358, 378–380, 388, 393, 396, 403, 412–413, 420, 426, 440, 447, 456–457, 464
Passarowitz
Congress of (1718) 99*n*5, 118, 188, 350, 380*n*27
Ottoman-Imperial Treaty of 432
Ottoman-Venetian Treaty of 435
Peloponnese 25, 48, 176, 207, 264*n*24, 268, 271, 277, 282, 294, 295–298, 330, 361, 364, 380, 393, 413, 434–435, 439, 460
Peter I (Tsar of Muscovy/Russia) 59, 79–82, 92, 132–135, 138, 153*n*5, 154, 160, 189, 202, 247, 252, 269*n*19, 270, 284, 324, 333, 340, 373*n*97, 386, 387, 435, 447
Petrovaradin (fortress in northern Serbia) 127*n*40, 144, 148, 153–155, 164, 180, 182, 190–191, 336, 338, 341, 344, 351, 357, 394, 458–459
Podolia 25, 61*n*88, 93, 146, 271, 274, 281, 288*n*119, 296, 309, 323, 365, 369–370, 432
Poland-Lithuania. *See* Polish-Lithuanian Commonwealth
Polish-Lithuanian Commonwealth 1, 7, 16, 25, 29*n*20, 30, 52, 58, 61, 73, 78, 84, 90–93, 96–97, 98, 108, 113, 119–123, 126, 132, 134, 136–138, 145, 148, 153–155, 157–158, 173–174, 176, 179–180, 184, 188–198, 203–204, 207, 222, 225, 238, 248, 258–259, 269–271, 273–274, 281, 283*n*90, 306, 313, 322–334, 365–370, 373, 380, 396, 428, 432–433, 460–461
Porte. *See* Ottoman Porte
Postnikov, Petr Vasil'evich (Muscovite secretary and interpreter) 174, 201, 205, 229, 354, 371, 373, 380, 383–384, 386–389, 393, 429–430, 433, 440, 447–448
Preveza (town in western Greece) 269, 271, 276, 364
Prince Eugene of Savoy (Imperial commander-in-chief) 39, 203, 305
Pufendorf, Samuel von 13
Pyrenees 288
Treaty of (1659) 106, 127, 131, 345

Radziwiłł, Karol Stanisław (Grand Chancellor of Lithuania) 145, 242, 332*n*130, 365, 394, 444
Ragusa 23, 112, 125*n*23, 268, 271, 310–321, 323, 327, 331, 375, 444, 457
Republic of. *See* Ragusa
Rāmī Meḥmed (Ottoman ambassador) 3, 15*n*47, 19*n*56, 44, 55*n*54, 56, 61, 69, 72, 80–81, 84, 113, 125, 159, 161, 164, 183, 187, 194, 197, 200–201, 202*n*19, 210, 215, 217, 220–221, 224, 230, 236, 240, 248, 251*n*221, 262, 266, 276, 297, 319, 330*n*112, 332, 337, 334, 352–353, 360–361, 372, 376, 378, 384, 390, 393, 396, 412, 419, 424*n*54, 431–432, 434, 439, 452, 454, 456
Rodostamov, Mikhail (Muscovite secretary) 380–381, 383
Rome 28, 38, 54
Church of 419
Papal College of Saint Athanasius in 34
Papal Court in 175
Ruzzini, Carlo (Venetian ambassador) 46*n*8, 47*n*12, 73–77, 89, 94–96, 111–112, 114, 117, 119, 123, 127, 148, 157, 162–164, 169–170, 176, 180, 182–184, 187–188, 194–195, 197, 204–205, 207, 214, 217–218, 220, 223, 228, 230, 234, 237–238, 242, 245, 247, 249, 252–253, 260–261, 276, 278–280, 298, 301, 321, 330, 342, 352–355, 359–365, 367–368, 374, 377–378, 382–383, 392, 410, 413–415, 434, 438–442, 444–448, 454, 456–459
Ryswick 47, 136, 162*n*73, 347, 464
Congress of 6, 44, 46, 141*n*118, 170, 173, 177, 182, 213, 447
Imperial-French Peace of 47–48, 57, 69–70, 277, 308
Treaty of. *See* Imperial-French Peace of

Rzeczpospolita. *See* Polish-Lithuanian Commonwealth

Sava (river) 155, 158, 236, 357
Schlik, Leopold von (Habsburg ambassador) 8*n*24, 19*n*59, 112, 115, 117, 119–120, 144, 154–156, 159*n*49, 160, 169, 182, 184–185, 187, 191–192, 195, 197, 204, 208, 210, 214, 215, 217, 219, 222–226, 230, 232, 234, 236–239, 242–248, 250, 253, 260, 264–266, 274, 278, 293–294, 298, 300–301, 305, 309, 321, 330, 332, 341, 351, 353–356, 358, 361–362, 371, 374, 379, 391, 393, 399, 400, 403, 411, 413–415, 419, 421, 426, 430–432, 439–444, 446–447, 451, 459
Schreyer, Georg Philipp (English secretary) 64–65, 82, 87, 122, 135, 139, 142, 155, 206, 291*n*130, 344, 380, 384, 445, 452
Second Northern War (1655–60) 4, 107, 157*n*38, 368
Sedlnitzky, – (Imperial ambassador) 66*n*16, 74*n*33, 80*n*69, 82*n*77, 93, 94
Selīm II Giray (Crimean khan) 203, 327, 368–369
Silāḥdār, Fındıḳlılı Meḥmed Aga (Ottoman chronicler and palace official) 25, 48
Sixteen Years' War (1683–99) 2*n*1, 4, 10, 15, 20, 26*n*3, 27, 34, 46, 53–54, 66, 91, 100, 107, 240, 251, 257, 269*n*18, 277, 315, 323, 386, 460*n*1
Spain 36, 106, 118, 127, 132–133, 288, 423*n*44, 447
  King of 91, 314, 319
Slankamen (fortress in northern Serbia) 37, 129, 139, 148, 336, 338, 445*n*30
Soranzo, Lorenzo (Venetian ambassador) 455–456
Sublime Porte. *See* Ottoman Porte
Sutton, Robert (English ambassador) 60
Süleymān (Ottoman prince and contender of the throne) 429
Süleymān the Magnificent (Ottoman Sultan) 56, 108, 324
Süleymān II (Ottoman Sultan) 25, 30, 38

Talmann, Michael (Habsburg interpreter) 385–386
Ṭemeşvar
  Fortress of 51, 145, 154*n*7, 234, 271, 281, 375
  Province of 57, 61, 246, 265, 271, 276, 281, 285, 296, 302–303, 357, 375, 431
  Banat of. *See* Province of
  Eyālet of. *See* Province of
  Region of. *See* Province of
The Hague 80*n*69, 81–82, 91, 117, 122, 420
Thirty Years' War (1618–48) 4, 33, 54*n*49, 105–106, 421
Thököly, Imre (Hungarian nobleman and 'King of Middle Hungary') 53, 203, 375
Till, Johannes (Habsburg secretary) 210, 232*n*132, 380–381, 383–384, 388, 434, 444
Tisza (river) 224, 236, 284, 285, 296, 303, 356, 397, 420
Transylvania 52–53, 61, 77, 79, 108, 112, 115, 124, 185, 209, 224, 251, 260, 262–265, 272, 284–285, 296, 301–302, 305, 308–310, 329–330, 391, 420, 431
  Prince of 106
  Principality of. *See* Transylvania

Ukraine 25, 61, 93, 271, 288*n*119, 305, 309, 365, 421, 432, 435
United Provinces 36, 37*n*62, 47, 62, 74, 81, 91, 103, 107–108, 118, 127, 130, 133, 162*n*73, 423*n*44
  States General of 71, 73, 141, 420
Utrecht 465
  Congress of 6, 173, 261*n*12, 462
Üsküdarī ʿAbdullāh Efendi (Ottoman chronicler and bureaucrat) 36*n*53, 37, 38*n*66, 108–109

Vasvár
  Treaty of (1664) 55*n*52, 215, 224, 426*n*70, 428*n*81, 431*n*97
Venice 14, 28, 30, 55*n*52, 61–62, 73, 75–76, 84, 96–97, 103, 112, 118–119, 122–123, 125, 132, 134, 153, 163, 175, 176–177, 179, 183, 196, 198–199, 204–205, 207, 236, 244, 252–253, 258, 259, 267–269, 271, 273, 280, 298, 301, 304, 308–309, 317, 320–321, 330–332, 359–364, 374, 376, 394,

Venice (*cont.*)
397–404, 411–415, 434–435, 438–440, 443–448, 451–453, 456–460
Republic of 1, 15, 25, 56, 77*n*52, 96, 115, 312, 315, 360, 372, 376, 400, 428
Venier, Girolamo (Venetian ambassador) 35
Vienna 1, 8*n*24, 14–15, 18*n*53, 25–26, 27*n*12, 29*n*19, 30, 32, 35–36, 39, 53–54, 56, 59–60, 63–65, 67, 70, 73, 75, 80, 82, 86–87, 90–91, 93–94, 97, 108–109, 111–112, 121–123, 127–129, 132, 134–139, 141–142, 144–145, 148, 154*n*7, 189–191, 217, 239, 247, 251, 274, 312, 315–317, 322–323, 332, 342–343, 357–359, 368, 379, 385–387, 392, 395, 397–398, 401, 409–411, 415, 430, 434, 439, 442–446, 457*n*43, 460
College of Oriental Languages in 385
Congress of (1689–90) 14, 25, 30–31, 31*n*30, 34, 36, 52, 57, 96*n*152, 103, 126, 135, 140, 141*n*118, 162, 213, 241, 244*n*189, 260, 270, 298, 324, 326, 348*n*61, 369, 416, 430, 431*n*95, 435, 461
Failed Congress. *See* Congress of (1689–90)
Villars, Claude Louis Hector de (French commander and ambassador) 70, 141–142
Vosnitsyn, Prokopii Bogdanovich (Muscovite ambassador) 14, 29*n*21, 61, 80, 111, 114, 135–138, 143–144, 148, 153–154, 160–161, 164, 173, 175, 177, 179–180, 182, 185, 189–202, 214, 218, 221, 228, 231–232, 238–239, 241, 247, 251–253, 273, 280, 297, 300, 325–326, 333, 341, 351, 354–355, 363, 371–374, 378–380, 387–389, 395, 415, 433, 435–436, 440–442, 447–448, 449–451, 456, 459

Wallachia 28, 38, 52, 90, 106, 216–217, 227–228, 271–272, 296, 301, 309*n*242, 310, 325, 368
Westphalia 6, 11–12, 343, 464
Congress of 5, 7, 14, 16, 44, 99*n*5, 105, 110, 118, 127*n*36, 152*n*1, 158, 170–171, 176, 193, 259, 303, 342, 420, 464
William III (King of England) 47, 57, 71, 75, 92–94, 117
Wolf, Peter (translator in Muscovite service) 383, 387

Zakynthos (Ionian island) 235*n*135, 330
Załuski, Andrzej Chryzostom (Polish clergyman and statesman) 146, 243
Zekan, Ivan (interpreter in Muscovite service) 387
Zsitvatorok 105, 110, 130, 140
Treaty of (1606) 13, 106, 127–128, 128*n*43, 173, 178
Peace of. *See* Treaty of
Żurawno
Battle of (1676) 368
Treaty of (1676) 29*n*20, 329
Zülfikār Efendi (Ottoman ambassador) 26, 31*n*30, 32, 55*n*53, 103, 104*n*28, 125, 170, 172*n*40, 241, 326, 378, 416, 423*n*38

www.ingramcontent.com/pod-product-compliance
Lightning Source LLC
LaVergne TN
LVHW010658300926
849161LV00005B/1159